The Sermons of John Wesley

A Collection for the Christian Journey

Edited by Kenneth J. Collins
and Jason E. Vickers

Abingdon Press
Nashville

THE SERMONS OF JOHN WESLEY
A COLLECTION FOR THE CHRISTIAN JOURNEY

This book is printed on acid-free paper.

Library of Congress Cataloging-in-Publication Data

The sermons of John Wesley : a collection for the Christian journey / edited by Kenneth J. Collins and Jason Vickers.

pages cm

ISBN 978-1-4267-4231-6 (pbk. : alk. paper) 1. Wesley, John, 1703-1791—Sermons. 2. Practical theology—Sermons. 3. Methodist Church—Doctrines—Sermons. 4. Wesleyan Church—Doctrines—Sermons. I. Collins, Kenneth J., editor of compilation.

BX8217.W54S47 2013

252'.07—dc23

2013012910

Scripture quotations are from the King James or Authorized Version of the Bible.

The Board of Directors of the Wesley Works Editorial Project has granted its approval for the editors of this collection to use the critically established texts of John Wesley's sermons as published in the Bicentennial Edition. The organization of the sermons and the introductions to them are the work of the editors of this collection; any views or interpretations expressed by the editors are their own.

13 14 15 16 17 18 19 20 21 22—10 9 8 7 6 5 4 3 2 1

MANUFACTURED IN THE UNITED STATES OF AMERICA

To the memory of Albert C. Outler

Contents

Abbreviations

B = Burwash, Nathanael. *Wesley's Fifty Two Standard Sermons.* Salem, Ohio: Schmul Publishing Co., 1967.

C = Cragg, Gerald R. *The Works of John Wesley.* Vol. 11, *The Appeals to Men of Reason and Religion and Certain Related Open Letters.* Bicentennial ed. Nashville: Abingdon Press, 1975.

D = Davies, Rupert E. *The Works of John Wesley.* Vol. 9, *The Methodist Societies, I: History, Nature, and Design.* Bicentennial ed. Nashville: Abingdon Press, 1989.

FB = Baker, Frank. *The Works of John Wesley.* Vols. 25–26, *Letters I & II.* Bicentennial ed. Nashville: Abingdon Press, 1980–82.

H = Henry, Matthew. *Matthew Henry's Commentary on the Whole Bible: Complete and Unabridged in One Volume.* Peabody, Mass.: Hendrickson, 2008.

HAR = Harrison, W. P., ed. *The Wesleyan Standards: Sermons by the Rev. John Wesley, A.M.* Nashville: Publishing House of The Methodist Episcopal Church, South, 1921.

HTZ = Heitzenrater, Richard P. "At Full Liberty: Doctrinal Standards in Early American Methodism." In *Mirror and Memory: Reflections on Early Methodism,* edited by Richard P. Heitzenrater, 189-204. Nashville: Kingswood Books, 1989.

J = Jackson, Thomas, ed. *The Works of Rev. John Wesley.* 14 vols. London: Wesleyan Methodist Book Room, 1829–31.

JAB = Bengel, John Albert. *New Testament Word Studies.* 2 vols. Grand Rapids, Mich.: Kregel, 1971.

NT = Wesley, John. *Explanatory Notes Upon the New Testament.* London: William Bowyer, 1755.

O = Outler, Albert C. *The Works of John Wesley.* Vols. 1–4, *Sermons.* Bicentennial ed. Nashville: Abingdon Press, 1984–87.

OD = Oden, Thomas C. *Doctrinal Standards in the Wesleyan Tradition.* Grand Rapids, Mich.: Francis Asbury Press of Zondervan Publishing House, 1988.

ODNB = *The Oxford Dictionary of National Biography.*

OH = Outler, Albert C., and Richard P. Heitzenrater. *John Wesley's Sermons: An Anthology.* Nashville: Abingdon Press, 1991.

OT = Wesley, John. *Notes Upon the Old Testament.* 3 vols. Edited by William M. Arnett. Salem, Ohio: Schmul Publishing Co., 1975.

R = Rack, Henry. *The Methodist Societies: The Minutes of Conference.* Nashville: Abingdon Press, 2011.

S = Sugden, Edward H., ed. *Wesley's Standard Sermons.* 2 vols. London: Epworth Press, 1921.

SOSO = Wesley, John. *Sermons on Several Occasions,* 1746–60, 1771, 1787–88.

SS = Wesley, John. *John Wesley's Sunday Service of the Methodists in North America.* Nashville: Quarterly Review, 1984.

T = Telford, John. *The Letters of the Rev. John Wesley.* 8 vols. London: Epworth Press, 1931.

WH = Ward, W. Reginald, and Richard P. Heitzenrater. *The Works of John Wesley.* Vols. 18–24, *Journals and Diaries I–VII.* Bicentennial ed. Nashville: Abingdon Press, 1988–2003.

WWS = Smith, Wanda Willard. *Register of John Wesley's Preaching.* Durham, N.C.: Duke University Divinity School, 2011. http://divinity.duke.edu/sites/default/files/documents/cswt/Register-04_Register_of_John_Wesley's_Preaching_Texts.pdf.

Note: *If readers notice numerous uses of the* O *abbreviation in the introductions to the sermons, that is only because, in most instances, it represents the voice of Wesley himself.*

General Introduction

The provision of resources for the theological and spiritual formation of believers has been a matter of deep and abiding concern in the life of the church across space and time. In the Western church, for example, this concern is on display in resources such as Augustine's *Confessions* and Ignatius's *Spiritual Exercises.* In the ancient Eastern church, this concern is perhaps best reflected in Chrysostom's *Baptismal Instructions.*

Like their Roman Catholic and Eastern Orthodox forebears, Protestants have developed significant resources for the theological and spiritual formation of believers. For example, Luther published numerous postils or homilies, an instructive series of sermons whose form was taken up by subsequent Lutheran leaders (Philipp Melanchthon, Martin Chemnitz, Andreas Osiander, and Johann Arndt) to communicate the genius of the faith. This rich history of employing sermons or homilies for theological and spiritual formation, so evident in the Lutheran tradition and present among Puritans as well (Richard Baxter readily comes to mind), was continued in the Anglican communion. Indeed, from the beginning, Anglicans have privileged the so-called Edwardian homilies of Thomas Cranmer in faith formation. However, they have also made ample use of sermons from other divines, including John Jewel, Richard Hooker, and Edward Stillingfleet.

While John Wesley was familiar with many resources used for formation in the ancient, medieval, and magisterial Protestant churches, he was most familiar with the formational materials and practices of his native Church of England. Thus when Wesley grew increasingly concerned about the theological and spiritual formation of the people called Methodists, he began assembling a collection of sermons for their edification. In these sermons, Wesley addressed a wide range of perennial concerns related to Christian living. For example, he dealt at length with the image of God; the origins, nature, and scope of sin; the need for repentance; the nature of faith; justification, regeneration, and sanctification; the place of works; temptations; Christian perfection; and the presence and work of the Holy Spirit in the midst of it all. In addressing these and many other concerns, Wesley provided Methodists with a ready resource for their theological and spiritual formation.

John Wesley's Sermon Collections

John Wesley drafted early sermons from the period 1725 to 1737, many of which he chose not to publish. In other words, these compositions ("On Mourning for the Dead" and "On Guardian Angels," for example) remained manuscript sermons and were omitted from the first collection of sermons that he produced in 1746.[1] In his preface to the *Sermons on Several Occasions* (SOSO) that year Wesley gives his readers a hint of some of the memorable changes that had taken place in his life during the years 1737–38 and that led to the creation of several vehicles for his practical theology: "The following sermons contain the substance of what I have been preaching for between eight and nine years last past" (O, 1:103). Not surprisingly, the pivotal sermon "Salvation by Faith," which Albert Outler referred to as Wesley's "evangelical manifesto" (O, 1:110) and which was preached before Oxford University shortly after Wesley's Aldersgate experience, marks the head of this early published collection.

In an attempt to provide the Methodists with a suitable means of grace for instruction and devotion and as an aid to right practice, Wesley published several editions of his sermons (in 1746, 1748, 1750, and 1760) such that by the year 1760 the collection embraced forty-three works. According to Outler, Wesley eventually included the sermon "Wandering Thoughts" in the second edition of volume III (which was published around 1762), and it therefore brought the number to forty-four sermons (O, 1:41).

Something of Wesley's practical theological design in publishing these sermons is revealed once again in his preface to the edition: "I have accordingly set down in the following sermons what I find in the Bible concerning *the way to heaven*; with a view to distinguish this way of God from all those which are the inventions of men" (O, 1:106). Similarly, Wesley exclaims: "Every serious man who peruses these will therefore see in the clearest manner what those doctrines are which I embrace and teach as the *essentials of true religion*" (O, 1:103). Moreover, operating out of a firm belief in the universal love of God manifested in Jesus Christ, Wesley viewed his audience quite broadly as embracing not simply those who *already* knew the religion of the heart, that is, faith working by love, but also those "who [were] just setting their faces toward heaven" (O, 1:106).

The Model Deed (1763)

As an effective administrator, Wesley realized the dangers of idiosyncratic and self-referential behavior among his preachers. He, therefore, executed a Model Deed in 1763 that brought greater order in terms of *what* was preached from a Methodist pulpit. As Henry Rack has pointed out, preaching-houses that were not grounded on this Model Deed "could cause trouble, as the Birstall and Dewsbury Chapel cases showed even after 1784" (R, 10:85). Edward Sugden, late professor of Queen's College, the University of Melbourne, cited the language of the Model Deed in his work as follows:

> Provided always that no person or person whomsoever shall any time hereafter be permitted to preach or expound God's Holy Word or perform any of the usual acts of Religious

> Worship . . . in the said Chapel . . . who shall maintain promulgate or teach any doctrine or practice contrary to what is contained in certain Notes on the New Testament commonly reputed to be the Notes of the said John Wesley and in the First Four Volumes of Sermons commonly reputed to be written and published by him. (S, 2:331)

Since the Model Deed was promulgated in 1763, the reference to the sermons in this document would include the forty-three of the 1760 edition plus the sermon "Wandering Thoughts" that was added in 1762, bringing the total to forty-four. In other words, when Wesley drafted this disciplinary instrument, he obviously viewed these forty-four sermons, and not his entire sermon corpus, as being of remarkable and distinct value in the ongoing life of Methodism.

When Wesley collected his works in 1770–71, he issued a new edition whose first four volumes were taken up by sermons, although nine more were now added, bringing the total to fifty-three (some later editions, published elsewhere, removed the sermon On the Death of George Whitefield to arrive at fifty-two). In the preface to this edition Wesley reveals that he wanted to "methodize these tracts, to range them under proper heads, placing those together which were on similar subjects and in such order that one might illustrate another" (S, 1:14). Beyond this, Wesley points out that "there is scarce any subject of importance in practical or controversial divinity, which is not treated more or less, either professedly or occasionally" (S, 1:14) therein, thereby highlighting the value of the collection for Christian formation. "His aims," Sugden observed, "were thus elucidation and completeness of presentation," indicating that Wesley's larger purpose in this endeavor included nothing less than the presentation of materials that would constitute a living tradition. Put another way, his ever-present goal in publishing the sermons was that the genius of Methodist life, faith, and practice might be suitably passed along from generation to generation. Indeed, Wesley himself drafted the following declaration that became a part of his introductory comments to the 1771 edition:

> Sermons on Several Occasions. First Series. Consisting of fifty-three discourses published in four volumes in the year 1771, and to which reference is made in the trust deeds of the Methodist Chapels as constituting, with Mr. Wesley's Notes on the New Testament, the standard doctrines of the Methodist Connection. (S, 2:336–37)

The nine additional sermons that filled out the 1771 edition are as follows:

The Witness of the Spirit, II—Rom. 8:16

On Sin in Believers—2 Cor. 5:17

The Repentance of Believers —Mark 1:15

The Great Assize—Rom. 14:10

The Lord Our Righteousness—Jer. 23:6

The Scripture Way of Salvation—Eph. 2:8

The Good Steward—Luke 16:2

The Reformation of Manners—Ps. 94:16

On the Death of George Whitefield—Num. 23:10

Remarkably, when Wesley brought forth a new edition (and the last one) of his sermons in 1787–88, it was identical to the volumes already published in 1746, 1748, 1750, and 1760, and it included the sermon "Wandering Thoughts" (S, 1:13). Wesley omitted the nine additional sermons of the 1771 edition just cited above. Sugden speculated that Wesley perhaps reverted to the composition of the earlier editions because he realized "the legal difficulty that would have arisen had he changed the standard of doctrine set out in the deeds executed before 1771, not that he had changed his mind as to the importance of the added sermons" (S, 1:14). In other words, Wesley knew that "the previous four volumes formed part of the legal standard of doctrine for his preachers; and he could not alter that without creating difficulties" (S, 1:14). Sugden also observed that after 1787 the form of the works in the Model Deed "was altered to 'the first four volumes of sermons'" (S, 1:13).

These observations help to illuminate the subsequent *publishing history* of the sermons in British Methodism, especially with regard to the preference for forty-four sermons and not fifty-two or fifty-three. In the twentieth century the British Conference actually went on record to maintain that the natural sense and proper intention of the phrase "the first four volumes of sermons" . . . referred to the 1787–88 edition of *Wesley's Works* (forty-four sermons), and not to Wesley's collected works of 1771 (S, 1:14; OD, 106). However, we agree with Outler's judgment that the omission of these eight sermons (if the one on Whitefield is excluded) in any published collection "would represent a serious loss" (O, 1:43–44), especially since it would shunt aside the two landmark sermons, "The Scripture Way of Salvation" and "The Lord Our Righteousness" (O, 1:42), which are so necessary for properly understanding Wesley's overall practical theology.

One of Wesley's more productive periods, homiletically speaking, was during the 1780s when he drafted more than sixty sermons, several of which contained his well-worked theme of real Christianity. Many of these sermons appeared in the *Arminian Magazine* that began publication in 1778 as a suitable contrast to the Calvinist *Gospel Magazine.* Accordingly, volumes V–VIII of the SOSO were filled with these sermons such that by the 1787–88 edition, Wesley's sermons numbered about one hundred (OH, 9). After Wesley's demise, George Story, who was at the time responsible for Methodist printing, gathered together Wesley's sermons written after 1788 and published them in a ninth volume. Through this effort, Wesley's published output of sermons expanded greatly and now totaled 151 (OH, 9).

The Publishing History of Wesley's Sermons: American, Canadian, and Australian Contexts

The publishing history of Wesley's sermons in the North American context is somewhat different from its British counterpart and more complicated in that it reflects the basic ambiguity entailed in the failure of the 1808 American Conference to state specifically, when Francis Ward had posed the question, what sermons constituted "our present and existing standards of doctrine" (HTZ, 197). By that late date, well after Wesley's death, the entire corpus of 151 sermons was no doubt published on occasion. However, other important editions emerged much later, and were widely circulated, that focused on the fifty-two sermons of the 1771 edition of Wesley's works (the sermon "On the Death of George Whitefield" was sometimes omitted).

Four subsequent editions of Wesley's sermons, not all of them North American, warrant significant attention: the first was that of Nathanael Burwash, dean of theology, Victoria College, Canada. His *Wesley's Doctrinal Standards, Part I, The Sermons,* or more popularly known as *Wesley's Fifty Two Standard Sermons,* was published in 1881 and was reprinted on numerous occasions for Canadian and American consumption. The second major collection that once again focused on fifty-three sermons (the one on Whitefield was this time included) was that of Edward Sugden in 1921, and it enjoyed a wide reading in Australia and beyond. The third major collection was produced in that same year by the Reverend W. P. Harrison, the American book editor of The Methodist Episcopal Church, South. Deeply appreciative of the work of Burwash, Harrison offered a revised edition of the fifty-two sermons specifically adapted for the use of students. Harrison's witness to the value of this particular arrangement of sermons is evident in his observation that it was the practice of the bishops of The Methodist Episcopal Church, South to include two volumes of Wesley's sermons (volume I, sermons I–XXVI; volume II, sermons XXVII–LII) for ministerial preparation in the Course of Study (HAR, 2:6). And so when North American and Australian Methodists of the last century were reading Wesley's sermons, it was likely some form of the fifty-two (three) sermons that went back to the 1771 edition of Wesley's works. The British, for their part, during the last century were likely reading a collection of forty-four sermons for the reasons already suggested.

The fourth and most recent edition of Wesley's sermons, however, departed from this dominant trend of focusing on either forty-four or fifty-two "standard sermons" in a rather dramatic way. In *John Wesley's Sermons: An Anthology,* Albert Outler and Richard P. Heitzenrater produced a collection that aimed (1) to broaden the list of sermons beyond the traditional lists and (2) to demonstrate how Wesley's theological emphases and wider concerns developed over time. With respect to the second aim, the editors organized the volume in a temporal sequence, beginning with "The Image of God" (1730) and concluding with "On Living without God" (1790). Suffice it to say, this volume has made a significant contribution in Wesley studies, giving scholars and students ready access to less familiar sermons and providing an impetus for a fresh interest in the matter of Wesley's theological concerns across time.

Readers, however, should note in light of this history that we are *not* making the case for what constituted standard sermons in the American context, though even the Plan of Union (1966–67) that led to the formation of The United Methodist Church in 1968 affirmed that the First Restrictive Rule of the Conference of 1808 would include "'as a minimum,' Wesley's forty-four *Sermons on Several Occasions* and his *Explanatory Notes Upon the New Testament*" (HTZ, 190).[2] Our purpose instead has been to lay the historical groundwork necessary for readers to understand why, after all is said and done, we have chosen to gather together the British forty-four (which clearly had Wesley's seal of approval), plus those eight additional sermons (we have omitted the one on George Whitefield) that were published in the 1771 edition of Wesley's works and that were republished again and again in the last century through the careful efforts of Sugden, Burwash, and Harrison.

Why a New Collection of Sermons Is Needed

Until recently, with the publication of the present work, readers of John Wesley's sermons basically had three options. First, they could try to find some edition of the fifty-two sermons whose publication has been erratic of late. Second, they could download sermons piecemeal from the Internet without suitable introductions, outlines, or a suggested ordering. Third, they could read the Outler and Heitzenrater volume, *John Wesley's Sermons: An Anthology*, which, while highly valuable for the purposes described above, was never intended primarily as a resource for theological and spiritual formation. Indeed, though the Outler and Heitzenrater volume (OH) is clearly valuable, especially for a graduate seminar, its arrangement and composition in our judgment are not best suited for use in active, full-orbed Christian discipleship. To illustrate, the OH volume is arranged *chronologically*, which makes it appropriate to discern the subtle shifts and nuances of Wesley's developing thought. In contrast, our volume is arranged *soteriologically*, following the *way* of salvation in general and the *ordo salutis* in particular, ever with an eye on the process of serious Christian formation. In other words, the focus is not so much on Wesley himself, in terms of his personal chronology or biography, as it is on the sermons themselves as evocative tools, as engaging instruments of transformation, in other words, as suitable and lively *means of grace*.

In addition, since the OH collection includes *seven* of the nine additional sermons from the 1771 edition of Wesley's sermons (the ones on Whitefield and The Reformation of Manners are deleted), its major differences from other collections are due in large part to which sermons of the British forty-four are left out. Consider then the following observations with respect to the composition of the OH anthology: (1) it *excludes* many of the forty-four sermons that Wesley viewed quite favorably as representing the substance of what he was preaching, (2) these same forty-four sermons were in fact protected by the Model Deed in 1763 and were subsequently given formal status in British Methodism, (3) these sermons have had a rich publishing history as a distinct and valuable body of material in the formative life of Methodism from the eighteenth century and beyond, and (4) these sermons have been and remain integral to Christian formation and substantive catechesis. The lists below reveal precisely the sermons of the forty-four that are omitted from the OH collection. We divide such deletions into three major sections to illustrate our larger point:

Sermons That the Outler-Heitzenrater Anthology Leaves Out (from the British Forty-Four)

(1) Faith and Assurance

6. The Righteousness of Faith—Rom. 10:5-8
8. The First-fruits of the Spirit—Rom. 8:1
11. The Witness of Our Own Spirit—2 Cor. 1:12
32. The Nature of Enthusiasm—Acts 26:24

(2) Wesley's Theological Ethics

16. Upon our Lord's Sermon on the Mount, Discourse the First—Matt. 5:1-4
17. Upon our Lord's Sermon on the Mount, Discourse the Second—Matt. 5:5-7
18. Upon our Lord's Sermon on the Mount, Discourse the Third—Matt. 5:8-12
22. Upon our Lord's Sermon on the Mount, Discourse the Seventh—Matt. 6:16-18
24. Upon our Lord's Sermon on the Mount, Discourse the Ninth—Matt. 6:24-34
25. Upon our Lord's Sermon on the Mount: Discourse the Tenth—Matt. 7:1-12
26. Upon our Lord's Sermon on the Mount, Discourse the Eleventh—Matt. 7:13-14
27. Upon our Lord's Sermon on the Mount, Discourse the Twelfth—Matt. 7:15-20
28. Upon our Lord's Sermon on the Mount, Discourse the Thirteenth—Matt. 7:21-27

(3) Challenges to the Christian Life

36. Wandering Thoughts—2 Cor. 10:5
37. Satan's Devices—2 Cor. 2:11
40. The Wilderness State—John 16:22
41. Heaviness through Manifold Temptations—1 Pet. 1:6
42. Self-denial—Luke 9:23
43. The Cure of Evil-speaking—Matt. 18:15-17

First of all, the issue of assurance was not only an emphasis of Wesley throughout much of his career; it also remains a vital part of contemporary Methodist witness to the broader catholic church. The reception of salvific graces, properly speaking, is marked by a *twofold* assurance that embraces the *direct* witness of the Holy Spirit that one is indeed forgiven and a child of God as well as the *indirect* witness, the assurance of our own spirit, as Wesley put it, to this same saving reality. The sermons "The First-fruits of the Spirit" and "The Witness of Our Own Spirit" fill out the indirect witness in a way that illustrates the balance and comprehensiveness of Methodist teaching, its conjunctive nature, if you will, on a topic so vital to mature Christian development.

Second, Wesley's series on the Sermon on the Mount, written from 1748 to 1750, is one of the best vehicles available to comprehend his basic Christian ethic; it displays, in other words, what form Christian graces should take on both personal and social levels. Moreover, the practical, ethical value of these sermons (How then shall we live?) can be appreciated once one realizes that these sermons treat, in an extensive way, the *moral law* that makes up such an integral part of Wesley's practical theology. Indeed, the *entirety* of the Sermon on the Mount, as Wesley clearly taught, and not simply the material reflected in SOM, Discourse the Fifth, is a suitable expression of the moral law, the holy law of love, whose Old Testament counterpart is seen in the Ten Commandments. It is difficult to find more practical ethical counsel in Wesley's writings apart from this material. Beyond this, the last sermons of this series (SOM, Discourses the Tenth through the Thirteenth) treat in a very realistic way some of the more perplexing obstacles to the Christian life.

Third, this last area of challenges to the Christian life (how such a graced life can *yet* go awry) is perhaps the greatest weakness, in our judgment, of the OH anthology from the standpoint of Christian formation. Indeed, not only has this assortment omitted much of the Sermon on the Mount series, but it has also eliminated those sermons that depict what may prove to be for some believers the darker, uncomfortable, and distressing aspects of a flesh-and-blood Christian journey, such sermons as "The Wilderness State" and "Heaviness through Manifold Temptations" in particular. Without these and many of the other sermons listed in the third section above, the OH anthology fails to offer a painstakingly realistic picture of what serious Christian formation actually looks like in its challenges, setbacks, and occasionally (though unnecessarily) defeats. Thus it is primarily with the work of formation and catechesis in mind that this present volume will include the *entirety* of the British forty-four sermons, but unlike this traditional collection, it will include those eight additional sermons of the 1771 edition of Wesley's works, many of which both Outler and Heitzenrater found so valuable.

Why the Traditional Collections of Burwash, Harrision, and Sugden Must Be Augmented

Though the fifty-two (three) sermons go a long way in expressing the heart of Wesley's practical theology, they nevertheless must be supplemented with several of his other sermons in order to offer a better and more accurate picture of his overall practical theology. Furthermore, since our social location today is removed from eighteenth-century British Methodism in terms of time and place, it is necessary to take up and reflect somewhat differing interests and concerns through the inclusion of other sermons. Our hope in joining together older interests with new ones is to take part, once again, in a living tradition. That is, our goal in embracing eight additional sermons beyond the fifty-two is to pass on the legacy of the Methodist tradition in a practical and relevant way to the current generation. The "new" sermons are as follows:

Eight Additional Sermons beyond the Fifty-Two

1. The General Deliverance—Rom. 8:19-22 [60]
2. The New Creation—Rev. 21:5 [64]
3. On Working Out Our Own Salvation—Phil 2:12-13 [85]
4. The Danger of Riches —1 Tim. 6:9 [87]
5. On Visiting the Sick—Matt. 25:36 [98]
6. The Duty of Constant Communion—Luke 22:19 [101]
7. Free Grace—Rom. 8:32 [110]
8. The Image of God—Gen. 1:27 [141]

These sermons were carefully chosen in conversation with Methodists around the world. They represent the interests and judgments of lay leaders, pastors, and scholars about how the Wesleyan way of salvation should be filled out in additional sermons that will have cash value, so to speak, for the practical tasks of ministry and for generous Christian development. Though space prohibits a discussion of the reasoning behind each selection, three nevertheless warrant additional consideration.

First of all, the sermon "The Danger of Riches" is necessary beyond the sermons "The Use of Money" and "The Good Steward" because Wesley recognized that the love of wealth, in its various forms, can so easily interlace itself in the human heart deflecting the love of God and neighbor in significant ways. During the 1780s as he was thinking of the future of Methodism and his legacy, Wesley feared that the Methodists would lose the power of religion to rest content merely in its form due to the corrupting power of riches. In fact, during this period he wrote three sermons specifically on wealth: "The Danger of Riches" being the earliest one (1781) followed by "On Riches" (1788) and "The Danger of Increasing Riches" (1790). This emphasis must be reflected in any representative collection of Wesley's sermons.

Second, the sermon "On Visiting the Sick" is one of the best windows on how Wesley considered the relation between temporal ministry, which focuses on the maintenance needs of the poor, and spiritual ministry, which unabashedly considers the eminent value of the human soul. As such, this sermon offers contemporary settings, both near and far, a number of Wesley's practical value judgments in terms of the proper relation between what our age has called personal and social action. In addition, this sermon is well focused on the ends, the goals, and the high calling of all ministry that bears the name of Christ, and it therefore deserves inclusion.

Third, the sermon "The General Deliverance" demonstrates clearly that Wesley's understanding of redemption was remarkably broad and embraced the animal realm as well. Such inclusion within the orbit of God's love and concern highlights the utter goodness, mercy, and providential care of the divine being for all sentient beings. This view accords quite well with current ecological interests and breaks out of the strictures of a mere anthropocentric understanding of redemption. Moreover, in underscoring the goodness and generosity of God, Wesley engages in the following remarkable speculation: What if the Almighty in the consummation of things invited the animal realm to become "Creatures capable of God? Capable of knowing, and loving, and enjoying the Author of their being" (O, 2:448)? How great then in Wesley's eyes is the extent of God's love and mercy!

With the inclusion of these eight additional sermons, helpful in filling out Wesley's practical theological judgment, the substance of our new collection can now be presented in the following chart:

Collections of John Wesley's Sermons			
British Forty-Four)	North American and Australian (Fifty-Two)	Additional Sermons New Collection	Total
44	+8	+8	60

The Arrangement of the Sermons

With an eye on serious Christian development, we have arranged the present collection in terms of the way of salvation in general and the *ordo salutis* in particular. In other words, the way of salvation, the *via salutis*, in its open and more general orientation, will embrace such elements as self-denial and good stewardship, for example, so necessary to Christian life and practice that are not specified in the Wesleyan *ordo salutis* (Outler's preferred terminology) as expressed, for example, in the summary sermon, "The Scripture Way of Salvation."[3] However, if the proffered way of salvation so envisioned does not gather up the *specifics* of the *ordo salutis* such as the two foci of redemption, for instance, in the form of justification/regeneration and entire sanctification as well as their attendant doctrines (such as repentance and works suitable for repentance) and their proper relations, then it is not Wesley's way of salvation that is actually being described. In this instance, the *way* so conceived would be too loose, far too amorphous for ready use in catechetical work.[4] In light of such considerations we employ both terminologies in this book to bring together Wesley's general counsels as well as his particular soteriological advice, and we have arranged the sermons accordingly, from the goodness of creation ("The Image of God") to the consummation in glorifying grace ("The New Creation") and every step along the way. The order is reflected in the following theological categories that are listed on the contents pages with each sermon:

- The Goodness of Creation
- The Fall
- Free Grace
- Awakening
- Prevenient Grace and Repentance
- Repentance and Converting Grace
- Repentance
- Justification
- Justification and Imputation
- Regeneration
- Assurance
- The Christian Life
- Challenges to the Christian Life
- The Sum of True Religion
- Illumination and Second Repentance
- Second Repentance
- Pressing on to Christian Perfection
- Christian Perfection
- The Extent of Redemption
- Judgment and Glorifying Grace
- Glorifying Grace

The process of ordering the sermons for this book was a lengthy one and involved the advice of Methodists from the United States, England, Germany, Kenya, South Korea, India, and Australia, among other places. We wanted to *listen* to a global, diverse community as to what arrangement of sermons would be most helpful to the tasks of ministry in general as well as for the hope and promise of formation in particular. We are especially grateful to the community of scholars and researchers who took part in the Wesleyan Studies Summer Seminar held in Wilmore in June 2012. Their advice and, on occasion, their correction have been invaluable. We especially would like to thank Dr. Phil Meadows of Cliff College, England, and Dr. Don Thorsen of Azusa Pacific University for their wonderful and at times memorable insights.

Of course, no order of sermons is perfect; each is subject to criticism. Yes, other arrangements are indeed possible; nevertheless, we believe that after a lengthy and informed process, we have arrived at one that will serve the global church well. Two particular sermons and their positioning, however, require further attention, a task that will acquaint readers with at least some of the reasoning behind this creative process. First of all, the sermon "Free Grace" is placed early on in the order, right after "Original Sin." We wanted to highlight that in Wesley's theology the universality of sin is matched by the universality of grace. That is, "Free Grace" underscores the *extent* of the *provision* that God has made for humanity in the atoning work of Jesus Christ. Moreover, "Free Grace" has been placed early, ahead of the sermon "On Working Out Our Own Salvation," for example, because it highlights that the grace of God, in some sense, must also be understood as a sheer gift, the work of God *alone.* "Thus is his grace free in all, that is, no way depending on any power or merit in man," Wesley writes, "but on God alone, who freely gave us his own Son, and 'with him freely giveth us all things'" (O, 3:545). In other words, Wesley's depiction of grace in this setting is sophisticated, informed by both Protestant (free grace) and catholic (co-operant, synergistic, responsible) understandings of grace in a carefully balanced conjunction. Our order therefore reflects such balance.

Second, the sermon "Catholic Spirit" is placed under the heading "Challenges to the Christian Life" not because such a spirit itself is problematic; rather it is the contrary uncatholic spirit that devolves upon the narrowness of opinion that may frustrate genuine communion among the people of God. This sermon is therefore placed right next to "A Caution against Bigotry" and with it shows some of the many ways that the universal love of God can be deflected by lesser interests that are often invested with far too much value, resulting in narrowness, parochialism, and even outright bigotry.

And finally, the first five sermons of the series "Upon our Lord's Sermon on the Mount" are positioned right after the challenges to the Christian life because they represent a very helpful summary of Christian experience. Beyond this, these same sermons display the very highest graces (think of the text "blessed are the pure in heart") as believers look to repenting of the carnal nature, through the ministrations of the Holy Spirit and the moral law, even to realize, by God's grace, nothing less than heart purity. These sermons, then, prepare the way for all that is to come.

Textual Considerations

The text of Wesley's sermons provided here represents the very best of scholarship, and it is drawn from the critical edition of *The Works of John Wesley* that was originally published in Albert Outler's four volumes of sermons. Outler's notes have been removed for the sake of space, though all of Wesley's original notes have been retained. Many of Wesley's observations were scriptural in nature, and the references for these are placed in the text in parentheses. Wesley's Greek and Hebrew citations have been carefully reproduced, and foreign phrases (Latin, for example) have been italicized.

The brief introductions to the sermons (though nowhere else) employ the following convention in formatting in terms of the title so that readers can quickly determine from what collection each sermon has been drawn:

British Forty-Four Sermons	No special formatting
Burwash, Harrison, and Sugden Additional Eight	*Italicized*
Eight "New" Sermons	Underlined

Moreover, the sermons are simply numbered from 1-60 in the table of contents to indicate the position of each entry in this volume. However, the number of each sermon drawn from the Bicentennial Edition of *The Works of John Wesley* is only retained (if readers care to consult this edition) at the heading of the sermon text itself in this current collection.

Appreciation

We would like to thank Christine Johnson, doctoral student at the University of Manchester in England, for her careful work in terms of preserving the accuracy of the text of the Bicentennial Edition of *The Works of John Wesley* that is reproduced in this present volume.

Also special thanks go to Asbury and United Theological Seminaries for their support of this project. Our hope is that this new collection of sermons, which has been years in the making, will serve the global Wesleyan community generously to the glory of God's love manifested in Jesus Christ through the power of the Holy Spirit!

Feast of St. Augustine of Hippo
August 28, 2012

Kenneth J. Collins
Jason Vickers

1. THE IMAGE OF GOD

November, 1730

An Introductory Comment

This sermon is a first in a couple of ways. It was John Wesley's first university sermon preached at St. Mary's on November 15, 1730 (O, 4:290), and due to its subject matter with its strong theme of creation, this sermon marks the very beginning of the way of salvation. Wesley preached on this same text about two dozen times, from London to Manchester and on to Armagh, Ireland, where he noted in his *Journal* late in his career on June 11, 1775, that he had preached to a huge congregation, "But I could not find the way to their hearts" (WH, 22:455). Following Matthew Henry, the great commentator, Wesley viewed verse 26, "Let us make man . . . ," in a trinitarian fashion, and he believed that the terms *image* and *likeness* referred to the very same reality (H, Gen. 1:26).

Wesley laid out his basic doctrine of humanity (anthropology) in this sermon by noting that human beings are a "compound of matter and spirit" (O, 4:296) and could not therefore be *reduced* to the "image of . . . the beasts that perish" (O, 4:292). Elsewhere he observed that *Homo sapiens* is not "mere matter, a clod of earth, a lump of clay, without sense or understanding; but a spirit like [the] Creator" (O, 2:400). Generally speaking, Wesley defined the *imago Dei* as "righteousness and true holiness" (O, 1:162), and he affirmed, "It was *free grace* that . . . stamped on that soul the image of God" (O, 1:117). Beyond this, Wesley specifically understood the image of God in a threefold manner along the lines of natural, political, and moral images, with an emphasis on the last. Human beings, then, are marked by understanding, will, and liberty and in their best sense by holiness and happiness.

The Image of God

1. A truth that honors human nature should not fail
    A. Some in every age have gladly received it
    B. Human beings were made in the image of God
2. Why, then, do human beings exhibit so many imperfections?
3. Many contend that humans were created in the image of beasts
4. God created human beings upright, but they rebelled against their Creator
5. I will explain the doctrine more distinctly by inquiring:
    A. How humans were made in the image of God
    B. How they lost that image
    C. How they may recover that image

I. Human beings were originally made in the image of God
1. They were given power to distinguish truth from falsehood
2. Far greater and nobler was their second endowment, a perfect will
3. God implanted perfect freedom in their nature
4. God crowned all of this with perfect happiness

II. How did human beings lose their perfection?
    A. Liberty required some trial so that they could have true choice
    B. Adam ate from the tree of the knowledge of good and evil
    C. Eating the forbidden fruit had numerous effects
1. The first effect was the loss of immortality
2. The understanding was destroyed, and error and ignorance increased
3. The perfect will became subject to imperfection, anger, and shame
4. The loss of freedom enslaved the mind to vice
5. The consequence of this enslavement was the reversal of happiness

III. Who shall recover us from the body of this death?
    A. Jesus Christ our Lord, who conquered death
1. The first step toward recovery is knowledge of our condition
2. This understanding directs us to reform our will by charity
3. The law of the Spirit makes us free from the law of sin and death

IV. Concluding remarks
1. Those who refuse the love of Christ are in a sad condition
2. The duty of Christians is to spread the love of Christ with unbelievers

Sermon 141: The Image of God, 1730

Genesis 1:27

In the first chapter of Genesis at the twenty-seventh verse it is thus written:

So God created man in his own image.

[1.] A truth that does so much honour to human nature, that gives so advantageous an account of it as this, could not fail, one would think, of being well entertained by all to whom that nature belonged. And accordingly some there have been in all ages who gladly received and firmly retained it; who asserted, not only that man was sprung from God, but that he was his likeness from whom he sprung; that the image of his divine Parent was still visible upon him, who had transfused as much of himself into this his picture as the materials on which he drew would allow.

[2.] But to this it has constantly been opposed: if man was made in the image of God, whence flow those numberless imperfections that stain and dishonour his nature? Why is his body exposed to sickness and pain, and at last to a total dissolution? Why is his soul still more disgraced and deformed by ignorance and error, by unruly passions, and what is worse than all, as it contains them all, by vice? A fine picture—this ignorant, wretched, guilty creature—of a wise, happy, and holy Creator!

[3.] I am ashamed to say there are [those] of our age and nation who greedily close with this old objection, and eagerly maintain that they were not made in the image of the living God, but of the beasts that perish; who heartily contend that it was not the divine but the brutal likeness in which they were created, and earnestly assert 'that they themselves are beasts' in a more literal sense than ever Solomon meant it. These consequently reject with scorn the account God has given of man, and affirm it to be contrary to reason and [to the account] itself, as well as it is to their practice.

[4.] The substance of his account is this: 'God created man upright; in the image of God created he him; but man found out to himself many inventions.' Abusing the liberty wherewith he was endowed, he rebelled against his Creator, and wilfully changed the image of the incorruptible God into sin, misery, and corruption. Yet his merciful, though rejected, Creator would not forsake even the depraved work of his own hands, but provided for him, and offered to him a means of being 'renewed after the image of him that created him'.

[5.] That it may appear whether this account of man is contrary to itself and reason or no, I shall endeavour to show the parts of it more distinctly, by inquiring: I, how man was made in the image of God; II, how he lost that image; and III, how he may recover it.

I. Man was originally made in the image of God.

1. First with regard to his understanding. He was endued, after the likeness of his Maker, with a power of distinguishing truth from falsehood; either by a simple view wherein he made the nearest approach to that all-seeing Nature, or by comparing one

thing with another (a manner of knowledge perhaps peculiar to himself) and often inferring farther truths from these preceding comparisons.

(1.) And in several properties of it, as well as in the faculty itself, man at first resembled God. His understanding was just; everything appeared to him according to its real nature. It never was betrayed into any mistake; whatever he perceived, he perceived as it was. He thought not at all of many things, but he thought wrong of none. (2.) And as it was just, it was likewise clear. Truth and evidence went hand in hand; as nothing appeared in a false light, so neither in a glimmering one. Light and darkness there were, but no twilight; whenever the shades of ignorance withdrew, in that moment the broader day appeared, the full blaze of knowledge shined. He was equally a stranger to error and doubt; either he saw not at all, or he saw plainly. (3.) And hence arose that other excellence of his understanding: being just and clear, it was swift in its motion. Nothing was then as quick as thought but that which alone is capable of it—spirit. How far anything of which we have any conception must fall short of expressing its swiftness will be readily seen by all who observe but one instance of it in our first father: in how short a space he 'gave names to all cattle, and to the fowls of the air, and to every beast of the field'. And names not arbitrarily imposed, but expressive of their inward natures. (4.) Sufficiently showing thereby not only the swiftness, but likewise the greatness of his understanding. For how extensive a view must he have had who could command so vast a prospect! What a comprehension was that, to take in at once almost an infinity of objects! Such doubtless it was that the visible creation would soon have been too small for its capacity.

2. And yet even this just, this clear, this swift, this comprehensive understanding was the least part of that image of God wherein man was originally made. Far greater and nobler was his second endowment, namely, a will equally perfect. It could not but be perfect while it followed the dictates of such an understanding. His affections were rational, even, and regular—if we may be allowed to say 'affections', for properly speaking he had but one: man was what God is, Love. Love filled the whole expansion of his soul; it possessed him without a rival. Every movement of his heart was love: it knew no other fervour. Love was his vital heat; it was the genial warmth that animated his whole frame. And the flame of it was continually streaming forth, directly to him from whom it came, and by reflection to all sensitive natures, inasmuch as they too were his offspring; but especially to those superior beings who bore not only the superscription, but likewise the image of their Creator.

3. What made his image yet plainer in his human offspring was, thirdly, the liberty he originally enjoyed; the perfect freedom implanted in his nature, and interwoven with all its parts. Man was made with an entire indifference, either to keep or change his first estate: it was left to himself what he would do; his own choice was to determine him in all things. The balance did not incline to one side or the other unless by his own deed. His Creator would not, and no creature besides himself could, weigh down either scale. So that, in this sense, he was the sole lord and sovereign judge of his own actions.

4. The result of all these—an unerring understanding, an uncorrupt will, and perfect freedom—gave the last stroke to the image of God in man, by crowning all these with happiness. Then indeed to live was to enjoy, when every faculty was in its perfection,

amidst abundance of objects which infinite wisdom had purposely suited to it, when man's understanding was satisfied with truth, as his will was with good; when he was at full liberty to enjoy either the Creator or the creation; to indulge in rivers of pleasure, ever new, ever pure from any mixture of pain.

II. How it was this wise, virtuous, happy creature was deprived of these perfections, how man lost the image of God, we are, secondly, to inquire. And the plain answer is this: the liberty of man necessarily required that he should have some trial; else he would have had no choice whether he would stand or no, that is, no liberty at all. In order to this necessary trial God said unto him, 'Of every tree of the garden thou mayst freely eat, but of the tree of the knowledge of good and evil, thou shalt not eat of it.' To secure him from transgressing this sole command, as far as could be done without destroying his liberty, the consequence was laid before him: 'In the day that thou eatest thereof thou shalt surely die.' Yet man did eat of it, and the consequence accordingly was death on him and all his descendants, and preparatory to death, sickness and pain, and folly and vice and slavery.

And 'tis easy to observe by what regular steps all these would succeed each other, if God did not miraculously prevent it, but suffer nature to take its course. But we should observe, first, that man even at his creation was a compound of matter and spirit; and that it was ordained by the original law that during this vital union neither part of the compound should act at all but together with its companion; that the dependence of each upon the other should be inviolably maintained; that even the operations of the soul should so far depend upon the body as to be exerted in a more or less perfect manner, as this was more or less aptly disposed.

This being observed, we may easily conceive how the forbidden fruit might work all those effects which are implied in the word 'death', as being introductory to, and paving the way for it. Which particulars of the following account are founded on Scripture and consequently certain, and which are built on conjecture and therefore proposed only as probable, it will not be hard to distinguish.

1. Its first effect must have been on his body, which, being before prepared for immortality, had no seeds of corruption within itself and adopted none from without. All its original particles were incorruptible, and therefore the additional ones taken in, being for pleasure rather than use, cannot be supposed ever to have cleaved to its native substance, ever to have adhered to any part of it, as none needed any reparation. By this means both the juices contained must have been still of the same consistence, and the vessels containing them have kept the same spring, and remained ever clear and open.

On the contrary, the fruit of that tree alone of whose deadly nature he was forewarned seems to have contained a juice, the particles of which were apt to cleave to whatever they touched. Some of these, being received into the human body, might adhere to the inner coats of the finer vessels; to which again other particles that before floated loose in the blood, continually joining, would naturally lay a foundation for numberless disorders in all parts of the machine. For death in particular; since, more foreign matter cleaving to the former every day, the solid parts of the body would every day lose something of their spring, and so be less able to contribute their necessary assistance to the circulation of the fluids. The smaller channels would gradually fill up, especially those that lie near the extremities, where the current, by reason of its distance from the fountain, was always more slow and languid. The whole tide, as the force that threw it forward abated, must [also] have abated its swiftness in proportion, till at length that force utterly failing, it ceased to move, and rested in death.

Indeed had Adam taken the antidote as well as the poison, had he again put forth his hand, and taken of the fruit of the Tree of Life, nothing of this could have followed. 'Tis sure this would have made him live for ever, naturally speaking, notwithstanding he had eaten death. 'Tis likely it would have done so by its thin, abstersive nature, particularly fitted to counteract the other, to wipe off its particles, wheresoever adhering, and so restore the eater to immortality.

However this be, thus much is certain: the moment wherein that fruit was tasted, the sentence of death passed on that body, which before was impassive and immortal. And this immortal having put on mortality, the next stroke fell on its companion: the soul felt a like change through all her powers, except only that she could not die. The instrument being now quite untuned, she could no longer make the same harmony: 'the corruptible body pressed down the soul', with which it soared so high during its incorruption.

2. His understanding first found the want of suitable organs; its notions were just no longer. It mistook falsehood for truth, and truth for falsehood. Error succeeded and increased ignorance. And no wonder, when it was no longer clear; when it not only saw through a glass, but darkly too, that glass being now grown thick and dull, having lost great part of its transparency. And hence it was that doubt perplexed it as well as error, that it could neither rest in knowledge nor ignorance. Through clouds like these its most laborious steps could win but little ground. With its clearness went its swiftness too; confusion and slowness came together. Instead of being able to find out the natures of ten thousand creatures almost in a moment, it became unable to trace out fully the nature of any one in many years. Nay, unable (so was the largeness of its capacity impaired, as well as the swiftness of its progress) with that apprehension for which the visible world was before but a scanty prospect, to take in at one view all the properties of any single creature therein.

3. How much the will suffered when its guide was thus blinded we may easily comprehend. Instead of the glorious one that possessed it whole *before*, it was *now* seized by legions of vile affections. Grief and anger and hatred and fear and shame, at once rushed in upon it; the whole train of earthly, sensual, and devilish passions fastened on and tore it in pieces. Nay, love itself, that ray of the Godhead, that balm of life, now became a torment. Its light being gone, it wandered about seeking rest and finding none; till at length, equally unable to subsist without any and to feel out its proper object, it reclined itself upon the painted trifles, the gilded poison of earthly enjoyments.

4. Indeed, what else could the human mind do when it had no freedom left? Liberty went away with virtue; instead of an indulgent master it was under a merciless tyrant. The subject of virtue became the slave of vice. It was not willingly that the creature obeyed vanity; the rule was now perforce; the sceptre of gold was changed into a rod of iron. Before,

the bands of love indeed drew him toward heaven; yet if he would, he could stoop down to earth. But now, he was so chained down to earth he could not so much as lift up his eyes toward heaven.

5. The consequence of his being enslaved to a depraved understanding and a corrupted will could be no other than the reverse of that happiness which flowed from them when in their perfection. Then were the days of man evil as well as few; then, when both his faculties were decayed, and bitterness poured on their earthly objects, and heavenly ones withdrawn, the mortal, foolish, vicious, enslaved creature was delivered over to his [un]sought-for misery.

How such a creature as this, as every fair inquirer finds by experience himself to be, could come from the hands of the good God, has been the just wonder of all ages. And let the infidel look to it; let him surmount the difficulty if he can upon any scheme beside the Christian. Upon this indeed it is no difficulty at all; all is rational, plain, and easy, while we observe, on the one hand, that not the good God but man himself made man what he is now; on the other, how he may recover what he wilfully lost, which is the subject of our third inquiry.

III. Who indeed shall recover us from the body of this death? Who shall restore our native immortality? We answer with the Apostle, 'I thank God, Jesus Christ our Lord!' 'As in Adam all died, so in Christ shall all be made alive'—all who accept of the means which he hath prepared, who walk by the rules which he hath given them. All these shall by dying conquer the first death, and shall never taste the second. The seeds of spiritual death they shall gradually expel, before this earthly tabernacle is dissolved, that this too, when it has been taken down and thoroughly purged, may be rebuilt 'eternal in the heavens'.

1. The first step to this glorious change is humility, a knowledge of ourselves, a just sense of our condition: which the evil spirit himself, either overruled by or mimicking the true God, recommended on the front of his temple in those celebrated words, 'Know Thyself', which a better prophet than he recommends to all those who would 'be transformed by the renewing of their minds'—'I say unto every man—not to think of himself more highly than he ought to think.'

'Tis almost needless to remark how conducive this is to the attainment of all other knowledge; or, in other words, how conducive it is to the improvement of the understanding. An erroneous opinion of ourselves naturally leads us into numberless errors; whereas to those who know their own folly (beside the natural advantage of it) the Lord of nature 'giveth the spirit of wisdom, and enlightens the eyes of their understanding, after the likeness in which they were created' (Eph. 1:17-18; [Col. 3:10]).

2. The understanding, thus enlightened by humility, immediately directs us to reform our will by charity. To root out of our souls all unmanly passions, and to give place to them, no, not an hour; to put away all malice, uncleanness, intemperance, 'all bitterness, wrath, and evil-speaking'; to collect the scattered beams of that affection which is truly human, truly divine, and fix them on that Sovereign Good 'in whom we live, move, and have our being'; for his sake, lastly, and after his example, to be 'kind one to another,

tender-hearted, forgiving one another, even as God, for Christ's sake, hath forgiven us' (Eph. 4:32).

3. Thus it is that the 'law of the Spirit of life makes us free from the law of sin and death'; thus it restores us, first to knowledge, and then to virtue, and freedom, and happiness. Thus are we 'delivered from the bondage of corruption into the glorious liberty of the sons of God'; into that liberty which not only implies the absence of all pain, unless what is necessary to future pleasure, but such a measure of present happiness as is a fit introduction to that which flows at God's right hand for evermore!

[IV.1.] One thing I would observe from what has been said—how extremely pitiable their condition is who are insensible of their innate disease, or refuse the only cure of it. 'Tis true, even those who are not invested with authority (such doubtless 'bear not the sword in vain') are apt to look upon these as the proper objects of anger, and not of compassion. Yet our Lord, when he beheld even that city which had killed the servants, and was about to murder the son, of its master, wept over it, and suffered all other passions to melt down into commiseration. Yet those whom we are often tempted to behold with passions of quite another nature, 'who are alienated from the image of God through the ignorance that is in them', are by our confession not more guilty than these, and little less unhappy. They are always sick, often in pain; destruction and unhappiness are in their ways; the way of peace have they not known, 'an evil disease cleaves to them'; their inward parts are very misery. Their understanding is darkened; clouds of ignorance and error are ever before their eyes, 'because the God of this world hath blinded their hearts', and infinitely increased its native corruption. Their love is fixed on mean, perishing, unsatisfying objects, and the frequent anguish that must flow from such a choice is sharpened by innumerable restless passions, that tear asunder their helpless prey. God help him who is a slave to such masters! Man cannot; he can only pity him! He can only, when he seeth such a one dragging his chain, and possibly talking loud of his own freedom, plunging through the flames of a fever into those that never shall be quenched, and perhaps dreaming he is in perfect health, recommend [him] to that All-sufficient Mercy to which all things are possible!

2. Yes, one step farther he may, he ought to go: he ought to acknowledge the riches of that mercy shown to himself, and indeed to all of us who have our education in a truly Christian country; who have all the opportunities of obtaining a better mind which the art of man and the wisdom of God can give; of obtaining this knowledge—knowledge, the basis of whatsoever things are pure, whatsoever things are honourable or lovely—[which] is held out to us with no sparing hand; we are suffered, courted, pressed to enjoy it. Others are glad if they can snatch a few drops from the rivulets that flow hence: we lie at the fountain-head of these living waters, and command all their various streams. The attainment of knowledge is the pleasure of many; of us, 'tis the business too. Our business it is to know in particular that we are all originally foolish and vicious, and that there is no truth in our whole religion more absolutely necessary to be known than this. Because if man be not naturally corrupt, then all religion, Jewish and Christian, is vain, seeing it is all built on this—all method[s] of cure presupposing the disease. We can scarce avoid

knowing how slight all objections against this fundamental truth must be while there is even this one argument for it: if man be naturally mortal, then he is naturally sinful; seeing one cause must work both sin and death. The seeds of natural being likewise the seeds of moral corruption, must undermine our understanding as well as our life, and the affections with the understanding. We are almost forced to know both the necessity and the divine efficacy of our religion; to see that if man be naturally corrupt, then Christianity is of God; seeing there is no other religion, as 'there is no other God which can deliver after this sort' from that corruption. We, lastly, have daily opportunities of knowing, if Christianity be of God, then of how glorious a privilege are they thought worthy who persuade others to accept of its benefits. Seeing when the author of it 'cometh in the clouds of heaven', and 'those that slept in the dust of the earth shall awake,' they who have saved others from sin and its attendant death 'shall shine as the brightness of the firmament'; they who have reprinted the image of God on many souls 'as the stars for ever'!

Now unto God the Father, God the Son, and God the Holy Ghost, be ascribed all honour and praise, now and for ever.

2. ORIGINAL SIN

1759

An Introductory Comment

In 1740 Dr. John Taylor, Hebrew scholar and president of the Presbyterian Theological College at Warrington (S, 2:207), published a treatise on original sin that Wesley judged to be problematic since it undermined one of the three essentials of the Christian faith (original sin, justification by faith, holiness of heart and life). "I verily believe no single person since Mahomet," Wesley exclaimed, "has given such a wound to Christianity as Dr. Taylor" (T, 4:48). Theologically perceptive, Wesley discerned a vital connection between original sin and the new birth broadly understood (the restoration of the image of God). That is, if the problem were misunderstood, then the solution would be as well. Accordingly, Wesley published one of his largest theological treatises ever, *The Doctrine of Original Sin,* in four parts in 1757, a work that was reduced to a more popular sermon form in a two penny pamphlet in 1759.

Referring to the disciples of Dr. Taylor as "silver-tongued Antichrists" (WH, 20:246), Wesley later articulated two basic elements of his largely Augustinian doctrine of original sin: (1) universality, "for all have sinned, and come short of the glory of God" (Rom. 3:23); and (2) total depravity, "every imagination of the thoughts of his heart was only evil continually" (Gen. 6:5). In terms of this last aspect Wesley followed Matthew Henry's *Commentary* fairly closely and employed the language of "bitter root" and "the corrupt spring" in his own observations on the text. In fact, Wesley maintained in his treatise "What Is an Arminian?" that there was little difference between him and George Whitefield on this essential doctrine —as well as that of justification by faith (J, 10:359). Differences did emerge, however, in that Wesley "sought to compound the Latin tradition of total depravity with the Eastern Orthodox view of sin as disease and salvation as therapeia psyches" (O, 2:171). Wesley preached on Genesis 6:5 eight times in 1759 and then once again in 1784 when the text dropped out of the sermon register.

Original Sin

1. The writings of many abound with descriptions of human dignity
2. On these accounts, human beings are but a little lower than angels
3. These accounts are very readily accepted by most people
4. These accounts are utterly irreconcilable with the scriptural

I. What were human beings like before the flood?

1. Before the flood God saw that 'the wickedness of man was great'
2. God saw all the imaginations of the thoughts of human hearts
3. God 'saw that all' this, the whole thereof, 'was evil'
4. 'God saw that the whole imagination of the heart was evil'

II. Are people the same now as they were before the flood?

1. Scripture gives us no reason to think otherwise
2. This account of the present state is confirmed by daily experience
3. When God opens our eyes, we see that we are without God
4. Without God, we would have no more religion than the beasts of the fields
5. Having no knowledge, we can have no love for God
6. We have by nature not only no love, but no fear of God
7. Thus all people are 'atheists in the world'
    A. In their natural state, every person is born an idolater
    B. Pride is idolatry; it is ascribing to ourselves what is due to God alone
8. Satan has stamped his own image on our *self-will*
9. People naturally love their own will and the world
10. The more this thirst is indulged, the more it increases
11. Another symptom of this fatal disease is the desire of praise

III. Inferences from what has been said

1. Heathenism is wholly ignorant of the entire deprivation of humanity
2. All who deny the depravity of the soul are heathens
3. God heals our atheism by the knowledge of himself and of Jesus Christ
4. If human beings were not fallen there would be no need of all this
5. The great end of religion is to renew our hearts in the image of God

Sermon 44: Original Sin, 1759

Genesis 6:5

And God saw that the wickedness of man was great in the earth, and that every imagination of the thoughts of his heart was only evil continually.

1. How widely different is this from the fair pictures of human nature which men have drawn in all ages! The writings of many of the ancients abound with gay descriptions of the dignity of man; whom some of them paint as having all virtue and happiness in his composition, or at least entirely in his power, without being beholden to any other being; yea, as self-sufficient, able to live on his own stock, and little inferior to God himself.

2. Nor have heathens alone, men who were guided in their researches by little more than the dim light of reason, but many likewise of them that bear the name of Christ, and to whom are entrusted the oracles of God, spoke as magnificently concerning the nature of man, as if it were all innocence and perfection. Accounts of this kind have particularly abounded in the present century; and perhaps in no part of the world more than in our own country. Here not a few persons of strong understanding, as well as extensive learning, have employed their utmost abilities to show what they termed 'the fair side of human nature'. And it must be acknowledged that if their accounts of him be just, man is still but 'a little lower than the angels', or (as the words may be more literally rendered), 'a little less than God'.

3. Is it any wonder that these accounts are very readily received by the generality of men? For who is not easily persuaded to think favourably of himself? Accordingly writers of this kind are almost universally read, admired, applauded. And innumerable are the converts they have made, not only in the gay but the learned world. So that it is now quite unfashionable to talk otherwise, to say anything to the disparagement of human nature; which is generally allowed, notwithstanding a few infirmities, to be very innocent and wise and virtuous.

4. But in the meantime, what must we do with our Bibles? For they will never agree with this. These accounts, however pleasing to flesh and blood, are utterly irreconcilable with the scriptural. The Scripture avers that 'by one man's disobedience all men were constituted sinners'; that 'in Adam all died', spiritually died, lost the life and the image of God; that fallen, sinful Adam then 'begat a son in his own likeness'; nor was it possible he should beget him in any other, for 'who can bring a clean thing out of an unclean?' That consequently *we*, as well as other men, 'were by nature' 'dead in trespasses and sins', 'without hope, without God in the world', and therefore 'children of wrath'; that every man may say, 'I was shapen in wickedness, and in sin did my mother conceive me;' that 'there is no difference, in that all have sinned, and come short of the glory of God,' of that glorious image of God wherein man was originally created. And hence, when 'the Lord looked down from heaven upon the children of men, he saw they were all gone out of the way, they were altogether become abominable, there was none righteous, no not one', none that truly 'sought after God'. Just agreeable, this, to what is declared by the Holy Ghost in the words above recited: 'God saw', when he looked down from heaven before,

'that the wickedness of man was great in the earth'; so great that 'every imagination of the thoughts of his heart was only evil continually'.

This is God's account of man: from which I shall take occasion, first, to show what men were before the flood; secondly, to inquire whether they are not the same now; and, thirdly, to add some inferences.

I.1. I am, first, by opening the words of the text, to show what men were before the flood. And we may fully depend on the account here given. For God saw it, and he cannot be deceived. He 'saw that the wickedness of man was great'. Not of this or that man; not of a few men only; not barely of the greater part, but of *man in general*, of men universally. The word includes the whole human race, every partaker of human nature. And it is not easy for us to compute their numbers, to tell how many thousands and millions they were. The earth then retained much of its primeval beauty and original fruitfulness. The face of the globe was not rent and torn as it is now; and spring and summer went hand in hand. 'Tis therefore probable it afforded sustenance for far more inhabitants than it is now capable of sustaining. And these must be immensely multiplied while men begat sons and daughters for seven or eight hundred years together. Yet among all this inconceivable number *only* Noah 'found favour with God'. He alone (perhaps including part of his household) was an exception from the universal wickedness, which by the just judgment of God in a short time after brought on universal destruction. All the rest were partakers in the same guilt, as they were in the same punishment.

2. 'God saw all the imaginations of the thoughts of his heart'—of his soul, his inward man, the spirit within him, the principle of all his inward and outward motions. He 'saw all the imaginations'. It is not possible to find a word of a more extensive signification. It includes whatever is formed, made, fabricated within; all that is or passes in the soul: every inclination, affection, passion, appetite; every temper, design, thought. It must of consequence include every word and action, as naturally flowing from the fountains, and being either good or evil according to the fountain from which they severally flow.

3. Now God 'saw that all' this, the whole thereof, 'was evil', contrary to moral rectitude; contrary to the nature of God, which necessarily includes all good; contrary to the divine will, the eternal standard of good and evil; contrary to the pure, holy image of God, wherein man was originally created, and wherein he stood when God, surveying the works of his hands, saw them all to be 'very good'; contrary to justice, mercy, and truth, and to the essential relations which each man bore to his Creator and his fellow creatures.

4. But was there not good mingled with the evil? Was there not light intermixed with the darkness? No, none at all: 'God saw that the whole imagination of the heart' of man 'was *only* evil.' It cannot indeed be denied but many of them, perhaps all, had good motions put into their hearts. For the spirit of God did then also 'strive with man', if haply he might repent; more especially during that gracious reprieve, the hundred and twenty years while the ark was preparing. But still 'in his flesh dwelt no good thing:' all his nature was purely evil. It was wholly consistent with itself, and unmixed with anything of any opposite nature.

5. However, it may still be matter of inquiry, 'Was there no intermission of this evil? Were there no lucid intervals, wherein something good might be found in the heart of man?' We are not here to consider what the grace of God might occasionally work in his soul. And abstracting from this, we have no reason to believe there was any intermission of that evil. For God, who 'saw the whole imagination of the thoughts of his heart to be *only* evil', saw likewise that it was always the same, that it 'was only evil *continually*'—every year, every day, every hour, every moment. He never deviated into good.

II. Such is the authentic account of the whole race of mankind, which he who knoweth what is in man, who searcheth the heart and trieth the reins, hath left upon record for our instruction. Such were all men before God brought the flood upon the earth. We are, secondly, to inquire whether they are the same now.

1. And this is certain, the Scripture gives us no reason to think any otherwise of them. On the contrary, all the above-cited passages of Scripture refer to those who lived after the flood. It was above a thousand years after that God declared by David concerning the children of men, 'They are all gone out of the way' of truth and holiness; 'there is none righteous, no, not one.' And to this bear all the prophets witness in their several generations. So Isaiah concerning God's peculiar people (and certainly the heathens were in *no better* condition): 'The whole head is sick, and the whole heart faint. From the sole of the foot even unto the head there is no soundness, but wounds and bruises and putrifying sores.' The same account is given by all the apostles, yea, by the whole tenor of the oracles of God. From all these we learn concerning man in his natural state, unassisted by the grace of God, that 'all the imaginations of the thoughts of his heart' are still 'evil, only evil', and that 'continually'.

2. And this account of the present state of man is confirmed by daily experience. It is true the natural man discerns it not. And this is not to be wondered at. So long as a man born blind continues so, he is scarce sensible of his want. Much less, could we suppose a place where all were born without sight, would they be sensible of the want of it. In like manner, so long as men remain in their natural blindness of understanding they are not sensible of their spiritual wants, and of this in particular. But as soon as God opens the eyes of their understanding they see the state they were in before; they are then deeply convinced that 'every man living', themselves especially, are by nature 'altogether vanity'; that is, folly and ignorance, sin and wickedness.

3. We see, when God opens our eyes, that we were before *ἄθεοι ἐν* [*τῷ*] *κόσμῳ*—'without God', or rather, 'atheists in the world'. We had by nature no knowledge of God, no acquaintance with him. It is true, as soon as we came to the use of reason we learned 'the invisible things of God, even his eternal power and godhead', from 'the things that are made'. From the things that are seen we inferred the existence of an eternal, powerful being that is not seen. But still, although we acknowledged his being, we had no acquaintance with him. As we know there is an emperor of China, whom yet we do not know, so we knew there was a King of all the earth; but yet we knew him not. Indeed we could not, by any of our natural faculties. By none of these could we attain the knowledge of

God. We could no more perceive him by our natural understanding than we could see him with our eyes. For 'no one knoweth the Father but the Son, and he to whom the Son willeth to reveal him. And no one knoweth the Son but the Father, and he to whom the Father revealeth him.'

4. We read of an ancient king who, being desirous to know what was the *natural language* of men, in order to bring the matter to a certain issue made the following experiment: he ordered two infants, as soon as they were born, to be conveyed to a place prepared for them, where they were brought up without any instruction at all, and without ever hearing an human voice. And what was the event? Why, that when they were at length brought out of their confinement, they spake no language at all, they uttered inarticulate sounds, like those of other animals. Were two infants in like manner to be brought up from the womb without being instructed in any religion, there is little room to doubt but (unless the grace of God interposed) the event would be just the same. They would have no religion at all: they would know no more of God than the beasts of the field, than the 'wild ass's colt'. Such is *natural religion*, abstracted from traditional, and from the influences of God's spirit!

5. And having no knowledge, we can have no love of God: we cannot love him we know not. Most men *talk* indeed of loving God, and perhaps imagine that they do. At least few will acknowledge they do not love him. But the fact is too plain to be denied. No man loves God by nature, no more than he does a stone, or the earth he treads upon. What we love, we delight in: but no man has naturally any delight in God. In our natural state we cannot conceive how anyone should delight in him. We take no pleasure in him at all; he is utterly tasteless to us. To love God! It is far above, out of our sight. We cannot naturally attain unto it.

6. We have by nature not only no love, but no fear of God. It is allowed, indeed, that most men have, sooner or later, a kind of senseless, irrational fear, properly called 'superstition'; though the blundering Epicureans gave it the name of 'religion'. Yet even this is not natural, but acquired; chiefly by conversation or from example. By nature 'God is not in all our thoughts.' We leave him to manage his own affairs, to sit quietly, as we imagine, in heaven, and leave us on earth to manage ours. So that we have no more of the fear of God before our eyes than of the love of God in our hearts.

7. Thus are all men 'atheists in the world'. But atheism itself does not screen us from *idolatry*. In his natural state every man born into the world is a rank idolater. Perhaps indeed we may not be such in the vulgar sense of the word. We do not, like the idolatrous heathens, worship molten or graven images. We do not bow down to the stock of a tree, to the work of our own hands. We do not pray to the angels or saints in heaven, any more than to the saints that are upon earth. But what then? We 'have set up our idols in our heart'; and to these we bow down, and worship them. We worship ourselves when we pay that honour to ourselves which is due to God only. Therefore all pride is idolatry; it is ascribing to ourselves what is due to God alone. And although pride was not made for man, yet where is the man that is born without it? But hereby we rob God of his unalienable right, and idolatrously usurp his glory.

8. But pride is not the only sort of idolatry which we are all by nature guilty of. Satan has stamped his own image on our heart in *self-will* also. 'I will', said he, before he was cast out of heaven, 'I will sit upon the sides of the north.' I will do my own will and pleasure, independently on that of my Creator. The same does every man born into the world say, and that in a thousand instances. Nay, and avow it, too, without ever blushing upon the account, without either fear or shame. Ask the man, 'Why did you do this?' He answers, 'Because I had a mind to it.' What is this but, 'Because it was my will;' that is, in effect, because the devil and I are agreed; because Satan and I govern our actions by one and the same principle. The will of God meantime is not in his thoughts, is not considered in the least degree; although it be the supreme rule of every intelligent creature, whether in heaven or earth, resulting from the essential, unalterable relation which all creatures bear to their Creator.

9. So far we bear the image of the devil, and tread in his steps. But at the next step we leave Satan behind, we run into an idolatry whereof he is not guilty: I mean *love of the world*, which is now as natural to every man as to love his own will. What is more natural to us than to seek happiness in the creature instead of the Creator? To seek that satisfaction in the works of his hands which can be found in God only? What more natural than the desire of the flesh? That is, of the pleasure of sense in every kind? Men indeed talk magnificently of despising these low pleasures, particularly men of learning and education. They affect to sit loose to the gratification of those appetites wherein they stand on a level with the beasts that perish. But it is mere affectation; for every man is conscious to himself that in this respect he is by nature a very beast. Sensual appetites, even those of the lowest kind, have, more or less, the dominion over him. They lead him captive, they drag him to and fro, in spite of his boasted reason. The man, with all his good breeding and other accomplishments, has no pre-eminence over the goat. Nay, it is much to be doubted whether the beast has not the pre-eminence over him! Certainly he has, if we may hearken to one of their modern oracles, who very decently tells us:

> Once in a season, beasts too taste of love:
> Only the beast of reason is its slave,
> And in that folly drudges all the year.

A considerable difference indeed, it must be allowed, there is between man and man, arising (beside that wrought by preventing grace) from difference of constitution and of education. But notwithstanding this, who that is not utterly ignorant of himself can here cast the first stone at another? Who can abide the test of our blessed Lord's comment on the seventh commandment: 'He that looketh upon a woman to lust after her hath committed adultery with her already in his heart'? So that one knows not which to wonder at most, the ignorance or the insolence of those men who speak with such disdain of them that are overcome by desires which every man has felt in his own breast! The desire of every pleasure of sense, innocent or not, being natural to every child of man.

10. And so is 'the desire of the eye', the desire of the pleasures of the imagination. These arise either from great, or beautiful, or uncommon objects—if the two former do

not coincide with the latter; for perhaps it would appear upon a diligent inquiry that neither *grand* nor *beautiful* objects please any longer than they are new; that when the novelty of them is over, the greatest part, at least, of the pleasure they give is over; and in the same proportion as they become familiar they become flat and insipid. But let us experience this ever so often, the same desire will remain still. The inbred thirst continues fixed in the soul. Nay, the more it is indulged, the more it increases, and incites us to follow after another and yet another object; although we leave every one with an abortive hope and a deluded expectation. Yea,

> The hoary fool, who many days
> Has struggled with continued sorrow,
> Renews his hope, and fondly lays
> The desperate bet upon tomorrow!
>
> Tomorrow comes! 'Tis noon! 'Tis night!
> This day like all the former flies:
> Yet on he goes, to seek delight
> Tomorrow, till tonight he dies!

11. A third symptom of this fatal disease, the love of the world, which is so deeply rooted in our nature, is 'the pride of life', the desire of praise, of 'the honor that cometh of men'. This the greatest admirers of human nature allow to be strictly natural—as natural as the sight or hearing, or any other of the external senses. And are they ashamed of it, even men of letters, men of refined and improved understanding? So far from it that they glory therein; they applaud themselves for their love of applause! Yea, eminent Christians, so called, make no difficulty of adopting the saying of the old, vain heathen, *Animi dissoluti est et nequam negligere quid de se homines sentiant*: 'Not to regard what men think of us is the mark of a wicked and abandoned mind.' So that to go calm and unmoved 'through honour and dishonour, through evil report and good report', is with them a sign of one that is indeed 'not fit to live; away with such a fellow from the earth.' But would one imagine that these men had ever heard of Jesus Christ or his apostles? Or that they knew who it was that said, 'How can ye believe, who receive honour one of another, and seek not that honour which cometh of God only?' But if this be really so; if it be impossible to believe, and consequently to please God, so long as we 'receive (or *seek*) honour one of another, and seek not the honour which cometh of God only'; then in what a condition are all mankind! The Christians as well as the heathens! Since they all seek 'honour one of another'! Since it is as natural for them so to do, themselves being the judges, as it is to see the light which strikes upon their eye, or to hear the sound which enters their ear; yea, since they account it the sign of a virtuous mind to seek the praise of men, and of a vicious one to be content with 'the honour which cometh of God only'!

III.1. I proceed to draw a few inferences from what has been said. And, first, from hence we may learn one grand, fundamental difference between Christianity, considered as a system of doctrines, and the most refined heathenism. Many of the ancient heathens have largely described the vices of particular men. They have spoken much against their covetousness or cruelty, their luxury or prodigality. Some have dared to say that 'no man is born without vices of one kind or another.' But still, as none of them were apprised of the fall of man, so none of them knew his total corruption. They knew not that all men were empty of all good, and filled with all manner of evil. They were wholly ignorant of the entire depravation of the whole human nature, of every man born into the world, in every faculty of his soul, not so much by those particular vices which reign in particular persons as by the general flood of atheism and idolatry, of pride, self-will, and love of the world. This, therefore, is the first, grand, distinguishing point between heathenism and Christianity. The one acknowledges that many men are infected with many vices, and even born with a proneness to them; but supposes withal that in some the natural good much overbalances the evil. The other declares that all men are 'conceived in sin', and 'shapen in wickedness'; that hence there is in every man a 'carnal mind which is enmity against God, which is not, cannot be, subject to his law', and which so infects the whole soul that 'there dwelleth in him, in his flesh', in his natural state, 'no good thing;' but 'all the imagination of the thoughts of his heart is evil', '*only* evil', and that 'continually.'

2. Hence we may, secondly, learn that all who deny this—call it 'original sin' or by any other title—are but heathens still in the fundamental point which differences heathenism from Christianity. They may indeed allow that men have many vices; that some are born with us; and that consequently we are not born altogether so wise or so virtuous as we should be; there being few that will roundly affirm we are born with as much propensity to good as to evil, and that every man is by nature as virtuous and wise as Adam was at his creation. But here is the shibboleth: Is man by nature filled with all manner of evil? Is he void of all good? Is he wholly fallen? Is his soul totally corrupted? Or, to come back to the text, is 'every imagination of the thoughts of his heart evil continually'? Allow this, and you are so far a Christian. Deny it, and you are but an heathen still.

3. We may learn from hence, in the third place, what is the proper nature of religion, of the religion of Jesus Christ. It is θεραπεία ψυχῆς, God's method of healing a soul which is *thus diseased*. Hereby the great Physician of souls applies medicine to heal *this sickness*; to restore human nature, totally corrupted in all its faculties. God heals all our atheism by the knowledge of himself, and of Jesus Christ whom he hath sent; by giving us faith, a divine evidence and conviction of God and of the things of God—in particular of this important truth: Christ loved *me*, and gave himself for *me*. By repentance and lowliness of heart the deadly disease of pride is healed; that of self-will by resignation, a meek and thankful submission to the will of God. And for the love of the world in all its branches the love of God is the sovereign remedy. Now this is properly religion, 'faith thus working by love', working the genuine, meek humility, entire deadness to the world, with a loving, thankful acquiescence in and conformity to the whole will and Word of God.

4. Indeed if man were not thus fallen there would be no need of all this. There would be no occasion for this work in the heart, this 'renewal in the spirit of our mind'. The 'superfluity of godliness' would then be a more proper expression than the 'superfluity of naughtiness'. For an outside religion without any godliness at all would suffice to all rational intents and purposes. It does accordingly suffice, in the judgment of those who deny

this corruption of our nature. They make very little more of religion than the famous Mr. Hobbes did of reason. According to him, reason is only 'a well-ordered train of words': according to them, religion is only a well-ordered train of words and actions. And they speak consistently with themselves; for if the inside be not 'full of wickedness', if this be clean already, what remains but to 'cleanse the outside of the cup'? Outward reformation, if their supposition be just, is indeed the one thing needful.

5. But ye have not so learned the oracles of God. Ye know that he who seeth what is in man gives a far different account both of nature and grace, of our fall and our recovery. Ye know that the great end of religion is to renew our hearts in the image of God, to repair that total loss of righteousness and true holiness which we sustained by the sin of our first parent. Ye know that all religion which does not answer this end, all that stops short of this, the renewal of our soul in the image of God, after the likeness of him that created it, is no other than a poor farce and a mere mockery of God, to the destruction of our own soul. O beware of all those teachers of lies who would palm this upon you for Christianity! Regard them not, though they should come unto you with 'all the deceivableness of unrighteousness', with all smoothness of language, all decency, yea, beauty and elegance of expression, all professions of earnest goodwill to you, and reverence for the Holy Scriptures. Keep to the plain, old 'faith, once delivered to the saints', and delivered by the Spirit of God to your hearts. Know your disease! Know your cure! Ye were born in sin; therefore 'ye must be born again', 'born of God'. By nature ye are wholly corrupted; by grace ye shall be wholly renewed. 'In Adam ye all died;' in the second Adam, 'in Christ, ye all are made alive.' You 'that were dead in sins hath he quickened'. He hath already given you a principle of life, even 'faith in him who loved *you*, and gave himself for *you*'! Now 'go on' 'from faith to faith', until your whole sickness be healed, and all that 'mind be in you which was also in Christ Jesus'!

3. FREE GRACE

1739

An Introductory Comment

Not long after George Whitefield encouraged Wesley to undertake field preaching, the latter casts lots to decide whether he should criticize predestination. "Preach and print" (FB, 25:640) was drawn among the four possibilities with the result that this present sermon was quickly published. Maintaining that salvation was *free for all*, meaning that all *may* be redeemed, Wesley rejected the decree of predestination as "blasphemy" (O, 3:555), for it made the Most High "more false, more cruel, more unjust" (O, 3:556) than the devil himself.

Though in much of this sermon Wesley explored the teaching of the grace of God as *free for all*, he also developed an understanding of grace as *free in all*, in other words that grace so understood does not depend on any power or merit in humanity, a theme in which he actually had much in common with Whitefield and the Calvinists. Moreover, in terms of the recipients of such grace, Wesley claimed that the free grace of God does not depend on "anything he has *done*, or anything he *is*" (O, 3:545). Such a boon of grace is a free *gift* from God and is therefore indicative of divine freedom, goodness, and mercy. Accordingly, the Methodist Conference a few years later concluded that in ascribing all good to the free grace of God, as it had done in its own teaching, we may "come to the very edge of Calvinism" (R, 10:153).

Wesley preached on the text for this sermon, Romans 8:32, only two times: once in 1738 and another in 1739, after which it dropped out of the sermon register. When Wesley lifted up the text the first time on May 9, 1738, at Great St. Helen's he was told afterward, "Sir, you must preach here no more" (WH, 18:237).

Free Grace

1. How freely does God love the world?
    A. When we were yet sinners, Christ died for us
2. The grace of God is free in all and free for all
3. It does not depend on any power or merit in human beings
4. But is it free for all, as well as in all?
    A. Some say, 'No, it is free only to those who God hath ordained'
5. This is the doctrine of predestination
    A. It holds that God elected a certain number of men to be justified
    B. God leaves everyone else to follow the imaginations of their own hearts
6. Is this all the predestination which you hold?
    A. If so, then you hold predestination in the full sense
7. You hold no decree of reprobation
8. Is not this what you mean by 'the election of grace'?
9. Call it whatever name you please, it comes to the same end
10. If this be so, then all preaching is in vain
    A. It is needless to them that are elected
11. This is a plain proof that the doctrine of predestination is not a doctrine of God
12. This doctrine destroys several branches of holiness
13. This doctrine destroys the comfort of religion
14. And as to the elect of God, what is their happiness?
15. The witness of the Spirit is obstructed by this doctrine
16. This doctrine is therefore not of God
17. The doctrine dooms many to everlasting burning
18. Predestinatioin destroys our zeal for good works
19. This doctrine overthrows revelation
20. Predestination makes revelation contradict itself
21. Contrary to predestination is the whole tenor of the New Testament
22. 'He willeth that all men should be saved'
23. This doctrine is full of blasphemy.
24. Predestination represents Jesus as a hypocrite and a deceiver
25. This doctrine also dishonours the Father; it destroys all of his attributes
26. Blasphemy is clearly contained in 'the horrible decree' of predestination
27. For this reason, 'I abhor the doctrine of predestination'
28. The enemy of God would rejoice to hear that these things were so
29. God says: 'I will set before' the sons of men 'life and death, blessings and curses'
30. Repent, and turn away from your transgressions

Sermon 110: Free Grace, 1739

Romans 8:32

To the Reader

Nothing but the strongest conviction, not only that what is here advanced is 'the truth as it is in Jesus', but also that I am indispensably obliged to declare this truth to all the world, could have induced me openly to oppose the sentiments of those whom I highly esteem for their works' sake: at whose feet may I be found in the day of the Lord Jesus!

Should any believe it his duty to reply hereto, I have only one request to make: let whatsoever you do be done in charity, in love, and in the spirit of meekness. Let your very disputing show that you have 'put on, as the elect of God, bowels of mercies, gentleness, long-suffering': that even according to this time it may be said, 'See how these Christians love one another.'

Romans 8:32

He that spared not his own Son, but delivered him up for us all, how shall he not with him also freely give us all things?

1. How freely does God love the world! While we were yet sinners, 'Christ died for the ungodly.' While we were 'dead in sin', God 'spared not his own Son, but delivered him up for us all.' And how 'freely with him' does he 'give us all things'! Verily, free grace is all in all!

2. The grace or love of God, whence cometh our salvation, is free in all, and free for all.

3. First, it is free in all to whom it is given. It does not depend on any power or merit in man; no, not in any degree, neither in whole, nor in part. It does not in any wise depend either on the good works or righteousness of the receiver; not on anything he has done, or anything he is. It does not depend on his endeavours. It does not depend on his good tempers, or good desires, or good purposes and intentions; for all these flow from the free grace of God. They are the streams only, not the fountain. They are the fruits of free grace, and not the root. They are not the cause, but the effects of it. Whatsoever good is in man, or is done by man, God is the author and doer of it. Thus is his grace free in all, that is, no way depending on any power or merit in man, but on God alone, who freely gave us his own Son, and 'with him freely giveth us all things'.

4. But is it free for all, as well as in all? To this some have answered: 'No: it is free only for those whom God hath ordained to life, and they are but a little flock. The greater part of mankind God hath ordained to death; and it is not free for them. Them God hateth; and therefore before they were born decreed they should die eternally. And this he absolutely decreed; because so was his good pleasure, because it was his sovereign will.

Accordingly, they are born for this: to be destroyed body and soul in hell. And they grow up under the irrevocable curse of God, without any possibility of redemption. For what grace God gives he gives only for this: to increase, not prevent, their damnation.'

5. This is that decree of predestination. But methinks I hear one say: 'This is not the predestination which I hold. I hold only "the election of grace". What I believe is no more than this, that God, before the foundation of the world, did elect a certain number of men to be justified, sanctified, and glorified. Now all these will be saved, and none else. For the rest of mankind God leaves to themselves: so they follow the imaginations of their own hearts, which are only evil continually, and, waxing worse and worse, are at length justly punished with everlasting destruction.'

6. Is this all the predestination which you hold? Consider; perhaps this is not all. Do not you believe 'God ordained them to this very thing'? If so, you believe the whole decree; you hold predestination in the full sense, which has been above described. But it may be you think you do not. Do not you then believe God hardens the hearts of them that perish? Do not you believe he (literally) hardened Pharaoh's heart, and that for this end he raised him up (or created him)? Why, this amounts to just the same thing. If you believe Pharaoh, or any one man upon the earth, was created for this end—to be damned—you hold all that has been said of predestination. And there is no need you should add that God seconds his decree, which is supposed unchangeable and irresistible, by hardening the hearts of those vessels of wrath whom that decree had before fitted for destruction.

7. Well, but it may be you do not believe even this. You do not hold any decree of reprobation. You do not think God decrees any man to be damned, nor hardens, irresistibly fits him for damnation. You only say, 'God eternally decreed that, all being dead in sin, he would say to some of the dry bones, "Live", and to others he would not; that consequently these should be made alive, and those abide in death—these should glorify God by their salvation, and those by their destruction.'

8. Is not this what you mean by 'the election of grace'? If it be, I would ask one or two questions. Are any who are not thus elected, saved? Or were any, from the foundation of the world? Is it possible any man should be saved unless he be thus elected? If you say 'No', you are but where you was. You are not got one hair's breadth further. You still believe that in consequence of an unchangeable, irresistible decree of God the greater part of mankind abide in death, without any possibility of redemption: inasmuch as none *can* save them but God; and he *will not* save them. You believe *he hath absolutely decreed not to save them*; and what is this but decreeing to damn them? It is, in effect, neither more nor less; it comes to the same thing. For if you are dead, and altogether unable to make yourself alive; then if God has absolutely decreed he will make others only alive, and not you, he hath absolutely decreed your everlasting death—you are absolutely consigned to damnation. So then, though you use softer words than some, you mean the selfsame thing. And God's decree concerning the election of grace, according to your own account of it, amounts to neither more nor less than what others call, 'God's decree of reprobation'.

9. Call it therefore by whatever name you please—'election', 'preterition', 'predestination', or 'reprobation'—it comes in the end to the same thing. The sense of all is plainly

this: 'By virtue of an eternal, unchangeable, irresistible decree of God, one part of mankind are infallibly saved, and the rest infallibly damned; it being impossible that any of the former should be damned, or that any of the latter should be saved.'

10. But if this be so, then is all preaching vain. It is needless to them that are elected. For they, whether with preaching or without, will infallibly be saved. Therefore the end of preaching, 'to save souls', is void with regard to them. And it is useless to them that are not elected. For they cannot possibly be saved. They, whether with preaching or without, will infallibly be damned. The end of preaching is therefore void with regard to them likewise. So that in either case, our preaching is vain, as your hearing is also vain.

11. This then is a plain proof that the doctrine of predestination is not a doctrine of God, because it makes void the ordinance of God; and God is not divided against himself. A second is that it directly tends to destroy that holiness which is the end of all the ordinances of God. I do not say, 'None who hold it are holy' (for God is of tender mercy to those who are unavoidably entangled in errors of any kind), but that the doctrine itself—that every man is either elected or not elected from eternity, and that the one must inevitably be saved, and the other inevitably damned—has a manifest tendency to destroy holiness in general, for it wholly takes away those first motives to follow after it, so frequently proposed in Scripture: the hope of future reward and fear of punishment, the hope of heaven and fear of hell. That 'these shall go away into everlasting punishment, and those into life eternal' is no motive to him to struggle for life who believes his lot is cast already: it is not reasonable for him so to do if he thinks he is unalterably adjudged either to life or death. You will say, 'But he knows not whether it is life or death.' What then? This helps not the matter. For if a sick man knows that he must unavoidably die or unavoidably recover, though he knows not which, it is not reasonable for him to take any physic at all. He might justly say (and so I have heard some speak, both in bodily sickness and in spiritual), 'If I am ordained to life, I shall live; if to death, I shall die. So I need not trouble myself about it.' So directly does this doctrine tend to shut the very gate of holiness in general, to hinder unholy men from ever approaching thereto, or striving to enter in thereat.

12. As directly does this doctrine tend to destroy several particular branches of holiness. Such are meekness and love: love, I mean, of our enemies, of the evil and unthankful. I say not that none who hold it have meekness and love (for as is the power of God, so is his mercy), but that it naturally tends to inspire or increase a sharpness or eagerness of temper which is quite contrary to the meekness of Christ—as then especially appears, when they are opposed on this head. And it as naturally inspires contempt or coldness toward those whom we suppose outcasts from God. 'Oh, (but you say) I suppose no particular man a reprobate.' You mean, you would not, if you could help it. You can't help sometimes applying your general doctrine to particular persons. The enemy of souls will apply it for you. You know how often he has done so. But you 'rejected the thought with abhorrence'. True; as soon as you could. But how did it sour and sharpen your spirit in the meantime! You well know it was not the spirit of love which you then felt towards that poor sinner, whom you supposed or suspected, whether you would or no, to have been hated of God from eternity.

13. Thirdly, this doctrine tends to destroy the comfort of religion, the happiness of Christianity. This is evident as to all those who believe themselves to be reprobated, or who only suspect or fear it. All the great and precious promises are lost to them. They afford them no ray of comfort. 'For they are not the elect of God; therefore they have neither lot nor portion in them.' This is an effectual bar to their finding any comfort or happiness, even in that religion whose 'ways' were designed to be 'ways of pleasantness, and all her paths peace'.

14. And as to you who believe yourselves the elect of God, what is your happiness? I hope, not a notion, a speculative belief, a bare opinion of any kind; but a feeling possession of God in your heart, wrought in you by the Holy Ghost; or, 'the witness of God's Spirit with your spirit, that you are a child of God'. This, otherwise termed 'the full assurance of faith', is the true ground of a Christian's happiness. And it does indeed imply a full assurance that all your past sins are forgiven, and that you are *now* a child of God. But it does not necessarily imply a full assurance of our future perseverance. I do not say, 'This is never joined to it,' but that it is not necessarily implied therein; for many have the one who have not the other.

15. Now, this witness of the Spirit experience shows to be much obstructed by this doctrine; and not only in those who, believing themselves reprobated, by this belief thrust it far from them, but even in them that have 'tasted of that good gift', who yet have soon lost it again, and fallen back into doubts, and fears, and darkness—'horrible darkness that might be felt'. And I appeal to any of you who hold this doctrine to say, between God and your own hearts, whether you have not often a return of doubts and fears concerning your election or perseverance? If you ask, 'Who has not?' I answer, 'Very few of those that hold this doctrine.' But many, very many of those that hold it not, in all parts of the earth; many of those who know and feel they are in Christ today, and 'take no thought for the morrow'; who 'abide in him' by faith from hour to hour, or rather from moment to moment. Many of these have enjoyed the uninterrupted witness of his Spirit, the continual light of his countenance, from the moment wherein they first believed, for many months or years to this day.

16. That assurance of faith which these enjoy excludes all doubt and fear. It excludes all kind of doubt and fear concerning their future perseverance; though it is not properly (as was said before) an assurance of what is future, but only of what *now* is. And this needs not for its support a speculative belief that whoever is once ordained to live, must live. For it is wrought from hour to hour by the mighty power of God, 'by the Holy Ghost which is given unto them'. And therefore that doctrine is not of God, because it tends to obstruct, if not destroy, this great work of the Holy Ghost, whence flows the chief comfort of religion, the happiness of Christianity.

17. Again, how uncomfortable a thought is this, that thousands and millions of men, without any preceding offence or fault of theirs, were unchangeably doomed to everlasting burnings! How peculiarly uncomfortable must it be to those who have put on Christ! To those who being filled with 'bowels of mercy, tenderness, and compassion', could even 'wish themselves accursed for their brethren's sake'.

18. Fourthly, this uncomfortable doctrine directly tends to destroy our zeal for good works. And this it does, first, as it naturally tends (according to what was observed before) to destroy our love to the greater part of mankind, namely, the evil and unthankful. For whatever lessens our love must so far lessen our desire to do them good. This it does, secondly, as it cuts off one of the strongest motives to all acts of bodily mercy, such as feeding the hungry, clothing the naked, and the like, viz., the hope of saving their souls from death. For what avails it to relieve their temporal wants who are just dropping into eternal fire? 'Well; but run and snatch them as brands out of the fire.' Nay, this you suppose impossible. They were appointed thereunto, you say, from eternity, before they had done either good or evil. You believe it is the will of God they should die. And 'who hath resisted his will?' But you say you 'do not know whether these are elected or not.' What then? If you know they are one or the other, that they are either elected or not elected, all your labour is void and vain. In either case your advice, reproof, or exhortation, is as needless and useless as our preaching. It is needless to them that are elected; for they will infallibly be saved without it. It is useless to them that are not elected; for with or without it they will infallibly be damned. Therefore you cannot, consistently with your principles, take any pains about their salvation. Consequently those principles directly tend to destroy your zeal for good works—for all good works, but particularly for the greatest of all, the saving of souls from death.

19. But, fifthly, this doctrine not only tends to destroy Christian holiness, happiness, and good works, but hath also a direct and manifest tendency to overthrow the whole Christian revelation. The point which the wisest of the modern unbelievers most industriously labour to prove is that the Christian revelation is not necessary. They well know, could they once show this, the conclusion would be too plain to be denied. 'If it be not necessary, it is not true.' Now this fundamental point you give up. For supposing that eternal, unchangeable decree, one part of mankind must be saved, though the Christian revelation were not in being, and the other part of mankind must be damned, notwithstanding that revelation. And what would an infidel desire more? You allow him all he asks. In making the gospel thus unnecessary to all sorts of men you give up the whole Christian cause. 'O tell it not in Gath! Publish it not in the streets of Askelon! Lest the daughters of the uncircumcised rejoice, lest the sons of unbelief triumph!'

20. And as this doctrine manifestly and directly tends to overthrow the whole Christian revelation, so it does the same thing, by plain consequence, in making that revelation contradict itself. For it is grounded on such an interpretation of some texts (more or fewer it matters not) as flatly contradicts all the other texts, and indeed the whole scope and tenor of Scripture. For instance: the asserters of this doctrine interpret that text of Scripture, 'Jacob have I loved, but Esau have I hated,' as implying that God in a literal sense hated Esau and all the reprobated from eternity. Now what can possibly be a more flat contradiction than this, not only to the whole scope and tenor of Scripture, but also to all those particular texts which expressly declare, 'God is love'? Again, they infer from that text, 'I will have mercy on whom I will have mercy' (Rom. 9:15), that God is love only to some men, viz., the elect, and that he hath mercy for those only: flatly contrary to which is the whole tenor of Scripture, as is that express declaration in particular, 'The Lord is

loving unto *every* man, and his mercy is over *all* his works' (Ps. 145:9). Again, they infer from that and the like texts, 'It is not of him that willeth, neither of him that runneth, but of God that showeth mercy,' that he showeth mercy only to those to whom he had respect from all eternity. 'Nay, but who replieth against God' now? You now contradict the whole oracles of God, which declare throughout, 'God is no respecter of persons' (Acts 10:34); 'There is no respect of persons with him' (Rom. 2:11). Again, from that text, 'The children being not yet born, neither having done good or evil, that the purpose of God according to election might stand, not of works, but of him that calleth, it was said unto her (unto Rebecca), The elder shall serve the younger'—you infer that our being predestinated or elect no way depends on the foreknowledge of God. Flatly contrary to this are all the Scriptures; and those in particular, 'elect according to the foreknowledge of God' (1 Pet. 1:2), [and] 'Whom he did foreknow, he also did predestinate' (Rom. 8:29).

21. And, 'The same Lord over all is rich in mercy to all that call upon him' (Rom. 10:12). But you say, 'No: he is such only to those for whom Christ died. And those are not all, but only a few, "whom God hath chosen out of the world"; for he died not for all, but only for those who were "chosen in him before the foundation of the world"' (Eph. 1:4). Flatly contrary to your interpretation of these Scriptures also is the whole tenor of the New Testament; as are in particular those texts: 'Destroy not him with thy meat for whom Christ died' (Rom. 14:15)—a clear proof that Christ died, not only for those that are saved, but also for them that perish; He is 'the Saviour of the world' (John 4:42); He is 'the Lamb of God, that taketh away the sins of the world' (John 1:29); 'He is the propitiation, not for our sins only, but also for the sins of the whole world' (1 John 2:2); 'He (the living God) is the Saviour of all men' (1 Tim. 4:10); 'He gave himself a ransom for all' (1 Tim. 2:6); 'He tasted death for every man' (Heb. 2:9).

22. If you ask, 'Why then are not all men saved?' the whole law and the testimony answer: first, not because of any decree of God, not because it is his pleasure they should die. For, 'as I live, saith the Lord God, I have no pleasure in the death of him that dieth' (Ezek. 18:32). Whatever be the cause of their perishing it cannot be his will, if the oracles of God are true; for they declare, 'He is not willing that any should perish, but that all should come to repentance' (2 Pet. 3:9). He 'willeth that all men should be saved'. And they, secondly, declare what is the cause why all men are not saved: namely, that they will not be saved. So our Lord expressly: 'They will not come unto me that they may have life' (John 5:40); 'The power of the Lord is present to heal them,' but they will not be healed. They 'reject the counsel', the merciful counsel 'of God against themselves', as did their stiff-necked forefathers. And therefore are they without excuse, because God would save them, but they will not be saved. This is the condemnation, 'How often would I have gathered you together, and ye would not' (Matt. 23:37).

23. Thus manifestly does this doctrine tend to overthrow the whole Christian revelation, by making it contradict itself; by giving such an interpretation of some texts as flatly contradicts all the other texts, and indeed the whole scope and tenor of Scripture—an abundant proof that it is not of God. But neither is this all. For, seventhly, it is a doctrine full of blasphemy; of such blasphemy as I should dread to mention but that the honour of our gracious God and the cause of his truth will not suffer me to be silent. In the cause

of God, then, and from a sincere concern for the glory of his great name, I will mention a few of the horrible blasphemies contained in this horrible doctrine. But first, I must warn every one of you that hears, as ye will answer it at the great day, not to charge me (as some have done) with blaspheming because I mention the blasphemy of others. And the more you are grieved with them that do thus blaspheme, see that ye 'confirm your love towards them' the more, and that your heart's desire and continual prayer to God be, 'Father, forgive them; for they know not what they do.'

24. This premised, let it be observed that this doctrine represents our Blessed Lord—'Jesus Christ the righteous', 'the only-begotten Son of the Father, full of grace and truth'—as an hypocrite, a deceiver of the people, a man void of common sincerity. For it cannot be denied that he everywhere speaks *as if he was* willing that all men should be saved. Therefore, to say *he was not* willing that all men should be saved is to represent him as a mere hypocrite and dissembler. It can't be denied that the gracious words which came out of his mouth are full of invitations to all sinners. To say, then, he did not *intend* to save all sinners is to represent him as a gross deceiver of the people. You cannot deny that he says, 'Come unto me, all ye that are weary and heavy laden.' If then you say he calls those that cannot come, those whom he knows to be unable to come, those whom he can make able to come but will not, how is it possible to describe greater insincerity? You represent him as mocking his helpless creatures by offering what he never intends to give. You describe him as saying one thing and meaning another; as pretending the love which he had not. Him 'in whose mouth was no guile' you make full of deceit, void of common sincerity. Then especially, when, drawing nigh the city, 'he wept over it', and said, 'O Jerusalem, Jerusalem, thou that killest the prophets, and stonest them that are sent unto thee, how often *would* I have gathered thy children together . . . and *ye would not*:' (ἠθέλησα . . . καὶ οὐκ ἠθελήσατε). Now if you say, 'They would', but 'he would not,' you represent him (which who could hear?) as weeping crocodile's tears, weeping over the prey which himself had doomed to destruction.

25. Such blasphemy this, as one would think might make the ears of a Christian tingle. But there is yet more behind; for just as it honours the Son, so doth this doctrine honour the Father. It destroys all his attributes at once. It overturns both his justice, mercy, and truth. Yea, it represents the most Holy God as worse than the devil; as both more false, more cruel, and more unjust. More false; because the devil, liar as he is, hath never said he 'willeth all men to be saved'. More unjust; because the devil cannot, if he would, be guilty of such injustice as you ascribe to God when you say that God condemned millions of souls to everlasting fire prepared for the devil and his angels for continuing in sin, which for want of that grace *he will not* give them, they cannot avoid. And more cruel; because that unhappy spirit 'seeketh rest and findeth none'; so that his own restless misery is a kind of temptation to him to tempt others. But God 'resteth in his high and holy place'; so that to suppose him of his own mere motion, of his pure will and pleasure, happy as he is, to doom his creatures, whether they will or no, to endless misery, is to impute such cruelty to him as we cannot impute even to the great enemy of God and man. It is to represent the most high God (he that hath ears to hear, let him hear!) as more cruel, false, and unjust than the devil.

26. This is the blasphemy clearly contained in 'the horrible decree' of predestination. And here I fix my foot. On this I join issue with every asserter of it. You represent God as worse than the devil—more false, more cruel, more unjust. But you say you will 'prove it by Scripture'. Hold! What will you prove by Scripture? That God is worse than the devil? It cannot be. Whatever that Scripture proves, it never can prove this. Whatever its true meaning be, this cannot be its true meaning. Do you ask, 'What is its true meaning, then?' If I say, 'I know not,' you have gained nothing. For there are many Scriptures the true sense whereof neither you nor I shall know till death is swallowed up in victory. But this I know, better it were to say it had no sense at all than to say it had such a sense as this. It cannot mean, whatever it mean besides, that the God of truth is a liar. Let it mean what it will, it cannot mean that the Judge of all the world is unjust. No Scripture can mean that God is not love, or that his mercy is not over all his works. That is, whatever it prove beside, no Scripture can prove predestination.

27. This is the blasphemy for which (however I love the persons who assert it) I abhor the doctrine of predestination: a doctrine upon the supposition of which, if one could possibly suppose it for a moment (call it election, reprobation, or what you please, for all comes to the same thing) one might say to our adversary the devil: 'Thou fool, why dost thou roar about any longer? Thy lying in wait for souls is as needless and useless as our preaching. Hearest thou not that God hath taken thy work out of thy hands? And that he doth it much more effectually? Thou, with all thy principalities and powers, canst only so assault that we may resist thee; but he can irresistibly destroy both body and soul in hell! Thou canst only entice; but his unchangeable decree to leave thousands of souls in death compels them to continue in sin till they drop into everlasting burnings. Thou temptest; he forceth us to be damned; for we cannot resist his will. Thou fool, why goest thou about any longer seeking whom thou mayest devour? Hearest thou not that God is the devouring lion, the destroyer of souls, the murderer of men? Moloch caused only children to pass through the fire; and that fire was soon quenched; or, the corruptible body being consumed, its torment was at an end. But God, thou art told, by his eternal decree, fixed before they had done good or evil, causes not only "children of a span long" but the parents also to pass through the fire of hell—that "fire which never shall be quenched"; and the body which is cast thereinto, being now incorruptible and immortal, will be ever consuming, and never consumed, but "the smoke of their torment", because it is God's good pleasure, "ascendeth up for ever and ever".'

28. O how would the enemy of God and man rejoice to hear these things were so! How would he cry aloud and spare not! How would he lift up his voice and say: 'To your tents, O Israel! Flee from the face of this God, or ye shall utterly perish. But whither will ye flee? Into heaven? He is there. Down to hell? He is there also. Ye cannot flee from an omnipresent, almighty tyrant. And whether ye flee or stay, I call heaven his throne, and earth his footstool to witness against you, ye shall perish, ye shall die eternally. Sing, O hell, and rejoice ye that are under the earth! For God, even the mighty God, hath spoken, and devoted to death thousands of souls, from the rising up of the sun unto the going down thereof. Here, O death, is thy sting! They shall not, cannot escape; for the mouth of the Lord hath spoken it. Here, O grave, is thy victory! Nations yet unborn, or ever they

have done good or evil, are doomed never to see the light of life, but thou shalt gnaw upon them for ever and ever. Let all those morning stars sing together who fell with Lucifer, son of the morning. Let all the sons of hell shout for joy! For the decree is past, and who shall disannul it?'

29. Yea, the decree is past. And so it was before the foundation of the world. But what decree? Even this: '"I will set before" the sons of men "life and death, blessing and cursing"; and the soul that chooseth life shall live, as the soul that chooseth death shall die.' This decree, whereby 'whom God did foreknow, he did predestinate,' was indeed from everlasting. This, whereby all who suffer Christ to make them alive are 'elect, according to the foreknowledge of God', now 'standeth fast, even as the moon, and as the faithful witness in heaven'. And when heaven and earth shall pass away, yet this shall not pass away; for it is as unchangeable and eternal as is the being of God that gave it. This decree yields the strongest encouragement to abound in all good works, and in all holiness; and it is a well-spring of joy, of happiness also, to our great and endless comfort. This is worthy of God. It is every way consistent with all the perfections of his nature. It gives us the noblest view both of his justice, mercy, and truth. To this agrees the whole scope of the Christian revelation, as well as all the parts thereof. To this Moses and all the prophets bear witness, and our blessed Lord and all his apostles. Thus Moses, in the name of his Lord: 'I call heaven and earth to record against you this day, that I have set before you life and death, blessing and cursing; therefore choose life, that thou and thy seed may live.' Thus Ezekiel (to cite one prophet for all): 'The soul that sinneth, it shall die. The son shall not bear (eternally) the iniquity of the father. The righteousness of the righteous shall be upon him, and the wickedness of the wicked shall be upon him' (Ezek. 18:20). Thus our blessed Lord: 'If any man thirst, let him come to me and drink' (John 7:37). Thus his great Apostle, St. Paul: 'God commandeth all men everywhere to repent' (Acts. 17:30). 'All men, everywhere'—every man in every place, without any exception, either of place or person. Thus St. James: 'If any of you lack wisdom, let him ask of God, who giveth to all men liberally and upbraideth not, and it shall be given him' (Jas. 1:5). Thus St. Peter: 'The Lord is . . . not willing that any should perish, but that all should come to repentance' (2 Pet. 3:9). And thus St. John: 'If any man sin, we have an advocate with the Father, . . . and he is the propitiation for our sins; and not for ours only, but for the sins of the whole world' (1 John 2:1-2).

30. O hear ye this, ye that forget God! Ye cannot charge your death upon him. 'Have I any pleasure at all that the wicked should die, saith the Lord God? Repent, and turn from all your transgressions; so iniquity shall not be your ruin. Cast away from you all your transgressions, whereby ye have transgressed; . . . for why will ye die, O house of Israel? For I have no pleasure in the death of him that dieth, saith the Lord God. Wherefore turn yourselves, and live ye' (Ezek. 18:23, etc). 'As I live, saith the Lord God, I have no pleasure in the death of the wicked, . . . Turn ye, turn ye from your evil ways; for why will ye die, O house of Israel?' (Ezek. 33:11).

4. 'AWAKE, THOU THAT SLEEPEST'

April 4, 1742

An Introductory Comment

Fulfilling an appointment at St. Mary's, Oxford, on April 4, 1742, Charles Wesley preached there "for the first and last time" (O, 1:112) given both the content and the delivery of his sermon. Emboldened by his evangelical conversion that had occurred much earlier on May 19, 1738, and having identified with the Great Evangelical Revival that was by now a transatlantic phenomenon, in part through the good graces of George Whitefield, Charles Wesley issued a clarion call for renewal to a people he so obviously judged to be a sleepy, self-satisfied congregation. At two o'clock in the afternoon on that day, John gathered a few people together to pray for the success of his brother's efforts (WH, 19:258).

Like his brother John (and Matthew Henry who had preceded them), Charles Wesley lifted up the characteristics of "stupor" or "stupidity" to explore the spiritual state of such sleepers, but then he specifically linked these attributes to what John was to describe later as the "natural state" in his sermon "The Spirit of Bondage and of Adoption," produced in 1746. With this linkage in place, Charles no doubt sallied forth trenchantly on the misgivings of "a sinner satisfied in his sins" (O, 1:143), the delusion of maintaining "a form of godliness, [but denying] the power thereof" (O, 1:144), and the futility of being satisfied with anything less than being restored in "the image of God" (O, 1:143). And when John preached on this same text, he observed: think not that "Because you do not commit gross sin, because you give alms, and go to the church and sacrament, . . . that you are serving God" (C, 11:64). Thus, the way forward out of this spiritual malaise as Charles understood it was nothing less than to "receive the Holy Spirit" and to embrace "This experimental knowledge . . . [which] is true Christianity" (O, 1:154).

'Awake, Thou That Sleepest'

I 1. Sleep is signified as the natural state of man
2. The state of nature is a state of darkness
3. Full of diseases, people believe they are in perfect health
4. The one who sleeps is a sinner satisfied in his sins
5. People who lack outward vices are usually most asleep
6. They have the form of godliness but deny the power
7. However highly esteemed they are, they are abominations
8. They abide in death, though they know it not
9. Before dead souls can live, they must know that they are dead
10. Those dead in sin do not have senses to discern good and evil
11. They ignore or even deny spiritual things

II. 1. God calls: 'Awake, thou that sleepest, and arise from the dead'
2. Never rest till you believe in Jesus, by the Spirit
3. I have a message from God: 'flee from the wrath to come'
4. May the angel of the Lord cause light to shine
5. Eternal happiness depends on this moment
6. Have you 'put off the old man and put on the new'?
7. Are you a Christian?
8. You cannot know that Christ is in you unless you are reprobate
9. If this offends, you are not a Christian
10. Have you received the Holy Ghost?
11. Do you see the need for inward change, spiritual birth, and holiness?
12. What reason do you give for the hope that is in you?

III. 1. Lastly, Christ will reveal himself to those who seek him
2. God will give himself to every awakened sinner that waits upon him
3. We are called to be 'an habitation of God through his Spirit'
4. The Spirit of Christ is that great gift promised to human beings
5. You may all be witnesses of the gift of the Holy Ghost
6. This experimental knowledge, and this alone, is true Christianity
7. The world cannot receive him, but utterly rejects the promise
8. Some say they deny only the *inspiration* and the *receiving* of the Holy Spirit
9. To deny these is to renounce the whole of Christian revelation
10. The 'wisdom of God' is foolishness to human beings
11. Among those who have kept themselves pure, how much sin is found
12. If the salt has lost its savor, it is good for nothing

13. Perhaps we are resisting the last effort of grace to save us
14. O God, 'in the midst of wrath remember mercy'
15. It is time for us to awake before the trumpet is blown

Sermon 3*:* 'Awake, Thou That Sleepest'

A Sermon preached on Sunday, April 4, 1742,

before the University of Oxford.

By Charles Wesley, M.A., Student of Christ Church.

Ephesians 5:14

Awake, thou that sleepest, and arise from the dead, and Christ shall give thee light.

In discoursing on these words I shall, with the help of God,

First, describe the sleepers to whom they are spoken;

Secondly, enforce the exhortation, 'Awake thou that sleepest, and arise from the dead'; and,

Thirdly, explain the promise made to such as do awake and arise—'Christ shall give thee light.'

I.1. And first, as to the sleepers here spoken to. By sleep is signified the natural state of man: that deep sleep of the soul into which the sin of Adam hath cast all who spring from his loins; that supineness, indolence, and stupidity, that insensibility of his real condition, wherein every man comes into the world, and continues till the voice of God awakes him.

2. Now 'they that sleep, sleep in the night.' The state of nature is a state of utter darkness, a state wherein 'darkness covers the earth, and gross darkness the people.' The poor unawakened sinner, how much knowledge soever he may have as to other things, has no knowledge of himself. In this respect 'he knoweth nothing yet as he ought to know.' He knows not that he is a fallen spirit, whose only business in the present world is to recover from his fall, to regain that image of God wherein he was created. He sees *no necessity* for 'the one thing needful', even that inward universal change, that 'birth from above' (figured out by baptism) which is the beginning of that total renovation, that sanctification of spirit, soul, and body, 'without which no man shall see the Lord'.

3. Full of all diseases as he is, he fancies himself in perfect health. Fast bound in misery and iron, he dreams that he is happy and at liberty. He says, 'Peace, peace,' while the devil as 'a strong man armed' is in full possession of his soul. He sleeps on still, and takes his rest, though hell is moved from beneath to meet him; though the pit, from whence there is no return, hath opened its mouth to swallow him up. A fire is kindled around him, yet he knoweth it not; yea, it burns him, yet he lays it not to heart.

4. By one who sleeps we are therefore to understand (and would to God we might all understand it!) a sinner satisfied in his sins, contented to remain in his fallen state, to live and die without the image of God; one who is ignorant both of his disease and of the only remedy for it; one who never was warned, or never regarded the warning voice of God 'to

flee from the wrath to come'; one that never yet saw he was in danger of hell-fire, or cried out in the earnestness of his soul, 'What must I do to be saved?'

5. If this sleeper be not outwardly vicious, his sleep is usually the deepest of all: whether he be of the Laodicean spirit, 'neither cold nor hot', but a quiet, rational, inoffensive, good-natured professor of the religion of his fathers; or whether he be zealous and orthodox, and 'after the most straitest sect of our religion lives a Pharisee'; that is, according to the scriptural account, one that *justifies himself*, one that labours 'to establish his own righteousness' as the ground of his acceptance with God.

6. This is he who 'having a form of godliness, denies the power thereof'; yea, and probably reviles it, wheresoever it is found, as mere extravagance and delusion. Meanwhile the wretched self-deceiver thanks God that he 'is not as other men are, adulterers, unjust, extortioners'. No, he doth no wrong to any man. He 'fasts twice in the week', uses all the means of grace, is constant at church and sacrament; yea, and 'gives tithes of all that he has', does all the good that he can. 'Touching the righteousness of the law', he is 'blameless': he wants nothing of godliness but the power; nothing of religion but the spirit; nothing of Christianity but the truth and the life.

7. But know ye not that however highly esteemed among men such a Christian as this may be, he is an abomination in the sight of God, and an heir of every woe which the Son of God yesterday, today, and for ever denounces against 'scribes and Pharisees, hypocrites'? He hath 'made clean the outside of the cup and the platter', but within is full of all filthiness. 'An evil disease cleaveth' still 'unto him,' so that 'his inward parts are very wickedness'. Our Lord fitly compares him to a 'painted sepulchre', which 'appears beautiful without', but nevertheless is 'full of dead men's bones and of all uncleanness'. The bones indeed are no longer dry; 'the sinews and flesh are come up upon them, and the skin covers them above: but there is no breath in them,' no Spirit of the living God. And 'if any man have not the Spirit of Christ, he is none of his.' 'Ye are Christ's', 'if so be that the Spirit of God dwell in you.' But if not, God knoweth that ye abide in death, even until now.

8. This is another character of the sleeper here spoken to. He abides in death, though he knows it not. He is dead unto God, 'dead in trespasses and sins'. 'For to be carnally minded is death.' Even as it is written, 'By one man sin entered into the world, and death by sin; and so death passed upon all men'—not only temporal death, but likewise spiritual and eternal. 'In the day thou eatest (said God to Adam) thou shalt surely die.' Not bodily (unless as he then became mortal) but spiritually: thou shalt lose the life of thy soul; thou shalt die to God, shalt be separated from him, thy essential life and happiness.

9. Thus first was dissolved the vital union of our soul with God, insomuch that 'in the midst of' natural 'life we are' now 'in' spiritual 'death'. And herein we remain till the Second Adam becomes a quickening spirit to us, till he raises the dead, the dead in sin, in pleasure, riches, or honours. But before any dead soul can live, he 'hears (hearkens to) the voice of the Son of God': he is made sensible of his lost estate, and receives the sentence of death in himself. He knows himself to be 'dead while he liveth', dead to God and all the things of God; having no more power to perform the actions of a living Christian than a dead body to perform the functions of a living man.

10. And most certain it is that one dead in sin has not 'senses exercised to discern' spiritual 'good and evil'. 'Having eyes, he sees not; he hath ears, and hears not.' He doth not 'taste and see that the Lord is gracious'. He 'hath not seen God at any time', nor 'heard his voice', nor 'handled the Word of life'. In vain is the name of Jesus 'like ointment poured forth', and 'all his garments smell of myrrh, aloes, and cassia'. The soul that sleepeth in death hath no perception of any objects of this kind. His heart is 'past feeling', and understandeth none of these things.

11. And hence, having no spiritual senses, no inlets of spiritual knowledge, the natural man receiveth not the things of the Spirit of God; nay, he is so far from receiving them that whatsoever is spiritually discerned is mere foolishness unto him. He is not content with being utterly ignorant of spiritual things, but he denies the very existence of them. And spiritual sensation itself is to him the foolishness of folly. 'How', saith he, 'can these things be?' How can any man *know* that he is alive to God? Even as you know that your body is now alive. Faith is the life of the soul: and if ye have this life abiding in you, ye want no marks to evidence it *to yourself*, but that ἔλεγχος Πνεύματος, that divine consciousness, that 'witness of God', which is more and greater than ten thousand human witnesses.

12. If he doth not now bear witness with thy spirit that thou art a child of God, O that he might convince thee, thou poor unawakened sinner, by his demonstration and power, that thou art a child of the devil! O that as I prophesy there might now be 'a noise and a shaking', and may 'the bones come together, bone to his bone'. Then 'come from the four winds, O breath, and breathe on these slain that they may live!' And do not ye harden your hearts and resist the Holy Ghost, who even now is come to 'convince you of sin', 'because you believe not on the name of the only-begotten Son of God'.

II.1. Wherefore, 'Awake, thou that sleepest, and arise from the dead.' God calleth thee now by my mouth; and bids thee know thyself, thou fallen spirit, thy true state and only concern below: 'What meanest thou, O sleeper? Arise! Call upon thy God, if so be thy God will think upon thee, that thou perish not.' A mighty tempest is stirred up round about thee, and thou art sinking into the depths of perdition, the gulf of God's judgments. If thou wouldst escape them, cast thyself into them. 'Judge thyself', and thou shalt 'not be judged of the Lord.'

2. Awake, awake! Stand up this moment, lest thou 'drink at the Lord's hand the cup of his fury'. Stir up thyself 'to lay hold on the Lord', 'the Lord thy righteousness, mighty to save!' 'Shake thyself from the dust.' At least, let the earthquake of God's threatenings shake thee. Awake and cry out with the trembling gaoler, 'What must I do to be saved?' And never rest till thou believest on the Lord Jesus, with a faith which is his gift, by the operation of his Spirit.

3. If I speak to any one of you more than to another it is to thee who thinkest thyself unconcerned in this exhortation. 'I have a message from God unto thee.' In his name I 'warn *thee* to flee from the wrath to come'. Thou unholy soul, see thy picture in condemned Peter, lying in the dark dungeon between the soldiers, bound with two chains,

the keepers before the door keeping the prison. The night is far spent, the morning is at hand when thou art to be brought forth to execution. And in these dreadful circumstances thou art fast asleep; thou art fast asleep in the devil's arms, on the brink of the pit, in the jaws of everlasting destruction.

4. O may 'the angel of the Lord come upon thee, and the light shine into thy prison'! And mayst thou feel the stroke of an almighty hand raising thee with, 'Arise up quickly, gird thyself, and bind on thy sandals, cast thy garment about thee, and follow me.'

5. Awake, thou everlasting spirit, out of thy dream of worldly happiness. Did not God create thee for himself? Then thou canst not rest till thou restest in him. Return, thou wanderer. Fly back to thy ark. 'This is not thy home.' Think not of building tabernacles here. Thou art but 'a stranger, a sojourner upon earth'; a creature of a day, but just launching out into an unchangeable state. Make haste; eternity is at hand. Eternity depends on this moment: an eternity of happiness, or an eternity of misery!

6. In what state is thy soul? Was God, while I am yet speaking, to require it of thee, art thou ready to meet death and judgment? Canst thou stand in his sight, 'who is of purer eyes than to behold iniquity'? Art thou 'meet to be partaker of the inheritance of the saints in light'? Hast thou 'fought a good fight and kept the faith'? Hast thou secured 'the one thing needful'? Hast thou recovered the image of God, even 'righteousness and true holiness'? Hast thou 'put off the old man and put on the new'? Art thou 'clothed upon with Christ'?

7. Hast thou oil in thy lamp? Grace in thy heart? Dost thou 'love the Lord thy God with all thy heart, and with all thy mind, and with all thy soul, and with all thy strength'? Is 'that mind in thee which was also in Christ Jesus'? Art thou a Christian indeed? That is, a new creature? Are 'old things passed away, and all things become new'?

8. Art thou 'partaker of the divine nature'? 'Knowest thou not that Christ is in thee, except thou be reprobate?' Knowest thou that 'God dwelleth in thee, and thou in God, by his Spirit which he hath given thee'? Knowest thou not that 'thy body is a temple of the Holy Ghost, which thou hast of God'? Hast thou 'the witness in thyself', 'the earnest of thine inheritance'? Art thou 'sealed by that Spirit of promise unto the day of redemption'? 'Hast thou received the Holy Ghost?' Or dost thou start at the question, not knowing whether there be any Holy Ghost?

9. If it offends thee, be thou assured that thou neither art a Christian nor desirest to be one. Nay, thy 'very prayer is turned into sin'; and thou hast solemnly mocked God this very day by praying for 'the inspiration of his Holy Spirit', when thou didst not believe there was any such thing to be received.

10. Yet on the authority of God's Word and our own Church I must repeat the question, 'Hast thou received the Holy Ghost?' If thou hast not thou art not yet a Christian; for a Christian is a man that is 'anointed with the Holy Ghost and with power'. Thou art not yet made a partaker of pure religion and undefiled. Dost thou know what religion is? That it is a participation of the divine nature, the life of God in the soul of man: 'Christ formed in the heart', 'Christ in thee, the hope of glory'; happiness and holiness; heaven begun upon earth; 'a kingdom of God within thee', 'not meat and drink', no outward

thing, 'but righteousness, and peace, and joy in the Holy Ghost'; an everlasting kingdom brought into thy soul, a 'peace of God that passeth all understanding'; a 'joy unspeakable and full of glory'?

11. Knowest thou that 'in Jesus Christ neither circumcision availeth anything, nor uncircumcision; but faith that worketh by love;' but a new creation? Seest thou the necessity of that inward change, that spiritual birth, that life from the dead, that holiness? And art thou thoroughly convinced that 'without it no man shall see the Lord'? Art thou labouring after it? 'Giving all diligence to make thy calling and election sure'? 'Working out thy salvation with fear and trembling'? 'Agonizing to enter in at the strait gate'? Art thou *in earnest* about thy soul? And canst thou tell the Searcher of hearts, 'Thou, O God, art the thing that I long for!' 'Lord, thou knowest all things! Thou knowest that I *would* love thee!'

12. Thou hopest to be saved. But what reason hast thou to give of the hope that is in thee? Is it because thou hast done no harm? Or because thou hast done much good? Or because thou art not like other men, but wise, or learned, or honest, and morally good? Esteemed of men, and of a fair reputation? Alas, all this will never bring thee to God. It is in his account lighter than vanity. Dost thou 'know Jesus Christ whom he hath sent'? Hath he taught thee that 'by grace we are saved through faith? And that not of ourselves: it is the gift of God; not of works, lest any man should boast'? Hast thou received the faithful saying as the whole foundation of thy hope, that 'Jesus Christ came into the world to save sinners'? Hast thou learned what that meaneth, 'I came not to call the righteous, but sinners to repentance'? 'I am not sent but to the lost sheep'? Art thou (he that heareth, let him understand!) lost, dead, *damned already*? Dost thou know thy deserts? Dost thou feel thy wants? Art thou 'poor in spirit'? Mourning for God and refusing to be comforted? Is the prodigal 'come to himself', and well content to be therefore thought 'beside himself' by those who are still feeding upon the husks which he hath left? Art thou willing to 'live godly in Christ Jesus'? And dost thou therefore 'suffer persecution'? Do 'men say all manner of evil against thee falsely, for the Son of man's sake'?

13. O that in all these questions ye may hear the voice that wakes the dead, and feel that hammer of the Word which 'breaketh the rock in pieces'! 'If ye will hear his voice today, while it is called today, harden not your hearts.' Now 'awake, thou that sleepest' in spiritual death, that thou sleep not in death eternal! Feel thy lost estate, and 'arise from the dead.' Leave thine old companions in sin and death. Follow thou Jesus, and 'let the dead bury their dead.' 'Save thyself from this untoward generation.' 'Come out from among them, and be thou separate, and touch not the unclean thing; and the Lord shall receive thee.' 'Christ shall give thee light.'

III.1. This promise I come, lastly, to explain. And how encouraging a consideration is this, that whosoever thou art who obeyest his call, thou canst not seek his face in vain. If thou even now 'awakest and arisest from the dead', he hath bound himself to 'give thee light'. 'The Lord shall give thee grace and glory'; the light of his grace here, and the light of his glory when thou receivest the 'crown that fadeth not away.' 'Thy light shall break forth as the morning,' and thy darkness be as the noonday. 'God, who commanded the light to shine out of darkness', shall 'shine in thy heart, to give the knowledge of the glory of God in the face of Jesus Christ.' 'On them that fear the Lord shall the Sun of righteousness arise with healing in his wings.' And 'in that day it shall be said unto thee', 'Arise, shine; for thy light is come, and the glory of the Lord is risen upon thee.' For Christ shall reveal himself in thee. And he is 'the true light'.

2. God is light, and will give himself to every awakened sinner that waiteth for him. And thou shalt then be a temple of the living God, and Christ shall 'dwell in thy heart by faith'. And, 'being rooted and grounded in love', thou shalt 'be able to comprehend with all saints what is the breadth, and length, and depth, and height' of that 'love of Christ which passeth knowledge, that thou mayest be filled with all the fullness of God.'

3. Ye see your calling, brethren. We are called to be 'an habitation of God through his Spirit'; and through his Spirit dwelling in us 'to be saints' here, 'and partakers of the inheritance of the saints in light'. So 'exceeding great are the promises which are given unto us', actually given unto us who believe. For by faith 'we receive, not the spirit of the world, but the Spirit which is of God'—the sum of all the promises—'that we may know the things that are freely given to us of God.'

4. The Spirit of Christ is that great gift of God which at sundry times and in divers manners he hath promised to man, and hath fully bestowed since the time that Christ was glorified. Those promises before made to the fathers he hath thus fulfilled: 'I will put my Spirit within you, and cause you to walk in my statutes' (Ezek. 36:27). 'I will pour water upon him that is thirsty, and floods upon the dry ground: I will pour my Spirit upon thy seed, and my blessing upon thine offspring' (Isa. 44:3).

5. Ye may all be living witnesses of these things, of remission of sins, and the gift of the Holy Ghost. 'If thou canst believe, all things are possible to him that believeth.' 'Who among you is there that feareth the Lord', and yet 'walketh on in darkness, and hath no light?' I ask thee in the name of Jesus, believest thou that 'his arm is not shortened at all'? That he is still 'mighty to save'? That he is 'the same yesterday, today, and for ever'? That 'he hath *now* power on earth to forgive sins'? 'Son, be of good cheer; thy sins are forgiven.' God, for Christ's sake, hath forgiven thee. Receive this, 'not as the word of man; but as it is, indeed, the word of God'; and thou art 'justified freely through faith'. Thou shalt be sanctified also through faith which is in Jesus, and shalt set to thy seal, even thine, 'that God hath given unto us eternal life, and this life is in his Son'.

6. Men and brethren, let me freely speak unto you, and 'suffer ye the word of exhortation', even from one the least esteemed in the church. Your conscience beareth you witness in the Holy Ghost that these things are so, 'if so be ye have tasted that the Lord is gracious'. 'This is eternal life, to know the only true God, and Jesus Christ whom he hath sent.' This experimental knowledge, and this alone, is true Christianity. He is a Christian who hath received the Spirit of Christ. He is not a Christian who hath not received him. Neither is it possible to have received him and not know it. For 'at that day' (when he cometh, saith the Lord) 'ye shall know that I am in my Father, and you in me, and I in you' (John 14:20). This is that 'Spirit of truth, whom the world cannot receive, because it seeth him not, neither knoweth him. But ye know him; for he dwelleth with you, and shall be in you.'

7. The world cannot receive him, but utterly rejecteth the promise of the Father, contradicting and blaspheming. But every spirit which confesseth not this is not of God. Yea, 'this is that spirit of antichrist, whereof ye have heard that it should come into the world; and even now it is in the world.' He is antichrist whosoever denies the inspiration of the Holy Ghost, or that the indwelling Spirit of God is the common privilege of all believers, the blessing of the gospel, the unspeakable gift, the universal promise, the criterion of a real Christian.

8. It nothing helps them to say, 'We do not deny the *assistance* of God's Spirit, but only this *inspiration*, this "receiving the Holy Ghost" and being *sensible* of it. It is only this *feeling* of the Spirit, this being *moved* by the Spirit, or *filled* with it, which we deny to have any place in sound religion.' But in 'only' denying this you deny the whole Scriptures, the whole truth and promise and testimony of God.

9. Our own excellent Church knows nothing of this devilish distinction; but speaks plainly of 'feeling the Spirit of Christ' (Article 17); of being 'moved by the Holy Ghost' (Office of consecrating Priests [i.e., deacons]), and knowing and 'feeling there is no other name than that of Jesus whereby we can receive any salvation' (Visitation of the Sick). She teaches us also to pray for the 'inspiration of the Holy Spirit' (Collect before the Holy Communion), yea, that we may be 'filled with the Holy Ghost' (Order of Confirmation). Nay, and every presbyter of hers professes to 'receive the Holy Ghost by the imposition of hands'. Therefore to deny any of these is in effect to renounce the Church of England, as well as the whole Christian revelation.

10. But 'the wisdom of God' was always 'foolishness with men'. No marvel, then, that the great mystery of the gospel should be now also 'hid from the wise and prudent', as well as in the days of old; that it should be almost universally denied, ridiculed, and exploded as mere frenzy, and all who dare avow it still branded with the names of madmen and enthusiasts. This is that 'falling away' which was to come—that general apostasy of all orders and degrees of men which we even now find to have overspread the earth. 'Run to and fro in the streets of Jerusalem, and see if you can find a man,' a man that loveth the Lord his God with all his heart, and serveth him with all his strength. How does our own land mourn (that we look no farther) under the overflowings of ungodliness! What villainies of every kind are committed day by day; yea, too often with impunity by those who sin with a high hand, and glory in their shame! Who can reckon up the oaths, curses, profaneness, blasphemies; the lying, slandering, evil speaking; the sabbath-breaking, gluttony, drunkenness, revenge; the whoredoms, adulteries, and various uncleanness; the frauds, injustice, oppression, extortion, which overspread our land as a flood?

11. And even among those who have kept themselves pure from those grosser abominations, how much anger and pride, how much sloth and idleness, how much softness and effeminacy, how much luxury and self-indulgence, how much covetousness and ambition, how much thirst of praise, how much love of the world, how much fear of man is to be found! Meanwhile, how little of true religion! For where is he that loveth either God or his neighbour, as he hath given us commandment? On the one hand are those who have not so much as the form of godliness; on the other, those who have the form only: there stands the open, there the painted sepulchre. So that, in very deed, whosoever

were earnestly to behold any public gathering together of the people (I fear those in our churches are not to be excepted) might easily perceive 'that the one part were Sadducees, and the other Pharisees': the one having almost as little concern about religion as if there were 'no resurrection, neither angel nor spirit'; and the other making it a mere lifeless form, a dull round of external performances without either true faith, or the love of God, or joy in the Holy Ghost.

12. Would to God I could except us of this place. 'Brethren, my heart's desire and prayer to God for you is that ye may be saved' from this overflowing of ungodliness, and that here may its proud waves be stayed! But is it so indeed? God knoweth, yea, and our own conscience, it is not. We have not kept ourselves pure. Corrupt are we also and abominable; and few are there that understand any more, few that worship God in spirit and in truth. We too are 'a generation that set not our hearts aright, and whose spirit cleaveth not steadfastly unto God'. He hath appointed us indeed to be 'the salt of the earth. But if the salt have lost its savour, it is thenceforth good for nothing but to be cast out, and to be trodden under foot of men.'

13. And 'shall I not visit for these things? saith the Lord. Shall not my soul be avenged on such a nation as this?' Yea, we know not how soon he may say to the sword, 'Sword, go through this land!' He hath given us long space to repent. He lets us alone this year also. But he warns and awakens us by thunder. His judgments are abroad in the earth. And we have all reason to expect that heaviest of all, even 'that he should come unto us quickly, and remove our candlestick out of its place, except we repent and do the first works'; unless we return to the principles of the Reformation, the truth and simplicity of the gospel. Perhaps we are now resisting the last effort of divine grace to save us. Perhaps we have wellnigh 'filled up the measure of our iniquities' by rejecting the counsel of God against ourselves, and casting out his messengers.

14. O God, 'in the midst of wrath remember mercy'! Be glorified in our reformation, not in our destruction. Let us 'hear the rod, and him that appointed it'. Now that 'thy judgments are abroad in the earth', let 'the inhabitants of the world learn righteousness'.

15. My brethren, it is high time for us to awake out of sleep; before 'the great trumpet of the Lord be blown', and our land become a field of blood. O may we speedily see the things that make for our peace, before they are hid from our eyes! 'Turn thou us, O good Lord, and let thine anger cease from us.' 'O Lord, look down from heaven, behold and visit this vine'; and cause us to know the time of our visitation. 'Help us, O God of our salvation, for the glory of thy name; O deliver us, and be merciful to our sins, for thy name's sake.' 'And so will we not go back from thee: O let us live, and we shall call upon thy name. Turn us again, O Lord God of hosts, show the light of thy countenance, and we shall be whole.'

'Now unto him that is able to do exceeding abundantly above all that we can ask or think, according to the power that worketh in us, unto him be glory in the church by Christ Jesus throughout all ages, world without end. Amen.'

5. THE SPIRIT OF BONDAGE AND OF ADOPTION

1746

An Introductory Comment

Though Wesley had preached on Romans 8:15 earlier at Baptist Mills, Bristol, in 1739, he chose this text once again for a sermon on top of his father's tomb on June 10, 1742 (S, 1:178). A few years later he brought this sermon into print since it explored his enduring theme of real Christianity, as the commentary on this passage found in his *Explanatory Notes Upon the New Testament* clearly illustrates.

By distinguishing the spirit of bondage, which is marked by the fear of death (O, 1:257; 4:34–35), from the Spirit of adoption, Wesley noted that those characterized by the former spirit cannot be termed the "sons of God. Yet some of them may be styled his servants" (O, 1:250). Much later in a letter to Thomas Davenport in 1781 Wesley specifically urged those who have received the spirit of bondage to "Look up! . . . He is nigh that justifieth!" (T, 7:95).

In some sense dependent on the typologies of Augustine (*The Enchiridion*) and more recently of Thomas Boston (*Human Nature in Its Fourfold State*) (O, 1:248) Wesley considered three stages along the *ordo salutis* (natural, legal, and evangelical), though he freely acknowledged that they are "frequently mixed" (O, 1:264–65). The terminology of "natural man" that surfaces in this present sermon (as well as in the work of Charles, 'Awake, Thou That Sleepest') must be distinguished from similar language when it is employed in the context of original sin in which the vocabulary of "wholly fallen" and "totally corrupted" predominates (O, 2:183–84). Simply put, the first context presupposes, at least in some sense, the ameliorating effects of prevenient grace; the latter does not. Broadly speaking, the transition from natural to legal and on to the evangelical stage highlights one that moves from ignorance through fear and onto the love of God and neighbor in rich liberty.

The Spirit of Bondage and of Adoption

I will distinguish the natural man from those under the law and those under grace

I. 1. The soul of the natural man is in deep sleep; his spiritual senses are not awake
2. Because he is *blind*, he is also *secure*; he has no fear
3. He is secure because he is ignorant of himself
4. This ignorance glares most in those who are men of learning
5. And what the world calls joy he may often possess
6. He imagines that he walks in such great *liberty*
7. Although he is a servant of sin, he is not troubled
8. How can the natural man be convinced of sin?

II. 1. God touches the hearts of those who are asleep in darkness
2. The inward, spiritual meaning of the law now begins to glare upon them
3. They see they are corrupt and abominable
4. They not only see, but feel, that they deserve to be cast into the fire
5. Here ends their false peace, their vain security
6. They feel the sorrow of heart
7. Now they truly strive to break loose from sin
8. But though they strive with all their might, sin retains the upper hand
9. This is what it means to be under the law
10. And they remain under the law until God answers their cries

III. 1. Now the miserable bondage ends; they are no longer under the law
2. They cried unto the Lord, and God delivered them
3. Heavenly, healing light now breaks in upon their souls
    A. They see the light of the love of God in the face of Jesus Christ
4. Here end both the guilt and the power of sin
5. Where the Spirit of the Lord is, there is liberty from sin
6. We receive the Spirit of adoption, whereby we cry, Abba, Father!
7. It is this Spirit which continually works in us
8. To sum:
    A. The natural man neither fears nor loves God.
    B. Those under the law fear God
    C. Those under grace love God

IV. 1. It is not right to divide man into sincere and insincere
2. Many do not discern their state because these states are often mingled
3. Many do not know how far they can go in a natural or legal state
4. Beware, then, that you do not come up short of your high calling

Sermon 9: The Spirit of Bondage and of Adoption, 1746

Romans 8:15

Ye have not received the spirit of bondage again unto fear; but ye have received the Spirit of adoption, whereby we cry, Abba, Father.

1. St. Paul here speaks to those who are the children of God by faith. Ye, saith he, who are indeed his children, have drunk into his Spirit. 'Ye have not received the spirit of bondage again unto fear;' but 'because ye are sons, God hath sent forth the Spirit of his Son into your hearts.' 'Ye have received the Spirit of adoption, whereby we cry, Abba, Father.'

2. The spirit of bondage and fear is widely distant from this loving Spirit of adoption. Those who are influenced only by slavish fear cannot be termed the sons of God. Yet some of them may be styled his servants, and 'are not far from the kingdom of heaven'.

3. But it is to be feared the bulk of mankind, yea, of what is called 'the Christian world', have not attained even this; but are still afar off, 'neither is God in all their thoughts.' A few names may be found of those who love God; a few more there are that fear him. But the greater part have neither the fear of God before their eyes, nor the love of God in their hearts.

4. Perhaps most of you, who by the mercy of God now partake of a better spirit, may remember the time when ye were as they, when ye were under the same condemnation. But at first ye knew it not, though ye were wallowing daily in your sins and in your blood; till in due time ye 'received the spirit of fear' (ye *received*; for this also is the gift of God); and afterwards fear vanished away, and the spirit of love filled your hearts.

5. One who is in the first state of mind, without fear or love, is in Scripture termed 'a natural man'. One who is under the spirit of bondage and fear is sometimes said to be 'under the law' (although that expression more frequently signifies one who is under the Jewish dispensation, who thinks himself obliged to observe all the rites and ceremonies of the Jewish law). But one who has exchanged the spirit of fear for the spirit of love is properly said to be 'under grace'.

Now because it highly imports us to know what spirit we are of, I shall endeavour to point out distinctly, first, the state of a 'natural man'; secondly, that of one who is 'under the law'; and thirdly, of one who is 'under grace'.

I.1. And, first, the state of a 'natural man'. This the Scripture represents as a state of sleep. The voice of God to him is, 'Awake, thou that sleepest.' For his soul is in a deep sleep. His spiritual senses are not awake; they discern neither spiritual good nor evil. The eyes of his understanding are closed; they are sealed together, and see not. Clouds and darkness continually rest upon them; for he lies in the valley of the shadow of death. Hence, having no inlets for the knowledge of spiritual things, all the avenues of his soul being shut up, he is in gross, stupid ignorance of whatever he is most concerned to know. He is utterly ignorant of God, knowing nothing concerning him as he ought to know. He is totally a stranger to the law of God, as to its true, inward, spiritual meaning. He has no conception of that evangelical holiness without which no man shall see the Lord; nor of the happiness which they only find whose 'life is hid with Christ in God'.

2. And for this very reason, because he is fast *asleep*, he is in some sense at *rest.* Because he is *blind*, he is also *secure*: he saith, 'Tush, . . . there shall no harm happen unto me.' The darkness which covers him on every side keeps him in a kind of peace—so far as peace can consist with the works of the devil, and with an earthly, devilish mind. He *sees* not that he stands on the edge of the pit; therefore he *fears* it not. He cannot tremble at the danger he does not know. He has not understanding enough to fear. Why is it that he is in no dread of God? Because he is totally ignorant of him: if not 'saying in his heart, There is no God', or that he 'sitteth on the circle of the heavens', 'and humbleth' not 'himself to behold the things' which are done on earth; yet satisfying himself as well, to all Epicurean intents and purposes, by saying, 'God is merciful;' confounding and swallowing up at once in that unwieldy idea of mercy all his holiness and essential hatred of sin, all his justice, wisdom, and truth. He is in no dread of the vengeance denounced against those who obey not the blessed law of God, because he understands it not. He imagines the main point is to *do thus*, to be *outwardly* blameless—and sees not that it extends to every temper, desire, thought, motion of the heart. Or he fancies that the obligation hereto is ceased, that Christ came to 'destroy the law and the prophets', to save his people *in*, not *from* their sins, to bring them to heaven without holiness; notwithstanding his own words, 'Not one jot or tittle of the law shall pass away till all things are fulfilled,' and, 'Not everyone that saith unto me, Lord, Lord, shall enter into the kingdom of heaven; but he that doth the will of my Father which is in heaven.'

3. He is secure, because he is utterly ignorant of himself. Hence he talks of 'repenting by and by'; he does not indeed exactly know when; but some time or other before he dies—taking it for granted that this is quite in his own power. For what should hinder his doing it if he will? If he does but once set a resolution, no fear but he will make it good.

4. But this ignorance never so strongly glares as in those who are termed 'men of learning'. If a natural man be one of these, he can talk at large of his rational faculties, of the freedom of his will and the absolute necessity of such freedom in order to constitute man a moral agent. He reads and argues, and proves to a demonstration that every man may do as he will, may dispose his own heart to evil or good as it seems best in his own eyes. Thus the god of this world spreads a double veil of blindness over his heart, lest by any means 'the light of the glorious gospel of Christ should shine' upon it.

5. From the same ignorance of himself and God there may sometimes arise in the natural man a kind of joy in congratulating himself upon his own wisdom and goodness. And what the world calls joy he may often possess. He may have pleasure in various kinds, either in gratifying the desires of the flesh, or the desire of the eye, or the pride of life—particularly if he has large possessions, if he enjoy an affluent fortune. Then he may 'clothe himself in purple and fine linen, and fare sumptuously every day'. And *so long as* he thus *doth well unto himself*, 'men will' doubtless 'speak good of' him. They will say he is a happy man; for indeed this is the sum of worldly happiness—to dress, and visit, and talk, and eat, and drink, and rise up to play.

6. It is not surprising if one in such circumstances as these, dozed with the opiates of flattery and sin, should imagine, among his other waking dreams, that he walks in great *liberty*. How easily may he persuade himself that he is at liberty from all 'vulgar errors' and from the 'prejudice' of education, judging exactly right, and keeping clear of all extremes. 'I am free (may he say) from all the *enthusiasm* of weak and narrow souls; from *superstition*, the disease of fools and cowards, always righteous overmuch; and from *bigotry*, continually incident to those who have not a free and generous way of thinking.' And too sure it is that he is altogether free from the 'wisdom which cometh from above', from holiness, from the religion of the heart, from the whole mind which was in Christ.

7. For all this time he is the servant of sin. He commits sin, more or less, day by day. Yet he is not troubled; he 'is in no bondage' (as some speak), he feels no condemnation. He contents himself (even though he should profess to believe that the Christian revelation is of God) with: 'Man is frail. We are all weak. Every man has his infirmity.' Perhaps he quotes Scripture: 'Why, does not Solomon say, "The righteous man falls into sin seven times a day"? And doubtless they are all hypocrites or enthusiasts who pretend to be better than their neighbours.' If at any time a serious thought fix upon him, he stifles it as soon as possible with, 'Why should I fear, since God is merciful, and Christ died for sinners?' Thus he remains a willing servant of sin, content with the bondage of corruption; inwardly and outwardly unholy, and satisfied therewith; not only not conquering sin, but not striving to conquer, particularly that sin which doth so easily beset him.

8. Such is the state of every 'natural man'; whether he be a gross, scandalous transgressor, or a more reputable and decent sinner, having the form though not the power of godliness. But how can such an one be 'convinced of sin'? How is he brought to *repent*? To be 'under the law'? To receive the 'spirit of bondage unto fear'? This is the point which is next to be considered.

II.1. By some awful providence, or by his Word applied with the demonstration of his Spirit, God touches the heart of him that lay asleep in darkness and in the shadow of death. He is terribly shaken out of his sleep, and awakes into a consciousness of his danger. Perhaps in a moment, perhaps by degrees, the eyes of his understanding are opened, and now first (the veil being in part removed) discern the real state he is in. Horrid light breaks in upon his soul; such light as may be conceived to gleam from the bottomless pit, from the lowest deep, from a lake of fire burning with brimstone. He at last sees the loving, the merciful God is also 'a consuming fire'; that he is a just God and a terrible, rendering to every man according to his works, entering into judgment with the ungodly for every idle word, yea, and for the imaginations of the heart. He now clearly perceives that the great and holy God is 'of purer eyes than to behold iniquity'; that he is an avenger of everyone who rebelleth against him, and repayeth the wicked to his face; and that 'it is a fearful thing to fall into the hands of the living God.'

2. The inward, spiritual meaning of the law of God now begins to glare upon him. He perceives the 'commandment is exceeding broad', and 'there is nothing hid from the light thereof.' He is convinced that every part of it relates not barely to outward sin or

obedience, but to what passes in the secret recesses of the soul, which no eye but God's can penetrate. If he now hears, 'Thou shalt not kill,' God speaks in thunder, 'He that hateth his brother is a murderer;' he that saith unto his brother, 'Thou fool, is obnoxious to hellfire.' If the law say, 'Thou shalt not commit adultery,' the voice of the Lord sounds in his ears, 'He that looketh on a woman to lust after her hath committed adultery with her already in his heart.' And thus in every point he feels the Word of God 'quick and powerful, sharper than a two-edged sword'. It pierces 'even to the dividing asunder of his soul and spirit, his joints and marrow'. And so much the more because he is conscious *to himself* of having neglected so great salvation; of having 'trodden under foot the Son of God' who would have saved him from his sins, and 'counted the blood of the covenant an unholy', a common, unsanctifying 'thing'.

3. And as he knows 'all things are naked and opened unto the eyes of him with whom we have to do,' so he sees himself naked, stripped of all the fig-leaves which he had sewed together, of all his poor pretences to religion or virtue, and his wretched excuses for sinning against God. He now sees himself like the ancient sacrifices, τετραχηλισμένον, 'cleft in sunder', as it were, from the neck downward, so that all within him stands confessed. His heart is bare, and he sees it is all sin, 'deceitful above all things, desperately wicked'; that it is altogether corrupt and abominable, more than it is possible for tongue to express; that there dwelleth there no good thing, but unrighteousness and ungodliness only; every motion thereof, every temper and thought, being only evil continually.

4. And he not only sees, but feels in himself, by an emotion of soul which he cannot describe, that for the sins of his heart, were his life without blame (which yet it is not, and cannot be; seeing 'an evil tree cannot bring forth good fruit'), he deserves to be cast into 'the fire that never shall be quenched'. He feels that 'the wages', the just reward, 'of sin', of his sin above all, 'is death;' even the second death, the death which dieth not, the destruction of body and soul in hell.

5. Here ends his pleasing dream, his delusive rest, his false peace, his vain security. His joy now vanishes as a cloud; pleasures once loved delight no more. They pall upon the taste; he loathes the nauseous sweet; he is weary to bear them. The shadows of happiness flee away, and sink into oblivion; so that he is stripped of all, and wanders to and fro seeking rest, but finding none.

6. The fumes of those opiates being now dispelled, he feels the anguish of a wounded spirit. He finds that sin let loose upon the soul (whether it be pride, anger, or evil desire; whether self-will, malice, envy, revenge, or any other) is perfect misery. He feels sorrow of heart for the blessings he has lost, and the curse which is come upon him; remorse for having thus destroyed himself, and despised his own mercies; fear, from a lively sense of the wrath of God, and of the consequences of his wrath; of the punishment which he has justly deserved, and which he sees hanging over his head; fear of death, as being to him the gate of hell, the entrance of death eternal; fear of the devil, the executioner of the wrath and righteous vengeance of God; fear of men, who if they were able to kill his body, would thereby plunge both body and soul into hell; fear, sometimes arising to such a height that the poor, sinful, guilty soul is terrified with everything, with nothing, with shades, with a leaf shaken of the wind. Yea, sometimes it may even border upon distraction, making

a man 'drunken, though not with wine', suspending the exercise of the memory, of the understanding, of all the natural faculties. Sometimes it may approach to the very brink of despair; so that he who trembles at the name of death may yet be ready to plunge into it every moment, to 'choose strangling rather than life'. Well may such a man 'roar', like him of old, 'for the very disquietness of his heart'. Well may he cry out, 'The spirit of a man may sustain his infirmities; but a wounded spirit who can bear?'

7. Now he truly desires to break loose from sin, and begins to struggle with it. But though he strive with all his might he cannot conquer; sin is mightier than he. He would fain escape; but he is so fast in prison that he cannot get forth. He resolves against sin, but yet sins on; he sees the snare, and abhors—and runs into it. So much does his boasted reason avail—only to enhance his guilt, and increase his misery! Such is the freedom of his will—free only to evil; free to 'drink in iniquity like water'; to wander farther and farther from the living God, and do more 'despite to the Spirit of grace'!

8. The more he strives, wishes, labours to be free, the more does he feel his chains, the grievous chains of sin, wherewith Satan binds and 'leads him captive at his will'. His servant he is, though he repine ever so much; though he rebel, he cannot prevail. He is still in bondage and fear by reason of sin: generally of some outward sin, to which he is peculiarly disposed either by nature, custom, or outward circumstances; but always of some inward sin, some evil temper or unholy affection. And the more he frets against it, the more it prevails; he may bite, but cannot break his chain. Thus he toils without end, repenting and sinning, and repenting and sinning again, till at length the poor sinful, helpless wretch is even at his wit's end, and can barely groan, 'O wretched man that I am, who shall deliver me from the body of this death?'

9. This whole struggle of one who is 'under the law', under the 'spirit of fear and bondage', is beautifully described by the Apostle in the foregoing chapter, speaking in the person of an awakened man. 'I (saith he) was alive without the law once.' I had much life, wisdom, strength, and virtue—so I thought. 'But when the commandment came, sin revived, and I died' (Rom. 7:9). When the commandment, in its spiritual meaning, came to my heart with the power of God my inbred sin was stirred up, fretted, inflamed, and all my virtue died away. 'And the commandment, which was ordained to life, I found to be unto death. For sin, taking occasion by the commandment, deceived me, and by it slew me' (Rom. 7:10-11). It came upon me unawares, slew all my hopes, and plainly showed, in the midst of life I was in death. 'Wherefore the law is holy, and the commandment holy, and just, and good' (Rom. 7:12): I no longer lay the blame on this, but on the corruption of my own heart. I acknowledge that 'the law is spiritual; but I am carnal, sold under sin' (Rom. 7:14). I now see both the spiritual nature of the law, and my own carnal devilish heart, 'sold under sin', totally enslaved (like slaves bought with money, who were absolutely at their master's disposal). 'For that which I do, I allow not; for what I would, I do not; but what I hate, that I do' (Rom. 7:15). Such is the bondage under which I groan; such the tyranny of my hard master. 'To will is present with me, but how to perform that which is good I find not. For the good that I would I do not; but the evil which I would not, that I do' (Rom. 7:18-19). 'I find a law', an inward constraining power, 'that when I would do good, evil is present with me. For I delight in' (or consent to) 'the law of God, after the inward man' (Rom. 7:21-22).

(In my mind: so the Apostle explains himself in the words that immediately follow; and so ὁ ἔσω ἄνθρωπος, 'the inward man', is understood in all other Greek writers.) 'But I see another law in my members', another constraining power, 'warring against the law of my mind', or inward man, 'and bringing me into captivity to the law', or power, 'of sin' (Rom. 7:23), dragging me as it were at my conqueror's chariot-wheels into the very thing which my soul abhors. 'O wretched man that I am, who shall deliver me from the body of this death!' (Rom. 7:24). Who shall deliver me from this helpless, dying life; from this bondage of sin and misery! Till this is done, 'I myself' (or rather, 'that I', αὐτὸς ἐγώ, *that man* I am now personating) 'with the mind', or inward man, 'serve the law of God'; my mind, my conscience, is on God's side: 'but with the flesh', with my body, 'the law of sin' (Rom. 7:25), being hurried away by a force I cannot resist.

10. How lively a portraiture is this of one 'under the law'! One who feels the burden he cannot shake off; who pants after liberty, power, and love, but is in fear and bondage still! Until the time that God answers the wretched man crying out, 'Who shall deliver me' from this bondage of sin, from this body of death?—'The grace of God, through Jesus Christ thy Lord.'

III.1. Then it is that this miserable bondage ends, and he is no more 'under the law, but under grace'. This state we are thirdly to consider; the state of one who has found 'grace', or favour in the sight of God, even the Father, and who has the 'grace', or power of the Holy Ghost, reigning in his heart; who has received, in the language of the Apostle, 'the Spirit of adoption, whereby he now cries, Abba, Father'.

2. 'He cried unto the Lord in his trouble, and God delivers him out of his distress.' His eyes are opened in quite another manner than before, even to see a loving, gracious God. While he is calling, 'I beseech thee show me thy glory,' he hears a voice in his inmost soul, 'I will make all my goodness pass before thee, and I will proclaim the name of the Lord; I will be gracious to whom I will be gracious, and I will show mercy to whom I will show mercy.' And it is not long before 'the Lord descends in the cloud, and proclaims the name of the Lord.' Then he sees (but not with eyes of flesh and blood) 'The Lord, the Lord God; merciful and gracious, long-suffering, and abundant in goodness and truth; keeping mercy for thousands, and forgiving iniquities and transgression and sin.'

3. Heavenly, healing light now breaks in upon his soul. He 'looks on him whom he had pierced', and 'God, who out of darkness commanded light to shine, shineth in his heart.' He sees 'the light of the glorious love of God, in the face of Jesus Christ'. He hath a divine 'evidence of things not seen' by sense, even of 'the deep things of God'; more particularly of the love of God, of his pardoning love to him that believes in Jesus. Overpowered with the sight, his whole soul cries out, 'My Lord, and my God!' For he sees all his iniquities laid on him who 'bare them in his own body on the tree'; he beholds the Lamb of God taking away his sins. How clearly now does he discern 'that God was in Christ, reconciling the world unto himself; . . . making him sin for us, who knew no sin, that we might be made the righteousness of God through him!' And that he himself is reconciled to God by that blood of the covenant!

4. Here end both the guilt and power of sin. He can now say, 'I am crucified with Christ. Nevertheless I live; yet not I, but Christ liveth in me. And the life which I now live in the flesh', even in this mortal body, 'I live by faith in the Son of God, who loved me and gave himself for me.' Here end remorse and sorrow of heart, and the anguish of a wounded spirit. 'God turneth his heaviness into joy.' He 'made sore', and now 'his hands bind up'. Here ends also that bondage unto fear; for 'his heart standeth fast, believing in the Lord.' He cannot fear any longer the wrath of God; for he knows it is now turned away from him, and looks upon him no more as an angry judge, but as a loving Father. He cannot fear the devil, knowing he has 'no power, except it be given him from above'. He fears not hell, being an heir of the kingdom of heaven. Consequently, he has no fear of death, by reason whereof he was in time past for so many years 'subject to bondage'. Rather, knowing that 'if the earthly house of this tabernacle be dissolved, he hath a building of God, a house not made with hands, eternal in the heavens, he groaneth earnestly, desiring to be clothed upon with that house which is from heaven.' He groans to shake off this house of earth, that 'mortality may be swallowed up of life'; knowing that 'God hath wrought him for the selfsame thing; who hath also given him the earnest of his Spirit.'

5. And 'where the Spirit of the Lord is, there is liberty'; liberty not only from guilt and fear, but from sin, from that heaviest of all yokes, that basest of all bondage. His labour is not now in vain. The snare is broken, and he is delivered. He not only strives, but likewise prevails; he not only fights, but conquers also. 'Henceforth he doth not serve sin (Rom. 6:6). He is dead unto sin and alive unto God. . . . Sin doth not now reign, even in his mortal body', nor doth he 'obey it in the desires thereof'. He does not 'yield his members as instruments of unrighteousness unto sin, but as instruments of righteousness unto God'. For 'being now made free from sin, he is become the servant of righteousness.'

6. Thus 'having peace with God, through our Lord Jesus Christ', 'rejoicing in hope of the glory of God', and having power over all sin, over every evil desire and temper, and word and work, he is a living witness of the 'glorious liberty of the sons of God': all of whom, being partakers of 'like precious faith', bear record with one voice, 'We have received the Spirit of adoption, whereby we cry, Abba, Father!'

7. It is this Spirit which continually 'worketh in them, both to will and to do of his good pleasure'. It is he that sheds the love of God abroad in their hearts, and the love of all mankind; thereby purifying their hearts from the love of the world, from the lust of the flesh, the lust of the eye, and the pride of life. It is by him they are delivered from anger and pride, from all vile and inordinate affections. In consequence, they are delivered from evil words and works, from all unholiness of conversation; doing no evil to any child of man, and being zealous of all good works.

8. To sum up all. The 'natural man' neither fears nor loves God; one 'under the law' fears, one 'under grace' loves him. The first has no light in the things of God, but walks in utter darkness. The second sees the painful light of hell; the third, the joyous light of heaven. He that sleeps in death has a false peace. He that is awakened has no peace at all. He that believes has true peace, the peace of God, filling and ruling his heart. The heathen, baptized or unbaptized, hath a fancied liberty, which is indeed licentiousness; the Jew (or one under the Jewish dispensation) is in heavy, grievous bondage; the Christian enjoys the

true glorious liberty of the sons of God, An unawakened child of the devil sins willingly; one that is awakened sins unwillingly; a child of God 'sinneth not, but keepeth himself, and the wicked one toucheth him not'. To conclude: the natural man neither conquers nor fights; the man under the law fights with sin, but cannot conquer; the man under grace fights and conquers, yea is 'more than conqueror, through him that loveth him'.

IV.1. From this plain account of the threefold state of man—the 'natural', the 'legal', and the 'evangelical'—it appears that it is not sufficient to divide mankind into sincere and insincere. A man may be sincere in any of these states; not only when he has the 'Spirit of adoption', but while he has the 'spirit of bondage unto fear'. Yea, while he has neither this fear, nor love. For undoubtedly there may be sincere heathens as well as sincere Jews or Christians. This circumstance, then, does by no means prove that a man is in a state of acceptance with God.

'Examine yourselves', therefore, not only whether ye are sincere, but 'whether ye be in the faith.' Examine narrowly; for it imports you much. What is the ruling principle in your soul? Is it the love of God? Is it the fear of God? Or is it neither one nor the other? Is it not rather the love of the world? The love of pleasure? Or gain? Of ease; or reputation? If so, you are not come so far as a Jew. You are but a *heathen* still. Have you heaven in your heart? Have you the Spirit of adoption, ever crying, 'Abba, Father'? Or do you cry unto God as 'out of the belly of hell', overwhelmed with sorrow and fear? Or are you a stranger to this whole affair, and cannot imagine what I mean? Heathen, pull off the mask. Thou hast never put on Christ. Stand barefaced. Look up to heaven; and own before him that liveth for ever and ever, thou hast no part either among the sons or servants of God.

Whosoever thou art, dost thou commit sin, or dost thou not? If thou dost, is it willingly, or unwillingly? In either case God hath told thee whose thou art—'He that committeth sin is of the devil.' If thou committest it willingly thou art his faithful servant. He will not fail to reward thy labour. If unwillingly, still thou art his servant. God deliver thee out of his hands!

Art thou daily fighting against all sin; and daily more than conqueror? I acknowledge thee for a child of God. O stand fast in thy glorious liberty. Art thou fighting, but not conquering; striving for the mastery, but not able to attain? Then thou art not yet a believer in Christ. But follow on; and thou shalt know the Lord. Art thou not fighting at all, but leading an easy, indolent, fashionable life? O how hast thou dared to name the name of Christ! Only to make it a reproach among the heathen? Awake, thou sleeper! Call upon thy God, before the deep swallow thee up.

2. Perhaps one reason why so many think of themselves more highly than they ought to think, why they do not discern what state they are in, is because these several states of soul are often mingled together, and in some measure meet in one and the same person. Thus experience shows that the legal state, or state of fear, is frequently mixed with the natural; for few men are so fast asleep in sin but they are sometimes more or less awakened. As the Spirit of God does not 'wait for the call of man', so at some times he *will* be heard. He puts them in fear, so that for a season at least the heathen 'know themselves to

be but men'. They feel the burden of sin, and earnestly desire to flee from the wrath to come. But not long. They seldom suffer the arrows of conviction to go deep into their souls; but quickly stifle the grace of God, and return to their wallowing in the mire.

In like manner the evangelical state, or state of love, is frequently mixed with the legal. For few of those who have the spirit of bondage and fear remain always without hope. The wise and gracious God rarely suffers this; for he remembereth that we are but dust. And he willeth not that 'the flesh should fail before him, or the spirit which he hath made'. Therefore, at such times as he seeth good he gives a dawning of light unto them that sit in darkness. He causes a part of his goodness to pass before them, and shows he is a 'God that heareth the prayer'. They see the promise which is by faith in Christ Jesus, though it be yet afar off; and hereby they are encouraged to 'run with patience the race which is set before them'.

3. Another reason why many deceive themselves is because they do not consider how far a man may go and yet be in a natural, or at best a legal state. A man may be of a compassionate and a benevolent temper; he may be affable, courteous, generous, friendly; he may have some degree of meekness, patience, temperance, and of many other moral virtues; he may feel many desires of shaking off all vice, and attaining higher degrees of virtue; he may abstain from much evil—perhaps from all that is grossly contrary to justice, mercy, or truth; he may do much good, may feed the hungry, clothe the naked, relieve the widow and fatherless; he may attend public worship, use prayer in private, read many books of devotion—and yet for all this he may be a mere natural man, knowing neither himself nor God; equally a stranger to the spirit of fear and to that of love; having neither repented nor believed the gospel.

But suppose there were added to all this a deep conviction of sin, with much fear of the wrath of God; vehement desires to cast off every sin, and to fulfil all righteousness; frequent rejoicing in hope, and touches of love often glancing upon the soul: yet neither do these prove a man to be 'under grace', to have true, living, Christian faith, unless the Spirit of adoption abide in his heart, unless he can continually cry, 'Abba, Father!'

4. Beware, then, thou who art called by the name of Christ, that thou come not short of the mark of thy high calling. Beware thou rest not, either in a natural state, with too many that are accounted 'good Christians', or in a legal state, wherein those who are 'highly esteemed of men' are generally content to live and die. Nay, but God hath prepared better things for thee, if thou follow on till thou attain. Thou art not called to fear and tremble, like devils, but to rejoice and love, like the angels of God. 'Thou shalt love the Lord thy God with all thy heart, and with all thy soul, and with all thy mind, and with all thy strength.' Thou shalt 'rejoice evermore.' Thou shalt 'pray without ceasing.' Thou shalt 'in everything give thanks.' Thou shalt do the will of God 'on earth, as it is done in heaven'. O 'prove' thou 'what is that good and acceptable and perfect will of God.' Now 'present' thyself 'a living sacrifice, holy, acceptable to God.' 'Whereunto thou hast already attained', 'hold fast', by 'reaching forth unto those things which are before'; until 'the God of peace . . . make thee perfect in every good work, working in thee that which is well-pleasing in his sight, through Jesus Christ, to whom be glory for ever and ever! Amen!'

6. THE WAY TO THE KINGDOM

1746

An Introductory Comment

Wesley employed the scriptural text of this sermon, "The kingdom of God is at hand: repent . . . and believe the gospel" (Mark 1:15), "one hundred and ninety times" in a nearly fifty-year span (O, 1:217). He specifically linked this text to the fruit of his evangelistic labors since 1738 in noting with its use among the poor of England "the word of God ran as fire among the stubble" (D, 9:223). The call to repentance, so prominent in this sermon, entails conviction of sin, self-knowledge as well as a sense of guilt and helplessness.

Interestingly enough, a second text (Rom. 14:17) emerges in this sermon as a point of ongoing attention. Wesley developed the theme "The Kingdom of God is not meat and drink; but righteousness, and peace, and joy in the Holy Ghost" at St. Mary's in Exeter with such effect that he was told, "Sir, you must not preach in the afternoon" (WH, 19:123–24). This text may also have informed the substance of Wesley's preaching atop his father's tombstone in the Epworth churchyard on June 6, 1742 (O, 1:217). By means of this second text, then, Wesley explored the vital topic of "true religion" and noted that it consists not in orthodoxy or right opinion, in "bare assent" to the truths of the gospel, or in any outward things such as forms of worship, rites, or ceremonies (O, 1:218–19). In fact, Wesley declared to the consternation of some of his more settled Anglican peers that one may use the means of grace, "abstain from outward evil, and do good" (O, 1:219) and yet have no religion. What, then, is true religion? It is best expressed in three particulars: "righteousness, and peace, and joy in the Holy Ghost" (O, 1:221). Put another way, true religion is nothing less than happiness and holiness in the Holy Spirit.

The Way to the Kingdom

I. 1. We will consider the nature of true religion or the kingdom of God

2–3. The 'kingdom of God' does not consist in any ritual observances

4. It does not consist in any *outward* thing, such as *forms* or *ceremonies*

5. True religion does not consist of any outward actions whatsoever

6. Neither does true religion consist of *orthodoxy* or *right opinions*

7. This alone is religion, truly so called:

A. righteousness, and peace, and joy in the Holy Ghost

B. The first great branch of righteousness is to love the Lord thy God

8. The second great branch of righteousness is to love thy neighbour as thyself

9. This is the sum of all Christian righteousness

10. But true religion implies happiness as well as holiness

11. With the peace of God, there is also joy in the Holy Ghost

12. Holiness and happiness, joined in one, are the kingdom of God

13. This is the kingdom of God that is at hand

II. 1. This is the way: walk in it.

A. Repent, and know yourself to be a sinner

2. Know the inbred corruption of your heart

3. Your sins are more than you are able to express

4. Do you not know that the wages of sin is death?

5. What will you do to appease the wrath of God, to atone for your sins?

6. Shake off that outward sin that so easily besets you

A. This cannot be done unless first your heart is changed

B. Art you able to change your own heart from all sin to all holiness?

7. If true sorrow accompany the conviction of sin, then you are not far from the kingdom of God

8. The gospel is that Jesus Christ came into the world to save sinners

9. Believe this by faith, and the kingdom of God is yours

10. Only beware that you understand the true nature of faith

A. Faith is not bare assent to the Bible or the articles of our creed

B. Faith is a sure trust in the mercy of God through Christ Jesus

11. Do you thus believe? Then the peace of God is in your heart

12. Do you now believe? Then the love of God is now shed abroad in your heart

13. This repentance is what the wisdom of the world has voted to be madness

Sermon 7: The Way to the Kingdom, 1746

Mark 1:15

The kingdom of God is at hand: repent ye, and believe the gospel.

These words naturally lead us to consider, first, the nature of true religion, here termed by our Lord 'the kingdom of God', which, saith he, 'is at hand'; and secondly, the way thereto, which he points out in those words, 'Repent ye, and believe the gospel.'

I. 1. We are, first, to consider the nature of true religion, here termed by our Lord 'the kingdom of God'. The same expression the great Apostle uses in his Epistle to the Romans, where he likewise explains his Lord's words, saying, 'The kingdom of God is not meat and drink; but righteousness, and peace, and joy in the Holy Ghost' (Rom. 14:17).

2. 'The kingdom of God', or true religion, 'is not meat and drink.' It is well known that not only the unconverted Jews, but great numbers of those who had received the faith of Christ, were notwithstanding 'zealous of the law' (Acts 21:20), even the ceremonial law of Moses. Whatsoever therefore they found written therein, either concerning meat and drink offerings, or the distinction between clean and unclean meats, they not only observed themselves, but vehemently pressed the same even on those 'among the Gentiles' (or heathens) 'who were turned to God'. Yea, to such a degree that some of them taught, wheresoever they came among them, 'Except ye be circumcised, and keep the law' (the whole ritual law), 'ye cannot be saved' (Acts 15:1, 24).

3. In opposition to these the Apostle declares, both here and in many other places, that true religion does not consist in *meat* and *drink*, or in any ritual observances; nor indeed in any outward thing whatever, in anything exterior to the heart; but whole substance thereof lying in 'righteousness, peace, and joy in the Holy Ghost'.

4. Not in any *outward thing*, such as *forms* or *ceremonies*, even of the most excellent kind. Supposing these to be ever so decent and significant, ever so expressive of inward things; supposing them ever so helpful, not only to the vulgar, whose thought reaches little farther than their sight, but even to men of understanding, men of strong capacities, as doubtless they may sometimes be; yea, supposing them, as in the case of the Jews, to be appointed by God himself; yet even during the period of time wherein that appointment remains in force, true religion does not principally consist therein—nay, strictly speaking, not at all. How much more must this hold concerning such rites and forms as are only of human appointment! The religion of Christ rises infinitely higher and lies immensely deeper than all these. These are good in their place; just so far as they are in fact subservient to true religion. And it were superstition to object against them while they are applied only as occasional helps to human weakness. But let no man carry them farther. Let no man dream that they have any intrinsic work; or that religion cannot subsist without them. This were to make them an abomination to the Lord.

5. The nature of religion is so far from consisting in these, in forms of worship, or rites and ceremonies, that it does not properly consist in any outward actions of what kind so ever. It is true a man cannot have any religion who is guilty of vicious, immoral actions; or

who does to others what he would not they should do to him if he were in the same circumstance. And it is also true that he can have no real religion who 'knows to do good, and doth it not'. Yet may a man both abstain from outward evil, and do good, and still have no religion. Yea, two persons may do the same outward work—suppose, feeding the hungry, or clothing the naked—and in the meantime one of these may be truly religious and the other have no religion at all; for the one may act from the love of God, and the other from the love of praise. So manifest it is that although true religion naturally leads to every good word and work, yet the real nature thereof lies deeper still, even in 'the hidden man of the heart'.

6. I say of the *heart.* For neither does religion consist in *orthodoxy* or *right opinions*; which, although they are not properly outward things, are not in the heart, but the understanding. A man may be orthodox in every point; he may not only espouse right opinions, but zealously defend them against all opposers; he may think justly concerning the incarnation of our Lord, concerning the ever blessed Trinity, and every other doctrine contained in the oracles of God. He may assent to all the three creeds—that called the Apostles', the Nicene, and the Athanasian—and yet 'tis possible he may have no religion at all, no more than a Jew, Turk, or pagan. He may be almost as orthodox as the devil (though indeed not altogether; for every man errs in something, whereas we can't well conceive him to hold any erroneous opinion) and may all the while be as great a stranger as he to the religion of the heart.

7. This alone is religion, truly so called: this alone is in the sight of God of great price. The Apostle sums it all up in three particulars—'righteousness, and peace, and joy in the Holy Ghost'. And first, *righteousness.* We cannot be at a loss concerning this if we remember the words of our Lord describing the two grand branches thereof, on which 'hang all the law and the prophets': 'Thou shalt love the Lord thy God with all thy heart, and with all thy mind, and with all thy soul, and with all thy strength. This is the first and great commandment' (Mark 12:30), the first and great branch of Christian righteousness. Thou shalt delight thyself in the Lord thy God; thou shalt seek and find all happiness in him. He shall be 'thy shield, and thy exceeding great reward', in time and in eternity. All thy bones shall say, 'Whom have I in heaven but thee? And there is none upon earth that I desire beside thee!' Thou shalt hear and fulfil his word who saith, 'My son, give me thy heart.' And having given him thy heart, thy inmost soul, to reign there without a rival, thou mayest well cry out in the fullness of thy heart, 'I will love thee, O Lord, my strength. The Lord is my strong rock and my defence: my Saviour, my God, and my might, in whom I will trust; my buckler, the horn also of my salvation, and my refuge.'

8. And the second commandment is like unto this; the second great branch of Christian righteousness is closely and inseparably connected therewith, even 'Thou shalt love thy neighbour as thyself.' 'Thou shalt love'—thou shalt embrace with the most tender goodwill, the most earnest and cordial affection, the most inflamed desires of preventing or removing all evil and of procuring for him every possible good—'thy neighbour'; that is, not only thy friend, thy kinsman, or thy acquaintance; not only the virtuous, the friendly, him that loves thee, that prevents or returns thy kindness; but every child of man, every human creature, every soul which God hath made: not excepting him whom thou never hast seen in the flesh, whom thou knowest not either by face or name; not except-

ing him whom that knowest to be evil and unthankful, him that still despitefully uses and persecutes thee. Him thou shalt 'love as thyself'; with the same invariable thirst after his happiness in every kind, the same unwearied care to screen him from whatever might grieve or hurt either his soul or body.

9. Now is not this love 'the fulfilling of the law'? The sum of all Christian righteousness? Of all inward righteousness; for it necessarily implies 'bowels of mercies, humbleness of mind' (seeing 'love is not puffed up'), 'gentleness, meekness, long-suffering' (for love 'is not provoked', but 'believeth, hopeth, endureth all things'): and of all outward righteousness, for 'love worketh no evil to his neighbour', either by word or deed. It cannot willingly either hurt or grieve anyone. And it is zealous of good works. Every lover of mankind, as he hath opportunity, 'doth good unto all men', being ('without partiality and without hypocrisy') 'full of mercy and good fruits'.

10. But true religion, or a heart right toward God and man, implies happiness as well as holiness. For it is not only righteousness, but also 'peace and joy in the Holy Ghost'. What peace? 'The peace of God', which God only can give, and the world cannot take away; the peace 'which passeth all understanding', all (barely) rational conception; being a supernatural sensation, a divine taste of 'the powers of the world to come'; such as the natural man knoweth not, how wise soever in the things of this world; nor, indeed, can he know it in his present state, 'because it is spiritually discerned'. It is a peace that banishes all doubt, all painful uncertainty, the Spirit of God 'bearing witness with the spirit' of a Christian that he is 'a child of God'. And it banishes fear, all such fear as hath torment; the fear of the wrath of God, the fear of hell, the fear of the devil, and in particular, the fear of death; he that hath the peace of God 'desiring' (if it were the will of God) 'to depart and to be with Christ'.

11. With this peace of God, wherever it is fixed in the soul, there is also 'joy in the Holy Ghost'; joy wrought in the heart by the Holy Ghost, by the ever-blessed Spirit of God. He it is that worketh in us that calm, humble rejoicing in God, through Christ Jesus, 'by whom we have now received the atonement', καταλλαγήν, the reconciliation with God; and that enables us boldly to confirm the truth of the royal Psalmist's declaration, 'Blessed is the man' (or rather, *happy*, אשדי חיש) 'whose unrighteousness is forgiven, and whose sin is covered.' He it is that inspires the Christian soul with that even, solid joy which arises from the testimony of the Spirit that he is a child of God; and that gives him to 'rejoice with joy unspeakable', 'in hope of the glory of God'—hope both of the glorious image of God, which is in part and shall be fully 'revealed in him', and of that crown of glory which fadeth not away, reserved in heaven for him.

12. This holiness and happiness, joined in one, are sometimes styled in the inspired writings, 'the kingdom of God' (as by our Lord in the text), and sometimes, 'the kingdom of heaven'. It is termed 'the kingdom of God' because it is the immediate fruit of God's reigning in the soul. So soon as ever he takes unto himself his mighty power, and sets up his throne in our hearts, they are instantly filled with this 'righteousness, and peace, and joy in the Holy Ghost'. It is called 'the kingdom of heaven' because it is (in a degree) heaven opened in the soul. For whosoever they are that experience this, they can aver before angels and men,

Everlasting life is won:
Glory is on earth begun;

according to the constant tenor of Scripture, which everywhere bears record, 'God hath given unto us eternal life, and this life is in his Son. He that hath the Son' (reigning in his heart) 'hath life,' even life everlasting (1 John 5:11-12). For 'this is life eternal, to know thee, the only true God, and Jesus Christ, whom thou hast sent . . .' (John 17:3). And they to whom this is given may confidently address God, though they were in the midst of a fiery furnace,

Thee . . . , Lord, safe-shielded by thy power,
Thee, Son of God, Jehovah, we adore,
In form of man descending to appear:
To thee be ceaseless hallelujahs given.
Praise, as in heaven thy throne, we offer here;
For where thy presence is displayed, is heaven.

13. And this 'kingdom of God', or of heaven, 'is at hand'. As these words were originally spoken they implied that 'the time' was then 'fulfilled', God being made 'manifest in the flesh', when he would set up his kingdom among men, and reign in the hearts of his people. And is not the time now fulfilled? For 'Lo (saith he), I am with you always', you who preach remission of sins in my name, 'even unto the end of the world' (Matt. 28:20). Wheresoever therefore the gospel of Christ is preached, this his 'kingdom is nigh at hand'. It is not far from every one of you. Ye may this hour enter thereinto, if so be ye hearken to his voice, 'Repent ye, and believe the gospel.'

II.1. This is the way: walk ye in it. And first, repent, that is, know yourselves. This is the first repentance, previous to faith, even conviction, or self-knowledge. Awake, then, thou that sleepest. Know thyself to be a sinner, and what manner of sinner thou art. Know that corruption of thy inmost nature, whereby thou art very far gone from original righteousness, whereby 'the flesh lusteth' always 'contrary to the Spirit', through that 'carnal mind which is enmity against God', which 'is not subject to the law of God, neither indeed can be'. Know that thou art corrupted in every power, in every faculty of thy soul, that thou art totally corrupted in every one of these, all the foundations being out of course. The eyes of thine understanding are darkened, so that they cannot discern God or the things of God. The clouds of ignorance and error rest upon thee, and cover thee with the shadow of death. Thou knowest nothing yet as thou oughtest to know, neither God, nor the world, nor thyself. Thy will is no longer the will of God, but is utterly perverse and distorted, averse from all good, from all which God loves, and prone to all evil, to every abomination which God hateth. Thy affections are alienated from God, and scattered abroad over the earth. All thy passions, both thy desires and aversions, thy joys and sorrows, thy hopes and fears, are out of frame, are either undue in their degree, or placed on undue objects. So that there is no soundness in thy soul, but 'from the crown of the head to the sole of the foot' (to use the strong expression of the prophet) there are only 'wounds, and bruises, and putrefying sores'.

2. Such is the inbred corruption of thy heart, of thy very inmost nature. And what manner of branches canst thou expect to grow from such an evil root? Hence springs unbelief, ever departing from the living God; saying, 'Who is the Lord that I should serve him?' 'Tush! Thou, God, carest not for it.' Hence independence, affecting to be like the Most High; hence pride, in all its forms, teaching thee to say, 'I am rich, and increased in good, and have need of nothing.' From this evil fountain flow forth the bitter streams of vanity, thirst of praise, ambition, covetousness, the lust of the flesh, the lust of the eye, and the pride of life. From this arise anger, hatred, malice, revenge, envy, jealousy, evil surmisings; from this, all the foolish and hurtful lusts that now 'pierce thee through with many sorrows', and if not timely prevented will at length 'drown thy soul in everlasting perdition'.

3. And what fruits can grow on such branches as these? Only such as are bitter and evil continually. Of pride cometh contention, vain boasting, seeking and receiving praise of men, and so robbing God of that glory which he cannot give unto another. Of the lust of the flesh come gluttony or drunkenness, luxury or sensuality, fornication, uncleanness, variously defiling that body which was designed for a temple of the Holy Ghost: of unbelief, every evil word and work. But the time would fail, shouldst thou reckon up all; all the idle words thou hast spoken, provoking the Most High, grieving the Holy One of Israel; all the evil works thou hast done, either wholly evil in themselves, or at least not done to the glory of God. For thy actual sins are more than thou art able to express, more than the hairs of thy head. Who can number the sands of the sea, or the drops of rain, or thy iniquities?

4. And knowest thou not that 'the wages of sin is death'?—death not only temporal, but eternal. 'The soul that sinneth, it shall die;' for the mouth of the Lord hath spoken it. It shall die the second death. This is the sentence, to 'be punished' with never-ending death, 'with everlasting destruction from the presence of the Lord, and from the glory of his power'. Knowest thou not that every sinner ἔνοχος ἐστι τῇ γεέννῃ τοῦ πυρός, not properly is 'in danger of hell-fire'—that expression is far too weak—but rather, 'is under the sentence of hell-fire'; doomed already, just dragging to execution? Thou art guilty of everlasting death. It is the just reward of thy inward and outward wickedness. It is just that the sentence should now take place. Dost thou see, dost thou feel this? Art thou thoroughly convinced that thou deservest God's wrath and everlasting damnation? Would God do thee any wrong if he now commanded the earth to open up and swallow thee up? If thou wert now to go down quick into the pit, into the fire that never shall be quenched? If God hath given thee truly to repent, thou hast a deep sense that these things are so; and that it is of his mere mercy thou art not consumed, swept away from the face of the earth.

5. And what wilt thou do to appease the wrath of God, to atone for all thy sins, and to escape the punishment thou hast so justly deserved? Alas, thou canst do nothing; nothing that will in any wise make amends to God for one evil work or word or thought. If thou couldst now do all things well, if from this very hour, till thy soul should return to God, thou couldst perform perfect, uninterrupted obedience, even this would not atone for what is past. The not increasing thy debt would not discharge it. It would still remain as great as ever. Yea, the present and future obedience of all the men upon earth, and all

the angels in heaven, would never make satisfaction to the justice of God for one single sin. How vain then was the thought of atoning for thy own sins by anything thou couldst do! It costeth far more to redeem one soul than all mankind is able to pay. So that were there no other help for a guilty sinner, without doubt he must have perished everlastingly.

6. But suppose perfect obedience for the time to come could atone for the sins that are past, this would profit thee nothing; for thou art not able to perform it; no, not in any one point. Begin now. Make the trial. Shake off that outward sin that so easily besetteth thee. Thou canst not. How then wilt thou change thy life from all evil to all good? Indeed, it is impossible to be done, unless first thy heart be changed. For so long as the tree remains evil, it cannot bring forth good fruit. But art thou able to change thy own heart from all sin to all holiness? To quicken a soul that is dead in sin? Dead to God and alive only to the world? No more than thou art able to quicken a dead body, to raise to life him that lieth in the grave. Yea, thou art not able to quicken thy soul in any degree, no more than to give any degree of life to the dead body. Thou canst do nothing, more or less, in this matter; thou art utterly without strength. To be deeply sensible of this, how helpless thou art, as well as how guilty and how sinful, this is that 'repentance not to be repented of' which is the forerunner of the kingdom of God.

7. If to this lively conviction of thy inward and outward sins, of thy utter guiltiness and helplessness, there be added suitable affections—sorrow of heart for having despised thy own mercies; remorse and self-condemnation, having the mouth stopped, shame to lift up thine eyes to heaven; fear of the wrath of God abiding on thee, of his curse hanging over thy head, and of the fiery indignation ready to devour those who forget God and obey not our Lord Jesus Christ; earnest desire to escape from that indignation, to cease from evil and learn to do well—then I say unto thee, in the name of the Lord, 'Thou art not far from the kingdom of God.' One step more and thou shalt enter in. Thou dost 'repent'. Now, 'believe the gospel'.

8. 'The gospel' (that is, good tidings, good news for guilty, helpless sinners) in the largest sense of the word means the whole revelation made to men by Jesus Christ; and sometimes the whole account of what our Lord did and suffered while he tabernacled among men. The substance of all is, 'Jesus Christ came into the world to save sinners;' or, 'God so loved the world that he gave his only begotten Son, to the end we might not perish, but have everlasting life;' or, 'He was bruised for our transgressions, he was wounded for our iniquities; the chastisement of our peace was upon him, and with his stripes we are healed.'

9. Believe this, and the kingdom of God is thine. By faith thou attainest the promise: 'He pardoneth and absolveth all that truly repent and unfeignedly believe his holy gospel.' As soon as ever God hath spoken to thy heart, 'Be of good cheer, thy sins are forgiven thee,' his kingdom comes; thou hast righteousness, and peace, and joy in the Holy Ghost.

10. Only beware thou do not deceive thy own soul with regard to the nature of this faith. It is not (as some have fondly conceived) a bare assent to the truth of the Bible, of the articles of our creed, or of all that is contained in the Old and New Testament. The devils believe this, as well as I or thou; and yet they are devils still. But it is, over and above

this, a sure trust in the mercy of God through Christ Jesus. It is a confidence in a pardoning God. It is a divine evidence or conviction that 'God was in Christ, reconciling the world to himself, not imputing to them their former trespasses;' and in particular that the Son of God hath loved me and given himself for me; and that I, even I, am now reconciled to God by the blood of the cross.

11. Dost thou thus believe? Then the peace of God is in thy heart, and sorrow and sighing flee away. Thou art no longer in doubt of the love of God; it is clear as the noonday sun. Thou criest out, 'My song shall be always of the loving-kindness of the Lord: with my mouth will I ever be telling of thy truth, from one generation to another.' Thou art no longer afraid of hell, or death, or him that had once the power of death, the devil: no, nor painfully afraid of God himself; only thou hast a tender, filial fear of offending him. Dost thou believe? Then thy 'soul doth magnify the Lord, and thy spirit rejoiceth in God thy Saviour'. Thou rejoicest in that thou hast 'redemption through his blood, even the forgiveness of sins'. Thou rejoicest in that 'Spirit of adoption which crieth in thy heart, Abba, Father!' Thou rejoicest in a 'hope full of immortality'; in reaching forth unto the 'mark of the prize of thy high calling'; in an earnest expectation of all the good things which God hath prepared for them that love him.

12. Dost thou now believe? Then 'the love of God is' now 'shed abroad in thy heart.' Thou lovest him, because he first loved us. And because thou lovest God, thou lovest thy brother also. And being filled with 'love, peace, joy', thou art also filled with 'long-suffering, gentleness, fidelity, goodness, meekness, temperance', and all the other fruits of the same Spirit—in a word, with whatever dispositions are holy, are heavenly or divine. For while thou 'beholdest with open (uncovered) face' (the veil now being taken away) 'the glory of the Lord', his glorious love, and the glorious image wherein thou wast created, thou art 'changed into the same image, from glory to glory, by the Spirit of the Lord'.

13. This repentance, this faith, this peace, joy, love; this change from glory to glory, is what the wisdom of the world has voted to be madness, mere enthusiasm, utter distraction. But thou, O man of God, regard them not: be thou moved by none of these things. Thou knowest in whom thou hast believed. See that no man take thy crown. Whereunto thou hast already attained, hold fast, and follow, till thou attain all the great and precious promises. And thou who hast not yet known him, let not vain men make thee ashamed of the gospel of Christ. Be thou in nothing terrified by those who speak evil of the things which they know not. God will soon turn thy heaviness into joy. O let not thy hands hang down. Yet a little longer, and he will take away thy fears, and give thee the spirit of a sound mind. 'He is nigh that justifieth:' 'Who is he that condemneth? It is Christ that died; yea, rather, that rose again; who is even now at the right hand of God, making intercession for thee.' Now cast thyself on the Lamb of God, with all thy sins, how many soever they be; and 'an entrance shall *now* be ministered unto *thee* into the kingdom of our Lord and Saviour Jesus Christ'!

7. ON WORKING OUT OUR OWN SALVATION

1785

An Introductory Comment

This late sermon, which made its appearance in print in the *Arminian Magazine* in 1785, explores a part of Wesley's sophisticated understanding of grace, especially in its catholic, synergistic (working together) emphases. It should be read in conjunction with the sermon "Free Grace" in which Wesley's Protestant conception of grace, richly drawn from the Anglican Reformation, is clearly on display. Wesley preached on the biblical text for this present sermon (Phil. 2:12-13) twice in 1732 and twice in 1734 (O, 3:199), the latter occurring at the Castle Prison in Oxford, at which point the text disappeared from the sermon register until 1781 at Norwich, an occasion upon which Wesley remarked, "Even the Calvinists were satisfied for the present" (WH, 23:192).

Wesley saw little difficulty in championing the two maxims of this sermon: (1) "God works; therefore you can work," underscoring *ability,* and (2) "God works; therefore you must work," highlighting *obligation* simply because he not only carefully laid out a doctrine of prevenient grace in this setting, in which conscience itself is viewed as a supernatural gift of God, but he also maintained that even in his most synergistic understanding of grace, of divine and human cooperation, God must be given "the whole glory of his own work" (O, 3:202) and in a way that "removes all imagination of merit from man" (O, 3:202). Moreover, such an estimate of the divine role in co-operant grace, as generous as it is, must yet be distinguished from that entailed in free grace, the work of God alone. This sermon is also remarkable in that it evidences the basic flow of the *ordo salutis* from the perspective of a diversity of graces: prevenient, convincing, and only "Afterwards [do] we experience the proper Christian salvation" (O, 3:204).

On Working Out Our Own Salvation

1. Some great truths were known in some measure to the heathen world
2. There are two grand doctrines of which heathens were totally ignorant
   A. The first relates to the eternal Son of God
   B. The second relates to the Spirit of God
3. Through the Incarnation and Scripture, these truths were revealed to all
4. The Apostle Paul demonstrated the connection between two things:
   A. That it is God that works in us
   B. That we should work out our salvation with fear and trembling

I. 1. The assertion that God works in us removes all thought of merit
   2. God works in you both to will and to do
      A. This expression has two interpretations, both of which are true
      B. To will may include the whole of inward religion
      C. To do the whole of outward religion
   3. The original words seem to favour the latter construction
   4. Nothing can so directly overcome pride as a deep conviction of this

II. 1. If God worketh in you, then work out your own salvation
   2. How are we to work out our salvation? With fear and trembling
   3. How easily may we transfer this to the business of life
   4. What steps does Scripture direct us to take?
      A. Isaiah gives us an answer: Cease to do evil; learn to do well

III. 1. Some reject that there is a connection between the former and the latter clause
   2. This is the reasoning of flesh and blood for two reasons
      A. God works; therefore you *can* work
      B. God works; therefore you *must* work
   3. If God did not work we could not work out our salvation
   4. This is no excuse for those who continue in sin, laying blame upon God
      A. They say the souls of men are dead in sin by *nature*
      B. But no man is entirely destitute of what is called natural conscience
      C. But this is not natural; it is more properly termed preventing grace
   5. Because God works in you, you can work out your own salvation
   6. You can do something, through Christ who is strengthening you
   7. God works in you; therefore you must work; you must be workers with him
   8. Go on in the work of faith, the patience of hope, and the labor of love

Sermon 85: On Working Out Our Own Salvation, 1785

Philippians 2:12-13

Work out your own salvation with fear and trembling; for it is God that worketh in you, both to will and to do of his good pleasure.

1. Some great truths, as the being and attributes of God, and the difference between moral good and evil, were known in some measure to the heathen world; the traces of them are to be found in all nations; so that in some sense it may be said to every child of man: 'He hath showed thee, O man, what is good; even to do justly, to love mercy, and to walk humbly with thy God.' With this truth he has in some measure 'enlightened everyone that cometh into the world'. And hereby they that 'have not the law', that have no written law, 'are a law unto themselves'. They show 'the work of the law', the substance of it, though not the letter, 'written in their hearts', by the same hand which wrote the commandments on the tables of stone; 'their conscience also bearing them witness', whether they act suitably thereto or not.

2. But there are two grand heads of doctrine, which contain many truths of the most important nature, of which the most enlightened heathens in the ancient world were totally ignorant; as are also the most intelligent heathens that are now on the face of the earth: I mean those which relate to the eternal Son of God, and the Spirit of God—to the Son, giving himself to be 'a propitiation for the sins of the world', and to the Spirit of God, renewing men in that image of God wherein they were created. For after all the pains which ingenious and learned men have taken (that great man the Chevalier Ramsay in particular), to find some resemblance of these truths in the immense rubbish of heathen authors, the resemblance is so exceeding faint as not to be discerned but by a very lively imagination. Beside that even this resemblance, faint as it was, is only to be found in the discourses of a very few, and those were the most improved and deeply thinking men in their several generations; while the innumerable multitudes that surrounded them were little better for the knowledge of the philosophers, but remained as totally ignorant, even of these capital truths, as were the beasts that perish.

3. Certain it is that these truths were never known to the vulgar, the bulk of mankind, to the generality of men in any nation, till they were brought to light by the gospel. Notwithstanding a spark of knowledge glimmering here and there, the whole earth was covered with darkness till the Sun of Righteousness arose and scattered the shades of night. Since this Day-spring from on high has appeared, a great light hath shined unto those who till then sat in darkness and in the shadow of death. And thousands of them in every age have known, 'that God so loved the world' as to 'give his only Son, to the end that whosoever believeth on him should not perish, but have everlasting life.' And being entrusted with the oracles of God, they have known that 'God hath also given us his Holy Spirit,' who 'worketh in us both to will and to do of his good pleasure'.

4. How remarkable are those words of the Apostle which precede these! 'Let this mind be in you, which was also in Christ Jesus: who, being in the form of God', the incommunicable nature of God from eternity, 'counted it no act of robbery' (that is the precise meaning of the word), no invasion of any other's prerogative, but his own

unquestionable right, 'to be equal with God.' The word implies both the *fullness* and the supreme *height* of the Godhead. To which are opposed the two words, he 'emptied', and he 'humbled himself'. He 'emptied himself' of that divine fullness, veiled his fullness from the eyes of men and angels, 'taking'—and by that very act emptying himself—'the form of a servant, being made in the likeness of man', a real man like other men. 'And being found in fashion as a man', a common man, without any peculiar beauty or excellency, 'he humbled himself' to a still greater degree, 'becoming obedient' to God, though equal with him, 'even unto death, yea the death of the cross'—the greatest instance both of humiliation and obedience.

Having proposed the example of Christ, the Apostle exhorts them to secure the salvation which Christ hath purchased for them: 'Wherefore work out your own salvation with fear and trembling; for it is God that worketh in you both to will and to do of his good pleasure.'

In these comprehensive words we may observe,

First, that grand truth, which ought never to be out of our remembrance, 'It is God that worketh in us, both to will and to do of his own good pleasure;'

Secondly, the improvement we ought to make of it: 'Work out your own salvation with fear and trembling;'

Thirdly, the connection between them: 'It is God that worketh in you;' therefore 'work out your own salvation.'

I.1. First, we are to observe that great and important truth which ought never to be out of our remembrance, 'It is God that worketh in us both to will and to do of his good pleasure.' The meaning of these words may be made more plain by a small transposition of them: 'It is God that of his good pleasure worketh in you both to will and to do.' This position of the words, connecting the phrase of 'his good pleasure' with the word 'worketh', removes all imagination of merit from man, and gives God the whole glory of his own work. Otherwise we might have had some room for boasting, as if it were our own desert, some goodness in us, or some good thing done by us, which first moved God to work. But this expression cuts off all such vain conceits, and clearly shows his motive to work lay wholly in himself—in his own mere grace, in his unmerited mercy.

2. It is by this alone he is impelled to work in man both to will and to do. The expression is capable of two interpretations, both of which are unquestionably true. First, 'to will' may include the whole of inward, 'to do' the whole of outward religion. And if it be thus understood, it implies that it is God that worketh both inward and outward holiness. Secondly, 'to will' may imply every good desire, 'to do' whatever results therefrom. And then the sentence means, God breathes into us every good desire, and brings every good desire to good effect.

3. The original words τὸ θέλειν and τὸ ἐνεργεῖν, seem to favour the latter construction; τὸ θέλειν, which we render 'to will', plainly including every good desire, whether relating to our tempers, words, or actions, to inward or outward holiness. And τὸ ἐνεργεῖν,

which we render 'to do', manifestly implies all that power from on high; all that energy which works in us every right disposition, and then furnishes us for every good word and work.

4. Nothing can so directly tend to hide pride from man as a deep, lasting conviction of this. For if we are thoroughly sensible that we have nothing which we have not received, how can we glory as if we had not received it? If we know and feel that the very first motion of good is from above, as well as the power which conducts it to the end—if it is God that not only infuses every good desire, but that accompanies and follows it, else it vanishes away—then it evidently follows that 'he who glorieth must glory in the Lord.'

II.1. Proceed we now to the second point: if God 'worketh in you', then 'work out your own salvation.' The original word rendered, 'work out', implies the doing a thing thoroughly. 'Your own'—for you yourselves must do this, or it will be left undone for ever. 'Your *own salvation*'—salvation begins with what is usually termed (and very properly) 'preventing grace'; including the first wish to please God, the first dawn of light concerning his will, and the first slight, transient conviction of having sinned against him. All these imply some tendency toward life, some degree of salvation, the beginning of a deliverance from a blind, unfeeling heart, quite insensible of God and the things of God. Salvation is carried on by 'convincing grace', usually in Scripture termed 'repentance', which brings a larger measure of self-knowledge, and a farther deliverance from the heart of stone. Afterwards we experience the proper Christian salvation, whereby 'through grace' we 'are saved by faith', consisting of those two grand branches, justification and sanctification. By justification we are saved from the guilt of sin, and restored to the favour of God: by sanctification we are saved from the power and root of sin, and restored to the image of God. All experience, as well as Scripture, shows this salvation to be both instantaneous and gradual. It begins the moment we are justified, in the holy, humble, gentle, patient love of God and man. It gradually increases from that moment, as a 'grain of mustard seed, which at first is the least of all seeds, but' gradually 'puts forth large branches', and becomes a great tree; till in another instant the heart is cleansed from all sin, and filled with pure love to God and man. But even that love increases more and more, till we 'grow up in all things into him that is our head', 'till we attain the measure of the stature of the fullness of Christ'.

2. But how are we to 'work out' this salvation? The Apostle answers, 'With fear and trembling'. There is another passage of St. Paul wherein the same expression occurs, which may give light to this: 'Servants, obey your masters according to the flesh,' according to the present state of things, although sensible that in a little time the servant will be free from his master, 'with fear and trembling'. This is a proverbial expression, which cannot be understood literally. For what master could bear, much less require, his servant to stand trembling and quaking before him? And the following words utterly exclude this meaning: 'in singleness of heart', with a single eye to the will and providence of God, 'not with eye-service, as men-pleasers, but as servants of Christ, doing the will of God from the heart'; doing whatever they do as the will of God, and therefore with their might (Eph. 6:5-6). It is easy to see that these strong expressions of the Apostle

clearly imply two things: first, that everything be done with the utmost earnestness of spirit, and with all care and caution—perhaps more directly referring to the former word, μετὰ φόβου, 'with fear'; secondly, that it be done with the utmost diligence, speed, punctuality, and exactness—not improbably referring to the latter word, μετὰ τρόμου, 'with trembling'.

3. How easily may we transfer this to the business of life, the working out our own salvation! With the same temper and in the same manner that Christian servants serve their masters that are upon earth, let other Christians labour to serve their Master that is in heaven: that is, first, with the utmost earnestness of spirit, with all possible care and caution; and, secondly, with the utmost diligence, speed, punctuality, and exactness.

4. But what are the steps which the Scripture directs us to take, in the working out of our own salvation? The prophet Isaiah gives us a general answer touching the first steps which we are to take: 'Cease to do evil; learn to do well.' If ever you desire that God should work in you that faith whereof cometh both present and eternal salvation, by the grace already given, fly from all sin as from the face of a serpent; carefully avoid every evil word and work; yea, abstain from all appearance of evil. And 'learn to do well'; be zealous of good works, of works of piety, as well as works of mercy. Use family prayer, and cry to God in secret. Fast in secret, and 'your Father which seeth in secret, he will reward you openly.' 'Search the Scriptures;' hear them in public, read them in private, and meditate therein. At every opportunity be a partaker of the Lord's Supper. 'Do this in remembrance of him,' and he will meet you at his own table. Let your conversation be with the children of God, and see that it 'be in grace, seasoned with salt'. As ye have time, do good unto all men, to their souls and to their bodies. And herein 'be ye steadfast, unmovable, always abounding in the work of the Lord.' It then only remains that ye deny yourselves and take up your cross daily. Deny yourselves every pleasure which does not prepare you for taking pleasure in God, and willingly embrace every means of drawing near to God, though it be a cross, though it be grievous to flesh and blood. Thus when you have redemption in the blood of Christ, you will 'go on to perfection'; till, 'walking in the light, as he is in the light', you are enabled to testify that 'he is faithful and just', not only 'to forgive your sins', but 'to cleanse you from all unrighteousness.'

III.1. 'But', say some, 'what connection is there between the former and the latter clause of this sentence? Is there not rather a flat opposition between the one and the other? If it is God that worketh in us both to will and to do, what need is there of our working? Does not his working thus supersede the necessity of our working at all? Nay, does it not render our working impracticable, as well as unnecessary? For if we allow that God does all, what is there left for us to do?'

2. Such is the reasoning of flesh and blood. And at first hearing it is exceeding plausible. But it is not solid, as will evidently appear if we consider the matter more deeply. We shall then see there is no opposition between these—'God works; therefore do ye work'—but on the contrary the closest connection, and that in two respects. For, first, God works; therefore you *can* work. Secondly, God works; therefore you *must* work.

3. First, God worketh in you; therefore you can work—otherwise it would be impossible. If he did not work it would be impossible for you to work out your own salvation. 'With man this is impossible—', saith our Lord, 'for a rich man to enter into the kingdom of heaven.' Yea, it is impossible for any man; for any that is born of a woman, unless God work in him. Seeing all men are by nature not only sick, but 'dead in trespasses, and sins', it is not possible for them to do anything well till God raises them from the dead. It was impossible for Lazarus to 'come forth' till the Lord had given him life. And it is equally impossible for us to 'come' out of our sins, yea, or to make the least motion toward it, till he who hath all power in heaven and earth calls our dead souls into life.

4. Yet this is no excuse for those who continue in sin, and lay the blame upon their Maker by saying: 'It is God only that must quicken us; for we cannot quicken our own souls.' For allowing that all the souls of men are dead in sin by *nature*, this excuses none, seeing there is no man that is in a state of mere nature; there is no man, unless he has quenched the Spirit, that is wholly void of the grace of God. No man living is entirely destitute of what is vulgarly called 'natural conscience'. But this is not natural; it is more properly termed 'preventing grace'. Every man has a greater or less measure of this, which waiteth not for the call of man. Everyone has sooner or later good desires, although the generality of men stifle them before they can strike deep root or produce any considerable fruit. Everyone has some measure of that light, some faint glimmering ray, which sooner or later, more or less, enlightens every man that cometh into the world. And everyone, unless he be one of the small number whose conscience is seared as with a hot iron, feels more or less uneasy when he acts contrary to the light of his own conscience. So that no man sins because he has not grace, but because he does not use the grace which he hath.

5. Therefore inasmuch as God works in you, you are now able to work out your own salvation. Since he worketh in you of his own good pleasure, without any merit of yours, both to will and to do, it is possible for you to fulfil all righteousness. It is possible for you to 'love God, because he hath first loved us', and to 'walk in love', after the pattern of our great Master. We know indeed that word of his to be absolutely true, 'Without me ye can do nothing.' But on the other hand we know, every believer can say, 'I can do all things through Christ that strengtheneth me.'

6. Meantime let us remember that God has joined these together in the experience of every believer. And therefore we must take care not to imagine they are ever to be put asunder. We must beware of that mock humility which teacheth us to say, in excuse for our wilful disobedience, 'Oh, I can do nothing,' and stops there, without once naming the grace of God. Pray think twice. Consider what you say. I hope you wrong yourself. For if it be really true that you can do nothing, then you have no faith. And if you have not faith you are in a wretched condition. Surely it is not so. You can do something, through Christ strengthening you. Stir up the spark of grace which is now in you, and he will give you more grace.

7. Secondly, God worketh in you; therefore you *must* work: you must be 'workers together with him' (they are the very words of the Apostle); otherwise he will cease working. The general rule on which his gracious dispensations invariably proceed is this: 'Unto him that hath shall be given; but from him that hath not', that does not improve the

grace already given, 'shall be taken away what he assuredly hath' (so the words ought to be rendered). Even St. Augustine, who is generally supposed to favour the contrary doctrine, makes that just remark, *Qui fecit nos sine nobis, non salvabit nos sine nobis*: 'he that made us without ourselves, will not save us without ourselves.' He will not save us unless we 'save ourselves from this untoward generation'; unless we ourselves 'fight the good fight of faith, and lay hold on eternal life'; unless we 'agonize to enter in at the strait gate,' 'deny ourselves, and take up our cross daily', and labour, by every possible means, to 'make our own calling and election sure'.

8. 'Labour' then, brethren, 'not for the meat that perisheth, but for that which endureth to everlasting life.' Say with our blessed Lord, though in a somewhat different sense, 'My Father worketh hitherto, and I work.' In consideration that he still worketh in you, be never 'weary of well-doing'. Go on, in virtue of the grace of God preventing, accompanying, and following you, in 'the work of faith, in the patience of hope, and in the labour of love'. 'Be ye steadfast and immovable; always abounding in the work of the Lord.' And 'the God of peace, who brought again from the dead the great Shepherd of the sheep',—Jesus—'make you perfect in every good work to do his will, working in you what is well-pleasing in his sight, through Jesus Christ, to whom be glory for ever and ever!'

8. THE MEANS OF GRACE

1746

An Introductory Comment

The means of grace are the ordinary channels whereby God might convey preventing, justifying, or sanctifying grace to humanity. The instituted means of grace, so celebrated in the church, include (1) prayer, (2) searching the Scriptures, (3) the Lord's Supper, (4) Christian conference, and (5) fasting. In this present sermon Wesley seeks a proper balance with respect to such means by neither undervaluing nor overvaluing them.

The first error occurred as early as September 1739 at the joint Moravian-Methodist society at Fetter Lane in London, when some began to teach the importance of leaving off using the means of grace until faith was received. John Wesley eventually corrected Philip Henry Molther, a Moravian champion of this view, but to no avail. Frustrated and ready to move to the Foundery, Wesley read a letter at the conclusion of a love feast at Fetter Lane on July 20, 1740, and criticized three teachings: (1) there is no such thing as weak faith, (2) one ought not to use the means of grace until all doubt and fear are gone, and (3) using the ordinances of God is salvation by works.

The second error of overvaluing the means had several examples among those Anglicans and others who rested content in "the form of godliness without the power" (O, 1:383). Cautioning some of his wayward peers in a letter to the Earl of Dartmouth in 1770, Wesley pointed out that though they were socially respectable by avoiding all known sin, doing much good, and employing the means of grace, they yet "had little of the life of God in their souls" (T, 5:173). Wesley had touched upon this theme in 1748 and reasoned, "He wants a religion of a nobler kind, a religion higher and deeper than this" (O, 1:497). Simply put, the means are not the end or goal of religion. Therefore "in using all means," Wesley observed, "seek God alone" (O, 1:396).

The Means of Grace

I. 1. Are there means ordained of God as the usual channels of grace?
2. Some associate religion with outward things rather than with a renewed heart
3. The means do not always lead to the end for which they were ordained
4. Many *abuse* the ordinances of God; far more *despise* them
5. Some talk as though outward religion were *absolutely nothing*
6. Experience shows how easily this notion spreads

II. 1. I propose to examine whether there are any means of grace
2. The value of religion depends on subservience to the end of religion
3. Apart from the Spirit of God, outward signs cannot profit at all
4. The use of all means will never atone for sin
5. Many Christians abuse the means of grace
6. They do not understand the great foundation, by grace ye are saved

III. 1. We should wait for the grace of God by means of prayer
2. Our Lord directs the use of this means and promises it will be effectual
3. The Lord declares that we may receive grace by this means
4. The Lord tells us to pray and faint not
5. We are to wait for the blessings of God in private prayer
6. All who desire grace should wait for it in prayer
7. All who desire grace should wait for it by searching the Scriptures
8. By this means, God not only gives but also increases true wisdom
9. The Holy Ghost expressly declares it is profitable
10. This is profitable both for Christians and for those still in darkness
11. All who desire an increase in grace are to partake of the Lord's Supper

IV. 1. People object that you cannot use these means without *trusting* in them
2. They also object that this is seeking salvation by works
3. Many strongly object that Christ is the only means of grace
4. They also object that Scripture directs us to *wait* for salvation
5. The Scriptures do not prove that we ought not to use these means

V. 1. How should we use the means of grace?
2. Some say we should follow the order given by God
3. Holy Writ gives no particular order to be observed
4. Remember that God is above all means
A. There is no power or merit in the means themselves
B. Look singly to the *power* of the Spirit and the *merits* of the Son

Sermon 16: The Means of Grace, 1746

Malachi 3:7

Ye are gone away from mine ordinances, and have not kept them.

[I].1. But are there any 'ordinances' now, since life and immortality were brought to light by the gospel? Are there, under the Christian dispensation, any 'means' ordained of God as the usual channels of his grace? This question could never have been proposed in the apostolical church unless by one who openly avowed himself to be a heathen, the whole body of Christians being agreed that Christ had ordained certain outward means for conveying his grace into the souls of men. Their constant practice set this beyond all dispute; for so long as 'all that believed were together, and had all things common' (Acts 2:44), 'they continued steadfastly in the teaching of the apostles, and in the breaking of bread, and in prayers' (Acts 2:42).

2. But in process of time, when 'the love of many waxed cold,' some began to mistake the *means* for the *end*, and to place religion rather in doing those outward works than in a heart renewed after the image of God. They forgot that 'the end of' every 'commandment is love, out of a pure heart, with faith unfeigned:' the loving the Lord their God with all their heart, and their neighbour as themselves; and the being purified from pride, anger, and evil desire, by a 'faith of the operation of God'. Others seemed to imagine that though religion did not principally consist in these outward means, yet there was something in them wherewith God was well-pleased, something that would still make them acceptable in his sight, though they were not exact in the weightier matters of the law, in justice, mercy, and the love of God.

3. It is evident, in those who abused them thus, they did not conduce to the end for which they were ordained. Rather, the things which should have been for their health were to them an occasion of falling. They were so far from receiving any blessing therein, that they only drew down a curse upon their head; so far from growing more heavenly in heart and life, that they were twofold more the children of hell than before. Others clearly perceiving that these means did not convey the grace of God to those children of the devil, began from this particular case to draw a general conclusion, 'that they were not means of conveying the grace of God.'

4. Yet the number of those who *abused* the ordinances of God was far greater than of those who *despised* them, till certain men arose, not only of great understanding (sometimes joined with considerable learning), but who likewise appeared to be men of love, experimentally acquainted with true, inward religion. Some of these were burning and shining lights, persons famous in their generations, and such as had well deserved of the church of Christ for standing in the gap against the overflowings of ungodliness.

It cannot be supposed that these holy and venerable men intended any more at first than to show that outward religion is nothing worth without the religion of the heart; that 'God is a Spirit, and they who worship him must worship him in spirit and truth;' that, therefore, external worship is lost labour without a heart devoted to God; that the outward ordinances of God then profit much when they advance inward holiness, but when they advance it not are unprofitable and void, are lighter than vanity; yea, that when they are used, as it were, *in the place* of this, they are an utter abomination to the Lord.

5. Yet is it not strange if some of these, being strongly convinced of that horrid profanation of the ordinances of God which had spread itself over the whole church, and wellnigh driven true religion out of the world, in their fervent zeal for the glory of God and the recovery of souls from that fatal delusion, spake as if outward religion were *absolutely nothing*, as if it had *no* place in the religion of Christ. It is not surprising at all if they should not always have expressed themselves with sufficient caution; so that unwary hearers might believe they condemned all outward means as altogether unprofitable, and as not designed of God to be the ordinary channels of conveying his grace into the souls of men.

Nay, it is not impossible some of these holy men did at length themselves fall into this opinion: in particular those who, not by choice, but by the providence of God, were cut off from all these ordinances—perhaps wandering up and down, having no certain abiding-place, or dwelling in dens and caves of the earth. These, experiencing the grace of God in themselves, though they were deprived of all outward means, might infer that the same grace would be given to them who of set purpose abstained from them.

6. And experience shows how easily this notion spreads, and insinuates itself into the minds of men: especially of those who are thoroughly awakened out of the sleep of death, and begin to feel the weight of their sins a burden too heavy to be borne. These are usually impatient of their present state, and trying every way to escape from it. They are always ready to catch at any new thing, any new proposal of ease or happiness. They have probably tried most outward means, and found no ease in them—it may be, more and more of remorse and fear and sorrow and condemnation. It is easy, therefore, to persuade these that it is better for them to abstain from all those means. They are already weary of striving (as it seems) in vain, of labouring in the fire; and are therefore glad of any pretence to cast aside that wherein their soul had no pleasure; to give over the painful strife, and sink down into an indolent inactivity.

II.1. In the following discourse I propose to examine at large whether there are any means of grace.

By 'means of grace' I understand outward signs, words, or actions ordained of God, and appointed for this end—to be the *ordinary* channels whereby he might convey to men preventing, justifying, or sanctifying grace.

I use this expression, 'means of grace', because I know none better, and because it has been generally used in the Christian church for many ages: in particular by our own church, which directs us to bless God both for the 'means of grace and hope of glory'; and teaches us that a sacrament is 'an outward sign of inward *grace*, and a *means* whereby we receive the same'.

The chief of these means are prayer, whether in secret or with the great congregation; searching the Scriptures (which implies reading, hearing, and meditating thereon) and receiving the Lord's Supper, eating bread and drinking wine in remembrance of him; and these we believe to be ordained of God as the ordinary channels of conveying his grace to the souls of men.

2. But we allow that the whole value of the means depends on their actual subservience to the end of religion; that consequently all these means, when separate from the end, are less than nothing, and vanity; that if they do not actually conduce to the knowledge and love of God they are not acceptable in his sight; yea, rather, they are an abomination before him; a stink in his nostrils; he is weary to bear them—above all if they are used as a kind of 'commutation' for the religion they were designed to subserve. It is not easy to find words for the enormous folly and wickedness of thus turning God's arms against himself, of keeping Christianity out of the heart by those very means which were ordained for the bringing it in.

3. We allow likewise that all outward means whatever, if separate from the Spirit of God, cannot profit at all, cannot conduce in any degree either to the knowledge or love of God. Without controversy, the help that is done upon earth, he doth it himself. It is he alone who, by his own almighty power, worketh in us what is pleasing in his sight. And all outward things, unless he work in them and by them, are mere weak and beggarly elements. Whosoever therefore imagines there is any intrinsic *power* in any means whatsoever does greatly err, not knowing the Scriptures, neither the power of God. We know that there is no inherent power in the words that are spoken in prayer, in the letter of Scripture read, the sound thereof heard, or the bread and wine received in the Lord's Supper; but that it is God alone who is the giver of every good gift, the author of all grace; that the whole power is of him, whereby through any of these there is any blessing conveyed to our soul. We know likewise that he is able to give the same grace, though there were no means on the face of the earth. In this sense we may affirm that with regard to God there is no such thing as means, seeing he is equally able to work whatsoever pleaseth him by any or by none at all.

4. We allow farther that the use of all means whatever will never atone for one sin; that it is the blood of Christ alone whereby any sinner can be reconciled to God; there being no other propitiation for our sins, no other fountain for sin and uncleanness. Every believer in Christ is deeply convinced that there is no *merit* but in him; that there is no *merit* in any of his own works; not in uttering the prayer, or searching the Scripture, or hearing the Word of God, or eating of that bread and drinking of that cup; so that if no more be intended by the expression some have used, 'Christ is the only means of grace,' than this—that he is the only *meritorious cause* of it—it cannot be gainsaid by any who know the grace of God.

5. Yet once more. We allow (though it is a melancholy truth) that a large proportion of those who are called Christians do to this day abuse the means of grace to the destruction of their souls. This is doubtless the case with all those who rest content in the form of godliness without the power. Either they fondly presume they are Christians already, because they do thus and thus, although Christ was never yet revealed in their hearts, nor the love of God shed abroad therein: or else they suppose they shall infallibly be so, barely because they use these means; idly dreaming (though perhaps hardly conscious thereof)

either that there is some kind of *power* therein whereby sooner or later (they know not when) they shall certainly be made holy; or that there is a sort of *merit* in using them, which will surely move God to give them holiness or accept them without it.

6. So little do they understand that great foundation of the whole Christian building, 'By grace ye are saved.' Ye are saved from your sins, from the guilt and power thereof, ye are restored to the favour and image of God, not for any works, merits, or deservings of yours, but by the free *grace*, the mere mercy of God through the merits of his well-beloved Son. Ye are thus saved, not by any power, wisdom, or strength which is in you or in any other creature, but merely through the grace or power of the Holy Ghost, which worketh all in all.

7. But the main question remains. We know this salvation is the gift and the work of God. But how (may one say, who is convinced he hath it not) may I attain thereto? If you say, 'Believe, and thou shalt be saved,' he answers, 'True; but how shall I believe?' You reply, 'Wait upon God.' 'Well. But how am I to wait? In the means of grace, or out of them? Am I to wait for the grace of God which bringeth salvation by using these means, or by laying them aside?'

8. It cannot possibly be conceived that the Word of God should give no direction in so important a point; or that the Son of God who came down from heaven for us men and for our salvation should have left us undetermined with regard to a question wherein our salvation is so nearly concerned.

And in fact he hath not left us undetermined; he hath shown us the way wherein we should go. We have only to consult the oracles of God, to inquire what is written there. And if we simply abide by their decision, there can no possible doubt remain.

III.1. According to this, according to the decision of Holy Writ, all who desire the grace of God are to wait for it in the means which he hath ordained; in using, not in laying them aside.

And first, all who desire the grace of God are to wait for it in the way of *prayer*. This is the express direction of our Lord himself. In his Sermon upon the Mount, after explaining at large wherein religion consists, and describing the main branches of it, he adds: 'Ask, and it shall be given you; seek, and ye shall find; knock, and it shall be opened unto you. For everyone that asketh, receiveth; and he that seeketh, findeth; and to him that knocketh, it shall be opened' (Matt. 7:7-8). Here we are in the plainest manner directed to ask in order to, or as a *means* of, receiving; to seek in order to find the grace of God, the pearl of great price; and to knock, to continue asking and seeking, if we would enter into his kingdom.

2. That no doubt might remain our Lord labours this point in a more peculiar manner. He appeals to every man's own heart: 'What man is there of you, who, if his son ask bread, will give him a stone? Or if he ask a fish, will he give him a serpent? If ye then, being evil, know how to give good gifts unto your children, how much more shall your Father which is in heaven'—the Father of angels and men, the Father of the spirits of all

flesh—'give good things to them that ask him?' (Matt. 7:9-11). Or, as he expresses himself on another occasion, including all good things in one, 'How much more shall your heavenly Father give the Holy Spirit to them that ask him?' (Luke 11:13). It should be particularly observed here that the persons directed to ask had not then received the Holy Spirit. Nevertheless our Lord directs them to use this means, and promises that it should be effectual; that upon asking they should receive the Holy Spirit from him whose mercy is over all his works.

3. The absolute necessity of using this means if we would receive any gift from God yet farther appears from that remarkable passage which immediately precedes these words: 'And he said unto them' (whom he had just been teaching how to pray) 'which of you shall have a friend, and shall go unto him at midnight, and shall say unto him, Friend, lend me three loaves; . . . and he from within shall answer, Trouble me not. . . . I cannot rise and give thee: I say unto you, though he will not rise and give him, because he is his friend, yet because of his importunity he will rise, and give him as many as he needeth. And I say unto you, ask and it shall be given you' (Luke 11:5, 7-9). 'Though he will not give him because he is his friend, yet because of his importunity he will rise and give him as many as he needeth.' How could our blessed Lord more plainly declare that we may receive of God by this means, by importunately asking, what otherwise we should not receive at all!

4. 'He spake also another parable to this end, that men ought always to pray, and not to faint,' till through this means they should receive of God whatsoever petition they asked of him: 'There was in a city a judge which feared not God, neither regarded man. And there was a widow in that city, and she came unto him, saying, Avenge me of my adversary. And he would not for a while; but afterward he said within himself, Though I fear not God, nor regard man, yet because this widow troubleth me I will avenge her, lest by her continual coming she weary me' (Luke 18:1-5). The application of this our Lord himself hath made. 'Hear what the unjust judge saith!' Because she continues to ask, because she will take no denial, therefore I will avenge her. 'And shall not God avenge his own elect which cry day and night unto him? I tell you he will avenge them speedily'—if they 'pray and faint not'.

5. A direction equally full and express to wait for the blessings of God in private prayer, together with a positive promise that by this means we shall obtain the request of our lips, he hath given us in those well-known words: 'Enter into thy closet; and when thou hast shut thy door, pray to thy Father which is in secret; and thy Father which seeth in secret shall reward thee openly' (Matt. 6:6).

6. If it be possible for any direction to be more clear, it is that which God hath given us by the Apostle with regard to prayer of every kind, public and private, and the blessing annexed thereto. 'If any of you lack wisdom, let him ask of God, that giveth to all men liberally' (if they ask; otherwise 'ye have not, because ye ask not', Jas. 4:2), 'and upbraideth not, and it shall be given him' (Jas. 1:5).

If it be objected, 'But this is no direction to unbelievers, to them who know not the pardoning grace of God; for the Apostle adds, "But let him ask in faith"; otherwise, "let him not think that he shall receive anything of the Lord."' I answer, the meaning of the word 'faith' in this place is fixed by the Apostle himself (as if it were on purpose to obviate this objection) in the words immediately following: 'Let him ask in faith, nothing wavering,' nothing *doubting*, μηδὲν διακρινόμενος—not doubting God heareth his prayer, and will fulfil the desire of his heart.

The gross, blasphemous absurdity of supposing 'faith' in this place to be taken in the full Christian meaning appears hence: it is supposing the Holy Ghost to direct a man who knows he has not this faith (which is here termed 'wisdom') to ask it of God, with a positive promise that 'it shall be given him'; and then immediately to subjoin that it shall not be given him unless he have it before he asks for it! But who can bear such a supposition? From this Scripture, therefore, as well as those cited above, we must infer that all who desire the grace of God are to wait for it in the way of prayer.

7. Secondly, all who desire the grace of God are to wait for it in 'searching the Scriptures'.

Our Lord's direction with regard to the use of this means is likewise plain and clear. 'Search the Scriptures', saith he to the unbelieving Jews, 'for [. . .] they [. . .] testify of me' (John 5:39). And for this very end did he direct them to search the Scriptures, that they might *believe in him.*

The objection that this is not a command, but only an assertion that they did 'search the Scriptures', is shamelessly false. I desire those who urge it to let us know how a command can be more clearly expressed than in those terms, 'Ερευνᾶτε τᾶς γραφάς. It is as peremptory as so many words can make it.

And what a blessing from God attends the use of this means appears from what is recorded concerning the Bereans, who, after hearing St. Paul, 'searched the Scriptures daily, whether those things were so. Therefore many of them believed'—found the grace of God in the way which he had ordained (Acts 17:11-12).

It is probable, indeed, that in some of those who had 'received the word with all readiness of mind', 'faith came (as the same Apostle speaks) by hearing,' and was only confirmed by *reading* the Scriptures. But it was observed above that under the general term of 'searching the Scriptures' both hearing, reading, and meditating are contained.

8. And that this is a means whereby God not only gives, but also confirms and increases true wisdom, we learn from the words of St. Paul to Timothy: 'From a child thou hast known the Holy Scriptures, which are able to make thee wise unto salvation, through faith which is in Christ Jesus' (2 Tim. 3:15). The same truth (namely, that this is the great means God has ordained for conveying his manifold grace to man) is delivered, in the fullest manner that can be conceived, in the words which immediately follow: 'All Scripture is given by inspiration of God' (consequently, all Scripture is infallibly true), 'and is profitable for doctrine, for reproof, for correction, for instruction in righteousness;' to the end 'that the man of God may be perfect, throughly furnished unto all good works' (2 Tim. 3:16-17).

9. It should be observed that this is spoken primarily and directly of the Scriptures which Timothy had 'known from a child'; which must have been those of the Old

Testament, for the New was not then wrote. How far then was St. Paul (though he was 'not a whit behind the very chief of the apostles', nor therefore, I presume, behind any man now upon earth) from making light of the Old Testament! Behold this, lest ye one day 'wonder and perish', ye who make so small account of one half of the oracles of God! Yea, and that half of which the Holy Ghost expressly declares that it is 'profitable', as a means ordained of God for this very thing, 'for doctrine, for reproof, for correction, for instruction in righteousness': to the end [that] 'the man of God may be perfect, throughly furnished unto all good works'.

10. Nor is this profitable only for the men of God, for those who walk already in the light of his countenance, but also for those who are yet in darkness, seeking him whom they know not. Thus St. Peter: 'We have also a more sure word of prophecy'—literally, 'And we have the prophetic word more sure' (καὶ ἔχομεν βεβαιότερον τὸν προφητικὸν λόγον), confirmed by our being 'eye-witnesses of his majesty', and 'hearing the voice which came from the excellent glory'—'unto which (prophetic word; so he styles the Holy Scriptures) ye do well that ye take heed, as unto a light that shineth in a dark place, until the day dawn, and the day-star arise in your hearts' (2 Pet. 1:19). Let all, therefore, who desire that day to dawn upon their hearts, wait for it in 'searching the Scriptures'.

11. Thirdly, all who desire an increase of the grace of God are to wait for it in partaking of the Lord's Supper. For this also is a direction himself hath given: 'The same night in which he was betrayed, he took bread, and brake it, and said, Take, eat; this is my body' (that is, the sacred sign of my body). 'This do in remembrance of me. Likewise he took the cup, saying, This cup is the New Testament' (or covenant) 'in my blood' (the sacred sign of that covenant): 'this do ye . . . in remembrance of me. For as often as ye eat this bread and drink this cup, ye do show forth the Lord's death till he come' (1 Cor. 11:23-26)—ye openly exhibit the same by these visible signs, before God, and angels, and men; ye manifest your solemn remembrance of his death, till he cometh in the clouds of heaven.

Only 'let a man (first) examine himself,' whether he understand the nature and design of this holy institution, and whether he really desire to be himself made conformable to the death of Christ; 'and so (nothing doubting) let him eat of that bread and drink of that cup' (1 Cor. 11:28).

Here then the direction first given by our Lord is expressly repeated by the Apostle: 'Let him eat,' 'let him drink' (ἐσθιέτω, πινέτω—both in the imperative mood); words not implying a bare permission only, but a clear explicit command; a command to all those either who already are filled with peace and joy in believing, or who can truly say, 'The remembrance of our sins is grievous unto us; the burden of them is intolerable.'

12. And that this is also an ordinary stated means of receiving the grace of God is evident from those words of the Apostle which occur in the preceding chapter: 'The cup of blessing which we bless, is it not the communion (or communication) of the blood of Christ? The bread which we break, is it not the communion of the body of Christ?' (1 Cor. 10:16). Is not the eating of that bread, and the drinking of that cup, the outward, visible means whereby God conveys into our souls all that spiritual grace, that righteousness, and peace, and joy in the Holy Ghost, which were purchased by the body of Christ

once broken and the blood of Christ once shed for us? Let all, therefore, who truly desire the grace of God, eat of that bread and drink of that cup.

IV.1. But as plainly as God hath pointed out the way wherein he will be inquired after, innumerable are the objections which men wise in their own eyes have from time to time raised against it. It may be needful to consider a few of these; not because they are of weight in themselves, but because they have so often been used, especially of late years, to turn the lame out of the way; yea, to trouble and subvert those who did run well, till Satan appeared as an angel of light.

The first and chief of these is, 'You cannot use these means (as you call them) without *trusting* in them.' I pray, where is this written? I expect you should show me plain Scripture for your assertion; otherwise I dare not receive it, because I am not convinced that you are wiser than God.

If it really had been as you assert, it is certain Christ must have known it. And if he had known it, he would surely have warned us; he would have revealed it long ago. Therefore, because he has not, because there is no tittle of this in the whole revelation of Jesus Christ, I am as fully assured your assertion is false as that this revelation is of God.

'However, leave them off for a short time to see whether you trusted in them or no.' So I am to disobey God in order to know whether I trust in obeying him! And do you avow this advice? Do you deliberately teach to 'do evil, that good may come'? O tremble at the sentence of God against such teachers! Their 'damnation is just'.

'Nay, if you are troubled when you leave them off, it is plain you trusted in them.' By no means. If I am troubled when I wilfully disobey God, it is plain his Spirit is still striving with me. But if I am not troubled at wilful sin, it is plain I am given up to a reprobate mind.

But what do you mean by '*trusting* in them'? Looking for the blessing of God therein? Believing that if I wait in this way I shall attain what otherwise I should not? So I do. And so I will, God being my helper, even to my life's end. By the grace of God I will *thus* trust in them till the day of my death; that is, I will believe that whatever God hath promised he is faithful also to perform. And seeing he hath promised to bless me in this way, I *trust* it shall be according to his Word.

2. It has been, secondly, objected, 'This is seeking salvation by works.' Do you know the meaning of the expression you use? What is 'seeking salvation by works'? In the writings of St. Paul it means either seeking to be saved by observing the ritual works of the Mosaic law, or expecting salvation for the sake of our own works, by the merit of our own righteousness. But how is either of these implied in my waiting in the way God has ordained, and expecting that he will meet me there because he has promised so to do?

I do expect that he will fulfil his Word, that he will meet and bless me in this way. Yet not for the sake of any works which I have done, nor for the merit of my righteousness; but merely through the merits and sufferings and love of his Son, in whom he is always well-pleased.

3. It has been vehemently objected, thirdly, that Christ is the only means of grace. I answer, this is mere playing upon words. Explain your term, and the objection vanishes away. When we say, 'Prayer is a means of grace,' we understand a channel through which the grace of God is conveyed. When you say, 'Christ is the means of grace,' you understand the sole price and purchaser of it; or, that 'no man cometh unto the Father, but through him.' And who denies it? But this is utterly wide of the question.

4. But does not the Scripture (it has been objected, fourthly) direct us to *wait* for salvation? Does not David say, 'My soul waiteth upon God; for of him cometh my salvation'? And does not Isaiah teach us the same thing, saying, 'O Lord, [. . .] we have waited for thee'? All this cannot be denied. Seeing it is the gift of God, we are undoubtedly to *wait* on him for salvation. But how shall we wait? If God himself has appointed a way, can you find a better way of waiting for him? But that he hath appointed a way hath been shown at large, and also what that way is. The very words of the Prophet which you cite put this out of the question. For the whole sentence runs thus: 'In the way of thy judgments' (or ordinances), 'O Lord, have we waited for thee' (Isa. 26:8). And in the very same way did David wait, as his own words abundantly testify: 'I have waited for thy saving health, O Lord, and have kept thy law.' 'Teach me, O Lord, the way of thy statutes, and I shall keep it unto the end.'

5. 'Yea', say some, 'but God has appointed another way—"Stand still and see the salvation of God."'

Let us examine the Scriptures to which you refer. The first of them, with the context, runs thus: 'And when Pharaoh drew nigh, the children of Israel lifted up their eyes . . . , and they were sore afraid. [. . .] And they said unto Moses, Because there were no graves in Egypt, hast thou taken us away to die in the wilderness? And Moses said unto the people, Fear ye not: stand still, and see the salvation of the Lord. [. . .] And the Lord said unto Moses, [. . .] Speak unto the children of Israel that they go forward. But lift thou up thy rod, and stretch out thine hand over the sea, and divide it. And the children of Israel shall go on dry ground through the midst of the sea' (Exod. 14:10-11, 13, 15-16).

This was the 'salvation' of God which they 'stood still' to see—by 'marching forward' with all their might!

The other passage wherein this expression occurs stands thus:

> 'There came some that told Jehoshaphat, saying, There cometh a great multitude against thee, from beyond the sea. [. . .] And Jehoshaphat feared, and set himself to seek the Lord, and proclaimed a fast throughout all Judah. And Judah gathered themselves together to ask help of the Lord; even out of all the cities they came to seek the Lord. And Jehoshaphat stood in the congregation, in the house of the Lord. . . . Then upon Jahaziel [. . .] came the Spirit of the Lord. . . . And he said, . . . Be not dismayed by reason of this great multitude. . . . Tomorrow go ye down against them; [. . .] ye shall not need to fight in this battle. Set yourselves: stand ye still, and see the salvation of the Lord. . . . And they rose early in the morning and went forth. [. . .] And when they began to sing and to praise, the Lord set ambushments against the children of Moab, Ammon, and Mount Seir, . . . and everyone helped to destroy another.' (2 Chron. 20:2-5, 14-17, 20, 22-23)

Such was the salvation which the children of Judah saw. But how does all this prove that we ought not to wait for the grace of God in the means which he hath ordained?

6. I shall mention but one objection more, which indeed does not properly belong to this head. Nevertheless, because it has been so frequently urged, I may not wholly pass it by.

'Does not St. Paul say, "If ye be dead with Christ, why are ye subject to *ordinances*?" (Col. 2:20). Therefore a Christian, one that is "dead with Christ", need not use the ordinances any more.'

So you say, 'If I am a Christian I am not subject to the ordinances of Christ!' Surely, by the absurdity of this you must see at the first glance that the ordinances here mentioned cannot be the ordinances of Christ! That they must needs be the Jewish ordinances, to which it is certain a Christian is no longer subject.

And the same undeniably appears from the words immediately following, 'Touch not, taste not, handle not'—all evidently referring to the ancient ordinances of the Jewish law.

So that this objection is the weakest of all. And in spite of all, that great truth must stand unshaken: that all who desire the grace of God are to wait for it in the means which he hath ordained.

V.1. But this being allowed—that all who desire the grace of God are to wait for it in the means he hath ordained—it may still be inquired how those means should be used, both as to the *order* and the *manner* of using them.

With regard to the former, we may observe there is a kind of order wherein God himself is generally pleased to use these means in bringing a sinner to salvation. A stupid, senseless wretch is going on in his own way, not having God in all his thoughts, when God comes upon him unawares, perhaps by an awakening sermon or conversation, perhaps by some awful providence; or it may be an immediate stroke of his convincing Spirit, without any outward means at all. Having now a desire to flee from the wrath to come, he purposely goes to *hear* how it may be done. If he finds a preacher who speaks to the heart, he is amazed, and begins 'searching the Scriptures', whether these things are so. The more he *hears* and *reads*, the more convinced he is; and the more he *meditates* thereon day and night. Perhaps he finds some other book which explains and enforces what he has heard and read in Scripture. And by all these means the arrows of conviction sink deeper into his soul. He begins also to *talk* of the things of God, which are ever uppermost in his thoughts; yea, and to talk with God, to *pray* to him, although through fear and shame he scarce knows what to say. But whether he can speak or no, he cannot but pray, were it only in 'groans which cannot be uttered'. Yet being in doubt whether 'the high and lofty One that inhabiteth eternity' will regard such a sinner as him, he wants to pray with those who know God, with the faithful 'in the great congregation'. But here he observes others go up to 'the table of the Lord'. He considers, Christ has said, 'Do this.' How is it that I do not? I am too great a sinner. I am not fit. I am not worthy. After struggling with these scruples a while, he breaks through. And thus he continues in God's way—in hearing, reading, meditating, praying, and partaking of the Lord's Supper—till God, in the manner that pleases him, speaks to his heart, 'Thy faith hath saved thee; go in peace.'

2. By observing this order of God we may learn what means to recommend to any particular soul. If any of these will reach a stupid, careless sinner, it is probably *hearing* or *conversation.* To such therefore we might recommend these, if he has ever any thought about salvation. To one who begins to feel the weight of his sins, not only hearing the Word of God but *reading* it too, and perhaps other *serious books,* may be a means of deeper conviction. May you not advise him also to *meditate* on what he reads, that it may have its full force upon his heart? Yea, and to *speak* thereof, and not be ashamed, particularly among those who walk in the same path. When trouble and heaviness take hold upon him, should you not then earnestly exhort him to pour out his soul before God? 'Always to pray and not to faint'? And when he feels the worthlessness of his own prayers, are you not to work together with God and remind him of going up into 'the house of the Lord', and praying with all them that fear him? But if he does this, the *dying word* of his Lord will soon be brought to his remembrance: a plain intimation that this is the time when we should second the motions of the blessed Spirit. And thus may we lead him step by step through all the means which God has ordained; not according to our own will, but just as the providence and the Spirit of God go before and open the way.

3. Yet as we find no command in Holy Writ for any particular order to be observed herein, so neither do the providence and the Spirit of God adhere to any, without variation: but the means into which different men are led, and in which they find the blessing of God, are varied, transposed, and combined together a thousand different ways. Yet still our wisdom is to follow the leadings of his providence and his Spirit; to be guided herein (more especially as to the means wherein we ourselves seek the grace of God) partly by his outward providence, giving us the opportunity of using sometimes one means, sometimes another; partly by our experience, which it is whereby his free Spirit is pleased most to work in our heart. And in the meantime the sure and general rule for all who groan for the salvation of God is this—whenever opportunity serves, use all the means which God has ordained. For who knows in which God will meet thee with the grace that bringeth salvation?

4. As to the *manner* of using them, whereon indeed it wholly depends whether they should convey any grace at all to the user, it behoves us, first, always to retain a lively sense that God is above all means. Have a care therefore of limiting the Almighty. He doth whatsoever and whensoever it pleaseth him. He can convey his grace, either in or out of any of the means which he hath appointed. Perhaps he will. 'Who hath known the mind of the Lord? Or who hath been his counsellor?' Look then every moment for his appearing! Be it at the hour you are employed in his ordinances; or before, or after that hour; or when you are hindered therefrom—he is not hindered. He is always ready; always able, always willing to save. 'It is the Lord, let him do what seemeth him good!'

Secondly, *before* you use any means let it be deeply impressed on your soul: There is no *power* in this. It is in itself a poor, dead, empty thing: separate from God, it is a dry leaf, a shadow. Neither is there any *merit* in my using this, nothing intrinsically pleasing to

God, nothing whereby I deserve any favour at his hands, no, not a drop of water to cool my tongue. But because God bids, therefore I do; because he directs me to wait in this way, therefore here I wait for his free mercy, whereof cometh my salvation.

Settle this in your heart, that the *opus operatum*, the mere work done, profiteth nothing; that there is no *power* to save but in the Spirit of God, no *merit* but in the blood of Christ; that consequently even what God ordains conveys no grace to the soul if you trust not in him alone. On the other hand, he that does truly trust in him cannot fall short of the grace of God, even though he were cut off from every outward ordinance, though he were shut up in the centre of the earth.

Thirdly, in using all means, seek God alone. In and through every outward thing look singly to the *power* of his Spirit and the *merits* of his Son. Beware you do not stick in the *work* itself; if you do, it is all lost labour. Nothing short of God can satisfy your soul. Therefore eye him in all, through all, and above all.

Remember also to use all means *as means*; as ordained, not for their own sake, but in order to the renewal of your soul in righteousness and true holiness. If therefore they actually tend to this, well; but if not, they are dung and dross.

Lastly, after you have used any of these, take care how you value yourself thereon; how you congratulate yourself as having done some great thing. This is turning all into poison. Think, 'If God was not there, what does this avail? Have I not been adding sin to sin? How long, O Lord! Save, or I perish! O lay not this sin to my charge!' If God was there, if his love flowed into your heart, you have forgot, as it were, the outward work. You see, you know, you feel, God is all in all. Be abased. Sink down before him. Give him all the praise. Let God 'in all things be glorified through Christ Jesus'. Let 'all your bones cry out', 'My song shall be always of the loving-kindness of the Lord: With my mouth will I ever be telling of thy truth, from one generation to another!'

9. THE DUTY OF CONSTANT COMMUNION

1787

An Introductory Comment

While he was a fellow at Lincoln College in 1732 Wesley edited the Anglican liturgist Robert Nelson's work, *The Great Duty of Frequenting the Christian Sacrifice*, for use by his students (O, 3:427). Fifty-five years later Wesley edited this work again, reducing its size, and published it as an "original sermon" in the *Arminian Magazine* (O, 3:427). In the interim Wesley had dropped Nelson's language of "sacrifice," which could suggest erroneous notions of priestcraft, and he accordingly remarked in his *Journal* on June 27, 1740, that "we come to his table, not to give him anything but to receive whatsoever he sees best for us" (WH, 19:159). Beyond this, Wesley repudiated the Roman Catholic understanding of transubstantiation (associated with an officiating priest) in his *Explanatory Notes on the New Testament* on the text for this sermon, Luke 22:19, by maintaining that the words of Christ, "This is my body," are a figurative, not literal, expression.

Viewing the Lord's Supper as an outward sign of an inward grace, Wesley urged the Methodists to take up the practice of the ancient church and to commune frequently. Since Wesley considered this means of grace as a "converting ordinance," whereby God would communicate prevenient, justifying, and sanctifying grace to recipients as needed, the only requirement to receive this sacrament was reflected in the language of the Book of Common Prayer itself, which Wesley reproduced in his *Sunday Service*: "Ye that do truly and earnestly repent of your sins. . . . Draw near with faith" (SS, 131). To substantiate this view, which had its critics, Wesley noted in his *Journal* on June 28, 1740, that at the first Lord's Supper Jesus "commanded those very men [the disciples] who were then unconverted, who had not yet 'received the Holy Ghost', who (in the full sense of the word) were not believers, to 'do this in remembrance of him'" (WH, 19:158). Given this counsel for the unconverted, then, the duty of all professing Christians was even clearer.

The Duty of Constant Communion

I. Every Christian should receive the Lord's Supper as often as possible

1. The first reason why is because it is the plain command of Christ
2. The second reason why is because the benefits of doing it are so great
3. The grace of God herein confirms to us thc pardon of our sins
4. Let those who desire to please God communicate every time they can
5. Eating bread and drinking wine are outward signs of inward grace
6. When possible, you should undergo self-examination and prayer

II. I will now answer objections against constantly receiving communion

1. I say constantly receiving, for the phrase 'frequent communion' is absurd
2. Observe that constantly communing is a command of God
3. Some will say, 'God does not command me to do this *as often as I can*'
   A. Are we not to obey every command of God as often as we can?
4. This great truth is proved from the absurdity of the contrary opinion
5. Consider the Lord's Supper as a mercy from God to human beings
   A. I ask, why do you not accept God's mercy as often as you can?
6. This yields a full answer to all the common objections

7.–8. Let us now see the particular excuses that people make for not obeying
   A. The most common excuse is, 'I am *unworthy*'
   B. Is that a reason for refusing mercy?

9.–10. You should not fear bringing *damnation* on yourself

11–12. Others plead that they cannot pretend to lead so holy a life

13. It requires neither more nor less obedience than you promised in baptism
14. A second objection is that business does not allow time for preparation
15. No business can hinder a person from the preparation which is necessary
16. A third objection is that it abates our reverence for the sacrament
17. Reverence for the sacrament may be of two sorts:
    A. Either owing purely to newness or owing to our faith

18.–19. I have communicated constantly . . . but I have not found the benefit
   A. We do this because God commands it, regardless of the benefit

20. Another objection is that the Church enjoins it only three times a year
    A. We obey the Church only for God's sake; receive it every time

21.–22. None of the objections usually made can be an excuse

Sermon 101: The Duty of Constant Communion, 1787
Luke 22:19

To the Reader

The following discourse was written above five and fifty years ago, for the use of my pupils at Oxford. I have added very little, but retrenched much; as I then used more words than I do now. But I thank God I have not yet seen cause to alter my sentiments in any point which is therein delivered. J. W.

Luke 22:19

Do this in remembrance of me.

It is no wonder that men who have no fear of God should never think of doing this. But it is strange that it should be neglected by any that do fear God, and desire to save their souls. And yet nothing is more common. One reason why any neglect it is, they are so much afraid of 'eating and drinking unworthily' that they never think how much greater the danger is when they do not eat or drink it at all. That I may do what I can to bring these well-meaning men to a more just way of thinking, I shall,

First, show that it is the duty of every Christian to receive the Lord's Supper as often as he can; and secondly, answer some objections.

I. I am to show that it is the duty of every Christian to receive the Lord's Supper as often as he can.

1. The first reason why it is the duty of every Christian so to do is because it is a plain command of Christ. That this is his command appears from the words of the text, 'Do this in remembrance of me:' by which, as the Apostles were obliged to bless, break, and give the bread to all that joined with them in those holy things, so were all Christians obliged to receive those signs of Christ's body and blood. Here therefore the bread and wine are commanded to be received, in remembrance of his death, to the end of the world. Observe, too, that this command was given by our Lord when he was just laying down his life for our sakes. They are therefore, as it were, his dying words to all his followers.

2. A second reason why every Christian should do this as often as he can is because the benefits of doing it are so great to all that do it in obedience to him; namely, the forgiveness of our past sins and the present strengthening and refreshing of our souls. In this world we are never free from temptations. Whatever way of life we are in, whatever

our condition be, whether we are sick or well, in trouble or at ease, the enemies of our souls are watching to lead us into sin. And too often they prevail over us. Now when we are convinced of having sinned against God, what surer way have we of procuring pardon from him than the 'showing forth the Lord's death', and beseeching him, for the sake of his Son's sufferings, to blot out all our sins?

3. The grace of God given herein confirms to us the pardon of our sins by enabling us to leave them. As our bodies are strengthened by bread and wine, so are our souls by these tokens of the body and blood of Christ. This is the food of our souls: this gives strength to perform our duty, and leads us on to perfection. If therefore we have any regard for the plain command of Christ, if we desire the pardon of our sins, if we wish for strength to believe, to love and obey God, then we should neglect no opportunity of receiving the Lord's Supper. Then we must never turn our backs on the feast which our Lord has prepared for us. We must neglect no occasion which the good providence of God affords us for this purpose. This is the true rule—so often are we to receive as God gives us opportunity. Whoever therefore does not receive, but goes from the holy table when all things are prepared, either does not understand his duty or does not care for the dying command of his Saviour, the forgiveness of his sins, the strengthening of his soul, and the refreshing it with the hope of glory.

4. Let everyone therefore who has either any desire to please God, or any love of his own soul, obey God and consult the good of his own soul by communicating every time he can; like the first Christians, with whom the Christian sacrifice was a constant part of the Lord's day's service. And for several centuries they received it almost every day. Four times a week always, and every saint's day beside. Accordingly those that joined in the prayers of the faithful never failed to partake of the blessed sacrament. What opinion they had of any who turned his back upon it we may learn from that ancient canon, 'If any believer join in the prayers of the faithful, and go away without receiving the Lord's Supper, let him be excommunicated, as bringing confusion into the church of God.'

5. In order to understand the nature of the Lord's Supper, it would be useful carefully to read over those passages in the Gospel and in the first Epistle to the Corinthians which speak of the institution of it. Hence we learn that the design of this sacrament is the continual remembrance of the death of Christ, by eating bread and drinking wine, which are the outward signs of the inward grace, the body and blood of Christ.

6. It is highly expedient for those who purpose to receive this, whenever their time will permit, to prepare themselves for this solemn ordinance by self-examination and prayer. But this is not absolutely necessary. And when we have not time for it, we should see that we have the habitual preparation which is absolutely necessary, and can never be dispensed with on any account or any occasion whatever. This is, first, a full *purpose* of heart to keep all the commandments of God. And secondly, a sincere *desire* to receive all his promises.

II. I am, in the second place, to answer the common objections against constantly receiving the Lord's Supper.

1. I say 'constantly' receiving. For as to the phrase of 'frequent communion', it is absurd to the last degree. If it means anything less than constant it means more than can be proved to be the duty of any man. For if we are not obliged to communicate 'constantly', by what argument can it be proved that we are obliged to communicate 'frequently'? Yea, more than once a year, or once in seven years? Or once before we die? Every argument brought for this either proves that we ought to do it *constantly*, or proves nothing at all. Therefore that indeterminate, unmeaning way of speaking ought to be laid aside by all men of understanding.

2. In order to prove that it is our duty to communicate constantly we may observe that the Holy Communion is to be considered either, (1), as a command of God, or (2), as a mercy to man.

First, as a command of God. God, our Mediator and Governor, from whom we have received our life and all things, on whose will it depends whether we shall be perfectly happy or perfectly miserable from this moment to eternity, declares to us that all who obey his commands shall be eternally happy; all who do not shall be eternally miserable. Now one of these commands is, 'Do this in remembrance of me.' I ask then, 'Why do you not do this, when you can do it if you will? When you have an opportunity before you, why do not you obey the command of God?'

3. Perhaps you will say, 'God does not command me to do this *as often as I can*;' that is, the words 'as often as you can' are not added in this particular place. What then? Are we not to obey every command of God as often as we can? Are not all the promises of God made to those, and those only, who 'give all diligence'; that is, to those who do all they can to obey his commandments? Our power is the one rule of our duty. Whatever we can do, that we ought. With respect either to this or any other command, he that when he may obey it if he will does not, will have no place in the kingdom of heaven.

4. And this great truth, that we are obliged to keep every command as far as we can, is clearly proved from the absurdity of the contrary opinion; for were we to allow that we are not obliged to obey every commandment of God as often as we can, we have no argument left to prove that any man is bound to obey any command at any time. For instance, should I ask a man why he does not obey one of the plainest commands of God—why, for instance, he does not help his parents—he might answer, 'I will not do it now, but I will at another time.' When that time comes, put him in mind of God's command again and he will say, 'I will obey it some time or other.' Nor is it possible ever to prove that he ought to do it now, unless by proving that he ought to do it as often as he can: and therefore he ought to do it now, because he can if he will.

5. Consider the Lord's Supper, secondly, as a mercy from God to man. As God, whose mercy is over all his works, and particularly over the children of men, knew there was but one way for man to be happy like himself, namely, by being like him in holiness; as he knew we could do nothing toward this of ourselves, he has given us certain means of obtaining his help. One of these is the Lord's Supper, which of his infinite mercy he hath given for this very end: that through this means we may be assisted to attain those blessings which he hath prepared for us; that we may obtain holiness on earth and everlasting glory in heaven.

I ask, then, why do you not accept of his mercy as often as ever you can? God now offers you his blessing: why do you refuse it? You have an opportunity of receiving his mercy: why do you not receive it? You are weak: why do not you seize upon every opportunity of increasing your strength? In a word: considering this as a command of God, he that does not communicate as often as he can has no piety; considering it as a mercy, he that does not communicate as often as he can has no wisdom.

6. These two considerations will yield a full answer to all the common objections which have been made against constant communion; indeed to all that ever were or can be made. In truth nothing can be objected against it but upon supposition that at this particular time, either the communion would be no mercy, or I am not commanded to receive it. Nay, should we grant it would be no mercy, that is not enough; for still the other reason would hold: whether it does you any good or none, you are to obey the command of God.

7. However, let us see the particular excuses which men commonly make for not obeying it. The most common is, 'I am *unworthy*; and "he that eateth and drinketh unworthily, eateth and drinketh damnation to himself." Therefore I dare not communicate, lest I should eat and drink my own damnation.'

The case is this. God offers you one of the greatest mercies on this side heaven, and commands you to accept it. Why do not you accept this mercy in obedience to his command? You say, 'I am unworthy to receive it.' And what then? You are unworthy to receive any mercy from God. But is that a reason for refusing all mercy? God offers you a pardon for all your sins. You are unworthy of it, 'tis sure, and he knows it: but since he is pleased to offer it nevertheless, will not you accept of it? He offers to deliver your soul from death. You are unworthy to live. But will you therefore refuse life? He offers to endue your soul with new strength. Because you are unworthy of it, will you deny to take it? What can God himself do for us farther, if we refuse his mercy, even because we are unworthy of it?

8. But suppose this were no mercy to us (to suppose which is indeed giving God the lie; saying, that is not good for man which he purposely ordered for his good), still I ask, Why do not you obey God's command? He says, 'Do this.' Why do you not? You answer, 'I am unworthy to do it.' What! Unworthy to obey God? Unworthy to do what God bids you do? Unworthy to obey God's command? What do you mean by this? That those who are unworthy to obey God ought not to obey him? Who told you so? If he were even 'an angel from heaven, let him be accursed'. If you think God himself has told you so by St. Paul, let us hear his words. They are these: 'He that eateth and drinketh unworthily, eateth and drinketh damnation to himself.'

Why, this is quite another thing. Here is not a word said of 'being unworthy' to eat and drink. Indeed he does speak of eating and drinking 'unworthily'; but that is quite a different thing—so he has told us himself. In this very chapter we are told that by eating and drinking unworthily is meant taking the holy sacrament in such a rude and disorderly way that one was 'hungry and another drunken'. But what is that to *you*? Is there any danger of *your* doing so? Of your eating and drinking *thus* 'unworthily'? However unworthy you are to communicate, there is no fear of your communicating thus. Therefore, whatever the punishment is of doing it thus unworthily, it does not concern *you*. You have no more reason from this text to disobey God than if there was no such text in the Bible. If you speak of 'eating and drinking unworthily' in the sense St. Paul uses the words you may as well say, 'I dare not communicate "for fear the church should fall" as for fear I should "eat and drink unworthily".'

9. If then you fear bringing *damnation* on yourself by this, you fear where no fear is. Fear it not for eating and drinking unworthily; for that, in St. Paul's sense, ye cannot do. But I will tell you for what you shall fear damnation: for not eating and drinking at all; for not obeying your Maker and Redeemer; for disobeying his plain command; for thus setting at nought both his mercy and authority. Fear ye this; for hear what his Apostle saith: 'Whosoever shall keep the whole law, and yet offend in one point, is guilty of all' (Jas. 2:10).

10. We see then how weak the objection is, 'I dare not receive (the Lord's Supper), because I am unworthy.' Nor is it any stronger, though the reason why you think yourself unworthy is that you have lately fallen into sin. It is true our Church forbids those 'who have done any grievous crime' to receive without repentance. But all that follows from this is that we should repent before we come; not that we should neglect to come at all.

To say, therefore, that 'a man may turn his back upon the altar because he has lately fallen into sin; that he may impose this penance upon himself', is talking without any warrant from Scripture. For where does the Bible teach to atone for breaking one commandment of God by breaking another? What advice is this—'Commit a new act of disobedience, and God will more easily forgive the past'!

11. Others there are who to excuse their disobedience plead that they are unworthy in another sense, that they 'cannot live up to it; they cannot pretend to lead so holy a life as constantly communicating would oblige them to do.' Put this into plain words. I ask: Why do not you accept the mercy which God commands you to accept? You answer, 'Because I cannot live up to the profession I must make when I receive it.' Then it is plain you ought never to receive it at all. For it is no more lawful to promise once what you know you cannot perform than to promise it a thousand times. You know, too, that it is one and the same promise whether you make it every year or every day. You promise to do just as much whether you promise ever so often or ever so seldom.

If therefore you cannot live up to the profession they make who communicate once a week, neither can you come up to the profession you make who communicate once a year. But cannot you, indeed? Then it had been good for you that you had never been born. For all that you profess at the Lord's table you must both profess and keep, or you cannot be saved. For you profess nothing there but this, that you will diligently keep his commandments. And cannot you keep up to this profession? Then you cannot enter into life.

12. Think then what you say, before you say you cannot live up to what is required of constant communicants. This is no more than is required of any communicants, yea, of everyone that has a soul to be saved. So that to say you cannot live up to this is neither better nor worse than renouncing Christianity. It is in effect renouncing your baptism, wherein you solemnly promised to keep all his commandments. You now fly from that

profession. You wilfully break one of his commandments, and to excuse yourself say you cannot keep his commandments! Then you cannot expect to receive the promises, which are made only to those that keep them.

13. What has been said on this pretence against constant communion is applicable to those who say the same thing in other words: 'We dare not do it, because it requires so perfect an obedience afterwards as we cannot promise to perform.' Nay, it requires neither more nor less perfect obedience than you promised in your baptism. You then undertook to keep the commandments of God by his help, and you promise no more when you communicate.

But observe upon the whole, this is not so properly an objection against constantly communicating as against communicating at all. For if we are not to receive the Lord's Supper till we are worthy of it, it is certain we ought never to receive it.

14. A second objection which is often made against constant communion is the having so much business as will not allow time for such a preparation as is necessary thereto. I answer: all the preparation that is absolutely necessary is contained in those words, 'Repent you truly of your sins past; have faith in Christ our Saviour' (and observe, that word is not here taken in its highest sense!); 'amend your lives, and be in charity with all men; so shall ye be meet partakers of these holy mysteries.' All who are thus prepared may draw near without fear, and receive the sacrament to their comfort. Now what business can hinder you from being thus prepared? From repenting of your past sins? From believing that Christ died to save sinners? From amending your lives, and being in charity with all men? No business can hinder you from this, unless it be such as hinders you from being in a state of salvation. If you resolve and design to follow Christ you are fit to approach the Lord's table. If you do not design this, you are only fit for the table and company of devils.

15. No business therefore can hinder any man from having that preparation which alone is necessary, unless it be such as unprepares him for heaven, as puts him out of a state of salvation. Indeed every prudent man will, when he has time, examine himself before he receives the Lord's Supper: whether he repents him truly of his former sins; whether he believes the promises of God; whether he fully designs to walk in his ways, and be in charity with all men. In this, and in private prayer, he will doubtless spend all the time he conveniently can. But what is this to *you* who have not time? What excuse is this for not obeying God? He commands you to come, and prepare yourself by prayer if you have time; if you have not, however, come. Make not reverence to God's command a pretence for breaking it. Do not rebel against him for fear of offending him. Whatever you do or leave undone besides, be sure to do what God bids you do. Examining yourself, and using private prayer, especially before the Lord's Supper, is good. But behold! 'To obey is better than' self-examination, 'and to hearken' than the prayer of an angel.

16. A third objection against constant communion is that it abates our reverence for the sacrament. Suppose it did? What then! Will you thence conclude that you are not to receive it constantly? This does not follow. God commands you, 'Do this.' You may do it now, but will not; and to excuse yourself say, 'If I do it so often, it will abate the reverence with which I do it now.' Suppose it did. Has God ever told you that when the obeying his

command abates your reverence to it then you may disobey it? If he has, you are guiltless; if not, what you say is just nothing to the purpose. The law is clear. Either show that the lawgiver makes this exception, or you are guilty before him.

17. Reverence for the sacrament may be of two sorts: either such as is owing purely to the newness of the thing, such as men naturally have for anything they are not used to; or such as is owing to our faith, or to the love or fear of God. Now the former of these is not properly a religious reverence, but purely natural. And this sort of reverence for the Lord's Supper the constantly receiving of it must lessen. But it will not lessen the true religious reverence, but rather confirm and increase it.

18. A fourth objection is, 'I have communicated constantly so long, but I have not found the benefit I expected.' This has been the case with many well-meaning persons, and therefore deserves to be particularly considered. And consider this first: whatever God commands us to do we are to do because he commands, whether we feel any benefit thereby or no. Now God commands, 'Do this in remembrance of me.' This therefore we are to do, because he commands, whether we find present benefit thereby or not. But undoubtedly we shall find benefit sooner or later, though perhaps insensibly. We shall be insensibly strengthened, made more fit for the service of God, and more constant in it. At least we are kept from falling back, and preserved from many sins and temptations. And surely this should be enough to make us receive this food as often as we can; though we do not presently feel the happy effects of it, as some have done, and we ourselves may when God sees best.

19. But suppose a man has often been at the sacrament, and yet received no benefit. Was it not his own fault? Either he was not rightly prepared, willing to obey all the commands, and to receive all the promises of God; or he did not receive it aright, trusting in God. Only see that you are duly prepared for it, and the oftener you come to the Lord's table the greater benefit you will find there.

20. A fifth objection which some have made against constant communion is that 'the Church enjoins it only three times a year.' The words of the Church are: 'Note, that every parishioner shall communicate at the least three times in the year.' To this I answer, first: What if the Church had not enjoined it at all? Is it not enough that God enjoins it? We obey the Church only for God's sake. And shall we not obey God himself? If then you receive three times a year because the Church commands it, receive every time you can because God commands it. Else your doing the one will be so far from excusing you for not doing the other that your own practice will prove your folly and sin, and leave you without excuse.

But, secondly, we cannot conclude from these words that the Church excuses him who receives only thrice a year. The plain sense of them is that he who does not receive thrice at least shall be cast out of the Church. But they do by no means excuse him who communicates no oftener. This never was the judgment of our Church. On the contrary, she takes all possible care that the sacrament be duly administered, wherever the Common Prayer is read, every Sunday and holiday in the year.

The Church gives a particular direction with regard to those that are in Holy Orders. 'In all cathedral and collegiate churches and colleges, where there are many priests and deacons, they shall all receive the communion with the priest, every Sunday at the least.'

21. It has been shown, first, that if we consider the Lord's Supper as a command of Christ, no man can have any pretence to Christian piety who does not receive it (not once a month, but) as often as he can; secondly, that if we consider the institution of it as a mercy to ourselves, no man who does not receive it as often as he can has any pretence to Christian prudence; thirdly, that none of the objections usually made can be any excuse for that man who does not at every opportunity obey his command and accept this mercy.

22. It has been particularly shown, first, that unworthiness is no excuse, because, though in one sense we are all unworthy, yet none of us need be afraid of being unworthy in St. Paul's sense, of 'eating and drinking unworthily'; secondly, that the not having time enough for preparation can be no excuse, since the only preparation which is absolutely necessary is that which no business can hinder; nor indeed anything on earth, unless so far as it hinders our being in a state of salvation; thirdly, that its abating our reverence is no excuse, since he who gave the command, 'Do this', nowhere adds, 'unless it abates your reverence;' fourthly, that our not profiting by it is no excuse, since it is our own fault in neglecting that necessary preparation which is in our own power; lastly, that the judgment of our own Church is quite in favour of constant communion. If those who have hitherto neglected it on any of these pretences will lay these things to heart, they will, by the grace of God, come to a better mind, and never more forsake their own mercies.

Oxon., Feb. 19, 1732

10. THE ALMOST CHRISTIAN

July 25, 1741

An Introductory Comment

With Wesley's earlier preaching before Oxford University well remembered, "Salvation by Faith" (June 11, 1738), both the curious and the earnest turned out in generous numbers to hear the Methodist leader in July 1741. Having been excluded from all the churches in London except four (S, 1:54), Wesley was informed by John Gambold, an Oxford Methodist who eventually joined the Moravians, that he would by no means be well received at St. Mary's. Undeterred by this advice, Wesley chose Acts 26:28 as his text, one that allowed him to apply the distinction between an almost and an altogether Christian to a difficult audience. About a month earlier Wesley had already employed this same text in London as he preached in the open air at Charles Square calling those assembled to repentance.

The characteristics of the almost Christian articulated by Wesley displayed not the life of an open, public sinner but one who was marked by a heathen honesty, a form of godliness, having "the *outside* of a real Christian" (O, 1:132), and who used the means of grace regularly. Beyond this, the almost Christian evidenced a deep sincerity, "a real design to serve God, a hearty desire to do his will" (O, 1:136), traits that would be recognized by Oxford dons and Methodists alike. Elsewhere in this sermon Wesley lifted up what would soon become (in 1743) the three basic counsels of the General Rules of the United Societies (avoid evil, do good, and employ the means of grace), and he referred to them as constituting not real Christianity but once again the characteristics of an almost Christian. And if an almost Christian is well below what justifying and regenerating graces mark a child of God, then the altogether Christian is exceedingly above them, having a faith that "purifies the heart" (O, 1:139) and that desires nothing but God (O, 1:140–41).

The Almost Christian

Since the Christian religion was in the world there have been almost Christians

A. First, what is implied by being almost Christian

B. Second, what it is to be *altogether* a Christian

I. 1. Now, in being almost a Christian is implied heathen honesty
2. Heathens paid some regard to truth as well as justice
3. They expected love and assistance from one another
4. Also implied in being almost a Christian is a form of godliness
5. Almost Christians endeavor to live peaceably with all
6. They do not confine themselves to kindness, but labor for the profit of many
7. They use the means of grace, frequenting the house of God
8. They also make use of family prayer and set apart time for private prayer
9. Almost Christians are even sincere
10. Their sincerity includes a real desire to serve God and to do God's will
11. It is possible to go thus far and yet be almost a Christian
12. I am content to be abased so you may be exalted
13. I did go this far for many years, doing all things sincerely

II. What more is implied in being altogether a Christian?
1. First is the love of God that engrosses the whole heart
2. Second is the love of neighbor
3. The last thing to be considered is faith in the Son of God
4. Faith which does not bring forth repentance, love, and good works is false
5. True faith is not only belief in the Scriptures, but trust in Christ
6. Whoever has this faith is not almost, but altogether a Christian
7. Who are the living witnesses of these things?
8. Are not many of you aware that you have never come this far?
9. Is the love of God shed abroad in your heart?
10. Awake, then, you who are asleep, and call upon your God
11. May we all experience what it means to be altogether Christians

Sermon 2: The Almost Christian

A Sermon preached at St. Mary's, Oxford, before the University, on July 25, 1741

Acts 26:28

Almost thou persuadest me to be a Christian.

And many there are who go thus far: ever since the Christian religion was in the world there have been many in every age and nation who were 'almost persuaded to be Christians'. But seeing it avails nothing before God to go *only thus far*, it highly imports us to consider,

First, what is implied in being *almost*,

Secondly, what in being *altogether* a Christian.

I.(I).1. Now in the being 'almost a Christian' is implied, first, heathen honesty. No one, I suppose, will make any question of this, especially since by heathen honesty here I mean, not that which is recommended in the writings of their philosophers only, but such as the common heathens expected of one another, and many of them actually practised. By the rules of this they were taught that they ought not to be unjust; not to take away their neighbour's goods, either by robbery or theft; not to oppress the poor, neither to use extortion toward any; not to cheat or overreach either the poor or rich in whatsoever commerce they had with them; to defraud no man of his right, and if it were possible to owe no man anything.

2. Again, the common heathens allowed that some regard was to be paid to truth as well as to justice. And accordingly they not only had him in abomination who was forsworn, who called God to witness to a lie, but him also who was known to be a slanderer of his neighbour, who falsely accused any man. And indeed little better did they esteem wilful liars of any sort, accounting them the disgrace of humankind, and the pests of society.

3. Yet again, there was a sort of love and assistance which they expected one from another. They expected whatever assistance anyone could give another without prejudice to himself. And this they extended, not only to those little offices of humanity which are performed without any expense or labour, but likewise to the feeding the hungry if they had food to spare, the clothing the naked with their own superfluous raiment, and in general the giving to any that needed such things as they needed not themselves. Thus far (in the lowest account of it) heathen honesty went, the first thing implied in the being 'almost a Christian'.

(II).4. A second thing implied in the being 'almost a Christian' is the having a form of godliness, of that godliness which is prescribed in the gospel of Christ—the having the *outside* of a real Christian. Accordingly the 'almost Christian' does nothing which the gospel forbids. He taketh not the name of God in vain, he blesseth and curseth not, he sweareth not at all, but his communication is 'Yea, yea,' 'nay, nay.' He profanes not the day of the Lord, nor suffers it to be profaned, even by the stranger that is within his gates. He not only avoids all actual adultery, fornication, and uncleanness, but every word or look that either directly or indirectly tends thereto: nay, and all idle words, abstaining both from all detraction, backbiting, talebearing, evil-speaking, and from 'all foolish talking and jesting' (εὐτραπελία), a kind of virtue in the heathen moralist's account. Briefly, from all conversation that is not 'good to the use of edifying', and that consequently 'grieves the Holy Spirit of God, whereby we are sealed to the day of redemption'.

5. He abstains from 'wine wherein is excess', from revellings and gluttony. He avoids, as much as in him lies, all strife and contention, continually endeavouring to live peaceably with all men. And if he suffer wrong, he avengeth not himself, neither returns evil for evil. He is no railer, no brawler, no scoffer, either at the faults or infirmities of his neighbour. He does not willingly wrong, hurt, or grieve any man; but in all things acts and speaks by that plain rule, 'Whatsoever thou wouldst not he should do unto thee, that do not thou to another.'

6. And in doing good he does not confine himself to cheap and easy offices of kindness, but labours and suffers for the profit of many, that by all means he may help some. In spite of toil or pain, 'whatsoever his hand findeth to do, he doth it with his might,' whether it be for his friends or for his enemies, for the evil or for the good. For, being 'not slothful in' this or in any 'business', 'as he hath opportunity he doth good', all manner of good, 'to all men', and to their souls as well as their bodies. He reproves the wicked, instructs the ignorant, confirms the wavering, quickens the good, and comforts the afflicted. He labours to awaken those that sleep, to lead those whom God hath already awakened to the fountain opened for sin and for uncleanness, that they may wash therein and be clean; and to stir up those who are saved through faith to adorn the gospel of Christ in all things.

7. He that hath the form of godliness uses also the means of grace; yea, all of them, and at all opportunities. He constantly frequents the house of God; and that not as the manner of some is, who come into the presence of the Most High either loaded with gold and costly apparel, or in all the gaudy vanity of dress, and either by their unseasonable civilities to each other or the impertinent gaiety of their behaviour disclaim all pretensions to the form as well as to the power of godliness. Would to God there were none, even among ourselves, who fall under the same condemnation: who come into his house, it may be, gazing about, or with all the signs of the most listless, careless indifference, though sometimes they may *seem* to use a prayer to God for his blessing on what they are entering upon; who during that awful service are either asleep or reclined in the most convenient posture for it; or, as though they supposed God was asleep, talking with one another, or looking round, as utterly void of employment. Neither let these be accused of the form of godliness. No: he who has even this behaves with seriousness and attention in every part of that solemn service. More especially when he approaches the table of the Lord it is not with a light or careless behaviour, but with an air, gesture, and deportment which speaks nothing else but 'God be merciful to me, a sinner!'

8. To this if we add the constant use of family prayer by those who are masters of families, and the setting times apart for private addresses to God, with a daily seriousness of behaviour—he who uniformly practises this outward religion has the form of

godliness. There needs but one thing more in order to his being 'almost a Christian', and that is, sincerity.

(III).9. By sincerity I mean a real, inward principle of religion from whence these outward actions flow. And indeed if we have not this we have not heathen honesty; no, not so much of it as will answer the demand of a heathen, Epicurean poet. Even this poor wretch, in his sober intervals, is able to testify:

Oderunt peccare boni virtutis amore;
Oderunt peccare mali formidine poenae.[1]

So that if a man only abstains from doing evil in order to avoid punishment,

Non pasces in cruce corvos[2]

saith the pagan—there, 'thou hast thy reward'. But even he will not allow such a harmless man as this to be so much as a *good heathen.* If then any man from the same motive (viz. to avoid punishment, to avoid the loss of his friends, or his gain, or his reputation) should not only abstain from doing evil but also do ever so much good—yea, and use all the means of grace—yet we could not with any propriety say, this man is even 'almost a Christian'. If he has no better principle in his heart he is only a hypocrite altogether.

10. Sincerity therefore is necessarily implied in the being 'almost a Christian': a real design to serve God, a hearty desire to do his will. It is necessarily implied that a man have a sincere view of pleasing God in all things: in all his conversation, in all his actions; in all he does or leaves undone. This design, if any man be 'almost a Christian', runs through the whole tenor of his life. This is the moving principle both in his doing good, his abstaining from evil, and his using the ordinances of God.

11. But here it will probably be inquired, Is it possible that any man living should go so far as this and nevertheless be *only* 'almost a Christian'? What more than this can be implied in the being 'a Christian altogether'? I answer, first, that it is possible to go thus far, and yet be but 'almost a Christian', I learn not only from the oracles of God, but also from the sure testimony of experience.

12. Brethren, 'great is my boldness toward you in this behalf.' And 'forgive me this wrong' if I declare my own folly upon the housetop, for yours and the gospel's sake. Suffer me then to speak freely of myself, even as of another man. I am content to be abased so ye may be exalted, and to be yet more vile for the glory of my Lord.

13. I did go thus far for many years, as many of this place can testify: using diligence to eschew all evil, and to have a conscience void of offence; redeeming the time, buying up every opportunity of doing all good to all men; constantly and carefully using all the public and all the private means of grace; endeavouring after a steady seriousness of behaviour at all times and in all places. And God is my record, before whom I stand, doing all this in sincerity; having a real design to serve God, a hearty desire to do his will in all things, to please him who had called me to 'fight the good fight', and to 'lay hold of eternal life'.

Yet my own conscience beareth me witness in the Holy Ghost that all this time I was but 'almost a Christian'.

II. If it be inquired, 'What more than this is implied in the being "altogether a Christian"?' I answer:

(I).1. First, the love of God. For thus saith his Word: 'Thou shalt love the Lord thy God with all thy heart, and with all thy soul, and with all thy mind, and with all thy strength.' Such a love of God is this as engrosses the whole heart, as takes up all the affections, as fills the entire capacity of the soul, and employs the utmost extent of all its faculties. He that thus loves the Lord his God, his spirit continually 'rejoiceth in God his Saviour'. 'His delight is in the Lord,' *his* Lord and his all, to whom 'in everything he giveth thanks'. All *his* 'desire is unto God, and to the remembrance of his name'. His heart is ever crying out, 'Whom have I in heaven but thee? and there is none upon earth that I desire beside thee.' Indeed, what can he desire beside God? Not the world, or the things of the world. For he is 'crucified to the world, and the world crucified to him'. He is crucified to the desire of the flesh, the desire of the eye, and the pride of life. Yea, he is dead to pride of every kind: for love 'is not puffed up', but he that dwelling in love 'dwelleth in God, and God in him', is less than nothing in his own eyes.

(II).2. The second thing implied in the being 'altogether a Christian' is the love of our neighbour. For thus said our Lord in the following words: 'Thou shalt love thy neighbour as thyself.' If any man ask, 'Who is my neighbour?' we reply, 'Every man in the world; every child of his who is "the Father of the spirits of all flesh".' Nor may we in any wise except our enemies, or the enemies of God and their own souls. But every Christian loveth these also as himself; yea, 'as Christ loved us'. He that would more fully understand what manner of love this is may consider St. Paul's description of it. It is 'long-suffering and kind. It envieth not. It is not rash or hasty in judging. It is not puffed up,' but maketh him that loves, the least, the servant of all. Love 'doth not behave itself unseemly', but 'becometh all things to all men'. She 'seeketh not her own', but only the good of others, that they may be saved. Love 'is not provoked'. It casteth out wrath, which he who hath is wanting in love. It 'thinketh no evil'. It 'rejoiceth not in iniquity, but rejoiceth in the truth'. It 'covereth all things, believeth all things, hopeth all things, endureth all things'.

(III).3. There is yet one thing more that may be separately considered, though it cannot actually be separate from the preceding, which is implied in the being 'altogether a Christian', and that is the ground of all, even faith. Very excellent things are spoken of this throughout the oracles of God. 'Everyone', saith the beloved disciple, 'that believeth, is born of God.' 'To as many as received him gave he power to become the sons of God, even to them that believe on his name.' And, 'This is the victory that overcometh the world, even our faith.' Yea, our Lord himself declares, 'He that believeth in the Son hath everlasting life;' and 'cometh not into condemnation, but is passed from death unto life'.

4. But here let no man deceive his own soul. It is diligently to be noted, the 'faith which bringeth not forth repentance' and love, and all good works, is not that 'right living

faith' which is here spoken of, 'but a dead and devilish one. . . . For even the devils believe that Christ was born of a virgin, that he wrought all kind of miracles, declaring himself very God; that for our sakes he suffered a most painful death, to redeem us from death everlasting; that he rose again the third day; that he ascended into heaven and sitteth at the right hand of the Father, and at the end of the world shall come again to judge both the quick and the dead. These articles of our faith the devils believe, and so they believe all that is written in the Old and New Testament. And yet for all this faith, they be but devils. They remain still in their damnable estate, lacking the very true Christian faith.'[3]

5. 'The right and true Christian faith is' (to go on in the words of our own Church) 'not only to believe that Holy Scripture and the articles of our faith are true, but also to have a sure trust and confidence to be saved from everlasting damnation by Christ'—it is a 'sure trust and confidence' which a man hath in God 'that by the merits of Christ his sins *are* forgiven, and he reconciled to the favour of God'—'whereof doth follow a loving heart to obey his commandments.'

6. Now whosoever has this faith which 'purifies the heart', by the power of God who dwelleth therein, from pride, anger, desire, 'from all unrighteousness', 'from all filthiness of flesh and spirit'; which fills it with love stronger than death both to God and to all mankind—love that doth the works of God, glorying to spend and to be spent for all men, and that endureth with joy, not only the reproach of Christ, the being mocked, despised, and hated of all men, but whatsoever the wisdom of God permits the malice of men or devils to inflict; whosoever has this faith, thus 'working by love', is not *almost* only, but *altogether* a Christian.

7. But who are the living witnesses of these things? I beseech you, brethren, as in the presence of that God before whom 'hell and destruction are without a covering: how much more the hearts of the children of men!'—that each of you would ask his own heart, 'Am I of that number? Do I so far practise justice, mercy, and truth, as even the rules of heathen honesty require? If so, have I the very *outside* of a Christian? The form of godliness? Do I abstain from evil, from whatsoever is forbidden in the written Word of God? Do I, whatever good my hand findeth to do, do it with my might? Do I seriously use all the ordinances of God at all opportunities? And is all this done with a sincere design and desire to please God in all things?'

8. Are not many of you conscious that you never came thus far? That you have not been even 'almost a Christian'? That you have not come up to the standard of heathen honesty? At least, not to the form of Christian godliness? Much less hath God seen sincerity in you, a real design of pleasing him in all things. You never so much as intended to devote all your words and works, your business, studies, diversions to his glory. You never even designed or desired that whatsoever you did should be done 'in the name of the Lord Jesus', and as such should be a 'spiritual sacrifice, acceptable to God through Christ.'

9. But supposing you had, do good designs and good desires make a Christian? By no means, unless they are brought to good effect. 'Hell is paved', saith one, 'with good intentions.' The great question of all, then, still remains. Is the love of God shed abroad in your heart? Can you cry out, 'My God and my all'? Do you desire nothing but him? Are you

happy in God? Is he your glory, your delight, your crown of rejoicing? And is this commandment written in your heart, 'that he who loveth God love his brother also'? Do you then love your neighbour as yourself? Do you love every man, even your enemies, even the enemies of God, as your own soul? As Christ loved you? Yea, dost thou believe that Christ loved *thee*, and gave himself for thee? Hast thou faith in his blood? Believest thou the Lamb of God hath taken away *thy* sins, and cast them as a stone into the depth of the sea? That he hath blotted out the handwriting that was against *thee*, taking it out of the way, nailing it to his cross? Hast *thou* indeed redemption through his blood, even the remission of *thy* sins? And doth his Spirit bear witness with *thy* spirit, that thou art a child of God?

10. The God and Father of our Lord Jesus Christ, who now standeth in the midst of us, knoweth that if any man die without this faith and this love, good it were for him that he had never been born. Awake, then, thou that sleepest, and call upon thy God: call in the day when he may be found. Let him not rest till he 'make his goodness to pass before thee, till he proclaim unto thee the name of the Lord'—'the Lord, the Lord God, merciful and gracious, long-suffering, and abundant in goodness and truth; keeping mercy for thousands, forgiving iniquity, and transgression, and sin.' Let no man persuade thee by vain words to rest short of this prize of thy high calling. But cry unto him day and night who 'while we were without strength died for the ungodly', until thou knowest in whom thou hast believed, and canst say, 'My Lord and my God.' Remember 'always to pray and not to faint', till thou also canst lift up thy hand unto heaven and declare to him that liveth for ever and ever, 'Lord, thou knowest all things; thou knowest that I love thee.'

11. May we all thus experience what it is to be not almost only, but altogether Christians! Being justified freely by his grace, through the redemption that is in Jesus, knowing we have peace with God through Jesus Christ, rejoicing in hope of the glory of God, and having the love of God shed abroad in our hearts by the Holy Ghost given unto us!

11. THE ORIGINAL, NATURE, PROPERTIES, AND USE OF THE LAW

1750

An Introductory Comment

This sermon was a "tract for the times" (O, 2:3), and there is no indication that Wesley ever preached on Romans 7:12 (WWS). Instead this sermon was principally a teaching tool used to defend against the antinomianism (lawlessness) of Nicholas von Zinzendorf, Philip Henry Molther, and August Spangenberg on the one hand, and the more pernicious form found in the writings of the Reverend William Cudworth on the other hand. Wesley had already spoken with Zinzendorf on these matters at Gray's Inn Walks in 1741. In 1745 Cudworth published a *Dialogue Between a Preacher of God's Righteousness and a Preacher of Inherent Righteousness* in which Wesley became the foil for inherent righteousness. Sensing the seriousness of these challenges, the second Methodist Conference held at Bristol on August 2, 1745, urged that "one or two more dialogues" (O, 2:2) should be written in response. To that end Wesley published *A Dialogue between an Antinomian and his Friend* and *A Second Dialogue between an Antinomian and his Friend* both in that same year. The first work treated the issues raised by Zinzendorf; the second, those by Cudworth.

The moral law (distinguished from the ceremonial law) displayed in this sermon, which is holy, just, and good, is strongly associated with prevenient grace and repentance. Indeed, the *content* of the moral law itself is in some measure "re-inscribed . . . on the heart of his dark, sinful creature" (O, 2:7) through the free and gracious action of God indicating not only Wesley's intuitionist tendencies (John 1:9) but also that a strictly empiricist reading of his doctrine of knowledge will quickly falter in the area of moral law. Precisely because Wesley intimately identified the moral law with the divine being (thereby unraveling the Euthyphro dilemma of Plato) he was able to affirm the third use of the law (*tertius usus*) in a way similar to Calvin and distinct from Luther: "each is continually sending me to the other,—the law to Christ and Christ to the law" (O, 2:18).

The Original, Nature, Properties, and Use of the Law

I. 1. The moral law predates Moses; it was given at creation
2. At creation, God gave human beings a law, a perfect model of truth
3. God gave free, intelligent creatures the law, engraven on their hearts
4. Human beings rebelled against God; they were alienated from God
5. But God once again gave them the law on tablets of stone
6. Thus God is now made known, when revealed by the Spirit

II. 1. The law and the commandment are not the ceremonial law
2. Neither is the law the Mosaic dispensation
3. The law is an incorruptible picture of the High and Holy One
4. The law of God is divine virtue and wisdom
5. The law of God is supreme, unchangeable reason
6. The law of God is a copy of the eternal mind, a transcript of the divine nature

III. 1. The moral law is holy, just, and good
2. It is pure, chaste, spotless, internally and essentially holy
3. Otherwise it could not be the immediate offspring of God
4. The Apostle denies that God is sin or the cause of sin
5. It is *just*; it renders all their due and prescribes exactly what is right
6. Is the will of God the cause of his law?
7. The difficulty arises from considering God's will as distinct from God
8. If the law depends on the nature and fitness of things, it must depend on God
9. Yet in every case God wills this or this because it is right
10. The law then is *good* as well as *just*
11. The law is like God, full of goodness and benignity
12. And it is *good* in its effects, as well as its nature

IV. 1. The first use of the law is to convince the world of sin
2. The second use of it is to bring us to Christ, that we may live
3. The third use of it is to keep us alive
4. Though believers are done with the law, it is still of unspeakable use
5. This agrees with the experience of every true believer
6. The more I look into the law, the more I feel how far I come short of it
7. I cannot spare the law one moment, no more than I can spare Christ
8. Love and value the law for him from whom it came and to whom it leads
9. Keep close to the law if you want to keep close to Christ
10. If the Lord has fulfilled his word, then stand fast in liberty

Sermon 34: The Original, Nature, Properties, and Use of the Law, 1750

Romans 7:12

Wherefore the law is holy, and the commandment holy, and just, and good.

1. Perhaps there are few subjects within the whole compass of religion so little understood as this. The reader of this Epistle is usually told, 'By "the law" St. Paul means the Jewish law;' and so, apprehending himself to have no concern therewith, passes on without farther thought about it. Indeed some are not satisfied with this account; but observing the Epistle is directed to the Romans, thence infer that the Apostle in the beginning of this chapter alludes to the old Roman law. But as they have no more concern with this than with the ceremonial law of Moses, so they spend not much thought on what they suppose is occasionally mentioned, barely to illustrate another thing.

2. But a careful observer of the Apostle's discourse will not be content with those slight explications of it. And the more he weighs the words, the more convinced he will be that St. Paul, by 'the law' mentioned in this chapter, does not mean either the ancient law of Rome or the ceremonial law of Moses. This will clearly appear to all who attentively consider the tenor of his discourse. He begins the chapter, 'Know ye not, brethren (for I speak to them that know the law)'—to them who have been instructed therein from their youth—'that the law hath dominion over a man as long as he liveth?' (Rom. 7:1). What? The law of Rome only, or the ceremonial law? No, surely; but the *moral* law. 'For', to give a plain instance, 'the woman that hath an husband is bound by the (moral) law to her husband as long as he liveth. But if her husband be dead, she is loosed from the law of her husband' (Rom. 7:2). 'So, then, if while her husband liveth she be married to another man, she shall be called an adulteress: but if her husband be dead she is free from that law, so that she is no adulteress, though she be married to another man' (Rom. 7:3). From this particular instance the Apostle proceeds to draw that general conclusion: 'Wherefore, my brethren', by a plain parity of reason, 'ye also are become dead to the law', the whole Mosaic institution, 'by the body of Christ' offered for you, and bringing you under a new dispensation: 'that ye should' without any blame 'be married to another, even to him who is raised from the dead', and hath thereby given proof of his authority to make the change, 'that ye should bring forth fruit unto God' (Rom. 7:4). And this we can do now, whereas before we could not: 'For when we were in the flesh', under the power of the flesh, that is, of corrupt nature (which was necessarily the case till we knew the power of Christ's resurrection), 'the motions of sins which were by the law', which were shown and inflamed by the Mosaic law, not conquered, 'did work in our members', broke out various ways, 'to bring forth fruit unto death' (Rom. 7:5). 'But now we are delivered from the law', from that whole moral as well as ceremonial economy; 'that being dead whereby we were held'—that entire institution being now as it were dead, and having no more authority over us than the husband when dead hath over his wife—'that we should serve' him who died for us and rose again 'in newness of spirit', in a new spiritual dispensation, 'and not in the oldness of the letter' (Rom. 7:6)—with a bare outward service, according to the letter of the Mosaic institution.

3. The Apostle having gone thus far in proving that the Christian had set aside the Jewish dispensation, and that the moral law itself, though it could never pass away, yet stood on a different foundation from what it did before, now stops to propose and answer an objection. 'What shall we say then? Is the law sin?' So some might infer from a misapprehension of those words, 'the motions of sin which were by the law'. 'God forbid!' saith the Apostle, that we should say so. 'Nay', the law is an irreconcilable enemy to sin, searching it out wherever it is. 'I had not known sin but by the law. I had not known lust', evil desire, to be sin, 'except the law had said, Thou shalt not covet' (Rom. 7:7). After opening this farther in the four following verses, he subjoins this general conclusion with regard more especially to the moral law, from which the preceding instance was taken: 'Wherefore the law is holy, and the commandment holy, and just, and good.'

4. In order to explain and enforce these deep words, so little regarded because so little understood, I shall endeavour to show, first, the original of this law; secondly, the nature thereof; thirdly, the properties, that it is 'holy, and just, and good'; and fourthly, the uses of it.

I.1. I shall, first, endeavour to show the original of the moral law, often called 'the law' by way of eminence. Now this is not, as some may possibly have imagined, of so late an institution as the time of Moses. Noah declared it to men long before that time, and Enoch before him. But we may trace its original higher still, even beyond the foundation of the world to that period, unknown indeed to men, but doubtless enrolled in the annals of eternity, when 'the morning stars' first 'sang together', being newly called into existence. It pleased the great Creator to make these his first-born sons intelligent beings, that they might know him that created them. For this end he endued them with understanding, to discern truth from falsehood, good from evil; and as a necessary result of this, with liberty, a capacity of choosing the one and refusing the other. By this they were likewise enabled to offer him a free and willing service: a service rewardable in itself, as well as most acceptable to their gracious Master.

2. To employ all the faculties which he had given them, particularly their understanding and liberty, he gave them a law, a complete model of all truth, so far as was intelligible to a finite being, and of all good, so far as angelic minds were capable of embracing it. It was also the design of their beneficent Governor herein to make way for a continual increase of their happiness; seeing every instance of obedience to that law would both add to the perfection of their nature and entitle them to an higher reward, which the righteous Judge would give in its season.

3. In like manner, when God in his appointed time had created a new order of intelligent beings, when he had raised man from the dust of the earth, breathed into him the breath of life, and caused him to become a living soul, endued with power to choose good or evil, he gave to this free, intelligent creature the same law as to his first-born children—not wrote indeed upon tables of stone, or any corruptible substance, but engraven on his heart by the finger of God, wrote in the inmost spirit both of men and of angels—to the

intent it might never be far off, never hard to be understood; but always at hand, and always shining with clear light, even as the sun in the midst of heaven.

4. Such was the original of the law of God. With regard to man, it was coeval with his nature. But with regard to the elder sons of God, it shone in its full splendour 'or ever the mountains were brought forth, or the earth and the round world were made'. But it was not long before man rebelled against God, and by breaking this glorious law wellnigh effaced it out of his heart; 'the eyes of his understanding' being *darkened* in the same measure as his soul was 'alienated from the life of God'. And yet God did not despise the work of his own hands; but being reconciled to man through the Son of his love, he in some measure re-inscribed the law on the heart of his dark, sinful creature. 'He' again 'showed thee, O man, what is good' (although not as in the beginning), 'even to do justly, and to love mercy, and to walk humbly with thy God.'

5. And this he showed not only to our first parents, but likewise to all their posterity, by 'that true light which enlightens every man that cometh into the world'. But notwithstanding this light, all flesh had in process of time 'corrupted their way before him'; till he chose out of mankind a peculiar people, to whom he gave a more perfect knowledge of his law. And the heads of this, because they were slow of understanding, he wrote on two tables of stone; which he commanded the fathers to teach their children through all succeeding generations.

6. And thus it is that the law of God is now made known to them that know not God. They hear, with the hearing of the ear, the things that were written aforetime for our instruction. But this does not suffice. They cannot by this means comprehend the height and depth and length and breadth thereof. God alone can reveal this by his Spirit. And so he does to all that truly believe, in consequence of that gracious promise made to all the Israel of God: 'Behold, the days come, saith the Lord, that I will make a new covenant with the house of Israel. . . . And this shall be the covenant that I will make. . . . I will put my law in their inward parts, and write it in their hearts; and I will be their God, and they shall be my people' (Jer. 31:31, 33).

II.1. The nature of that law which was originally given to angels in heaven and man in paradise, and which God has so mercifully promised to write afresh in the hearts of all true believers, was the second thing I proposed to show. In order to which I would first observe that although 'the law' and 'the commandment' are sometimes differently taken (the commandment meaning but a part of the law) yet in the text they are used as equivalent terms, implying one and the same thing. But we cannot understand here, either by one or the other, the ceremonial law. 'Tis not the ceremonial law whereof the Apostle says, in the words above recited, 'I had not known sin but by the law:' this is too plain to need a proof. Neither is it the ceremonial law which saith, in the words immediately subjoined, 'Thou shalt not covet.' Therefore the ceremonial law has no place in the present question.

2. Neither can we understand by the law mentioned in the text the Mosaic dispensation. 'Tis true the word is sometimes so understood: as when the Apostle says, speaking to the Galatians, 'The covenant which was confirmed before' (namely with Abraham the

father of the faithful), 'the law', i.e. the Mosaic dispensation, 'which was four hundred and thirty years after, cannot disannul' (Gal. 3:17). But it cannot be so understood in the text; for the Apostle never bestows so high commendations as these upon that imperfect and shadowy dispensation. He nowhere affirms the Mosaic to be a *spiritual* law; or that it is 'holy, and just, and good'. Neither is it true that God 'will write that law in the hearts' of them whose 'iniquities he remembers no more'. It remains that 'the law', eminently so termed, is no other than the moral law.

3. Now this law is an incorruptible picture of the high and holy One that inhabiteth eternity. It is he whom in his essence no man hath seen or can see, made visible to men and angels. It is the face of God unveiled; God manifested to his creatures as they are able to bear it; manifested to give and not to destroy life; that they may see God and live. It is the heart of God disclosed to man. Yea, in some sense we may apply to this law what the Apostle says of his Son—it is 'the streaming forth' or outbeaming 'of his glory, the express image of his person'.

4. 'If virtue', said the ancient heathen, 'could assume such a shape as that we could behold her with our eyes, what wonderful love would she excite in us!' If virtue could do this! It is done already. The law of God is all virtues in one, in such a shape as to be beheld with open face by all those whose eyes God hath enlightened. What is the law but divine virtue and wisdom assuming a visible form? What is it but the original ideas of truth and good, which were lodged in the uncreated mind from eternity, now drawn forth and clothed with such a vehicle as to appear even to human understanding?

5. If we survey the law of God in another point of view, it is supreme, unchangeable reason; it is unalterable rectitude; it is the everlasting fitness of all things that are or ever were created. I am sensible what a shortness, and even impropriety, there is in these and all other human expressions, when we endeavour by these faint pictures to shadow out the deep things of God. Nevertheless we have no better, indeed no other way, during this our infant state of existence. As 'we' now 'know' but 'in part', so we are constrained to 'prophesy', i.e. speak of the things of God, 'in part' also. 'We cannot order our speech by reason of darkness' while we are in this house of clay. While I am 'a child' I must 'speak as a child'. But I shall soon 'put away childish things'. For 'when that which is perfect is come, that which is in part shall be done away.'

6. But to return. The law of God (speaking after the manner of men) is a copy of the eternal mind, a transcript of the divine nature; yea, it is the fairest offspring of the everlasting Father, the brightest efflux of his essential wisdom, the visible beauty of the Most High. It is the delight and wonder of cherubim and seraphim and all the company of heaven, and the glory and joy of every wise believer, every well instructed child of God upon earth.

III.1. Such is the nature of the ever-blessed law of God. I am, in the third place, to show the properties of it. Not all, for that would exceed the wisdom of an angel; but those only which are mentioned in the text. These are three: It is 'holy, just, and good'. And first, 'the law is holy.'

2. In this expression the Apostle does not appear to speak of its effects, but rather of its nature. As St. James, speaking of the same thing under another name, says, 'The wisdom from above' (which is no other than this law, written in our heart) 'is first pure (Jas. 3:17), ἁγνή—chaste, spotless, internally and essentially holy. And consequently, when it is transcribed into the life, as well as the soul, it is (as the same Apostle terms it), θρησκεία καθαρὰ καὶ ἀμίαντος, 'pure religion and undefiled' (Jas. 1:27); or, the pure, clean, unpolluted worship of God.

3. It is indeed in the highest degree pure, chaste, clean, holy. Otherwise it could not be the immediate offspring, and much less the express resemblance of God, who is essential holiness. It is pure from all sin, clean and unspotted from any touch of evil. It is a chaste virgin, incapable of any defilement, of any mixture with that which is unclean or unholy. It has no fellowship with sin of any kind; for 'what communion hath light with darkness?' As sin is in its very nature enmity to God, so his law is enmity to sin.

4. Therefore it is that the Apostle rejects with such abhorrence that blasphemous supposition that the law of God is either sin itself or the cause of sin. 'God forbid' that we should suppose it is the cause of sin because it is the discoverer of it; because it detects the hidden things of darkness, and drags them out into open day. 'Tis true, by this means (as the Apostle observes, verse 13) 'sin appears to be sin.' All its disguises are torn away, and it appears in its native deformity. 'Tis true likewise that 'sin by the commandment becomes exceeding sinful.' Being now committed against light and knowledge, being stripped even of the poor plea of ignorance, it loses its excuse as well as disguise, and becomes far more odious both to God and man. Yea, and it is true that 'sin worketh death by that which is good,' which in itself is pure and holy. When it is dragged out to light it rages the more: when it is restrained it bursts out with greater violence. Thus the Apostle, speaking in the person of one who was convinced of sin but not yet delivered from it, 'sin taking occasion by the commandment', detecting and endeavouring to restrain it, disdained the restraint, and so much the more 'wrought in me all manner of concupiscence' (verse 8)—all manner of foolish and hurtful desire, which that commandment sought to restrain. Thus 'when the commandment came, sin revived' (verse 9). It fretted and raged the more. But this is no stain on the commandment. Though it is abused it cannot be defiled. This only proves that 'the heart' of man 'is desperately wicked.' But 'the law' of God 'is holy' still.

5. And it is, secondly, *just.* It renders to all their due. It prescribes exactly what is right, precisely what ought to be done, said, or thought, both with regard to the Author of our being, with regard to ourselves, and with regard to every creature which he has made. It is adapted in all respects to the nature of things, of the whole universe and every individual. It is suited to all the circumstances of each, and to all their mutual relations, whether such as have existed from the beginning, or such as commenced in any following period. It is exactly agreeable to the fitnesses of things, whether essential or accidental. It clashes with none of these in any degree, nor is ever unconnected with them. If the word be taken in that sense, there is nothing *arbitrary* in the law of God: although still the whole and every part thereof is totally dependent upon his will, so that 'Thy will be done' is the supreme universal law both in earth and heaven.

6. 'But is the will of God the cause of his law? Is his will the original of right and wrong? Is a thing therefore right because God wills it? Or does he will it because it is right?'

I fear this celebrated question is more curious than useful. And perhaps in the manner it is usually treated of it does not so well consist with the regard that is due from a creature to the Creator and Governor of all things. 'Tis hardly decent for man to call the supreme God to give an account to him! Nevertheless, with awe and reverence we may speak a little. The Lord pardon us if we speak amiss!

7. It seems, then, that the whole difficulty arises from considering God's will as distinct from God. Otherwise it vanishes away. For none can doubt but God is the cause of the law of God. But the will of God is God himself. It is God considered as willing thus or thus. Consequently, to say that the will of God, or that God himself, is the cause of the law, is one and the same thing.

8. Again: if the law, the immutable rule of right and wrong, depends on the nature and fitnesses of things, and on their essential relations to each other (I do not say their eternal relations; because the eternal relations of things existing in time is little less than a contradiction); if, I say, this depends on the nature and relations of things, then it must depend on God, or the will of God; because those things themselves, with all their relations, are the work of his hands. By his will, 'for his pleasure' alone, they all 'are and were created'.

9. And yet it may be granted (which is probably all that a considerate person would contend for) that in every particular case God wills this or this (suppose that men should honour their parents) because it is right, agreeable to the fitness of things, to the relation wherein they stand.

10. The law then is right and just concerning all things. And it is *good* as well as *just.* This we may easily infer from the fountain whence it flowed. For what was this but the goodness of God? What but goodness alone inclined him to impart that divine copy of himself to the holy angels? To what else can we impute his bestowing upon man the same transcript of his own nature? And what but tender love constrained him afresh to manifest his will to fallen man? Either to Adam or any of his seed, who like him were 'come short of the glory of God'? Was it not mere love that moved him to publish his law, after the understandings of men were darkened? And to send his prophets to declare that law to the blind, thoughtless children of men? Doubtless his goodness it was which raised up Enoch and Noah to be preachers of righteousness; which caused Abraham, his friend, and Isaac and Jacob, to bear witness to his truth. It was his goodness alone which, when 'darkness' had 'covered the earth, and thick darkness the people', gave a written law to Moses, and through him to the nation whom he had chosen. It was his love which explained these living oracles by David and all the prophets that followed; until, when the fullness of time was come, he sent his only-begotten Son, 'not to destroy the law, but to fulfil', to confirm every jot and tittle thereof, till having wrote it in the hearts of all his children, and put all his enemies under his feet, 'he shall deliver up' his mediatorial 'kingdom to the Father', 'that God may be all in all'.

11. And this law which the goodness of God gave at first, and has preserved through all ages, is, like the fountain from whence it springs, full of goodness and benignity. It is mild and kind; it is (as the Psalmist expresses it) 'sweeter than honey and the honeycomb'. It is winning and amiable. It includes 'whatsoever things are lovely or of good report. If there be any virtue, if there be any praise' before God and his holy angels, they are all comprised in this: wherein are hid all the treasures of the divine wisdom and knowledge and love.

12. And it is *good* in its effects, as well as in its nature. As the tree is, so are its fruits. The fruits of the law of God written in the heart are 'righteousness and peace and assurance for ever'. Or rather, the law itself is righteousness, filling the soul with a peace that passeth all understanding, and causing us to rejoice evermore in the testimony of a good conscience toward God. It is not so properly a pledge as an 'earnest of our inheritance', being a part of the purchased possession. It is God made manifest in our flesh, and bringing with him eternal life; assuring us by that pure and perfect love that we are 'sealed unto the day of redemption'; that he will 'spare us, as a man spareth his own son that serveth him, in the day when he maketh up his jewels', and that there remaineth for us 'a crown of glory which fadeth not away'.

IV.1. It remains only to show, in the fourth and last place, the uses of the law. And the first use of it, without question, is to convince the world of sin. This is indeed the peculiar work of the Holy Ghost, who can work it without any means at all, or by whatever means it pleaseth him, however insufficient in themselves, or even improper to produce such an effect. And accordingly, some there are whose hearts have been broken in pieces in a moment, either in sickness or in health, without any visible cause, or any outward means whatever. And others (one in an age) have been awakened to a sense of 'the wrath of God abiding on them' by hearing that 'God was in Christ, reconciling the world unto himself'. But it is the ordinary method of the Spirit of God to convict sinners by the law. It is this which, being set home on the conscience, generally breaketh the rocks in pieces. It is more especially this part of 'the word of God' which 'is' ζῶν [. . .] καὶ ἐνεργής, 'quick and powerful', full of life and energy, 'and sharper than any two-edged sword'. This, in the hand of God and of those whom he hath sent, 'pierces' through all the folds of a deceitful heart, and 'divides asunder even the soul and spirit', yea, as it were, the very 'joints and marrow'. By this is the sinner discovered to himself. All his fig leaves are torn away, and he sees that he is 'wretched, and poor, and miserable, and blind, and naked'. The law flashes conviction on every side. He feels himself a mere sinner. He has nothing to pay. His 'mouth is stopped,' and he stands 'guilty before God'.

2. To slay the sinner is then the first use of the law; to destroy the life and strength wherein he trusts, and convince him that he is dead while he liveth; not only under sentence of death, but actually dead unto God, void of all spiritual life, 'dead in trespasses and sins'. The second use of it is to bring him unto life, unto Christ, that he may live. 'Tis true, in performing both these offices it acts the part of a severe schoolmaster. It drives us by force, rather than draws us by love. And yet love is the spring of all. It is the spirit of love which, by this painful means, tears away our confidence in the flesh, which leaves us

no broken reed whereon to trust, and so constrains the sinner, stripped of all, to cry out in the bitterness of his soul, or groan in the depth of his heart,

> I give up every plea beside
> 'Lord, I am damned—but thou hast died.'

3. The third use of the law is to keep us alive. It is the grand means whereby the blessed Spirit prepares the believer for larger communications of the life of God.

I am afraid this great and important truth is little understood, not only by the world, but even by many whom God hath taken out of the world, who are real children of God by faith. Many of these lay it down as an unquestioned truth that when we come to Christ we have done with the law; and that in *this* sense, 'Christ is the end of the law . . . to everyone that believeth.' 'The end of the law'. So he is, 'for righteousness', for justification, 'to everyone that believeth'. Herein the law is at an end. It justifies none, but only brings them to Christ; who is also, in another respect, 'the end' or scope 'of the law'—the point at which it continually aims. But when it has brought us to him it has yet a farther office, namely, to keep us with him. For it is continually exciting all believers, the more they see of its height and depth and length and breadth, to exhort one another so much the more:

> Closer and closer let us cleave
> To his beloved embrace;
> Expect his fullness to receive,
> And grace to answer grace.

4. Allowing then that every believer has done with the law, as it means the Jewish ceremonial law, or the entire Mosaic dispensation (for these Christ 'hath taken out of the way'); yea, allowing we have done with the moral law as a means of procuring our justification (for we are 'justified freely by his grace, through the redemption that is in Jesus'); yet in another sense we have not done with this law. For it is still of unspeakable use, first, in convincing us of the sin that yet remains both in our hearts and lives, and thereby keeping us close to Christ, that his blood may cleanse us every moment; secondly, in deriving strength from our Head into his living members, whereby he empowers them to do what his law commands; and thirdly, in confirming our hope of whatsoever it commands and we have not yet attained, of receiving grace upon grace, till we are in actual possession of the fullness of his promises.

5. How clearly does this agree with the experience of every true believer! While he cries out: 'O what love have I unto thy law! All the day long is my study in it,' he sees daily in that divine mirror more and more of his own sinfulness. He sees more and more clearly that he is still a sinner in all things; that neither his heart nor his ways are right before God; and that every moment sends him to Christ. This shows him the meaning of what is written: 'Thou shalt make a plate of pure gold, and grave upon it, Holiness to the Lord. And it shall be upon Aaron's forehead' (the type of our great High Priest) 'that Aaron may bear the iniquities of the holy things, which the children of Israel shall hallow

in all their holy gifts' (so far are our prayers or holy things from atoning for the rest of our sins); 'and it shall be always upon his forehead, that they may be accepted before the Lord' (Exod. 28:36, 38).

6. To explain this by a single instance. The law says, 'Thou shalt not kill,' and hereby (as our Lord teaches) forbids not only outward acts but every unkind word or thought. Now the more I look into this perfect law, the more I feel how far I come short of it; and the more I feel this, the more I feel my need of his blood to atone for all my sin, and of his Spirit to purify my heart, and make me 'perfect and entire, lacking nothing'.

7. Therefore I cannot spare the law one moment, no more than I can spare Christ; seeing I now want it as much to keep me to Christ as ever I wanted it to bring me to him. Otherwise this 'evil heart of unbelief' would immediately 'depart from the living God'. Indeed each is continually sending me to the other—the law to Christ, and Christ to the law. On the one hand, the height and depth of the law constrain me to fly to the love of God in Christ; on the other, the love of God in Christ endears the law to me 'above gold or precious stones'; seeing I know every part of it is a gracious promise, which my Lord will fulfil in its season.

8. Who art thou then, O man, that 'judgest the law, and speakest evil of the law'? That rankest it with sin, Satan, and death, and sendest them all to hell together? The Apostle James esteemed 'judging' or 'speaking evil of the law' so enormous a piece of wickedness that he knew not how to aggravate the guilt of judging our brethren more than by showing it included this. So now, says he, 'thou art not a doer of the law but a judge!' A judge of that which God hath ordained to judge thee. So thou hast set up thyself in the judgment seat of Christ, and cast down the rule whereby he will judge the world! O take knowledge what advantage Satan hath gained over thee! And for the time to come never think or speak lightly of, much less dress up as a scarecrow, this blessed instrument of the grace of God. Yea, love and value it for the sake of him from whom it came, and of him to whom it leads. Let it be thy glory and joy, next to the cross of Christ. Declare its praise, and make it honourable before all men.

9. And if thou art throughly convinced that it is the offspring of God, that it is the copy of all his imitable perfections, and that it 'is holy, and just, and good', but especially to them that believe; then instead of casting it away as a polluted thing, see that thou cleave to it more and more. Never let the law of mercy and truth, of love to God and man, of lowliness, meekness, and purity forsake thee. 'Bind it about thy neck: write it on the table of thy heart.' Keep close to the law if thou wilt keep close to Christ; hold it fast; let it not go. Let this continually lead thee to the atoning blood, continually confirm thy hope, till all 'the righteousness of the law is fulfilled in thee', and thou art 'filled with all the fullness of God'.

10. And if thy Lord hath already fulfilled his word, if he hath already 'written his law in thy heart', then 'stand fast in the liberty wherewith Christ hath made thee free.' Thou art not only made free from Jewish ceremonies, from the guilt of sin and the fear of hell (these are so far from being the whole, that they are the least and lowest part of Christian liberty), but what is infinitely more, from the power of sin, from serving the devil, from

offending God. O stand fast in this liberty, in comparison of which all the rest is not even worthy to be named. Stand fast in loving God with all thy heart and serving him with all thy strength. This is perfect freedom; thus to keep his law and to walk in all his commandments blameless. 'Be not entangled again with the yoke of bondage.' I do not mean of Jewish bondage; nor yet of bondage to the fear of hell: these, I trust, are far from thee. But beware of being entangled again with the yoke of sin, of any inward or outward transgression of the law. Abhor sin far more than death or hell; abhor sin itself far more than the punishment of it. Beware of the bondage of pride, of desire, of anger; of every evil temper or word or work. 'Look unto Jesus', and in order thereto 'look' more and more 'into the perfect law, the law of liberty', and 'continue therein'; so shalt thou daily 'grow in grace, and in the knowledge of our Lord Jesus Christ.'

12. THE RIGHTEOUSNESS OF FAITH

1746

An Introductory Comment

Wesley preached on the text of this sermon (Rom. 10:5-8) on June 12, 1742, from his father's tombstone in Epworth. While he was proclaiming the Word of God "several dropped down as dead; and among the rest such a cry was heard" (WH, 19:276). Wesley's exposition that day was based on a distinction between a "covenant of works" (known only to Adam and Eve) and a "covenant of grace." Sugden referred to the former as a "theological fiction, which made its first appearance in the seventeenth century" (S, 1:131), and among the creeds it was found only in the Westminster Confession (S, 1:131). Since this first distinction informed in some sense Wesley's articulation of "the righteousness of the law" and "the righteousness of faith" and since he affirmed that the Mosaic covenant was a gracious one (O, 1:202–3), the unavoidable conclusion is that the Jews had improperly turned the gracious Mosaic law into a covenant of works.

Wesley developed the contrast between the righteousness of the law (perfect in degree, uninterrupted) and that of faith so strongly in this sermon that he came to the very edge of Calvinism (as suggested in the earlier Conference *Minutes*) and offered an "unnuanced" expression of *sola fide* (O, 1:202). Sinners do not have to be or do anything *first* in order to receive the righteousness of faith ("Do not imagine that these things are to be done now, in order to procure thy pardon and salvation"; NT, Rom. 10:5-8). That is, this greater righteousness can be received immediately. "Now, at this instant, in the present moment, and in thy present state," Wesley declared, ". . . believe the gospel" (O, 1:216). Moreover, the objections of the sinner ("I am not good enough"; "But I am not *contrite enough*"; O, 1:214) were likewise cast aside. Such a faith is saved from antinomianism (lawlessness), however, in that it must issue in freedom "from the guilt and power of sin" (O, 1:204).

The Righteousness of Faith

1.–2. Paul does not oppose the covenant of Moses and the covenant of Christ; he opposes the covenant of grace with the covenant of works

3.–4. Many are ignorant that Christ is the end of the law for all who believe

I. 1. The covenant of works given in paradise required perfect obedience

2. It required that people fulfill all righteousness, inward and outward

3. This inward and outward holiness should be perfect in *degree*

4. Obedience to the covenant of works had to be uninterrupted

5. People were to desire nothing but God in thought, word, and deed

6. God established the new covenant with sinful humans through Jesus Christ

7. By the righteousness of faith is meant the condition of justification in Christ

8. This covenant does not say, 'Perform unsinning obedience and live'

9. It says, 'Believe in the Lord Jesus Christ, and thou shalt be saved'

10. This condition of life is plain, easy, and always at hand

11. The covenant of works supposes us to be now holy and happy.

12. The covenant of works requires perfection; the covenant of grace only faith

13. In the covenant of grace, God has already *paid the price for us*

14. The first covenant required what is now far off, namely, unsinning obedience

II. 1. Those who trust in the law still suppose we are in a state of innocence

2. They do not consider the manner of obedience or righteousness required

3. They should consider that the law requires all things in the perfect degree

4. They desire to be tried where no flesh can be justified

5. Is it not folly for fallen human beings to seek life by this righteousness?

6. This proves the wisdom of submitting to God by faith

7. The righteousness of faith is the method of reconciliation chosen by God

8. This reconciliation was wholly a matter of grace

III. 1. The best end a fallen creature can pursue is the recovery of the image of God

2. We can do nothing but sin until we are reconciled

3. Do not say, 'I am not *contrite enough*: I am not sensible enough of my sins'

4. Nor say, 'I must *do* something more before I come to Christ'

5. Why would you wait for *more sincerity* before your sins are forgiven?

6. The Lord did not say, 'Do this; perfectly obey all my commands and live,' but 'Believe in the Lord Jesus Christ, and thou shalt be saved'

Sermon 6: The Righteousness of Faith, 1746

Romans 10:5-8

Moses describeth the righteousness which is of the law, that the man which doeth those things shall live by them.

But the righteousness which is of faith speaketh on this wise: Say not in thine heart, Who shall ascend into heaven? (that is, to bring Christ down from above;)

Or, Who shall descend into the deep? (that is, to bring Christ again from the dead.)

But what saith it? The word is nigh thee, even in thy mouth and in thy heart; that is, the word of faith which we preach.

1. The Apostle does not here oppose the covenant given by Moses to the covenant given by Christ. If we ever imagined this it was for want of observing that the latter as well as the former part of these words were spoken by Moses himself to the people of Israel, and that concerning the covenant which then was (Deut. 30:11, 12, 14). But it is the covenant of *grace* which God through Christ hath established with men in all ages (as well before, and under the Jewish dispensation, as since God was manifest in the flesh), which St. Paul here opposes to the covenant of *works*, made with Adam while in paradise, but commonly supposed to be the only covenant which God had made with man, particularly by those Jews of whom the Apostle writes.

2. Of these it was that he so affectionately speaks in the beginning of this chapter. 'My heart's desire and prayer to God for Israel is, that they may be saved. For I bear them record that they have a zeal for God, but not according to knowledge. For they, being ignorant of God's righteousness' (of the justification that flows from his mere grace and mercy, freely forgiving our sins through the Son of his love, through the redemption which is in Jesus), 'and seeking to establish their own righteousness' (their own holiness, antecedent to faith in 'him that justifieth the ungodly', as the ground of their pardon and acceptance), 'have not submitted themselves unto the righteousness of God', and consequently seek death in the error of their life.

3. They were ignorant that 'Christ is the end of the law for righteousness to everyone that believeth;' that by the oblation of himself once offered he had put an end to the first law or covenant (which indeed was not given by God to Moses, but to Adam in his state of innocence), the strict tenor whereof, without any abatement, was, 'Do this and live;' and at the same time purchased for us that better covenant, 'Believe and live:' 'Believe and thou shalt be saved;' now saved both from the guilt and power of sin, and of consequence from the wages of it.

4. And how many are equally ignorant now, even among those who are called by the name of Christ? How many who have now a 'zeal for God', yet have it not 'according to knowledge', but are still 'seeking to establish their own righteousness' as the ground of their pardon and acceptance, and therefore vehemently refuse to 'submit themselves unto the righteousness of God'? Surely my heart's desire and prayer to God for you, brethren, is that ye may be saved. And in order to remove this grand stumbling-block out of your way I will endeavour to show, first, what 'the righteousness' is 'which is of the law', and what

'the righteousness which is of faith'; secondly, the folly of trusting in 'the righteousness . . . of the law', and the wisdom of 'submitting to that which is of faith'.

I.1. And, first, 'The righteousness which is of the law saith, The man which doth these things shall live by them.' Constantly and perfectly observe all these things, to do them, and then thou shalt live for ever. This law or covenant (usually called the covenant of *works*) given by God to man in paradise, required an obedience perfect in all its parts, entire and wanting nothing, as the condition of his eternal continuance in the holiness and happiness wherein he was created.

2. It required that man should fulfil all righteousness, inward and outward, negative and positive: that he should not only abstain from every idle word, and avoid every evil work, but should keep every affection, every desire, every thought, in obedience to the will of God; that he should continue holy, as he which had created him was holy, both in heart and in all manner of conversation; that he should be pure in heart, even as God is pure, perfect as his Father in heaven was perfect; that he should love the Lord his God with all his heart, with all his soul, with all his mind, and with all his strength; that he should love every soul which God had made even as God had loved him; that by this universal benevolence he should 'dwell in God (who is love) and God in him'; that he should serve the Lord his God with all his strength, and in all things singly aim at his glory.

3. These were the things which the righteousness of the law required, that he who did them might live thereby. But it farther required that this entire obedience to God, this inward and outward holiness, this conformity both of heart and life to his will, should be perfect in *degree*. No abatement, no allowance could possibly be made for falling short in any degree as to any jot or tittle either of the outward or the inward law. If every commandment relating to outward things was obeyed, yet that was not sufficient unless every one was obeyed with all the strength, in the highest measure and most perfect manner. Nor did it answer the demand of this covenant to love God with every power and faculty, unless he were loved with the full capacity of each, with the whole possibility of the soul.

4. One thing more was indispensably required by the righteousness of the law, namely that this universal obedience, this perfect holiness both of heart and life, should be perfectly uninterrupted also, should continue without any intermission from the moment wherein God created man, and breathed into his nostrils the breath of life, until the days of his trial should be ended, and he should be confirmed in life everlasting.

5. The righteousness, then, which is of the law speaketh on this wise. 'Thou, O man of God, stand fast in love, in the image of God wherein thou art made. If thou wilt remain in life, keep the commandments which are now written in thy heart. Love the Lord thy God with all thy heart. Love as thyself every soul that he hath made. Desire nothing but God. Aim at God in every thought, in every word and work. Swerve not in one motion of body or soul from him, thy mark, and the prize of thy high calling. And let all that is in thee praise his holy name, every power and faculty of thy soul, in every kind, in every degree, and at every moment of thine existence. "This do, and thou shalt live;" thy light

shall shine, thy love shall flame more and more, till thou art received up into the house of God in the heavens, to reign with him for ever and ever.'

6. 'But the righteousness which is of faith speaketh on this wise: Say not in thine heart, Who shall ascend into heaven? that is, to bring down Christ from above' (as though it were some impossible task which God required thee previously to perform in order to thine acceptance); 'or, Who shall descend into the deep? that is, to bring up Christ from the dead' (as though that were still remaining to be done for the sake of which thou wert to be accepted). 'But what saith it? The word' (according to the tenor of which thou mayest now be accepted as an heir of life eternal) 'is nigh thee, even in thy mouth and in thy heart; that is, the word of faith which we preach', the new covenant which God hath now established with sinful man through Christ Jesus.

7. By 'the righteousness which is of faith' is meant that condition of justification (and in consequence of present and final salvation, if we endure therein unto the end) which was given by God to *fallen man* through the merits and mediation of his only begotten Son. This was in part revealed to Adam soon after his fall, being contained in the original promise made to him and his seed concerning the seed of the woman, who should 'bruise the serpent's head' (Gen. 3:15). It was a little more clearly revealed to Abraham by the angel of God from heaven, saying, 'By myself have I sworn, saith the Lord', that 'in thy seed shall all the nations of the earth be blessed.' It was yet more fully made known to Moses, to David, and to the prophets that followed; and through them to many of the people of God in their respective generations. But still the bulk even of these were ignorant of it; and very few understood it clearly. Still 'life and immortality' were not so 'brought to light' to the Jews of old as they are now unto us 'by the gospel'.

8. Now this covenant saith not to sinful man, 'Perform unsinning obedience and live.' If this were the term, he would have no more benefit by all which Christ hath done and suffered for him than if he was required, in order to life, to 'ascend into heaven and bring down Christ from above'; or to 'descend into the deep', into the invisible world, and 'bring up Christ from the dead'. It doth not require any impossibility to be done (although to mere man what it requires would be impossible, but not to man assisted by the Spirit of God); this were only to mock human weakness. Indeed, strictly speaking, the covenant of *grace* doth not require us to *do* anything at all, as absolutely and indispensably necessary in order to our justification, but only to *believe* in him who for the sake of his Son and the propitiation which he hath made, 'justifieth the ungodly that worketh not', and 'imputes his faith to him for righteousness'. Even so Abraham 'believed in the Lord; and he counted it to him for righteousness' (Gen. 15:6). 'And he received the sign of circumcision, a seal of the righteousness of faith . . . ; that he might be the father of all them that believe . . . ; that righteousness might be imputed unto them also' (Rom. 4:11). 'Now it was not written for his sake alone that it (i.e. faith) was imputed to him; but for us also, to whom it shall be imputed' (to whom faith shall be imputed for righteousness, shall stand in the stead of perfect obedience, in order to our acceptance with God) 'if we believe on him who raised up Jesus our Lord from the dead; who was delivered' to death 'for our offences, and was raised again for our justification' (Rom. 4:23-25), 'for the assurance of the remission of our sins, and of a second life to come to them that believe.'

9. What saith then the covenant of forgiveness, of unmerited love, of pardoning mercy? 'Believe in the Lord Jesus Christ, and thou shalt be saved.' In the day thou believest, thou shalt surely live. Thou shalt be restored to the favour of God; and in his pleasure is life. Thou shalt be saved from the curse and from the wrath of God. Thou shalt be quickened from the death of sin into the life of righteousness. And if thou endure to the end, believing in Jesus, thou shalt never taste the second death, but having suffered with the Lord shalt also live and reign with him for ever and ever.

10. Now 'this word is nigh thee'. This condition of life is plain, easy, always at hand. 'It is in thy mouth and in thy heart' through the operation of the Spirit of God. The moment 'thou believest in thine heart in him whom God hath raised from the dead, and confessest with thy mouth the Lord Jesus as thy Lord and thy God, thou shalt be saved' from condemnation, from the guilt and punishment of thy *former* sins, and shalt have power to serve God in true holiness all the *remaining* days of thy life.

11. What is the difference then between the 'righteousness which is of the law' and the 'righteousness which is of faith'? Between the first covenant, or the covenant of works, and the second, the covenant of grace? The essential, unchangeable difference is this: the one supposes him to whom it is given to be already holy and happy, created in the image and enjoying the favour of God; and prescribes the condition whereon he may continue therein, in love and joy, life and immortality. The other supposes him to whom it is given to be now unholy and unhappy; fallen short of the glorious image of God, having the wrath of God abiding on him, and hastening through sin, whereby his soul is dead, to bodily death and death everlasting. And to man in this state it prescribes the condition whereon he may regain the pearl he has lost; may recover the favour, and the image of God, may retrieve the life of God in his soul, and be restored to the knowledge and the love of God, which is the beginning of life eternal.

12. Again, the covenant of works, in order to man's *continuance* in the favour of God, in his knowledge and love, in holiness and happiness, required of perfect man a *perfect* and uninterrupted *obedience* to every point of the law of God; whereas the covenant of grace, in order to man's *recovery* of the favour and life of God, requires only *faith*—living faith in him who through God justifies him that *obeyed not.*

13. Yet again: the covenant of works required of Adam and all his children to *pay the price themselves,* in consideration of which they were to receive all the future blessings of God. But in the covenant of grace, seeing we have nothing to pay, God 'frankly forgives us all'; provided only that we believe in him who hath *paid the price for us;* who hath given himself a 'propitiation for our sins, for the sins of the whole world'.

14. Thus the first covenant required what is now *afar off* from all the children of men, namely, unsinning obedience, which is far from those who are 'conceived and born in sin'; whereas the second requires what is nigh at hand, as though it should say, Thou art sin: God is love. Thou by sin art fallen short of the glory of God; yet there is mercy with him. Bring then all thy sins to the pardoning God, and they shall vanish away as a cloud. If thou wert not ungodly there would be no room for him to justify thee as ungodly. But

now draw near, in full assurance of faith. He speaketh, and it is done. Fear not, only believe; for even the just God 'justifieth all that believe in Jesus'.

II.1. These things considered, it will be easy to show, as I proposed to do in the second place, the folly of trusting in the 'righteousness which is of the law', and the wisdom of 'submitting to the righteousness which is of faith'.

The folly of those who still trust in the 'righteousness which is of the law', the terms of which are, 'Do this and live', may abundantly appear from hence. They set out wrong. Their very first step is a fundamental mistake. For before they can ever think of claiming any blessing on the terms of this covenant, they must suppose themselves to be in his state with whom this covenant was made. But how vain a supposition is this, since it was made with Adam in a state of innocence. How weak therefore must that whole building be which stands on such a foundation! And how foolish are they who thus build on the sand! Who seem never to have considered that the covenant of works was not given to man when he was dead in trespasses and sins, but when he was alive to God, when he knew no sin, but was holy as God is holy; who forget that it was never designed for the *recovery* of the favour and life of God once lost, but only for the *continuance* and increase thereof, till it should be complete in life everlasting.

2. Neither do they consider, who are thus 'seeking to establish their own righteousness which is of the law', what manner of obedience or righteousness that is which the law indispensably requires. It must be perfect and entire in every point, or it answers not the demand of the law. But which of you is able to perform such obedience? Or, consequently, to live thereby? Who among you fulfils every jot and tittle even of the outward commandments of God? Doing nothing, great or small, which God forbids? Leaving nothing undone which he enjoins? Speaking no 'idle word'? Having your conversation always 'meet to minister grace to the hearers'? And 'whether you eat or drink, or whatever you do, doing all to the glory of God'? And how much less are you able to fulfil all the inward commandments of God? Those which require that every temper and motion of your soul should be holiness unto the Lord? Are you able to 'love God with all your heart'? To love all mankind as your own soul? To 'pray without ceasing'? 'In everything to give thanks'? To have God always before you? And to keep every affection, desire, and thought in obedience to his law?

3. You should farther consider that the righteousness of the law requires, not only the obeying every command of God, negative and positive, internal and external, but likewise in the perfect degree. In every instance whatever the voice of the law is, 'Thou shalt serve the Lord thy God with all thy strength.' It allows no abatement of any kind. It excuses no defect. It condemns every coming short of the full measure of obedience, and immediately pronounces a curse on the offender. It regards only the invariable rules of justice, and saith, 'I know not to show mercy.'

4. Who then can appear before such a Judge, who is 'extreme to mark what is done amiss'? How weak are they who desire to be tried at the bar where 'no flesh living can be justified'!—none of the offspring of Adam. For suppose we did now keep every

commandment with all our strength; yet one single breach which ever was utterly destroys our whole claim to life. If we have ever offended, in any one point, this righteousness is at an end. For the law condemns all who do not perform uninterrupted as well as perfect obedience. So that according to the sentence of this, for him who hath once sinned, in any degree, 'there remaineth only a fearful looking for of fiery indignation which shall devour the adversaries' of God.

5. Is it not then the very foolishness of folly for fallen man to seek life by this righteousness? For man, who was 'shapen in wickedness', and 'in sin did his mother conceive him'; man, who is by nature all 'earthly, sensual, devilish'; altogether 'corrupt and abominable'; in whom, till he find grace, 'dwelleth no good thing'; nay, who cannot of himself think one good thought? Who is indeed all sin, a mere lump of ungodliness, and who commits sin in every breath he draws; whose actual transgressions, in word and deed, are more in number than the hairs of his head! What stupidity, what senselessness must it be for such an unclean, guilty, helpless worm as this to dream of seeking acceptance by 'his own righteousness', of living by 'the righteousness which is of the law'!

6. Now whatsoever considerations prove the folly of trusting in the 'righteousness which is of the law' prove equally the wisdom of submitting to 'the righteousness which is of God by faith'. This were easy to be shown with regard to each of the preceding considerations. But to waive this, the wisdom of the first step hereto, the disclaiming our own righteousness, plainly appears from hence, that it is acting according to truth, to the real nature of things. For what is it more than to acknowledge with our heart as well as lips the true state wherein we are? To acknowledge that we bring with us into the world a corrupt, sinful nature; more corrupt indeed than we can easily conceive, or find words to express? That hereby we are prone to all that is evil, and averse from all that is good; that we are full of pride, self-will, unruly passions, foolish desires; vile and inordinate affections; lovers of the world, lovers of pleasure more than lovers of God? That our lives have been no better than our hearts, but many ways ungodly and unholy, insomuch that our actual sins, both in word and deed, have been as the stars of heaven for multitude? That on all these accounts we are displeasing to him who is of purer eyes than to behold iniquity, and deserve nothing from him but indignation and wrath and death, the due wages of sin? That we cannot by any of our righteousness (for indeed we have none at all) nor by any of our works (for they are as the tree from which they grow) appease the wrath of God, or avert the punishment we have justly deserved? Yea, that if left to ourselves we shall only wax worse and worse, sink deeper and deeper into sin, offend God more and more both with our evil works and with the evil tempers of our carnal mind, till we fill up the measure of our iniquities, and bring upon ourselves swift destruction? And is not this the very state wherein by nature we are? To acknowledge this, then, both with our heart and lips, that is, to disclaim our own righteousness, 'the righteousness which is of the law', is to act according to the real nature of things, and consequently is an instance of true wisdom.

7. The wisdom of submitting to 'the righteousness of faith' appears farther from this consideration, that it is 'the righteousness of God'. I mean here, it is that method of reconciliation with God which hath been chosen and established by God himself, not only as he is the God of wisdom, but as he is the sovereign Lord of heaven and earth, and of

every creature which he hath made. Now as it is not meet for man to say unto God, 'What dost thou?'—as none who is not utterly void of understanding will contend with one that is mightier than he, with him whose kingdom ruleth over all—so it is true wisdom, it is a mark of a sound understanding, to acquiesce in whatever he hath chosen, to say in this as in all things, 'It is the Lord; let him do what seemeth him good.'

8. It may be farther considered that it was of mere grace, of free love, of undeserved mercy, that God hath vouchsafed to sinful man any way of reconciliation with himself; that we were not cut away from his hand, and utterly blotted out of his remembrance. Therefore whatever method he is pleased to appoint, of his tender mercy, of his unmerited goodness, whereby his enemies, who have so deeply revolted from him, so long and obstinately rebelled against him, may still find favour in his sight, it is doubtless our wisdom to accept it with all thankfulness.

9. To mention but one consideration more. It is wisdom to aim at the best end by the best means. Now the best end which any creature can pursue is happiness in God. And the best end a fallen creature can pursue is the recovery of the favour and image of God. But the best, indeed the only means under heaven given to man whereby he may regain the favour of God, which is better than life itself, or the image of God, which is the true life of the soul, is the submitting to the 'righteousness which is of faith', the believing in the only-begotten Son of God.

III.1. Whosoever therefore thou art who desirest to be forgiven and reconciled to the favour of God, do not say in thy heart, 'I must *first do this*: I must *first* conquer every sin, break off every evil word and work, and do all good to all men; or I must *first* go to Church, receive the Lord's Supper, hear more sermons, and say more prayers.' Alas, my brother, thou art clean gone out of the way. Thou art still 'ignorant of the righteousness of God', and art 'seeking to establish thy own righteousness' as the ground of thy reconciliation. Knowest thou not that thou canst do nothing but sin till thou art reconciled to God? Wherefore then dost thou say, I must do this and this *first*, and then I shall believe? Nay, but *first believe*. Believe in the Lord Jesus Christ, the propitiation for thy sins. Let this good foundation *first* be laid, and then thou shalt do all things well.

2. Neither say in thy heart, 'I can't be accepted yet because I am not *good enough*.' Who is good enough, who ever was, to merit acceptance at God's hands? Was ever any child of Adam good enough for this? Or will any, till the consummation of all things? And as for thee, thou art not good at all; there dwelleth in thee no good thing. And thou never wilt be till thou believe in Jesus. Rather thou wilt find thyself worse and worse. But is there any need of being worse in order to be accepted? Art thou not *bad enough* already? Indeed thou art, and that God knoweth. And thou thyself canst not deny it. Then delay not. All things are now ready. 'Arise, and wash away thy sins.' The fountain is open. Now is the time to wash thee white in the blood of the Lamb. Now he shall 'purge thee as with hyssop, and thou shalt be clean; he shall wash thee, and thou shalt be whiter than snow'.

3. Do not say, 'But I am not *contrite enough*: I am not sensible enough of my sins.' I know it. I would to God thou wert more sensible of them, more contrite a thousandfold

than thou art. But do not stay for this. It may be God will make thee so, not before thou believest, but by believing. It may be thou wilt not weep much till thou lovest much, because thou hast had much forgiven. In the meantime, look unto Jesus. Behold how he loveth thee! What could he have done more for thee which he hath not done?

> O Lamb of God, was ever pain,
> Was ever love like thine!

Look steadily upon him till he looks on thee, and breaks thy hard heart. Then shall thy 'head be waters, and thy eyes fountains of tears'.

4. Nor yet do thou say, 'I must *do* something more before I come to Christ.' I grant, supposing thy Lord should delay his coming, it were meet and right to wait for his appearing in doing, so far as thou hast power, whatsoever he hath commanded thee. But there is no necessity for making such a supposition. How knowest thou that he will delay? Perhaps he will appear as the day-spring from on high, before the morning light. O do not set him a time. Expect him every hour. Now, he is nigh! Even at the door!

5. And to what end wouldst thou wait for *more sincerity* before thy sins are blotted out? To make thee more worthy of the grace of God? Alas, thou art still 'establishing thy own righteousness'. He will have mercy, not because thou art worthy of it, but because his compassions fail not; not because thou art righteous, but because Jesus Christ hath atoned for thy sins.

Again, if there be anything good in *sincerity*, why dost thou expect it *before* thou hast faith?—seeing faith itself is the only root of whatever is really good and holy.

Above all, how long wilt thou forget that whatsoever thou dost, or whatsoever thou hast, before thy sins are forgiven thee, it avails nothing with God toward the procuring of thy forgiveness? Yea, and that it must all be cast behind thy back, trampled under foot, made no account of, or thou wilt never find favour in God's sight? Because until then thou canst not ask it as a mere sinner, guilty, lost, undone, having nothing to plead, nothing to offer to God but only the merits of his well-beloved Son, 'who loved *thee*, and gave himself for *thee*'.

6. To conclude. Whosoever thou art, O man, who hast the sentence of death in thyself, who feelest thyself a condemned sinner, and hast the wrath of God abiding on thee: unto thee said the Lord, not 'Do this; perfectly obey all my commands and live:' but, 'Believe in the Lord Jesus Christ, and thou shalt be saved'. 'The word of faith is nigh unto thee.' Now, at this instant, in the present moment, and in thy present state, sinner as thou art, just as thou art, believe the gospel, and 'I will be merciful unto thy unrighteousness, and thy iniquities will I remember no more.'

13. SALVATION BY FAITH

June 11, 1738

An Introductory Comment

Wesley's turn to preach at St. Mary's, Oxford, came up shortly after his Aldersgate experience. Taking one of his most popular texts, Ephesians 2:8, Wesley delivered in the afternoon to a curious congregation what Outler has called his "positive evangelical manifesto" (O, 1:110). Earlier that morning he had preached on the same text at Gambold's church in Stanton Harcourt, no doubt with good effect. The sermon itself is remarkable in many respects, due to its strong Reformation themes, and bears comparison with the later composition, "The Scripture Way of Salvation," produced in 1765, whose major divisions are the same (S, 1:36).

As Wesley exposited the text "By grace ye are saved through faith," he did so, for the most part, in terms not of co-operant grace but of free grace that highlights the divine role in redemption: "All the blessings which God hath bestowed upon man are of his mere grace, bounty, or favour; his free, undeserved favour" (O, 1:117). And again, Wesley exclaimed, "We are justified freely by his grace, through the redemption that is in Jesus Christ" (O, 1:455). Indeed, Wesley's own notes on the text of this sermon, produced much later in 1754–55, underscore that faith *receives* the gift of salvation with an "empty hand," language that reverberates with the meanings of *sola fide*, properly understood. Not surprisingly, Martin Luther is celebrated in this sermon as "the glorious champion of the Lord of Hosts" (O, 1:129), though upon reading more of the German Reformer's works (and encountering several difficulties especially in terms of the moral law), Wesley eventually removed such honorific language in the 1746 edition of the SOSO (O, 1:129n119). The basic teaching of this sermon, in its celebration of grace and faith, clearly avoided antinomianism (lawlessness) in its affirmation that saving faith, once again, ever delivers from both the *guilt* and the *power* of sin (O, 1:124).

Salvation by Faith

1.–2. All the blessings which God has bestowed upon humans are of mere grace

3. If sinful people find favour with God, it is grace upon grace

I. What faith it is through which we are saved

1. It is not the faith of a heathen

2. It is not the faith of a devil, though this goes farther than that of a heathen

3. It is not the faith the apostles had while Christ was yet upon earth

4. What faith is it then through which we are saved?

A. It may be answered: it is a faith in Christ, and God through Christ

5. And herein it differs from that faith which the apostles themselves had

A. It acknowledges the necessity and merit of his death and resurrection

II. What salvation is to be had by this faith?

1. Whatever else it may imply, it is a present salvation

2. We are saved from sin; this is the salvation which is through faith

3. From the guilt of all past sin

A. There is no condemnation now to them which believe in Christ Jesus

4. And being saved from guilt, we are saved from fear

5. Whosoever believeth is born of God

6. Those who are born of God do not sin; sin cannot reign in any who believe

7. Salvation through faith is salvation from sin and the consequences of sin

III. The usual objection to this is:

1. To preach salvation or justification by faith is to preach against good works

2. This is no new objection, but as old as St. Paul's time

A. We establish the law by calling all to that righteous way of living

B. In that way, the law may be fulfilled in them

3. But does not preaching this way lead people into pride?

A. We answer, accidentally it may. But we must remember God's mercy

4. But will speaking of the mercy of God not encourage people to sin?

A. It may and will. But their blood is upon their own heads

5. Yet to the same truth, a quite contrary objection is made:

A. If people cannot be saved by all that they can do, they will despair

B. True, they will despair of being saved by their own works

6. But this, it is said, is an uncomfortable doctrine

7. Then we are told that salvation by faith ought not to be preached at all

8. At this time we will speak that by grace ye are saved through faith

9. The adversary rages whenever salvation by faith is declared

Sermon 1: Salvation by Faith

A Sermon preached at St. Mary's, Oxford, before the University, on June 11, 1738

Ephesians 2:8

By grace ye are saved through faith.

1. All the blessings which God hath bestowed upon man are of his mere grace, bounty, or favour: his free, undeserved favour, favour altogether undeserved, man having no claim to the least of his mercies. It was free grace that 'formed man of the dust of the ground, and breathed into him a living soul', and stamped on that soul the image of God, and 'put all things under his feet'. The same free grace continues to us, at this day, life, and breath, and all things. For there is nothing we are, or have, or do, which can deserve the least thing at God's hand. 'All our works thou, O God, hast wrought in us.' These therefore are so many more instances of free mercy: and whatever righteousness may be found in man, this also is the gift of God.

2. Wherewithal then shall a sinful man atone for any the least of his sins? With his own works? No. Were they ever so many or holy, they are not his own, but God's. But indeed they are all unholy and sinful themselves, so that every one of them needs a fresh atonement. Only corrupt fruit grows on a corrupt tree. And his heart is altogether corrupt and abominable, being 'come short of the glory of God', the glorious righteousness at first impressed on his soul, after the image of his great Creator. Therefore having nothing, neither righteousness nor works, to plead, his 'mouth is utterly stopped before God'.

3. If then sinful man find favour with God, it is 'grace upon grace' (χάριν ἀντὶ χάριτος). If God vouchsafe still to pour fresh blessings upon us—yea, the greatest of all blessings, salvation—what can we say to these things but 'Thanks be unto God for his unspeakable gift!' And thus it is. Herein 'God commendeth his love toward us, in that, while we were yet sinners, Christ died' to save us. 'By grace', then, 'are ye saved through faith.' Grace is the source, faith the condition, of salvation.

Now, that we fall not short of the grace of God, it concerns us carefully to inquire:

I. What faith it is through which we are saved.

II. What is the salvation which is through faith.

III. How we may answer some objections.

I. What faith it is through which we are saved.

1. And, first, it is not barely the faith of a heathen. Now God requireth of a heathen to believe 'that God is, and that he is a rewarder of them that diligently seek him;' and that he is to be sought by 'glorifying him as God by giving him thanks for all things', and by a careful practice of moral virtue, of justice, mercy, and truth, toward their fellow-creatures. A Greek or Roman, therefore, yea, a Scythian or Indian, was without excuse if he did not believe thus much: the being and attributes of God, a future state of reward and punishment, and the obligatory nature of moral virtue. For this is barely the faith of a heathen.

2. Nor, secondly, is it the faith of a devil, though this goes much farther than that of a heathen. For the devil believes, not only that there is a wise and powerful God, gracious to reward and just to punish, but also that Jesus is the Son of God, the Christ, the Saviour of the world. So we find him declaring in express terms: 'I know thee who thou art, the Holy One of God' (Luke 4:34). Nor can we doubt but that unhappy spirit believes all those words which came out of the mouth of the Holy One; yea, and whatsoever else was written by those holy men of old, of two of whom he was compelled to give that glorious testimony, 'These men are the servants of the most high God, who show unto you the way of salvation.' Thus much then the great enemy of God and man believes, and trembles in believing, that 'God was made manifest in the flesh;' that he will 'tread all enemies under his feet'; and that 'all Scripture was given by inspiration of God.' Thus far goeth the faith of a devil.

3. Thirdly, the faith through which we are saved, in that sense of the word which will hereafter be explained, is not barely that which the apostles themselves had while Christ was yet upon earth; though they so believed on him as to 'leave all and follow him'; although they had then power to work miracles, 'to heal all manner of sickness, and all manner of disease'; yea, they had then 'power and authority over all devils': and which is beyond all this, were sent by their Master to 'preach the kingdom of God'. Yet after their return from doing all these mighty works their Lord himself terms them, 'a faithless generation'. He tells them 'they could not cast out a devil, because of their unbelief.' And when long after, supposing they had some already, they said unto him, 'Increase our faith,' he tells them plainly that of this faith they had none at all, no, not as a grain of mustard seed: 'The Lord said, If ye had faith as a grain of mustard seed, ye might say unto this sycamine tree, Be thou plucked up by the roots, and be thou planted in the sea; and it should obey you.'

4. What faith is it then through which we are saved? It may be answered: first, in general, it is a faith in Christ—Christ, and God through Christ, are the proper object of it. Herein therefore it is sufficiently, absolutely, distinguished from the faith either of ancient or modern heathens. And from the faith of a devil it is fully distinguished by this—it is not barely a speculative, rational thing, a cold, lifeless assent, a train of ideas in the head; but also a disposition of the heart. For thus saith the Scripture, 'With the heart man believeth unto righteousness.' And, 'If thou shalt confess with thy mouth the Lord Jesus, and shalt believe with thy *heart* that God hath raised him from the dead, thou shalt be saved.'

5. And herein does it differ from that faith which the apostles themselves had while our Lord was on earth, that it acknowledges the necessity and merit of his death, and the power of his resurrection. It acknowledges his death as the only sufficient means of redeeming man from death eternal, and his resurrection as the restoration of us all to life and immortality; inasmuch as he 'was delivered for our sins, and rose again for our justification'. Christian faith is then not only an assent to the whole gospel of Christ, but also a full reliance on the blood of Christ, a trust in the merits of his life, death, and resurrection; a recumbency upon him as our atonement and our life, as *given for us*, and *living in us*. It is a sure confidence which a man hath in God, that through the merits of Christ *his* sins are forgiven, and *he* reconciled to the favour of God; and in consequence hereof a closing

with him and cleaving to him as our 'wisdom, righteousness, sanctification, and redemption' or, in one word, our salvation.

II. What salvation it is which is through this faith is the second thing to be considered.

1. And, first, whatsoever else it imply, it is a present salvation. It is something attainable, yea, actually attained on earth, by those who are partakers of this faith. For thus saith the Apostle to the believers at Ephesus, and in them to the believers of all ages, not, 'Ye *shall be*' (though that also is true), but 'Ye *are* saved through faith.'

2. Ye are saved (to comprise all in one word) from sin. This is the salvation which is through faith. This is that great salvation foretold by the angel before God brought his first-begotten into the world: 'Thou shalt call his name Jesus, for he shall save his people from their sins.' And neither here nor in other parts of Holy Writ is there any limitation or restriction. All his people, or as it is elsewhere expressed, all that believe in him, he will save from all their sins: from original and actual, past and present sin, of the flesh and of the spirit. Through faith that is in him they are saved both from the guilt and from the power of it.

3. First, from the guilt of all past sin. For whereas 'all the world is guilty before God'; insomuch that should he 'be extreme to mark what is done amiss, there is none that could abide it'; and whereas 'by the law is only the knowledge of sin', but no deliverance from it, so that 'by fulfilling the deeds of the law no flesh can be justified in his sight'; now 'the righteousness of God, which is by faith of Jesus Christ', 'is manifested unto all that believe'. Now they are 'justified freely by his grace through the redemption that is in Jesus Christ. Him God hath set forth to be a propitiation through faith in his blood, to declare his righteousness for (or by) the remission of the sins that are past.' Now hath Christ 'taken away the curse of the law, being made a curse for us'. He hath 'blotted out the handwriting that was against us, taking it out of the way, nailing it to his cross'. 'There is therefore no condemnation now to them which believe in Christ Jesus.'

4. And being saved from guilt, they are saved from fear. Not indeed from a filial fear of offending, but from all servile fear, from that 'fear which hath torment', from fear of punishment, from fear of the wrath of God, whom they now no longer regard as a severe master, but as an indulgent Father. 'They have not received again the spirit of bondage, but the Spirit of adoption, whereby they cry, Abba, Father: the Spirit itself also bearing witness with their spirit, that they are the children of God.' They are also saved from the fear, though not from the possibility, of falling away from the grace of God, and coming short of the great and precious promises. They are 'sealed with the Holy Spirit of promise, which is the earnest of their inheritance'. Thus have they 'peace with God through our Lord Jesus Christ. . . . They rejoice in hope of the glory of God. . . . And the love of God is shed abroad in their hearts through the Holy Ghost which is given unto them.' And hereby they are 'persuaded' (though perhaps not all at all times, nor with the same fullness of persuasion) 'that neither death, nor life, nor things present, nor things to come, nor height, nor depth, nor any other creature, shall be able to separate them from the love of God, which is in Christ Jesus our Lord.'

5. Again, through this faith they are saved from the power of sin as well as from the guilt of it. So the Apostle declares, 'Ye know that he was manifested to take away our sins, and in him is no sin. Whosoever abideth in him sinneth not' (1 John 3:5-6). Again, 'Little children, let no man deceive you. . . . He that committeth sin is of the devil.' 'Whosoever believeth is born of God.' And, 'Whosoever is born of God doth not commit sin; for his seed remaineth in him: and he cannot sin, because he is born of God.' Once more, 'We know that whosoever is born of God sinneth not; but he that is begotten of God keepeth himself, and that wicked one toucheth him not' (1 John 5:18).

6. He that is by faith born of God sinneth not, (1), by any habitual sin, for all habitual sin is sin reigning; but sin cannot reign in any that believeth. Nor, (2), by any wilful sin; for his will, while he abideth in the faith, is utterly set against all sin, and abhorreth it as deadly poison. Nor, (3), by any sinful desire; for he continually desireth the holy and perfect will of God; and any unholy desire he by the grace of God stifleth in the birth. Nor, (4), doth he sin by infirmities, whether in act, word, or thought; for his infirmities have no concurrence of his will; and without this they are not properly sins. Thus, 'He that is born of God doth not commit sin.' And though he cannot say he *hath not sinned*, yet now *'he sinneth not'.*

7. This then is the salvation which is through faith, even in the present world: a salvation from sin and the consequences of sin, both often expressed in the word 'justification', which, taken in the largest sense, implies a deliverance from guilt and punishment, by the atonement of Christ actually applied to the soul of the sinner now believing on him, and a deliverance from the power of sin, through Christ 'formed in his heart'. So that he who is thus justified or saved by faith is indeed 'born again'. He is 'born again of the Spirit' unto a new 'life which is hid with Christ in God'. And as a 'newborn babe he gladly receives the ἄδολον, the sincere milk of the word, and grows thereby'; 'going on in the might of the Lord his God', 'from faith to faith', 'from grace to grace', 'until at length he comes unto a perfect man, unto the measure of the stature of the fullness of Christ'.

III. The first usual objection to this is,

1. That to preach salvation or justification by faith only is to preach against holiness and good works. To which a short answer might be given: it would be so if we spake, as some do, of a faith which was separate from these. But we speak of a faith which is not so, but necessarily productive of all good works and all holiness.

2. But it may be of use to consider it more at large: especially since it is no new objection, but as old as St. Paul's time, for even then it was asked, 'Do we not make void the law through faith?' We answer, first, all who preach not faith do manifestly make void the law, either directly and grossly, by limitations and comments that eat out all the spirit of the text; or indirectly, by not pointing out the only means whereby it is possible to perform it. Whereas, secondly, 'We establish the law', both by showing its full extent and spiritual meaning, and by calling all to that living way whereby 'the righteousness of the law may be fulfilled in them'. These, while they trust in the blood of Christ alone, use all the ordinances which he hath appointed, do all the 'good works which he had before prepared

that they should walk therein', and enjoy and manifest all holy and heavenly tempers, even the same 'mind that was in Christ Jesus'.

3. But does not preaching this faith lead men into pride? We answer, accidentally it may. Therefore ought every believer to be earnestly cautioned (in the words of the great Apostle): 'Because of unbelief the first branches were broken off, and thou standest by faith. Be not high-minded, but fear. If God spared not the natural branches, take heed lest he spare not thee. Behold therefore the goodness and severity of God: on them which fell, severity; but toward thee, goodness, if thou continue in his goodness: otherwise thou also shalt be cut off.' And while he continues therein, he will remember those words of St. Paul, foreseeing and answering this very objection: 'Where is boasting, then? It is excluded. By what law? Of works? Nay; but by the law of faith' (Rom. 3:27). If a man were justified by his works, he would have whereof to glory. But there is no glorying for him 'that worketh not, but believeth on him that justifieth the ungodly' (Rom. 4:5). To the same effect are the words both preceding and following the text: 'God, who is rich in mercy, . . . even when we were dead in sins, hath quickened us together with Christ (by grace ye are saved), . . . that he might show the exceeding riches of his grace in his kindness toward us through Christ Jesus. For by grace ye are saved through faith: and that not of yourselves' (Eph. 2:4-5, 7-8). Of yourselves cometh neither your faith nor your salvation. 'It is the gift of God,' the free, undeserved gift—the faith through which ye are saved, as well as the salvation which he of his own good pleasure, his mere favour, annexes thereto. That ye believe is one instance of his grace; that believing, ye are saved, another. 'Not of works, lest any man should boast.' For all our works, all our righteousness, which were before our believing, merited nothing of God but condemnation, so far were they from deserving faith, which therefore, whenever given, is not 'of works'. Neither is salvation of the works we do when we believe. For 'it is' then 'God that worketh in us'. And, therefore, that he giveth us a reward for what he himself worketh only commendeth the riches of his mercy, but leaveth us nothing whereof to glory.

4. However, may not the speaking thus of the mercy of God, as saving or justifying freely by faith only, encourage men in sin? Indeed it may and will; many will 'continue in sin, that grace may abound'. But their blood is upon their own head. The goodness of God ought to lead them to repentance, and so it will those who are sincere of heart. When they know there is yet forgiveness with him, they will cry aloud that he would blot out their sins also through faith which is in Jesus. And if they earnestly cry and faint not, if they seek him in all the means he hath appointed, if they refuse to be comforted till he come, he 'will come, and will not tarry'. And he can do much work in a short time. Many are the examples in the Acts of the Apostles of God's working this faith in men's hearts as quick as lightning falling from heaven. So in the same hour that Paul and Silas began to preach the gaoler *repented*, *believed*, and *was baptized*—as were three thousand by St. Peter on the day of Pentecost, who all repented and believed at his first preaching. And, blessed be God, there are now many living proofs that he is still thus 'mighty to save'.

5. Yet to the same truth, placed in another view, a quite contrary objection is made: 'If a man cannot be saved by all that he can do, this will drive men to despair.' True, to despair of being saved by their own works, their own merits or righteousness. And so it

ought; for none can trust in the merits of Christ till he has utterly renounced his own. He that 'goeth about to establish his own righteousness' cannot receive the righteousness of God. The righteousness which is of faith cannot be given him while he trusteth in that which is of the law.

6. But this, it is said, is an uncomfortable doctrine. The devil spoke like himself, that is, without either truth or shame, when he dared to suggest to men that it is such. 'Tis the only comfortable one, 'tis 'very full of comfort', to all self-destroyed, self-condemned sinners. That 'whosoever believeth on him shall not be ashamed'; that 'the same Lord over all is rich unto all that call upon him'—here is comfort, high as heaven, stronger than death! What! Mercy for all? For Zaccheus, a public robber? For Mary Magdalene, a common harlot? Methinks I hear one say, 'Then I, even I, may hope for mercy!' And so thou mayst, thou afflicted one, whom none hath comforted! God will not cast out thy prayer. Nay, perhaps he may say the next hour, 'Be of good cheer, thy sins are forgiven thee;' so forgiven that they shall reign over thee no more; yea, and that 'the Holy Spirit shall bear witness with thy spirit that thou art a child of God.' O glad tidings! Tidings of great joy, which are sent unto all people. 'Ho, everyone that thirsteth, come ye to the waters; come ye and buy without money, and without price.' Whatsoever your sins be, 'though red, like crimson', though 'more than the hairs of your head', 'return ye unto the Lord, and he will have mercy upon you, and to our God, for he will abundantly pardon.'

7. When no more objections occur, then we are simply told that salvation by faith only ought not to be preached as the first doctrine, or at least not to be preached to all. But what saith the Holy Ghost? 'Other foundation can no man lay than that which is laid, even Jesus Christ.' So, then, 'that whosoever believeth on him shall be saved' is and must be the foundation of all our preaching; that is, must be preached first. 'Well, but not to all.' To whom then are we not to preach it? Whom shall we except? The poor? Nay, they have a peculiar right to have the gospel preached unto them. The unlearned? No. God hath revealed these things unto unlearned and ignorant men from the beginning. The young? By no means. 'Suffer these' in any wise 'to come unto Christ, and forbid them not.' The sinners? Least of all. He 'came not to call the righteous, but sinners to repentance'. Why then, if any, we are to except the rich, the learned, the reputable, the moral men. And 'tis true, they too often except themselves from hearing; yet we must speak the words of our Lord. For thus the tenor of our commission runs: 'Go and preach the gospel to every creature.' If any man wrest it or any part of it to his destruction, he must bear his own burden. But still, 'as the Lord liveth, whatsoever the Lord saith unto us, that we will speak.'

8. At this time more especially will we speak, that 'by grace ye are saved through faith:' because never was the maintaining this doctrine more seasonable than it is at this day. Nothing but this can effectually prevent the increase of the Romish delusion among us. 'Tis endless to attack one by one all the errors of that Church. But salvation by faith strikes at the root, and all fall at once where this is established. It was this doctrine (which our Church justly calls 'the strong rock and foundation of the Christian religion') that first drove popery out of these kingdoms, and 'tis this alone can keep it out. Nothing but this can give a check to that immorality which hath overspread the land as a flood. Can you

empty the great deep drop by drop? Then you may reform us by dissuasives from particular vices. But let 'the righteousness which is of God by faith' be brought in, and so shall its proud waves be stayed. Nothing but this can stop the mouths of those who 'glory in their shame', 'and openly deny the Lord that bought them'. They can talk as sublimely of the law as he that hath it written by God in his heart. To hear them speak on this head might incline one to think they were not far from the kingdom of God. But take them out of the law into the gospel; begin with the righteousness of faith, with 'Christ, the end of the law to everyone that believeth', and those who but now appeared almost if not altogether Christians stand confessed the sons of perdition, as far from life and salvation (God be merciful unto them!) as the depth of hell from the height of heaven.

9. For this reason the adversary so rages whenever 'salvation by faith' is declared to the world. For this reason did he stir up earth and hell to destroy those who first preached it. And for the same reason, knowing that faith alone could overturn the foundations of his kingdom, did he call forth all his forces, and employ all his arts of lies and calumny, to affright that glorious champion of the Lord of Hosts, Martin Luther, from reviving it. Nor can we wonder thereat. For as that man of God observes, 'How would it enrage a proud strong man armed to be stopped and set at nought by a little child, coming against him with a reed in his hand!'—especially when he knew that little child would surely overthrow him and tread him under foot. 'Even so, Lord Jesus!' Thus hath thy strength been ever 'made perfect in weakness'! Go forth then, thou little child that believest in him, and his 'right hand shall teach thee terrible things'! Though thou art helpless and weak as an infant of days, the strong man shall not be able to stand before thee. Thou shalt prevail over him, and subdue him, and overthrow him, and trample him under thy feet. Thou shalt march on under the great Captain of thy salvation, 'conquering and to conquer', until all thine enemies are destroyed, and 'death is swallowed up in victory'.

Now thanks be to God which giveth us the victory through our Lord Jesus Christ, to whom, with the Father and the Holy Ghost, be blessing and glory, and wisdom, and thanksgiving, and honour, and power, and might, for ever and ever. Amen.

14. JUSTIFICATION BY FAITH

1746

An Introductory Comment

At the heart of John Wesley's doctrine of salvation, "Justification by Faith" was a "landmark sermon" (O, 1:182) and one of the eight that he considered to be *articulus stantis vel cadentis ecclesiae* (the Christian church stands or falls with it). It was likely preached the first time on May 28, 1738, at the Long Acre Chapel in London and several years later on top of his father's tomb at Epworth on June 8, 1742 (S, 1:112). It did not appear in print until 1746.

Dispelling the notion that sanctification in any sense can be the basis of justification ("The one implies what God *does for us* through his Son; the other, what he *works in us* by his Spirit"; O, 1:187), Wesley insisted in his notes upon the text of this sermon, Romans 4:5, that God justifies not the righteous but the *ungodly*, who receive "the seal of the Spirit" (WH, 19:25), and yet the Almighty remains just in doing so. Elsewhere Wesley affirmed that he thought on justification, which is quite simply the forgiveness of sins that are past, "just as Mr. Calvin does. In this respect I do not differ from him a hair's breadth" (T, 4:298). In fact, Wesley demonstrated the significant influence of both the English and the Continental Reformation on his thinking in this sermon by affirming that faith is the "*only necessary* condition" (O, 1:196) of justification and pointing out that it is the glory of God's "free grace" (O, 1:199) to justify the ungodly. Not surprisingly, Wesley had already published Robert Barnes's *Treatise on Justification by Faith Only, According to the Doctrine of the Eleventh Article of the Church of England* in 1739.

Wesley's estimate of works prior to justifying grace was somewhat different from Calvinist conceptions due to his doctrine of prevenient grace. That is, though such works were not good "strictly speaking" (O, 1:192), they nevertheless were in some sense good.

Justification by Faith

1. How a sinner may be justified is a question of great importance
2. And yet how little has this important question been understood

I. The general ground of this doctrine of justification
1. People were made in the image of God; they were holy and perfect
2. God gave a perfect law and required perfect obedience to it
3. There was one positive law: do not eat of the fruit of the tree
4. Human beings were happy and holy in their original state
5. But they disobeyed God; they ate of the tree
6. Thus sin entered into the world and death with it
7. Humanity was in this state when God sent God's only begotten Son
8. Through the death of Christ, God reconciled the world to himself
9. This is the general ground of the whole doctrine of justification

II. 1. To be justified is not to be made righteous; this is *sanctification*
2. Neither is it the clearing of humanity from Satan's accusation
3. It is not clearing from the accusation brought against us by *the law*
4. Least of all does it imply that God is *deceived* in those whom God justifies
5. The plain scriptural notion of justification is pardon, the forgiveness of sins

III. 1. God justifies the ungodly
2. Some contend that people must be sanctified before they can be justified
3. Does the good Shepherd seek and save only those that are found already?
4. Those who are sick are the ones who need a physician
5. People may do good works before justification; they are not good in themselves
6. If God does not justify the ungodly, then Christ has died in vain

IV. 1. But on what terms are we justified? We are justified by faith alone
2. Faith is a divine, supernatural evidence or conviction of things not seen
3. Faith is a sure trust and confidence that God forgives us for Christ's merits
4. Faith is the *condition* of justification; there is no justification without faith
5. Faith is the *only necessary* condition of justification
6. Not assenting to this proposition must arise from not understanding it
7. We should not call into question the condition of justification
8. The condition of faith makes people humble
9. Ungodly sinners, go straight to God with all your ungodliness

Sermon 5: Justification by Faith, 1746

Romans 4:5

To him that worketh not, but believeth on him that justifieth the ungodly, his faith is counted to him for righteousness.

1. How a sinner may be justified before God, the Lord and Judge of all, is a question of no common importance to every child of man. It contains the foundation of all our hope, inasmuch as while we are at enmity with God there can be no true peace, no solid joy, either in time or in eternity. What peace can there be while our own heart condemns us? And much more he that 'is greater than our heart, and knoweth all things'? What solid joy, either in this world or that to come, while 'the wrath of God abideth on us'?

2. And yet how little hath this important question been understood! What confused notions have many had concerning it! Indeed not only confused, but often utterly false, contrary to the truth as light to darkness; notions absolutely inconsistent with the oracles of God, and with the whole analogy of faith. And hence, erring concerning the very foundation, they could not possibly build thereon; at least, not 'gold, silver, or precious stones', which would endure when 'tried as by fire', but only 'hay and stubble', neither acceptable to God nor profitable to man.

3. In order to do justice, as far as in me lies, to the vast importance of the subject, to save those that seek the truth in sincerity from 'vain jangling' and 'strife of words', to clear the confusedness of thought into which so many have already been led thereby, and to give them true and just conceptions of this great mystery of godliness, I shall endeavour to show,

First, what is the general ground of this whole doctrine of justification;

Secondly, what justification is;

Thirdly, who they are that are justified; and,

Fourthly, on what terms they are justified.

I. I am first to show what is the general ground of this whole doctrine of justification.

1. In the image of God was man made; holy as he that created him is holy, merciful as the author of all is merciful, perfect as his Father in heaven is perfect. As God is love, so man dwelling in love dwelt in God, and God in him. God made him to be 'an image of his own eternity', an incorruptible picture of the God of glory. He was accordingly pure, as God is pure, from every spot of sin. He knew not evil in any kind or degree, but was inwardly and outwardly sinless and undefiled. He 'loved the Lord his God with all his heart, and with all his mind, and soul, and strength'.

2. To man thus upright and perfect God gave a perfect law, to which he required full and perfect obedience. He required full obedience in every point, and this to be performed without any intermission from the moment man became a living soul till the time of his trial should be ended. No allowance was made for any falling short. As, indeed,

there was no need of any, man being altogether equal to the task assigned, and thoroughly furnished for every good word and work.

3. To the entire law of love which was written in his heart (against which, perhaps, he could not sin directly) it seemed good to the sovereign wisdom of God to superadd one positive law: 'Thou shalt not eat of the fruit of the tree that groweth in the midst of the garden;' annexing that penalty thereto, 'In the day thou eatest thereof, thou shalt surely die.'

4. Such then was the state of man in paradise. By the free, unmerited love of God he was holy and happy; he knew, loved, enjoyed God, which is (in substance) life everlasting. And in this life of love he was to continue for ever if he continued to obey God in all things. But if he disobeyed him in any he was to forfeit all. 'In that day (said God) thou shalt surely die.'

5. Man did disobey God; he 'ate of the tree of which God commanded him, saying, Thou shalt not eat of it.' And in that day he was condemned by the righteous judgment of God. Then also the sentence whereof he was warned before began to take place upon him. For the moment he tasted that fruit he died. His soul died, was separated from God; separate from whom the soul has no more life than the body has when separate from the soul. His body likewise became corruptible and mortal, so that death then took hold on this also. And being already dead in spirit, dead to God, dead in sin, he hastened on to death everlasting, to the destruction both of body and soul in the fire never to be quenched.

6. Thus 'by one man sin entered into the world, and death by sin. And so death passed upon all men,' as being contained in him who was the common father and representative of us all. Thus 'through the offence of one' all are dead, dead to God, dead in sin, dwelling in a corruptible, mortal body, shortly to be dissolved, and under the sentence of death eternal. For as 'by one man's disobedience all were made sinners', so by that offence of one 'judgment came upon all men to condemnation' (Rom. 5:12, etc.).

7. In this state we were, even all mankind, when 'God so loved the world that he gave his only begotten Son, to the end we might not perish but have everlasting life.' In the fullness of time he was made man, another common head of mankind, a second general parent and representative of the whole human race. And as such it was that 'he bore our griefs', the Lord 'laying upon him the iniquities of us all'. Then 'was he wounded for our transgressions, and bruised for our iniquities.' 'He made his soul an offering for sin.' He poured out his blood for the transgressors. He 'bare our sins in his own body on the tree', that 'by his stripes we might be healed'. And 'by that one oblation of himself once offered' he 'hath redeemed me and all mankind'; having thereby 'made a full, perfect, and sufficient sacrifice and satisfaction for the sins of the whole world'.

8. In consideration of this, that the Son of God hath 'tasted death for every man', God hath now 'reconciled the world to himself, not imputing to them their former trespasses'. And thus, 'as by the offence of one judgment came upon all men to condemnation, even so by the righteousness of one the free gift came upon all men unto justification.' So that for the sake of his well-beloved Son, of what he hath done and suffered for us, God now vouchsafes on one only condition (which himself also enables us to perform)

both to remit the punishment due to our sins, to reinstate us in his favour, and to restore our dead souls to spiritual life, as the earnest of life eternal.

9. This therefore is the general ground of the whole doctrine of justification. By the sin of the first Adam, who was not only the father but likewise the representative of us all, we all 'fell short of the favour of God', we all became 'children of wrath'; or, as the Apostle expresses it, 'Judgment came upon all men to condemnation.' Even so by the sacrifice for sin made by the second Adam, as the representative of us all, God is so far reconciled to all the world that he hath given them a new covenant. The plain condition whereof being once fulfilled, 'there is no more condemnation for us', but we are 'justified freely by his grace through the redemption that is in Jesus Christ'.

II.1. But what is it to be 'justified'? What is 'justification'? This was the second thing which I proposed to show. And it is evident from what has been already observed that it is not the being made actually just and righteous. This is *sanctification*; which is indeed in some degree the immediate *fruit* of justification, but nevertheless is a distinct gift of God, and of a totally different nature. The one implies what God *does for us* through his Son; the other what he *works in us* by his Spirit. So that although some rare instances may be found wherein the term 'justified' or 'justification' is used in so wide a sense as to include sanctification also, yet in general use they are sufficiently distinguished from each other both by St. Paul and the other inspired writers.

2. Neither is that far-fetched conceit that justification is the clearing us from accusation, particularly that of Satan, easily provable from any clear text of Holy Writ. In the whole scriptural account of this matter, as above laid down, neither that accuser nor his accusation appears to be at all taken in. It cannot indeed be denied that he is the 'accuser of men', emphatically so called. But it does in no wise appear that the great Apostle hath any reference to this, more or less, in all that he hath written touching justification either to the Romans or the Galatians.

3. It is also far easier to take for granted than to prove from any clear Scripture testimony that justification is the clearing us from the accusation brought against us by *the law.* At least, if this forced, unnatural way of speaking mean either more or less than this, that whereas we have transgressed the law of God and thereby deserved the damnation of hell, God does not inflict on those who are justified the punishment which they had deserved.

4. Least of all does justification imply that God is *deceived* in those whom he justifies; that he thinks them to be what in fact they are not, that he accounts them to be otherwise than they are. It does by no means imply that God judges concerning us contrary to the real nature of things, that he esteems us better than we really are, or believes us righteous when we are unrighteous. Surely no. The judgment of the all-wise God is always according to truth. Neither can it ever consist with his unerring wisdom to think that I am innocent, to judge that I am righteous or holy, because another is so. He can no more in this manner confound me with Christ than with David or Abraham. Let any man to whom God hath given understanding weigh this without prejudice, and he cannot but perceive that such a notion of justification is neither reconcilable to reason nor Scripture.

5. The plain scriptural notion of justification is pardon, the forgiveness of sins. It is that act of God the Father whereby, for the sake of the propitiation made by the blood of his Son, he 'showeth forth his righteousness (or mercy) by the remission of the sins that are past'. This is the easy, natural account of it given by St. Paul throughout his whole Epistle. So he explains it himself, more particularly in this and in the following chapter. Thus in the next verses but one to the text, 'Blessed are they (saith he) whose iniquities are forgiven, and whose sins are covered. Blessed is the man to whom the Lord will not impute sin.' To him that is justified or forgiven God 'will not impute sin' to his condemnation. He will not condemn him on that account either in this world or in that which is to come. His sins, all his past sins, in thought, word, and deed, 'are covered', are blotted out; shall not be remembered or mentioned against him, any more than if they had not been. God will not inflict on that sinner what he deserved to suffer, because the Son of his love hath suffered for him. And from the time we are 'accepted through the Beloved', 'reconciled to God through his blood', he loves and blesses and watches over us for good, even as if we had never sinned.

Indeed the Apostle in one place seems to extend the meaning of the word much farther, where he says: 'Not the hearers of the law, but the doers of the law shall be justified.' Here he appears to refer our justification to the sentence of the great day. And so our Lord himself unquestionably doth when he says, 'By thy words thou shalt be justified;' proving thereby that 'for every idle word men shall speak they shall give an account in the day of judgment.' But perhaps we can hardly produce another instance of St. Paul's using the word in that distant sense. In the general tenor of his writings it is evident he doth not; and least of all in the text before us, which undeniably speaks, not of those who have already 'finished their course', but of those who are now just setting out, just beginning 'to run the race which is set before them'.

III.1. But this is the third thing which was to be considered, namely, who are they that are justified? And the Apostle tells us expressly, the ungodly: he, that is, God, 'justifieth the ungodly'; the ungodly of every kind and degree, and none but the ungodly. As 'they that are righteous need no repentance,' so they need no forgiveness. It is only sinners that have any occasion for pardon: it is sin alone which admits of being forgiven. Forgiveness therefore has an immediate reference to sin and (in this respect) to nothing else. It is our 'unrighteousness' to which the pardoning God is 'merciful'; it is our 'iniquity' which he 'remembereth no more'.

2. This seems not to be at all considered by those who so vehemently contend that man must be sanctified, that is, holy, before he can be justified; especially by such of them as affirm that universal holiness or obedience must precede justification (unless they mean that justification at the last day which is wholly out of the present question); so far from it, that the very supposition is not only flatly impossible (for where there is no love of God there is no holiness, and there is no love of God but from a sense of his loving us) but also grossly, intrinsically absurd, contradictory to itself. For it is not a *saint* but a *sinner* that is *forgiven*, and under the notion of a sinner. God *justifieth* not the godly, but the *ungodly*; not those that are holy already, but the unholy. Upon what condition he doth this will

be considered quickly; but whatever it is, it cannot be holiness. To assert this is to say the Lamb of God takes away only those sins which were taken away before.

3. Does then the good Shepherd seek and save only those that are found already? No. He seeks and saves that which is lost. He pardons those who need his pardoning mercy. He saves from the guilt of sin (and at the same time from the power) sinners of every kind, of every degree: men who till then were altogether ungodly; in whom the love of the Father was not; and consequently in whom dwelt no good thing, no good or truly Christian temper, but all such as were evil and abominable—pride, anger, love of the world, the genuine fruits of that 'carnal mind which is enmity against God'.

4. These 'who are sick', the 'burden of whose sins is intolerable', are they that 'need a physician'; these who are guilty, who groan under the wrath of God, are they that need a pardon. These who are 'condemned already', not only by God but also by their own conscience, as by a thousand witnesses, of all their ungodliness, both in thought, and word, and work, cry aloud for him that 'justifieth the ungodly' 'through the redemption that is in Jesus'—'the ungodly and him that worketh not', that worketh not before he is justified anything that is good, that is truly virtuous or holy, but only evil continually. For his heart is necessarily, essentially evil, till the love of God is shed abroad therein. And while the tree is corrupt so are the fruits, 'for an evil tree cannot bring forth good fruit'.

5. If it be objected, 'Nay, but a man, before he is justified, may feed the hungry, or clothe the naked; and these are good works,' the answer is easy. He *may* do these, even before he is justified. And these are in one sense 'good works'; they are 'good and profitable to men'. But it does not follow that they are, strictly speaking, good in themselves, or good in the sight of God. All truly 'good works' (to use the words of our Church) 'follow after justification', and they are therefore 'good and acceptable to God in Christ', because they 'spring out of a true and living faith'. By a parity of reason all 'works done before justification are not good', in the Christian sense, 'forasmuch as they spring not of faith in Jesus Christ' (though from some kind of faith in God they may spring), 'yea, rather for that they are not done as God hath willed and commanded them to be done, we doubt not' (how strange soever it may appear to some) 'but they have the nature of sin.'

6. Perhaps those who doubt of this have not duly considered the weighty reason which is here assigned why no works done before justification can be truly and properly good. The argument runs thus:

No works are good which are not done as God hath willed and commanded them to be done:

But no works done before justification are done as God hath willed and commanded them to be done:

Therefore no works done before justification are good.

The first proposition is self-evident. And the second, that no works done before justification are done as God hath willed and commanded them to be done, will appear equally plain and undeniable if we only consider God hath willed and commanded that 'all our works should be done in charity' (ἐν ἀγάπῃ), in love, in that love to God which produces love to all mankind. But none of our works can be done in this love while the love of the Father (of God as our Father) is not in us. And this love cannot be in us till we receive the 'Spirit of adoption, crying in our hearts, Abba, Father'. If therefore God doth not 'justify the ungodly', and him that (in this sense) 'worketh not', then hath Christ died in vain; then, notwithstanding his death, can no flesh living be justified.

IV.1. But on what terms then is he justified who is altogether 'ungodly,' and till that time 'worketh not'? On one alone, which is faith. He 'believeth in him that justifieth the ungodly', and 'he that believeth is not condemned'; yea, he 'is passed from death unto life'. For 'the righteousness (or mercy) of God is by faith of Jesus Christ unto all and upon all them that believe; . . . whom God hath set forth to be a propitiation through faith in his blood', that 'he might be just, and (consistently with his justice) the justifier of him which believeth in Jesus. . . . Therefore we conclude that a man is justified by faith without the deeds of the law'—without previous obedience to the moral law, which indeed he could not till now perform. That it is the moral law, and that alone, which is here intended, appears evidently from the words that follow: 'Do we then make void the law through faith? God forbid! Yea, we establish the law.' What law do we establish by faith? Not the ritual law; not the ceremonial law of Moses. In no wise; but the great, unchangeable law of love, the holy love of God and of our neighbour.

2. Faith in general is a divine, supernatural ἔλεγχος, 'evidence' or conviction 'of things not seen', not discoverable by our bodily senses as being either past, future, or spiritual. Justifying faith implies, not only a divine evidence or conviction that 'God was in Christ, reconciling the world unto himself', but a sure trust and confidence that Christ died for *my* sins, that he loved *me*, and gave himself for *me*. And at what time soever a sinner thus believes, be it in early childhood, in the strength of his years, or when he is old and hoary-haired, God justifieth that ungodly one; God for the sake of his Son pardoneth and absolveth him who had in him till then no good thing. Repentance indeed God had given him before. But that repentance was neither more nor less than a deep sense of the want of all good, and the presence of all evil. And whatever good he hath or doth from that hour when he first believes in God through Christ, faith does not *find* but *bring*. This is the fruit of faith. First the tree is good, and then the fruit is good also.

3. I cannot describe the nature of this faith better than in the words of our own Church: 'The only instrument of salvation' (whereof justification is one branch) 'is faith: that is [. . .] a sure trust and confidence [. . .] that God both hath and will forgive our sins, that he hath accepted us again into his favour, [. . .] for the merits of Christ's death and Passion. . . . But here we must take heed that we do not halt with God through an inconstant, wavering faith. [. . .] Peter coming to Christ upon the water, because he fainted in faith, was in danger of drowning. So we, if we begin to waver or doubt, it is to be feared that we should sink as Peter did, not into the water but into the bottomless pit of hell-fire' (Second Sermon on the Passion [*Homilies*]).

Therefore have 'a sure and constant faith, not only that the death of Christ is available for [. . .] all the world, [. . .] but [. . .] that he hath made [. . .] a full and sufficient sacrifice for *thee*, a perfect cleansing of *thy* sins, so that [. . .] thou mayst say with the Apostle, [. . .] he loved *thee*, and gave himself for *thee*. For this is [. . .] to make Christ *thine own*, and to apply his merits unto *thyself*' (Sermon on the Sacrament, First Part [*Homilies*]).

4. By affirming that this faith is the term or *condition* of justification I mean, first, that there is no justification without it. 'He that believeth not is condemned already;' and so long as he believeth not that condemnation cannot be removed, 'but the wrath of God abideth on him'. As 'there is no other name given under heaven than that of Jesus of Nazareth,' no other merit whereby a condemned sinner can ever be saved from the guilt of sin; so there is no other way of obtaining a share in his merit than 'by faith in his name'. So that as long as we are without this faith we are 'strangers to the covenant of promise', we are 'aliens from the commonwealth of Israel', and 'without God in the world'. Whatsoever virtues (so called) a man may have—I speak of those unto whom the gospel is preached; 'for what have I to do to judge them that are without?'—whatsoever good works (so accounted) he may do, it profiteth not: he is still a 'child of wrath', still under the curse, till he believes in Jesus.

5. Faith therefore is the *necessary* condition of justification. Yea, and the *only necessary* condition thereof. This is the second point carefully to be observed: that the very moment God giveth faith (for 'it is the gift of God') to the 'ungodly', 'that worketh not', that 'faith is counted to him for righteousness'. He hath no righteousness at all antecedent to this, not so much as negative righteousness or innocence. But 'faith is imputed to him for righteousness' the very moment that he believeth. Not that God (as was observed before) thinketh him to be what he is not. But as 'he made Christ to be sin for us' (that is, treated him as a sinner, punished him for our sins), so he counteth us righteous from the time we believe in him (that is, he doth not punish us for our sins, yea, treats us as though we were guiltless and righteous).

6. Surely the difficulty of assenting to this proposition, that faith is the *only condition* of justification, must arise from not understanding it. We mean thereby thus much: that it is the only thing without which none is justified, the only thing that is immediately, indispensably, absolutely requisite in order to pardon. As on the one hand, though a man should have everything else, without faith, yet he cannot be justified; so on the other, though he be supposed to want everything else, yet if he hath faith he cannot but be justified. For suppose a sinner of any kind or degree, in a full sense of his total ungodliness, of his utter inability to think, speak, or do good, and his absolute meetness for hell-fire—suppose, I say, this sinner, helpless and hopeless, casts himself wholly on the mercy of God in Christ (which indeed he cannot do but by the grace of God)—who can doubt but he is forgiven in that moment? Who will affirm that any more is *indispensably required* before that sinner can be justified?

Now if there ever was one such instance from the beginning of the world (and have there not been, and are there not ten thousand times ten thousand?) it plainly follows that faith is, in the above sense, the sole condition of justification.

7. It does not become poor, guilty, sinful worms, who receive whatsoever blessings they enjoy (from the least drop of water that cools our tongue to the immense riches of glory in eternity) of grace, of mere favour, and not of debt, to ask of God the reasons of his conduct. It is not meet for us to call him in question 'who giveth account to none

of his ways'; to demand, 'Why didst thou make faith the condition, the only condition of justification? Wherefore didst thou decree, "He that believeth", and he only, "shall be saved"?' This is the very point on which St. Paul so strongly insists in the ninth chapter of this Epistle, *viz.*, that the terms of pardon and acceptance must depend, not on us, but 'on him that calleth us'; that there is no 'unrighteousness with God' in fixing his own terms, not according to ours, but his own good pleasure: who may justly say, 'I will have mercy on whom I will have mercy,' namely, on him who believeth in Jesus. 'So then it is not of him that willeth, nor of him that runneth', to choose the condition on which he shall find acceptance, 'but of God that showeth mercy,' that accepteth none at all but of his own free love, his unmerited goodness. 'Therefore hath he mercy on whom he will have mercy,' *viz.*, on those who believe on the Son of his love; 'and whom he will', that is, those who believe not, 'he hardeneth'—leaves at last to the hardness of their hearts.

8. One reason, however, we may humbly conceive, of God's fixing this condition of justification—'If thou believest in the Lord Jesus Christ thou shalt be saved'—was to 'hide pride from man'. Pride had already destroyed the very angels of God, had cast down a 'third part of the stars of heaven'. It was likewise in great measure owing to this, when the tempter said, 'Ye shall be as gods,' that Adam fell from his own steadfastness and brought sin and death into the world. It was therefore an instance of wisdom worthy of God to appoint such a condition of reconciliation for him and all his posterity as might effectually humble, might abase them to the dust. And such is faith. It is peculiarly fitted for this end. For he that cometh unto God by this faith must fix his eye singly on his own wickedness, on his guilt and helplessness, without having the least regard to any supposed good in himself, to any virtue or righteousness whatsoever. He must come as a *mere sinner* inwardly and outwardly, self-destroyed and self-condemned, bringing nothing to God but ungodliness only, pleading nothing of his own but sin and misery. Thus it is, and thus alone, when his 'mouth is stopped', and he stands utterly 'guilty before God', that he can 'look unto Jesus' as the whole and sole 'propitiation for his sins'. Thus only can he be 'found in him' and receive the 'righteousness which is of God by faith'.

9. Thou ungodly one who hearest or readest these words, thou vile, helpless, miserable sinner, I charge thee before God, the judge of all, go straight unto him with all thy ungodliness. Take heed thou destroy not thy own soul by pleading thy righteousness, more or less. Go as altogether ungodly, guilty, lost, destroyed, deserving and dropping into hell, and thou shalt then find favour in his sight, and know that he justifieth the ungodly. As such thou shalt be brought unto the 'blood of sprinkling' as an undone, helpless, damned sinner. Thus 'look unto Jesus'! There is 'the Lamb of God, who taketh away *thy* sins'! Plead thou no works, no righteousness of thine own; no humility, contrition, sincerity! In no wise. That were, in very deed, to deny the Lord that bought thee. No. Plead thou singly the blood of the covenant, the ransom paid for thy proud, stubborn, sinful soul. Who art thou that now seest and feelest both thine inward and outward ungodliness? Thou art the man! I want thee for my Lord. I challenge *thee* for a child of God by faith. The Lord hath need of thee. Thou who feelest thou art just fit for hell art just fit to advance his glory: the glory of his free grace, justifying the ungodly and him that worketh not. O come quickly. Believe in the Lord Jesus; and *thou*, even *thou*, art reconciled to God.

15. THE LORD OUR RIGHTEOUSNESS

1765

An Introductory Comment

Another landmark sermon, "The Lord Our Righteousness," represents "the end of Wesley's efforts to avoid an open rift with the Calvinists" (O, 1:446). This larger theological dispute went back to the controversy with George Whitefield over the publication of "Free Grace" in 1739. It was renewed in 1758 when Wesley published *A Preservative against Unsettled Notions in Religion* in the face of a likely forthcoming publication from James Hervey, a former Oxford Methodist. As an earlier student of John Wesley (he unofficially taught him Hebrew; see ODNB), Hervey asked him to express his judgment in terms of the three-volume work *Theron and Aspasio* in which Theron represented the views of Arminians and Aspasio those of Hervey himself. Eventually Wesley was frank in his criticisms, which in turn roiled Hervey, who then composed a reply in the form of a series of long letters. Gravely ill, Hervey left instructions that these letters should not be published. Nevertheless, a surreptitious edition of the work emerged shortly after Hervey's death that contained numerous errors, and so Hervey's brother published a corrected, official edition of *Eleven Letters from the late Rev. Mr. Hervey to the Rev. Mr. John Wesley* in 1765. The present sermon was Wesley's quick, though largely irenic, reply.

Wesley pointed out, among other things, that the phrase "the imputed righteousness of Christ" is not actually found in the Bible (S, 2:421). Instead the language "[faith is] imputed to him for righteousness" (Rom. 4:22) is employed, which suggests that imputation, properly understood, means "neither more nor less than that we are justified by faith, not by works; or that every believer is forgiven and accepted merely for the sake of what Christ has done and suffered" (O, 1:458). Wesley preached this sermon on November 24, 1765, at the West Street Chapel in London and urged his assistants to retain a copy (S, 2:423).

The Lord Our Righteousness

1. How dreadful are the contests among the children of God
2. Every lover of God and neighbor should want to remedy this evil
3. A step toward this end is rightly to understand each other
4. Another step is this: he should be called, 'The Lord our righteousness'
5. Might not one expect all those who name the name of Christ to agree?
6. The children of God need a clear understanding on this point

I. Divine righteousness is twofold, either his divine or human righteousness
  1. Divine righteousness is Christ's eternal holiness; this is not imputed to us
  2. Christ's human righteousness includes the image of God
  3. It also includes the fact that he did not sin
  4. His obedience implied not only doing but suffering the will of God

II. But when and how is the Lord's righteousness *imputed* to us?
  1. The righteousness of Christ is imputed to believers, not to unbelievers
  2. Believers do not all speak alike, but they are of the same sentiment
  3. People may differ from us in their expressions but be of the same faith
  4. It is faith and not the absence of wrong opinions that brings righteousness
  5. Righteousness is imputed to believers on the basis of Christ's merits
  6.–9. Examples of this doctrine were published across three decades
  10. We are justified by faith, not works; faith in what Christ has done and suffered
  11. Believers are clothed with righteousness when they repent and trust in Christ
  12. *Inherent* righteousness is the *fruit* of our acceptance with God
  13. The righteousness of Christ is the sole *foundation* of our hope
    A. By faith, the Holy Spirit enables us to build on this foundation
    B. In the moment that God gives this faith, we are accepted
  14. The righteousness of Christ is imputed to every believer
  15. Rome denies Christ's righteousness as the sole basis for justification
    A. But there are many in that church who feel what they cannot express
  16. With these we may rank those called *mystics*
  17. Let people repent as criminals at Christ's feet, relying solely on his merits
  18. Can we not all agree on this?
  19. The righteousness of Christ should not be used as a cover for unrighteousness
  20. Christ's righteousness is imputed to us so that we may live godly lives

Sermon 20: The Lord Our Righteousness, 1765

Jeremiah 23:6

This is his name whereby he shall be called, The Lord our righteousness.

1. How dreadful and how innumerable are the contests which have arisen about religion! And not only among the children of this world, among those who knew not what true religion was; but even among the children of God, those who had experienced 'the kingdom of God within them', who had tasted of 'righteousness, and peace, and joy in the Holy Ghost'. How many of these in all ages, instead of joining together against the common enemy, have turned their weapons against each other, and so not only wasted their precious time but hurt one another's spirits, weakened each other's hands, and so hindered the great work of their common Master! How many of the weak have hereby been offended! How many of the 'lame turned out of the way'! How many sinners confirmed in their disregard of all religion, and their contempt of those that profess it! And how many of 'the excellent ones upon earth' have been constrained to 'weep in secret places'!

2. What would not every lover of God and his neighbour do, what would he not suffer, to remedy this sore evil? To remove contention from the children of God? To restore or preserve peace among them? What but a good conscience would he think too dear to part with in order to promote this valuable end? And suppose we cannot 'make these wars to cease in all the world', suppose we cannot reconcile all the children of God to each other; however, let each do what he can, let him contribute if it be but two mites toward it. Happy are they who are able in any degree to promote 'peace and goodwill among men'! Especially among good men; among those that are all listed under the banner of 'the Prince of Peace'; and are therefore peculiarly engaged, 'as much as lies in them, to live peaceably with all men'.

3. It would be a considerable step toward this glorious end if we could bring good men to understand one another. Abundance of disputes arise purely from the want of this, from mere misapprehension. Frequently neither of the contending parties understands what his opponent means; whence it follows that each violently attacks the other while there is no real difference between them. And yet it is not always an easy matter to convince them of this. Particularly when their passions are moved: it is then attended with the utmost difficulty. However, it is not impossible; especially when we attempt it, not trusting in ourselves, but having all our dependence upon him with whom all things are possible. How soon is he able to disperse the cloud, to shine upon their hearts, and to enable them both to understand each other and 'the truth as it is in Jesus'!

4. One very considerable article of this truth is contained in the words above recited, 'This is his name whereby he shall be called, The Lord our righteousness:' a truth this which enters deep into the nature of Christianity, and in a manner supports the whole frame of it. Of this undoubtedly may be affirmed what Luther affirms of a truth closely connected with it: it is *articulus stantis vel cadentis ecclesiae*—the Christian church stands or falls with it. It is certainly the pillar and ground of that faith of which alone cometh salvation—of that *catholic* or universal faith which is found in all the children of God, and which 'unless a man keep whole and undefiled, without doubt he shall perish everlastingly'.

5. Might not one therefore reasonably expect, that however they differed in others, all those who name the name of Christ should agree in this point? But how far is this from being the case! There is scarce any wherein they are so little agreed, wherein those who all profess to follow Christ seem so widely and irreconcilably to differ. I say 'seem', because I am throughly convinced that many of them only seem to differ. The disagreement is more in words than in sentiments: they are much nearer in judgment than in language. And a wide difference in language there certainly is, not only between Protestants and Papists, but between Protestant and Protestant; yea, even between those who all believe justification by faith, who agree as well in this as every other fundamental doctrine of the gospel.

6. But if the difference be more in *opinion* than real *experience*, and more in *expression* than in *opinion*, how can it be that even the children of God should so vehemently contend with each other on the point? Several reasons may be assigned for this: the chief is their not understanding one another, joined with too keen an attachment to their *opinions* and particular modes of *expression*.

In order to remove this, at least in some measure, in order to our understanding one another on this head, I shall by the help of God endeavour to show,

I. What is the righteousness of Christ;

II. When, and in what sense, it is imputed to us;

And conclude with a short and plain application.

And, I. What is the righteousness of Christ? It is twofold, either his divine or his human righteousness.

1. His divine righteousness belongs to his divine nature, as he is ὁ ὤν, 'He that existeth, over all, God, blessed for ever:' the supreme, the eternal, 'equal with the Father as touching his godhead, though inferior to the Father as touching his manhood'. Now this is his eternal, essential, immutable holiness; his infinite justice, mercy, and truth: in all which 'he and the Father are one.'

But I do not apprehend that the divine righteousness of Christ is immediately concerned in the present question. I believe few, if any, do now contend for the *imputation* of *this* righteousness to us. Whoever believes the doctrine of imputation understands it chiefly, if not solely, of his human righteousness.

2. The *human righteousness* of Christ belongs to him in his human nature, as he is 'the mediator between God and man, the man Christ Jesus'. This is either *internal* or *external*. His internal righteousness is the image of God stamped on every power and faculty of his soul. It is a copy of his divine righteousness, as far as it can be imparted to a human spirit. It is a transcript of the divine purity, the divine justice, mercy, and truth. It includes love, reverence, resignation to his Father; humility, meekness, gentleness; love to lost mankind, and every other holy and heavenly temper: and all these in the highest degree, without any defect, or mixture of unholiness.

3. It was the least part of his *external righteousness* that he did nothing amiss; that he knew no outward sin of any kind, 'neither was guile found in his mouth'; that he never spoke one improper word, nor did one improper action. Thus far it is only a *negative* righteousness, though such an one as never did nor ever can belong to anyone that is born of a woman, save himself alone. But even his outward righteousness was *positive* too. 'He did all things well.' In every word of his tongue, in every work of his hands, he did precisely the 'will of him that sent him'. In the whole course of his life he did the will of God on earth as the angels do it in heaven. All he acted and spoke was exactly right in every circumstance. The whole and every part of his obedience was complete. 'He fulfilled all righteousness.'

4. But his obedience implied more than all this. It implied not only doing, but suffering: suffering the whole will of God from the time he came into the world till 'he bore our sins in his own body upon the tree;' yea, till having made a full atonement for them 'he bowed his head and gave up the ghost.' This is usually termed the *passive* righteousness of Christ, the former, his *active* righteousness. But as the active and passive righteousness of Christ were never in fact separated from each other, so we never need separate them at all, either in speaking or even in thinking. And it is with regard to both these conjointly that Jesus is called, 'the Lord our righteousness'.

II. But when is it that any of us may truly say, 'the Lord our righteousness'? In other words, when is it that the righteousness of Christ is *imputed* to us, and in what sense is it imputed?

1. Look through all the world, and all the men therein are either believers or unbelievers. The first thing then which admits of no dispute among reasonable men is this: to all believers the righteousness of Christ is imputed; to unbelievers it is not.

'But when is it imputed?' When they believe. In that very hour the righteousness of Christ is theirs. It is imputed to every one that believes, as soon as he believes: faith and the righteousness of Christ are inseparable. For if he believes according to Scripture, he believes in the righteousness of Christ. There is no true faith, that is, justifying faith, which hath not the righteousness of Christ for its object.

2. It is true believers may not all speak alike; they may not all use the same language. It is not to be expected that they should; we cannot reasonably require it of them. A thousand circumstances may cause them to vary from each other in the manner of expressing themselves. But a difference of expression does not necessarily imply a difference of sentiment. Different persons may use different expressions, and yet mean the same thing. Nothing is more common than this, although we seldom make sufficient allowance for it. Nay, it is not easy for the same persons, when they speak of the same thing at a considerable distance of time, to use exactly the same expressions, even though they retain the same sentiments. How then can we be rigorous in requiring others to use just the same expressions with us?

3. We may go a step farther yet. Men may differ from us in their opinions as well as their expressions, and nevertheless be partakers with us of the same precious faith. 'Tis possible they may not have a *distinct apprehension* of the very blessing which they enjoy.

Their *ideas* may not be so *clear*, and yet their experience may be as sound as ours. There is a wide difference between the natural faculties of men, their understandings in particular. And that difference is exceedingly increased by the manner of their education. Indeed, this alone may occasion an inconceivable difference in their opinions of various kinds. And why not upon this head as well as on any other? But still, though their opinions as well as expressions may be confused and inaccurate, their hearts may cleave to God through the Son of his love, and be truly interested in his righteousness.

4. Let us then make all that allowance to others which, were we in their place, we would desire for ourselves. Who is ignorant (to touch again on that circumstance only) of the amazing power of education? And who that knows it can expect, suppose, a member of the Church of Rome either to think or speak clearly on this subject? And yet if we had heard even dying Bellarmine cry out, when he was asked, 'Unto which of the saints wilt thou turn?'—'*Fidere meritis Christi tutissimum*: It is safest to trust in the merits of Christ'—would we have affirmed that notwithstanding his wrong opinions he had no share in his righteousness?

5. 'But in what sense is this righteousness imputed to believers?' In this: all believers are forgiven and accepted, not for the sake of anything in them, or of anything that ever was, that is, or ever can be done by them, but wholly and solely for the sake of what Christ hath done and suffered for them. I say again, not for the sake of anything in them or done by them, of their own righteousness or works. 'Not for works of righteousness which we have done, but of his own mercy he saved us.' 'By grace ye are saved through faith. . . . Not of works, lest any man should boast;' but wholly and solely for the sake of what Christ hath done and suffered for us. We are 'justified freely by his grace, through the redemption that is in Jesus Christ'. And this is not only the means of our *obtaining* the favour of God, but of our continuing therein. It is thus we come to God at first: it is by the same we come unto him ever after. We walk in one and the same 'new and living way' till our spirit returns to God.

6. And this is the doctrine which I have constantly believed and taught for near eight and twenty years. This I published to all the world in the year 1738, and ten or twelve times since, in those words, and many others to the same effect, extracted from the *Homilies* of our Church:

> These things must necessarily go together in our justification: upon God's part his great mercy and grace, upon Christ's part the satisfaction of God's justice, and on our part faith in the merits of Christ. So that the grace of God doth not shut out the righteousness of God in our justification, but only shutteth out the righteousness of man, as to *deserving* our justification.
>
> That we are justified by faith alone is spoken to take away clearly all merit of our works, and wholly to ascribe the *merit* and *deserving* of our justification to Christ only. Our justification comes freely of the mere mercy of God. For whereas all the world was not able to pay any part toward our ransom, it pleased him, without any of our deserving, to prepare for us Christ's body and blood, whereby our ransom might be paid, and his justice satisfied. Christ therefore is now the righteousness of all them that truly believe in him.

7. The hymns published a year or two after this, and since republished several times (a clear testimony that my judgment was still the same) speak full to the same purpose. To

cite all the passages to this effect would be to transcribe a great part of the volumes. Take one for all, which was reprinted seven years ago, five years ago, two years ago, and some months since:

> Jesu, thy blood and righteousness
> My beauty are, my glorious dress:
> Midst flaming worlds in these arrayed
> With joy shall I lift up my head.

The whole expresses the same sentiment from the beginning to the end.

8. In the sermon on justification published nineteen, and again seven or eight years ago, I express the same thing in these words:

> In consideration of this, that the Son of God hath 'tasted death for every man', God hath now 'reconciled the world unto himself, not imputing to them their former trespasses'. [. . .] So that for the sake of his well-beloved Son, of what he hath done and suffered for us, God now vouchsafes on one only condition (which himself also enables us to perform) both to remit the punishment due to our sins, to reinstate us in his favour, and to restore our dead souls to spiritual life, as the earnest of life eternal. ([*Sermons on Several Occasions* (1746), I], p. 87)

9. This is more largely and particularly expressed in the *Treatise on Justification* which I published last year:

> If we take the phrase of 'imputing Christ's righteousness' for the bestowing (as it were) the righteousness of Christ, including his obedience, as well passive as active, in the return of it—that is, in the privileges, blessings, and benefits purchased by it—so a believer may be said to be justified by the *righteousness of Christ imputed.* The meaning is, God justifies the believer for the sake of Christ's righteousness, and not for any righteousness of his own. [. . .] So Calvin: 'Christ by his obedience procured and merited for us grace or favour with God the Father' (*Institutes* [Vol. I], II.xvii. [3; cf. LCC, Vol. XX.530–31]). Again, 'Christ by his obedience procured or purchased righteousness for us.' And yet again: 'All such expressions as these—that we are justified by the grace of God, that Christ is our righteousness, that righteousness was procured for us by the death and resurrection of Christ—import the same thing:' namely, that the righteousness of Christ, both his active and passive righteousness, is the meritorious cause of our justification, and has procured for us at God's hand that upon our believing we should be accounted righteous by him. (p. 5)

10. But perhaps some will object, 'Nay, but you affirm that "faith is imputed to us for righteousness."' St. Paul affirms this over and over; therefore I affirm it too. Faith is imputed for righteousness to every believer; namely, faith in the righteousness of Christ. But this is exactly the same thing which has been said before. For by that expression I mean neither more nor less than that we are justified by faith, not by works; or that every believer is forgiven and accepted merely for the sake of what Christ has done and suffered.

11. 'But is not a believer invested or clothed with the righteousness of Christ?' Un-

doubtedly he is. And accordingly the words above-recited are the language of every believing heart:

> Jesu, thy blood and righteousness
> My beauty are, my glorious dress.

That is, for the sake of thy active and passive righteousness I am forgiven and accepted of God.

'But must not we put off the filthy rags of our own righteousness before we can put on the spotless righteousness of Christ?' Certainly we must; that is, in plain terms, we must 'repent' before we can 'believe the gospel'. We must be cut off from dependence upon ourselves before we can truly depend upon Christ. We must cast away all confidence in our own righteousness, or we cannot have a true confidence in his. Till we are delivered from trusting in anything that we do, we cannot throughly trust in what he has done and suffered. First 'we receive the sentence of death in ourselves;' then we trust in him that lived and died for us.

12. 'But do not you believe *inherent* righteousness?' Yes, in its proper place; not as the *ground* of our acceptance with God, but as the *fruit* of it; not in the place of *imputed* righteousness, but as consequent upon it. That is, I believe God *implants* righteousness in every one to whom he has *imputed* it. I believe 'Jesus Christ is made of God unto us sanctification' as well as righteousness; or that God sanctifies, as well as justifies, all them that believe in him. They to whom the righteousness of Christ is imputed are made righteous by the spirit of Christ, are renewed in the image of God 'after the likeness wherein they were created, in righteousness and true holiness'.

13. 'But do not you put faith in the room of Christ, or of his righteousness?' By no means. I take particular care to put each of these in its proper place. The righteousness of Christ is the whole and sole *foundation* of all our hope. It is by faith that the Holy Ghost enables us to build upon this foundation. God gives this faith. In that moment we are accepted of God; and yet not for the sake of that faith, but of what Christ has done and suffered for us. You see, each of these has its proper place, and neither clashes with the other: we believe, we love; we endeavour to walk in all the commandments of the Lord blameless. Yet,

> While thus we bestow
> Our moments below,
> Ourselves we forsake,
> And refuge in Jesus's righteousness take.
> His passion alone,
> The foundation we own:
> And pardon we claim,
> And eternal redemption in Jesus's name.

14. I therefore no more deny the righteousness of Christ than I deny the godhead of Christ. And a man may full as justly charge me with denying the one as the other.

Neither do I deny *imputed righteousness*: this is another unkind and unjust accusation. I always did, and do still continually affirm, that the righteousness of Christ is imputed to every believer. But who do deny it? Why, all *infidels*, whether baptized or unbaptized; all who affirm the glorious gospel of our Lord Jesus Christ to be a *cunningly* devised fable; all Socinians and Arians; all who deny the supreme godhead of the Lord that bought them. They of consequence deny his divine righteousness, as they suppose him to be a mere creature. And they deny his human righteousness as imputed to any man, seeing they believe everyone is accepted *for his own righteousness*.

15. The human righteousness of Christ, at least the imputation of it as the whole and sole meritorious cause of the justification of a sinner before God, is likewise denied by the members of the Church of Rome—by all of them who are true to the principles of their own church. But undoubtedly there are many among them whose experience goes beyond their principles; who, though they are far from expressing themselves justly, yet feel what they know not how to express. Yea, although their conceptions of this great truth be as crude as their expressions, yet 'with their heart they believe'; they rest on Christ alone, both 'unto' present and eternal 'salvation'.

16. With these we may rank those even in the Reformed Churches who are usually termed *mystics*. One of the chief of these in the present century (at least in England) was Mr. Law. It is well known that he absolutely and zealously denied the imputation of the righteousness of Christ; as zealously as Robert Barclay, who scruples not to say, 'Imputed righteousness, imputed nonsense!' The body of the people known by the name of Quakers espouse the same sentiment. Nay, the generality of those who profess themselves members of the Church of England are either totally ignorant of the matter and know nothing about *imputed righteousness*, or deny this and justification by faith together as destructive of good works. To these we may add a considerable number of the people vulgarly styled Anabaptists, together with thousands of Presbyterians and Independents lately enlightened by the writings of Dr. Taylor. On the last I am not called to pass any sentence: I leave them to him that made them. But will anyone dare to affirm that all mystics (such as was Mr. Law in particular), all Quakers, all Presbyterians or Independents, and all members of the Church of England, who are not clear in their opinions or expressions, are void of all Christian experience? That consequently they are all in a state of damnation, 'without hope, without God in the world'? However confused their ideas may be, however improper their language, may there not be many of them whose heart is right toward God and who effectually know 'the Lord our righteousness'?

17. But, blessed be God, we are not among those who are so dark in their conceptions and expressions. We no more deny the *phrase* than the *thing*; but we are unwilling to obtrude it on other men. Let them use either this or such other expressions as they judge to be more exactly scriptural, provided their *heart* rests only on what Christ hath done and suffered for pardon, grace, and glory. I cannot express this better than in Mr. Hervey's words, worthy to be wrote in letters of gold: 'We are not solicitous as to any *particular set of phrases*. Only let men be humbled as repenting criminals at Christ's feet, let them rely as devoted pensioners on his merits, and they are undoubtedly in the way to a blessed immortality.'

18. Is there any need, is there any possibility of saying more? Let us only abide by this declaration, and all the contention about this or that 'particular phrase' is torn up by the roots. Keep to this: 'All who are humbled as repenting criminals at Christ's feet and rely as devoted pensioners on his merits are in the way to a blessed immortality.' And what room for dispute? Who denies this? Do we not all meet on this ground? What then shall we wrangle about? A man of peace here proposes terms of accommodation to all the contending parties. We desire no better. We accept of the terms. We subscribe to them with heart and hand. Whoever refuses so to do, set a mark upon that man! He is an enemy of peace, and a troubler of Israel, a disturber of the church of God.

19. In the meantime what we are afraid of is this: lest any should use the phrase, 'the righteousness of Christ', or, 'the righteousness of Christ is "imputed to me",' as a cover for his unrighteousness. We have known this done a thousand times. A man has been reproved, suppose, for drunkenness. 'Oh, said he, I pretend to no righteousness of *my own*: Christ is *my righteousness*.' Another has been told that 'the extortioner, the unjust, shall not inherit the kingdom of God.' He replies with all assurance, 'I am unjust in myself, but I have a spotless righteousness in Christ.' And thus though a man be as far from the practice as from the tempers of a Christian, though he neither has the mind which was in Christ nor in any respect walks as he walked, yet he has armour of proof against all conviction in what he calls the 'righteousness of Christ'.

20. It is the seeing so many deplorable instances of this kind which makes us sparing in the use of these expressions. And I cannot but call upon all of you who use them frequently, and beseech you in the name of God our Saviour, whose you are and whom you serve, earnestly to guard all that hear you against this accursed abuse of it. O warn them (it may be they will hear *your* voice) against 'continuing in sin that grace may abound'! Warn them against making 'Christ the minister of sin'! Against making void that solemn decree of God, 'without holiness no man shall see the Lord,' by a vain imagination of being *holy in Christ*. O warn them that if they remain unrighteous, the righteousness of Christ will profit them nothing! Cry aloud (is there not a cause?) that for this very end the righteousness of Christ is imputed to us, that 'the righteousness of the law may be fulfilled in us,' and that we may 'live soberly, religiously, and godly in this present world.'

It remains only to make a short and plain application. And first I would address myself to you who violently oppose these expressions, and are ready to condemn all that use them as antinomians. But is not this bending the bow too much the other way? Why should you condemn all who do not speak just as you do? Why should you quarrel with *them* for using the phrases they like, any more than they with *you* for taking the same liberty? Or if they do quarrel with you upon that account, do not imitate the bigotry which you blame. At least allow *them* the liberty which they ought to allow *you*. And why should you be angry at an *expression*? 'Oh, it has been abused.' And what expression has not? However, the abuse may be removed, and at the same time the use remain. Above all be sure to retain the important sense which is couched under that expression. All the blessings I enjoy, all I hope for in time and in eternity, are given wholly and solely for the sake of what Christ has done and suffered for me.

I would, secondly, add a few words to you who are fond of these expressions. And permit me to ask, Do not I allow enough? What can any reasonable man desire more? I allow the whole *sense* which you contend for: that we have every blessing 'through the righteousness of God our Saviour'. I allow *you* to use whatever expressions you choose, and that a thousand times over; only guarding them against that dreadful abuse which you are as deeply concerned to prevent as I am. I myself frequently use the expression in question, 'imputed righteousness'; and often put this and the like expressions into the mouth of a whole congregation. But allow me liberty of conscience herein: allow me the right of private judgment. Allow me to use it just as often as I judge it preferable to any other expression. And be not angry with me if I cannot judge it proper to use any one expression every two minutes. *You* may if you please; but do not condemn me because I do not. Do not for this represent me as a Papist, or 'an enemy to the righteousness of Christ'. Bear with *me*, as I do with *you*; else how shall we 'fulfil the law of Christ'? Do not make tragical outcries, as though I was 'subverting the very foundations of Christianity'. Whoever does this does me much wrong: the Lord lay it not to his charge! I lay, and have done for many years, the very same foundation with you. And indeed 'other foundation can no man lay than that which is laid, even Jesus Christ.' I build inward and outward holiness thereon, as you do, even by faith. Do not therefore suffer any distaste, or unkindness, no, nor any shyness or coldness in your heart. If there were *a difference of opinion*, where is our religion if we cannot *think and let think*? What hinders but you may forgive *me* as easily as I may forgive *you*? How much more when there is only *a difference of expression*? Nay, hardly so much as that—all the dispute being only whether a particular mode of expression shall be used *more or less frequently*! Surely we must earnestly desire to contend with one another before we can make this a bone of contention! O let us not any more for such very trifles as these give our common enemies room to blaspheme! Rather let us at length cut off occasion from them that seek occasion! Let us at length (O why was it not done before?) join hearts and hands in the service of our great Master. As we have 'one Lord, one faith, one hope of our calling', let us all strengthen each other's hands in God, and with one heart and one mouth declare to all mankind, 'the Lord our righteousness'.

16. THE NEW BIRTH

1760

An Introductory Comment

Wesley had preached on John 3:7 more than sixty times before this sermon was printed in 1760 (WWS). He deemed the new birth to be an essential doctrine of the Christian faith (FB, 26:148) since it was strongly associated with that of original sin: "Know your disease! Know your cure! Ye were born in sin: Therefore, "ye must be born again" (O, 2:185). Outler considered this sermon to reflect some of the basic tensions created by the Revival in the form of "the claims of nominal Christians to baptismal regeneration and the claims of the evangelicals to 'conversion'" (O, 2:186).

As a "miraculous or supernatural work" (T, 4:332), not to be confused with human working, the new birth was distinguished by Wesley from (a) baptism ("that the one is an external, the other an internal work"; O, 2:197), (b) the "form, notions and externals" of religion (T, 7:217), and (c) the means of grace themselves ("Go to church twice a day, go to the Lord's table every week . . . still you must be born again"; O, 2:00–201). As such, the new birth for Wesley not only marked the beginning of spiritual life, properly speaking ("must in the nature of the thing have a first moment"; T, 4:332), but was also conjoined with the doctrine of justification (in the Christian sense), never one without the other: "In the moment we are justified . . . we are also 'born of the Spirit'" (O, 2:187), the one work God does *for us;* the other God does *in us.*

Since Wesley affirmed that the new birth is "the gate," "the entrance" (O, 2:198) to holiness, it thereby begins the process of sanctification. Moreover, since he closely associated happiness and holiness in his overall theology, Wesley maintained that regeneration is therefore *necessary* to embark upon the path that leads to real and lasting happiness.

The New Birth

1. If any doctrines within Christianity may be termed fundamental they are:
    - A. The doctrine of justification
    - B. The doctrine of the new birth
2. It is of great importance that we understand these two doctrines
    - A. We must give an account of the new birth, answering three questions
    - B. First, why must we be born again?
    - C. Secondly, how we must be born again?
    - D. Thirdly, what is the nature of the new birth?

I. 1. The foundation of this doctrine is this: people were made in the image of God
2. But people did not abide in honor
    - A. They ate of the tree of which God commanded them not to eat
    - B. God told them, 'In the day that thou eatest . . . thou shalt surely die'
3. This death must be understood as the loss of the life and image of God
4. In Adam all died, all humankind, all the children of men
    - A. Hence, being born in sin we must be born again of the Spirit

II. 1. How must we be born again? What is the nature of the new birth?
2. We cannot give a philosophical account of how this is done
3. However, we can give a plain scriptural account of the nature of the new birth
4. While people are in a mere natural state, they have no knowledge of God
    - A. As soon as they are born of God there is a total change
    - B. They are now capable of hearing the inward voice of God
5. From that point, the nature of the new birth is manifest
    - A. It is the change that happens when God brings the soul to life

III. 1. Why must we be born again?
    - A. It is necessary for holiness
2. Without holiness no man shall see the Lord
3. Also, unless a person be born again, she cannot be happy in this world
    - A. For it is not possible for a person who is not holy to be happy

IV. A few inferences which follow from these observations
1. It follows that baptism is not the new birth
2. It follows that the new birth does not always accompany baptism
3. It follows that the new birth is not the same as sanctification
4. Finally, attending the ordinances of God is not the same thing as the new birth

Sermon 45: The New Birth, 1760

John 3:7

Ye must be born again.

1. If any doctrines within the whole compass of Christianity may be properly termed fundamental they are doubtless these two—the doctrine of justification, and that of the new birth: the former relating to that great work which God does *for us*, in forgiving our sins; the latter to the great work which God does *in us*, in renewing our fallen nature. In order of time neither of these is before the other. In the moment we are justified by the grace of God through the redemption that is in Jesus we are also 'born of the Spirit'; but in order of thinking, as it is termed, justification precedes the new birth. We first conceive his wrath to be turned away, and then his Spirit to work in our hearts.

2. How great importance, then, must it be of to every child of man throughly to understand these fundamental doctrines! From a full conviction of this, many excellent men have wrote very largely concerning justification, explaining every point relating thereto, and opening the Scriptures which treat upon it. Many likewise have wrote on the new birth—and some of them largely enough—but yet not so clearly as might have been desired, nor so deeply and accurately; having either given a dark, abstruse account of it, or a slight and superficial one. Therefore a full and at the same time a clear account of the new birth seems to be wanting still. Such as may enable us to give a satisfactory answer to these three questions: First, why must we be born again? What is the foundation of this doctrine of the new birth? Secondly, how must we be born again? What is the nature of the new birth? And thirdly, wherefore must we be born again? To what end is it necessary? These questions, by the assistance of God, I shall briefly and plainly answer, and then subjoin a few inferences which will naturally follow.

I.1. And, first, why must we be born again? What is the foundation of this doctrine? The foundation of it lies near as deep as the creation of the world, in the scriptural account whereof we read, 'And God', the three-one God, 'said, Let us make man in our image, after our likeness. So God created man in his own image, in the image of God created he him' (Gen. 1:26-27). Not barely in his *natural image*, a picture of his own immortality, a spiritual being endued with understanding, freedom of will, and various affections; nor merely in his *political image*, the governor of this lower world, having 'dominion over the fishes of the sea, and over the fowl of the air, and over the cattle, and over all the earth'; but chiefly in his *moral image*, which, according to the Apostle, is 'righteousness and true holiness' (Eph. 4:24). In this image of God was man made. 'God is love:' accordingly man at his creation was full of love, which was the sole principle of all his tempers, thoughts, words, and actions. God is full of justice, mercy, and truth: so was man as he came from the hands of his Creator. God is spotless purity: and so man was in the beginning pure from every sinful blot. Otherwise God could not have pronounced *him* as well as all the other works of his hands, 'very good' (Gen. 1:31). This he could not have been had he not been pure from sin, and filled with righteousness and true holiness. For there is no medium. If we suppose an intelligent creature not to love God, not to be righteous and holy, we necessarily suppose him not to be good at all; much less to be 'very good'.

2. But although man was made in the image of God, yet he was not made immutable. This would have been inconsistent with that state of trial in which God was pleased to place him. He was therefore created able to stand, and yet liable to fall. And this God himself apprised him of, and gave him a solemn warning against it. Nevertheless 'man did not abide in honour.' He fell from his high estate. He 'ate of the tree whereof the Lord had commanded him, Thou shalt not eat thereof.' By this wilful act of disobedience to his Creator, this flat rebellion against his sovereign, he openly declared that he would no longer have God to rule over him; that he would be governed by his own will, and not the will of him that created him, and that he would not seek his happiness in God, but in the world, in the works of his hands. Now God had told him before, 'In the day that thou eatest' of that fruit 'thou shalt surely die.' And the word of the Lord cannot be broken. Accordingly in that day he did die: he died to God, the most dreadful of all deaths. He lost the life of God: he was separated from him in union with whom his spiritual life consisted. The body dies when it is separated from the soul, the soul when it is separated from God. But this separation from God Adam sustained in the day, the hour, he ate of the forbidden fruit. And of this he gave immediate proof; presently showing by his behaviour that the love of God was extinguished in his soul, which was now 'alienated from the life of God'. Instead of this he was now under the power of servile fear, so that he fled from the presence of the Lord. Yea, so little did he retain even of the knowledge of him who filleth heaven and earth that he endeavoured to 'hide himself from the Lord God, among the trees of the garden' (Gen. 3:8). So had he lost both the knowledge and the love of God, without which the image of God would not subsist. Of this therefore he was deprived at the same time, and became unholy as well as unhappy. In the room of this he had sunk into pride and self-will, the very image of the devil, and into sensual appetites and desires, the image of the beasts that perish.

3. If it be said, 'Nay, but that threatening, "In the day that thou eatest thereof thou shalt surely die," refers to temporal death, and that alone, to the death of the body only;' the answer is plain: to affirm this is flatly and palpably to make God a liar—to aver that the God of truth positively affirmed a thing contrary to truth. For it is evident Adam did not *die* in this sense 'in the day that he ate thereof'. He lived, in the sense opposite to this death, above nine hundred years after; so that this cannot possibly be understood of the death of the body without impeaching the veracity of God. It must therefore be understood of spiritual death, the loss of the life and image of God.

4. And 'in Adam all died,' all humankind, all the children of men who were then in Adam's loins. The natural consequence of this is that everyone descended from him comes into the world spiritually dead, dead to God, wholly 'dead in sin'; entirely void of the life of God, void of the image of God, of all that 'righteousness and holiness' wherein Adam was created. Instead of this every man born into the world now bears the image of the devil, in pride and self-will; the image of the beast, in sensual appetites and desires. This then is the foundation of the new birth—the entire corruption of our nature. Hence it is that being 'born in sin' we 'must be born again'. Hence everyone that is born of a woman must be born of the Spirit of God.

II.1. But how must a man be born again? What is the nature of the new birth? This is the second question. And a question it is of the highest moment that can be conceived. We ought not, therefore, in so weighty a concern, to be content with a slight inquiry, but to examine it with all possible care, and to ponder it in our hearts, till we fully understand this important point, and clearly see how we are to be born again.

2. Not that we are to expect any minute, philosophical account of the *manner how* this is done. Our Lord sufficiently guards us against any such expectation by the words immediately following the text: wherein he reminds Nicodemus of as indisputable a fact as any in the whole compass of nature—which, notwithstanding, the wisest man under the sun is not able fully to explain. 'The wind bloweth where it listeth', not by thy power or wisdom, 'and thou hearest the sound thereof.' Thou art absolutely assured, beyond all doubt, that it doth blow. 'But thou canst not tell whence it cometh, neither whither it goeth.' The precise manner how it begins and ends, rises and falls, no man can tell. 'So is everyone that is born of the Spirit.' Thou mayst be as absolutely assured of the fact as of the blowing of the wind; but the precise manner how it is done, how the Holy Spirit works this in the soul, neither thou nor the wisest of the children of men is able to explain.

3. However, it suffices for every rational and Christian purpose that without descending into curious, critical inquiries, we can give a plain scriptural account of the nature of the new birth. This will satisfy every reasonable man who desires only the salvation of his soul. The expression, 'being born again', was not first used by our Lord in his conversation with Nicodemus. It was well known before that time, and was in common use among the Jews when our Saviour appeared among them. When an adult heathen was convinced that the Jewish religion was of God, and desired to join therein, it was the custom to baptize him first, before he was admitted to circumcision. And when he was baptized he was said to be 'born again': by which they meant that he who was before a child of the devil was now adopted into the family of God, and accounted one of his children. This expression therefore which Nicodemus, being 'a teacher in Israel', ought to have understood well, our Lord uses in conversing with him; only in a stronger sense than he was accustomed to. And this might be the reason of his asking, 'How can these things be?' They cannot be literally. 'A man' cannot 'enter a second time into his mother's womb and be born'. But they may, spiritually. A man may be 'born from above', 'born of God', 'born of the Spirit'—in a manner which bears a very near analogy to the natural birth.

4. Before a child is born into the world he has eyes, but sees not; he has ears, but does not hear. He has a very imperfect use of any other sense. He has no knowledge of any of the things of the world, nor any natural understanding. To that manner of existence which he then has we do not even give the name of life. It is then only when a man is born that we say, he begins to live. For as soon as he is born he begins to see the light and the various objects with which he is encompassed. His ears are then opened, and he hears the sounds which successively strike upon them. At the same time all the other organs of sense begin to be exercised upon their proper objects. He likewise breathes and lives in a manner wholly different from what he did before. How exactly does the parallel hold in all these instances! While a man is in a mere natural state, before he is born of God, he has, in a spiritual sense, eyes and sees not; a thick impenetrable veil lies upon them. He

has ears, but hears not; he is utterly deaf to what he is most of all concerned to hear. His other spiritual senses are all locked up; he is in the same condition as if he had them not. Hence he has no knowledge of God, no intercourse with him; he is not at all acquainted with him. He has no true knowledge of the things of God, either of spiritual or eternal things. Therefore, though he is a living man, he is a dead Christian. But as soon as he is born of God there is a total change in all these particulars. The 'eyes of his understanding are opened' (such is the language of the great Apostle). And he who of old 'commanded light to shine out of darkness shining on his heart', he sees 'the light of the glory of God', his glorious love, 'in the face of Jesus Christ'. His ears being opened, he is now capable of hearing the inward voice of God, saying, 'Be of good cheer, thy sins are forgiven thee:' 'Go and sin no more.' This is the purport of what God speaks to his heart; although perhaps not in these very words. He is now ready to hear whatsoever 'he that teacheth man knowledge' is pleased from time to time to reveal to him. He 'feels in his heart' (to use the language of our Church) 'the mighty working of the Spirit of God'. Not in a gross, carnal sense, as the men of the world stupidly and wilfully misunderstand the expression, though they have been told again and again, we mean thereby neither more nor less than this: he feels, is inwardly sensible of, the graces which the Spirit of God works in his heart. He feels, he is conscious of, a 'peace which passeth all understanding'. He many times feels such a joy in God as is 'unspeakable and full of glory'. He feels 'the love of God shed abroad in his heart by the Holy Ghost which is given unto him'. And all his spiritual senses are then 'exercised to discern' spiritual 'good and evil'. By the use of these he is daily increasing in the knowledge of God, of Jesus Christ whom he hath sent, and of all the things pertaining to his inward kingdom. And now he may properly be said *to live*: God having quickened him by his Spirit, he is alive to God through Jesus Christ. He lives a life which the world knoweth not of, a 'life' which 'is hid with Christ in God'. God is continually breathing, as it were, upon his soul, and his soul is breathing unto God. Grace is descending into his heart, and prayer and praise ascending to heaven. And by this intercourse between God and man, this fellowship with the Father and the Son, as by a kind of spiritual respiration, the life of God in the soul is sustained: and the child of God grows up, till he comes to 'the full measure of the stature of Christ'.

5. From hence it manifestly appears what is the nature of the new birth. It is that great change which God works in the soul when he brings it into life: when he raises it from the death of sin to the life of righteousness. It is the change wrought in the whole soul by the almighty Spirit of God when it is 'created anew in Christ Jesus', when it is 'renewed after the image of God', 'in righteousness and true holiness', when the love of the world is changed into the love of God, pride into humility, passion into meekness; hatred, envy, malice, into a sincere, tender, disinterested love for all mankind. In a word, it is that change whereby the 'earthly, sensual, devilish' mind is turned into 'the mind which was in Christ'. This is the nature of the new birth. 'So is everyone that is born of the Spirit.'

III.1. It is not difficult for any who has considered these things to see the necessity of the new birth, and to answer the third question: Wherefore, to what ends, is it necessary that we should be born again? It is very easily discerned that this is necessary, first, in order to holiness. For what is holiness, according to the oracles of God? Not a bare external religion, a round of outward duties, how many soever they be, and how exactly soever performed. No; gospel holiness is no less than the image of God stamped upon the heart. It is no other than the whole mind which was in Christ Jesus. It consists of all heavenly affections and tempers mingled together in one. It implies such a continual, thankful love to him who hath not withheld from us his Son, his only Son, as makes it natural, and in a manner necessary to us, to love every child of man; as fills us with 'bowels of mercies, kindness, gentleness, long-suffering'. It is such a love of God as teaches us to be blameless in all manner of conversation; as enables us to present our souls and bodies, all we are and all we have, all our thoughts, words, and actions, a continual sacrifice to God, acceptable through Christ Jesus. Now this holiness can have no existence till we are renewed in the image of our mind. It cannot commence in the soul till that change be wrought, till by the power of the highest overshadowing us we are brought 'from darkness to light, from the power of Satan unto God'; that is, till we are born again; which therefore is absolutely necessary in order to holiness.

2. But 'without holiness no man shall see the Lord,' shall see the face of God in glory. Of consequence the new birth is absolutely necessary in order to eternal salvation. Men may indeed flatter themselves (so desperately wicked and so deceitful is the heart of man!) that they may live in their sins till they come to the last gasp, and yet afterward live with God. And thousands do really believe that they have found a 'broad way which leadeth' not 'to destruction'. What danger, say they, can a woman be in, that is so *harmless* and so *virtuous*? What fear is there that so *honest* a man, one of so strict *morality*, should miss of heaven? Especially if over and above all this they constantly attend on church and sacrament. One of these will ask with all assurance, 'What, shall not I do as well as my neighbours?' Yes, as well as your unholy neighbours; as well as your neighbours that die in their sins. For you will all drop into the pit together, into the nethermost hell. You will all lie together in the lake of fire, 'the lake of fire burning with brimstone'. Then at length you will see (but God grant you may see it before!) the necessity of holiness in order to glory—and consequently of the new birth, since none can be holy except he be born again.

3. For the same reason, except he be born again none can be happy even in this world. For it is not possible in the nature of things that a man should be happy who is not holy. Even the poor ungodly poet could tell us,

Nemo malus felix—

no wicked man is happy. The reason is plain: all unholy tempers are uneasy tempers. Not only malice, hatred, envy, jealousy, revenge, create a present hell in the breast, but even the softer passions, if not kept within due bounds, give a thousand times more pain than pleasure. Even 'hope', when 'deferred' (and how often must this be the case!) 'maketh the heart sick.' And every desire which is not according to the will of God is liable to 'pierce us through with many sorrows'. And all those general sources of sin, pride, self-will, and idolatry, are, in the same proportion as they prevail, general sources of misery. Therefore as long as these reign in any soul happiness has no place there. But they must reign till the bent of our nature is changed, that is, till we are born again. Consequently the new birth is absolutely necessary in order to happiness in this world, as well as in the world to come.

IV. I proposed in the last place to subjoin a few inferences which naturally follow from the preceding observations.

1. And, first, it follows that baptism is not the new birth: they are not one and the same thing. Many indeed seem to imagine they are just the same; at least, they speak as if they thought so. But I do not know that this opinion is publicly avowed by any denomination of Christians whatever. Certainly it is not by any within these kingdoms, whether of the Established Church, or dissenting from it. The judgment of the latter is clearly declared in their *Larger Catechism*: '*Q.* What are the parts of a sacrament? *A.* The parts of a sacrament are two: the one, an outward and sensible sign [. . .]; the other, an inward and spiritual grace thereby signified: [. . .] *Q.* What is baptism? *A.* Baptism is a sacrament [. . .] wherein Christ hath ordained the washing with water [. . .] to be a sign and seal of [. . .] regeneration by his Spirit' (*Qq.* 163, 165). Here it is manifest [that] baptism, the sign, is spoken of as distinct from regeneration, the thing signified.

In the Church Catechism likewise the judgment of our Church is declared with the utmost clearness. 'What meanest thou by this word, "sacrament"? I mean an outward and visible sign of an inward and spiritual grace. [. . .] What is the outward part or form in baptism? Water, wherein the person is baptized, "In the name of the Father, Son, and Holy Ghost". What is the inward part or thing signified? A death unto sin, and a new birth unto righteousness.' Nothing therefore is plainer than that, according to the Church of England, baptism is not the new birth.

But indeed the reason of the thing is so clear and evident as not to need any other authority. For what can be more plain than that the one is an external, the other an internal work? That the one is a visible, the other an invisible thing, and therefore wholly different from each other: the one being an act of man, purifying the body, the other a change wrought by God in the soul. So that the former is just as distinguishable from the latter as the soul from the body, or water from the Holy Ghost.

2. From the preceding reflections we may, secondly, observe that as the new birth is not the same thing with baptism, so it does not always accompany baptism; they do not constantly go together. A man may possibly be 'born of water', and yet not be 'born of the Spirit'. There may sometimes be the outward sign where there is not the inward grace. I do not now speak with regard to infants: it is certain, our Church supposes that all who are baptized in their infancy are at the same time born again. And it is allowed that the whole office for the baptism of infants proceeds upon this supposition. Nor is it an objection of any weight against this that we cannot comprehend how this work can be wrought in infants: for neither can we comprehend *how* it is wrought in a person of riper years. But whatever be the case with infants, it is sure all of riper years who are baptized are not at the same time born again. 'The tree is known by its fruits.' And hereby it appears too plain to be denied that divers of those who were children of the devil before they were baptized continue the same after baptism: 'For the works of' their

'father they do'; they continue servants of sin, without any pretence either to inward or outward holiness.

3. A third inference which we may draw from what has been observed is that the new birth is not the same with sanctification. This is indeed taken for granted by many; particularly by an eminent writer in his late treatise on 'the nature and grounds of Christian regeneration'. To waive several other weighty objections which might be made to that tract, this is a palpable one: it all along speaks of regeneration as a progressive work carried on in the soul by slow degrees from the time of our first turning to God. This is undeniably true of sanctification; but of regeneration, the new birth, it is not true. This is a part of sanctification, not the whole; it is the gate of it, the entrance into it. When we are born again, then our sanctification, our inward and outward holiness, begins. And thenceforward we are gradually to 'grow up in him who is our head'. This expression of the Apostle admirably illustrates the difference between one and the other, and farther points out the exact analogy there is between natural and spiritual things. A child is born of a woman in a moment, or at least in a very short time. Afterward he gradually and slowly grows till he attains the stature of a man. In like manner a child is born of God in a short time, if not in a moment. But it is by slow degrees that he afterward grows up to the measure of the full stature of Christ. The same relation therefore which there is between our natural birth and our growth there is also between our new birth and our sanctification.

4. One point more we may learn from the preceding observations. But it is a point of so great importance as may excuse the considering it the more carefully, and prosecuting it at some length. What must one who loves the souls of men, and is grieved that any of them should perish, say to one whom he sees living in sabbath-breaking, drunkenness, or any other wilful sin? What can he say, if the foregoing observations are true, but 'you must be born again.' 'No', says a zealous man, 'that cannot be. How can you talk so uncharitably to the man? Has he not been baptized already? He cannot be born again now.' Can he not be born again? Do you affirm this? Then he cannot be saved. Though he be as old as Nicodemus was, yet, 'except he be born again, he cannot see the kingdom of God.' Therefore in saying, 'he cannot be born again,' you in effect deliver him over to damnation. And where lies the uncharitableness now? On my side, or on yours? I say, 'He may be born again, and so become an heir of salvation.' You say, 'He cannot be born again.' And if so, he must inevitably perish. So you utterly block up his way to salvation, and send him to hell out of mere charity!

But perhaps the sinner himself, to whom in real charity we say, 'You must be born again,' has been taught to say, 'I defy your new doctrine; I need not be born again. I was born again when I was baptized. What! Would you have me deny my baptism?' I answer, first, there is nothing under heaven which can excuse a lie. Otherwise I should say to an open sinner, 'If you have been baptized, do not own it.' For how highly does this aggravate your guilt! How will it increase your damnation! Was you devoted to God at eight days old, and have you been all these years devoting yourself to the devil? Was you, even before you had the use of reason, consecrated to God the Father, the Son, and the Holy Ghost? And have you, ever since you had the use of it, been flying in the face of God, and consecrating yourself to Satan? Does the abomination of desolation, the love of the world, pride, anger, lust, foolish desire, and a whole train of vile affections, stand where it ought not? Have you set up all these accursed things in that soul which was once a 'temple of the Holy Ghost'? Set apart for 'an habitation of God through the Spirit'? Yea, solemnly given up to him? And do you glory in this, that you once belonged to God? O, be ashamed! Blush! Hide yourself in the earth! Never boast more of what ought to fill you with confusion, to make you ashamed before God and man! I answer, secondly, you have already denied your baptism; and that in the most effectual manner. You have denied it a thousand and a thousand times; and you do so still day by day. For in your baptism you renounced the devil and all his works. Whenever therefore you give place to him again, whenever you do any of the works of the devil, then you deny your baptism. Therefore you deny it by every wilful sin; by every act of uncleanness, drunkenness, or revenge; by every obscene or profane word; by every oath that comes out of your mouth. Every time you profane the day of the Lord you thereby deny your baptism; yea, every time you do anything to another which you would not he should do to you. I answer, thirdly, be you baptized or unbaptized, you must be born again. Otherwise it is not possible you should be inwardly holy: and without inward as well as outward holiness you cannot be happy even in this world; much less in the world to come. Do you say, 'Nay, but I do no harm to any man; I am honest and just in all my dealings; I do not curse, or take the Lord's name in vain; I do not profane the Lord's day; I am no drunkard, I do not slander my neighbour, nor live in any wilful sin'? If this be so, it were much to be wished that all men went as far as you do. But you must go farther yet, or you cannot be saved. Still you must be born again. Do you add, 'I do go farther yet; for I not only do no harm, but do all the good I can.' I doubt that fact; I fear you have had a thousand opportunities of doing good which you have suffered to pass by unimproved, and for which therefore you are accountable to God. But if you had improved them all, if you really had done all the good you possibly could to all men, yet this does not at all alter the case. Still you must be born again. Without this nothing will do any good to your poor, sinful, polluted soul. 'Nay, but I constantly attend all the ordinances of God: I keep to my church and sacrament.' It is well you do. But all this will not keep you from hell, except you be born again. Go to church twice a day, go to the Lord's table every week, say ever so many prayers in private; hear ever so many sermons, good sermons, excellent sermons, the best that ever were preached; read ever so many good books—still you must be born again. None of these things will stand in the place of the new birth. No, nor anything under heaven. Let this, therefore, if you have not already experienced this inward work of God, be your continual prayer, 'Lord, add this to all thy blessings: let me be "born again". Deny whatever thou pleasest, but deny not this: let me be "born from above". Take away whatsoever seemeth thee good, reputation, fortune, friends, health. Only give me this: to be "born of the Spirit"! To be received among the children of God. Let me be born, "not of corruptible seed, but incorruptible, by the Word of God, which liveth and abideth for ever". And then let me daily "grow in grace, and in the knowledge of our Lord and Saviour Jesus Christ"!'

17. THE MARKS OF THE NEW BIRTH

1748

An Introductory Comment

This is one of the four major sermons in the collection in which Wesley highlights the reality of the new birth. Not only does he explore the characteristics of regeneration in terms of the theological virtues of faith, hope, and love, but he also underscores the two key fruits of saving faith (peace and power) that he had learned from Peter Böhler in May 1738 (WH, 18:247–48). Outler claimed, in terms of this particular sermon, that Wesley was "in search of a doctrine of regeneration that would take seriously the realities of evangelical conversions" (O, 1:415–16). And Burwash maintained that the modern Christian church "owes its understanding of regeneration [so defined] to Methodism" (B, 173).

Elsewhere Wesley affirmed that the new birth is not a human work—indeed the manner of the Spirit's operations in bringing it about is "inexplicable" (NT, John 3:8) but represents *a free gift* of God (O, 2:343) and therefore, like justification, is to be received by grace through faith. The joint witness to the realization of this saving grace is evident in the testimony of (1) our own spirit and (2) the Spirit of God (O, 1:423), the latter understood in terms of the transition from the spirit of bondage to the Spirit of adoption (O, 1:423).

Though Wesley clearly taught that "our Church supposes all who are baptized in their infancy are at the same time born again" (S, 1:281), his emphasis in this sermon is elsewhere—not on what they once were, but on what they now *are.* "How many are the baptized gluttons and drunkards, the baptized liars and common swearers, the baptized railers and evil-speakers, the baptized whoremongers, thieves, extortioners!" he asked. And even more pointedly Wesley concluded: if "there is no new birth but in baptism [then this], is to seal you all under damnation, to consign you to hell, without any help, without hope" (O, 1:429).

The Marks of the New Birth

1. What is meant by the being born again? What is the new birth?
    A. I propose to lay down the marks of it

I. 1. The first mark is faith
2. Faith is not only assent to divine truth
3. Faith is also a disposition which God hath wrought in the heart
4. The immediate and constant fruit of this faith is power over sin
    A. And over inward sin
5. Whosoever is born of God doth not commit sin
6. By this plain mark are they distinguished
7. Another fruit of living faith is peace

II. 1. A second scriptural mark is hope
2. This implies:
    A. The testimony of our own spirit
    B. The testimony of the Spirit of God
3. You have not received the spirit of bondage
4. You have received the Spirit of adoption
5. When the Comforter comes, your heart shall rejoice

III. 1. A third scriptural mark, and the greatest of all, is love
2. Those who are born again love the Lord Jesus Christ in sincerity
3. The necessary fruit of this love of God is the love of neighbor
4. This is the love of God: that we keep his commandments
5. A second fruit of the love of God is universal obedience

IV. 1. These are the marks of the new birth
2. Who then is born of God?
    A. The question is not what you were in baptism
3. Do not say, 'I *was once* baptized'
4. Those who say there is no new birth but in baptism are sealed under damnation
5. Do not lean on the broken reed that you *were* born again in baptism
6. May everyone receive again that Spirit of adoption and cry out, 'Abba, Father!'

Sermon 18: The Marks of the New Birth, 1748

John 3:8

So is everyone that is born of the Spirit.

1. How is everyone that is 'born of the Spirit'? That is, 'born again', 'born of God'? What is meant by the being 'born again'? The being 'born of God'? Or, being 'born of the Spirit'? What is implied in the being a 'son' or a 'child of God'? Or, having the 'Spirit of adoption'? That these privileges, by the free mercy of God, are ordinarily annexed to baptism (which is thence termed by our Lord in the preceding verse the being 'born of water and of the Spirit') we know; but we would know what these privileges are. What is 'the new birth'?

2. Perhaps it is not needful to give a definition of this, seeing the Scripture gives none. But as the question is of the deepest concern to every child of man (since 'except a man be born again', 'born of the Spirit', he 'cannot see the kingdom of God'), I propose to lay down the marks of it in the plainest manner, just as I find them laid down in Scripture.

I.1. The first of these (and the foundation of all the rest) is faith. So St. Paul, 'Ye are all the children of God by faith in Christ Jesus' (Gal. 3:26). So St. John, 'To them gave he power' (ἐξουσίαν, right, or privilege, it might rather be translated) 'to become the sons of God, even to them that believe on his name: which were born', when they believed, ('not of blood, nor of the will of the flesh', not by natural generation, 'nor of the will of man', like those children adopted by men, in whom no inward change is thereby wrought, 'but) of God' (John 1:12-13). And again in his General Epistle, 'Whosoever believeth that Jesus is the Christ is born of God' (1 John 5:1).

2. But it is not a barely notional or speculative faith that is here spoken of by the apostles. It is not a bare assent to this proposition, 'Jesus is the Christ;' nor indeed to all the propositions contained in our creed, or in the Old and New Testament. It is not merely 'an assent to any, or all these credible things, as credible'. To say this were to say (which who could hear?) that the devils were born of God. For they have their faith. They trembling believe both that Jesus is the Christ and that all Scripture, having been given by inspiration of God, is true as God is true. It is not only 'an assent to divine truth, upon the testimony of God', or 'upon the evidence of miracles'. For they also heard the words of his mouth, and knew him to be a faithful and true witness. They could not but receive the testimony he gave, both of himself and of the Father which sent him. They saw likewise the mighty works which he did, and thence believed that he 'came forth from God'. Yet notwithstanding this faith they are still 'reserved in chains of darkness unto the judgment of the great day'.

3. For all this is no more than a dead faith. The true, living, Christian faith, which whosoever hath is 'born of God', is not only an assent, an act of the understanding, but a disposition which God hath wrought in his heart; 'a sure trust and confidence in God that through the merits of Christ his sins are forgiven, and he reconciled to the favour of God'. This implies that a man first *renounce himself*; that, in order to be 'found in Christ', to be

accepted through him, he totally reject all 'confidence in the flesh'; that, 'having nothing to pay', having no trust in his own works or righteousness of any kind, he come to God as a lost, miserable, self-destroyed, self-condemned, undone, helpless sinner, as one whose 'mouth' is utterly 'stopped', and who is altogether 'guilty before God'. Such a sense of sin (commonly called 'despair' by those who speak evil of the things they know not), together with a full conviction, such as no words can express, that of Christ only cometh our salvation, and an earnest desire of that salvation must precede a living faith: a trust in him who 'for us paid our ransom by his death, and for us fulfilled the law of his life'. This faith, then, whereby we are born of God, is 'not only a belief of all the articles of our faith, but also a true confidence of the mercy of God, through our Lord Jesus Christ'.

4. An immediate and constant fruit of this faith whereby we are born of God, a fruit which can in no wise be separated from it, no, not for an hour, is power over sin: power over outward sin of every kind; over every evil word and work; for wheresoever the blood of Christ is thus applied it 'purgeth the conscience from dead works'. And over inward sin; for it 'purifieth the heart' from every unholy desire and temper. This fruit of faith St. Paul has largely described in the sixth chapter of his Epistle to the Romans: 'How shall we (saith he) who' by faith 'are dead to sin, live any longer therein?' 'Our old man is crucified with Christ, that the body of sin might be destroyed, that henceforth we should not serve sin.' 'Likewise reckon ye yourselves to be dead unto sin, but alive unto God through Jesus Christ our Lord. . . . Let not sin therefore reign', even 'in your mortal body, [. . .] but yield yourselves unto God, as those that are alive from the dead. [. . .] For sin shall not have dominion over you. . . . God be thanked that ye were the servants of sin . . . , but being made free'—the plain meaning is, God be thanked that though ye were in the time past the servants of sin, yet now—'being free from sin, ye are become the servants of righteousness.'

5. The same invaluable privilege of the sons of God is as strongly asserted by St. John; particularly with regard to the former branch of it, namely, power over outward sin. After he had been crying out as one astonished at the depth of the riches of the goodness of God, 'Behold what manner of love the Father hath bestowed upon us, that we should be called the sons of God! [. . .] Beloved, now are we the sons of God; and it doth not yet appear what we shall be; but we know that when he shall appear we shall be like him; for we shall see him as he is'—he soon adds, 'Whosoever is born of God doth not commit sin; for his seed remaineth in him, and he cannot sin because he is born of God' (1 John 3:1-2, 9). But some men will say, 'True; "whosoever is born of God doth not commit sin" (1 John 3:6) *habitually*.' *Habitually*! Whence is that? I read it not. It is not written in the Book. God plainly saith, he 'doth not commit sin'. And thou addest, 'habitually'! Who art thou that *mendest* the oracles of God? That 'addest to the words of this Book'? Beware, I beseech thee, lest God 'add to thee all the plagues that are written therein'! Especially when the comment thou addest is such as quite swallows up the text: so that by this μεθοδεία πλάνης, this artful method of deceiving, the precious promise is utterly lost; by this κυβεία ἀνθρώπων, this tricking and shuffling of men, the Word of God is made of none effect. O beware thou that thus takest from the words of this Book, that taking away the whole meaning and spirit from them leavest only what may indeed be termed a dead letter, lest God take away thy part out of the book of life!

6. Suffer we the Apostle to interpret his own words by the whole tenor of his discourse. In the fifth verse of this chapter he had said, 'Ye know that he (Christ) was manifested to take away our sins; and in him is no sin.' What is the inference he draws from this? 'Whosoever abideth in him sinneth not; whosoever sinneth hath not seen him, neither known him.' To his enforcement of this important doctrine he premises an highly necessary caution: 'Little children, let no man deceive you' (for many will endeavour so to do; to persuade you that you may be unrighteous, that you may commit sin, and yet be children of God). 'He that doth righteousness is righteous, even as he is righteous. He that committeth sin is of the devil; for the devil sinneth from the beginning.' Then follows, 'Whosoever is born of God doth not commit sin; for his seed remaineth in him: and he cannot sin, because he is born of God. In this (adds the Apostle) the children of God are manifest, and the children of the devil' (1 John 3:7-10). By this plain mark (the committing or not committing sin) are they distinguished from each other. To the same effect are those words in his fifth chapter. 'We know that whosoever is born of God sinneth not; but he that is begotten of God keepeth himself, and that wicked one toucheth him not' (1 John 3:18).

7. Another fruit of this living faith is peace. For 'being justified by faith', having all our sins blotted out, 'we have peace with God, through our Lord Jesus Christ' (Rom. 5:1). This indeed our Lord himself, the night before his death, solemnly bequeathed to all his followers. 'Peace (saith he) I leave with you;' (you who 'believe in God', and 'believe also in me') 'my peace I give unto you. Not as the world giveth, give I unto you. Let not your heart be troubled, neither let it be afraid' (John 14:27). And again, 'These things have I spoken unto you, that in me ye might have peace' (John 16:33). This is that 'peace of God which passeth all understanding'; that serenity of soul which it hath not entered into the heart of a natural man to conceive, and which it is not possible for even the spiritual man to utter. And it is a peace which all the powers of earth and hell are unable to take from him. Waves and storms beat upon it, but they shake it not; for it is founded upon a rock. It keepeth the hearts and minds of the children of God at all times and in all places. Whether they are in ease or in pain, in sickness or health, in abundance or want, they are happy in God. In every state they have learned to be content, yea, to give thanks unto God through Christ Jesus; being well assured that 'whatsoever is, is best;' because it is his will concerning them. So that in all the vicissitudes of life their 'heart standeth fast, believing in the Lord'.

II.1. A second scriptural mark of those who are born of God is hope. Thus St. Peter, speaking to all the children of God who were then 'scattered abroad', saith, 'Blessed be the God and Father of our Lord Jesus Christ, who according to his abundant mercy hath begotten us again unto a lively hope' (1 Pet. 1:3). Ἐλπίδα ζῶσαν, a *lively* or *living* hope, saith the Apostle: because there is also a *dead* hope (as well as a dead faith), a hope which is not from God but from the enemy of God and man—as evidently appears by its fruits. For as it is the offspring of pride, so it is the parent of every evil word and work. Whereas every man that hath in him this living hope is 'holy as he that calleth him is holy'. Every man that can truly say to his brethren in Christ, 'Beloved, now are we the sons of God; [. . .] and we shall see him as he is'—'purifieth himself, even as he is pure'.

2. This hope (termed in the Epistle to the Hebrews πληροφορία πίστεως [Heb. 10:22], and elsewhere πληροφορία ἐλπίδος [Heb. 6:11]—in our translation, the 'full assurance of faith', and the 'full assurance of hope'; expressions the best which our language could afford, although far weaker than those in the original), as described in Scripture, implies, (1): the testimony of our own spirit or conscience that we walk 'in simplicity and godly sincerity'; but, secondly and chiefly, the testimony of the Spirit of God, 'bearing witness with', or to, 'our spirit, that we are the children of God; and if children, then heirs; heirs of God, and joint-heirs with Christ'.

3. Let us well observe what is here taught us by God himself touching this glorious privilege of his children. Who is it that is here said to 'bear witness'? Not our spirit only, but another; even the Spirit of God. He it is who 'beareth witness with our spirit'. What is it he beareth witness of? 'That we are the children of God; and if children, then heirs; heirs of God, and joint-heirs with Christ'—'if so be that we suffer with him' (if we deny ourselves, if we take up our cross daily, if we cheerfully endure persecution or reproach for his sake) 'that we may be also glorified together.' And in whom doth the Spirit of God bear this witness? In all who are the children of God. By this very argument does the Apostle prove in the preceding verses that they are so: 'As many', saith he, 'as are led by the Spirit of God, they are the sons of God. For ye have not received the spirit of bondage again to fear; but ye have received the Spirit of adoption, whereby we cry, Abba, Father!' It follows, 'The Spirit itself beareth witness with our spirit, that we are the children of God' (Rom. 8:14-16).

4. The variation of the phrase in the fifteenth verse is worthy our observation. '*Ye* have received the Spirit of adoption, whereby *we* cry, Abba, Father!' *Ye*—as many [as] are the sons of God—have, in virtue of your sonship, received that selfsame Spirit of adoption whereby *we* cry, Abba, Father. *We*, the apostles, prophets, teachers (for so the word may not improperly be understood); we, through whom you have believed, the 'ministers of Christ, and stewards of the mysteries of God'. As *we* and *you* have one Lord, so we have one Spirit; as we have one faith, so have we one hope also. We and you are sealed with one 'Spirit of promise', the earnest of *yours* and of *our* inheritance: the same Spirit bearing witness with yours and with our spirit, 'that we are the children of God'.

5. And thus is the Scripture fulfilled: 'Blessed are they that mourn, for they shall be comforted.' For 'tis easy to believe that though sorrow may precede this witness of God's Spirit with our spirit (indeed *must* in some degree while we groan under fear and a sense of the wrath of God abiding on us), yet as soon as any man feeleth it in himself his 'sorrow is turned into joy'. Whatsoever his pain may have been before, yet as soon as that 'hour is come, he remembereth the anguish no more, for joy' that he is born of God. It may be many of *you* have now sorrow, because you are 'aliens from the commonwealth of Israel', because you are conscious to yourselves that you have not this Spirit, that you are 'without hope and without God in the world'. But when the Comforter is come, then 'your heart shall rejoice'; yea, 'your joy shall be full', 'and that joy no man taketh from you' (John 16:22). 'We joy in God', will ye say, 'through our Lord Jesus Christ, by whom we have now received the atonement' (Rom. 5:11): 'by whom we have access into this grace'; this state of grace, of favour, of reconciliation with God, 'wherein we stand, and rejoice

in hope of the glory of God.' Ye, saith St. Peter, whom God 'hath begotten again unto a lively hope', 'are kept by the power of God unto salvation. . . . Wherein ye greatly rejoice, though now for a season, if need be, ye are in heaviness through manifold temptations; that the trial of your faith . . . may be found unto praise, and honour, and glory, at the appearing of Jesus Christ, . . . in whom, though now ye see him not, ye rejoice with joy unspeakable, and full of glory' (1 Pet. 1:3-8). Unspeakable indeed! It is not for the tongue of man to describe this joy in the Holy Ghost. It is 'the hidden manna, [. . .] which no man knoweth save he that receiveth it'. But this we know, it not only remains, but overflows, in the depth of affliction. 'Are the consolations of God small' with his children, when all earthly comforts fail? Not so. But when sufferings most abound, the consolation of his Spirit doth much more abound: insomuch that the sons of God 'laugh at destruction when it cometh'; at want, pain, hell and the grave; as knowing him who 'hath the keys of death and hell', and will shortly 'cast them into the bottomless pit'; as hearing even now the 'great voice out of heaven' saying, 'Behold, the tabernacle of God is with men, and he will dwell with them, and they shall be his people, and God himself shall be with them, and be their God. And God shall wipe away all tears from their eyes, and there shall be no more death, neither sorrow, nor crying; neither shall there be any more pain; for the former things are passed away' (Rev. 21:3-4).

III.1. A third scriptural mark of those who are born of God, and the greatest of all, is love: even 'the love of God shed abroad in their hearts by the Holy Ghost which is given unto them' (Rom. 5:5). 'Because they are sons, God hath sent forth the Spirit of his Son into their hearts, crying, Abba Father!' (Gal. 4:6). By this Spirit, continually looking up to God as their reconciled and loving Father, they cry to him for their daily bread, for all things needful whether for their souls or bodies. They continually pour out their hearts before him, knowing 'they have the petitions which they ask of him' (1 John 5:15). Their delight is in him. He is the joy of their heart, 'their shield, and their exceeding great reward'. The desire of their soul is toward him; it is their 'meat and drink to do his will'; and they are 'satisfied as with marrow and fatness, while their mouth praiseth him with joyful lips' (Ps. 63:5).

2. And in this sense also 'everyone who loveth him that begat, loveth him that is begotten of him' (1 John 5:1). His spirit rejoiceth in God his Saviour. He 'loveth the Lord Jesus Christ in sincerity'. He is so 'joined unto the Lord' as to be 'one spirit'. His soul hangeth upon him, and chooseth him as altogether lovely, 'the chiefest among ten thousand'. He knoweth, he feeleth, what that means, 'My Beloved is mine, and I am his' (Cant. 2:16). 'Thou art fairer than the children of men; full of grace are thy lips, because God hath anointed thee for ever!' (Ps. 45:2).

3. The necessary fruit of this love of God is the love of our neighbour, of every soul which God hath made; not excepting our enemies, not excepting those who are now 'despitefully using and persecuting us'; a love whereby we love every man *as ourselves*—as we love our own souls. Nay, our Lord has expressed it still more strongly, teaching us to 'love one another even as he hath loved us'. Accordingly the commandment written in the hearts of all those that love God is no other than this, 'As I have loved you, so love ye one

another.' Now 'herein perceive we the love of God, in that he laid down his life for us. We ought', then, as the Apostle justly infers, 'to lay down our lives for our brethren' (1 John 3:16). If we feel ourselves ready to do this, then do we truly love our neighbour. Then 'we know that we have passed from death unto life, because we' thus 'love our brethren' (1 John 3:14). 'Hereby know we' that we are born of God, 'that we dwell in him, and he in us, because he hath given us of his loving Spirit' (1 John 4:13). 'For love is of God, and everyone that' thus 'loveth is born of God, and knoweth God' (1 John 4:7).

4. But some may possibly ask, 'Does not the Apostle say, "This is the love of God, that we keep his commandments"?' (1 John 5:3). Yea; and this is the love of our neighbour also, in the same sense as it is the love of God. But what would you infer from hence? That the keeping the outward commandments is all that is implied in loving God with all your heart, with all your mind, and soul, and strength, and in loving your neighbour as yourself? That the love of God is not an affection of the soul, but merely an *outward service*? And that the love of our neighbour is not a disposition of the heart, but barely a course of *outward works*? To mention so wild an interpretation of the Apostle's words is sufficiently to confute it. The plain indisputable meaning of that text is: 'this is the' sign or proof of the 'love of God', of our keeping the first and great commandment—to keep the rest of his commandments. For true love, if it be once shed abroad in our heart, will constrain us so to do; since whosoever loves God with all his heart cannot but serve him with all his strength.

5. A second fruit then of the love of God (so far as it can be distinguished from it) is universal obedience to him we love, and conformity to his will; obedience to all the commands of God, internal and external; obedience of the heart and of the life, in every temper and in all manner of conversation. And one of the tempers most obviously implied herein is the being 'zealous of good works'; the hungering and thirsting to do good, in every possible kind, unto all men; the rejoicing to 'spend and be spent for them', for every child of man, not looking for any recompense in this world, but only in the resurrection of the just.

IV.1. Thus have I plainly laid down those marks of the new birth which I find laid down in Scripture. Thus doth God himself answer that weighty question what it is to be born of God. Such, if the appeal be made to the oracles of God, is 'everyone that is born of the Spirit'. This it is, in the judgment of the Spirit of God, to be a son or a child of God. It is so to believe in God through Christ as 'not to commit sin', and to enjoy, at all times and in all places, that 'peace of God which passeth all understanding'. It is so to *hope* in God through the Son of his love as to have not only the 'testimony of a good conscience', but also 'the Spirit of God bearing witness with your spirits that ye are the children of God': whence cannot but spring the 'rejoicing evermore in him through whom ye have received the atonement'. It is so to *love* God, who hath thus loved you, as you never did love any creature: so that ye are constrained to love all men as yourselves; with a love not only ever burning in your hearts, but flaming out in all your actions and conversations, and making your whole life one 'labour of love', one continued obedience to those commands, 'Be ye merciful, as God is merciful;' 'Be ye holy, as I the Lord am holy;' 'Be ye perfect, as your Father which is in heaven is perfect.'

2. Who then are ye that are *thus* born of God? Ye 'know the things which are given to you of God'. Ye well know that ye are the children of God, and 'can assure your hearts before him'. And every one of you who has observed these words cannot but feel and know of a truth whether at this hour (answer to God and not to man!) you are thus a child of God or no! The question is not what you was made in baptism (do not evade!) but what you are now. Is the Spirit of adoption now in your heart? To your own heart let the appeal be made. I ask not whether you *was* born of water and the Spirit. But *are* you *now* the temple of the Holy Ghost which dwelleth in you? I allow you was 'circumcised with the circumcision [. . .] of Christ' (as St. Paul emphatically terms baptism). But does the Spirit of Christ and of glory *now* rest upon you? Else 'your circumcision is become uncircumcision'.

3. Say not then in your heart, I *was once* baptized; therefore I *am now* a child of God. Alas, that consequence will by no means hold. How many are the baptized gluttons and drunkards, the baptized liars and common swearers, the baptized railers and evil-speakers, the baptized whoremongers, thieves, extortioners! What think you? Are these now the children of God? Verily I say unto you, whosoever you are, unto whom any of the preceding characters belong, 'Ye are of your father the devil, and the works of your father ye do.' Unto you I call in the name of him whom you crucify afresh, and in his words to your circumcised predecessors, 'Ye serpents, ye generation of vipers, how can you escape the damnation of hell?'

4. How indeed, except ye be born again! For ye are now dead in trespasses and sins. To say then that ye cannot be born again, that there is no new birth but in baptism, is to seal you all under damnation, to consign you to hell, without any help, without hope. And perhaps some may think this just and right. In their zeal for the Lord of Hosts they may say, 'Yea, cut off the sinners, the Amalekites! Let these Gibeonites be utterly destroyed! They deserve no less.' No; nor I, nor you—mine and your desert, as well as theirs, is hell. And it is mere mercy, free undeserved mercy, that *we* are not now in unquenchable fire. You will say, 'But we are washed, we were born again of water and of the Spirit.' So *were* they. This therefore hinders not at all, but that ye may *now* be even as they. Know ye not that 'what is highly esteemed of men is an abomination in the sight of God'? Come forth, ye 'saints of the world', ye that are honoured of men, and see who will cast the first stone at them, at these wretches not fit to live upon the earth, these common harlots, adulterers, murderers. Only learn ye first what that meaneth, 'He that hateth his brother is a murderer' (1 John 3:15)—'He that looketh on a woman to lust after her hath committed adultery with her already in his heart' (Matt. 5:28)—'Ye adulterers and adulteresses, know ye not that the friendship of the world is enmity with God?' (Jas. 4:4).

5. 'Verily, verily, I say unto you, ye also must be born again.' 'Except' ye also 'be born again, ye cannot see the kingdom of God.' Lean no more on the staff of that broken reed, that ye *were* born again in baptism. Who denies that ye were then made 'children of God, and heirs of the kingdom of heaven'? But notwithstanding this, ye are now children of the devil; therefore ye must be born again. And let not Satan put it into your heart to cavil at a word, when the thing is clear. Ye have heard what are the marks of the children of God; all ye who have them not on your souls, baptized or unbaptized, must needs receive

them, or without doubt ye will perish everlastingly. And if ye have been baptized, your only hope is this: that those who were made the children of God by baptism, but are now the children of the devil, may yet again receive 'power to become the sons of God'; that they may receive again what they have lost, even the 'Spirit of adoption, crying in their hearts, Abba, Father'!

6. Amen, Lord Jesus! May everyone who prepareth his heart yet again to seek thy face receive again that Spirit of adoption, and cry out, Abba, Father! Let him now again have power to believe in thy name as to become a child of God; as to know and feel he hath 'redemption in thy blood, even the forgiveness of sins', and that he 'cannot commit sin, because he is born of God'. Let him be now 'begotten again unto a living hope', so as to 'purify himself, as thou art pure'! And 'because he is a son', let the Spirit of love and of glory rest upon him, cleansing him 'from all filthiness of flesh and spirit', and teaching him to 'perfect holiness in the fear of God'!

18. THE GREAT PRIVILEGE OF THOSE THAT ARE BORN OF GOD

1748

An Introductory Comment

Though Wesley preached on the text of this sermon (1 John 3:9) only three times (the first in September 1739; the second in January 1740; and the last in November 1756; WWS), the content of this sermon complements the material found in "The Marks of the New Birth," whose text was preached more than a dozen times. This additional sermon on the great privilege of the children of God, deemed necessary by Wesley, clarifies the issue at hand by offering a careful definition of sin and thereby distinguishing between voluntary and involuntary transgressions against the moral law of God (O, 1:436).

Articulating the liberties of those born of God, broadly speaking, Wesley furthermore distinguished between freedom from the *guilt* of sin, in terms of justification, and from the *power* of sin, with respect to the new birth (O, 1:431–32). Wesley was likely informed in these judgments, in part, by his reading of the works of Matthew Henry, who maintained that a "vital union with the Lord Jesus broke the power of sin in the heart" (H, 1 John 3:9), and by John Albert Bengel, who affirmed in a similar fashion that the "new birth and sin *cannot* coexist" (JAB, 1 John 3:9).

Such a privilege, then, marking a "great change" in the soul (O, 1:432), suggests an ongoing dependence upon God. In other words, such a gift will remain in place so long as the believer "keepeth himself" (O, 1:438), to use Wesley's words. Indeed, toward the end of this sermon, Wesley cautioned his readers to avoid those behaviors that could lead to a loss of saving faith, the "unquestionable progress from grace to sin" (O, 1:440), what in effect would be a reversal of what Outler calls the *ordo salutis*. Unlike some of his Calvinist contemporaries, Wesley freely acknowledged that those who were genuinely born of God may yet fall away.

The Great Privilege of those that are Born of God

1. Being born of God is often equated with being justified
2. Justification and new birth are in point of time inseparable from each other
    - A. They are easily distinguished from each other as not being the same
    - B. Justification implies only a relative, the new birth a real, change
3. Not discerning this has led to great confusion of thought
    - A. Especially the phrase 'Whosoever is born of God doth not commit sin'

I.

1. Being born of God implies an inward and not merely an outward change
2. When we undergo this great change we are born again
    - A. Consider natural birth to understand spiritual birth
3. The child which is not yet born subsists by air but *feels* it not
4. The child does not have the senses to hold commerce with the world
5. No sooner is the child born than he exists in a quite different manner
6. So it is with those that are born of God
7. Before this change, they do not have knowledge of the invisible world
8. But when they are born of God, the manner of their existence changes
9. The eyes of their understanding are opened, and they see
10. Their ears are open, and the voice of God no longer calls in vain

II.

1. It remains to inquire in what sense they do not commit sin
2. By sin I here mean outward sin
3. Those born of God nevertheless do commit sin
4. David was born of God, but he committed adultery and murder
5. This happens even after the Holy Ghost is given
6. How then can those born of God not commit sin?
7. Those born of God must keep themselves, abiding daily in the faith

III.

1. From the preceding considerations we may answer the question:
    - A. Does sin precede or follow the loss of faith?
    - B. I answer: Some sin must necessarily precede the loss of faith
        - i. But the loss of faith must precede the committing outward sin
2. We may learn also what the life of God in the soul of a believer is
    - A. It implies the continual inspiration of God's Holy Spirit
3. And we may infer the absolute necessity of this re-action of the soul
4. Let us learn, lastly, to follow that direction: 'Be not high-minded, but fear'

Sermon 19: The Great Privilege of those that are Born of God, 1748

1 John 3:9

Whosoever is born of God doth not commit sin.

1. It has been frequently supposed that the being born of God was all one with the being justified; that the new birth and justification were only different expressions denoting the same thing: it being certain on the one hand that whoever is justified is also born of God, and on the other that whoever is born of God is also justified; yea, that both these gifts of God are given to every believer in one and the same moment. In one point of time his sins are blotted out and he is born of God.

2. But though it be allowed that justification and the new birth are in point of time inseparable from each other, yet are they easily distinguished as being not the same, but things of a widely different nature. Justification implies only a relative, the new birth a real, change. God in justifying us does something *for* us: in begetting us again he does the work *in* us. The former changes our outward relation to God, so that of enemies we become children; by the latter our inmost souls are changed, so that of sinners we become saints. The one restores us to the favour, the other to the image of God. The one is the taking away the guilt, the other the taking away the power, of sin. So that although they are joined together in point of time, yet are they of wholly distinct natures.

3. The not discerning this, the not observing the wide difference there is between being justified and being born again, has occasioned exceeding great confusion of thought in many who have treated on this subject; particularly when they have attempted to explain this great privilege of the children of God, to show how 'whosoever is born of God doth not commit sin.'

4. In order to apprehend this clearly it may be necessary, first, to consider what is the proper meaning of that expression, 'whosoever is born of God'; and, secondly, to inquire in what sense he 'doth not commit sin'.

I.1. First, we are to consider what is the proper meaning of that expression, 'whosoever is born of God'. And in general, from all the passages of Holy Writ wherein this expression, the being 'born of God', occurs, we may learn that it implies not barely the being baptized, or any outward change whatever; but a vast inward change; a change wrought in the soul by the operation of the Holy Ghost, a change in the whole manner of our existence; for from the moment we are 'born of God' we live in quite another manner than we did before; we are, as it were, in another world.

2. The ground and reason of the expression is easy to be understood. When we undergo this great change we may with much propriety be said 'to be born again', because there is so near a resemblance between the circumstances of the natural and of the spiritual birth; so that to consider the circumstances of the natural birth is the most easy way to understand the spiritual.

3. The child which is not yet born subsists indeed by the air, as does everything which has life; but *feels* it not, nor anything else, unless in a very dull and imperfect manner. It *hears* little, if at all, the organs of hearing being as yet closed up. It *sees* nothing, having its eyes fast shut, and being surrounded with utter darkness. There are, it may be, some faint beginnings of life when the time of its birth draws nigh, and some motion consequent thereon, whereby it is distinguished from a mere mass of matter. But it has no *senses*; all these avenues of the soul are hitherto quite shut up. Of consequence it has scarce any intercourse with this visible world, nor any knowledge, conception, or idea of the things that occur therein.

4. The reason why he that is not yet born is wholly a stranger to the visible world is not because it is afar off—it is very nigh; it surrounds him on every side—but partly because he has not those senses (they are not yet opened in his soul) whereby alone it is possible to hold commerce with the material world; and partly because so thick a veil is cast between, through which he can discern nothing.

5. But no sooner is the child born into the world than he exists in a quite different manner. He now *feels* the air with which he is surrounded, and which pours into him from every side, as fast as he alternately breathes it back, to sustain the flame of life. And hence springs a continual increase of strength, of motion, and of sensation; all the bodily senses being now awakened and furnished with their proper objects.

His eyes are now opened to perceive the light, which silently flowing in upon them discovers not only itself but an infinite variety of things with which before he was wholly unacquainted. His ears are unclosed, and sounds rush in with endless diversity. Every sense is employed upon such objects as are peculiarly suitable to it. And by these inlets the soul, having an open intercourse with the visible world, acquires more and more knowledge of sensible things, of all the things which are under the sun.

6. So it is with him that is born of God. Before that great change is wrought, although he subsists by him in whom all that have life 'live and move and have their being', yet he is not *sensible* of God. He does not *feel*, he has no inward consciousness of his presence. He does not perceive that divine breath of life without which he cannot subsist a moment. Nor is he sensible of any of the things of God. They make no impression upon his soul. God is continually calling to him from on high, but he heareth not; his ears are shut; so that 'the voice of the charmer' is lost to him, 'charm he never so wisely'. He seeth not the things of the Spirit of God, the eyes of his understanding being closed, and utter darkness covering his whole soul, surrounding him on every side. It is true he may have some faint dawnings of life, some small beginnings of spiritual motion; but as yet he has no spiritual senses capable of discerning spiritual objects. Consequently, he 'discerneth not the things of the Spirit of God. He cannot know them; because they are spiritually discerned.'

7. Hence he has scarce any knowledge of the invisible world, as he has scarce any intercourse with it. Not that it is afar off. No; he is in the midst of it: it encompasses him round about. The 'other world', as we usually term it, is not far from every one of us. It is above, and beneath, and on every side. Only the natural man discerneth it not; partly because he has no spiritual senses, whereby alone we can discern the things of God; partly because so thick a veil is interposed as he knows not how to penetrate.

8. But when he is born of God, born of the Spirit, how is the manner of his existence changed! His whole soul is now sensible of God, and he can say by sure experience, 'Thou art about my bed, and about my path;' I feel thee in 'all my ways'. 'Thou besettest me behind and before, and layest thy hand upon me.' The Spirit or breath of God is immediately inspired, breathed into the new-born soul; and the same breath which comes from, returns to God. As it is continually received by faith, so it is continually rendered back by love, by prayer, and praise, and thanksgiving—love and praise and prayer being the breath of every soul which is truly born of God. And by this new kind of spiritual respiration, spiritual life is not only sustained but increased day by day, together with spiritual strength and motion and sensation; all the senses of the soul being now awake, and capable of 'discerning' spiritual 'good and evil'.

9. 'The eyes of his understanding' are now open, and he 'seeth him that is invisible'. He sees what is 'the exceeding greatness of his power' and of his love toward them that believe. He sees that God is merciful to him a sinner; that he is reconciled through the Son of his love. He clearly perceives both the pardoning love of God and all his 'exceeding great and precious promises'. 'God, who commanded the light to shine out of the darkness, hath shined' and doth shine 'in his heart, to enlighten him with the knowledge of the glory of God in the face of Jesus Christ.' All the darkness is now passed away, and he abides in the light of God's countenance.

10. His ears are now opened, and the voice of God no longer calls in vain. He hears and obeys the heavenly calling: he 'knows the voice of his shepherd'. All his spiritual senses being now awakened, he has a clear intercourse with the invisible world. And hence he knows more and more of the things which before it 'could not enter into his heart to conceive'. He now knows what the peace of God is; what is joy in the Holy Ghost; what the love of God which is shed abroad in the hearts of them that believe through Christ Jesus. Thus the veil being removed which before interrupted the light and voice, the knowledge and love of God, he who is born of the Spirit, 'dwelling in love, dwelleth in God and God in him'.

II.1. Having considered the meaning of that expression, 'whosoever is born of God', it remains in the second place to inquire in what sense he 'doth not commit sin'.

Now one who is so born of God as hath been above described, who continually receives into his soul the breath of life from God, the gracious influence of his Spirit, and continually renders it back; one who thus believes and loves, who by faith perceives the continual actings of God upon his spirit, and by a kind of spiritual re-action returns the grace he receives in unceasing love, and praise, and prayer; not only 'doth not commit sin' while he thus 'keepeth himself', but so long as this 'seed remaineth in him he cannot sin', because he is born of God.

2. By 'sin' I here understand outward sin, according to the plain, common acceptation of the word: an actual, voluntary 'transgression of the law'; of the revealed, written law of God; of any commandment of God acknowledged to be such at the time that it is transgressed. But 'whosoever is born of God', while he abideth in faith and love and in

the spirit of prayer and thanksgiving, not only 'doth not', but 'cannot' thus 'commit sin'. So long as he thus believeth in God through Christ and loves him, and is pouring out his heart before him, he cannot voluntarily transgress any command of God, either by speaking or acting what he knows God hath forbidden—so long that 'seed' which 'remaineth in him' (that loving, praying, thankful faith) compels him to refrain from whatsoever he knows to be an abomination in the sight of God.

3. But here a difficulty will immediately occur, and one that to many has appeared insuperable, and induced them to deny the plain assertion of the Apostle, and give up the privilege of the children of God.

It is plain, in fact, that those whom we cannot deny to have been truly 'born of God' (the Spirit of God having given us in his Word this infallible testimony concerning them) nevertheless not only could but did commit sin, even gross, outward sin. They did transgress the plain, known laws of God, speaking or acting what they knew he had forbidden.

4. Thus David was unquestionably born of God or ever he was anointed king over Israel. He knew in whom he had believed; he was strong in faith, giving glory to God. 'The Lord', saith he, 'is my shepherd; therefore can I lack nothing. He shall feed me in green pastures, and lead me forth beside the waters of comfort. [. . .] Yea, though I walk through the valley of the shadow of death, I will fear no evil; for thou art with me' (Ps. 23:1, 2, 4). He was filled with love, such as often constrained him to cry out, 'I will love thee, O Lord, my God; the Lord is my stony rock, and my defence; the horn also of my salvation, and my refuge' (Ps. 18:1, 2). He was a man of prayer, pouring out his soul before God in all circumstances of life; and abundant in praises and thanksgiving. 'Thy praise', saith he, 'shall be ever in my mouth' (Ps. 34:1). 'Thou art my God, and I will thank thee; thou art my God, and I will praise thee' (Ps. 118:28). And yet such a child of God could and did commit sin; yea, the horrid sins of adultery and murder.

5. And even after the Holy Ghost was more largely given, after 'life and immortality were brought to light by the gospel', we want not instances of the same melancholy kind, which were also doubtless written for our instruction. Thus he who (probably from his selling all that he had, and bringing the price for the relief of his poor brethren) was 'by the apostles' themselves 'surnamed Barnabas', that is, 'the son of consolation' (Acts 4:36-37); who was so honoured at Antioch as to be selected with Saul out of all the disciples to carry their 'relief unto the brethren in Judea' (Acts 11:29): this Barnabas, who at his return from Judea was by the peculiar direction of the Holy Ghost solemnly 'separated' from the other 'prophets and teachers' 'for the work whereunto God had called him' (Acts 13:1-2), even to accompany the great Apostle among the Gentiles, and to be his fellow-labourer in every place; nevertheless was afterward so 'sharp' in his 'contention' with St. Paul (because he 'thought it not good to take with them' John in his 'visiting the brethren' a second time, 'who had departed from them from Pamphylia, and went not with them to the work') that he himself also departed from the work; that he 'took John, and sailed unto Cyprus' (Acts 15:35, 38, 39), forsaking him to whom he had been in so immediate a manner joined by the Holy Ghost.

6. An instance more astonishing than both these is given by St. Paul in his Epistle

to the Galatians. 'When Peter', the aged, the zealous, the first of the apostles, one of the three most highly favoured by his Lord, 'was come to Antioch, I withstood him to the face, because he was to be blamed. For before that certain came from James he did eat with the Gentiles'—the heathens converted to the Christian faith—as having been peculiarly taught of God that he 'should not call any man common or unclean' (Acts 10:28). But 'when they were come, [. . .] he separated himself, fearing them which were of the circumcision. And the other Jews dissembled likewise with him; insomuch that Barnabas also was carried away with their dissimulation. But when I saw that they walked not uprightly according to the truth of the gospel, I said unto Peter before them all, If thou, being a Jew, livest after the manner of the Gentiles', not regarding the ceremonial law of Moses, 'why compellest thou the Gentiles to live as do the Jews?' (Gal. 2:12-14). Here is also plain undeniable sin, committed by one who was undoubtedly 'born of God'. But how can this be reconciled with the assertion of St. John, if taken in the obvious literal meaning, that 'whosoever is born of God doth not commit sin'?

7. I answer, what has been long observed is this: so long as 'he that is born of God keepeth himself' (which he is able to do, by the grace of God) 'the wicked one toucheth him not.' But if he keepeth not himself, if he abide not in the faith, he may commit sin even as another man.

It is easy therefore to understand how any of these children of God might be moved from his own steadfastness, and yet the great truth of God, declared by the Apostle, remain steadfast and unshaken. He did not keep himself by that grace of God which was sufficient for him. He fell step by step, first into negative, inward sin—not 'stirring up the gift of God' which was in him, not 'watching unto prayer', not 'pressing on to the mark of the prize of his high calling'; then into positive, inward sin—inclining to wickedness with his heart, giving way to some evil desire or temper. Next he lost his faith, his sight of a pardoning God, and consequently his love of God. And being then weak and like another man he was capable of committing even outward sin.

8. To explain this by a particular instance. David was born of God, and saw God by faith. He loved God in sincerity. He could truly say, 'Whom have I in heaven but thee? And there is none upon earth' (neither person or thing) 'that I desire in comparison to thee!' But still there remained in his heart that corruption of nature which is the seed of all evil.

He was 'walking upon the roof of his house' (2 Sam. 11:2), probably praising the God whom his soul loved, when he looked and saw Bathsheba. He felt a temptation, a thought which tended to evil. The Spirit of God did not fail to convince him of this. He doubtless heard and knew the warning voice. But he yielded in some measure to the thought, and the temptation began to prevail over him. Hereby his spirit was sullied. He saw God still; but it was more dimly than before. He loved God still; but not in the same degree, not with the same strength and ardour of affection. Yet God checked him again, though his spirit was grieved; and his voice, though fainter and fainter, still whispered, 'Sin lieth at the door;' 'look unto me, and be thou saved.' But he would not hear. He looked again, not unto God, but unto the forbidden object, till nature was superior to grace, and kindled lust in his soul.

The eye of his mind was now closed again, and God vanished out of his sight. Faith, the divine, supernatural intercourse with God, and the love of God ceased together. He then rushed on as a horse into the battle, and knowingly committed the outward sin.

9. You see the unquestionable progress from grace to sin. Thus it goes on, from step to step. (1). The divine seed of loving, conquering faith remains in him that is 'born of God'. 'He keepeth himself', by the grace of God, and 'cannot commit' sin; (2). A temptation arises, whether from the world, the flesh, or the devil, it matters not; (3). The Spirit of God gives him warning that sin is near, and bids him more abundantly watch unto prayer; (4). He gives way in some degree to the temptation, which now begins to grow pleasing to him; (5). The Holy Spirit is grieved; his faith is weakened, and his love of God grows cold; (6). The Spirit reproves him more sharply, and saith, 'This is the way; walk thou in it.' (7). He turns away from the painful voice of God and listens to the pleasing voice of the tempter; (8). Evil desire begins and spreads in his soul, till faith and love vanish away; (9). He is then capable of committing outward sin, the power of the Lord being departed from him.

10. To explain this by another instance. The Apostle Peter was full of faith and of the Holy Ghost; and hereby keeping himself he had a conscience void of offence toward God and toward man.

Walking thus in simplicity and godly sincerity, 'before that certain came from James he did eat with the Gentiles', knowing that what God had cleansed was not common or unclean.

But 'when they were come' a temptation arose in his heart to 'fear those of the circumcision' (the Jewish converts who were zealous for circumcision and the other rites of the Mosaic law) and regard the favour and praise of these men more than the praise of God.

He was warned by the Spirit that sin was near. Nevertheless, he yielded to it in some degree, even to sinful fear of man, and his faith and love were proportionably weakened.

God reproved him again for giving place to the devil. Yet he would not hearken to the voice of his Shepherd, but gave himself up to that slavish fear, and thereby quenched the Spirit.

Then God disappeared, and faith and love being extinct he committed the outward sin. 'Walking not uprightly, not according to the truth of the gospel', he 'separated himself' from his Christian brethren, and by his evil example, if not advice also, 'compelled' even 'the Gentiles to live after the manner of the Jews'; to entangle themselves again with that 'yoke of bondage' from which 'Christ had set them free'.

Thus it is unquestionably true that he who is born of God, keeping himself, doth not, cannot commit sin; and yet if he keepeth not himself he may commit all manner of sin with greediness.

III.1. From the preceding considerations we may learn, first, to give a clear and incontestable answer to a question which has frequently perplexed many who were sincere of heart. Does sin precede or follow the loss of faith? Does a child of God first commit sin, and thereby lose his faith? Or does he lose his faith first, before he can commit sin?

I answer: some sin, of omission at least, must necessarily precede the loss of faith—some inward sin. But the loss of faith must precede the committing outward sin.

The more any believer examines his own heart, the more will he be convinced of this: that 'faith working by love' excludes both inward and outward sin from a soul 'watching unto prayer'; that nevertheless we are even then liable to temptation, particularly to the sin that did easily beset us; that if the loving eye of the soul be steadily fixed on God the temptation soon vanishes away. But if not, if we are ἐξελκόμενοι (as the Apostle James speaks), 'drawn out' of God by our 'own desire', and δελεαζόμενοι, 'caught by the bait' of present or promised pleasure: then that 'desire conceived' in us 'brings forth sin'; and having by that inward sin destroyed our faith, it casts us headlong into the snare of the devil, so that we may commit any outward sin whatever.

2. From what has been said we may learn, secondly, what the life of God in the soul of a believer is, wherein it properly consists, and what is immediately and necessarily implied therein. It immediately and necessarily implies the continual inspiration of God's Holy Spirit: God's breathing into the soul, and the soul's breathing back what it first receives from God; a continual action of God upon the soul, and re-action of the soul upon God; an unceasing presence of God, the loving, pardoning God, manifested to the heart, and perceived by faith; and an unceasing return of love, praise, and prayer, offering up all the thoughts of our hearts, all the words of our tongues, all the works of our hands, all our body, soul, and spirit, to be an holy sacrifice, acceptable unto God in Christ Jesus.

3. And hence we may, thirdly, infer the absolute necessity of this re-action of the soul (whatsoever it be called) in order to the continuance of the divine life therein. For it plainly appears God does not continue to act upon the soul unless the soul re-acts upon God. He prevents us indeed with the blessings of his goodness. He first loves us, and manifests himself unto us. While we are yet afar off he calls us to himself, and shines upon our hearts. But if we do not then love him who first loved us; if we will not hearken to his voice; if we turn our eye away from him, and will not attend to the light which he pours upon us: his Spirit will not always strive; he will gradually withdraw, and leave us to the darkness of our own hearts. He will not continue to breathe into our soul unless our soul breathes toward him again; unless our love, and prayer, and thanksgiving return to him, a sacrifice wherewith he is well pleased.

4. Let us learn, lastly, to follow that direction of the great Apostle: 'Be not high-minded, but fear.' Let us fear sin more than death or hell. Let us have a jealous (though not painful) fear, lest we should lean to our own deceitful hearts. 'Let him that standeth take heed lest he fall.' Even he who now standeth fast in the grace of God, in the faith that 'overcometh the world', may nevertheless fall into inward sin, and thereby 'make shipwreck of his faith'. And how easily then will outward sin regain its dominion over him! Thou, therefore, O man of God, watch always, that thou mayest always hear the voice of God. Watch that thou mayest pray without ceasing, at all times and in all places pouring out thy heart before him. So shalt thou always believe, and always love, and never commit sin.

19. THE FIRST-FRUITS OF THE SPIRIT

1746

An Introductory Comment

As in his other major sermons on the new birth, Wesley underscored freedom from the guilt and power of sin in this present work as marking the qualitatively distinct graces of a child of God (O, 1:244). In fact, he borrowed the very adjectives from Bengel's commentary on Romans 8:1, the text of this sermon, in terms of "deliverance and liberty" and made them his own designations as well (NT, John 8:1). Moreover, when Wesley preached on this text in June 1745 at St. Just, he noted "all our hearts were in a flame" (WH, 20:72), and on another occasion at Short's Gardens he observed that "thoughts and words crowded in so fast upon me" (WH, 19:190), such that his sermon did not go beyond the first verse: "Who walk not after the flesh, but after the Spirit" (WH, 19:190).

Sugden was correct in pointing out that this sermon, in a real sense, was a "first sketch for 'On Sin in Believers'" (S, 1:162). In other words, as early as 1746 Wesley carefully distinguished between the *guilt, power,* and *being* of sin. Thus, those who have the first-fruits of the Spirit are indeed both justified (freedom from the guilt of sin) and born of God (freedom from its power) though the *being* of sin remains. In other words, believers "feel the root of bitterness" (O, 1:236) as well as the "corruption of nature" (O, 1:236) that remains. Since the carnal nature or original sin is yet present in the hearts of the children of God, they must repent once again, this time in terms not of actual *sins* but of inbred *sin.* Accordingly, Wesley concluded this sermon on an optimistic note by urging believers to "wait in peace for that hour when 'the God of peace shall sanctify thee wholly'" (O, 1:247).

The First-fruits of the Spirit

I. 1. First, I will show who those are that are in Christ Jesus
   A. Are they not those who believe in his name?
2. Whosoever abideth in him sinneth not
3. Those who are of Christ have crucified the flesh
4. They walk after the Spirit in their hearts and in their lives
5. They are also led by the Spirit into all holiness of conversation

II. 1. Second, I will show how there is no condemnation
   A. To believers there is no condemnation on account of past sins
2. There is no sense of guilt or dread
3. Some say that a believer may lose sight of God's mercy
   A. I answer, then he is not a believer; for faith implies light
4. They are not condemned, secondly, for any present sins
5. They are not condemned, thirdly, for inward sin, even though it remains
6. And yet for all this they are not condemned
7. Fourthly, although they are convinced of sin, there is no condemnation
8. They are not condemned, fifthly, for sins of infirmity
9. Last, there is no condemnation for things not in their power to help
10. Believers may grieve because they cannot do what their souls long for
11. It is more difficult to determine sins of surprise
12. There may be sins of surprise which bring guilt and condemnation
13. But there may be sudden assaults from the world that we can hardly foresee

III. 1. It remains only to draw some practical inferences
   A. First, if there is no condemnation, then why are you fearful?
2. Faith cancels all that is past; there is no condemnation to you
3. Second, do all who abide in Christ walk after the Spirit?
   A. Whoever sins has no part in this matter
4. Third, is there no condemnation of *inward sin* still remaining?
   A. So long as you do not give in to it, fret not
5. Fourth, if we are not condemned for sins of infirmity, then beware that:
   A. Satan gain no advantage over you
6. Last, if you who believe falter, then grieve unto the Lord
   A. It shall be a precious balm; pour out your heart before him

Sermon 8: The First-fruits of the Spirit, 1746

Romans 8:1

There is therefore now no condemnation to them
which are in Christ Jesus, who walk not
after the flesh, but after the Spirit.

1. By 'them which are in Christ Jesus' St. Paul evidently means those who truly believe in him; those who 'being justified by faith, have peace with God, through our Lord Jesus Christ'. They who thus believe do no longer 'walk after the flesh', no longer follow the motions of corrupt nature, but 'after the Spirit'. Both their thoughts, words, and works are under the direction of the blessed Spirit of God.

2. 'There is therefore now no condemnation to' these. There is no condemnation to them from God, for he hath 'justified them freely by his grace, through the redemption that is in Jesus'. He hath forgiven all their iniquities, and blotted out all their sins. And there is no condemnation to them from within, for they 'have received, not the spirit of the world, but the Spirit which is of God, that they might know the things which are freely given to them of God' (1 Cor. 2:12): 'which Spirit beareth witness with their spirits that they are the children of God'. And to this is added 'the testimony of their conscience, that in simplicity and godly sincerity, not with fleshly wisdom, but by the grace of God, they have had their conversation in the world' (2 Cor. 1:12).

3. But because this Scripture has been so frequently misunderstood, and that in so dangerous a manner; because such multitudes of 'unlearned and unstable men' (οἱ ἀμαθεῖς καὶ ἀστήρικτοι, men untaught of God, and consequently unestablished in 'the truth which is after godliness') have 'wrested it to their own destruction'; I propose to show as clearly as I can, first, who those are 'which are in Christ Jesus, and walk not after the flesh, but after the Spirit'; and secondly, how 'there is no condemnation to' these. I shall conclude with some practical inferences.

I.1. First, I am to show who those are that 'are in Christ Jesus'. And are they not those who believe in his name? Those who are 'found in him, not having their own righteousness, but the righteousness which is of God by faith'? These, who 'have redemption through his blood', are properly said to be 'in him', for *they* 'dwell in Christ and Christ in them'. They are 'joined unto the Lord in one Spirit'. They are engrafted into him as branches into the vine. They are united, as members to their head, in a manner which words cannot express, nor could it before enter into their hearts to conceive.

2. Now 'whosoever abideth in him sinneth not,' 'walketh not after the flesh'. The flesh, in the usual language of St. Paul, signifies corrupt nature. In this sense he uses the word, writing to the Galatians, 'The works of the flesh are manifest' (Gal. 5:19); and a little before, 'Walk in the Spirit, and ye shall not fulfil the lust (or desire) of the flesh' (Gal. 5:16). To prove which, namely, that those who 'walk by the Spirit do not fulfil the lust of the flesh', he immediately adds, 'For the flesh lusteth against the spirit; but the spirit lusteth against the flesh (for these are contrary to each other), that ye may not do the things

which ye would.' So the words are literally translated (ἵνα μὴ ἃ ἂν θέλητε, ταῦτα ποιῆτε); not, 'So that ye cannot do the things that ye would,' as if the flesh overcame the spirit—a translation which hath not only nothing to do with the original text of the Apostle, but likewise makes his whole argument nothing worth, yea, asserts just the reverse of what he is proving.

3. 'They who are of Christ', who 'abide in him', 'have crucified the flesh with its affections and lusts.' They abstain from all those works of the flesh: from 'adultery and fornication'; from 'uncleanness and lasciviousness'; from 'idolatry, witchcraft, hatred, variance'; from 'emulations, wrath, strife, sedition, heresies, envyings, murders, drunkenness, revellings'—from every design, and word, and work to which the corruption of nature leads. Although they feel the root of bitterness in themselves, yet are they endued with power from on high to trample it continually under foot, so that it cannot 'spring up to trouble them': insomuch that every fresh assault which they undergo only gives them fresh occasion of praise, of crying out, 'Thanks be unto God, who giveth us the victory, through Jesus Christ our Lord.'

4. They now 'walk after the Spirit' both in their hearts and lives. They are taught of him to love God and their neighbour with a love which is as 'a well of water, springing up into everlasting life'. And by him they are led into every holy desire, into every divine and heavenly temper, till every thought which arises in their heart is holiness unto the Lord.

5. They who 'walk after the Spirit' are also led by him into all holiness of conversation. Their speech is 'always in grace, seasoned with salt', with the love and fear of God. 'No corrupt communication comes out of their mouth, but (only) that which is good;' that which is 'to the use of edifying', which is 'meet to minister grace to the hearers'. And herein likewise do they exercise themselves day and night to do only the things which please God; in all their outward behaviour to follow him who 'left us an example that we might tread in his steps'; in all their intercourse with their neighbour to walk in justice, mercy, and truth; and 'whatsoever they do', in every circumstance of life, to 'do all to the glory of God.'

6. These are they who indeed 'walk after the Spirit'. Being filled with faith and with the Holy Ghost, they possess in their hearts, and show forth in their lives, in the whole course of their words and actions, the genuine fruits of the Spirit of God, namely, 'love, joy, peace, long-suffering, gentleness, goodness, fidelity, meekness, temperance', and whatsoever else is lovely or praiseworthy. They 'adorn in all things the gospel of God our Saviour'; and give full proof to all mankind that they are indeed actuated by the same Spirit 'which raised up Jesus from the dead'.

II.1. I proposed to show, in the second place, how 'there is no condemnation to them which are' thus 'in Christ Jesus', and thus 'walk, not after the flesh, but after the Spirit.'

And, first, to believers in Christ walking thus 'there is no condemnation' on account of their past sins. God condemneth them not for any of these; they are as though they had never been; they are 'cast as a stone into the depth of the sea', and he remembereth them no more. God having 'set forth his Son to be a propitiation for them, through faith in his blood, hath declared unto them his righteousness, for the remission of the sins that are past'. He layeth therefore none of these to their charge; their memorial is perished with them.

2. And there is no condemnation in their own breast, no sense of guilt, or dread of the wrath of God. They 'have the witness in themselves'; they are conscious of their interest in the blood of sprinkling. They 'have not received again the spirit of bondage unto fear', unto doubt and racking uncertainty; but they 'have received the Spirit of adoption, crying in their hearts, Abba, Father'. Thus 'being justified by faith, they have the peace' of God ruling in their hearts, flowing from a continual sense of his pardoning mercy, and 'the answer of a good conscience toward God'.

3. If it be said, 'But sometimes a believer in Christ may lose his sight of the mercy of God; sometimes such darkness may fall upon him that he no longer sees him that is invisible, no longer feels that witness in himself of his part in the atoning blood; and then he is inwardly condemned, he hath again "the sentence of death in himself".' I answer, supposing it so to be, supposing him not to see the mercy of God, then he is not a believer; for faith implies light, the light of God shining upon the soul. So far therefore as anyone loses this light, he for the time loses his faith. And no doubt a true believer in Christ may lose the light of faith. And so far as this is lost he may for a time fall again into condemnation. But this is not the case of them who now 'are in Christ Jesus', who now believe in his name. For so long as they believe and walk after the Spirit neither God condemns them nor their own heart.

4. They are not condemned, secondly, for any present sins, for now transgressing the commandments of God. For they do not transgress them; they do not 'walk after the flesh, but after the Spirit'. This is the continual proof of their 'love of God, that they keep his commandments': even as St. John bears witness, 'Whosoever is born of God doth not commit sin. For his seed remaineth in him, and he cannot sin, because he is born of God;' he cannot so long as that seed of God, that loving, holy faith, remaineth in him. So long as 'he keepeth himself' herein 'that wicked one toucheth him not.' Now it is evident he is not condemned for the sins which he doth not commit at all. They therefore who are thus 'led by the Spirit are not under the law' (Gal. 5:18): not under the curse or condemnation of it, for it condemns none but those who break it. Thus that law of God, 'Thou shalt not steal,' condemns none but those who do steal. Thus, 'Remember the sabbath day to keep it holy' condemns those only who do not keep it holy. But 'against' the fruits of the Spirit 'there is no law' (Gal. 5:23). As the Apostle more largely declares in those memorable words of his former Epistle to Timothy, 'We know that the law is good if a man use it lawfully; knowing this' (if while he uses the law of God, in order either to convince or direct, he know and remember this), ὅτι δικαίῳ νόμος οὐ κεῖται (not 'that the law is not made for a righteous man', but) 'that the law does not lie against a righteous man' (it has no force against him, no power to condemn him), 'but against the lawless and disobedient, against the ungodly and sinners, against the unholy and profane; . . . according to the glorious gospel of the blessed God' (1 Tim. 1:8-9, 11).

5. They are not condemned, thirdly, for inward sin, even though it does now remain. That the corruption of nature does still remain, even in those who are the children of God

by faith; that they have in them the seeds of pride and vanity, of anger, lust and evil desire, yea, sin of every kind, is too plain to be denied, being matter of daily experience. And on this account it is that St. Paul, speaking to those whom he had just before witnessed to be 'in Christ Jesus' (1 Cor. 1:2), to have been 'called of God into the fellowship (or participation) of his Son Jesus Christ' (1 Cor. 1:9), yet declares, 'Brethren, I could not speak unto you as unto spiritual, but as unto carnal; even as unto babes in Christ' (1 Cor. 3:1). 'Babes in Christ'—so we see they were 'in Christ'; they were believers in a low degree. And yet how much of sin remained in them! Of that 'carnal mind' which 'is not subject to the law of God'!

6. And yet for all this they are not condemned. Although they feel the flesh, the evil nature in them; although they are more sensible day by day that their 'heart *is* deceitful, and desperately wicked'; yet so long as they do not yield thereto, so long as they give no place to the devil, so long as they maintain a continual war with all sin, with pride, anger, desire, so that the flesh hath not dominion over them, but they still 'walk after the Spirit': there is 'no condemnation to them which are in Christ Jesus'. God is well-pleased with their sincere though imperfect obedience; and they 'have confidence toward God', knowing they are his 'by the Spirit which he hath given them' (1 John 3:24).

7. Nay, fourthly, although they are continually convinced of sin cleaving to all they do; although they are conscious of not fulfilling the perfect law, either in their thoughts, or words, or works; although they know they do not love the Lord their God with all their heart, and mind, and soul, and strength; although they feel more or less of pride or self-will stealing in and mixing with their best duties; although even in their more immediate intercourse with God, when they assemble themselves with the great congregation, and when they pour out their souls in secret to him who seeth all the thoughts and intents of the heart, they are continually ashamed of their wandering thoughts, or of the deadness and dullness of their affections—yet there is no condemnation to them still, either from God or from their own heart. The consideration of these manifold defects only gives them a deeper sense that they have always need of that blood of sprinkling which speaks for them in the ears of God, and that advocate with the Father who 'ever liveth to make intercession for them.' So far are these from driving them away from him in whom they have believed, that they rather drive them the closer to him, whom they feel the want of every moment. And at the same time, the deeper sense they have of this want the more earnest desire do they feel, and the more diligent they are, as they 'have received the Lord Jesus, so to walk in him'.

8. They are not condemned, fifthly, for 'sins of infirmity', as they are usually called. (Perhaps it were advisable rather to call them *infirmities,* that we may not seem to give any countenance to sin, or to extenuate it in any degree by thus coupling it with infirmity.) But if we must retain so ambiguous and dangerous an expression, by 'sins of infirmity' I would mean such involuntary failings as the saying a thing we believe true, though in fact it prove to be false; or the hurting our neighbour without knowing or designing it, perhaps when we designed to do him good. Though these are deviations from the holy and acceptable and perfect will of God, yet they are not properly sins, nor do they bring any guilt on the conscience of 'them which are in Christ Jesus'. They separate not between

God and them, neither intercept the light of his countenance, as being no ways inconsistent with their general character of 'walking not after the flesh, but after the Spirit'.

9. Lastly, 'there is no condemnation' to them for anything whatever which it is not in their power to help; whether it be of an inward or outward nature, and whether it be doing something or leaving something undone. For instance, the Lord's Supper is to be administered, but you do not partake thereof. Why do you not? You are confined by sickness; therefore you cannot help omitting it—and for the same reason you are not condemned. There is no guilt, because there is no choice. As there is 'a willing mind, it is accepted, according to that a man hath, not according to that he hath not'.

10. A believer indeed may sometimes be *grieved* because he cannot do what his soul longs for. He may cry out, when he is detained from worshipping God in the great congregation, 'Like as the hart panteth after the water brooks, so panteth my soul after thee, O God. My soul is athirst for God, yea even for the living God. When shall I come to appear in the presence of God?' He may earnestly desire (only still saying in his heart, 'Not as I will, but as thou wilt') to 'go again with the multitude, and bring them forth into the house of God'. But still, if he cannot go, he feels no condemnation, no guilt, no sense of God's displeasure; but can cheerfully yield up those desires with, 'O my soul, put thy trust in God: for I will yet give him thanks, who is the help of my countenance and my God.'

11. It is more difficult to determine concerning those which are usually styled 'sins of surprise': as when one who commonly in patience possesses his soul on a sudden and violent temptation speaks or acts in a manner not consistent with the royal law, 'Thou shalt love thy neighbour as thyself.' Perhaps it is not easy to fix a general rule concerning transgressions of this nature. We cannot say either that men are, or that they are not, condemned for sins of surprise in general. But it seems whenever a believer is by surprise overtaken in a fault there is more or less condemnation as there is more or less concurrence of his will. In proportion as a sinful desire or word or action is more or less voluntary, so we may conceive God is more or less displeased, and there is more or less guilt upon the soul.

12. But if so, then there may be some sins of surprise which bring much guilt and condemnation. For in some instances our being surprised is owing to some wilful and culpable neglect; or to a sleepiness of soul which might have been prevented, or shaken off before the temptation came. A man may be previously warned, either of God or man, that trials and danger are at hand, and yet may say in his heart, 'A little more slumber, a little more folding of the hands to rest.' Now if such an one afterwards fall, though unawares, into the snare which he might have avoided, that he fell unawares is no excuse—he might have foreseen and have shunned the danger. The falling even by surprise, in such an instance as this, is in effect a wilful sin; and as such must expose the sinner to condemnation both from God and his own conscience.

13. On the other hand, there may be sudden assaults either from the world, or the god of this world, and frequently from our own evil hearts, which we did not, and hardly could foresee. And by these even a believer, while weak in faith, may possibly be borne down, suppose into a degree of anger, or thinking evil of another, with scarce any concurrence of his will. Now in such a case the jealous God would undoubtedly show him that

he had done foolishly. He would be convinced of having swerved from the perfect law, from the mind which was in Christ, and consequently *grieved* with a godly sorrow, and lovingly *ashamed* before God. Yet need he not come into condemnation. God layeth not folly to his charge, but hath compassion upon him, even 'as a father pitieth his own children'. And his heart condemneth him not; in the midst of that sorrow and shame he can still say, 'I will trust and not be afraid. For the Lord Jehovah is my strength and my song; he is also become my salvation.'

III.1. It remains only to draw some practical inferences from the preceding considerations.

And, first, if there be 'no condemnation to them which are in Christ Jesus', and 'walk not after the flesh, but after the Spirit', on account of their past sins; then 'Why art thou fearful, O thou of little faith?' Though thy sins were once more in number than the sand, what is that to thee now thou art in Christ Jesus? 'Who shall lay anything to the charge of God's elect? It is God that justifieth: who is he that condemneth?' All the sins thou hast committed from thy youth up until the hour when thou wast 'accepted in the Beloved' are driven away as chaff, are gone, are lost, swallowed up, remembered no more. Thou art now 'born of the Spirit'; wilt thou be troubled or afraid for what was done before thou wert born? Away with thy fears! Thou art not called to fear, but to the 'spirit of love and of a sound mind'. Know thy calling. Rejoice in God thy Saviour, and give thanks to God thy Father through him.

2. Wilt thou say, 'But I have again committed sin, since I had redemption through his blood; and therefore it is that "I abhor myself, and repent in dust and ashes"'? It is meet thou shouldst abhor thyself; and it is God who hath wrought thee to this selfsame thing. But dost thou now believe? Hath he again enabled thee to say, 'I know that my Redeemer liveth'; 'and the life which I now live, I live by faith in the Son of God'? Then that faith again cancels all that is past, and there is no condemnation to thee. At whatsoever time thou truly believest in the name of the Son of God, all thy sins antecedent to that hour vanish away as the morning dew. Now, then, 'Stand thou fast in the liberty wherewith Christ hath made thee free.' He hath once more made thee free from the power of sin, as well as from the guilt and punishment of it. O 'be not entangled again with the yoke of bondage'! Neither the vile, devilish bondage of sin, of evil desires, evil tempers, or words, or works, the most grievous yoke on this side hell; nor the bondage of slavish tormenting fear, of guilt and self-condemnation.

3. But, secondly, do all they which abide 'in Christ Jesus walk not after the flesh, but after the Spirit'? Then we cannot but infer that whosoever now committeth sin hath no part or lot in this matter. He is even now condemned by his own heart. But 'if our heart condemn us', if our own conscience beareth witness that we are guilty, undoubtedly God doth; for he 'is greater than our heart, and knoweth all things'; so that we cannot deceive him, if we can ourselves. And think not to say, 'I was justified once; my sins were once forgiven me.' I know not that; neither will I dispute whether they were or no. Perhaps, at this distance of time, 'tis next to impossible to know with any tolerable degree of certainty

whether that was a true, genuine work of God, or whether thou didst only deceive thy own soul. But this I know with the utmost degree of certainty, 'He that committeth sin is of the devil.' Therefore thou art of thy father the devil. It cannot be denied; for the works of thy father thou dost. O flatter not thyself with vain hopes. Say not to thy soul, 'Peace, peace!' For there is no peace. Cry aloud! Cry unto God out of the deep, if haply he may hear thy voice. Come unto him as at first, as wretched and poor, as sinful, miserable, blind, and naked. And beware thou suffer thy soul to take no rest till his pardoning love be again revealed, till he 'heal thy backslidings', and fill thee again with the 'faith that worketh by love'.

4. Thirdly, is there no condemnation to them which 'walk after the Spirit' by reason of *inward sin* still remaining, so long as they do not give way thereto; nor by reason of *sin cleaving* to all they do? Then fret not thyself because of ungodliness, though it still remain in thy heart. Repine not because thou still comest short of the glorious image of God; nor yet because pride, self-will, or unbelief, cleave to all thy words and works. And be not afraid to know all the evil of thy heart, to know thyself as also thou art known. Yea, desire of God that thou mayst not think of thyself more highly than thou oughtest to think. Let thy continual prayer be:

> Show me, as my soul can bear,
> The depth of inbred sin:
> All the unbelief declare,
> The pride that lurks within!

But when he heareth thy prayer, and unveils thy heart, when he shows thee throughly what spirit thou art of; then beware that thy faith fail thee not, that thou suffer not thy shield to be torn from thee. Be abased. Be humbled in the dust. See thyself nothing, less than nothing, and vanity. But still, 'let not thy heart be troubled, neither let it be afraid.' Still hold fast, 'I', even I, 'have an advocate with the Father, Jesus Christ the righteous.' And 'as the heavens are higher than the earth, so is his love higher than even my sins.' Therefore God is merciful to thee a sinner! Such a sinner as thou art! God is love; and Christ hath died. Therefore the Father himself loveth thee. Thou art his child. Therefore he will withhold from thee no manner of thing that is good. Is it good that the whole body of sin which is now crucified in thee should be destroyed? It shall be done. Thou shalt be 'cleansed from all filthiness both of flesh and spirit'. Is it good that nothing should remain in thy heart but the pure love of God alone? Be of good cheer! 'Thou shalt love the Lord thy God with all thy heart and mind and soul and strength.' 'Faithful is he that hath promised, who also will do it.' It is thy part patiently to continue in the work of faith, and in the labour of love; and in cheerful peace, in humble confidence, with calm, and resigned, and yet earnest expectation to wait till 'the zeal of the Lord of Hosts shall perform this'.

5. Fourthly, if they that 'are in Christ and walk after the Spirit' are not condemned for *sins of infirmity*, as neither for *involuntary failings*, nor for anything whatever which they are not able to help; then beware, O thou that hast faith in his blood, that Satan

herein 'gain no advantage over thee'. Thou art still foolish and weak, blind and ignorant; more weak than any words can express, more foolish than it can yet enter into thy heart to conceive, knowing nothing yet as thou oughtest to know. Yet let not all thy weakness and folly, or any fruit thereof which thou art not yet able to avoid, shake thy faith, thy filial trust in God, or disturb thy peace or joy in the Lord. The rule which some give as to wilful sins, and which in that case may perhaps be dangerous, is undoubtedly wise and safe if it be applied only to the case of weakness and infirmities. Art thou fallen, O man of God? Yet do not lie there, fretting thyself and bemoaning thy weakness; but meekly say, 'Lord, I shall fall thus every moment unless thou uphold me with thy hand.' And then, arise! Leap and walk. Go on thy way. 'Run with patience the race set before thee.'

6. Lastly, since a believer need not come into condemnation, even though he be *surprised* into what his soul abhors (suppose his being surprised is not owing to any carelessness or wilful neglect of his own); if thou who believest art thus overtaken in a fault, then grieve unto the Lord: it shall be a precious balm. Pour out thy heart before him, and show him of thy trouble. And pray with all thy might to him who is 'touched with the feeling of thy infirmities' that he would stablish and strengthen and settle thy soul, and suffer thee to fall no more. But still he condemneth thee not. Wherefore shouldst thou fear? Thou hast no need of any 'fear that hath torment'. Thou shalt love him that loveth thee, and it sufficeth: more love will bring more strength. And as soon as thou lovest him with all thy heart thou shall be 'perfect and entire, lacking nothing'. Wait in peace for that hour when 'the God of peace shall sanctify thee wholly, so that thy whole spirit and soul and body may be preserved blameless unto the coming of our Lord Jesus Christ'!

20. THE WITNESS OF THE SPIRIT, I

1746

An Introductory Comment

In this second of five sermons that treat some aspect of Christian assurance, Wesley expressed this vital doctrine in a way that steers a middle course between "enthusiasm" or fanaticism on the one hand and "rationalism" on the other (O, 1:268). Emboldened by his "great experience of realized salvation" (S, 1:200) at Aldersgate, Wesley considered the sources of the witness of the Holy Spirit as found in the works of Chrysostom, Origen, Athanasius, and Augustine as well as in the Liturgy and Homilies of the Church of England (B, 92). Though the Anglican Articles themselves were nevertheless vague in this regard (Article XVII, for example, simply refers to "sons of God by adoption") as Sugden pointed out (S, 1:200), Bishop Pearson's *Exposition of the Creed* clearly referred to a direct witness of the Spirit (S, 1:200).

Though Wesley modified his views on Christian assurance in 1739 and during the early 1740s (throwing off some of the unreasonable expectations of the English Moravians), he nevertheless affirmed throughout the remainder of his ministry that the witness of the Holy Spirit, affirmed by the Apostle Paul in Romans 8:16, the text of this sermon, is the *common* privilege of the children of God. Indeed, not only did Wesley distinguish the spirit of bondage from the Spirit of adoption in this sermon, but he also pointed out in his notes on this text, produced in 1755, that the Spirit bears witness "with the spirit of every true believer" (NT, Rom. 8:16).

Moreover, this first discourse suggests that Wesley's theory of religious knowledge was far more sophisticated than that of some of his Anglican peers. In this context at least Outler affirmed that Wesley was frankly "intuitionist" (O, 1:267). Indeed, as to the manner of the direct witness of the Holy Spirit, Wesley exclaimed it "is too wonderful and excellent for me" (O, 1:276). Again, "He . . . cannot explain it to one who hath [it] not" (O, 1:283).

The Witness of the Spirit, I

I. 1. In every believer there is both the testimony of God's Spirit and ours
   2. The foundation is in the text describing the marks of the children of God
      A. If people are led into holy tempers or actions they are the sons of God
   3. Agreeable to this are the declarations of John in his first epistle
   4. Those who have these marks are the children of God
   5. But how does it appear that we have these marks?
      A. How does it appear that you are alive?
      B. By this same consciousness you know if your soul is alive to God
   6. This is properly called the testimony of our own spirit, or of our conscience
   7. But what is the testimony of God's Spirit which is conjoined to this?
      A. The testimony of the Spirit is an inward impression on the soul
   8. The testimony of the Spirit of God must be antecedent to our own
   9. We love God because God first loved us
   10. It is God working in us that clearly shows what God has wrought
   11. We perceive that we are children of God when we love and rejoice in God
   12. I will not attempt to explain how the divine testimony is manifested

II. 1. God's Spirit and our spirit may be distinguished
   2. How is this testimony of God's Spirit and our spirit to be distinguished?
   3. The Holy Scriptures abound with marks whereby they may be distinguished
   4. By those marks, one who presumes the gift of God can know he believes a lie
   5. Again, the Scriptures describe being born of God
   6. By these marks may we easily distinguish a child of God from a self-deceiver
   7. A true lover of God hastens to do God's will on earth as it is done in heaven
   8. If you do not bear those marks, you are a self-deceiver
   9. But how may one who has the real witness distinguish it from falsehood?
      A. The difference is immediately perceived by our spiritual senses
   10. Giving a more philosophical answer is a demand that cannot be answered
   11. He who has the witness cannot explain it to one who does not
   12. But how shall I know that my spiritual senses are rightly disposed?
   13. By these fruits you can distinguish God's voice from the devil's delusion
   14. Thanks be unto God for his unspeakable gift

Sermon 10: The Witness of the Spirit, I, 1746

Romans 8:16

The Spirit itself beareth witness with our spirit,
that we are the children of God.

1. How many vain men, not understanding what they speak, neither whereof they affirmed, have wrested this Scripture to the great loss if not the destruction of their souls! How many have mistaken the voice of their own imagination for this 'witness of the Spirit' of God, and thence idly presumed they were the children of God while they were doing the works of the devil! These are truly and properly *enthusiasts*; and, indeed, in the worst sense of the word. But with what difficulty are they convinced thereof, especially if they have drank deep into that spirit of error! All endeavours to bring them to the knowledge of themselves they will then account 'fighting against God'. And that vehemence and impetuosity of spirit which they call 'contending earnestly for the faith' sets them so far above all the usual methods of conviction that we may well say, 'With men it is impossible.'

2. Who can then be surprised if many reasonable men, seeing the dreadful effects of this delusion, and labouring to keep at the utmost distance from it, should sometimes lean toward another extreme? If they are not forward to believe any who speak of having this witness concerning which others have so grievously erred; if they are almost ready to set all down for 'enthusiasts' who use the expressions which have been so terribly abused? Yea, if they should question whether the witness or testimony here spoken of be the privilege of *ordinary* Christians, and not rather one of those *extraordinary* gifts which they suppose belonged only to the apostolic age?

3. But is there any necessity laid upon us of running either into one extreme or the other? May we not steer a middle course? Keep a sufficient distance from that spirit of error and enthusiasm without denying the gift of God and giving up the great privilege of his children? Surely we may. In order thereto, let us consider, in the presence and fear of God,

First: What is this 'witness (or testimony) of our spirit'? What is the 'testimony of God's Spirit'? And how does he 'bear witness with our spirit that we are the children of God'?

Secondly: How is this joint testimony of God's Spirit and our own clearly and solidly distinguished from the presumption of a natural mind, and from the delusion of the devil?

I.1. Let us first consider, what is the 'witness' or 'testimony of our spirit'? But here I cannot but desire all those who are for swallowing up the testimony of the Spirit of God in the rational testimony of our own spirit to observe that in this text the Apostle is so far from speaking of the testimony of our own spirit *only*, that it may be questioned whether he speaks of it *at all*—whether he does not speak *only* of the testimony of God's Spirit. It does not appear but the original text may fairly be understood thus. The Apostle had just said, in the preceding verse, 'Ye have received the Spirit of adoption, whereby we cry, Abba, Father,' and immediately subjoins, Αὐτὸ τὸ πνεῦμα (some copies read τὸ αὐτὸ πνεῦμα) συμμαρτυρεῖ τῷ πνεύματι ἡμῶν, ὅτι ἐσμὲν τέκνα θεοῦ; which may be translated, 'The same Spirit beareth witness to our spirit that we are the children of God' (the preposition σύν only denoting that he witnesses this *at the same time* that he enables us to cry, 'Abba, Father!'). But I contend not; seeing so many other texts, with the experience of all real Christians, sufficiently evince that there is in every believer both the testimony of God's Spirit, and the testimony of his own, that he is a child of God.

2. With regard to the latter, the foundation thereof is laid in those numerous texts of Scripture which describe the marks of the children of God; and that so plain that he which runneth may read them. These are also collected together, and placed in the strongest light, by many both ancient and modern writers. If any need farther light he may receive it by attending on the ministry of God's Word, by meditating thereon before God in secret, and by conversing with those who have the knowledge of his ways. And by the reason or understanding that God has given him—which religion was designed not to extinguish, but to perfect, according to that [word] of the Apostle, 'Brethren, be not children in understanding; in malice (or wickedness) be ye children; but in understanding be ye men' (1 Cor. 14:20). Every man applying those scriptural marks to himself may know whether he is a child of God. Thus if he know, first, 'As many as are led by the Spirit of God' into all holy tempers and actions, 'they are the sons of God' (for which he has the infallible assurance of Holy Writ); secondly, I am thus 'led by the Spirit of God'—he will easily conclude, 'Therefore I am a "son of God".'

3. Agreeable to this are all those plain declarations of St. John in his First Epistle, 'Hereby we know that we do know him, if we keep his commandments' (1 John 2:3). 'Whoso keepeth his word, in him verily is the love of God perfected; hereby know we that we are in him' (1 John 2:5)—that we are indeed the children of God. 'If ye know that he is righteous, ye know that everyone that doth righteousness is born of him' (1 John 2:29). 'We know that we have passed from death unto life, because we love the brethren' (1 John 3:14). 'Hereby we know that we are of the truth, and shall assure our hearts before him;' namely, because we 'love' one another not 'in word, neither in tongue; but in deed and in truth' (1 John 3:18). 'Hereby know we that we dwell in him, . . . because he hath given us of his (loving) Spirit' (1 John 4:13). And, 'Hereby we know that he abideth in us, by the (obedient) spirit which he hath given us' (1 John 3:24).

4. It is highly probable there never were any children of God, from the beginning of the world unto this day, who were farther advanced in the grace of God and the knowledge of our Lord Jesus Christ than the Apostle John at the time when he wrote these words, and the 'fathers in Christ' to whom he wrote. Notwithstanding which, it is evident both the Apostle himself and all those pillars in God's temple were very far from despising these marks of their being the children of God; and that they applied them to their own souls for the confirmation of their faith. Yet all this is no other than rational evidence: the 'witness of our spirit', our reason or understanding. It all resolves into this: those who have these marks, they are the children of God. But we have these marks: therefore we are children of God.

5. But how does it appear that we have these marks? This is a question which still remains. How does it appear that we do love God and our neighbour? And that we keep

his commandments? Observe that the meaning of the question is, How does it appear to *ourselves*—not to *others*. I would ask him then that proposes this question, How does it appear to you that you are alive? And that you are now in ease and not in pain? Are you not immediately conscious of it? By the same immediate consciousness you will know if your soul is alive to God; if you are saved from the pain of proud wrath, and have the ease of a meek and quiet spirit. By the same means you cannot but perceive if you love, rejoice, and delight in God. By the same you must be directly assured if you love your neighbour as yourself; if you are kindly affectioned to all mankind, and full of gentleness and longsuffering. And with regard to the outward mark of the children of God, which is (according to St. John) the keeping his commandments, you undoubtedly know in your own breast if, by the grace of God, it belongs to you. Your conscience informs you from day to day if you do not take the name of God within your lips unless with seriousness and devotion, with reverence and godly fear; if you remember the sabbath day to keep it holy; if you honour your father and mother; if you do to all as you would they should do unto you; if you possess your body in sanctification and honour; and if, whether you eat or drink, you are temperate therein, and do all to the glory of God.

6. Now this is properly the 'testimony of our own spirit', even the testimony of our conscience, that God hath given us to be holy of heart, and holy in outward conversation. It is a consciousness of our having received, in and by the Spirit of adoption, the tempers mentioned in the Word of God as belonging to his adopted children; even a loving heart toward God and toward all mankind, hanging with childlike confidence on God our Father, desiring nothing but him, casting all our care upon him, and embracing every child of man with earnest, tender affection, so as to be ready to lay down our life for our brother, as Christ laid down his life for us—a consciousness that we are inwardly conformed by the Spirit of God to the image of his Son, and that we walk before him in justice, mercy, and truth; doing the things which are pleasing in his sight.

7. But what is that testimony of God's Spirit which is superadded to and conjoined with this? How does he 'bear witness with our spirit that we are the children of God'? It is hard to find words in the language of men to explain 'the deep things of God'. Indeed there are none that will adequately express what the children of God experience. But perhaps one might say (desiring any who are taught of God to correct, to soften or strengthen the expression), the testimony of the Spirit is an inward impression on the soul, whereby the Spirit of God directly 'witnesses to my spirit that I am a child of God'; that Jesus Christ hath loved me, and given himself for me; that all my sins are blotted out, and I, even I, am reconciled to God.

8. That this 'testimony of the Spirit of God' must needs, in the very nature of things, be antecedent to the 'testimony of our own spirit' may appear from this single consideration: we must be holy of heart and holy in life before we can be conscious that we are so, before we can have 'the testimony of our spirit' that we are inwardly and outwardly holy. But we must love God before we can be holy at all; this being the root of all holiness. Now we cannot love God till we know he loves us: 'We love him, because he first loved us.' And we cannot know his pardoning love to us till his Spirit witnesses it to our spirit. Since therefore this 'testimony of his Spirit' must precede the love of God and all holiness,

of consequence it must precede our inward consciousness thereof, or the 'testimony of our spirit' concerning them.

9. Then, and not till then—when the Spirit of God beareth that witness to our spirit, 'God hath loved thee and given his own Son to be the propitiation for thy sins;' 'the Son of God hath loved thee, and hath washed thee from thy sins in his blood'—'we love God, because he first loved us,' and for his sake we 'love our brother also'. And of this we cannot but be conscious to ourselves: we 'know the things that are freely given to us of God'; we know that we love God and keep his commandments; and hereby also 'we know that we are of God.' This is that testimony of our own spirit which, so long as we continue to love God and keep his commandments, continues joined with the testimony of God's Spirit, 'that we are the children of God'.

10. Not that I would by any means be understood by anything which has been spoken concerning it to exclude the operation of the Spirit of God, even from the 'testimony of our own spirit'. In no wise. It is he that not only worketh in us every manner of thing that is good, but also shines upon his own work, and clearly shows what he has wrought. Accordingly this is spoken of by St. Paul as one great end of our receiving the Spirit, 'that we may know the things which are freely given to us of God'; that he may strengthen the testimony of our conscience touching our 'simplicity and godly sincerity', and give us to discern in a fuller and stronger light that we now do the things which please him.

11. Should it still be inquired, 'How does the Spirit of God "bear witness with our spirit that we are the children of God" so as to exclude all doubt, and evince the reality of our sonship?'—the answer is clear from what has been observed above. And, first, as to the witness of our spirit: the soul as intimately and evidently perceives when it loves, delights, and rejoices in God, as when it loves and delights in anything on earth; and it can no more doubt whether it loves, delights, and rejoices, or no, than whether it exists, or no. If therefore this be just reasoning:

He that now loves God—that delights and rejoices in him with an humble joy, an holy delight, and an obedient love—is a child of God;

But I thus love, delight, and rejoice in God;
Therefore I am a child of God;

then a Christian can in no wise doubt of his being a child of God. Of the former proposition he has as full an assurance as he has that the Scriptures are of God. And of his thus loving God he has an inward proof, which is nothing short of self-evidence. Thus the 'testimony of our own spirit' is with the most intimate conviction manifested to our hearts; in such a manner as beyond all reasonable doubt to evince the reality of our sonship.

12. The *manner* how the divine testimony is manifested to the heart I do not take upon me to explain. 'Such knowledge is too wonderful and excellent for me; I cannot attain unto it.' 'The wind bloweth; and I hear the sound thereof'; but I cannot 'tell how it cometh, or whither it goeth'. As no one knoweth the things of a man save the spirit of a man that is in him, so the *manner* of the things of God knoweth no one save the Spirit of God. But the fact we know: namely, that the Spirit of God does give a believer such a testimony of his adoption that while it is present to the soul he can no more doubt the

reality of his sonship than he can doubt of the shining of the sun while he stands in the full blaze of his beams.

II.1. How this joint testimony of God's Spirit and our spirit may be clearly and solidly distinguished from the presumption of a natural mind, and from the delusion of the devil, is the next thing to be considered. And it highly imports all who desire the salvation of God to consider it with the deepest attention, as they would not deceive their own souls. An error in this is generally observed to have the most fatal consequences; the rather, because he that errs seldom discovers his mistake till it is too late to remedy it.

2. And, first, How is this testimony to be distinguished from the presumption of a natural mind? It is certain, one who was never convinced of sin is always ready to flatter himself, and to think of himself, especially in spiritual things, more highly than he ought to think. And hence it is in no wise strange if one who is vainly puffed up by his fleshly mind, when he hears of this privilege of true Christians, among whom he undoubtedly ranks himself, should soon work himself up into a persuasion that he is already possessed thereof. Such instances now abound in the world, and have abounded in all ages. How then may the real testimony of the Spirit with our spirit be distinguished from this damning presumption?

3. I answer, the Holy Scriptures abound with marks whereby the one may be distinguished from the other. They describe in the plainest manner the circumstances which go before, which accompany, and which follow, the true, genuine testimony of the Spirit of God with the spirit of a believer. Whoever carefully weighs and attends to these will not need to put darkness for light. He will perceive so wide a difference with respect to all these, between the real and the pretended witness of the Spirit, that there will be no danger—I might say, no possibility—of confounding the one with the other.

4. By these, one who vainly presumes on the gift of God might surely know, if he really desired it, that he hath been hitherto 'given up to a strong delusion' and suffered to 'believe a lie'. For the Scriptures lay down those clear, obvious marks as preceding, accompanying, and following that gift, which a little reflection would convince him, beyond all doubt, were never found in his soul. For instance, the Scripture describes repentance, or conviction of sin, as constantly going before this witness of pardon. So, 'Repent; for the kingdom of heaven is at hand' (Matt. 3:2). 'Repent ye, and believe the Gospel' (Mark 1:15). 'Repent, and be baptized every one of you . . . for the remission of sins' (Acts 2:38). 'Repent ye therefore, and be converted, that your sins may be blotted out' (Acts 3:19). In conformity whereto our Church also continually places repentance before pardon or the witness of it: 'He pardoneth and absolveth all them that truly repent and unfeignedly believe his holy gospel.' 'Almighty God . . . hath promised forgiveness of sins to all them who with hearty repentance and true faith turn unto him.' But he is a stranger even to this repentance. He hath never known 'a broken and a contrite heart'. 'The remembrance of his sins' was never 'grievous unto' him, nor 'the burden of them intolerable'. In repeating those words he never meant what he said; he merely paid a compliment to God. And were it only from the want of this previous work of God

he hath too great reason to believe that he hath grasped a mere shadow, and never yet known the real privilege of the sons of God.

5. Again, the Scriptures describe the being born of God, which must precede the witness that we are his children, as a vast and mighty change, a change 'from darkness to light', as well as 'from the power of Satan unto God'; as a 'passing from death unto life', a resurrection from the dead. Thus the Apostle to the Ephesians: 'You hath he quickened, who were dead in trespasses and sins' (Eph. 2:1). And again, 'When we were dead in sins, he hath quickened us together with Christ; . . . and hath raised us up together, and made us sit together in heavenly places in Christ Jesus' (Eph. 2:5, 6). But what knoweth he concerning whom we now speak of any such change as this? He is altogether unacquainted with this whole matter. This is a language which he does not understand. He tells you he always was a Christian. He knows no time when he had need of such a change. By this also, if he give himself leave to think, may he know that he is not born of the Spirit; that he has never yet known God, but has mistaken the voice of nature for the voice of God.

6. But waiving the consideration of whatever he has or has not experienced in time past, by the present marks may we easily distinguish a child of God from a presumptuous self-deceiver. The Scriptures describe that joy in the Lord which accompanies the witness of his Spirit as an humble joy, a joy that abases to the dust; that makes a pardoned sinner cry out, 'I am vile! What am I or my father's house?—Now mine eye seeth thee I abhor myself in dust and ashes!' And wherever lowliness is, there is meekness, patience, gentleness, long-suffering. There is a soft, yielding spirit, a mildness and sweetness, a tenderness of soul which words cannot express. But do these fruits attend that *supposed* testimony of the Spirit in a presumptuous man? Just the reverse. The more confident he is of the favour of God, the more is he lifted up. The more does he exalt himself, the more haughty and assuming is his whole behaviour. The stronger witness he imagines himsel to have, the more overbearing is he to all around him, the more incapable of receiving any reproof, the more impatient of contradiction. Instead of being more meek, and gentle, and teachable, more 'swift to hear, and slow to speak', he is more slow to hear and swift to speak, more unready to learn of anyone, more fiery and vehement in his temper, and eager in his conversation. Yea, perhaps, there will sometimes appear a kind of fierceness in his air, his manner of speaking, his whole deportment, as if he were just going to take the matter out of God's hands, and himself to 'devour the adversaries'.

7. Once more: the Scriptures teach, 'This is the love of God' (the sure mark thereof) 'that we keep his commandments' (1 John 5:3). And our Lord himself saith, 'He that keepeth my commandments, he it is that loveth me' (John 14:21). Love rejoices to obey, to do in every point whatever is acceptable to the Beloved. A true lover of God hastens to do his will on earth as it is done in heaven. But is this the character of the presumptuous pretender to the love of God? Nay, but his love gives him a liberty to disobey, to break, not keep, the commandments of God. Perhaps when he was in fear of the wrath of God he did labour to do his will. But now, looking on himself as 'not under the law', he thinks he is no longer obliged to observe it. He is therefore less zealous of good works, less careful to abstain from evil, less watchful over his own heart, less jealous over his tongue. He is less earnest to deny himself, and to take up his cross daily. In a word, the whole form of

his life is changed since he has fancied himself to be 'at liberty'. He is no longer 'exercising himself unto godliness': 'wrestling not only with flesh and blood, but with principalities and powers', 'enduring hardships', 'agonizing to enter in at the strait gate'. No; he has found an easier way to heaven: a broad, smooth, flowery path, in which he can say to his soul, 'Soul, take thy ease; eat, drink, and be merry.' It follows with undeniable evidence that he has not the true testimony of his own spirit. He cannot be conscious of having those marks which he hath not, that lowliness, meekness, and obedience. Nor yet can the Spirit of the God of truth bear witness to a lie; or testify that he is a child of God when he is manifestly a child of the devil.

8. Discover thyself, thou poor self-deceiver! Thou who art confident of being a child of God; thou who sayest, 'I have the witness in myself,' and therefore defiest all thy enemies. Thou art weighed in the balance and found wanting, even in the balance of the sanctuary. The Word of the Lord hath tried thy soul, and proved thee to be reprobate silver. Thou art not lowly of heart; therefore thou hast not received the Spirit of Jesus unto this day. Thou art not gentle and meek; therefore thy joy is nothing worth: it is not joy in the Lord. Thou dost not keep his commandments; therefore thou lovest him not, neither art thou partaker of the Holy Ghost. It is consequently as certain and as evident as the oracles of God can make it, his Spirit doth not bear witness with thy spirit that thou art a child of God. O cry unto him, that the scales may fall off thine eyes; that thou mayst know thyself as thou art known; that thou mayst receive the sentence of death in thyself, till thou hear the voice that raises the dead, saying, 'Be of good cheer; thy sins are forgiven; thy faith hath made thee whole.'

9. 'But how may one who has the real witness in himself distinguish it from presumption?' How, I pray, do you distinguish day from night? How do you distinguish light from darkness? Or the light of a star, or glimmering taper, from the light of the noonday sun? Is there not an inherent, obvious, essential difference between the one and the other? And do you not immediately and directly perceive that difference, provided your senses are rightly disposed? In like manner, there is an inherent, essential difference between spiritual light and spiritual darkness; and between the light wherewith the sun of righteousness shines upon our heart, and that glimmering light which arises only from 'sparks of our own kindling'. And this difference also is immediately and directly perceived, if our spiritual senses are rightly disposed.

10. To require a more minute and philosophical account of the *manner* whereby we distinguish these, and of the *criteria* or intrinsic marks whereby we know the voice of God, is to make a demand which can never be answered; no, not by one who has the deepest knowledge of God. Suppose, when Paul answered before Agrippa, the wise Roman had said: 'Thou talkest of hearing the voice of the Son of God. How dost thou know it was his voice? By what *criteria*, what intrinsic marks, dost thou know the voice of God? Explain to me the *manner* of distinguishing this from a human or angelic voice.' Can you believe the Apostle himself would have once attempted to answer so idle a demand? And yet doubtless the moment he heard that voice he knew it was the voice of God. But *how* he knew this who is able to explain? Perhaps neither man nor angel.

11. To come yet closer: suppose God were now to speak to any soul, 'Thy sins are forgiven thee.' He must be willing that soul should know his voice; otherwise he would speak in vain. And he is able to effect this, for whenever he wills, to do is present with him. And he does effect it. That soul is absolutely assured, 'This voice is the voice of God.' But yet he who hath that witness in himself cannot explain it to one who hath not. Nor indeed is it to be expected that he should. Were there any natural medium to prove, or natural method to explain the things of God to unexperienced men, then the natural man might discern and know the things of the Spirit of God. But this is utterly contrary to the assertion of the Apostle that 'he cannot know them, because they are spiritually discerned;' even by spiritual senses which the natural man hath not.

12. 'But how shall I know that my spiritual senses are rightly disposed?' This also is a question of vast importance; for if a man mistake in this he may run on in endless error and delusion. 'And how am I assured that this is not my case; and that I do not mistake the voice of the Spirit?' Even by the 'testimony of your own spirit'; by 'the answer of a good conscience toward God'. By the fruits which he hath wrought in your spirit you shall know the 'testimony of the Spirit of God'. Hereby you shall know that you are in no delusion; that you have not deceived your own soul. The immediate fruits of the Spirit ruling in the heart are 'love, joy, peace'; 'bowels of mercies, humbleness of mind, meekness, gentleness, long-suffering'. And the outward fruits are the doing good to all men, the doing no evil to any, and the walking in the light—a zealous, uniform obedience to all the commandments of God.

13. By the same fruits shall you distinguish this voice of God from any delusion of the devil. That proud spirit cannot humble thee before God. He neither can nor would soften thy heart and melt it first into earnest mourning after God and then into filial love. It is not the adversary of God and man that enables thee to love thy neighbour; or to put on meekness, gentleness, patience, temperance, and the whole armour of God. He is not divided against himself, or a destroyer of sin, his own work. No; it is none but the Son of God who cometh to 'destroy the works of the devil'. As surely therefore as holiness is of God, and as sin is the work of the devil, so surely the witness thou hast in thyself is not of Satan, but of God.

14. Well then mayst thou say, 'Thanks be unto God for his unspeakable gift!' Thanks be unto God who giveth me to 'know in whom I have believed'; who 'hath sent forth the Spirit of his Son into my heart, crying Abba, Father', and even now 'bearing witness with my spirit that I am a child of God'! And see that not only thy lips, but thy life show forth his praise. He hath sealed thee for his own; 'glorify him then in thy body and thy spirit which are' his. Beloved, if thou 'hast this hope in thyself, purify thyself as he is pure'. While thou 'beholdest what manner of love the Father hath given thee, that thou shouldst be called a child of God', 'cleanse thyself from all filthiness of flesh and Spirit, perfecting holiness in the fear of God;' and let all thy thoughts, words, and works be a spiritual sacrifice, holy, acceptable to God through Christ Jesus!

21. THE WITNESS OF THE SPIRIT, II

1767

An Introductory Comment

More than twenty years after Wesley published his first discourse on the witness of the Spirit, he brought forth a second. Several Anglicans such as Edmund Gibson, bishop of London, Thomas Herring, archbishop of York, and Richard Smalbroke, bishop of Lichfield and Coventry (O, 1:267), had been critical of Wesley's theological emphases in this area. Moreover, many of the anti-Methodist publications of the period written by such people as John Parkhurst, biblical lexicographer, Theophilus Evans, rector at Llangamarch, Brecknockshire, and William Warburton, bishop of Gloucester, targeted the whole matter of assurance. "Anglicans tended to interpret assurance," as Outler pointed out, "in terms of their *hope* of salvation rather than an inner certainty" (O, 1:286n). Indeed, Susanna Wesley had "scarce heard such a thing mentioned" (S, 1:200) until she was steeped in years. Wesley, therefore, was determined to underscore that the witness of the Holy Spirit, promised in Romans 8:16, the text of this sermon as well, was immediate *and* direct (B, 92).

Much of this present sermon treats the numerous objections raised against the specific doctrine of Christian assurance in seven key refutations. Well aware of the fanaticism of people like William Cudworth and James Relly, Wesley developed a balanced view, so typical of his theological style, that avoided lifeless formality *and* debasing excess. However, so earnest was Wesley to uphold the direct witness of the Spirit, in the face of its distortions, that he maintained whoever denies this teaching in effect denies justification by faith (O, 1:292). Such an emphasis is also evident in Wesley's affirmation that the direct witness must be *antecedent* to the witness of our own spirit (O, 1:289–90). He concluded this "apologetic" sermon with two key inferences that embraced the fruit of the Spirit (indirect evidence) and the direct witness of the Spirit, each in its proper place.

The Witness of the Spirit, II

I. 1. The witness of the Spirit is a peculiar privilege of the children of God
  2. It is necessary to explain and defend this truth from danger
  3. Little on this subject has been written with much clearness
  4. Methodists should be concerned to understand and defend this doctrine

II. 1. The witness of the Spirit is the record that we have eternal life
  2.–3. It is the Spirit witnessing to my spirit that I am a child of God
  4. God works upon the soul by direct or immediate influence
  5. That there is a testimony of the Spirit is acknowledged by all parties
  6. Neither is it questioned whether there is an *indirect* witness
  7. There cannot be any real testimony without the fruit of the Spirit
  8. The point in question is whether there is a *direct* testimony of the Spirit

III. 1. The testimony of our spirit is consciousness of the fruit of the Spirit
  2. Some think the witness of the Spirit is consciousness of our own works
  3. The verse preceding suggests otherwise
  4. God has sent forth the Spirit to enable us to cry, 'Abba, Father'
  5. The testimony of God's Spirit must be antecedent to that of our own Spirit
  6. The experience of the children of God confirms this scriptural doctrine
  7. This is also confirmed by those who are convinced of sin
  8. All who deny the existence of such testimony deny justification by faith
  9. The experience of the children of the world confirms that of God's children

IV. An abundance of objections have been made to this, including:
  1. Experience is not sufficient to prove a doctrine not founded on Scripture
  2. Madmen have imagined they have experienced this
  3.–7. Others insist that the fruit of the Spirit is the direct witness of the Spirit
  8.–10. The direct witness of the Spirit does not secure us from delusions

V. 1.–2. Over against these objections, we have shown that the testimony of the Spirit is an inward impression by which God testifies to believers that they are children of God
  3. Two inferences may be drawn from this:
    A. First, do not rest in a testimony of the Spirit separate from the fruit of it
  4. Second, do not rest in any supposed fruit of the Spirit without its witness

Sermon 11: The Witness of the Spirit, II, 1767

Romans 8:16

The Spirit itself beareth witness with our spirit,
that we are the children of God.

I.1. None who believes the Scriptures to be the Word of God can doubt the *importance* of such a truth as this: a truth revealed therein not once only, not obscurely, not incidentally, but frequently, and that in express terms; but solemnly and of set purpose, as denoting one of the peculiar privileges of the children of God.

2. And it is the more necessary to explain and defend this truth, because there is a danger on the right hand and on the left. If we deny it, there is a danger lest our religion degenerate into mere formality; lest, 'having a form of godliness', we neglect if not 'deny, the power of it'. If we allow it, but do not understand what we allow, we are liable to run into all the wildness of enthusiasm. It is therefore needful in the highest degree to guard those who fear God from both these dangers by a scriptural and rational illustration and confirmation of this momentous truth.

3. It may seem something of this kind is the more needful because so little has been wrote on the subject with any clearness, unless some discourses on the wrong side of the question, which explain it quite away. And it cannot be doubted but these were occasioned, at least in great measure, by the crude, unscriptural, irrational explications of others, who 'knew not what they spake, nor whereof they affirmed'.

4. It more clearly concerns the Methodists, so called, clearly to understand, explain, and defend this doctrine, because it is one grand part of the testimony which God has given them to bear to all mankind. It is by his peculiar blessing upon them in searching the Scriptures, confirmed by the experience of his children, that this great evangelical truth has been recovered, which had been for many years wellnigh lost and forgotten.

II.1. But what is 'the witness of the Spirit'? The original word, μαρτυρία, may be rendered either (as it is in several places) 'the witness', or less ambiguously 'the testimony' or 'the record': so it is rendered in our translation, 'This is the record' (the testimony, the sum of what God testifies in all the inspired writings), 'that God hath given unto us eternal life, and this life is in his Son' (1 John 5:11). The testimony now under consideration is given by the Spirit of God to and with our spirit. He is the person testifying. What he testifies to us is 'that we are the children of God'. The immediate result of this testimony is 'the fruit of the Spirit'; namely, 'love, joy, peace; longsuffering, gentleness, goodness'. And without these the testimony itself cannot continue. For it is inevitably destroyed, not only by the commission of any outward sin, or the omission of known duty, but by giving way to any inward sin—in a word, by whatever grieves the Holy Spirit of God.

2. I observed many years ago:

It is hard to find words in the language of men to explain the deep things of God. Indeed there are none that will adequately express what the Spirit of God works in his children. But perhaps

> one might say (desiring any who are taught of God to correct, soften, or strengthen the expression), by 'the testimony of the Spirit' I mean an inward impression of the soul, whereby the Spirit of God immediately and directly witnesses to my spirit that I am a child of God, that 'Jesus Christ hath loved me, and given himself for me;' that all my sins are blotted out, and I, even I, am reconciled to God. (*Sermons,* Vol. 1 ['The Witness of the Spirit, I'])

3. After twenty years' farther consideration I see no cause to retract any part of this. Neither do I conceive how any of these expressions may be altered so as to make them more intelligible. I can only add, that if any of the children of God will point out any other expressions which are more clear, and more agreeable to the Word of God, I will readily lay these aside.

4. Meantime let it be observed, I do not mean hereby that the Spirit of God testifies this by any outward voice; no, nor always by an inward voice, although he may do this sometimes. Neither do I suppose that he always applies to the heart (though he often may) one or more texts of Scripture. But he so works upon the soul by his immediate influence, and by a strong though inexplicable operation, that the stormy wind and troubled waves subside, and there is a sweet calm; the heart resting as in the arms of Jesus, and the sinner being clearly satisfied that God is reconciled, that all his 'iniquities are forgiven, and his sins covered'.

5. Now what is the matter of dispute concerning this? Not whether there be a witness or testimony of the Spirit? Not whether the Spirit does testify with our spirit that we are the children of God? None can deny this without flatly contradicting the Scripture, and charging a lie upon the God of truth. Therefore that there is a testimony of the Spirit is acknowledged by all parties.

6. Neither is it questioned whether there is an *indirect* witness or testimony that we are the children of God. This is nearly, if not exactly, the same with 'the testimony of a good conscience toward God', and is the result of reason or reflection on what we feel in our own souls. Strictly speaking, it is a conclusion drawn partly from the Word of God, and partly from our own experience. The Word of God says everyone who has the fruit of the Spirit is a child of God. Experience, or inward consciousness, tells me that I have the fruit of the Spirit. And hence I rationally conclude: therefore I am a child of God. This is likewise allowed on all hands, and so is no matter of controversy.

7. Nor do we assert that there can be any real testimony of the Spirit without the fruit of the Spirit. We assert, on the contrary, that the fruit of the Spirit immediately springs from this testimony. Not always, indeed, in the same degree, even when the testimony is first given, and much less afterwards. Neither joy nor peace are always at one stay; no, nor love; as neither is the testimony itself always equally strong and clear.

8. But the point in question is whether there be any *direct testimony* of the Spirit at all; whether there be any other testimony of the Spirit than that which arises from a consciousness of the fruit.

III.1. I believe there is, because that is the plain, natural meaning of the text, 'The Spirit itself beareth witness with our spirit, that we are the children of God.' It is manifest, here are two witnesses mentioned, who together testify the same thing—the Spirit of God, and our own spirit. The late Bishop of London, in his sermon on this text, seems astonished that anyone can doubt of this, which appears upon the very face of the words. Now 'the testimony of our own spirit', says the bishop, is one which is 'the consciousness of our own sincerity'; or, to express the same thing a little more clearly, the consciousness of the fruit of the Spirit. When our spirit is conscious of this—of love, joy, peace, long-suffering, gentleness, goodness—it easily infers from these premises that we are the children of God.

2. It is true, that great man supposes the other witness to be 'the consciousness of our own good works'. This, he affirms, is 'the testimony of God's Spirit'. But this is included in the testimony of our own spirit; yea, and in sincerity, even according to the common sense of the word. So the Apostle: 'Our rejoicing is this, the testimony of our conscience, that in simplicity and godly sincerity [. . .] we have had our conversation in the world:' where, it is plain, sincerity refers to our words and actions at least as much as to our inward dispositions. So that this is not another witness, but the very same that he mentioned before, the consciousness of our good works being only one branch of the consciousness of our sincerity. Consequently here is only one witness still. If therefore the text speaks of two witnesses, one of these is not the consciousness of good works, neither of our sincerity, all this being manifestly contained in 'the testimony of our own spirit'.

3. What then is the other witness? This might easily be learned, if the text itself were not sufficiently clear, from the verse immediately preceding: 'Ye have received, not the spirit of bondage, but the Spirit of adoption, whereby we cry, Abba, Father.' It follows, 'The Spirit itself beareth witness with our spirit, that we are the children of God.'

4. This is farther explained by the parallel text, 'Because ye are sons, God hath sent forth the Spirit of his Son into your hearts, crying Abba, Father' (Gal. 4:6). Is not this something *immediate* and *direct*, not the result of reflection or argumentation? Does not this Spirit cry 'Abba, Father', in our hearts the moment it is given—antecedently to any reflection upon our sincerity; yea, to any reasoning whatsoever? And is not this the plain, natural sense of the words, which strikes anyone as soon as he hears them? All these texts, then, in their most obvious meaning, describe a direct testimony of the Spirit.

5. That 'the testimony of the Spirit of God' must, in the very nature of things, be antecedent to 'the testimony of our own spirit', may appear from this single consideration: we must be holy in heart and life before we can be conscious that we are so. But we must love God before we can be holy at all, this being the root of all holiness. Now we cannot love God till we know he loves us: 'We love him, because he first loved us.' And we cannot know his love to us till his Spirit witnesses it to our spirit. Till then we cannot believe it; we cannot say, 'The life which I now live, I live by faith in the Son of God, who loved me, and gave himself for me.'

> Then, only then we feel
> Our interest in his blood,
> And cry, with joy unspeakable,
> Thou art my Lord, my God.

Since therefore the testimony of his Spirit must precede the love of God and all holiness, of consequence it must precede our consciousness thereof.

6. And here properly comes in, to confirm this scriptural doctrine, the experience of the children of God—the experience not of two or three, not of a few, but of a great multitude which no man can number. It has been confirmed, both in this and in all ages, by 'a cloud of' living and dying 'witnesses'. It is confirmed by *your* experience and *mine.* The Spirit itself bore witness to my spirit that I was a child of God, gave me an *evidence* hereof, and I immediately cried, 'Abba, Father!' And this I did (and so did you) before I reflected on, or was conscious of, any fruit of the Spirit. It was from this testimony received that love, joy, peace, and the whole fruit of the Spirit flowed. First I heard,

'Thy sins are forgiven! Accepted thou art!'
I listened, and heaven sprung up in my heart.

7. But this is confirmed, not only by the experience of the children of God—thousands of whom can declare that they never did know themselves to be in the favour of God till it was directly witnessed to them by his Spirit—but by all those who are convinced of sin, who feel the wrath of God abiding on them. These cannot be satisfied with anything less than a direct testimony from his Spirit that he is 'merciful to their unrighteousness, and remembers their sins and iniquities no more'. Tell any of these, 'You are to know you are a child by reflecting on what he has wrought in you, on your love, joy, and peace;' and will he not immediately reply, 'By all this I know I am a child of the devil. I have no more love to God than the devil has; my carnal mind is enmity against God. I have no joy in the Holy Ghost; my soul is sorrowful even unto death. I have no peace; my heart is a troubled sea; I am all storm and tempest.' And which way can these souls possibly be comforted but by a divine testimony (not that they are good, or sincere, or conformable to the Scripture in heart and life, but) that God 'justifieth the ungodly'—him that, till the moment he is justified, is all ungodly, void of all true holiness? 'Him that worketh not', that worketh nothing that is truly good till he is conscious that he is accepted, 'not for any works of righteousness which he hath done', but by the mere free mercy of God? Wholly and solely for what the Son of God hath done and suffered for him? And can it be otherwise if 'a man is justified by faith, without the works of the law'? If so, what inward or outward goodness can he be conscious of antecedent to his justification? Nay, is not the 'having nothing to pay', that is, the being conscious that 'there dwelleth in us no good thing,' neither inward nor outward goodness, essentially, indispensably necessary before we can be 'justified freely through the redemption that is in Jesus Christ'? Was ever any man justified since his coming into the world, or can any man ever be justified till he is brought to that point,

I give up every plea, beside
'Lord, I am damned—but thou hast died!'

8. Everyone therefore who denies the existence of such a testimony does, in effect, deny justification by faith. It follows that either he never experienced this, either he never was justified, or that he has forgotten (as St. Peter speaks) τοῦ καθαρισμοῦ τῶν πάλαι [αὐτοῦ] ἁμαρτιῶν, 'the purification from his former sins', the experience he then had himself, the manner wherein God wrought in his own soul, when his former sins were blotted out.

9. And the experience even of the children of the world here confirms that of the children of God. Many of these have a desire to please God: some of them take much pains to please him. But do they not, one and all, count it the highest absurdity for any to talk of *knowing* his sins are forgiven? Which of *them* even pretends to any such thing? And yet many of them are conscious of their own sincerity. Many of them undoubtedly have, in a degree, the testimony of their own spirit, a consciousness of their own uprightness. But this brings them no consciousness that they are forgiven, no knowledge that they are the children of God. Yea, the more sincere they are, the more uneasy they generally are for want of knowing it: plainly showing that this cannot be known in a satisfactory manner by the bare testimony of our own spirit, without God's directly testifying that we are his children.

IV. But abundance of objections have been made to this, the chief of which it may be well to consider.

1. It is objected, first, 'Experience is not sufficient to prove a doctrine which is not founded on Scripture.' This is undoubtedly true, and it is an important truth. But it does not affect the present question, for it has been shown that this doctrine is founded on Scripture. Therefore experience is properly alleged to confirm it.

2. 'But madmen, French prophets, and enthusiasts of every kind have imagined they experienced this witness.' They have so, and perhaps not a few of them did, although they did not retain it long. But if they did not, this is no proof at all that others have not experienced it: as a madman's *imagining* himself a king does not prove that there are no *real* kings.

'Nay, many who pleaded strongly for this have utterly decried the Bible.' Perhaps so, but this was no necessary consequence: thousands plead for it who have the highest esteem for the Bible.

'Yea, but many have fatally deceived themselves hereby, and got above all conviction.'

And yet a scriptural doctrine is no worse, though men abuse it to their own destruction.

3. 'But I lay it down as an undoubted truth, the fruit of the Spirit is the witness of the Spirit.' Not undoubted; thousands doubt of, yea flatly deny it: but to let that pass, 'If this witness be sufficient there is no need of any other. But it is sufficient, unless in one of these cases: (1). The *total absence* of the fruit of the Spirit.' And this is the case when the

direct witness is first given. '(2). The *not perceiving it.* But to contend for it in this case is to contend for being in the favour of God and not knowing it.' True, not knowing it at that time any otherwise than by the testimony which is given for that end. And this we do contend for: we contend that the direct witness may shine clear, even while the indirect one is under a cloud.

4. It is objected, secondly: 'the design of the witness contended for is to prove that the profession we make is genuine. But it does not prove this.' I answer, the proving this is not the design of it. It is antecedent to our making any profession at all, but that of being lost, undone, guilty, helpless sinners. It is designed to assure those to whom it is given that they are the children of God; that they are 'justified freely by his grace, through the redemption that is in Jesus Christ'. And this does not suppose that their preceding thoughts, words, and actions are conformable to the rule of the Scripture. It supposes quite the reverse, namely, that they are sinners all over, sinners both in heart and life. Were it otherwise God would 'justify the godly', and their own works would be 'counted to them for righteousness'. And I cannot but fear that a supposition of our being justified by works is at the root of all these objections. For whoever cordially believes that God *imputes* to all that are justified 'righteousness without works', will find no difficulty in allowing the witness of his Spirit preceding the fruit of it.

5. It is objected, thirdly: 'One evangelist says, "Your heavenly Father will give the Holy Spirit to them that ask him." The other evangelist calls the same thing "good gifts", abundantly demonstrating that the Spirit's way of bearing witness is by giving good gifts.' Nay, here is nothing at all about 'bearing witness', either in one text or the other. Therefore till this demonstration is more abundantly demonstrated, I let it stand as it is.

6. It is objected, fourthly: 'The Scripture says, "The tree is known by its fruit;" "Prove all things;" "Try the spirits;" "Examine yourselves."' Most true: therefore let every man who believes he 'hath the witness in himself' *try* whether it be of God. If the fruit follow, it is; otherwise, it is not. For certainly 'the tree is known by its fruit.' Hereby we *prove* if it be of God. 'But the direct witness is never referred to in the Book of God.' Not as standing alone, not as a single witness, but as connected with the other; as giving a *joint testimony*, testifying *with our spirit* that we are children of God. And who is able to prove that it is not *thus* referred to in this very Scripture: 'Examine yourselves whether ye be in the faith; prove your own selves. Know ye not your own selves that Jesus Christ is in you?' It is by no means clear that they did not know this by a *direct* as well as a *remote* witness. How is it proved that they did not know it, first, by inward consciousness, and then by love, joy, and peace?

7. 'But the testimony arising from the internal and external change is constantly referred to in the Bible.' It is so. And we constantly refer thereto to confirm the testimony of the Spirit.

'Nay, all the marks *you* have given whereby to distinguish the operations of God's Spirit from delusion refer to the change wrought in us and upon us.' This likewise is undoubtedly true.

8. It is objected, fifthly, that 'the direct witness of the Spirit does not secure us from the greatest delusions. And is that a witness fit to be trusted whose testimony cannot be

depended on, that is forced to fly to something else to prove what it asserts?' I answer: to secure us from all delusion, God gives us two witnesses that we are his children. And this they testify conjointly. Therefore 'what God hath joined together, let not man put asunder.' And while they are joined we cannot be deluded: their testimony can be depended on. They are fit to be trusted in the highest degree, and need nothing else to prove what they assert.

'Nay, the direct witness only asserts, but does not prove anything.' By two witnesses shall every word be established. And when the Spirit 'witnesses with our spirit', as God designs it to do, then it fully proves that we are children of God.

9. It is objected, sixthly: 'You own the change wrought is a sufficient testimony, unless in the case of severe trials, such as that of our Saviour upon the cross. But none of us can be tried in that manner.' But you or I may be tried in such a manner, and so may any other child of God, that it will be impossible for us to keep our filial confidence in God without the direct witness of his Spirit.

10. It is objected, lastly, 'The greatest contenders for it are some of the proudest and most uncharitable of men.' Perhaps some of the *hottest* contenders for it are both proud and uncharitable. But many of the *firmest* contenders for it are eminently meek and lowly in heart, and, indeed, in all other respects also,

True followers of their lamb-like Lord.

The preceding objections are the most considerable that I have heard, and I believe contain the strength of the cause. Yet I apprehend whoever calmly and impartially considers those objections and the answers together, will easily see that they do not destroy, no, nor weaken the evidence of that great truth, that the Spirit of God does *directly* as well as *indirectly* testify that we are children of God.

V.1. The sum of all is this: the testimony of the Spirit is an inward impression on the souls of believers, whereby the Spirit of God directly testifies to their spirit that they are children of God. And it is not questioned whether there is a testimony of the Spirit, but whether there is any *direct testimony*, whether there is any other than that which arises from a consciousness of the fruit of the Spirit. We believe there is: because this is the plain, natural meaning of the text, illustrated both by the preceding words and by the parallel passage in the Epistle to the Galatians; because, in the nature of the thing, the testimony must precede the fruit which springs from it, and because this plain meaning of the Word of God is confirmed by the experience of innumerable children of God; yea, and by the experience of all who are convinced of sin, who can never rest till they have a direct witness; and even of the children of the world who, not having the witness in themselves, one and all declare none can *know* his sins forgiven.

2. And whereas it is objected that experience is not sufficient to prove a doctrine unsupported by Scripture; that madmen and enthusiasts of every kind have imagined such a witness; that the design of that witness is to prove our profession genuine, which design it does not answer; that the Scripture says, 'The tree is known by its fruit,' 'Examine your-

selves: . . . prove your own selves,' and meantime the direct witness is never referred to in all the Book of God; that it does not secure us from the greatest delusions; and, lastly, that the change wrought in us is a sufficient testimony, unless in such trials as Christ alone suffered—we answer, (1). Experience is sufficient to *confirm* a doctrine which is grounded on Scripture. (2). Though many fancy they experience what they do not, this is no prejudice to real experience. (3). The design of that witness is to assure us we are children of God; and this design it does answer. (4). The true witness of the Spirit is known by its fruit—love, peace, joy—not indeed preceding, but following it. (5). It cannot be proved that the direct as well as the indirect witness is not referred to in that very text, 'Know ye not your own selves . . . that Jesus Christ is in you?' (6). The Spirit of God, 'witnessing with our spirit', does secure us from all delusion. And, lastly, we are all liable to trials wherein the testimony of our own spirit is not sufficient, wherein nothing less than the direct testimony of God's Spirit can assure us we are his children.

3. Two inferences may be drawn from the whole. The first: let none ever presume to rest in any supposed testimony of the Spirit which is separate from the fruit of it. If the Spirit of God does really testify that we are children of God, the immediate consequence will be the fruit of the Spirit, even 'love, joy, peace, long-suffering, gentleness, goodness, fidelity, meekness, temperance'. And however this fruit may be clouded for a while during the time of strong temptation, so that it does not appear to the tempted person while 'Satan is sifting him as wheat,' yet the substantial part of it remains, even under the thickest cloud. It is true, joy in the Holy Ghost may be withdrawn during the hour of trial. Yea, the soul may be 'exceeding sorrowful' while 'the hour and power of darkness' continues. But even this is generally restored with increase, and he rejoices 'with joy unspeakable and full of glory'.

4. The second inference is: let none rest in any supposed fruit of the Spirit without the witness. There may be foretastes of joy, of peace, of love—and those not delusive, but really from God—long before we have the witness in ourselves, before the Spirit of God witnesses with our spirits that we have 'redemption in the blood of Jesus, even the forgiveness of sins'. Yea, there may be a degree of long-suffering, of gentleness, of fidelity, meekness, temperance (not a shadow thereof, but a real degree, by the preventing grace of God) before we are 'accepted in the Beloved', and consequently before we have a testimony of our acceptance. But it is by no means advisable to rest here; it is at the peril of our souls if we do. If we are wise we shall be continually crying to God, until his Spirit cry in our heart, 'Abba, Father!' This is the privilege of all the children of God, and without this we can never be assured that we are his children. Without this we cannot retain a steady peace, nor avoid perplexing doubts and fears. But when we have once received this 'Spirit of adoption', that 'peace which passes all understanding', and which expels all painful doubt and fear, will 'keep our hearts and minds in Christ Jesus'. And when this has brought forth its genuine fruit, all inward and outward holiness, it is undoubtedly the will of him that calleth us to give us always what he has once given. So that there is no need that we should ever more be deprived of either the testimony of God's Spirit or the testimony of our own, the consciousness of our walking in all righteousness and true holiness.

Newry, April 4, 1767

22. THE NATURE OF ENTHUSIASM

1750

An Introductory Comment

By midcentury many Anglican leaders were steeled in their opposition to Wesley's emphasis on the Holy Spirit. Earlier, in 1739, Bishop Joseph Butler accused Wesley of "pretending to extraordinary revelations" and called it a "horrid thing—a very horrid thing" (O, 2:44). In that same year, the Reverend Charles Wheatly fulminated against the Methodists from St. Paul's Cathedral and labeled them "rapturous enthusiasts" (S, 2:84). And in the year in which this sermon was published Wesley began his two-part reply to Bishop George Lavington's *The Enthusiasm of Methodists and Papists Compared* (S, 2:85). Beyond this, Dr. Joseph Trapp, Anglican cleric and gifted writer, preached four sermons in various London churches against "the doctrines and practices of certain modern enthusiasts" (S, 2:84).

Wesley turned the tables on his critics, so to speak, in this sermon by arguing that enthusiasm or fanaticism, rightly understood, is the heady false confidence that emerges among those "who imagine they have the *grace* which they have not" (O, 2:50). A second form of this madness is evident as those so deceived imagine they have gifts from God that they so obviously lack, or worse yet, they hope to attain the end of religion, which is holiness (holy love), apart from employing suitable means. In other words, this extended reply to his critics was yet another way by which Wesley developed his well-worked theme of nominal as opposed to *real* Christianity. "Talk of righteousness and peace and joy in the Holy Ghost," he pointed out, and such detractors will conclude, "Thou art beside thyself" (O, 2:46).

Wesley preached the text of this sermon, Acts 26:24, on five occasions (WWS) to a good end by affirming the necessity of the religion of the heart whereby the Holy Spirit transforms the inner person in the holy affections of love, a transformation that marks the character of a Methodist.

The Nature of Enthusiasm

1.–2. There is a sort of religion, often called Christianity, which is practiced

A. It is a religion of outward duties performed in a decent, regular manner

B. But if you talk about peace and joy in the Holy Ghost, they will say:

C. Thou art beside thyself

3. What the world accounts as madness is the testimony of the Spirit

4.–7. They term this madness *enthusiasm*

8. Some people use this term to denote the inspiration of prophets or apostles

9. Others use it to describe uncommon vigour of thought or spirit

10. But neither captures the sense in which it is usually used

11. Enthusiasm is undoubtedly a disorder of the mind

12. Enthusiasm is a form of madness, not an ordinary but a religious madness

13.–17. There are innumerable sorts of enthusiasts

A. The first sort is those who imagine they have *grace* when they do not

18. A second sort is those who imagine they have *gifts* from God but do not

19.–20. To this class belong those who believe they are influenced by the Spirit

21. And those who expect to be directed by God in *extraordinary* ways

22. We are not to know God's will by waiting for supernatural dreams

23. Scripture gives a rule to know God's will in every case

24. Knowing God's will is determined in part by reason and experience

25. The assistance of God's Spirit is supposed during the process of inquiry

26. This is the plain, scriptural, rational way to know the will of God

27. A third form is those who try to attain the ends without using the means

28.–29. I should also mention what is often accounted a fourth type

30. We must guard against every form of enthusiasm with utmost diligence

31. Together with pride, there will arise an unadvisable and unconvincible spirit

32. Being against the grace of God, the enthusiast is left to his own guidance

33. Do not use the word *enthusiasm* until you understand it

34. Beware of judging or calling anyone an enthusiast upon common report

35. Beware you are not entangled with enthusiasm

36. Beware you are not a fiery, persecuting enthusiast

37. Beware you do not run with the common herd of enthusiasts

38. Beware of imagining you have *gifts* from God which you do not have

39. Beware of imagining you can obtain the ends with the means conducive to it

Sermon 37: The Nature of Enthusiasm, 1750

Acts 26:24

And Festus said with a loud voice, Paul, thou art beside thyself.

1. And so say all the world, the men who know not God, of all that are of Paul's religion, of everyone who is so a follower of him as he was of Christ. It is true there is a sort of religion—nay, and it is called Christianity too—which may be practised without any such imputation, which is generally allowed to be consistent with common sense. That is, a religion of form, a round of outward duties performed in a decent, regular manner. You may add orthodoxy thereto, a system of right opinions; yea, and some quantity of heathen morality. And yet not many will pronounce that 'much *religion* hath made you mad.' But if you aim at the religion of the heart, if you talk of righteousness and peace and joy in the Holy Ghost, then it will not be long before *your* sentence is passed: 'Thou art beside thyself.'

2. And it is no compliment which the men of the world pay you herein. They for once mean what they say. They not only affirm but cordially believe that every man is beside himself who says the love of God is shed abroad in his heart by the Holy Ghost given unto him, and that God has enabled him to rejoice in Christ with joy unspeakable and full of glory. If a man is indeed alive to God, and dead to all things here below; if he continually sees him that is invisible, and accordingly walks by faith and not by sight; then they account it a clear case—beyond all dispute 'much *religion* hath made him mad.'

3. It is easy to observe that the determinate thing which the world accounts madness is that utter contempt of all temporal things, and steady pursuit of things eternal; that divine conviction of things not seen; that rejoicing in the favour of God; that happy, holy love of God; and that testimony of his Spirit with our spirit that we are the children of God. That is, in truth, the whole spirit and life and power of the religion of Jesus Christ.

4. They will, however, allow [that] in other respects the man acts and talks like one in his senses. In other things he is a reasonable man: 'tis in these instances only his head is touched. It is therefore acknowledged that the madness under which he labours is of a particular kind. And accordingly they are accustomed to distinguish it by a particular name—*enthusiasm.*

5. A term this which is exceeding frequently used, which is scarce ever out of some men's mouths. And yet it is exceeding rarely understood, even by those who use it most. It may be therefore not unacceptable to serious men, to all who desire to understand what they speak or hear, if I endeavour to explain the meaning of this term, to show what 'enthusiasm' is. It may be an encouragement to those who are unjustly charged therewith; and may possibly be of use to some who are justly charged with it—at least to others who might be so were they not cautioned against it.

6. As to the word itself, it is generally allowed to be of Greek extraction. But whence the Greek word ἐνθουσιασμός is derived none has yet been able to show. Some have endeavoured to derive it from ἐν Θεῷ, 'in God', because all enthusiasm has reference to him. But this is quite forced, there being small resemblance between the word derived and

those they strive to derive it from. Others would derive it from ἐν θυσίᾳ, 'in sacrifice', because many of the enthusiasts of old were affected in the most violent manner during the time of sacrifice. Perhaps it is a fictitious word, invented from the noise which some of those made who were so affected.

7. It is not improbable that one reason why this uncouth word has been retained in so many languages was because men were no better agreed concerning the meaning than concerning the derivation of it. They therefore adopted the Greek word because they did not understand it: they did not translate it into their own tongues because they knew not how to translate it, it having been always a word of loose, uncertain sense, to which no determinate meaning was affixed.

8. It is not therefore at all surprising that it is so variously taken at this day, different persons understanding it in different senses quite inconsistent with each other. Some take it in a good sense, for a divine impulse or impression superior to all the natural faculties, and suspending for the time, either in whole or in part, both the reason and the outward senses. In this meaning of the word both the prophets of old and the apostles were proper 'enthusiasts'; being at divers times so filled with the Spirit, and so influenced by him who dwelt in their hearts, that the exercise of their own reason, their senses, and all their natural faculties, being suspended, they were wholly actuated by the power of God, and 'spake' only 'as they were moved by the Holy Ghost'.

9. Others take the word in an indifferent sense, such as is neither morally good nor evil. Thus they speak of the enthusiasm of the poets, of Homer and Virgil in particular. And this a late eminent writer extends so far as to assert, there is no man excellent in his profession, whatsoever it be, who has not in his temper a strong tincture of enthusiasm. By enthusiasm these appear to understand an uncommon vigour of thought, a peculiar fervour of spirit, a vivacity and strength not to be found in common men; elevating the soul to greater and higher things than cool reason could have attained.

10. But neither of these is the sense wherein the word enthusiasm is most usually understood. The generality of men, if no farther agreed, at least agree thus far concerning it, that it is something evil; and this is plainly the sentiment of all those who call the religion of the heart enthusiasm. Accordingly I shall take it in the following pages as an evil—a misfortune, if not a fault.

11. As to the nature of enthusiasm, it is undoubtedly a disorder of the mind, and such a disorder as greatly hinders the exercise of reason. Nay, sometimes it wholly sets it aside: it not only dims but shuts the eyes of the understanding. It may therefore well be accounted a species of madness: of madness rather than of folly, seeing a fool is properly one who draws wrong conclusions from right premises, whereas a madman draws right conclusions, but from wrong premises. And so does an enthusiast. Suppose his premises true, and his conclusions would necessarily follow. But here lies his mistake: his premises are false. He imagines himself to be what he is not. And therefore, setting out wrong, the farther he goes the more he wanders out of the way.

12. Every enthusiast then is properly a madman. Yet his is not an ordinary, but a religious madness. By religious I do not mean that it is any part of religion. Quite the

reverse: religion is the spirit of a sound mind, and consequently stands in direct opposition to madness of every kind. But I mean it has religion for its object; it is conversant about religion. And so the enthusiast is generally talking of religion, of God or of the things of God; but talking in such a manner that every reasonable Christian may discern the disorder of his mind. Enthusiasm in general may then be described in some such manner as this: a religious madness arising from some falsely imagined influence or inspiration of God; at least from imputing something to God which ought not to be imputed to him, or expecting something from God which ought not to be expected from him.

13. There are innumerable sorts of enthusiasm. Those which are most common, and for that reason most dangerous, I shall endeavour to reduce under a few general heads, that they may be more easily understood and avoided.

The first sort of enthusiasm which I shall mention is that of those who imagine they have the *grace* which they have not. Thus some imagine, when it is not so, that they have 'redemption' through Christ, 'even the forgiveness of sin'. These are usually such as 'have no root in themselves', no deep repentance or thorough conviction. Therefore 'they receive the word with joy.' And 'because they have no deepness of earth', no deep work in their heart, therefore the seed 'immediately springs up'. There is immediately a superficial change which, together with that light joy, striking in with the pride of their unbroken heart and with their inordinate self-love, easily persuades them they have already 'tasted the good word of God, and the powers of the world to come'.

14. This is properly an instance of the first sort of enthusiasm; it is a kind of madness, arising from the imagination that they have that grace which in truth they have not; so that they only deceive their own souls. Madness it may justly be termed, for the reasonings of these poor men are right, were their premises good; but as those are a mere creature of their own imagination, so all that is built on them falls to the ground. The foundation of all their reveries is this: they imagine themselves to have faith in Christ. If they had this they would be 'kings and priests to God', possessed of 'a kingdom which cannot be moved'. But they have it not. Consequently all their following behaviour is as wide of truth and soberness as that of the ordinary madman who, fancying himself an earthly king, speaks and acts in that character.

15. There are many other enthusiasts of this sort. Such, for instance, is the fiery zealot for religion; or (more probably) for the opinions and modes of worship which he dignifies with that name. This man also strongly imagines himself to be a believer in Jesus, yea, that he is a champion for the faith which was once delivered to the saints. Accordingly all his conduct is formed upon that vain imagination. And allowing his supposition to be just, he would have some tolerable plea for his behaviour; whereas now it is evidently the effect of a distempered brain, as well as of a distempered heart.

16. But the most common of all the enthusiasts of this kind are those who imagine themselves Christians and are not. These abound not only in all parts of our land, but in most parts of the habitable earth. That they are not Christians is clear and undeniable, if we believe the oracles of God. For Christians are holy; these are unholy. Christians love God; these love the world. Christians are humble; these are proud. Christians are gentle;

these are passionate. Christians have the mind which was in Christ; these are at the utmost distance from it. Consequently they are no more Christians than they are archangels. Yet they imagine themselves so to be; and they can give several reasons for it. For they have been *called so* ever since they can remember. They were 'christened' many years ago. They embrace the 'Christian opinions' vulgarly termed the Christian or catholic faith. They use the 'Christian modes of worship', as their fathers did before them. They live what is called a good 'Christian life', as the rest of their neighbours do. And who shall presume to think or say that these men are not Christians? Though without one grain of true faith in Christ, or of real, inward holiness! Without ever having tasted the love of God, or been 'made partakers of the Holy Ghost'!

17. Ah, poor self-deceivers! Christians ye are not. But you are enthusiasts in an high degree. Physicians, heal yourselves. But first know your disease: your whole life is enthusiasm, as being all suitable to the imagination that you have received that grace of God which you have not. In consequence of this grand mistake, you blunder on day by day, speaking and acting under a character which does in no wise belong to you. Hence arises that palpable, glaring inconsistency that runs through your whole behaviour, which is an awkward mixture of real heathenism and imaginary Christianity. Yet still, as you have so vast a majority on your side, you will always carry it by mere dint of numbers that you are the only men in your senses, and all are lunatics who are not as you are. But this alters not the nature of things. In the sight of God and his holy angels—yea, and all the children of God upon earth—you are mere madmen, mere enthusiasts all. Are you not? Are you not 'walking in a vain shadow', a shadow of religion, a shadow of happiness? Are you not still 'disquieting yourselves in vain'? With misfortunes as imaginary as your happiness or religion? Do you not fancy yourselves great or good? Very knowing, and very wise! How long? Perhaps till death brings you back to your senses—to bewail your folly for ever and ever!

18. A second sort of enthusiasm is that of those who imagine they have such *gifts* from God as they have not. Thus some have imagined themselves to be endued with a power of working miracles, of healing the sick by a word or a touch, of restoring sight to the blind; yea, even of raising the dead, a notorious instance of which is still fresh in our own history. Others have undertaken to prophesy, to foretell things to come, and that with the utmost certainty and exactness. But a little time usually convinces these enthusiasts. When plain facts run counter to their predictions, experience performs what reason could not, and sinks them down into their senses.

19. To the same class belong those who in preaching or prayer imagine themselves to be so influenced by the Spirit of God as in fact they are not. I am sensible indeed that without him we can do nothing, more especially in our public ministry; that all our preaching is utterly vain unless it be attended with his power, and all our prayer, unless his Spirit therein help our infirmities. I know if we do not both preach and pray by the Spirit it is all but lost labour, seeing the help that is done upon earth, he doth it himself, who worketh all in all. But this does not affect the case before us. Though there is a real influence of the Spirit of God, there is also an imaginary one; and many there are who mistake the one for the other. Many suppose themselves to be under that influence when they are not, when it is far from them. And many others suppose they are more under

that influence than they really are. Of this number, I fear, are all they who imagine that God dictates the very words they speak, and that consequently it is impossible they should speak anything amiss, either as to the matter or manner of it. It is well known how many enthusiasts of this sort also have appeared during the present century; some of whom speak in a far more authoritative manner than either St. Paul or any of the apostles.

20. The same sort of enthusiasm, though in a lower degree, is frequently found in men of a private character. They may likewise imagine themselves to be influenced or directed by the Spirit when they are not. I allow, 'if any man have not the Spirit of Christ, he is none of his;' and that if ever we either think, speak, or act aright, it is through the assistance of that blessed Spirit. But how many impute things to him, or expect things from him, without any rational or scriptural ground! Such are they who imagine they either do or shall receive 'particular directions' from God, not only in points of importance, but in things of no moment, in the most trifling circumstances of life. Whereas in these cases God has given us our own reason for a guide; though never excluding the 'secret assistance' of his Spirit.

21. To this kind of enthusiasm they are peculiarly exposed who expected to be directed of God, either in spiritual things or in common life, in what is justly called an *extraordinary* manner. I mean by visions or dreams, by strong impressions or sudden impulses on the mind. I do not deny that God has of old times manifested his will in this manner, or that he can do so now. Nay, I believe he does, in some very rare instances. But how frequently do men mistake herein! How are they misled by pride and a warm imagination to ascribe such impulses or impressions, dreams or visions, to God, as are utterly unworthy of him! Now this is all pure enthusiasm, all as wide of religion as it is of truth and soberness.

22. Perhaps some may ask, 'Ought we not then to inquire what is *the will of God* in all things? And ought not his will to be the rule of our practice? Unquestionably it ought. But how is a sober Christian to make this inquiry? To know what is 'the will of God'? Not by waiting for supernatural dreams. Not by expecting God to reveal it in visions. Not by looking for any 'particular impressions', or sudden impulses on his mind. No; but by consulting the oracles of God. 'To the law and to the testimony.' This is the general method of knowing what is 'the holy and acceptable will of God'.

23. 'But how shall I know what is the will of God in such and such a particular case? The thing proposed is in itself of an indifferent nature, and so left undetermined in Scripture.' I answer, the Scripture itself gives you a general rule, applicable to all particular cases: 'The will of God is our sanctification.' It is his will that we should be inwardly and outwardly holy; that we should *be good and do good* in every kind, and in the highest degree whereof we are capable. Thus far we tread upon firm ground. This is as clear as the shining of the sun. In order therefore to know what is the will of God in a particular case we have only to apply this general rule.

24. Suppose, for instance, it were proposed to a reasonable man to marry, or to enter into a new business. In order to know whether this is the will of God, being assured, 'It is the will of God concerning me that I should be as holy and do as much good as I can,' he has only to inquire, 'In which of these states can I be most holy, and do the most good?' And this is to be determined partly by reason and partly by experience. Experience tells

him what advantages he has in his present state, either for being or doing good; and reason is to show what he certainly or probably will have in the state proposed. By comparing these he is to judge which of the two may most conduce to his being and doing good; and as far as he knows this, so far he is certain what is the will of God.

25. Meantime the assistance of his Spirit is supposed during the whole process of the inquiry. Indeed 'tis not easy to say in how many ways that assistance is conveyed. He may bring many circumstances to our remembrance; may place others in a stronger and clearer light; may insensibly open our mind to receive conviction, and fix that conviction upon our heart. And to a concurrence of many circumstances of this kind in favour of what is acceptable in his sight he may superadd such an unutterable peace of mind, and so uncommon a measure of his love, as will leave us no possibility of doubting that *this*, even *this*, is his will concerning us.

26. This is the plain, scriptural, rational way to know what is the will of God in a particular case. But considering how seldom this way is taken, and what a flood of enthusiasm must needs break in on those who endeavour to know the will of God by unscriptural, irrational ways, it were to be wished that the expression itself were far more sparingly used. The using it as some do, on the most trivial occasions, is a plain breach of the third commandment. It is a gross way of taking the name of God in vain, and betrays great irreverence toward him. Would it not be far better then to use other expressions, which are not liable to such objections? For example: instead of saying on any particular occasion, 'I want to know what is the will of God,' would it not be better to say, 'I want to know what will be most for my improvement, and what will make me most useful.' This way of speaking is clear and unexceptionable. It is putting the matter on a plain, scriptural issue, and that without any danger of enthusiasm.

27. A third very common sort of enthusiasm (if it does not coincide with the former) is that of those who think to attain the end without using the means, by the immediate power of God. If indeed those means were providentially withheld they would not fall under this charge. God can, and sometimes does in cases of this nature, exert his own immediate power. But they who expect this when they have those means and will not use them are proper enthusiasts. Such are they who expect to understand the Holy Scriptures without reading them and meditating thereon; yea, without using all such helps as are in their power, and may probably conduce to that end. Such are they who *designedly* speak in the public assembly without any premeditation. I say 'designedly', because there may be such circumstances as at some times make it unavoidable. But whoever *despises* that great means of speaking profitably is so far an enthusiast.

28. It may be expected that I should mention what some have accounted a fourth sort of enthusiasm, namely, the imagining those things to be owing to the providence of God which are not owing thereto. But I doubt. I know not what things they are which are not owing to the providence of God; in ordering, or at least in governing, of which this is not either directly or remotely concerned. I expect nothing but sin; and even in the sins of others I see the providence of God to *me*. I do not say, his *general providence*, for this I take to be a sounding word which means just nothing. And if there be a *particular providence* it must extend to all persons and all things. So our Lord understood it, or he could never

have said, 'Even the hairs of your head are all numbered.' And, 'Not a sparrow falleth to the ground' without 'the will of your Father which is in heaven.' But if it be so, if God presides *universis tanquam singulis, et singulis tanquam universis*—over the whole universe as over every single person, over every single person as over the whole universe—what is it (except only our own sins) which we are not to ascribe to the providence of God? So that I cannot apprehend there is any room here for the charge of enthusiasm.

29. If it be said the charge lies here: 'When you impute *this* to providence you imagine yourself the peculiar favourite of heaven,' I answer, you have forgot some of the last words I spoke: *Praesidet universis tanquam singulis*—his providence is over all men in the universe as much as over any single person. Don't you see that he who believing this imputes anything which befalls him to providence does not therein make himself any more the favourite of heaven than he supposes every man under heaven to be? Therefore you have no pretence upon this ground to charge him with enthusiasm.

30. Against every sort of this it behoves us to guard with the utmost diligence, considering the dreadful effects it has so often produced, and which indeed naturally result from it. Its immediate offspring is pride; it continually increases this source from whence it flows, and hereby it alienates us more and more from the favour and from the life of God. It dries up the very springs of faith and love, of righteousness and true holiness; seeing all these flow from grace. But 'God resisteth the proud and giveth grace' only 'to the humble.'

31. Together with pride there will naturally arise an unadvisable and unconvincible spirit; so that into whatever error or fault the enthusiast falls there is small hope of his recovery. For reason will have little weight with him (as has been justly and frequently observed) who imagines he is led by an higher guide, by the immediate wisdom of God. And as he grows in pride, so he must grow in unadvisableness, and in stubbornness also. He must be less and less capable of being convinced, less susceptible of persuasion; more and more attached to his own judgment and his own will, till he is altogether fixed and immovable.

32. Being thus fortified both against the grace of God and against all advice and help from man, he is wholly left to the guidance of his own heart, and of the king of the children of pride. No marvel then that he is daily more rooted and grounded in contempt of all mankind, in furious anger, in every unkind disposition, in every earthly and devilish temper. Neither can we wonder at the terrible outward effects which have flowed from such dispositions in all ages; even all manner of wickedness, all the works of darkness, committed by those who called themselves Christians while they wrought with greediness such things as were hardly named even among the heathens.

Such is the nature, such the dreadful effects, of that many-headed monster, enthusiasm! From the consideration of which we may now draw some plain inferences with regard in our own practice.

33. And, first, if enthusiasm be a term, though so frequently used yet so rarely understood, take *you* care not to talk of you know not what, not to use the word till you understand it. As in all other points, so likewise in this, learn to think before you speak. First, know the meaning of this hard word; and then use it if need require.

34. But if so few, even among men of education and learning, much more among the

common sort of men, understand this dark, ambiguous word, or have any fixed notion of what it means, then, secondly, beware of judging or calling any man an enthusiast upon common report. This is by no means a sufficient ground for giving any name of reproach to any man; least of all is it a sufficient ground for so black a term of reproach as this. The more evil it contains, the more cautious you should be how you apply it to anyone; to bring so heavy an accusation without full proof being neither consistent with justice nor mercy.

35. But if enthusiasm be so great an evil, beware you are not entangled therewith yourself. Watch and pray that you fall not into the temptation. It easily besets those who fear or love God. O beware you do not think of yourself more highly than you ought to think. Do not imagine you have attained that grace of God to which you have not attained. You may have much joy; you may have a measure of love, and yet not have living faith. Cry unto God that he would not suffer you, blind as you are, to go out of the way; that you may never fancy yourself a believer in Christ till Christ is revealed in you, and till his Spirit witnesses with your spirit that you are a child of God.

36. Beware you are not a fiery, persecuting enthusiast. Do not imagine that God has called you (just contrary to the spirit of him you style your Master) to destroy men's lives, and not to save them. Never dream of forcing men into the ways of God. Think yourself, and let think. Use no constraint in matters of religion. Even those who are farthest out of the way never 'compel to come in' by any other means than reason, truth, and love.

37. Beware you do not run with the common herd of enthusiasts, fancying you are a Christian when you are not. Presume not to assume that venerable name unless you have a clear, scriptural title thereto; unless you have the mind which was in Christ, and walk as he also walked.

38. Beware you do not fall into the second sort of enthusiasm, fancying you have those *gifts* from God which you have not. Trust not in visions or dreams, in sudden impressions or strong impulses of any kind. Remember, it is not by these you are to know what is 'the will of God' on any particular occasion, but by applying the plain Scripture rule, with the help of experience and reason, and the ordinary assistance of the Spirit of God. Do not lightly take the name of God in your mouth: do not talk of 'the will of God' on every trifling occasion. But let your words as well as your actions be all tempered with reverence and godly fear.

39. Beware, lastly, of imagining you shall obtain the end without using the means conducive to it. God *can* give the end without any means at all; but you have no reason to think he *will.* Therefore constantly and carefully use all these means which he has appointed to be the ordinary channels of his grace. Use every means which either reason or Scripture recommends as conducive (through the free love of God in Christ) either to the obtaining or increasing any of the gifts of God. Thus expect a daily growth in that pure and holy religion which the world always did, and always will, call enthusiasm; but which to all who are saved from real enthusiasm—from merely nominal Christianity—is the wisdom of God and the power of God, the glorious image of the Most High, righteousness and peace, a fountain of living water, springing up into everlasting life!

23. THE WITNESS OF OUR OWN SPIRIT

1746

An Introductory Comment

This last of the several sermons on the topic of assurance was never preached but was expressly produced for publication in order to serve as a teaching tool (S, 1:219). In it Wesley considered the indirect witness of our own spirit in contrast to the direct witness of God's Spirit. This former witness, at least in this sermon, is expressed for the most part in terms of the faculty of conscience, a faculty that Wesley nevertheless judged to be not a natural but a supernatural one, that is, as a species of prevenient grace (O, 2:156–57nn).

Exploring conscience in terms of *simplicity* (with respect to the intention itself) and *sincerity* (in terms of the execution of it), Wesley outlined the constitution of a "good conscience" in terms of four key elements: (1) "a right understanding of the Word of God," (2) "a true knowledge of ourselves," (3) "an agreement of our hearts and lives," and (4) "an inward perception of this agreement" (O, 1:303–4). Naturally, Scripture is of considerable value for a rightly ordered conscience since according to Wesley it functions in an illuminative and normative way as nothing less than the touchstone of the faith (J, 9:502-03).

Beyond this sermon Wesley considered other elements that make up the indirect witness in terms of such things as recognizing "the marks of the children of God" (O, 1:271), keeping the commandments (O, 1:272), and having received "the tempers mentioned in the Word of God" (O, 1:274), as well as the fruit of the Spirit (J, 5:126). All of this is "rational evidence" (O, 1:272) by means of which the proper conclusion can be made, demonstrating its indirect nature: "we have these marks: therefore we are children of God" (O, 1:272). Though Wesley affirmed that the indirect witness is valuable in keeping believers from fanaticism, he nevertheless maintained that by itself it is insufficient (O, 1:297).

The Witness of Our Own Spirit

1. Rejoice in the Lord always; and again I say, rejoice
2. I will show what is the nature and ground of a Christian's joy
   A. It is that happy peace arising from the testimony of conscience
3. What are we to understand by 'conscience'?
4. God has made us thinking beings capable of perceiving what is present
   A. This is what we mean when we say we are conscious beings
   B. But what we term 'conscience' usually implies more than this
   C. Its main business is to approve or disprove, to acquit or condemn
5. Some have given a new name to this but 'conscience' is preferable
6. What is the *rule* whereby people are to judge right and wrong?
   A. The rule of heathens is the law written in their hearts
   B. The Christian rule of right and wrong is the Word of God
7. If people are directed thereby, then they have a good conscience
   A. To this is required a right understanding of the Word of God
   B. There is also required a true knowledge of ourselves
8. A conscience void of offense must be laid on the right foundation
9. This extends to all of our actions and words, outward and inward
10. We are in conversation with the world, even with the ungodly
11. We have our conversation in the world in simplicity and godly sincerity
    A. Simplicity means all actions and conversation shall be full of light
12. We have our conversation in the world, secondly, in godly sincerity
    A. Simplicity regards the intention itself, sincerity the execution of it
13. Godly sincerity should not be mistaken for heathen sincerity
14. We cannot gain this sincerity by good sense, good nature, or good breeding
15. It can be attained only by the knowledge of Jesus Christ our Lord
16. This is the ground of a Christian's joy
    A. I rejoice because he gives to feel in myself the mind that was in Christ
17. We may infer, first, that this is not a *natural* joy
18. We may infer, second, this does not arise from *blindness of conscience*
19. Neither does it arise from *dullness* or *callousness of conscience*
20. Christian joy is joy in obedience
    A. It is joy in obedience in loving God and keeping God's commandments

Sermon 12: The Witness of Our Own Spirit, 1746

2 Corinthians 1:12

This is our rejoicing, the testimony of our conscience, that in simplicity and godly sincerity, not with fleshly wisdom, but by the grace of God, we have had our conversation in the world.

1. Such is the voice of every true believer in Christ, so long as he abides in faith and love. 'He that followeth me', saith our Lord, 'walketh not in darkness.' And while he hath the light he rejoiceth therein. 'As he hath received the Lord Jesus Christ, so he walketh in him.' And while he walketh in him, the exhortation of the Apostle takes place in his soul day by day: 'Rejoice in the Lord always; and again I say, rejoice.'

2. But that we may not build our house upon the sand (lest when the rains descend, and the winds blow, and the floods arise and beat upon it, it fall, and great be the fall thereof) I intend, in the following discourse, to show what is the nature and ground of a Christian's joy. We know, in general, it is that happy peace, that calm satisfaction of spirit, which arises from such a testimony of his conscience as is here described by the Apostle. But in order to understand this the more throughly, it will be requisite to weigh all his words; whence will easily appear both what we are to understand by 'conscience', and what by the 'testimony' thereof; and also how he that hath this testimony rejoiceth evermore.

3. And, first, what are we to understand by 'conscience'? What is the meaning of this word that is in everyone's mouth? One would imagine it was an exceeding difficult thing to discover this, when we consider how large and numerous volumes have been from time to time wrote on this subject; and how all the treasures of ancient and modern learning have been ransacked in order to explain it. And yet it is to be feared it has not received much light from all those elaborate inquiries. Rather, have not most of those writers puzzled the cause, 'darkening counsel by words without knowledge', perplexing a subject plain in itself, and easy to be understood? For set aside but hard words, and every man of an honest heart will soon understand the thing.

4. God has made us thinking beings, capable of perceiving what is present, and of reflecting or looking back on what is past. In particular we are capable of perceiving whatsoever passes in our own hearts or lives; of knowing whatsoever we feel or do; and that either while it passes, or when it is past. This we mean when we say man is a 'conscious' being: he hath a 'consciousness' or inward perception both of things present and past relating to himself, of his own tempers and outward behaviour. But what we usually term 'conscience' implies somewhat more than this. It is not barely the knowledge of our present, or the remembrance of our preceding life. To remember, to bear witness either of past or present things is only one, and the least, office of conscience. Its main business is to excuse or accuse, to approve or disapprove, to acquit or condemn.

5. Some late writers indeed have given a new name to this, and have chose to style it a 'moral sense'. But the old word seems preferable to the new, were it only on this account, that it is more common and familiar among men, and therefore easier to be understood. And to Christians it is undeniably preferable on another account also; namely, because

it is scriptural; because it is the word which the wisdom of God hath chose to use in the inspired writings.

And according to the meaning wherein it is generally used there, particularly in the epistles of St. Paul, we may understand by conscience a faculty or power, implanted by God in every soul that comes into the world, of perceiving what is right or wrong in his own heart or life, in his tempers, thoughts, words, and actions.

6. But what is the *rule* whereby men are to judge of right and wrong; whereby their conscience is to be directed? The rule of heathens (as the Apostle teaches elsewhere) is 'the law written in their hearts'. 'These (saith he) not having the (outward) law, are a law unto themselves: who show the work of the law', that which the outward law prescribes, 'written in their heart' by the finger of God; 'their conscience also bearing witness' whether they walk by this rule or not; 'and their thoughts the meanwhile accusing, or even excusing', acquitting, defending them (ἢ καὶ ἀπολογουμένων) (Rom. 2:14-15). But the Christian rule of right and wrong is the Word of God, the writings of the Old and New Testament: all which the prophets and 'holy men of old' wrote 'as they were moved by the Holy Ghost'; 'all' that 'Scripture' which was 'given by inspiration of God', and which is indeed 'profitable for doctrine', or teaching the whole will of God; 'for reproof' of what is contrary thereto; 'for correction' of error; and 'for instruction (or training us up) in righteousness' (2 Tim. 3:16).

This 'is a lantern unto a' Christian's 'feet, and a light in all his paths'. This alone he receives as his rule of right or wrong, of whatever is really good or evil. He esteems nothing good but what is here enjoined, either directly or by plain consequence. He accounts nothing evil but what is here forbidden, either in terms or by undeniable inference. Whatever the Scripture neither forbids nor enjoins (either directly or by plain consequence) he believes to be of an indifferent nature, to be in itself neither good nor evil: this being the whole and sole outward rule whereby his conscience is to be directed in all things.

7. And if it be directed thereby in fact, then hath he 'the answer of a good conscience toward God'. A 'good conscience' is what is elsewhere termed by the Apostle a 'conscience void of offence'. So what he at one time expresses thus, 'I have lived in all good conscience before God until this day' (Acts 23:1), he denotes at another by that expression, 'Herein do I exercise myself, to have always a conscience void of offence toward God and toward man' (Acts 24:16). Now in order to this there is absolutely required, first, a right understanding of the Word of God; of his 'holy and acceptable and perfect will' concerning us, as it is revealed therein. For it is impossible we should walk by a rule if we do not know what it means. There is, secondly, required (which how few have attained!) a true knowledge of ourselves; a knowledge both of our hearts and lives, of our inward tempers and outward conversation: seeing, if we know them not, it is not possible that we should compare them with our rule. There is required, thirdly, an agreement of our hearts and lives, of our tempers and conversation, of our thoughts and words and works with that rule, with the written Word of God. For without this, if we have any conscience at all, it can be only an evil conscience. There is, fourthly, required an inward perception of this agreement with our rule. And this habitual perception, this inward consciousness itself, is properly a 'good conscience'; or (in the other phrase of the Apostle) 'A conscience void of offence toward God and toward man'.

8. But whoever desires to have a conscience thus void of offence, let him see that he lay the right foundation. Let him remember, 'Other foundation' of this 'can no man lay than that which is laid, even Jesus Christ.' And let him also be mindful that no man buildeth on him but by a living faith, that no man is a partaker of Christ until he can clearly testify, 'The life which I now live . . . I live by faith in the Son of God,' in him who is now *revealed* in my heart, 'who loved me, and gave himself for me'. Faith alone is that evidence, that conviction, that demonstration of things invisible, whereby the eyes of our understanding being opened, and divine light poured in upon them, we 'see the wondrous things of' God's 'law', the excellency and purity of it; the height and depth and length and breadth thereof, and of every commandment contained therein. It is by faith that beholding 'the light of . . . the glory of God in the face of Jesus Christ' we perceive, as in a glass, all that is in ourselves, yea, the inmost motions of our souls. And by this alone can that blessed love of God be 'shed abroad in our hearts', which enables us so to love one another as Christ loved us. By this is that gracious promise fulfilled unto all the Israel of God, 'I will put my laws into their minds, and write (or engrave) them in their hearts' (Heb. 8:10); hereby producing in their souls an entire agreement with his holy and perfect law, and 'bringing into captivity every thought to the obedience of Christ'.

And as an evil tree cannot bring forth good fruit, so a good tree cannot bring forth evil fruit. As the heart therefore of a believer, so likewise his life is throughly conformed to the rule of God's commandments. In a consciousness whereof he can give glory to God, and say with the Apostle, 'This is our rejoicing, the testimony of our conscience, that in simplicity and godly sincerity, not with fleshly wisdom, but by the grace of God, we have had our conversation in the world.'

9. 'We have had our conversation.' The Apostle in the original expresses this by one single word (ἀνεστράφημεν). But the meaning thereof is exceeding broad, taking in our whole deportment, yea, every inward as well as outward circumstance, whether relating to our soul or body. It includes every motion of our heart, of our tongue, of our hands and bodily members. It extends to all our actions and words; to the employment of all our powers and faculties; to the manner of using every talent we have received, with respect either to God or man.

10. 'We have had our conversation in the world;' even in the world of the ungodly: not only among the children of God—that were, comparatively, a little thing—but among the children of the devil, among those that 'lie in wickedness', ἐν τῷ πονηρῷ, 'in the wicked one'. What a world is this! How throughly impregnated with the spirit it continually breathes! As our God is good and doth good, so the god of this world and all his children are evil, and do evil (so far as they are suffered) to all the children of God. Like their father they are always lying in wait, or 'walking about, seeking whom they may devour'; using fraud or force, secret wiles or open violence, to destroy those who are not of the world; continually warring against our souls, and by old or new weapons and devices of every kind, labouring to bring them back into the snare of the devil, into the broad road that leadeth to destruction.

11. 'We have had our whole conversation in such a world, in simplicity and godly sincerity.' First, 'in simplicity'. This is what our Lord recommends under the name of a

'single eye'. 'The light of the body (saith he) is the eye. If therefore thine eye be single, thy whole body shall be full of light.' The meaning whereof is this: what the eye is to the body, that the intention is to all the words and actions. If therefore this eye of thy soul be single, all thy actions and conversation shall be 'full of light', of the light of heaven, of love and peace and joy in the Holy Ghost.

We are then simple of heart when the eye of our mind is singly fixed on God; when in all things we aim at God alone, as our God, our portion, our strength, our happiness, our exceeding great reward, our all in time and eternity. This is simplicity: when a steady view, a single intention of promoting his glory, of doing and suffering his blessed will, runs through our whole soul, fills all our heart, and is the constant spring of all our thoughts, desires, and purposes.

12. 'We have had our conversation in the world', secondly, 'in godly sincerity.' The difference between simplicity and sincerity seems to be chiefly this: simplicity regards the intention itself, sincerity the execution of it. And this sincerity relates not barely to our words, but to our whole conversation, as described above. It is not here to be understood in that narrow sense wherein St. Paul himself sometimes uses it, for speaking the truth, or abstaining from guile, from craft and dissimulation, but in a more extensive meaning, as actually hitting the mark which we aim at by simplicity. Accordingly it implies in this place that we do in fact speak and do all to the glory of God; that all our words are not only pointed at this, but actually conducive thereto; that all our actions flow on in an even stream, uniformly subservient to this great end; and that in our whole lives we are moving straight toward God, and that continually—walking steadily on in the highway of holiness, in the paths of justice, mercy, and truth.

13. This sincerity is termed by the Apostle 'godly sincerity', or the sincerity of God (εἰλικρινείᾳ Θεοῦ) to prevent our mistaking or confounding it with the sincerity of the heathens (for they had also a kind of sincerity among them, for which they professed no small veneration); likewise to denote the object and end of this, as of every Christian virtue; seeing whatever does not ultimately tend to God sinks among 'the beggarly elements of the world'. By styling it 'the sincerity of God' he also points out the author of it, the 'Father of lights, from whom every good and perfect gift descendeth'; which is still more clearly declared in the following words, 'not with fleshly wisdom, but by the grace of God'.

14. 'Not with fleshly wisdom': as if he had said, 'We cannot thus converse in the world by any natural strength of understanding, neither by any naturally acquired knowledge or wisdom. We cannot gain this simplicity or practise this sincerity by the force either of good sense, good nature, or good breeding. It overshoots all our native courage and resolution, as well as all our precepts of philosophy. The power of custom is not able to train us up to this, nor the most exquisite rules of human education. Neither could I, Paul, ever attain hereto, notwithstanding all the advantages I enjoyed, so long as I was "in the flesh" (in my natural state) and pursued it only by "fleshly", natural, "wisdom".'

And yet surely, if any man could, Paul himself might have attained thereto by that wisdom. For we can hardly conceive any who was more highly favoured with all the gifts both of nature and education. Besides his natural abilities, probably not inferior to those of any person then upon the earth, he had all the benefits of learning, studying at the university of Tarsus, afterwards 'brought up at the feet of Gamaliel', the person of the greatest account both for knowledge and integrity that was then in the whole Jewish nation. And he had all the possible advantages of religious education, being a Pharisee, the son of a Pharisee, trained up in the very straitest sect or profession, distinguished from all others by a more eminent strictness. And herein he had 'profited above many others who were his equals in years, being more abundantly zealous' of whatever he thought would please God, and 'as touching the righteousness of the law, blameless'. But it could not be that he should hereby attain this simplicity and godly sincerity. It was all but lost labour; in a deep, piercing sense of which he was at length constrained to cry out: 'The things which were gain to me, those I counted loss for Christ. . . . Yea, doubtless, and I count all things but loss for the excellency of the knowledge of Christ Jesus my Lord' (Phil. 3:7-8).

15. It could not be that ever he should attain to this but by the 'excellent knowledge of Jesus Christ our Lord'; or 'by the grace of God'—another expression of nearly the same import. By 'the grace of God' is sometimes to be understood that free love, that unmerited mercy, by which I, a sinner, through the merits of Christ am now reconciled to God. But in this place it rather means that power of God the Holy Ghost which 'worketh in us both to will and to do of his good pleasure'. As soon as ever the grace of God (in the former sense, his pardoning love) is manifested to our soul, the grace of God (in the latter sense, the power of his Spirit) takes place therein. And now we can perform, through God, what to man was impossible. Now we can order our conversation aright. We can do all things in the light and power of that love, through Christ which strengtheneth us. We now have 'the testimony of our conscience', which we could never have by fleshly wisdom, 'that in simplicity and godly sincerity . . . we have our conversation in the world'.

16. This is properly the ground of a Christian's joy. We may now therefore readily conceive how he that hath this testimony in himself 'rejoiceth evermore'. '"My soul" (may he say) "doth magnify the Lord, and my spirit rejoiceth in God my Saviour." I rejoice in him who, of his own unmerited love, of his own free and tender mercy, "hath called me into this state of salvation" wherein through his power I now stand. I rejoice because his Spirit beareth witness to my spirit that I am bought with the blood of the Lamb, and that believing in him, "I am a member of Christ, a child of God, and an inheritor of the kingdom of heaven." I rejoice because the sense of God's love to me hath by the same Spirit wrought in me to love him, and to love for his sake every child of man, every soul that he hath made. I rejoice because he gives me to feel in myself "the mind that was in Christ": simplicity, a single eye to him in every motion of my heart; power always to fix the loving eye of my soul on him who "loved me, and gave himself for me", to aim at him alone, at his glorious will, in all I think or speak or do; purity, desiring nothing more but God, "crucifying the flesh with its affections and lusts", "setting my affections on things above, not on things of the earth"; holiness, a recovery of the image of God, a renewal of soul after his likeness; and godly sincerity, directing all my words and works so as to conduce to his glory. In this I likewise rejoice, yea and will rejoice, because my conscience beareth me witness in the Holy Ghost, by the light he continually pours in upon it, that "I walk worthy of the vocation wherewith" I am "called"; that I "abstain from all appearance of

evil", "fleeing from sin as from the face of a serpent"; that as I have opportunity I do all possible good, in every kind, to all men; that I follow my Lord in all my steps, and do what is acceptable in his sight. I rejoice because I both see and feel, through the inspiration of God's Holy Spirit, that all my works are wrought in him, yea, and that it is he who worketh all my works in me. I rejoice in seeing, through the light of God which shines in my heart, that I have power to walk in his ways, and that through his grace I turn not therefrom, to the right hand or to the left.'

17. Such is the ground and the nature of that joy whereby a Christian rejoiceth evermore. And from all this we may easily infer, first, that this is not a *natural* joy. It does not arise from any natural cause: not from any sudden flow of spirits. This may give a transient start of joy. But the Christian 'rejoiceth always'. It cannot be owing to bodily health or ease, to strength and soundness of constitution. For it is equally strong in sickness and pain; yea, perhaps far stronger than before. Many Christians have never experienced any joy to be compared with that which then filled their soul, when the body was wellnigh worn out with pain, or consumed away with pining sickness. Least of all can it be ascribed to outward prosperity, to the favour of men, or plenty of worldly goods. For then chiefly when their faith has been tried as with fire, by all manner of outward afflictions, have the children of God rejoiced in him 'whom unseen they loved', even 'with joy unspeakable'. And never surely did men rejoice like those who were used as 'the filth and offscouring of the world'; who wandered to and fro, being in want of all things, in hunger, in cold, in nakedness; who 'had trials', not only 'of cruel mockings', but 'moreover of bonds and imprisonments'; yea, who at last 'counted not their lives dear unto themselves, so they might finish their course with joy'.

18. From the preceding considerations we may, secondly, infer that the joy of a Christian does not arise from any *blindness of conscience*, from his not being able to discern good from evil. So far from it that he was an utter stranger to this joy till the eyes of his understanding were opened, that he knew it not until he had spiritual senses, fitted to discern spiritual good and evil. And now the eye of his soul waxeth not dim. He was never so sharpsighted before. He has so quick a perception of the smallest things as is quite amazing to the natural man. As a mote is visible in the sunbeam, so to him who is walking in the light, in the beams of the uncreated sun, every mote of sin is visible. Nor does he close the eyes of his conscience any more. That sleep is departed from him. His soul is always broad awake: no more slumber or folding of the hands in rest! He is always standing on the tower, and hearkening what his Lord will say concerning him; and always rejoicing in this very thing, in 'seeing him that is invisible'.

19. Neither does the joy of a Christian arise, thirdly, from any *dullness* or *callousness of conscience*. A kind of joy, it is true, may arise from this in those whose 'foolish hearts are darkened'; whose heart is callous, unfeeling, dull of sense, and consequently without spiritual understanding. Because of their senseless, unfeeling hearts, they may rejoice even in committing sin; and this they may probably call 'liberty'! Which is indeed mere drunkenness of soul; a fatal numbness of spirit, the stupid insensibility of a seared conscience. On the contrary, a Christian has the most exquisite sensibility, such as he would not have conceived before. He never had such a tenderness of conscience as he has had since the

love of God has reigned in his heart. And this also is his glory and joy, that God hath heard his daily prayer:

> O that my tender soul might fly
> The first abhorred approach of ill:
> Quick as the apple of an eye
> The slightest touch of sin to feel.

20. To conclude. Christian joy is joy in obedience—joy in loving God and keeping his commandments. And yet not in keeping them as if we were thereby to fulfil the terms of the *covenant of works*; as if by any works or righteousness of ours we were to *procure* pardon and acceptance with God. Not so: we are already pardoned and accepted through the mercy of God in Christ Jesus—not as if we were by our own obedience to *procure* life, life from the death of sin. This also we have already through the grace of God. 'Us hath he quickened, who were dead in sin.' And now we are 'alive to God, through Jesus Christ our Lord'. But we rejoice in walking according to the *covenant of grace*, in holy love and happy obedience. We rejoice in knowing that 'being justified through his grace', we have 'not received that grace of God in vain'; that God having freely (not for the sake of our willing or running, but through the blood of the Lamb) reconciled us to himself, we run in the strength which he hath given us the way of his commandments. He hath 'girded us with strength unto the war', and we gladly 'fight the good fight of faith'. We rejoice, through him who liveth in our hearts by faith, to 'lay hold of eternal life'. This is our rejoicing; that as our 'Father worketh hitherto', so (not by our own might or wisdom, but through the power of his Spirit freely given in Christ Jesus) we also work the works of God. And may he work in us whatsoever is well-pleasing in his sight, to whom be the praise for ever and ever!

24. SCRIPTURAL CHRISTIANITY

August 24, 1744

An Introductory Comment

As a teaching fellow at Oxford, John Wesley was required to preach before the university at St. Mary's when his turn came up on August 24, 1744. His text for the occasion was Acts 4:31, "They were all filled with the Holy Ghost," which he employed one other time at Owston Ferry on June 29, 1784 (WWS). This particular language for Wesley does not always refer to entire sanctification but at times marks the transition of the sinner from ungodliness to the beginning of holiness in which "the energy of Satan ends" (O, 2:68). Such is its usage here, which explains, in part, the animated and overwhelmingly negative reaction of the university officials to Wesley's prophetic foray. This sermon, then, marks Wesley's transition from the life of a tenured don, with all its privileges, to that of a bold, and at times incautious, itinerant field preacher who was in earnest to reach the masses (O, 1:115).

Defining scriptural Christianity as "heart religion" and "the religion of love" (WH 21:20) that is ever associated with the Holy Spirit (B, 28), Wesley was intent in 1744 upon applying the same pointed questioning to his Oxford congregation that Spangenberg had employed earlier with respect to him so effectively in Georgia (O, 1:176n). After a number of trenchant and embarrassing accusations, Wesley concluded his sermon by calling the youth in that place "a generation of *triflers,* triflers with God, with one another, and with your own souls" (O, 1:179). William Blackstone, the famous judge and author, recorded of the event: "His [Wesley's] notes were demanded by the Vice-Chancellor [William Hodges], but on mature deliberation it has been thought proper to punish him by a mortifying neglect" (S, 1:90). And Wesley himself noted in his *Journal*: "I preached for the last time before the University of Oxford. I am now clear of the blood of these men. I have fully delivered my own soul" (WH, 20:36–37).

Scriptural Christianity

1. Those gathered at Pentecost were filled with the Holy Ghost
2. We are not informed that any *extraordinary* gifts were given
3. It was for a more excellent purpose that they were all filled with the Holy Ghost
4. It was to give them the mind of Christ and the fruits of the Spirit
5. Let us take a closer view of these extraordinary gifts

I. 1. Christianity began to exist when they called 'Jesus Lord, by the Holy Ghost'
2. This is the very essence of faith, a love of God the Father, through the Son
3. They magnified the Lord, and they rejoiced in the Saviour
4. The love of God was also shed abroad in their hearts by the Holy Ghost
5.–6. Loving God, they could not but love each other also
7. It was impossible for them knowingly to do harm to anyone
8. They daily increased in the strength, knowledge, and love of God
9. They not only abstained from doing evil; they sought to do good
10. Such was Christianity in its rise; such were Christians in ancient days

II. 1. The Lord declared, 'Ye are the salt of the earth'
2. A few saw the whole world lying in wickedness
3.–4. They warned people to flee from the wrath to come
5.–7. And their labour was not in vain
8. The pillars of hell were shaken, and the kingdom of God spread
9. But the tares soon began to appear with the wheat

III. 1.–2. But shall we not see greater things than these?
3. When the fullness of time has come, the prophecies will be accomplished
4.–6. With righteousness or justice, mercy will also be found

IV. Having considered all of this, I close with a practical application
1.–3. I would ask, 'Where does this Christianity now exist?'
A. We have never yet seen a Christian country upon earth
4. I appeal to your conscience, guided by the Word of God
5. Are you filled with the Holy Ghost?
6.–7. Are you filled with the fruits of the Spirit?
8. Many of us are consecrated to God, called to minister in holy things
9. What shall we say concerning the youth of this place?
10. May you not be a generation of *triflers*
11. Are you convinced that scriptural Christianity should be restored?

Sermon 4: Scriptural Christianity

A Sermon preached at St. Mary's, Oxford, before the University, August 24, 1744

Acts 4:31

To the Reader.

It was not my design when I wrote ever to print the latter part of the following sermon. But the false and scurrilous accounts of it which have been published almost in every corner of the nation constrain me to publish the whole, just as it was preached, that men of reason may judge for themselves.

OCTOBER 20 JOHN WESLEY

1744

Acts 4:31

And they were all filled with the Holy Ghost.

1. The same expression occurs in the second chapter, where we read, 'When the day of Pentecost was fully come, they were all' (the apostles, with the women, and the mother of Jesus, and his brethren) 'with one accord in one place. And suddenly there came a sound from heaven, as of a rushing mighty wind. . . . And there appeared unto them cloven tongues, like as of fire, and it sat upon each of them. And they were all filled with the Holy Ghost' (Acts 2:1-4). One immediate effect whereof was, they 'began to speak with other tongues' (Acts 2:4); insomuch that both the 'Parthians, Medes, Elamites', and the other strangers who 'came together' 'when this was noised abroad', 'heard them speak' in their several 'tongues, the wonderful works of God' (Acts 2:6, 9, 11).

2. In this chapter we read that when the apostles and brethren had been praying and praising God, 'the place was shaken where they were assembled together, and they were all filled with the Holy Ghost' (Acts 4:31). Not that we find any visible appearance here, such as had been in the former instance: nor are we informed that the *extraordinary* gifts of the Holy Ghost were then given to all or any of them, such as 'the gifts of healing, of working other miracles, of prophecy, of discerning spirits', the speaking with 'divers kinds of tongues', and 'the interpretation of tongues' (1 Cor. 12:9-10).

3. Whether these gifts of the Holy Ghost were designed to remain in the church throughout all ages, and whether or not they will be restored at the nearer approach of the 'restitution of all things', are questions which it is not needful to decide. But it is needful to observe this, that even in the infancy of the church God divided them with a sparing hand. 'Were all' even then 'prophets?' Were 'all workers of miracles? Had all the gifts of healing? Did all speak with tongues?' No, in no wise. Perhaps not one in a thousand.

Probably none but the teachers in the church, and only some of them (1 Cor. 12:28-30). It was therefore for a more excellent purpose than this that 'they were all filled with the Holy Ghost.'

4. It was to give them (what none can deny to be essential to all Christians in all ages) 'the mind which was in Christ', those holy 'fruits of the Spirit' which whosoever hath not 'is none of his'; to fill them with 'love, joy, peace, long-suffering, gentleness, goodness'; to endue them with 'faith' (perhaps it might be rendered 'fidelity'), with 'meekness and temperance'; to enable them to 'crucify the flesh with its affections and lusts' (Gal. 5:22-24), its passions and desires; and, in consequence of that *inward change*, to fulfil all *outward* righteousness, 'to walk as Christ also walked', in the 'work of faith, the patience of hope, the labour of love' (1 Thess. 1:3).

5. Without busying ourselves then in curious, needless inquiries touching those *extraordinary* gifts of the Spirit, let us take a nearer view of these his *ordinary* fruits, which we are assured will remain throughout all ages: of that great work of God among the children of men which we are used to express by one word, 'Christianity'; not as it implies a set of opinions, a system of doctrines, but as it refers to men's hearts and lives. And this Christianity it may be useful to consider under three distinct views:

I. As beginning to exist in individuals.

II. As spreading from one to another.

III. As covering the earth.

I design to close these considerations with a plain practical application.

I. And first, let us consider Christianity in its rise, as beginning to exist in individuals.

[1.] Suppose then one of those who heard the Apostle Peter preaching 'repentance and remission of sins' was 'pricked to the heart', was convinced of sin, repented, and then 'believed in Jesus'. By this 'faith of the operation of God', which was the very 'substance', or subsistence, 'of things hoped for', the demonstrative 'evidence of invisible things' (Heb. 11:1), he instantly 'received the Spirit of adoption, whereby he (now) cried Abba, Father' (Rom. 8:15). Now first it was that he could 'call Jesus Lord, by the Holy Ghost' (1 Cor. 12:3), 'the Spirit itself bearing witness with his spirit that he was a child of God' (Rom. 8:16). Now it was that he could truly say, 'I live not, but Christ liveth in me; and the life which I now live in the flesh I live by faith in the Son of God, who loved me and gave himself for me' (Gal. 2:20).

2. This then was the very essence of his faith, a divine ἔλεγχος (evidence or conviction) of the love of God the Father, through the Son of his love, to him a sinner, now 'accepted in the beloved'. And 'being justified by faith, he had peace with God' (Rom. 5:1), yea, 'the peace of God ruling in his heart'; a peace 'which, passing all understanding' (πάντα νοῦν, all barely rational conception), 'kept his heart and mind' from all doubt and fear, through the 'knowledge of him in whom he had believed'. He could not therefore 'be afraid of any evil tidings'; for his 'heart stood fast, believing in the Lord'. He feared

not what man could do unto him, knowing 'the very hairs of his head were all numbered'. He feared not all the powers of darkness, whom God was daily 'bruising under his feet'. Least of all was he afraid to die; nay, he 'desired to depart and be with Christ' (Phil. 1:23); who 'through death had destroyed him that had the power of death, even the devil, and delivered them who through fear of death were all their lifetime', till then, 'subject to bondage' (Heb. 2:14-15).

3. 'His soul' therefore 'magnified the Lord, and his spirit rejoiced in God his Saviour.' He rejoiced in him 'with joy unspeakable', who 'had reconciled him to God, even the Father'; 'in whom he had redemption through his blood, the forgiveness of sins.' He rejoiced in that 'witness of God's Spirit with his spirit that he was a child of God'; and more abundantly 'in hope of the glory of God'; in hope of the glorious image of God, the full 'renewal of his soul in righteousness and true holiness'; and in hope of that 'crown of glory', that 'inheritance incorruptible, undefiled, and that fadeth not away'.

4. 'The love of God' was also 'shed abroad in his heart by the Holy Ghost which was given unto him' (Rom. 5:5). 'Because he was a son, God had sent forth the Spirit of his Son into his heart, crying Abba, Father!' (Gal. 4:6). And that filial love of God was continually increased by the 'witness he had in himself' (1 John 5:10) of God's pardoning love to him, by 'beholding what manner of love it was which the Father had bestowed upon him, that he should be called a child of God' (1 John 3:1). So that God was the desire of his eyes, and the joy of his heart; his portion in time and in eternity.

5. He that thus 'loved God' could not but 'love his brother also'; and 'not in word only, but in deed and in truth'. 'If God', said he, 'so loved us, we ought also to love one another' (1 John 4:11); yea, every soul of man, as the 'mercy' of God 'is over all his works' (Ps. 145:9). Agreeably hereto, the affection of this lover of God embraced all mankind for his sake; not excepting those whom he had never seen in the flesh, or those of whom he knew nothing more than that they were 'the offspring of God', for whose souls his Son had died; not excepting the *evil* and *unthankful*, and least of all his enemies, those who 'hated, or persecuted, or despitefully used' him for his Master's sake. These had a peculiar place both in his heart and his prayers. He loved them 'even as Christ loved us'.

6. And 'love is not puffed up' (1 Cor. 13:4). It abases to the dust every soul wherein it dwells. Accordingly he was 'lowly of heart', little and mean and vile in his own eyes. He neither sought nor received the 'praise of men', 'but that which cometh of God only'. He was meek and long-suffering, gentle to all, and easy to be entreated. Faithfulness and truth never forsook him; they were 'bound about his neck, and wrote on the table of his heart'. By the same Spirit he was enabled to be 'temperate in all things', 'refraining his soul even as a weaned child'. He was 'crucified to the world, and the world crucified to him'—superior to 'the desire of the flesh, the desire of the eye, and the pride of life.' By the same almighty love was he saved both from passion and pride, from lust and vanity, from ambition and covetousness, and from every temper which was not in Christ.

7. It may be easily believed, he who had this love in his heart would 'work no evil to his neighbour'. It was impossible for him knowingly and designedly to do harm to any man. He was at the greatest distance from cruelty and wrong, from any unjust or unkind

action. With the same care did he 'set a watch before his mouth, and keep the door of his lips', lest he should offend in tongue either against justice, or against mercy or truth. He 'put away all lying', falsehood, and fraud; 'neither was guile found in his mouth'. He 'spake evil of no man'; nor did an unkind word ever come out of his lips.

8. And as he was deeply sensible of the truth of that word, 'without me ye can do nothing', and consequently of the need he had to be 'watered' of God 'every moment'; so he 'continued daily' in all the ordinances of God, the stated channels of his grace to man: 'in the apostles' doctrine' or teaching, receiving that food of the soul with all readiness of heart; 'in the breaking of bread', which he found to be 'the communion of the body of Christ'; and 'in the prayers' and praises offered up by the great congregation. And thus he daily 'grew in grace', increasing in strength, in the knowledge and love of God.

9. But it did not satisfy him barely to abstain from doing evil. His soul was athirst to do good. The language of his heart continually was, 'My Father worketh hitherto, and I work.' My Lord 'went about doing good'; and shall not I 'tread in his steps'? 'As he had opportunity', therefore, if he could do no good of a higher kind, he fed the hungry, clothed the naked, helped the fatherless or stranger, visited and assisted them that were sick or in prison. He 'gave all his goods to feed the poor'. He rejoiced to labour or to suffer for them; and whereinsoever he might profit another, there especially to 'deny himself'. He counted nothing too dear to part with for them, as well remembering the word of his Lord, 'Inasmuch as ye have done it unto one of the least of these my brethren, ye have done it unto me' (Matt. 25:40).

10. Such was Christianity in its rise. Such was a Christian in ancient days. Such was every one of those who, 'when they heard' the threatenings of 'the chief priests and elders', 'lifted up their voice to God with one accord, . . . and were all filled with the Holy Ghost. . . . The multitude of them that believed were of one heart and of one soul' (so did the love of him in whom they had believed constrain them to love one another). 'Neither said any of them that ought of the things which he possessed was his own; but they had all things common.' So fully were they crucified to the world and the world crucified to them. 'And they continued steadfastly . . .' 'with one accord . . .' 'in the apostles' doctrine, and in the breaking of bread, and in prayers.' 'And great grace was upon them all; neither was there any among them that lacked: for as many as were possessors of lands or houses sold them, and brought the prices of the things that were sold, and laid them down at the apostles' feet; and distribution was made unto every man according as he had need' (Acts 4:31-35).

II.1. Let us take a view, in the second place, of this Christianity as spreading from one to another, and so gradually making its way into the world. For such was the will of God concerning it, who 'did not light a candle to put it under a bushel, but that it might give light to all that were in the house'. And this our Lord had declared to his first disciples, 'Ye are the salt of the earth, . . . the light of the world,' at the same time that he gave that general command, 'Let your light so shine before men that they may see your good works, and glorify your Father which is in heaven' (Matt. 5:13-16).

2. And, indeed, supposing a few of these lovers of mankind to see 'the whole world lying in wickedness', can we believe they would be unconcerned at the sight? At the misery of those for whom their Lord died? Would not their bowels yearn over them, and their hearts 'melt away for very trouble'? Could they then stand idle all the day long? Even were there no command from him whom they loved? Rather, would they not labour, by all possible means, to 'pluck some of these brands out of the burning'? Undoubtedly they would: they would spare no pains to bring back whomsoever they could of those poor 'sheep that had gone astray' 'to the great Shepherd and Bishop of their souls' (1 Pet. 2:25).

3. So the Christians of old did. They laboured, having opportunity, to 'do good unto all men' (Gal. 6:10), warning them to 'flee from the wrath to come'; now, now, to 'escape the damnation of hell'. They declared, 'The times of ignorance God winked at; but now he calleth all men everywhere to repent' (Acts 17:30). They cried aloud, 'Turn ye, turn ye from your evil ways'; 'so iniquity shall not be your ruin' (Ezek. 18:30). They 'reasoned' with them 'of temperance and righteousness', or justice, of the virtues opposite to their reigning sins, and 'of judgment to come' (Acts 24:25), of the wrath of God which would surely be executed on evil-doers in that day when he should judge the world.

4. They endeavoured herein to speak to every man severally as he had need. To the careless, to those who lay unconcerned in darkness and in the shadow of death, they thundered, 'Awake, thou that sleepest; . . . arise from the dead, and Christ shall give thee light.' But to those who were already awakened out of sleep, and groaning under a sense of the wrath of God, their language was, 'We have an advocate with the Father; . . . he is the propitiation for our sins.' Meantime those who had believed they 'provoked to love and to good works'; to 'patient continuance in well-doing'; and to 'abound more and more' in that 'holiness, without which no man can see the Lord' (Heb. 12:14).

5. And their labour was not in vain in the Lord. His 'word ran and was glorified'. It 'grew mightily and prevailed'. But so much the more did offences prevail also. The world in general were offended, 'because they testified of it that the works thereof were evil' (John 7:7). The men of pleasure were offended, not only because these men were 'made', as it were, 'to reprove their thoughts' ('He professeth', said they, 'to have the knowledge of God; he calleth himself the child of the Lord;' 'his life is not like other men's; his ways are of another fashion; he abstaineth from our ways, as from filthiness; he maketh his boast that God is his Father'; Wisd. 2:13-16), but much more because so many of their companions were taken away and would no more 'run with them to the same excess of riot' (1 Pet. 4:4). The men of reputation were offended, because as the gospel spread they declined in the esteem of the people; and because many no longer dared to 'give them flattering titles', or to pay man the homage due to God only. The men of trade called one another together and said, 'Sirs, ye know that by this craft we have our wealth. But ye see and hear that these men have persuaded and turned away much people; . . . so that this our craft is in danger to be set at nought' (Acts 19:25-27). Above all the men of religion, so called—the men of *outside* religion, 'the saints of the world'—were offended, and ready at every opportunity to cry out, 'Men of Israel, help!' (Acts 21:28). 'We have found these men pestilent fellows, movers of sedition throughout the world' (Acts 24:5). 'These are the men that teach all men everywhere against the people and against the law' (Acts 21:28).

6. Thus it was that the heavens grew black with clouds, and the storm gathered amain. For the more Christianity spread, 'the more hurt was done', in the account of those who received it not; and the number increased of those who were more and more enraged at these 'men who (thus) turned the world upside down' (Acts 17:6); insomuch that they more and more cried out, 'Away with such fellows from the earth; it is not fit that they should live'; yea, and sincerely believed that 'whosoever' should 'kill them would do God service'.

7. Meanwhile they did not fail to 'cast out their name as evil' (Luke 6:22); so that this 'sect was everywhere spoken against' (Acts 28:22). 'Men said all manner of evil of them', even as had been done of 'the prophets that were before them' (Matt 5:11, 12). And whatever any would affirm, others would believe; so that offences grew as the stars of heaven for multitude. And hence arose, at the time foreordained of the Father, persecution in all its forms. Some, for a season, suffered only shame and reproach; some, 'the spoiling of their goods' (Heb. 10:34); some 'had trial of mocking and scourging'; some 'of bonds and imprisonment' (Heb. 11:36); and others 'resisted unto blood'.

8. Now it was that the pillars of hell were shaken, and the kingdom of God spread more and more. Sinners were everywhere 'turned from darkness to light, and from the power of Satan unto God'. He gave his children 'such a mouth, and such wisdom, as all their adversaries could not resist'. And their lives were of equal force with their words. But above all, their sufferings spake to all the world. They 'approved themselves' the servants of God 'in afflictions, in necessities, in distresses; in stripes, in imprisonments, in tumults, in labours' (2 Cor. 6:4-5); 'in perils in the sea, in perils in the wilderness; in weariness and painfulness, in hunger and thirst, in cold and nakedness'. And when, having 'fought the good fight', they were 'led as . . . sheep to the slaughter', and 'offered upon the sacrifice and service of their faith', then the blood of each found a voice, and the heathen owned, 'He being dead, yet speaketh.'

9. Thus did Christianity spread itself in the earth. But how soon did the tares appear with the wheat! And 'the mystery of iniquity' work as well as 'the mystery of godliness'! How soon did Satan find a seat, even 'in the temple of God'! Till 'the woman fled into the wilderness', and 'the faithful were (again) minished from the children of men.' Here we tread a beaten path: the still increasing corruptions of the succeeding generations have been largely described from time to time, by those witnesses God raised up, to show that he had 'built his church upon a rock, and the gates of hell should not' wholly 'prevail against her' (Matt. 16:18).

III.1. But shall we not see greater things than these? Yea, greater than have been yet from the beginning of the world? Can Satan cause the truth of God to fail? Or his promises to be of none effect? If not, the time will come when Christianity will prevail over all, and cover the earth. Let us stand a little, and survey (the third thing which was proposed) this strange sight, a *Christian world.* 'Of this the prophets of old inquired and searched diligently:' of this 'the Spirit which was in them testified' (1 Pet. 1:10, 11, etc.): 'It shall come to pass in the last days, that the mountain of the Lord's house shall be established in the top of the mountains, and shall be exalted above the hills, and all nations shall flow unto it. . . . And they shall beat their swords into ploughshares, and their spears into pruning-hooks. Nation shall not lift up sword against nation; neither shall they learn war any more' (Isa. 2:2, 4). 'In that day there shall be a root of Jesse, which shall stand for an ensign of the people. To it shall the Gentiles seek, and his rest shall be glorious. And it shall come to pass in that day, that the Lord shall set his hand again to recover the remnant of his people; . . . and he shall set up an ensign for the nations, and shall assemble the outcasts of Israel, and gather together the dispersed of Judah, from the four corners of the earth' (Isa. 11:10-12). 'The wolf shall (then) dwell with the lamb, and the leopard shall lie down with the kid; and the calf, and the young lion, and the fatling together; and a little child shall lead them. . . . They shall not hurt nor destroy (saith the Lord) in all my holy mountain: for the earth shall be full of the knowledge of the Lord, as the waters cover the sea' (Isa. 11:6, 9).

2. To the same effect are the words of the great Apostle, which it is evident have never yet been fulfilled: 'Hath God cast away his people? God forbid. . . . But through their fall, salvation is come to the Gentiles. And if the diminishing of them be the riches of the Gentiles, how much more their fullness? . . . For I would not, brethren, that ye should be ignorant of this mystery; . . . that blindness in part is happened to Israel, until the fullness of the Gentiles be come in: and so all Israel shall be saved' (Rom. 11:1, 11-12, 25-26).

3. Suppose now the fullness of time to be come, and the prophecies to be accomplished—what a prospect is this! All is 'peace, quietness, and assurance forever'. Here is no din of arms, no 'confused noise', no 'garments rolled in blood'. 'Destructions are come to a perpetual end:' wars are ceased from the earth. Neither is there any intestine jar remaining: no brother rising up against brother; no country or city divided against itself, and tearing out its own bowels. Civil discord is at an end for evermore, and none is left either to destroy or hurt his neighbour. Here is no oppression to 'make (even) the wise man mad'; no extortion to 'grind the face of the poor'; no robbery or wrong; no rapine or injustice; for all are 'content with such things as they possess'. Thus 'righteousness and peace have kissed each other' (Ps. 85:10); they have 'taken root and filled the land'; righteousness flourishing out of the earth, and 'peace looking down from heaven'.

4. And with righteousness or justice, mercy is also found. The earth is no longer 'full of cruel habitations'. 'The Lord hath destroyed both the bloodthirsty' and malicious, the envious and revengeful man. Were there any provocation, there is none that now knoweth to 'return evil for evil': but indeed there is none doth evil, no not one; for all are 'harmless as doves'; and being 'filled with peace and joy in believing', and united in one body, by one Spirit, they all 'love as brethren'; they are all 'of one heart, and of one soul, neither saith any of them that ought of the things which he possesseth is his own'. There is none among them that lacketh; for every man loveth his neighbour as himself. And all walk by one rule: 'Whatever ye would that men should do unto you, even so do unto them.'

5. It follows that no unkind word can ever be heard among them—no 'strife of tongues', no contention of any kind, no railing, or evil speaking—but everyone 'opens his mouth with wisdom, and in his tongue there is the law of kindness'. Equally incapable are they of fraud or guile: their 'love is without dissimulation'; their words are always the just

expression of their thoughts, opening a window into their breast, that whosoever desires may look into their hearts and see that only love and God are there.

6. Thus, where 'the Lord God omnipotent taketh to himself his mighty power, and reigneth', doth he 'subdue all things to himself', cause every heart to overflow with love, and fill every mouth with praise. 'Happy are the people that are in such a case; yea, blessed are the people who have the Lord for their God' (Ps. 144:15). 'Arise, shine (saith the Lord), for thy light is come, and the glory of the Lord is risen upon thee. . . . Thou hast known that I the Lord am thy Saviour and thy Redeemer, the mighty God of Jacob. . . . I have made thy officers peace, and thy exactors righteousness. Violence shall no more be heard in thy land, wasting nor destruction within thy borders; but thou shalt call thy walls "Salvation", and thy gates "Praise". . . . Thy people are all righteous; they shall inherit the land for ever, the branch of my planting, the work of my hands, that I may be glorified' (Isa. 60:1, 16-18, 21). 'The sun shall no more be thy light by day; neither for brightness shall the moon give light unto thee: but the Lord shall be unto thee an everlasting light, and thy God thy glory' (Isa. 60:19).

IV. Having thus briefly considered Christianity as beginning, as going on, and as covering the earth, it remains only that I should close the whole with a plain practical application.

1. And first I would ask, Where does this Christianity now exist? Where, I pray, do the Christians live? Which is the country, the inhabitants whereof are 'all (thus) filled with the Holy Ghost'? Are all 'of one heart and of one soul'? Cannot suffer one among them to 'lack anything', but continually give 'to every man as he hath need'? Who one and all have the love of God filling their hearts, and constraining them to love their neighbour as themselves? Who have all 'put on bowels of mercies, humbleness of mind, gentleness, long-suffering'? Who offend not in any kind, either by word or deed, against justice, mercy, or truth, but in every point do unto all men as they would these should do unto them? With what propriety can we term any a Christian country which does not answer this description? Why then, let us confess we have never yet seen a Christian country upon earth.

2. I beseech you, brethren, by the mercies of God, if ye do account *me* a madman or a fool, yet 'as a fool bear with me.' It is utterly needful that someone should use great plainness of speech toward you. It is more especially needful at *this* time; for who knoweth but it is the *last*? Who knoweth how soon the righteous judge may say, 'I will no more be entreated for this people'? 'Though Noah, Daniel, and Job, were in this land, they should but deliver their own souls.' And who will use this plainness if I do not? Therefore I, even I, will speak. And I adjure you, by the living God, that ye steel not your breasts against receiving a blessing at *my* hands. Do not say in your heart, *Non persuadebis, etiamsi persuaseris*; or, in other words, Lord, thou shalt not 'send by whom thou wilt send'! Let me rather perish in my blood than be saved by this man!

3. 'Brethren, I am persuaded better things of you, though I thus speak.' Let me ask you, then, in tender love, and in the spirit of meekness, Is this city a *Christian* city? Is Christianity, *scriptural* Christianity, found here? Are we, considered as a community of

men, so 'filled with the Holy Ghost' as to enjoy in our hearts, and show forth in our lives, the genuine fruits of that Spirit? Are all the magistrates, all heads and governors of colleges and halls, and their respective societies (not to speak of the inhabitants of the town), 'of one heart and of one soul'? Is 'the love of God shed abroad in our hearts'? Are our tempers the same that were in him? And are our lives agreeable thereto? Are we 'holy as he which hath called us is holy, in all manner of conversation'?

4. I entreat you to observe that here are no *peculiar notions* now under consideration; that the question moved is not concerning *doubtful opinions* of one kind or another; but concerning the undoubted, fundamental branches (if there be any such) of our *common Christianity*. And for the decision thereof I appeal to your own conscience, guided by the Word of God. He therefore that is not condemned by his own heart, let him go free.

5. In the fear, then, and in the presence of the great God before whom both you and I shall shortly appear, I pray you that are in authority over us, whom I reverence for your office' sake, to consider (and not after the manner of dissemblers with God), are you 'filled with the Holy Ghost'? Are ye lively portraitures of him whom ye are appointed to represent among men? 'I have said, Ye are gods,' ye magistrates and rulers; ye are by office so nearly allied to the God of heaven! In your several stations and degrees ye are to show forth unto us 'the Lord our Governor'. Are all the thoughts of your hearts, all your tempers and desires, suitable to your high calling? Are all your words like unto those which come out of the mouth of God? Is there in all your actions dignity and love? A greatness which words cannot express, which can flow only from an heart full of God—and yet consistent with the character of 'man that is a worm, and the son of man that is a worm'!

6. Ye venerable men who are more especially called to form the tender minds of youth, to dispel thence the shades of ignorance and error, and train them up to be wise unto salvation, are you 'filled with the Holy Ghost'? With all those 'fruits of the Spirit' which your important office so indispensably requires? Is your heart whole with God? Full of love and zeal to set up his kingdom on earth? Do you continually remind those under your care that the one rational end of all our studies is to know, love, and serve 'the only true God, and Jesus Christ whom he hath sent'? Do you inculcate upon them day by day that 'love alone never faileth'? Whereas, 'whether there be tongues, they shall fail', or philosophical 'knowledge, it shall vanish away'; and that without love all learning is but splendid ignorance, pompous folly, vexation of spirit. Has all you teach an actual tendency to the love of God, and of all mankind for his sake? Have you an eye to this end in whatever you prescribe touching the kind, the manner, and the measure of their studies; desiring and labouring that wherever the lot of these young soldiers of Christ is cast they may be so many 'burning and shining lights', 'adorning the gospel of Christ in all things'? And permit me to ask, Do you put forth all your strength in the vast work you have undertaken? Do you labour herein with all your might? Exerting every faculty of your soul? Using every talent which God hath lent you, and that to the uttermost of your power?

7. Let it not be said that I speak here as if all under your care were intended to be clergymen. Not so; I only speak as if they were all intended to be Christians. But what example is set them by us who enjoy the beneficence of our forefathers; by fellows, students, scholars; more especially those who are of some rank and eminence? Do ye, brethren,

abound in the fruits of the Spirit, in lowliness of mind, in self-denial and mortification, in seriousness and composure of spirit, in patience, meekness, sobriety, temperance, and in unwearied, restless endeavours to do good in every kind unto all men, to relieve their outward wants, and to bring their souls to the true knowledge and love of God? Is this the general character of fellows of colleges? I fear it is not. Rather, have not pride and haughtiness of spirit, impatience and peevishness, sloth and indolence, gluttony and sensuality, and even a proverbial uselessness, been objected to us, *perhaps* not always by our enemies, nor *wholly* without ground? O that God would roll away this reproach from us, that the very memory of it might perish for ever!

8. Many of us are more immediately consecrated to God, called to 'minister in holy things'. Are we then patterns to the rest, 'in word, in conversation, in charity; in spirit, in faith, in purity'? (1 Tim. 4:12). Is there written on our forehead and on our heart, 'Holiness to the Lord'? From what motives did we enter upon this office? Was it indeed with a single eye 'to serve God, trusting that we were inwardly moved by the Holy Ghost to take upon us this ministration, for the promoting of his glory, and the edifying of his people'? And have we 'clearly determined, by God's grace, to give ourselves wholly to this office? Do we forsake and set aside, as much as in us lies, all worldly cares and studies? Do we apply ourselves wholly to this one thing, and draw all our cares and studies this way'? Are we 'apt to teach'? Are we 'taught of God', that we may be able to teach others also? Do we know God? Do we know Jesus Christ? Hath God 'revealed his Son in us'? And hath he 'made us able ministers of the new covenant'? Where then are 'the seals of our apostleship'? Who that 'were dead in trespasses and sins' have been quickened by our word? Have we a burning zeal to save souls from death, so that for their sake we often forget even to eat our bread? Do we speak plain, 'by manifestation of the truth commending ourselves to every man's conscience in the sight of God'? (2 Cor. 4:2). Are we dead to the world and the things of the world, 'laying up all our treasure in heaven'? 'Do we lord it over God's heritage'? Or are we the least, the 'servants of all'? When we bear the reproach of Christ, does it sit heavy upon us, or do we rejoice therein? When we are 'smitten on the one cheek', do we resent it? Are we impatient of affronts? Or do we 'turn the other also'; 'not resisting the evil', but 'overcoming evil with good'? Have we a bitter zeal, inciting us to strive sharply and passionately with them 'that are out of the way'? Or is our zeal the flame of love? So as to direct all our words with sweetness, lowliness, and meekness of wisdom?

9. Once more: what shall we say concerning the youth of this place? Have *you* either the form or the power of Christian godliness? Are you humble, teachable, advisable; or stubborn, self-willed, heady, and high-minded? Are you obedient to your superiors as to parents; or do you despise those to whom you owe the tenderest reverence? Are you diligent in your easy business, pursuing your studies with all your strength? Do you 'redeem the time', crowding as much work into every day as it can contain? Rather, are ye not conscious to yourselves that you waste away day after day, either in reading what has no tendency to Christianity, or in gaming, or in—you know not what? Are you better managers of your fortune than of your time? Do you, out of principle, take care to 'owe no man anything'? Do you 'remember the sabbath day to keep it holy'; to spend it in the more immediate worship of God? When you are in his house do you consider that God is there?

Do you behave 'as seeing him that is invisible'? Do you know how to 'possess your bodies in sanctification and honour'? Are not drunkenness and uncleanness found among you? Yea, are there not of you who 'glory in their shame'? Do not many of you 'take the name of God in vain', perhaps habitually, without either remorse or fear? Yea, are there not a multitude of you that are forsworn? I fear, a swiftly increasing multitude. Be not surprised, brethren: before God and this congregation I own myself to have been of that number; solemnly swearing to 'observe all those customs' which I then knew nothing of, 'and those statutes' which I did not so much as read over, either then, or for some years after. What is perjury, if this is not? But if it be, O what a weight of sin, yea, sin of no common dye, lieth upon us! And doth not 'the Most High regard it'?

10. May it not be one of the consequences of this that so many of you are a generation of *triflers*; triflers with God, with one another, and with your own souls? For how few of you spend, from one week to another, a single hour in private prayer? How few have any thought of God in the general tenor of your conversation? Who of you is in any degree acquainted with the work of his Spirit? His supernatural work in the souls of men? Can you bear, unless now and then in a church, any talk of the Holy Ghost? Would you not take it for granted if one began such a conversation that it was either 'hypocrisy' or 'enthusiasm'? In the name of the Lord God Almighty I ask, What religion are *you* of? Even the talk of Christianity ye cannot, will not, bear! O my brethren! What a Christian city is this? 'It is time for thee, Lord, to lay to thine hand!'

11. For indeed what probability—what possibility rather (speaking after the manner of men)—is there that Christianity, scriptural Christianity, should be again the religion of this place? That all orders of men among us should speak and live as men 'filled with the Holy Ghost'? By whom should this Christianity be restored? By those of you that are in authority? Are you convinced then that this is scriptural Christianity? Are you desirous it should be restored? And do ye not count your fortune, liberty, life, dear unto yourselves, so ye may be instrumental in the restoring it? But suppose ye have this desire, who hath any power proportioned to the effect? Perhaps some of you have made a few faint attempts, but with how small success! Shall Christianity then be restored by young, unknown, inconsiderable men? I know not whether ye yourselves could suffer it. Would not some of you cry out, 'Young man, in so doing thou reproachest us!' But there is no danger of your being put to the proof, so hath 'iniquity overspread us like a flood'. Whom then shall God send? The famine, the pestilence (the last messengers of God to a guilty land), or the sword? 'The armies of the' Romish 'aliens', to reform us into our first love? Nay, rather 'let us fall into thy hand, O Lord, and let us not fall into the hand of man.'

Lord, save, or we perish! Take us out of the mire, that we sink not! O help us against these enemies! For vain is the help of man. Unto thee all things are possible. According to the greatness of thy power, preserve thou those that are appointed to die. And preserve us in the manner that seemest thee good; not as we will, but as thou wilt!

25. UPON OUR LORD'S SERMON ON THE MOUNT, DISCOURSE THE SIXTH

1748

An Introductory Comment

Many preachers in the eighteenth century would consider Matthew 6:1-15 as too large a text for pulpit exposition. Earlier Wesley had preached on parts of this material (Matt. 6:10 and 6:11, for example) at Kingswood in December 1740 (WWS). A decade later, to the month and year, the much larger text emerged as Wesley's vehicle for exhortation at the Foundery (WWS).

Drawing from many of the insights culled from reading the medieval classic *The Imitation of Christ* as a young man, Wesley underscored in this present sermon the value of purity of intention that should inform works of mercy and piety. In other words, a holy and pure intention, with an eye on the church's high calling, should ever be the motivation in serving the poor in so many different ways. And in terms of works of piety Wesley was well aware of Matthew Henry's counsel, expressed in his own commentary, that "we must do better than the scribes and Pharisees in avoiding heart sins . . . [and] in maintaining and keeping up heart religion" (H, Matt. 6:1).

During the first century the three principal duties of the Jewish religion entailed praying, fasting, and almsgiving (S, 1:423). In the Sermon on the Mount, then, Christ explains each one of these familiar duties in terms of a proper intention, with an eye to the glory of God. This was also the setting in which Jesus taught his disciples how to pray the Lord's Prayer. In commenting on this material, Wesley observed that "we do not pray to inform God of our wants" (NT, Matt. 6:8). Omniscient as God is, the Most High "cannot be informed of anything which he knew not before" (NT, Matt. 6:8). Instead, the chief thing lacking, Wesley pointed out, is once again "a fit disposition on our part to receive his grace and blessing" (NT, Matt. 6:8).

Upon our Lord's Sermon on the Mount, Discourse the Sixth

1.–2. In the preceding chapter our Lord described inward religion
A. In this chapter he shows how our actions may be made holy
1. This is done by a pure and holy intention

I. 1. First, with regard to mercy, which includes feeding the hungry
A. As well as clothing the naked, helping the stranger, visiting the prisoner
2. Take heed not to do these things with a view toward your own glory
3.–4. When you give alms, do not sound a trumpet
A. Do these works in as secret a manner as possible

II. 1. From works of mercy our Lord proceeds to works of piety
A. Hypocrisy is the first thing we are to guard against in prayer
B. Some pray that they may be seen of men
2. Having an eye to praise cuts us off from reward in heaven
3. When you pray, enter into your closet
4. When you pray, do not use vain repetitions
5. The end of praying is not to inform God
A. But rather to inform ourselves, to fix a sense of dependence on God

III. 1. After having taught the purpose of prayer our Lord gives an example
2. This prayer contains all we can reasonably pray for
3. It consists of three parts: the preface, the petition, and the doxology
A. It also points out the tempers with which we are to approach God
4.–5. 'Our Father' signals that God is loving to his children
6. 'Which art in heaven' reminds us that we are under the eye of the Lord
7. 'Hallowed be thy name'; God's name contains all the divine attributes
8. We next pray that God's kingdom will come
9.–10. We then pray for an active conformity to God's will
11.–12. We pray for things which are most needful
13.–14. We pray for forgiveness and for the ability to forgive
15. We beseech God not to lead us into temptation
16. The conclusion of the prayer is a solemn thanksgiving

Sermon 26: Upon our Lord's Sermon on the Mount

Discourse the Sixth, 1748

Matthew 6:1-15

Take heed that ye do not your alms before men, to be seen of them; otherwise ye have no reward of your Father which is in heaven.

Therefore when thou dost thine alms, do not sound a trumpet before thee, as the hypocrites do in the synagogues and in the streets, that they may have praise of men. Verily, I say unto you, they have their reward.

But when thou dost alms, let not thy left hand know what thy right hand doth: that thine alms may be in secret; and thy Father which seeth in secret, himself shall reward thee openly.

And when thou prayest, thou shalt not be as the hypocrites are; for they love to pray standing in the synagogues and in the corners of the streets, that they may be seen of men. Verily I say unto you, They have their reward.

But thou, when thou prayest, enter into thy closet, and when thou hast shut the door, pray to thy Father which is in secret; and thy Father which seeth in secret, he shall reward thee openly.

But when ye pray, use not vain repetitions, as the heathen do; for they think that they shall be heard for their much speaking.

Be not ye therefore like unto them; for your Father knoweth what things ye have need of before you ask him.

After this manner therefore pray ye: Our Father, which art in heaven, hallowed be thy name. Thy kingdom come. Thy will be done on earth as it is in heaven. Give us this day our daily bread. And forgive us our trespasses, as we forgive them that trespass against us. And lead us not into temptation, but deliver us from evil. For thine is the kingdom and the power and the glory, for ever and ever. Amen.

For if ye forgive men their trespasses, your heavenly Father will also forgive you.

But if ye forgive not men their trespasses, neither will your Father forgive your trespasses.

1. In the preceding chapter our Lord has described inward religion in its various branches. He has laid before us those dispositions of soul which constitute real Christianity: the inward tempers contained in that holiness 'without which no man shall see the Lord'—the affections which, when flowing from their proper fountain, from a living faith in God through Christ Jesus, are intrinsically and essentially good, and acceptable to God. He proceeds to show in this chapter how all our actions likewise, even those that are indifferent in their own nature, may be made holy and good and acceptable to God, by a pure and holy intention. Whatever is done without this, he largely declares, is of no value before God. Whereas whatever outward works are thus consecrated to God, they are, in his sight, of great price.

2. The necessity of this purity of intention he shows, first, with regard to those which are usually accounted religious actions, and indeed are such when performed with a right

intention. Some of these are commonly termed works of piety; the rest, works of charity or mercy. Of the latter sort he particularly names almsgiving; of the former, prayer and fasting. But the directions given for these are equally to be applied to every work, whether of charity or mercy.

I.1. And, first, with regard to works of mercy. 'Take heed', saith he, 'that ye do not your alms before men, to be seen of them. Otherwise ye have no reward of your Father which is in heaven.' 'That ye do not your alms'—although this only is named, yet is every work of charity included, everything which we give, or speak, or do, whereby our neighbour may be profited, whereby another man may receive any advantage, either in his body or soul. The feeding the hungry, the clothing the naked, the entertaining or assisting the stranger, the visiting those that are sick or in prison, the comforting the afflicted, the instructing the ignorant, the reproving the wicked, the exhorting and encouraging the well-doer; and if there be any other work of mercy, it is equally included in this direction.

2. 'Take heed that ye do not your alms before men, to be seen of them.' The thing which is here forbidden is not barely the doing good in the sight of men. This circumstance alone, that others see what we do, makes the action neither worse nor better, but the doing it before men, 'to be seen of them'—with this view, from this intention only. I say, 'from this intention only', for this may in some cases be a part of our intention; we may design that some of our actions should be seen, and yet they may be acceptable to God. We may intend that our 'light' should 'shine before men', when our conscience bears us witness in the Holy Ghost that our ultimate end in designing they should 'see our good works' is 'that they may glorify our Father which is in heaven'. But take heed that ye do not the least thing with a view to your own glory. Take heed that a regard to the praise of men have no place at all in your works of mercy. If ye seek your own glory, if you have any design to gain the honour that cometh of men, whatever is done with this view is nothing worth; it is not done unto the Lord; he accepteth it not; 'ye have no reward' for this 'of our Father which is in heaven'.

3. 'Therefore when thou dost thine alms, do not sound a trumpet before thee, as the hypocrites do in the synagogues and in the streets, that they may have praise of men.' The word 'synagogue' does not here mean a place of worship, but any place of public resort, such as the market-place or exchange. It was a common thing among the Jews who were men of large fortunes, particularly among the Pharisees, to cause a trumpet to be sounded before them in the most public parts of the city when they were about to give any considerable alms. The pretended reason for this was to call the poor together to receive it, but the real design that they might have praise of men. But be not thou like unto them. Do not thou cause a trumpet to be sounded before thee. Use no ostentation in doing good. Aim at the honour which cometh of God only. 'They' who seek the praise of men 'have their reward.' They shall have no praise of God.

4. 'But when thou dost alms, let not thy left hand know what thy right hand doth.' This is a proverbial expression, the meaning of which is, do it in as secret a manner as is possible: as secret as is consistent with the doing it at all (for it must not be left undone:

omit no opportunity of doing good, whether secretly or openly) and with the doing it in the most effectual manner. For here is also an exception to be made. When you are fully persuaded in your own mind that by your not concealing the good which is done either you will yourself be enabled, or others excited, to do the more good, then you may not conceal it: then let your light appear, and 'shine to all that are in the house'. But unless where the glory of God and the good of mankind oblige you to the contrary, act in as private and unobserved a manner as the nature of the thing will admit: 'That thy alms may be in secret; and thy Father which seeth in secret, he shall reward thee openly.' Perhaps in the present world—many instances of this stand recorded in all ages—but infallibly in the world to come, before the general assembly of men and angels.

II.1. From works of charity or mercy our Lord proceeds to those which are termed works of piety. 'And when thou prayest', saith he, 'thou shalt not be as the hypocrites are; for they love to pray standing in the synagogues, and in the corners of the streets, that they may be seen of men.' 'Thou shalt not be as the hypocrites are.' Hypocrisy then, or insincerity, is the first thing we are to guard against in prayer. Beware not to speak what thou dost not mean. Prayer is the lifting up of the heart to God: all words of prayer without this are mere hypocrisy. Whenever therefore thou attemptest to pray, see that it be thy one design to commune with God, to lift up thy heart to him, to pour out thy soul before him. Not 'as the hypocrites', who 'love', or are wont, 'to pray standing in the synagogues', the exchange or market-places, 'and in the corners of the streets', wherever the most people are, 'that they may be seen of men': this was the sole design, the motive and end, of the prayers which they there repeated. 'Verily I say unto you, They have their reward.' They are to expect none from your Father which is in heaven.

2. But it is not only the having an eye to the praise of men which cuts us off from any reward in heaven, which leaves us no room to expect the blessing of God upon our works, whether of piety or mercy; purity of intention is equally destroyed by a view to any temporal reward whatever. If we repeat our prayers, if we attend the public worship of God, if we relieve the poor, with a view to gain or interest, it is not a whit more acceptable to God than if it were done with a view to praise. Any temporal view, any motive whatever on this side eternity, any design but that of promoting the glory of God, and the happiness of men for God's sake, makes every action, however fair it may appear to men, an abomination unto the Lord.

3. 'But when thou prayest, enter into thy closet; and when thou hast shut the door, pray to thy Father which is in secret.' There is a time when thou art openly to glorify God, to pray and praise him in the great congregation. But when thou desirest more largely and more particularly to make thy requests known unto God, whether it be in the evening or in the morning or at noonday, 'enter into thy closet and shut the door.' Use all the privacy thou canst. (Only leave it not undone, whether thou hast any closet, any privacy, or no. Pray to God if it be possible when none seeth but he; but if otherwise, pray to God.) Thus 'pray to thy Father which is in secret;' pour out thy heart before him; 'and thy Father which seeth in secret, he shall reward thee openly.'

4. 'But when ye pray', even in secret, 'use not vain repetitions, as the heathen do.' Μὴ βατταλογήσητε. Do not use abundance of words without any meaning. Say not the same thing over and over again; think not the fruit of your prayers depends on the length of them, like the heathens; 'for they think they shall be heard for their much speaking.'

The thing here reproved is not simply the length, no more than the shortness of our prayers. But, first, length without meaning: the speaking much, and meaning little or nothing; the using (not all repetitions; for our Lord himself prayed thrice, repeating the same words; but) vain repetitions, as the heathens did, reciting the names of their gods over and over; as they do among Christians (vulgarly so called) and not among the Papists only, who say over and over the same string of prayers without ever feeling what they speak. Secondly, the thinking to be heard for our much speaking: the fancying God measures prayers by their length, and is best pleased with those which contain the most words, which sound the longest in his ears. These are such instances of superstition and folly as all who are named by the name of Christ should leave to the heathens, to them on whom the glorious light of the gospel hath never shined.

5. 'Be not ye therefore like unto them.' Ye who have tasted of the grace of God in Christ Jesus are throughly convinced 'your Father knoweth what things ye have need of before ye ask him.' So that the end of your praying is not to inform God, as though he knew not your wants already; but rather to inform yourselves, to fix the sense of those wants more deeply in your hearts, and the sense of your continual dependence on him who only is able to supply all your wants. It is not so much to move God—who is always more ready to give than you to ask—as to move yourselves, that you may be willing and ready to receive the good things he has prepared for you.

III.1. After having taught the true nature and ends of prayer our Lord subjoins an example of it: even that divine form of prayer which seems in this place to be proposed by way of pattern chiefly, as the model and standard of all our prayers—'After this manner therefore pray ye.' Whereas elsewhere he enjoins the use of these very words: 'He said unto them, When ye pray, say. . . ' (Luke 11:2).

2. We may observe in general concerning this divine prayer, first, that it contains all we can reasonably or innocently pray for. There is nothing which we have need to ask of God, nothing which we can ask without offending him, which is not included either directly or indirectly in this comprehensive form. Secondly, that it contains all we can reasonably or innocently desire; whatever is for the glory of God, whatever is needful or profitable, not only for ourselves, but for every creature in heaven and earth. And indeed our prayers are the proper test of our desires, nothing being fit to have a place in our desires which is not fit to have a place in our prayers; what we may not pray for, neither should we desire. Thirdly, that it contains all our duty to God and man; whatsoever things are pure and holy, whatsoever God requires of the children of men, whatsoever is acceptable in his sight, whatsoever it is whereby we may profit our neighbour, being expressed or implied therein.

3. It consists of three parts: the preface, the petitions, and the doxology or conclusion. The preface, 'Our Father which art in heaven', lays a general foundation for prayer; comprising what we must first know of God before we can pray in confidence of being heard. It likewise points out to us all those tempers with which we are to approach to God, which are most essentially requisite if we desire either our prayers or our lives should find acceptance with him.

4. 'Our *Father*.' If he is a Father, then he is good, then he is loving to his children. And here is the first and great reason for prayer. God is willing to bless; let us ask for a blessing. 'Our *Father*'—our Creator, the Author of our being; he who raised us from the dust of the earth, who breathed into us the breath of life, and we became living souls. But if he made us, let us ask, and he will not withhold any good thing from the work of his own hands. 'Our *Father*'—our Preserver, who day by day sustains the life he has given; of whose continuing love we now and every moment receive life and breath and all things. So much the more boldly let us come to him, and 'we shall find mercy and grace to help in time of need.' Above all, the Father of our Lord Jesus Christ, and of all that believe in him; who justifies us 'freely by his grace, through the redemption that is in Jesus'; who hath 'blotted out all our sins', 'and healed all our infirmities'; who hath received us for 'his own children, by adoption and grace', 'and because we are sons, hath sent forth the Spirit of his Son into our hearts, crying Abba, Father;' 'who hath begotten us again of incorruptible seed', and 'created us anew in Christ Jesus'. Therefore we know that he heareth us always; therefore we 'pray' to him 'without ceasing'. We pray, because we love. And 'we love him, because he first loved us.'

5. '*Our* Father'—not *mine* only who now cry unto him; but *ours*, in the most extensive sense. The 'God and Father of the spirits of all flesh'; the Father of angels and men (so the very heathens acknowledged him to be, Πατὴρ ἀνδρῶν τε θεῶν τε), the Father of the universe, of all the families both in heaven and earth. Therefore with him there is no respect of persons. He loveth all that he hath made. He 'is loving unto every man, and his mercy is over all his works'. And 'the Lord's delight is in them that fear him, and put their trust in his mercy;' in them that trust in him through the Son of his love, knowing they are 'accepted in the Beloved'. But 'if God so loved us, we ought also to love one another.' Yea, all mankind; seeing 'God so loved the world, that he gave his only-begotten Son', even to die the death, that they 'might not perish, but have everlasting life'.

6. 'Which art in heaven'—high and lifted up; God over all, blessed for ever. Who, sitting on the circle of the heavens, beholdeth all things both in heaven and earth. Whose eye pervades the whole sphere of created being; yea, and of uncreated night; unto whom 'known are all his works', and all the works of every creature, not only 'from the beginning of the world' (a poor, low, weak translation) but ἀπ' αἰῶνος, from all eternity, from everlasting to everlasting. Who constrains the host of heaven, as well as the children of men, to cry out with wonder and amazement, O the depth!—'the depth of the riches both of the wisdom and of the knowledge of God!' 'Which art in heaven'—the Lord and ruler of all, superintending and disposing all things; who art the King of kings and Lord of lords, the blessed and only potentate; who art strong and girded about with power, doing whatsoever pleaseth thee! The Almighty, for whensoever thou willest, to do is

present with thee. 'In heaven'—eminently there. Heaven is thy throne, the place where thine honour particularly dwelleth. But not there alone; for thou fillest heaven and earth, the whole expanse of space. Heaven and earth are full of thy glory. Glory be to thee, O Lord, most high!

Therefore should we 'serve the Lord with fear, and rejoice unto him with reverence'. Therefore should we think, speak, and act, as continually under the eye, in the immediate presence of the Lord, the King.

7. 'Hallowed be thy name.' This is the first of the six petitions whereof the prayer itself is composed. The name of God is God himself—the nature of God so far as it can be discovered to man. It means, therefore, together with his existence, all his attributes or perfections—his eternity, particularly signified by his great and incommunicable name Jehovah, as the Apostle John translates it, τὸ καὶ τὸ Ὠ, ἀρχὴ καὶ τέλος, ὁ ὢν καὶ ὁ ἦν καὶ ὁ ἐρχόμενος, 'the Alpha and Omega, the Beginning and the End; he which is, and which was, and which is to come.' His 'fullness of being', denoted by his other great name, 'I am that I am;' his omnipresence;—his omnipotence;—who is indeed the only agent in the material world, all matter being essentially dull and inactive, and moving only as it is moved by the finger of God. And he is the spring of action in every creature, visible and invisible, which could neither act nor exist without the continued influx and agency of his almighty power;—his wisdom, clearly deduced from the things that are seen, from the goodly order of the universe;—his Trinity in Unity and Unity in Trinity, discovered to us in the very first line of his Written Word, ברא אלחים—literally 'the Gods created', a plural noun joined with a verb of the singular number; as well as in every part of his subsequent revelations, given by the mouth of all his holy prophets and apostles;—his essential purity and holiness;—and above all his love, which is the very brightness of his glory.

In praying that God, or his 'name', may 'be hallowed' or glorified, we pray that he may be known, such as he is, by all that are capable thereof, by all intelligent beings, and with affections suitable to that knowledge: that he may be duly honoured and feared and loved by all in heaven above and in the earth beneath; by all angels and men, whom for that end he has made capable of knowing and loving him to eternity.

8. 'Thy kingdom come.' This has a close connection with the preceding petition. In order that the name of God may be hallowed, we pray that his kingdom, the kingdom of Christ, may come. This kingdom then comes to a particular person when he 'repents and believes the gospel'; when he is taught of God not only to know himself but to know Jesus Christ and him crucified. As 'this is life eternal, to know the only true God, and Jesus Christ whom he hath sent', so it is the kingdom of God begun below, set up in the believer's heart. The Lord God omnipotent then reigneth, when he is known through Christ Jesus. He taketh unto himself his mighty power; that he may subdue all things unto himself. He goeth on in the soul conquering and to conquer, till he hath put all things under his feet, till 'every thought' is 'brought into captivity to the obedience of Christ'.

When therefore God shall 'give his Son the heathen for his inheritance, and the utmost parts of the earth for his possession'; when 'all kingdoms shall bow before him, and all nations shall do him service'; when 'the mountain of the Lord's house', the church of Christ, 'shall be established in the top of the mountains'; when 'the fullness of the Gentiles shall come in, and all Israel shall be saved'—then shall it be seen that 'the Lord is King, and hath put on glorious apparel', appearing to every soul of man as King of kings, and Lord of lords. And it is meet for all those who 'love his appearing' to pray that he would hasten the time; that this his kingdom, the kingdom of grace, may come quickly, and swallow up all the kingdoms of the earth; that all mankind receiving him for their king, truly believing in his name, may be filled with righteousness and peace and joy, with holiness and happiness, till they are removed hence into his heavenly kingdom, there to reign with him for ever and ever.

For this also we pray in those words, 'Thy kingdom come.' We pray for the coming of his everlasting kingdom, the kingdom of glory in heaven, which is the continuation and perfection of the kingdom of grace on earth. Consequently this, as well as the preceding petition, is offered up for the whole intelligent creation, who are all interested in this grand event, the final renovation of all things by God's putting an end to misery and sin, to infirmity and death, taking all things into his own hands, and setting up the kingdom which endureth throughout all ages.

Exactly answerable to this are those awful words in the prayer at the burial of the dead: 'Beseeching thee, that it may please thee, of thy gracious goodness, shortly to accomplish the number of thine elect, and to hasten thy kingdom; that we, with all those that are departed in the true faith of thy holy name, may have our perfect consummation and bliss, both in body and soul, in thy everlasting glory.'

9. 'Thy will be done on earth, as it is in heaven.' This is the necessary and immediate consequence wherever the kingdom of God is come; wherever God dwells in the soul by faith, and Christ reigns in the heart by love.

It is probable many, perhaps the generality of men, at the first view of these words are apt to imagine they are only an expression of, or petition for, resignation; for a readiness to suffer the will of God, whatsoever it be concerning us. And this is unquestionably a divine and excellent temper, a most precious gift of God. But this is not what we pray for in this petition, at least not in the chief and primary sense of it. We pray, not so much for a passive as for an active conformity to the will of God in saying, 'Thy will be done on earth as it is done in heaven.'

How is it done by the angels of God in heaven? Those who now circle his throne rejoicing? They do it *willingly*; they love his commandments, and gladly hearken to his words. It is their meat and drink to do his will; it is their highest glory and joy. They do it *continually*; there is no interruption in their willing service. They rest not day nor night, but employ every hour (speaking after the manner of men—otherwise our measures of duration, days and nights and hours, have no place in eternity) in fulfilling his commands, in executing his designs, in performing the counsel of his will. And they do it *perfectly*. No sin, no defect belongs to angelic minds. It is true, 'the stars are not pure in his sight,' even the morning stars that sing together before him. 'In his sight', that is, in comparison of him, the very angels are not pure. But this does not imply that they are not pure *in themselves*. Doubtless they are; they are without spot and blameless. They are altogether devoted to his will, and perfectly obedient in all things.

If we view this in another light, we may observe the angels of God in heaven do *all* the will of God. And they do nothing else, nothing but what they are absolutely assured is his will. Again, they do all the will of God *as* he willeth, in the manner which pleases him, and no other. Yea, and they do this only *because* it is his will; for this and no other reason.

10. When therefore we pray that the 'will of God' may 'be done on earth as it is in heaven', the meaning is that all the inhabitants of the earth, even the whole race of mankind, may do the will of their Father which is in heaven as *willingly* as the holy angels; that these may do it *continually*, even as they, without any interruption of their willing service. Yea, and that they may do it *perfectly*; that 'the God of peace, through the blood of the everlasting covenant, may make them perfect in every good work to do his will, and work in them all which is well-pleasing in his sight'.

In other words, we pray that we, and all mankind, may do the whole will of God in all things; and nothing else, not the least thing but what is the holy and acceptable will of God. We pray that we may do the whole will of God *as* he willeth, in the manner that pleases him; and lastly, that we may do it *because* it is his will; that this may be the sole reason and ground, the whole and only motive, of whatsoever we think, or whatsoever we speak, or do.

11. 'Give us this day our daily bread.' In the three former petitions we have been praying for all mankind. We come now more particularly to desire a supply for our own wants. Not that we are directed, even here, to confine our prayer altogether to ourselves; but this and each of the following petitions may be used for the whole church of Christ upon earth.

By 'bread' we may understand all things needful, whether for our souls or bodies: τὰ πρὸς ζωὴν καὶ εὐσέβειαν, 'the things pertaining to life and godliness'. We understand not barely the outward bread, what our Lord terms 'the meat which perisheth'; but much more the spiritual bread, the grace of God, the food 'which endureth unto everlasting life'. It was the judgment of many of the ancient Fathers that we are here to understand the sacramental bread also; daily received in the beginning by the whole church of Christ, and highly esteemed, till the love of many waxed cold, as the grand channel whereby the grace of his Spirit was conveyed to the souls of all the children of God.

'Our daily bread.' The word we render 'daily' has been differently explained by different commentators. But the most plain and natural sense of it seems to be this, which is retained in almost all translations, as well ancient as modern: what is sufficient for this day, and so for each day as it succeeds.

12. 'Give us'; for we claim nothing of right, but only of free mercy. We deserve not the air we breathe, the earth that bears, or the sun that shines upon us. All our desert, we own, is hell. But God loves us freely. Therefore we ask him to *give* what we can no more *procure* for ourselves than we can *merit* it at his hands.

Not that either the goodness or the power of God is a reason for us to stand idle. It is his will that we should use all diligence in all things, that we should employ our utmost endeavours, as much as if our success were the natural effect of our own wisdom and strength. And then, as though we had done nothing, we are to depend on him, the giver of every good and perfect gift.

'This day'; for we are to take no thought for the morrow. For this very end has our wise Creator divided life into these little portions of time, so clearly separated from each other; that we might look on every day as a fresh gift of God, another life which we may devote to his glory; and that every evening may be as the close of life, beyond which we are to see nothing but eternity.

13. 'And forgive us our trespasses, as we forgive them that trespass against us.' As nothing but sin can hinder the bounty of God from flowing forth upon every creature, so this petition naturally follows the former; that all hindrances being removed, we may the more clearly trust in the God of love for every manner of thing which is good.

'Our trespasses.' The word properly signifies 'our debts'. Thus our sins are frequently represented in Scripture; every sin laying us under a fresh debt to God, to whom we already owe, as it were, ten thousand talents. What then can we answer when he shall say, 'Pay me that thou owest'? We are utterly insolvent; we have nothing to pay; we have wasted all our substance. Therefore if he deal with us according to the rigour of his law, if he exact what he justly may, he must command us to be 'bound hand and foot', 'and delivered over to the tormentors'.

Indeed we are already bound hand and foot by the chains of our own sins. These, considered with regard to ourselves, are chains of iron and fetters of brass. They are wounds wherewith the world, the flesh, and the devil, have gashed and mangled us all over. They are diseases that drink up our blood and spirits, that bring us down to the chambers of the grave. But considered, as they are here, with regard to God, they are debts, immense and numberless. Well, therefore, seeing we have nothing to pay, may we cry unto him that he would 'frankly forgive' us all.

The word translated 'forgive' implies either to forgive a debt, or to unloose a chain. And if we attain the former, the latter follows of course: if our debts are forgiven, the chains fall off our hands. As soon as ever, through the free grace of God in Christ, we 'receive forgiveness of sins', we receive likewise 'a lot among those which are sanctified, by faith which is in him'. Sin has lost its power; it has no dominion over those who 'are under grace', that is, in favour with God. As 'there is now no condemnation for them that are in Christ Jesus', so they are freed from sin as well as from guilt. 'The righteousness of the law is fulfilled in them', and they 'walk not after the flesh, but after the Spirit'.

14. 'As we forgive them that trespass against us.' In these words our Lord clearly declares both on what condition and in what degree or manner we may look to be forgiven of God. All our trespasses and sins are forgiven us *if* we forgive, and *as* we forgive, others. First, God forgives us *if* we forgive others. This is a point of the utmost importance. And our blessed Lord is so jealous lest at any time we should let it slip out of our thoughts that he not only inserts it in the body of his prayer, but presently after repeats it twice over: 'If', saith he, 'ye forgive men their trespasses, your heavenly Father will also forgive you. But if ye forgive not men their trespasses, neither will your Father forgive your trespasses' (Matt. 6:14-15). Secondly, God forgives us *as* we forgive others. So that if any malice or

bitterness, if any taint of unkindness or anger remains, if we do not clearly, fully, and from the heart, forgive all men their trespasses, we far cut short the forgiveness of our own. God cannot clearly and fully forgive us. He may show us some degree of mercy. But we will not suffer him to blot out all our sins, and forgive all our iniquities.

In the meantime, while we do not from our hearts forgive our neighbour his trespasses, what manner of prayer are we offering to God whenever we utter these words? We are indeed setting God at open defiance: we are daring him to do his worst. 'Forgive us our trespasses, as we forgive them that trespass against us!' That is, in plain terms, 'Do not thou forgive us at all; we desire no favour at thy hands. We pray that thou wilt keep our sins in remembrance, and that thy wrath may abide upon us.' But can you seriously offer such a prayer to God? And hath he not yet cast you quick into hell? O tempt him no longer! Now, even now, by his grace, forgive as you would be forgiven! Now have compassion on thy fellow-servant, as God hath had and will have pity on thee!

15. 'And lead us not into temptation, but deliver us from evil.' 'Lead us not into temptation.' The word translated 'temptation' means trial of any kind. And so the English word 'temptation' was formerly taken in an indifferent sense, although now it is usually understood of solicitation to sin. St. James uses the word in both these senses: first in its general, then its restrained acceptation. He takes it in the former sense when he saith, 'Blessed is the man that endureth temptation; for when he is tried', or approved of God, 'he shall receive the crown of life' (Jas. 1:12). He immediately adds, taking the word in the latter sense: 'Let no man say when he is tempted, I am tempted of God; for God cannot be tempted with evil, neither tempteth he any man. But every man is tempted, when he is drawn away of his own lust,' or desire, ἐξελκόμενος, drawn out of God, in whom alone he is safe, 'and enticed', caught as a fish with a bait. Then it is, when he is thus 'drawn away and enticed', that he properly 'enters into temptation'. The temptation covers him as a cloud; it overspreads his whole soul. Then how hardly shall he escape out of the snare! Therefore we beseech God 'not to lead us into temptation', that is (seeing 'God tempteth no man') not to suffer us to be led into it. 'But deliver us from evil'; rather 'from the evil one'; ἀπὸ τοῦ πονηροῦ. Ὁ πονηρός is unquestionably 'the wicked one', emphatically so called, the prince and god of this world, who works with mighty power in the children of disobedience. But all those who are the children of God by faith are delivered out of his hands. He may fight against them; and so he will. But he cannot conquer, unless they betray their own souls. He may torment for a time, but he cannot destroy; for God is on their side, who will not fail in the end to 'avenge his own elect, that cry unto him day and night': 'Lord, when we are tempted, suffer us not to enter into temptation. Do thou make a way for us to escape, that the wicked one touch us not.'

16. The conclusion of this divine prayer, commonly called the doxology, is a solemn thanksgiving, a compendious acknowledgement of the attributes and works of God. 'For thine is the kingdom'—the sovereign right of all things that are or ever were created; yea, thy kingdom is an everlasting kingdom, and thy dominion endureth throughout all ages. 'The power'—the executive power whereby thou governest all things in thy everlasting kingdom, whereby thou dost whatsoever pleaseth thee, in all places of thy dominion. 'And the glory'—the praise due from every creature for thy power, and the mightiness of thy

kingdom, and for all thy wondrous works which thou workest from everlasting, and shalt do, world without end, 'for ever and ever! Amen.' So be it!

I believe it will not be unacceptable to the serious reader, to subjoin

A
Paraphrase
on the
Lord's Prayer

I

Father of all, whose powerful voice
Called forth this universal frame,
Whose mercies over all rejoice,
Through endless ages still the same:
Thou by thy word upholdest all;
Thy bounteous LOVE to all is showed,
Thou hear'st thy every creature call,
And fillest every mouth with good.

II

In heaven thou reign'st, enthroned in light,
Nature's expanse beneath thee spread;
Earth, air, and sea before thy sight,
And hell's deep gloom are open laid.
Wisdom, and might, and love are thine,
Prostrate before thy face we fall,
Confess thine attributes divine,
And hail the sovereign Lord of all.

III

Thee, sovereign Lord, let all confess
That moves in earth, or air, or sky,
Revere thy power, thy goodness bless,
Tremble before thy piercing eye.
All ye who owe to him your birth
In praise your every hour employ;
Jehovah reigns! Be glad, O earth,
And shout, ye morning stars, for joy.

IV

Son of thy sire's eternal love,
Take to thyself thy mighty power;
Let all earth's sons thy mercy prove,
Let all thy bleeding grace adore.

The triumphs of thy love display;
   In every heart reign thou alone,
Till all thy foes confess thy sway,
   And glory ends what grace begun.

V

Spirit of grace, and health, and power,
   Fountain of light and love below,
Abroad thine healing influence shower,
   O'er all the nations let it flow.
Inflame our hearts with perfect love,
   In us the work of faith fulfil;
So not heaven's hosts shall swifter move
   Than we on earth to do thy will.

VI

Father, 'tis thine each day to yield
   Thy children's wants a fresh supply;
Thou cloth'st the lilies of the field,
   And hearest the young ravens cry.
On thee we cast our care; we live
   Through thee, who know'st our every need;
O feed us with thy grace, and give
   Our souls this day the living bread.

VII

Eternal, spotless Lamb of God,
   Before the world's foundation slain,
Sprinkle us ever with thy blood,
   O cleanse and keep us ever clean.
To every soul (all praise to thee!)
   Our bowels of compassion move:
And all mankind by this may see
   God is in us; for God is love.

VIII

Giver and Lord of life, whose power
   And guardian care for all are free;
To thee in fierce temptation's hour
   From sin and Satan let us flee.
Thine, Lord, we are, and ours thou art;
   In us be all thy goodness showed;
Renew, enlarge, and fill our heart
   With peace, and joy, and heaven, and God.

IX

Blessing and honour, praise and love,
  Co-equal, co-eternal Three,
In earth below, in heaven above,
  By all thy works be paid to Thee.
Thrice holy, thine the kingdom is,
  The power omnipotent is thine;
And when created nature dies,
  Thy never-ceasing glories shine.

26. UPON OUR LORD'S SERMON ON THE MOUNT, DISCOURSE THE SEVENTH

1748

An Introductory Comment

In the first five books of the Bible the only fast that is prescribed is on the tenth day of the seventh month, the Day of Atonement (S, 1:448). Other fasts were taken up after the people returned from the Babylonian captivity. The Pharisees of the first century, for example, practiced a weekly discipline on Mondays and Thursdays (S, 1:448), though the early church, according to the *Didache,* chose Wednesdays and Fridays as the regular fast days (S, 1:448) to distinguish its practice from that of the Jews (S, 1:448).

The Methodists continued the Wednesday and Friday fasts of the ancient church as a suitable means of grace through which they might draw nearer to God. And in 1763 Wesley recalled in the pages of the 'Large' *Minutes* that God had led the Methodists to this vital channel of grace early on at Oxford (S, 1:449). The homily 'On Fasting,' a part of the Anglican heritage since the sixteenth century, was reproduced by John Wesley with but a few slight omissions (O, 1:599n) in order to encourage this weekly practice. General fasts, of course, were also held among the Methodists, most notably the one that occurred on the first Friday after New Year's Day (S, 1:449) each year.

Wesley defended the employment of fasting as a suitable means of grace in the face of the Moravian quietism that broke out in the Fetter Lane Society in 1739 through the teaching of Molther and Bray (WH, 19:13134.). In this present sermon, produced several years after that controversy had run its course, Wesley points out that the discipline of fasting has attracted extreme views: some that undervalue it and others that overvalue it, often to the detriment of the body. Rightly understood, fasting should "remove the food of lust and sensuality," be an "help to prayer," and increase the awareness of God (O, 1:600).

Upon our Lord's Sermon on the Mount, Discourse the Seventh

1. Satan longs to separate inward from outward religion
    A. Many disregard all outward duties
2. It is by this device that Satan sets faith and works at variance
3. He also opposes the ends and means of religion
4. Of all the means of grace, fasting is subject to the greatest extremes

I. 1.–2. All the prophets take fasting to mean abstaining from food
    3. As to the degree of fasting, some fasted for days
    4. Some may fast by eating little, by reason of sickness or bodily health
    5.–6. The lowest kind of fasting is the abstaining from pleasant food

II. 1. What are the grounds and ends of fasting?
    2. The natural ground of fasting concerns those under deep affliction
        A. They should abstain not only from pleasant, but needful food
    3. Many are sensible that they have sinned by abusing these things
    4. They remember how fullness of bread increased carelessness and unholiness
    5. Another reason for fasting is punishment for abusing the gifts of God
    6.–9. A more weighty reason for fasting is that it is an help to prayer
    10.–11. The apostles fasted with prayer when they desired the blessing of God
    12. Above all, we have reason to fast because of the command of Christ
        A. Yet, there are an abundance of objections men have raised against it

III. 1.–2. The most plausible is that Christians should fast from sin, not food
        A. That a Christian ought to abstain from sin is most true
        B. But how does it follow from hence that he ought not abstain from food?
    3.–4. Another objection is that fasting does not avail much
        A. The fault does not lay in the *means*, but in the *manner* of using it
    5.–7. If fasting indeed be of so great importance, is it not best to fast always?
        A. This type of fasting is not scriptural fasting

IV. 1. I am, in the last place, to show in what manner we are to fast
        A. Let it be done unto the Lord, with our eyes singly fixed on him
    2.–3. Let us beware of fancying that we *merit* anything of God by this
    4. The body may sometimes be afflicted too much for fasting
    5. Let us care to afflict our souls as well as our bodies
    6.–7. With fasting let us always join fervent prayer

Sermon 27: Upon our Lord's Sermon on the Mount

Discourse the Seventh, 1748

Matthew 6:16-18

Moreover, when ye fast, be not as the hypocrites, of a sad countenance; for they disfigure their faces, that they may appear unto men to fast. Verily I say unto you, They have their reward.

But thou, when thou fastest, anoint thy head, and wash thy face;

That thou appear not unto men to fast, but unto thy Father which is in secret; and thy Father, which seeth in secret, shall reward thee openly.

1. It has been the endeavour of Satan from the beginning of the world to put asunder what God had joined together; to separate inward from outward religion; to set one of these at variance with the other. And herein he has met with no small success among those who were 'ignorant of his devices'.

Many in all ages, having a zeal for God, but not according to knowledge, have been strictly attached to the 'righteousness of the law', the performance of outward duties, but in the meantime wholly regardless of inward righteousness, 'the righteousness which is of God by faith'. And many have run into the opposite extreme, disregarding all outward duties, perhaps even 'speaking evil of the law, and judging the law', so far as it enjoins the performance of them.

2. It is by this very device of Satan that faith and works have been so often set at variance with each other. And many who had a real zeal for God have for a time fallen into the snare on either hand. Some have magnified faith to the utter exclusion of good works, not only from being the cause of our justification (for we know that man is 'justified freely by the redemption which is in Jesus') but from being the necessary fruit of it—yea, from having any place in the religion of Jesus Christ. Others, eager to avoid this dangerous mistake, have run as much too far the contrary way; and either maintained that good works were the cause, at least the previous condition, of justification, or spoken of them as if they were all in all, the whole religion of Jesus Christ.

3. In the same manner have the end and the means of religion been set at variance with each other. Some well-meaning men have seemed to place all religion in attending the prayers of the church, in receiving the Lord's Supper, in hearing sermons, and reading books of piety; neglecting meantime the end of all these, the love of God and their neighbour. And this very thing has confirmed others in the neglect, if not contempt, of the ordinances of God, so wretchedly abused to undermine and overthrow the very end they were designed to establish.

4. But of all the means of grace there is scarce any concerning which men have run into greater extremes than that of which our Lord speaks in the above-mentioned words; I mean religious fasting. How have some exalted this beyond all Scripture and reason! And others utterly disregarded it, as it were revenging themselves by undervaluing as much as the former had overvalued it. Those have spoken of it as if it were all in all; if not the end

itself, yet infallibly connected with it: these as if it were just nothing, as if it were a fruitless labour which had no relation at all thereto. Whereas it is certain the truth lies between them both. It is not all; nor yet is it nothing. It is not the end; but it is a precious means thereto, a means which God himself has ordained; and in which therefore, when it is duly used, he will surely give us his blessing.

In order to set this in the clearest light I shall endeavour to show, first, what is the nature of fasting, and what the several sorts and degrees thereof; secondly, what are the reasons, grounds, and ends of it; thirdly, how we may answer the most plausible objections against it; and fourthly, in what manner it should be performed.

I.1. I shall endeavour to show, first, what is the nature of fasting, and what the several sorts and degrees thereof. As to the nature of it, all the inspired writers, both in the Old Testament and the New, take the word to 'fast' in one single sense, for not to eat, to abstain from food. This is so clear that it would be labour lost to quote the words of David, Nehemiah, Isaiah, and the prophets which followed, or of our Lord and his apostles; all agreeing in this: that to fast is not to eat for a time prescribed.

2. To this other circumstances were usually joined by them of old, which had no necessary connection with it. Such were the neglect of their apparel, the laying aside those ornaments which they were accustomed to wear; the putting on mourning, the strewing ashes upon their head, or wearing sackcloth next their skin. But we find little mention made in the New Testament of any of these indifferent circumstances; nor does it appear that any stress was laid upon them by the Christians of the purer ages, however some penitents might voluntarily use them as outward signs of inward humiliation. Much less did the apostles or the Christians cotemporary with them beat or tear their own flesh. Such 'discipline' as this was not unbecoming the priests or worshippers of Baal. The gods of the heathens were but devils; and it was doubtless acceptable to their devil-god when his priests 'cried aloud, and cut themselves after their manner, till the blood gushed out upon them' (1 Kgs. 18:28). But it cannot be pleasing to him, nor become his followers, who 'came not to destroy men's lives, but to save them'.

3. As to the degrees or measures of fasting, we have instances of some who have fasted several days together. So Moses, Elijah, and our blessed Lord, being endued with supernatural strength for that purpose, are recorded to have fasted without intermission 'forty days and forty nights'. But the time of fasting more frequently mentioned in Scripture is one day, from morning till evening. And this was the fast commonly observed among the ancient Christians. But beside these they had also their half-fasts (*semi-jejunia*, as Tertullian styles them) on the fourth and sixth days of the week (Wednesday and Friday) throughout the year; on which they took no sustenance till three in the afternoon, the time when they returned from the public service.

4. Nearly related to this is what our Church seems peculiarly to mean by the term 'abstinence'; which may be used when we cannot fast entirely, by reason of sickness or bodily weakness. This is the eating little; the abstaining in part; the taking a smaller quantity of food than usual. I do not remember any scriptural instance of this. But neither can I con-

demn it, for the Scripture does not. It may have its use, and receive a blessing from God.

5. The lowest kind of fasting, if it can be called by that name, is the abstaining from pleasant food. Of this we have several instances in Scripture, besides that of Daniel and his brethren: who from a peculiar consideration, namely, that they might 'not defile themselves with the portion of the king's meat, nor with the wine which he drank' (a 'daily provision' of which 'the king had appointed for them'), 'requested' and obtained of 'the prince of the eunuchs' 'pulse to eat, and water to drink' (Dan. 1:5, etc.). Perhaps from a mistaken imitation of this might spring the very ancient custom of abstaining from flesh and wine during such times as were set apart for fasting and abstinence; if it did not rather arise from a supposition that these were the most pleasant food, and a belief that it was proper to use what was least pleasing at those times of solemn approach to God.

6. In the Jewish church there were some *stated* fasts. Such was the fast of the seventh month, appointed by God himself to be observed by all Israel under the severest penalty. 'The Lord spake unto Moses, saying, [. . .] on the tenth day of the seventh month there shall be a day of atonement; [. . .] and ye shall afflict your souls . . . to make an atonement for you before the Lord your God. For whatsoever soul it be that shall not be afflicted in that same day, he shall be cut off from among his people' (Lev. 23:26-29). In after ages several other stated fasts were added to these. So mention is made by the prophet Zechariah of the fast, not only 'of the seventh', but also of 'the fourth, of the fifth, and of the tenth month' (Zech. 8:19).

In the ancient Christian church there were likewise stated fasts, and those both annual and weekly. Of the former sort was that before Easter, observed by some for eight and forty hours; by others, for an entire week; by many for two weeks; taking no sustenance till the evening of each day. Of the latter, those of the fourth and sixth days of the week, observed (as Epiphanius writes, remarking it as an undeniable fact) ἐν ὅλῃ τῇ οἰκουμένῃ—'in the whole habitable earth', at least in every place where any Christians made their abode. The annual fasts in our Church are 'The forty days of Lent, the Ember days at the four seasons', the Rogation days, and the vigils or eves of several solemn festivals: the weekly, 'all Fridays in the year, except Christmas Day'.

But beside those which were fixed, in every nation fearing God there have always been occasional fasts appointed from time to time as the particular circumstances and occasions of each required. So when 'the children of Moab and the children of Ammon [. . .] came against Jehoshaphat to battle, [. . .] Jehoshaphat set himself to seek the Lord, and proclaimed a fast throughout all Judah' (2 Chr. 20:1, 3). And so 'in the fifth year of Jehoiakim the son of Josiah, in the ninth month', when they were afraid of the King of Babylon, the princes of Judah 'proclaimed a fast before the Lord to all the people of Jerusalem' (Jer. 36:9).

And in like manner particular persons who take heed unto their ways, and desire to walk humbly and closely with God, will find frequent occasion for private seasons of thus afflicting their souls before their Father which is in secret. And it is to this kind of fasting that the directions here given do chiefly and primarily refer.

II.1. I proceed to show, in the second place, what are the grounds, the reasons, and ends of fasting.

And first, men who are under strong emotions of mind, who are affected with any vehement passion such as sorrow or fear, are often swallowed up therein, and even 'forget to eat their bread'. At such seasons they have little regard for food, not even what is needful to sustain nature; much less for any delicacy or variety, being taken up with quite different thoughts. Thus when Saul said, 'I am sore distressed; for the Philistines make war against me, and God is departed from me'; it is recorded, 'He had eaten no bread all the day, nor all the night' (1 Sam. 28:15, 20). Thus those who were in the ship with St. Paul, 'when no small tempest lay upon them', and all 'hope that they should be saved was taken away', 'continued fasting, having taken nothing' (Acts 27:33), no regular meal, for fourteen days together. And thus 'David, [. . .] and all the men that were with him', when they heard that 'the people were fled from the battle, and that many of the people were fallen and dead, and Saul and Jonathan his son were dead also', 'mourned, and wept, and fasted until even, for Saul, and Jonathan, and for the house of Israel' (2 Sam. 1:12).

Nay, many times they whose minds are deeply engaged are impatient of any interruption, and even loathe their needful food, as diverting their thoughts from what they desire should engross their whole attention. Even as Saul, when on the occasion mentioned before he had 'fallen all along upon the earth, and there was no strength in him', yet 'said, I will not eat', till 'his servants, together with the woman, compelled him.'

2. Here then is the natural ground of fasting. One who is under deep affliction, overwhelmed with sorrow for sin, and a strong apprehension of the wrath of God, would without any rule, without knowing or considering whether it were a command of God or not, 'forget to eat his bread', abstain not only from pleasant, but even from needful food. Like St. Paul, who after he was 'led into Damascus, was three days without sight, and neither did eat nor drink' (Acts 9:9).

Yea, when the storm rose high, when 'an horrible dread overwhelmed' one who had long been without God in the world, his soul would 'loathe all manner of meat'; it would be unpleasing and irksome to him. He would be impatient of anything that should interrupt his ceaseless cry, 'Lord, save! or I perish.'

How strongly is this expressed by our Church in the first part of the homily on fasting!

> When men feel in themselves the heavy burden of sin, see damnation to be the reward of it, and behold with the eye of their mind the horror of hell, they tremble, they quake, and are inwardly touched with sorrowfulness of heart, and cannot but accuse themselves, and open their grief unto Almighty God, and call unto him for mercy. This being done seriously, their mind is so occupied (taken up), partly with sorrow and heaviness, partly with an earnest desire to be delivered from this danger of hell and damnation, that all desire of meat and drink is laid apart, and loathsomeness (or loathing) of all worldly things and pleasure cometh in place; so that nothing then liketh them more than to weep, to lament, to mourn, and both with words and behaviour of body to show themselves weary of life.

3. Another reason or ground of fasting is this. Many of those who now fear God are deeply sensible how often they have sinned against him by the abuse of these lawful things. They know how much they have sinned by excess of food; how long they have transgressed the holy law of God with regard to temperance, if not sobriety too; how they have indulged their sensual appetites, perhaps to the impairing even their bodily health, certainly to the no small hurt of their soul. For hereby they continually fed and increased that sprightly folly, that airiness of mind, that levity of temper, that gay inattention to things of the deepest concern, that giddiness and carelessness of spirit, which were no other than drunkenness of soul, which stupefied all their noblest faculties, no less than excess of wine or strong drink. To remove therefore the effect they remove the cause; they keep at a distance from all excess. They abstain, as far as is possible, from what had well-nigh plunged them in everlasting perdition. They often wholly refrain; always take care to be sparing and temperate in all things.

4. They likewise well remember how fullness of bread increased not only carelessness and levity of spirit but also foolish and unholy desires, yea, unclean and vile affections. And this experience puts beyond all doubt. Even a genteel, regular sensuality is continually sensualizing the soul, and sinking it into a level with the beasts that perish. It cannot be expressed what an effect variety and delicacy of food have on the mind as well as the body; making it just ripe for every pleasure of sense, as soon as opportunity shall invite. Therefore on this ground also every wise man will refrain his soul, and keep it low; will wean it more and more from all those indulgences of the inferior appetites which naturally tend to chain it down to earth, and to pollute as well as debase it. Here is another perpetual reason for fasting: to remove the food of lust and sensuality, to withdraw the incentives of foolish and hurtful desires, of vile and vain affections.

5. Perhaps we need not altogether omit (although I know not if we should do well to lay any great stress upon it) another reason for fasting which some good men have largely insisted on: namely, the punishing themselves for having abused the good gifts of God, by sometimes wholly refraining from them; thus exercising a kind of holy revenge upon themselves for their past folly and ingratitude, in turning the things which should have been for their health into an occasion of falling. They suppose David to have had an eye to this when he said, 'I wept and chastened' or punished 'my soul with fasting;' and St. Paul, when he mentions 'what revenge' godly sorrow occasioned in the Corinthians.

6. A fifth and more weighty reason for fasting is that it is an help to prayer; particularly when we set apart larger portions of time for private prayer. Then especially it is that God is often pleased to lift up the souls of his servants above all the things of earth, and sometimes to rap them up, as it were, into the third heaven. And it is chiefly as it is an help to prayer that it has so frequently been found a means in the hand of God of confirming and increasing not one virtue, not chastity only (as some have idly imagined, without any ground either from Scripture, reason, or experience), but also seriousness of spirit, earnestness, sensibility, and tenderness of conscience; deadness to the world, and consequently the love of God and every holy and heavenly affection.

7. Not that there is any natural or necessary connection between fasting and the blessings God conveys thereby. But he will have mercy as he will have mercy: he will convey whatsoever seemeth him good, by whatsoever means he is pleased to appoint. And he hath in all ages appointed this to be a means of averting his wrath, and obtaining whatever blessings we from time to time stand in need of.

How powerful a means this is to avert the wrath of God we may learn from the remarkable instance of Ahab. 'There was none like him, who did sell himself'—wholly give himself up, like a slave bought with money—'to work wickedness.' Yet when he 'rent his clothes, and put sackcloth upon his flesh, and fasted, [. . .] and went softly, the word of the Lord came to Elijah, saying, Seest thou how Ahab humbleth himself before me? Because he humbleth himself before me, I will not bring the evil in his days.'

It was for this end, to avert the wrath of God, that Daniel sought God 'with fasting and sackcloth and ashes'. This appears from the whole tenor of his prayer, particularly from the solemn conclusion of it: 'O Lord, according to all thy righteousnesses (or mercies), [. . .] let thy anger be turned away from thy holy mountain. . . . Hear the prayer of thy servant, and cause thy face to shine upon thy sanctuary that is desolate. . . . O Lord, hear! O Lord, forgive! O Lord, hearken and do, [. . .] for thine own sake' (Dan. 9:3, 16-19).

8. But it is not only from the people of God that we learn when his anger is moved to seek him by fasting and prayer; but even from the heathens. When Jonah had declared, 'Yet forty days, and Nineveh shall be destroyed, the people of Nineveh proclaimed a fast, and put on sackcloth, from the greatest of them unto the least. For the King of Nineveh arose from his throne, and laid his robe from him, and covered him with sackcloth, and sat in ashes. And he caused it to be proclaimed and published through Nineveh, Let neither man nor beast, herd nor flock, taste anything. Let them not feed, nor drink water.' (Not that the beasts had sinned, or could repent; but that by their example man might be admonished, considering that for his sin the anger of God was hanging over all creatures.) 'Who can tell if God will turn and repent, and turn away from his fierce anger, that we perish not?'And their labour was not in vain. The fierce anger of God was turned away from them. 'God saw their works' (the fruits of that repentance and faith which he had wrought in them by his prophet), 'and God repented of the evil that he had said he would do unto them; and he did it not' (Jonah 3:4-7, 9, 10).

9. And it is a means not only of turning away the wrath of God, but also of obtaining whatever blessings we stand in need of. So when the other tribes were smitten before the Benjamites, 'all the children of Israel went up unto the house of the Lord, and wept, and fasted that day until even.' And then the Lord said, 'Go up again; for tomorrow I will deliver them into thine hand' (Judg. 20:26, 28). So Samuel 'gathered all Israel together' when they were in bondage to the Philistines, 'and they fasted on that day before the Lord'. And when 'the Philistines drew near to battle against Israel, the Lord thundered upon them with a great thunder, and discomfited them, and they were smitten before Israel' (1 Sam. 7:5, 6, 10). So Ezra: 'I proclaimed a fast at the river Ahava, that we might afflict ourselves before our God, to seek of him a right way for us, and for our little ones; . . . and he was entreated of us' (Ezra 8:21, 23). So Nehemiah: 'I [. . .] fasted and prayed

before the God of heaven, and said, [. . .] Prosper, I pray thee, thy servant this day, and grant him mercy in the sight of this man' (Neh. 1:4, 11). And God granted him mercy in the sight of the king.

10. In like manner the apostles always joined fasting with prayer when they desired the blessing of God on any important undertaking. Thus we read (Acts thirteen): 'There were in the church that was at Antioch certain prophets and teachers. . . . As they ministered to the Lord and fasted' (doubtless for direction in this very affair) 'the Holy Ghost said, Separate me Barnabas and Saul for the work whereunto I have called them. And when they had' (a second time) 'fasted and prayed, and laid their hands on them, they sent them away' (Acts 13:1-3).

Thus also Paul and Barnabas themselves, as we read in the following chapter, when they 'returned again to Lystra, Iconium, and Antioch, confirming the souls of the disciples; [. . .] and when they had ordained them elders in every church, and had prayed with fasting, commended them to the Lord' (Acts 14:23).

Yea, that blessings are to be obtained in the use of his means which are no otherwise attainable our Lord expressly declares in his answer to his disciples, asking, 'Why could not we cast him out? Jesus said unto them, Because of your unbelief; for verily I say unto you, if ye have faith as a grain of mustard seed, ye shall say unto this mountain, Remove hence to yonder place, and it shall remove; and nothing shall be impossible unto you. Howbeit, this kind' (of devils) 'goeth not out but by prayer and fasting' (Matt. 17:19-21)— these being the appointed means of attaining that faith whereby the very devils are subject unto you.

11. These were the *appointed* means; for it was not merely by the light of reason, or of natural conscience (as it is called), that the people of God have been in all ages directed to use fasting as a means to these ends. But they have been from time to time taught it of God himself, by clear and open revelations of his will. Such is that remarkable one by the prophet Joel: 'Therefore thus saith the Lord, Turn you unto me with all your heart, and with fasting, and with weeping, and with mourning. . . . Who knoweth if the Lord will return and repent, and leave a blessing behind him? [. . .] Blow the trumpet in Zion, sanctify a fast, call a solemn assembly. . . . Then will the Lord be jealous over his land, and will spare his people. Yea, [. . .] I will send you corn and wine and oil. . . . I will no more make you a reproach among the heathen' (Joel 2:12, 14, 15, 18-19).

Nor are they only temporal blessings which God directs his people to expect in the use of these means. For at the same time that he promised to those who should seek him with fasting, and weeping, and mourning, 'I will render you the [y]ears which the grasshopper hath eaten, the canker-worm, and the caterpillar, and the palmer-worm, my great army,' he subjoins: 'So shall ye eat and be satisfied, and praise the name of the Lord your God. . . . Ye shall also know that I am in the midst of Israel, and that I am the Lord your God.' And then immediately follows the great gospel promise: 'I will pour out my Spirit upon all flesh, and your sons and your daughters shall prophesy, your old men shall dream dreams, and your young men shall see visions. And also upon the servants and upon the handmaids in those days will I pour out my Spirit.'

12. Now whatsoever reasons there were to quicken those of old in the zealous and constant discharge of this duty, they are of equal force still to quicken us. But above all these we have a peculiar reason for being 'in fastings often', namely the command of him by whose name we are called. He does not indeed in this place *expressly* enjoin either fasting, giving of alms, or prayer. But his directions how to fast, to give alms, and to pray, are of the same force with such injunctions. For the commanding us to do anything *thus* is an unquestionable command to do that thing; seeing it is impossible to perform it *thus* if it be not performed *at all.* Consequently the saying, Give alms, pray, fast in *such a manner*, is a clear command to perform all those duties; as well as to perform them in that *manner* which shall in no wise lose its reward.

And this is a still farther motive and encouragement to the performance of this duty; even the promise which our Lord has graciously annexed to the due discharge of it: 'Thy Father, which seeth in secret, shall reward thee openly.' Such are the plain grounds, reasons, and ends of fasting; such our encouragement to persevere therein, notwithstanding abundance of objections which men, wiser than their Lord, have been continually raising against it.

III.1. The most plausible of these I come now to consider. And, first, it has been frequently said, 'Let a Christian fast from sin, and not from food: this is what God requires at his hands.' So he does; but he requires the other also. Therefore this ought to be done, and that not left undone.

View your argument in its full dimensions, and you will easily judge of the strength of it:

If a Christian ought to abstain from sin, then he ought not to abstain from food;

But a Christian ought to abstain from sin;

Therefore he ought not to abstain from food.

That a Christian ought to abstain from sin is most true. But how does it follow from hence that he ought not to abstain from food? Yea, let him do both the one and the other. Let him, by the grace of God, always abstain from sin; and let him often abstain from food, for such reasons and ends as experience and Scripture plainly show to be answered thereby.

2. 'But is it not better' (as it has, secondly, been objected) 'to abstain from pride and vanity, from foolish and hurtful desires, from peevishness, and anger, and discontent, than from food?' Without question it is. But here again we have need to remind you of our Lord's words, 'These things ought ye to have done, and not to leave the other undone.' And indeed the latter is only in order to the former; it is a means to that great end. We abstain from food with this view, that by the grace of God, conveyed into our souls through this outward means, in conjunction with all the other channels of his grace

which he hath appointed, we may be enabled to abstain from every passion and temper which is not pleasing in his sight. We refrain from the one that, being endued with power from on high, we may be able to refrain from the other. So that your argument proves just the contrary to what you designed. It proves that we ought to fast. For if we ought to abstain from evil tempers and desires, then we ought thus to abstain from food; since these little instances of self-denial are the ways God hath chose wherein to bestow that great salvation.

3. 'But we do not find it so in fact.' (This is a third objection.) 'We have fasted much and often. But what did it avail? We were not a whit better: we found no blessing therein. Nay, we have found it an hindrance rather than an help. Instead of preventing anger, for instance, or fretfulness, it has been a means of increasing them to such a height that we could neither bear others nor ourselves.' This may very possibly be the case. 'Tis possible either to fast or pray in such a manner as to make you much worse than before; more unhappy, and more unholy. Yet the fault does not lie in the means itself, but in the *manner* of using it. Use it still, but use it in a different manner. Do what God commands *as* he commands it, and then doubtless his promise shall not fail; his blessing shall be withheld no longer; but 'when thou fastest in secret, he that seeth in secret shall reward thee openly.'

4. 'But is it not mere superstition' (so it has been, fourthly, objected) 'to imagine that God regards such little things as these?' If you say it is, you condemn all the generation of God's children. But will you say, These were all weak superstitious men? Can you be so hardy as to affirm this both of Moses and Joshua, of Samuel and David, of Jehoshaphat, Ezra, Nehemiah, and all the prophets? Yea, of a greater than all—the Son of God himself? It is certain both our Master and all these his servants did imagine that fasting is not a little thing, and that he who is higher than the highest doth regard it. Of the same judgment, it is plain, were all his apostles, after they were 'filled with the Holy Ghost and with wisdom'. When they had 'the unction of the Holy One', 'teaching' them 'all things', they still 'approved themselves the ministers of God, by fastings', as well as 'by the armour of righteousness on the right hand and on the left'. After 'the bridegroom was taken from them, then did they fast in those days'. Nor would they attempt anything (as we have seen above) wherein the glory of God was nearly concerned, such as the sending forth labourers into the harvest, without solemn fasting as well as prayer.

5. 'But if fasting be indeed of so great importance, and attended with such a blessing, is it not best', say some, fifthly, 'to fast always? Not to do it now and then, but to keep a continual fast? To use as much abstinence at all times as our bodily strength will bear?' Let none be discouraged from doing this. By all means use as little and plain food, exercise as much self-denial herein at all times, as your bodily strength will bear. And this may conduce, by the blessing of God, to several of the great ends above-mentioned. It may be a considerable help not only to chastity, but also to heavenly-mindedness; to the weaning your affections from things below, and setting them on things above. But this is not fasting, scriptural fasting; it is never termed so in all the Bible. It in some measure answers some of the ends thereof, but still it is another thing. Practise it by all means; but not so as thereby to set aside a command of God, and an instituted means of averting his judgments, and obtaining the blessings of his children.

6. Use continually then as much abstinence as you please; which taken thus is no other than Christian temperance. But this need not at all interfere with your observing solemn times of fasting and prayer. For instance: your habitual abstinence or temperance would not prevent your fasting in secret if you was suddenly overwhelmed with huge sorrow and remorse, and with horrible fear and dismay. Such a situation of mind would almost constrain you to fast; you would loathe your dainty food; you would scarce endure even to take such supplies as were needful for the body, till God lifted you up 'out of the horrible pit, and set your feet upon a rock, and ordered your goings'. The same would be the case if you was in agony of desire, vehemently wrestling with God for his blessing. You would need none to instruct you not to eat bread till you had obtained the request of your lips.

7. Again, had you been at Nineveh when it was proclaimed throughout the city, 'Let neither man nor beast, herd nor flock, taste anything. Let them not feed, nor drink water; but let them cry mightily unto God:' would your continual fast have been any reason for not bearing part in that general humiliation? Doubtless it would not. You would have been as much concerned as any other not to taste food on that day.

No more would abstinence, or the observing a continual fast, have excused any of the children of Israel from fasting on the tenth day of the seventh month, the great annual day of atonement. There was no exception for these in that solemn decree, 'Whatsoever soul it shall be that shall not be afflicted' (shall not fast) 'in that day, he shall be cut off from among his people.'

Lastly, had you been with the brethren in Antioch at the time when they fasted and prayed before the sending forth of Barnabas and Saul, can you possibly imagine that your temperance or abstinence would have been a sufficient cause for not joining therein? Without doubt, if you had not, you would soon have been cut off from the Christian community. You would have deservedly been cast out from among them 'as bringing confusion into the church of God'.

IV.1. I am, in the last place, to show in what manner we are to fast, that it may be an acceptable service unto the Lord. And, first, let it be done *unto the Lord*, with our eye singly fixed on him. Let our intention herein be this, and this alone, to glorify our Father which is in heaven; to express our sorrow and shame for our manifold transgressions of his holy law; to wait for an increase of purifying grace, drawing our affections to things above; to add seriousness and earnestness to our prayers; to avert the wrath of God, and to obtain all the great and precious promises which he hath made to us in Christ Jesus.

Let us beware of mocking God, of turning our fast as well as our prayer into an abomination unto the Lord, by the mixture of any temporal view, particularly by seeking the praise of men. Against this our blessed Lord more peculiarly guards us in the words of the text: 'Moreover, when ye fast, be ye not as the hypocrites' (such were too many who were called the people of God), 'of a sad countenance'; sour, affectedly sad, putting their looks into a peculiar form; 'for they disfigure their faces', not only by unnatural distortions, but also by covering them with dust and ashes, 'that they may appear unto men to fast'. This is their chief, if not only design. 'Verily, I say unto you, they have their reward'—even the admiration and praise of men. 'But thou, when thou fastest, anoint thy head, and wash thy face'—do as thou art accustomed to do at other times—'that thou appear not unto men to fast' (let this be no part of thy intention: if they know it without any desire of thine it matters not; thou art neither the better nor the worse), 'but unto thy Father which is in secret; and thy Father which seeth in secret shall reward thee openly.'

2. But if we desire this reward, let us beware, secondly, of fancying we *merit* anything of God by our fasting. We cannot be too often warned of this; inasmuch as a desire to 'establish our own righteousness', to procure salvation of *debt*, and not of *grace*, is so deeply rooted in all our hearts. Fasting is only a way which God hath ordained wherein we wait for his *unmerited* mercy; and wherein, without any desert of ours, he hath promised *freely* to give us his blessing.

3. Not that we are to imagine the performing the bare outward act will receive any blessing from God. 'Is it such a fast that I have chosen?' saith the Lord. 'A day for a man to afflict his soul? Is it to bow down his head as a bulrush, and to spread sackcloth and ashes under him?' Are these outward acts, however strictly performed, all that is meant by a man's 'afflicting his soul'? 'Wilt thou call this a fast, and an acceptable day to the Lord?' No, surely. If it be a mere external service, it is all but lost labour. Such a performance may possibly afflict the body. But as to the soul, it profiteth nothing.

4. Yea, the body may sometimes be afflicted too much, so as to be unfit for the works of our calling. This also we are diligently to guard against; for we ought to preserve our health, as a good gift of God. Therefore care is to be taken, whenever we fast, to proportion the fast to our strength. For we may not offer God murder for sacrifice, or destroy our bodies to help our souls.

But at these solemn seasons we may, even in great weakness of body, avoid that other extreme for which God condemns those who of old expostulated with him for not accepting their fast. 'Wherefore have we fasted, say they, and thou seest not?' 'Behold, in the day of your fast you find pleasure,' saith the Lord. If we cannot wholly abstain, we may at least abstain from pleasant food; and then we shall not seek his face in vain.

5. But let us take care to afflict our souls as well as our bodies. Let every season, either of public or private fasting, be a season of exercising all those holy affections which are implied in a broken and contrite heart. Let it be a season of devout mourning, of godly sorrow for sin: such a sorrow as that of the Corinthians, concerning which the Apostle saith, 'I rejoice, not that ye were made sorry, but that ye sorrowed to repentance. For ye were made sorry after a godly manner, that ye might receive damage by us in nothing.' 'For godly sorrow' (ἡ [γὰρ] κατὰ θεὸν λύπη), the sorrow which is according to God, which is a precious gift of his Spirit, lifting the soul to God from whom it flows, 'worketh repentance to salvation, not to be repented of'. Yea, and let our sorrowing after a godly sort work in us the same inward and outward repentance; the same entire change of heart, renewed after the image of God, in righteousness and true holiness; and the same change of life, till we are holy as he is holy in all manner of conversation. Let it work in us the same *carefulness* to be found in him without spot and blameless; the same 'clearing of

ourselves' by our lives rather than words, by our abstaining from all appearance of evil; the same *indignation*, vehement abhorrence of every sin; the same *fear* of our own deceitful hearts; the same *desire* to be in all things conformed to the holy and acceptable will of God; the same *zeal* for whatever may be a means of his glory, and of our growth in the knowledge of our Lord Jesus Christ; and the same *revenge* against Satan and all his works, against all filthiness both of flesh and spirit (2 Cor. 7:9-11) .

6. And with fasting let us always join fervent prayer, pouring out our whole souls before God, confessing our sins with all their aggravations, humbling ourselves under his mighty hand, laying open before him all our wants, all our guiltiness and helplessness. This is a season for enlarging our prayers, both in behalf of ourselves and of our brethren. Let us now bewail the sins of our people, and cry aloud for the city of our God: that the Lord may build up Zion, and cause his face to shine on her desolations. Thus we may observe the men of God in ancient times always joined prayer and fasting together; thus the apostles in all the instances cited above; and thus our Lord joins them in the discourse before us.

7. It remains only, in order to our observing such a fast as is acceptable to the Lord, that we add alms thereto: works of mercy, after our power, both to the bodies and souls of men. 'With such sacrifices' also 'God is well pleased.' Thus the angel declares to Cornelius, fasting and praying in his house, 'Thy prayers and thine alms are come up for a memorial before God' (Acts 10:4). And this God himself expressly and largely declares: 'Is not this the fast that I have chosen: . . . to undo the heavy burdens, to let the oppressed go free, and that ye break every yoke? Is it not to deal thy bread to the hungry, and that thou bring the poor that are cast out to thy house? When thou seest the naked, that thou cover him, and that thou hide not thyself from thy own flesh? Then shall thy light break forth as the morning, and thine health shall spring forth speedily; and thy righteousness shall go before thee; the glory of the Lord shall be thy reward. Then shalt thou call, and the Lord shall answer; thou shalt cry, and he shall say, Here I am. . . . If (when thou fastest) thou draw out thy soul to the hungry, and satisfy the afflicted soul; then shall thy light rise in obscurity, and thy darkness be as the noonday. And the Lord shall guide thee continually, and satisfy thy soul in drought, and make thy bones fat: and thou shalt be like a watered garden, and like a spring . . . whose waters fail not' (Isa. 58:6-11).

27. UPON OUR LORD'S SERMON ON THE MOUNT, DISCOURSE THE EIGHTH

1748

An Introductory Comment

Wesley preached on Matthew 6:22 at Epworth in August 1761, and in November 1760, he had exposited the passage Matthew 6:20 at the Foundery in London. This present sermon begins with verses 22 and 23 ("If therefore thine eye be single") in its explication and makes them the basis for the counsel of verses 19 through 21 ("Lay not up for yourselves treasures upon earth"). Sugden maintained that in this particular approach Wesley, along with William Law (a few excerpts from *A Serious Call* appear in this sermon), took the notion of a single eye to mean simply purity of intention, whereas ancient Jewish usage suggests that an evil eye refers to stinginess, a lack of generosity and liberality (S, 1:471). With Sugden's helpful correction in mind the order does not have to be reversed, and verses 22 and 23 flow readily from 19 through 21.

Developing a well-worked theme among the Methodists, Wesley contended that the fullness of light that results from a single eye is none other than happiness and holiness. He then proceeded to make a practical application of this basic truth, however derived, in his exposition of the caution "Lay not up for yourselves treasures upon earth . . . ," which forms the bulk of this sermon. Indeed, so concerned was Wesley that the Methodists would lose the *power* of religion to be left with its *form,* he not only expressed this same caution against the aggregation of wealth in the General Rules of the United Societies (by doing no harm), but he also included it in his *Character of a Methodist* and *Plain Account of Christian Perfection.* Simply put, laying up treasures on the earth is exceedingly dangerous in that it robs both God and the poor and corrupts such ill-directed souls with many vain and harmful desires (O, 1:628).

Upon our Lord's Sermon on the Mount, Discourse the Eighth

1. Our Lord shows purity of intention is needed in ordinary business
   A. This concerns giving alms, fasting, or prayer
2. If therefore thine eye is single, thy whole body shall be full of light
3. 'Full of light' implies, first, true, divine knowledge
4. The second thing which we may here understand by 'light' is holiness
5. This light implies, thirdly, happiness as well as holiness
6. There is no medium between a single and an evil eye
7. We will be full of ignorance and error concerning the things of God
   A. And we will be full of ungodliness and unrighteousness
8. There is no peace for those who do not know God
9. Therefore, lay not up for yourselves treasures upon earth

10.–11. Many hear these words and do not realize they are condemned

12.–13. We may now discern what is forbidden here
   A. It is labouring for more than is required

14. It is hard for those who have riches to enter into the kingdom of God

15.–16. And if you do not succeed, what is the fruit of your efforts to be rich?

17. And if someone asks, 'What must I do to be saved?'
   A. The answer is clear: sell everything

18.–20. Trust not in uncertain riches, not for help or for happiness

21. Trust in the living God for happiness as well as for help
22. Do not seek to *increase in goods*

23.–26. If you ask, 'But what must we do with our goods?'
   A. If you threw them into the sea they would be better bestowed
   B. There are two methods of throwing them away which are worst
   C. The first is laying them up for your posterity
   D. The second is laying them upon yourselves in folly or superfluity

27. We charge you who are rich in this world to be habitually doing good
28. Lay a good foundation, a foundation which is Jesus Christ

Sermon 28: Upon our Lord's Sermon on the Mount

Discourse the Eighth, 1748

Matthew 6:19-23

Lay not up for yourselves treasures upon earth, where moth and rust doth corrupt, and where thieves break through and steal:

But lay up for yourselves treasures in heaven, where neither moth nor rust doth corrupt, and where thieves do not break through nor steal;

For where your treasure is, there will your heart be also.

The light of the body is the eye: if therefore thine eye be single, thy whole body shall be full of light.

But if thine eye be evil, thy whole body shall be full of darkness. If therefore the light that is in thee be darkness, how great is that darkness!

1. From those which are commonly termed 'religious actions', and which are real branches of true religion where they spring from a pure and holy intention and are performed in a manner suitable thereto, our Lord proceeds to the actions of 'common life', and shows that the same purity of intention is as indispensably required in our ordinary business as in giving alms, or fasting, or prayer.

And without question the same purity of intention 'which makes our alms and devotions acceptable must also make our labour or employment a proper offering to God. If a man [. . .] pursues his business that he may raise himself to a state of honour and riches in the world, he is no longer serving God in his employment, [. . .] and has no more title to a reward from God than he who gives alms that he may be *seen*, or prays that he may be *heard* of men. For vain and earthly designs are no more allowable in our employments than in our alms and devotions.[. . .] They are not only evil when they mix with our good works', with our religious actions, 'but they have the same evil nature [. . .] when they enter into the common business of our employments. If it were allowable to pursue them in our worldly employments, it would be allowable to pursue them in our devotions. But as our alms and devotions are not an acceptable service but when they proceed from a pure intention, so our common employment cannot be reckoned a service to him but when it is performed with the same piety of heart.'

2. This our blessed Lord declares in the liveliest manner in those strong and comprehensive words which he explains, enforces, and enlarges upon throughout this whole chapter. 'The light of the body is the eye. If therefore thine eye be single, thy whole body shall be full of light: but if thine eye be evil, thy whole body shall be full of darkness.' The eye is the intention: what the eye is to the body, the intention is to the soul. As the one guides all the motions of the body, so does the other those of the soul. This eye of the soul is then said to be 'single' when it looks at one thing only; when we have no other design but to 'know God, and Jesus Christ whom he hath sent'; to know him with suitable affections, loving him as he hath loved us; to please God in all things; to serve God (as we love him) with all our heart and mind and soul and strength; and to enjoy God in all and above all things, in time and in eternity.

3. 'If thine eye be' thus 'single', thus fixed on God, 'thy whole body shall be full of light.' 'Thy whole body'—all that is guided by the intention, as the body is by the eye. All thou art, all thou dost: thy desires, tempers, affections; thy thoughts and words and actions. The whole of these 'shall be full of light'; full of true, divine knowledge. This is the first thing we may here understand by light. 'In his light thou shalt see light.' 'He which' of old 'commanded light to shine out of darkness, shall shine in thy heart.' He shall enlighten the eyes of thy understanding with the knowledge of the glory of God. His Spirit shall reveal unto thee the deep things of God. The inspiration of the Holy One shall give thee understanding, and cause thee to know wisdom secretly. Yea, the anointing which thou receivest of him 'shall abide in thee and teach thee of all things'.

How does experience confirm this? Even after God hath opened the eyes of our understanding, if we seek or desire anything else than God, how soon is our foolish heart darkened! Then clouds again rest upon our souls. Doubts and fears again overwhelm us. We are tossed to and fro, and know not what to do, or which is the path wherein we should go. But when we desire and seek nothing but God, clouds and doubts vanish away. We 'who were sometime darkness are now light in the Lord'. The night now shineth as the day; and we find 'the path of the upright is light.' God showeth us the path wherein we should go, and 'maketh plain the way before our face'.

4. The second thing which we may here understand by 'light' is holiness. While thou seekest God in all things thou shalt find him in all, the fountain of all holiness, continually filling thee with his own likeness, with justice, mercy, and truth. While thou lookest unto Jesus and him alone thou shalt be filled with the mind that was in him. Thy soul shall be renewed day by day after the image of him that created it. If the eye of thy mind be not removed from him, if thou endurest 'as seeing him that is invisible', and seeking nothing else in heaven or earth, then as thou beholdest the glory of the Lord thou shalt be 'transformed into the same image, from glory to glory, by the Spirit of the Lord'.

And it is also matter of daily experience that 'by grace we are thus saved through faith.' It is by faith that the eye of the mind is opened to see the light of the glorious love of God. And as long as it is steadily fixed thereon, on God in Christ, reconciling the world unto himself, we are more and more filled with the love of God and man, with meekness, gentleness, long-suffering; with all the fruits of holiness, which are, through Christ Jesus, to the glory of God the Father.

5. This light which fills him who has a single eye implies, thirdly, happiness as well as holiness. Surely 'light is sweet, and a pleasant thing it is to see the sun.' But how much more to see the sun of righteousness continually shining upon the soul! And if there be any consolation in Christ, if any comfort of love, if any peace that passeth all understanding, if any rejoicing in hope of the glory of God, they all belong to him whose eye is single. Thus is his 'whole body full of light'. He walketh in the light as God is in the light, rejoicing evermore, praying without ceasing, and in everything giving thanks, *enjoying* whatever is the will of God concerning him in Christ Jesus.

6. 'But if thine eye be evil, thy whole body shall be full of darkness.' 'If thine eye be evil': we see there is no medium between a single and an evil eye. If the eye be not single,

then it is evil. If the intention in whatever we do be not singly to God, if we seek anything else, then our 'mind and conscience are defiled'.

Our eye therefore is evil if in anything we do we aim at any other end than God; if we have any view but to know and to love God, to please and serve him in all things; if we have any other design than to enjoy God, to be happy in him both now and for ever.

7. If thine eye be not singly fixed on God, 'thy whole body shall be full of darkness.' The veil shall still remain on thy heart. Thy mind shall be more and more blinded by 'the God of this world, lest the light of the glorious gospel of Christ should shine upon thee'. Thou wilt be full of ignorance and error touching the things of God, not being able to receive or discern them. And even when thou hast some desire to serve God, thou wilt be full of uncertainty as to the manner of serving him; finding doubts and difficulties on every side, and not seeing any way to escape.

Yea, if thine eye be not single, if thou seek any of the things of earth, thou shalt be full of ungodliness and unrighteousness, thy desires, tempers, affections, being all out of course, being all dark, and vile, and vain. And thy conversation will be evil as well as thy heart, not 'seasoned with salt', or 'meet to minister grace unto the hearers', but idle, unprofitable, corrupt, grievous to the Holy Spirit of God.

8. Both 'destruction and unhappiness are in thy ways;' for 'the way of peace hast thou not known.' There is no peace, no settled, solid peace, for them that know not God. There is no true nor lasting content for any who do not seek him with their whole heart. While thou aimest at any of the things that perish, 'all that cometh is vanity.' Yea, not only vanity, but 'vexation of spirit', and that both in the pursuit and the enjoyment also. Thou walkest indeed in a vain shadow, and disquietest thyself in vain. Thou walkest in darkness that may be felt. 'Sleep on;' but thou canst not 'take thy rest.' The dreams of life can give pain, and that thou knowest; but ease they cannot give. There is no rest in this world or the world to come, but only in God, the centre of spirits.

'If the light which is in thee be darkness, how great is that darkness!' If the intention which ought to enlighten the whole soul, to fill it with knowledge, and love, and peace, and which in fact does so as long as it is single, as long as it aims at God alone—if this be darkness; if it aim at anything beside God, and consequently cover the soul with darkness instead of light, with ignorance and error, with sin and misery—O how great is that darkness! It is the very smoke which ascends out of the bottomless pit! It is the essential night which reigns in the lowest deep, in the land of the shadow of death.

9. Therefore 'lay not up for yourselves treasures upon earth, where moth and rust doth corrupt, and where thieves break through and steal.' If you do, it is plain your eye is evil; it is not singly fixed on God.

With regard to most of the commandments of God, whether relating to the heart or life, the heathens of Africa or America stand much on a level with those that are called Christians. The Christians observe them (a few only being excepted) very near as much as the heathens. For instance: the generality of the natives of England, commonly called Christians, are as sober and as temperate as the generality of the heathens near the Cape of Good Hope. And so the Dutch or French Christians are as humble and as chaste as the

Choctaw or Cherokee Indians. It is not easy to say, when we compare the bulk of the nations in Europe with those in America, whether the superiority lies on the one side or the other. At least the American has not much the advantage. But we cannot affirm this with regard to the command now before us. Here the heathen has far the pre-eminence. He desires and seeks nothing more than plain food to eat and plain raiment to put on. And he seeks this only from day to day. He reserves, he lays up nothing; unless it be as much corn at one season of the year as he will need before that season returns. This command, therefore, the heathens, though they know it not, do constantly and punctually observe. They 'lay up for themselves no treasures upon earth'; no stores of purple or fine linen, of gold or silver, which either 'moth or rust may corrupt', or 'thieves break through and steal'. But how do the Christians observe what they profess to receive as a command of the most high God? Not at all; not in any degree; no more than if no such command had ever been given to man. Even the *good* Christians, as they are accounted by others as well as themselves, pay no manner of regard thereto. It might as well be still hid in its original Greek for any notice they take of it. In what Christian city do you find one man of five hundred who makes the least scruple of laying up just as much treasure as he can? Of increasing his goods just as far as he is able? There are indeed those who would not do this unjustly; there are many who will neither rob nor steal; and some who will not defraud their neighbour; nay, who will not gain either by his ignorance or necessity. But this is quite another point. Even these do not scruple the thing, but the manner of it. They do not scruple the 'laying up treasures upon earth', but the laying them up by dishonesty.

They do not start at disobeying Christ, but at a breach of heathen morality. So that even these honest men do no more obey this command than a highwayman or a housebreaker. Nay, they never designed to obey it. From their youth up it never entered into their thoughts. They were bred up by their Christian parents, masters, and friends, without any instruction at all concerning it; unless it were this, to break it as soon and as much as they could, and to continue breaking it to their life's end.

10. There is no one instance of spiritual infatuation in the world which is more amazing than this. Most of these very men read or hear the Bible read, many of them every Lord's day. They have read or heard these words an hundred times, and yet never suspect that they are themselves condemned thereby, any more than by those which forbid parents to offer up their sons or daughters unto Moloch.

O that God would speak to these miserable self-deceivers with his own voice, his mighty voice! That they may at last awake out of the snare of the devil, and the scales may fall from their eyes!

11. Do you ask what it is to 'lay up treasures on earth'? It will be needful to examine this thoroughly. And let us, first, observe what is not forbidden in this command, that we may then clearly discern what is.

We are not forbidden in this command, first, to 'provide things honest in the sight of all men,' to provide wherewith we may 'render unto all their due,' whatsoever they can justly demand of us. So far from it that we are taught of God to 'owe no man anything'. We ought therefore to use all diligence in our calling, in order to owe no man anything:

this being no other than a plain law of common justice which our Lord came 'not to destroy but to fulfil'.

Neither, secondly, does he here forbid the providing for ourselves such things as are needful for the body; a sufficiency of plain, wholesome food to eat, and clean raiment to put on. Yea, it is our duty, so far as God puts it into our power, to provide these things also; to the end we may 'eat our own bread', and be 'burdensome to no man'.

Nor yet are we forbidden, thirdly, to provide for our children and for those of our own household. This also it is our duty to do, even upon principles of heathen morality. Every man ought to provide the plain necessaries of life both for his own wife and children, and to put them into a capacity of providing these for themselves when he is gone hence and is no more seen. I say, of providing *these*, the plain necessaries of life—not delicacies, not superfluities—and that by their *diligent labour*; for it is no man's duty to furnish them any more than himself with the means either of luxury or idleness. But if any man provides not thus far for his own children (as well as for 'the widows of his own house', of whom primarily St. Paul is speaking in those well-known words to Timothy), 'he hath' practically 'denied the faith, and is worse than an infidel,' or heathen.

Lastly, we are not forbidden in these words to lay up from time to time what is needful for the carrying on our worldly business in such a measure and degree as is sufficient to answer the foregoing purposes: in such a measure as, first, to 'owe no man anything'; secondly, to procure for ourselves the necessaries of life; and, thirdly, to furnish those of our own house with them while we live, and with the means of procuring them when we are gone to God.

12. We may now clearly discern (unless we are unwilling to discern it) what that is which is forbidden here. It is the designedly procuring more of this world's goods than will answer the foregoing purposes; the labouring after a larger measure of worldly substance, a larger increase of gold and silver; the laying up any more than these ends require is what is here expressly and absolutely forbidden. If the words have any meaning at all, it must be this, for they are capable of no other. Consequently whoever he is that, owing no man anything, and having food and raiment for himself and his household, together with a sufficiency to carry on his worldly business so far as answers these reasonable purposes—whosoever, I say, being already in these circumstances, seeks a still larger portion on earth—he lives in an open habitual denial of the Lord that bought him. He hath practically 'denied the faith, and is worse than an' African or American 'infidel'.

13. Hear ye this, all ye that dwell in the world, and love the world wherein ye dwell. Ye may be 'highly esteemed of men'; but ye are an 'abomination in the sight of God'. How long shall your souls cleave to the dust? How long will ye load yourselves with thick clay? When will ye awake and see that the open, speculative heathens are nearer the kingdom of heaven than you? When will ye be persuaded to choose the better part; that which cannot be taken away from you? When will ye seek only to 'lay up treasures in heaven', renouncing, dreading, abhorring all other? If you aim at 'laying up treasures on earth' you are not *barely* losing your time and spending your strength for that which is not bread: for what is the fruit if you succeed? You have murdered your own soul. You have extinguished the

last spark of spiritual life therein. Now indeed, in the midst of life you are in death. You are a living man, but a dead Christian. 'For where your treasure is, there will your heart be also.' Your heart is sunk into the dust; your soul cleaveth to the ground. Your affections are set, not on things above, but on things of the earth; on poor husks that may poison, but cannot satisfy an everlasting spirit made for God. Your love, your joy, your desire are all placed on the things which perish in the using. You have thrown away the treasure in heaven: God and Christ are lost. You have gained riches, and hell-fire.

14. O 'how hardly shall they that have riches enter into the kingdom of God!' When our Lord's disciples were astonished at his speaking thus he was so far from retracting it that he repeated the same important truth in stronger terms than before. 'It is easier for a camel to go through the eye of a needle, than for a rich man to enter into the kingdom of God.' How hard is it for them whose very word is applauded not to be wise in their own eyes! How hard for them not to think themselves better than the poor, base, uneducated herd of men! How hard not to seek happiness in their riches, or in things dependent upon them; in gratifying the desire of the flesh, the desire of the eye, or the pride of life! O ye rich, how can ye escape the damnation of hell? Only, with God all things are possible.

15. And even if you do not succeed, what is the fruit of your *endeavouring* to lay up treasures on earth? 'They that will be rich' (οἱ βουλόμενοι πλοτεῖν, they that desire, that endeavour after it, whether they succeed or no) 'fall into a temptation and a snare', a gin, a trap of the devil, 'and into many foolish and hurtful lusts'—ἐπιθυμίας [πολλὰς] ἀνοήτους, desires with which reason hath nothing to do, such as properly belong, not to rational and immortal beings, but only to the brute beasts which have no understanding; 'which drown men in destruction and perdition', in present and eternal misery. Let us but open our eyes, and we may daily see the melancholy proofs of this: men who desiring, resolving to be rich, 'coveting after money, the root of all evil, have already pierced themselves through with many sorrows', and anticipated the hell to which they are going.

The cautiousness with which the Apostle here speaks is highly observable. He does not affirm this absolutely of *the rich*; for a man may possibly be rich without any fault of his, by an overruling providence, preventing his own choice. But he affirms it of οἱ βουλόμενοι πλουτεῖν, 'those who desire' or seek 'to be rich'. Riches, dangerous as they are, do not always 'drown men in destruction and perdition'. But the *desire of riches* does: those who calmly desire and deliberately seek to attain them, whether they do, in fact, gain the world or no, do infallibly lose their own souls. These are they that sell him who bought them with his blood, for a few pieces of gold or silver. These enter into a covenant with death and hell: and their covenant shall stand. For they are daily making themselves meet to partake of their inheritance with the devil and his angels.

16. O who shall warn this generation of vipers to flee from the wrath to come! Not those who lie at their gate, or cringe at their feet, desiring to be fed with the crumbs that fall from their tables. Not those who court their favour or fear their frown: none of those who mind earthly things. But if there be a Christian upon earth, if there be a man who hath overcome the world, who desires nothing but God, and fears none but him that is able to destroy both body and soul in hell—thou, O man of God, speak and spare not; lift up thy voice like a trumpet. Cry aloud, and show these honourable sinners the desperate

condition wherein they stand. It may be one in a thousand may have ears to hear, may arise and shake himself from the dust; may break loose from these chains that bind him to the earth, and at length lay up treasures in heaven.

17. And if it should be that one of these, by the mighty power of God, awoke and asked, What must I do to be saved? the answer, according to the oracles of God, is clear, full, and express. God doth not say to thee, 'Sell all that thou hast.' Indeed he who seeth the hearts of men saw it needful to enjoin this in one peculiar case, that of the *young, rich ruler*. But he never laid it down for a general rule to all rich men, in all succeeding generations. His general direction is, first, 'Be not highminded.' 'God seeth not as man seeth.' He esteems thee not for thy riches, for thy grandeur or equipage, for any qualification or accomplishment which is directly or indirectly owing to thy wealth, which can be bought or procured thereby. All these are with him as dung and dross: let them be so with thee also. Beware thou think not thyself to be one jot wiser or better for all these things. Weigh thyself in another balance: estimate thyself only by the measure of faith and love which God hath given thee. If thou hast more of the knowledge and love of God than he, thou art on this account, and no other, wiser and better, more valuable and honourable than him who is with the dogs of thy flock. But if thou hast not this treasure those art more foolish, more vile, more truly contemptible—I will not say, than the lowest servant under thy roof but—than the beggar laid at thy gate, full of sores.

18. Secondly, 'Trust not in uncertain riches.' Trust not in them for help; and trust not in them for happiness.

First, trust not in them for help. Thou art miserably mistaken if thou lookest for this in gold or silver. These are no more able to set thee *above the world* than to set thee above the devil. Know that both the world and the prince of this world laugh at all such preparations against them. These will little avail in the day of trouble—even if they remain in the trying hour. But it is not certain that they will; for how oft do they 'make themselves wings and fly away'? But if not, what support will they afford, even in the ordinary troubles of life? The desire of thy eyes, the wife of thy youth, thy son, thine only son, or the friend which was as thy own soul, is taken away at a stroke. Will thy riches reanimate the breathless clay, or call back its late inhabitant? Will they secure thee from sickness, diseases, pain? Do these visit the poor only? Nay; he that feeds thy flocks or tills thy ground has less sickness and pain than thou. He is more rarely visited by these unwelcome guests: and if they come there at all they are more easily driven away from the little cot than from 'the cloud-topped palaces'. And during the time that thy body is chastened with pain, or consumes away with pining sickness, how do thy treasures help thee? Let the poor heathen answer:

Ut lippum pictae tabulae, fomenta podagrum,
Auriculas citharae collecta sorde dolentes.

19. But there is at hand a greater trouble than all these. *Thou* art to die. *Thou* art to sink into dust; to return to the ground from which thou wast taken, to mix with common clay. *Thy* body is to go to the earth as it was, while thy spirit returns to God that gave it. And the time draws on: the years slide away with a swift though silent pace. Perhaps your

day is far spent: the noon of life is past, and the evening shadows begin to rest upon you. You feel in yourself sure approaching decay. The springs of life wear away apace. Now what help is there in your riches? Do they sweeten death? Do they endear that solemn hour? Quite the reverse. 'O death, how bitter art thou to a man that liveth at rest in his possessions!' How unacceptable to him is that awful sentence. 'This night shall thy soul be required of thee!' Or will they prevent the unwelcome stroke, or protract the dreadful hour? Can they deliver your soul that it should not see death? Can they restore the years that are past? Can they add to your appointed time a month, a day, an hour, a moment? Or will the good things you have chosen for your portion here follow you over the great gulf? Not so: naked came you into this world; naked must you return.

Linquenda tellus, et domus et placens
Uxor: nec harum quas seris arborum
Te, praeter invisam cupressum,
Ulla brevem dominum sequetur.

Surely, were not these truths too plain to be *observed*, because they are too plain to be *denied*, no man that is to die could possibly 'trust' for help 'in uncertain riches'.

20. And trust not in them for happiness. For here also they will be found 'deceitful upon the weights'. Indeed this every reasonable man may infer from what has been observed already. For if neither thousands of gold and silver, nor any of the advantages or pleasures purchased thereby, can prevent our being miserable, it evidently follows they cannot make us happy. What happiness can they afford to him who in the midst of all is constrained to cry out,

To my new courts sad thought does still repair,
And round my gilded roofs hangs hovering care.

Indeed experience is here so full, strong, and undeniable, that it makes all other arguments needless. Appeal we therefore to fact. Are the rich and great the only happy men? And is each of them more or less happy in proportion to his measure of riches? Are they happy at all? I had wellnigh said, they are of all men most miserable! Rich man, for once, speak the truth from thy heart. Speak, both for thyself, and for thy brethren:

Amidst our plenty something still . . .
To me, to thee, to him is wanting!
That cruel something unpossessed
Corrodes and leavens all the rest.

Yea, and so it will, till thy wearisome days of vanity are shut up in the night of death.

Surely then, to trust in riches for happiness is the greatest folly of all that are under the sun! Are you not convinced of this? Is it possible you should still expect to find happiness in money or all it can procure? What! Can silver and gold, and eating and drinking, and horses and servants, and glittering apparel, and diversions and pleasures (as they are called) make thee happy? They can as soon make thee immortal.

21. These are all dead show. Regard them not. 'Trust' thou 'in the living God;' so shalt thou be safe under the shadow of the Almighty; his faithfulness and truth shall be thy shield and buckler. He is a very present help in time of trouble; such an help as can never fail. Then shalt thou say, if all thy other friends die, 'The Lord liveth, and blessed be my strong helper!' He shall remember thee when thou liest sick upon thy bed; when vain is the help of man; when all the things of earth can give no support, he will 'make all thy bed in thy sickness'. He will sweeten thy pain; the consolations of God shall cause thee to clap thy hands in the flames. And even when this house of earth is wellnigh shaken down, when it is just ready to drop into the dust, he will teach thee to say, 'O death, where is thy sting? O grave, where is thy victory? [. . .] Thanks be unto God, who giveth me the victory, through my Lord Jesus Christ.'

O trust in him for happiness as well as for help. All the springs of happiness are in him. Trust in him 'who giveth us all things richly to enjoy', παρέχοντι [ἡμῖν] πλουσίως πάντα εἰς ἀπόλαυσιν; who of his own rich and free mercy holds them out to us as in his own hand, that receiving them as his gift, and as pledges of his love, we may 'enjoy all' that we possess. It is his love gives a relish to all we taste, puts life and sweetness into all, while every creature leads us up to the great Creator, and all earth is a scale to heaven. He transfuses the joys that are at his own right hand into all he bestows on his thankful children; who, having fellowship with the Father and his Son Jesus Christ, enjoy him in all and above all.

22. Thirdly, seek not to *increase in goods*. 'Lay not up for thyself treasures upon earth.' This is a flat, positive command, full as clear as 'Thou shalt not commit adultery.' How then is it possible for a rich man to grow richer without denying the Lord that bought him? Yea, how can any man who has already the necessaries of life gain or aim at more, and be guiltless? 'Lay not up', saith our Lord, 'treasures upon earth.' If in spite of this you do and will lay up money or goods, what 'moth or rust' may 'corrupt, or thieves break through and steal'; if you will add house to house, or field to field, why do you call yourself a Christian? You do not obey Jesus Christ. You do not design it. Why do you name yourself by his name? 'Why call ye me, Lord, Lord', saith he himself, 'and do not the things which I say?'

23. If you ask, 'But what must we do with our goods, seeing we have more than we have occasion to use, if we must not lay them up? Must we throw them away?' I answer: if you threw them into the sea, if you were to cast them into the fire and consume them, they would be better bestowed than they are now. You cannot find so mischievous a manner of throwing them away as either the laying them up for your posterity or the laying them out upon yourselves in folly and superfluity. Of all possible methods of 'throwing them away' these two are the very worst—the most opposite to the gospel of Christ, and the most pernicious to your own soul.

How pernicious to your own soul the latter of these is has been excellently shown by a late writer:

> If we waste our money we are not only guilty of wasting a talent which God has given us, [. . .] but we do ourselves this farther harm: we turn this useful talent into a powerful means of corrupting ourselves; because so far as it is spent wrong, so far it is spent in the support of some wrong temper, in gratifying some vain and unreasonable desires, which as Christians we are obliged to renounce.
>
> As wit and fine parts cannot be only trifled away, but will expose those that have them to greater follies, so money cannot be only trifled away, but if it is not used according to reason and religion, will make people live a more silly and extravagant life than they would have done without it. If therefore you don't spend your money in doing good to others, you must spend it to the hurt of yourself. You act like one that refuses the cordial to his sick friend which he cannot drink himself without inflaming his blood. For this is the case of superfluous money; if you give it to those who want it it is a cordial; if you spend it upon yourself in something that you do not want it only inflames and disorders your mind.[. . .]
>
> In using riches where they have no real use, nor we any real want, we only use them to our great hurt, in creating unreasonable desires, in nourishing ill tempers, in indulging in foolish passions, and supporting a vain turn of mind. For high eating and drinking, fine clothes and fine houses, state and equipage, gay pleasures and diversions, do all of them naturally hurt and disorder our heart. They are the food and nourishment of all the folly and weakness of our nature.[. . .] They are all of them the support of something that ought not to be supported. They are contrary to that sobriety and piety of heart which relishes divine things. They are so many weights upon our mind, that makes us less able and less inclined to raise our thoughts and affections to things above.
>
> So that money thus spent is not merely wasted or lost, but it is spent to bad purposes and miserable effects; to the corruption and disorder of our hearts; to the making us unable to follow the sublime doctrines of the gospel. It is but like keeping money from the poor to buy poison for ourselves.

24. Equally inexcusable are those who *lay up* what they do not need for any reasonable purposes:

> If a man had hands and eyes and feet that he could give to those that wanted them; if he should lock them up in a chest [. . .] instead of giving them to his brethren that were blind and lame, should we not justly reckon him an inhuman wretch? If he should rather choose to amuse himself with hoarding them up than entitle himself to an eternal reward by giving them to those that wanted eyes and hands, might we not justly reckon him mad?
>
> Now money has very much the nature of eyes and feet. If therefore we lock it up in chests [. . .] while the poor and distressed want it for their necessary uses [. . .] we are not far from the cruelty of him that chooses rather to hoard up the hands and eyes than to give them to those that want them. If we choose to lay it up rather than to entitle ourselves to an eternal reward by disposing of our money well, we are guilty of his madness that rather chooses to lock up eyes and hands than to make himself for ever blessed by giving them to those that want them.

25. May not this be another reason why rich men shall so hardly enter into the kingdom of heaven? A vast majority of them are under a curse, under the peculiar curse of God; inasmuch as in the general tenor of their lives they are not only robbing God continually, embezzling and wasting their Lord's goods, and by that very means corrupting

their own souls; but also robbing the poor, the hungry, the naked, wronging the widow and the fatherless, and making themselves accountable for all the want, affliction, and distress which they may but do not remove. Yea, doth not the blood of all those who perish for want of what they either lay up or lay out needlessly, cry against them from the earth? O what account will they give to him who is ready to judge both the quick and the dead!

26. The true way of employing what you do not want yourselves you may, fourthly, learn from those words of our Lord which are the counterpart of what went before: 'Lay up for yourselves treasures in heaven, where neither moth nor rust doth corrupt, and where thieves do not break through and steal.' Put out whatever thou canst spare upon better security than this world can afford. Lay up thy treasures in the bank of heaven; and God shall restore them in that day. 'He that hath pity upon the poor lendeth unto the Lord,' and look, 'what he layeth out, it shall be paid him again.' Place that, saith he, unto my account. Howbeit, 'thou owest me thine own self also!'

Give to the poor with a single eye, with an upright heart, and write, 'So much given to God.' For 'Inasmuch as ye did it unto one of the least of these my brethren, ye have done it unto me.'

This is the part of a 'faithful and wise steward': not to sell either his houses or lands, or principal stock, be it more or less, unless some peculiar circumstance should require it; and not to desire or endeavour to increase it, any more than to squander it away in vanity; but to employ it wholly to those wise and reasonable purposes for which his Lord has lodged it in his hands. The wise steward, after having provided his own household with what is needful for life and godliness, 'makes' himself 'friends with' all that remains from time to time of the 'mammon of unrighteousness; that when he fails they may receive him into everlasting habitations;' that whensoever his earthly tabernacle is dissolved, they who were before carried into Abraham's bosom, after having eaten his bread, and worn the fleece of his flock, and praised God for the consolation, may welcome him into paradise, and to 'the house of God, eternal in the heavens'.

27. We 'charge you', therefore, 'who are rich in this world', as having authority from our great Lord and Master, ἀγαδοεργεῖν—'to be habitually doing good', to live in a course of good works. 'Be ye merciful as your Father which is in heaven is merciful,' who doth good and ceaseth not. 'Be ye merciful'—'How far?' *After your power*, with all the ability which God giveth. Make this your only measure of doing good, not any beggarly maxims or customs of the world. We charge you to 'be rich in good works'; as you have much, to *give plenteously*. Freely ye have received; freely give; so as to lay up no treasure but in heaven. Be ye 'ready to distribute' to everyone according to his necessity. Disperse abroad, give to the poor: deal your bread to the hungry. Cover the naked with a garment, entertain the stranger, carry or send relief to them that are in prison. Heal the sick; not by miracle, but through the blessing of God upon your seasonable support. Let the blessing of him that was ready to perish through pining want come upon thee. Defend the oppressed, plead the cause of the fatherless, and make the widow's heart sing for joy.

28. We exhort *you* in the name of the Lord Jesus Christ to be 'willing to communicate', κοινωνικούς εἶναι; to be of the same spirit (though not in the same outward state)

with those believers of ancient times, who 'remained steadfast' ἐν τῇ κοινωνίᾳ, in that blessed and holy 'fellowship' wherein 'none said that anything was his own, but they had all things common.' Be a steward, a faithful and wise steward, of God and of the poor; differing from them in these two circumstances only, that your wants are first supplied out of the portion of your Lord's goods which remains in your hands, and that you have the blessedness of giving. Thus 'lay up for yourselves a good foundation', not in the world which now is, but rather 'for the time to come, that ye may lay hold on eternal life.' The great foundation indeed of all the blessings of God, whether temporal or eternal, is the Lord Jesus Christ, his righteousness and blood, what he hath done, and what he hath suffered for us. And 'other foundation', in this sense, 'can no man lay'; no, not an apostle, no, not an angel from heaven. But through his merits, whatever we do in his name is a foundation for a good reward in the day when 'every man shall receive his own reward, according to his own labour.' Therefore 'labour' thou, 'not for the meat that perisheth, but for that which endureth unto everlasting life.' Therefore 'whatsoever thy hand' now 'findeth to do, do it with thy might'. Therefore let

> No fair occasion pass unheeded by;
> Snatching the golden moments as they fly,
> Thou by few fleeting years ensure eternity!

'By patient continuance in well-doing, seek' thou 'for glory and honour and immortality.' In a constant, zealous performance of all good works wait thou for that happy hour when 'the King shall say, [. . .] I was an hungered, and ye gave me meat; I was thirsty, and ye gave me drink. I was a stranger, and ye took me in, naked, and ye clothed me. I was sick, and ye visited me; I was in prison, and ye came unto me.' 'Come, ye blessed of my Father, receive the kingdom prepared for you from the foundation of the world!'

28. UPON OUR LORD'S SERMON ON THE MOUNT, DISCOURSE THE NINTH

1748

An Introductory Comment

Early in his career Wesley preached on the text Matthew 6:33 at Binsey and Buckland, in 1725, for example, and also much later in 1783 at Bristol. The entire passage for this sermon, verses 24-34, is remarkably lengthy, even by Wesley's standards, and his exposition therefore often focused on two principal points: (1) the danger of riches (a well-developed theme) and (2) the importance of seeking the kingdom of God and the righteousness of the Most High.

In his *Notes Upon the New Testament* Wesley considered the word *mammon* in terms of riches or money in particular and more generally with respect to "anything loved or sought, without reference to God" (NT, Matt. 6:24). In exploring verse 31 he cautioned the Methodists against doing themselves harm by harassing and oppressing their minds with "that burden of anxiety" (NT, Matt. 6:31) that accompanies wealth. Moreover, in his sermon "On Family Religion," Wesley counseled against seeking riches for one's children in marriage, especially since "riches and happiness seldom dwell together" (O, 3:345). Accordingly, the double-minded person, who wants to hold onto God and mammon simultaneously, has "religion enough to make him miserable, but not enough to make him happy" (O, 1:637–38).

Facing the lure of wealth as a significant temptation, the heart (made up of various dispositions and tempers) must be rightly directed to God as the end, the goal, the very completion of its being. Put another way, to believe in God, Wesley reasoned, "implies to trust in God as our happiness; as the centre of spirits" (O, 1:635). Righteousness, then, is intimately connected with both the kingdom of God and inward religion in that it is, to use Wesley's words, "the fruit of God's reigning in the heart" (O, 1:642).

Upon our Lord's Sermon on the Mount, Discourse the Ninth

1.–4. The Lord states: 'no man can serve two masters . . . ye cannot serve God and mammon'; Mammon was a heathen god

A. Mammon means here riches

5. To believe is the first thing we are to understand by serving God

A. The second is to love God

6. A third thing is to resemble or imitate God

7. One more thing is obeying and glorifying God

8. What is meant by 'serving mammon'?

A. It implies the trusting in the world for our happiness

9. It implies, secondly, loving the world or desiring it for its own sake

10. It implies, thirdly, to resemble and to be conformed to the world

11. It implies, lastly, to obey the world by conforming to its customs and maxims

12.–14. Do you not see that you cannot *comfortably* serve both?

15. You shall worship the Lord your God, and him only shall you serve

16. Our Lord does not say we should be unconcerned about this life

17. He does forbid us to worry about tomorrow

18. If God gave you life, will God not give you food and raiment?

19. Therefore, take no thought, saying, 'What shall we eat?'

20.–23. Instead, seek ye first the kingdom of God

24. Do not think about how to lay up treasures on earth

A. Also take no thought for things which are needful for the body

25. Do not make the care of future things a pretence for neglecting duty

26. There is another way of taking thought for the morrow

A. It is possible to take thought in a wrong manner with spiritual things

27. Take no thought for the temptations of tomorrow

28. Let the morrow therefore take thought for the things of itself

29. Gladly suffer whatsoever God permits this day

Sermon 29: Upon our Lord's Sermon on the Mount

Discourse the Ninth, 1748

Matthew 6:24-34

No man can serve two masters; for either he will hate the one and love the other, or else he will hold to the one and despise the other. Ye cannot serve God and mammon.

Therefore I say unto you, Take no thought for your life, what ye shall eat, or what ye shall drink; nor yet for your body, what ye shall put on. Is not the life more than meat, and the body than raiment?

Behold the fowls of the air: for they sow not, neither do they reap, nor gather into barns; yet your heavenly Father feedeth them. Are ye not much better than they?

Which of you by taking thought can add one cubit unto his stature?

And why take ye thought for raiment? Consider the lilies of the field, how they grow; they toil not, neither do they spin:

And yet I say unto you, that even Solomon in all his glory was not arrayed like one of these.

Wherefore, if God so clothe the grass of the field, which today is, and tomorrow is cast into the oven, shall he not much more clothe you, O ye of little faith?

Therefore take no thought, saying, What shall we eat? or, What shall we drink? or, Wherewithal shall we be clothed?

(For after all these things do the Gentiles seek); for your heavenly Father knoweth that ye have need of all these things.

But first seek ye the kingdom of God and his righteousness; and all these things shall be added unto you.

Take therefore no thought for the morrow; for the morrow shall take thought for the things of itself: sufficient unto the day is the evil thereof.

1. It is recorded of the nations whom the King of Assyria, after he had carried Israel away into captivity, placed in the cities of Samaria: 'They feared the Lord, and served their own gods.' 'These nations', saith the inspired writer, 'feared the Lord,' performed an outward service to him (a plain proof that they had a fear of God, though not according to knowledge) 'and served their graven images, both their children, and their children's children; as did their fathers, so did they unto this day' (2 Kgs. 17:33, 41).

How nearly does the practice of most modern Christians resemble this of the ancient heathens! 'They fear the Lord': they also perform an outward service to him, and hereby show they have some fear of God; but they likewise 'serve their own gods'. There are those who 'teach them' (as there were who taught the Assyrians) 'the manner of the God of the land'; the God whose name the country bears to this day, and who was once worshipped there with an holy worship. 'Howbeit', they do not serve him alone; they do not fear him enough for this; but 'every nation maketh gods of their own, every nation in the cities wherein they dwell.' 'These nations fear the Lord', they have not laid aside the outward form of worshipping him. But 'they serve their graven images,' silver and gold, the work of men's hands. Money, pleasure, and praise, the gods of this world, more than divide their service with the God of Israel. This is the manner both of 'their children and their children's children; as did their fathers, so do they unto this day.'

2. But although, speaking in a loose way, after the common manner of men, those poor heathens were said to 'fear the Lord', yet we may observe the Holy Ghost immediately adds, speaking according to the truth and real nature of things: 'They fear not the Lord, neither do after the law and commandment which the Lord commanded the children of Jacob. With whom the Lord made a covenant, and charged them, saying, Ye shall not fear other gods nor serve them. . . . But the Lord your God ye shall fear, and he shall deliver you out of the hand of all your enemies.'

The same judgment is passed by the unerring Spirit of God, and indeed by all, the eyes of whose understanding he hath opened to discern the things of God, upon these poor Christians, commonly so called. If we speak according to the truth and real nature of things, 'they fear not the Lord, neither do they serve him.' For they do not 'after the covenant the Lord hath made with them, neither after the law and commandment which he hath commanded them', saying, Thou shalt worship the Lord thy God, and him only shalt thou serve. 'They serve other gods' unto this day. And 'no man can serve two masters.'

3. How vain is it for any man to aim at this—to attempt the serving of two masters! Is it not easy to foresee what must be the unavoidable consequence of such an attempt? 'Either he will hate the one, and love the other; or else he will hold to the one, and despise the other.' The two parts of this sentence, although separately proposed, are to be understood in connection with each other; for the latter part is a consequence of the former. He will naturally 'hold to' him whom he loves. He will so cleave to him as to perform to him a willing, faithful, and diligent service. And in the meantime he will so far at least 'despise' the master he hates as to have little regard to his commands, and to obey them, if at all, in a slight and careless manner. Therefore, whatsoever the wise men of the world may suppose, 'Ye cannot serve God and mammon.'

4. Mammon was the name of one of the heathen gods, who was supposed to preside over riches. It is here understood of riches themselves, gold and silver, or in general, money; and by a common figure of speech, of all that may be purchased thereby, such as ease, honour, and sensual pleasure.

But what are we here to understand by 'serving God'; and what by 'serving mammon'?

We cannot 'serve God' unless we believe in him. This is the only true foundation of serving him. Therefore believing in God as 'reconciling the world to himself' through Christ Jesus, the believing in him as a loving, pardoning God, is the first great branch of his service.

And thus to believe in God implies to *trust* in him as our strength, without whom we can do nothing, who every moment endues us with power from on high, without which it is impossible to please him; as our help, our only help in time of trouble, who compasseth us about with songs of deliverance; as our shield, our defender, and the lifter up of our head above all our enemies that are round about us.

It implies to trust in God as our happiness; as the centre of spirits, the only rest of our souls; the only good who is adequate to all our capacities, and sufficient to satisfy all the desires he hath given us.

It implies (what is nearly allied to the other) to trust in God as our end; to have an eye to him in all things; to use all things only as means of enjoying him; wheresoever we are, or whatsoever we do, to see him that is invisible looking on us well-pleased, and to refer all things to him in Christ Jesus.

5. Thus to believe is the first thing we are to understand by 'serving God'. The second is, to love him.

Now, to love God in the manner the Scripture describes, in the manner God himself requires of us, and by requiring engages to work in us, is to love him as the one God; that is, 'with all our heart, and with all our soul, and with all our mind, and with all our strength'. It is to desire God alone for his own sake, and nothing else but with reference to him; to rejoice in God; to delight in the Lord; not only to seek, but find happiness in him; to enjoy God as the chiefest among ten thousand; to rest in him as our God and our all—in a word, to have such a possession of God as makes us always happy.

6. A third thing we are to understand by 'serving God' is to resemble or imitate him.

So the ancient Father: *Optimus Dei cultus, imitari quem colis*—'It is the best worship or service of God, to imitate him you worship.'

We here speak of imitating or resembling him in the spirit of our minds. For here the true Christian imitation of God begins. God is a Spirit; and they that imitate or resemble him must do it in spirit and in truth.

Now God is love; therefore they who resemble him in the spirit of their minds are transformed into the same image. They are merciful even as he is merciful. Their soul is all love. They are kind, benevolent, compassionate, tender-hearted; and that not only to the good and gentle, but also to the froward. Yea, they are, like him, loving unto every man, and their mercy extends to all his works.

7. One thing more we are to understand by 'serving God', and that is, the obeying him; the glorifying him with our bodies as well as with our spirits; the keeping his outward commandments; the zealously doing whatever he hath enjoined; the carefully avoiding whatever he hath forbidden; the performing all the ordinary actions of life with a single eye and a pure heart—offering them all in holy, fervent love, as sacrifices to God through Jesus Christ.

8. Let us consider now what we are to understand, on the other hand, by 'serving mammon'. And first, it implies the *trusting* in riches, in money, or the things purchasable thereby, as our strength, the means whereby we shall perform whatever cause we have in hand; the trusting in them as our help, by which we look to be comforted in or delivered out of trouble.

It implies the trusting in the world for happiness; the supposing that 'a man's life consisteth' (the comfort of his life) 'in the abundance of the things which he possesseth;' the looking for rest in the things that are seen; for content, in outward plenty; the expecting that satisfaction in the things of the world which can never be found out of God.

And if we do this we cannot but make the world our end; the ultimate end, if not of all, at least of many of our undertakings, many of our actions and designs—in which we shall aim only at an increase of wealth; at the obtaining pleasure or praise; at the gaining a larger measure of temporal things, without any reference to things eternal.

9. The 'serving mammon' implies, secondly, loving the world; desiring it for its own sake; the placing our joy in the things thereof, and setting our hearts upon them; the seeking (what indeed it is impossible we should find) our happiness therein; the resting with the whole weight of our souls upon the staff of this broken reed, although daily experience shows it cannot support, but will only 'enter into our hand and pierce it'.

10. To resemble, to be conformed to the world, is the third thing we are to understand by 'serving mammon'; to have not only designs, but desires, tempers, affections suitable to those of the world; to be of an earthly, sensual mind, chained down to the things of earth; to be self-willed, inordinate lovers of ourselves; to think highly of our own attainments; to desire and delight in the praise of men; to fear, shun, and abhor reproach; to be impatient of reproof, easy to be provoked, and swift to return evil for evil.

11. To 'serve mammon' is, lastly, to obey the world, by outwardly conforming to its maxims and customs; to walk as other men walk, in the common road, in the broad, smooth, beaten path; to be in the fashion; to follow a multitude; to do like the rest of our neighbours; that is, to do the will of the flesh and the mind, to gratify our appetites and inclinations—to sacrifice to ourselves, to aim at our own ease and pleasure in the general course both of our words and actions.

Now what can be more undeniably clear than that we 'cannot' thus 'serve God and mammon'?

12. Does not every man see that he cannot *comfortably* serve both? That to trim between God and the world is the sure way to be disappointed in both, and to have no rest either in one or the other? How uncomfortable a condition must he be in, who, having the fear but not the love of God, who, serving him, but not with all his heart, has only the toils and not the joys of religion! He has religion enough to make him miserable, but not enough to make him happy: his religion will not let him enjoy the world, and the world will not let him enjoy God. So that by halting between both he loses both, and has no peace either in God or the world.

13. Does not every man see that he cannot serve both *consistently* with himself? What more glaring inconsistency can be conceived than must continually appear in his whole behaviour who is endeavouring to obey both these masters, striving to 'serve God and mammon'! He is indeed a 'sinner that goeth two ways'—one step forward and another backward. He is continually building up with one hand and pulling down with the other. He loves sin, and he hates it: he is always seeking, and yet always fleeing from God. He would, and he would not. He is not the same man for one day, no, not for an hour togeth-

er. He is a motley mixture of all sorts of contrarieties; a heap of contradictions jumbled in one. Oh, be consistent with thyself, one way or the other. Turn to the right hand or to the left. If 'mammon' be God, serve thou him; if the Lord, then serve him. But never think of serving either at all unless it be with thy whole heart.

14. Does not every reasonable, every thinking man see that he cannot *possibly* 'serve God and mammon'? Because there is the most absolute contrariety, the most irreconcilable enmity, between them. The contrariety between the most opposite things on earth, between fire and water, darkness and light, vanishes into nothing when compared to the contrariety between God and mammon. So that in whatsoever respect you serve the one, you necessarily renounce the other. Do you believe in God through Christ? Do you *trust* in him as your strength, your help, your shield, and your exceeding great reward? As your happiness? Your end in all, above all things? Then you cannot *trust* in riches. It is absolutely impossible you should, so long as you have this faith in God. Do you thus 'trust in riches'? Then you have denied the faith. You do not trust in the living God. Do you *love* God? Do you seek and find happiness in him? Then you cannot love the world, neither the things of the world. You are crucified to the world and the world crucified to you. Do you 'love the world'? Are your affections set on things beneath? Do you seek happiness in earthly things? Then it is impossible you should love God. Then the love of the Father is not in you. Do you *resemble* God? Are you merciful, as your Father is merciful? Are you transformed by the renewal of your mind into the image of him that created you? Then you cannot be conformed to the present world. You have renounced all its affections and lusts. Are you conformed to the world? Does your soul still bear the image of the earthly? Then you are not renewed in the spirit of your mind. You do not bear the image of the heavenly. Do you *obey God*? Are you zealous to do his will on earth as the angels do in heaven? Then it is impossible you should *obey mammon*. Then you set the world at open defiance. You trample its customs and maxims under foot, and will neither follow nor be led by them. Do you follow the world? Do you live like other men? Do you please men? Do you please yourself? Then you cannot be a servant of God. You are of your master and father, the devil.

15. Therefore thou shalt worship the Lord thy God, and him only shalt thou serve. Thou shalt lay aside all thoughts of obeying two masters, of serving God and mammon. Thou shalt propose to thyself no end, no help, no happiness, but God. Thou shalt seek nothing in earth or heaven but him; thou shalt aim at nothing but to know, to love, and enjoy him. And because this is all your business below, the only view you can reasonably have, the one design you are to pursue in all things, 'Therefore I say unto you' (as our Lord continues his discourse) 'Take no thought for your life, what ye shall eat, or what ye shall drink; nor yet for your body, what ye shall put on.' A deep and weighty direction, which it imports us well to consider and throughly to understand.

16. Our Lord does not here require that we should be utterly without thought, even touching the concerns of this life. A giddy, careless temper is at the farthest remove from the whole religion of Jesus Christ. Neither does he require us to be 'slothful in business', to be slack and dilatory therein. This likewise is contrary to the whole spirit and genius of his religion. A Christian abhors sloth as much as drunkenness, and flees from idleness

as he does from adultery. He well knows that there is one kind of thought and care with which God is well-pleased; which is absolutely needful for the due performance of those outward works unto which the providence of God has called him.

It is the will of God that every man should labour to 'eat his own bread'; yea, and that every man should provide for his own, for them of his own household. It is likewise his will that we should 'owe no man anything', but 'provide things honest in the sight of all men'. But this cannot be done without taking some thought, without having some care upon our minds; yea, often not without long and serious thought, not without much and earnest care. Consequently this care to provide for ourselves and our household, this thought how to render to all their dues, our blessed Lord does not condemn. Yea, it is good and acceptable in the sight of God our Saviour.

It is good and acceptable to God that we should so take thought concerning whatever we have in hand as to have a clear comprehension of what we are about to do, and to plan our business before we enter upon it. And it is right that we should carefully consider from time to time what steps we are to take therein; as well as that we should prepare all things beforehand for the carrying it on in the most effectual manner. This care, termed by some, 'the care of the head', it was by no means our Lord's design to condemn.

17. What he here condemns is 'the care of the heart': the anxious, uneasy care; the care that hath torment; all such care as does hurt, either to the soul or body. What he forbids is that care which sad experience shows wastes the blood and drinks up the spirits; which anticipates all the misery it fears, and comes to torment us before the time. He forbids only that care which poisons the blessings of today by fear of what may be tomorrow; which cannot enjoy the present plenty through apprehensions of future want. This care is not only a sore disease, a grievous sickness of soul, but also an heinous offence against God, a sin of the deepest dye. It is an high affront to the gracious Governor and wise Disposer of all things; necessarily implying that the great Judge does not do right, that he does not order all things well. It plainly implies that he is wanting either in wisdom, if he does not know what things we stand in need of, or in goodness, if he does not provide those things for all who put their trust in him. Beware, therefore, that you take not thought in this sense: be ye anxiously careful for nothing. Take no uneasy thought. This is a plain, sure rule—*uneasy* care is *unlawful* care. With a single eye to God, do all that in you lies to provide things honest in the sight of all men. And then give up all into better hands: leave the whole event to God.

18. 'Take no thought' of this kind, no uneasy thought, even 'for your life, what ye shall eat, or what ye shall drink, nor yet for your body, what ye shall put on. Is not the life more than meat, and the body than raiment?' If then God gave you life, the greater gift, will he not give you food to sustain it? If he hath given you the body, how can ye doubt but he will give you raiment to cover it? More especially if you give yourselves up to him, and serve him with your whole heart. 'Behold', see before your eyes, 'the fowls of the air: for they sow not, neither do they reap, nor gather into barns;' and yet they lack nothing, 'yet your heavenly Father feedeth them. Are ye not much better than they?' Ye that are creatures capable of God? Are ye not of more account in the eyes of God? Of a higher rank in the scale of beings? 'And which of you by taking thought can add one cubit to his

stature?' What profit have you then from this anxious thought? It is every way fruitless and unavailing.

'And why take ye thought for raiment?' Have ye not a daily reproof wherever you turn your eyes? 'Consider the lilies of the field, how they grow; they toil not, neither do they spin. And yet I say unto you, that even Solomon in all his glory was not arrayed like one of these. Wherefore if God so clothe the grass of the field, which today is, and tomorrow is cast into the oven', is cut down, burnt up, and seen no more, 'shall he not much more clothe you, O ye of little faith?' You, whom he made to endure for ever and ever, to be pictures of his own eternity! Ye are indeed of little faith. Otherwise ye could not doubt of his love and care; no, not for a moment.

19. 'Therefore take no thought, saying, What shall we eat,' if we lay up no treasure upon earth? 'What shall we drink,' if we serve God with all our strength, if our eye be singly fixed on him? 'Wherewithal shall we be clothed,' if we are not conformed to the world, if we disoblige those by whom we might be profited? 'For after all these things do the Gentiles seek,' the heathens who know not God. But ye are sensible, 'your heavenly Father knoweth that ye have need of all these things.' And he hath pointed out to you an infallible way of being constantly supplied therewith. 'Seek ye first the kingdom of God, and his righteousness, and all these things shall be added unto you.'

20. 'Seek ye first the kingdom of God.' Before ye give place to any other thought or care let it be your concern that the God and Father of our Lord Jesus Christ, who 'gave his only-begotten Son, to the end that believing in him ye might not perish, but have everlasting life', may reign in your heart, may manifest himself in your soul, and dwell and rule there: 'that he may cast down every high thing which exalteth itself against the knowledge of God, and bring into captivity every thought to the obedience of Christ.' Let God have the sole dominion over you. Let him reign without a rival. Let him possess all your heart, and rule alone. Let him be your one desire, your joy, your love; so that all that is within you may continually cry out, 'The Lord God omnipotent reigneth.'

'Seek the kingdom of God and his righteousness.' Righteousness is the fruit of God's reigning in the heart. And what is righteousness but love? The love of God and of all mankind, flowing from faith in Jesus Christ, and producing humbleness of mind, meekness, gentleness, long-suffering, patience, deadness to the world; and every right disposition of heart toward God and toward man. And by these it produces all holy actions, whatsoever are lovely or of good report; whatsoever works of faith and labour of love are acceptable to God and profitable to man.

'His righteousness.' This is all *his* righteousness still: it is his own free *gift* to us, for the sake of Jesus Christ the righteous, through whom alone it is purchased for us. And it is his *work*: it is he alone that worketh it in us by the inspiration of his Holy Spirit.

21. Perhaps the well observing this may give light to some other Scriptures which we have not always so clearly understood. St. Paul, speaking in his Epistle to the Romans concerning the unbelieving Jews, saith, 'They, being ignorant of God's righteousness, and going about to establish their own righteousness, have not submitted themselves unto the righteousness of God.' I believe this may be one sense of the words: they were 'ignorant

of God's righteousness', not only of the righteousness of Christ, imputed to every believer, whereby all his sins are blotted out, and he is reconciled to the favour of God; but (which seems here to be more immediately understood) they were ignorant of that inward righteousness, of that holiness of heart, which is with the utmost propriety termed 'God's righteousness', as being both his own free gift through Christ, and his own work, by his almighty Spirit. And because they were ignorant of this they 'went about to establish their own righteousness'. They laboured to establish that outside righteousness which might very properly be termed 'their own'; for neither was it wrought by the Spirit of God nor was it owned or accepted of him. They might work this themselves, by their own natural strength; and when they had done, it was a stink in his nostrils. And yet, trusting in this, they would 'not submit themselves unto the righteousness of God'. Yea, they hardened themselves against that faith whereby alone it was possible to attain it. 'For Christ is the end of the law for righteousness to everyone that believeth.' Christ, when he said, 'It is finished,' put an end to that law—to the law of external rites and ceremonies—that he might 'bring in a better righteousness' through his blood, by that one oblation of himself once offered, even the image of God, into the inmost soul of 'everyone that believeth'.

22. Nearly related to these are those words of the Apostle in his Epistle to the Philippians: 'I count all things but dung that I may win Christ,' an entrance into his everlasting kingdom, 'and be found in him', believing in him, 'not having mine own righteousness, which is of the law, but that which is through the faith of Christ, the righteousness which is of God by faith'—'not having my own righteousness, which is of the law', a barely external righteousness, the outside religion I formerly had when I hoped to be accepted of God because I was, 'touching the righteousness which is in the law, blameless'—'but that which is through the faith of Christ, the righteousness which is of God by faith:' that holiness of heart, that renewal of the soul in all its desires, tempers, and affections, 'which is of God'. It is the work of God and not of man, 'by faith'; through the faith of Christ, through the revelation of Jesus Christ in us, and by faith in his blood; whereby alone we obtain the remission of our sins, and an inheritance among those that are sanctified.

23. 'Seek ye first' this 'kingdom of God' in your hearts, this 'righteousness', which is the gift and work of God, the image of God renewed in your souls—'and all these things' shall be added unto you: all things needful for the body; such a measure of all as God sees most for the advancement of his kingdom. These 'shall be added', they shall be thrown in, over and above. In seeking the peace and the love of God you shall not only find what you more immediately seek, even the kingdom that cannot be moved; but also what you seek not, not at all for its own sake, but only in reference to the other. You shall find in your way to the kingdom all outward things, so far as they are expedient for you. This care God hath taken upon himself: cast you all your care upon him. He knoweth your wants; and whatsoever is lacking he will not fail to supply.

24. 'Therefore take no thought for the morrow.' Not only, take ye no thought how to lay up treasures on earth, how to increase in worldly substance; take no thought how to procure more food than you can eat, or more raiment than you can put on; or more money than is required from day to day for the plain, reasonable purposes of life: but take no *uneasy* thought even concerning those things which are absolutely needful for the

body. Do not trouble yourself now with thinking what you shall do at a season which is yet afar off. Perhaps that season will never come; or it will be no concern of yours—before then you will have passed through all the waves, and be landed in eternity. All those distant views do not belong to *you*, who are but a creature of a day. Nay, what have you to do with 'the morrow', more strictly speaking? Why should you perplex yourself without need? God provides for you today what is needful to sustain the life which he hath given you. It is enough. Give yourself up into his hands. If you live another day he will provide for that also.

25. Above all, do not make the care of future things a pretence for neglecting present duty. This is the most fatal way of 'taking thought for the morrow'. And how common is it among men! Many, if we exhort them to keep a conscience void of offence, to abstain from what they are convinced is evil, do not scruple to reply: 'How then must we live? Must we not take care of ourselves and of our families?' And this they imagine to be a sufficient reason for continuing in known, wilful sin. They say, and perhaps think, they would serve God now were it not that they should by and by lose their bread. They would prepare for eternity; but they are afraid of wanting the necessaries of life. So they serve the devil for a morsel of bread; they rush into hell for fear of want; they throw away their poor souls lest they should some time or other fall short of what is needful for their bodies.

It is not strange that they who thus take the matter out of God's hand should be so often disappointed of the very things they seek; that while they throw away heaven to secure the things of earth they lose the one, but do not gain the other. The jealous God, in the wise course of his providence, frequently suffers this. So that they who will not cast their care on God, who, taking thought for temporal things, have little concern for things eternal, lose the very portion which they have chosen. There is a visible blast on all their undertakings: whatsoever they do it doth not prosper. Insomuch that after they have forsaken God for the world they lose what they sought, as well as what they sought not. They fall short of the kingdom of God and his righteousness; nor yet are other things added unto them.

26. There is another way of 'taking thought for the morrow', which is equally forbidden in these words. It is possible to take thought in a wrong manner, even with regard to spiritual things; to be so careful about what may be by and by as to neglect what is now required at our hands. How insensibly do we slide into this if we are not continually watching unto prayer! How easily are we carried away in a kind of waking dream, projecting distant schemes, and drawing fine scenes in our own imagination! We think what good we will do when we are in such a place, or when such a time is come! How useful we will be, how plenteous in good works, when we are easier in our circumstances! How earnestly we will serve God when once such an hindrance is out of the way!

Or, perhaps, you are now in heaviness of soul: God as it were hides his face from you. You see little of the light of his countenance; you cannot taste his redeeming love. In such a temper of mind how natural is it to say, 'O how I will praise God when the light of his countenance shall be again lifted up upon my soul! How will I exhort others to praise him when his love is again shed abroad in my heart! Then I will do thus and thus: I will speak for God in all places; I will not be ashamed of the gospel of Christ. Then I will redeem the time, I will use to the uttermost every talent I have received.' Do not believe thyself. Thou wilt not do it then unless thou dost it now. 'He that is faithful in that which is little', of whatsoever kind it be, whether it be worldly substance or the fear or love of God, 'will be faithful in that which is much.' But if thou now hidest one talent in the earth, thou wilt then hide five. That is, if ever they are given; but there is small reason to expect they ever will. Indeed 'unto him that hath', that is, uses what he hath, 'shall be given, and he shall have more abundantly. But from him that hath not', that is, uses not the grace which he hath already received, whether in a larger or smaller degree, 'shall be taken away even that which he hath.'

27. And 'take no thought' for the temptations of tomorrow. This also is a dangerous snare. Think not, 'When such a temptation comes, what shall I do, how shall I stand? I feel I have not power to resist: I am not able to conquer that enemy.' Most true: you have not *now* the power which you do not *now* stand in need of. You are not able at *this time* to conquer that enemy; and at *this time* he does not assault you. With the grace you have now you could not withstand the temptations which you have not. But when the temptation comes the grace will come. In greater trials you will have greater strength. When sufferings abound, the consolations of God will in the same proportion abound also. So that in every situation the grace of God will be sufficient for you. He doth not suffer you 'to be tempted' today 'above that ye are able to bear. And in every temptation he will make a way to escape.' 'As thy day, so thy strength shall be.'

28. 'Let the morrow' therefore 'take thought for the things of itself.' That is, when the morrow comes, then think of it. Live thou today. Be it thy earnest care to improve the present hour. This is your own, and it is your all. The past is as nothing, as though it had never been. The future is nothing to you. It is not yours; perhaps it never will be. There is no depending on what is yet to come; for you 'know not what a day may bring forth'. Therefore live today: lose not an hour; use this moment; for it is your portion. 'Who knoweth the things which have been before him,' 'or which shall be after him under the sun?' The generations that were from the beginning of the world, where are they now? Fled away, forgotten. They *were*: they lived their day; they were shook off of the earth, as leaves off of their trees. They mouldered away into common dust. Another and another race succeeded; then they 'followed the generation of their fathers, and shall never' more 'see the light.' Now is thy turn upon the earth. 'Rejoice, O young man, in the days of thy youth.' Enjoy the very, very now; by enjoying him 'whose years fail not'. Now let thine eye be singly fixed on him, in 'whom is no variableness, neither shadow of turning'. Now give him thy heart; now stay thyself on him; now be thou holy as he is holy. Now lay hold of the blessed opportunity of doing his acceptable and perfect will. Now 'rejoice to suffer the loss of all things, so thou mayst win Christ.'

29. Gladly suffer today, for his name's sake, whatsoever he permits this day to come upon thee. But look not at the sufferings of tomorrow. 'Sufficient unto the day is the evil thereof.' Evil it is, speaking after the manner of men; whether it be reproach or want, pain or sickness. But in the language of God, all is blessing: 'It is a precious balm,' prepared by the wisdom of God, and variously dispensed among his children according to the various sicknesses of their souls. And he gives in one day sufficient for that day, proportioned to

the want and strength of the patient. If therefore thou snatchest today what belongs to the morrow, if thou addest this to what is given thee already, it will be more than thou canst bear: this is the way, not to heal, but to destroy thy own soul. Take therefore just as much as he gives thee today: today do and suffer his will. Today give up thyself, thy body, soul, and spirit, to God, through Christ Jesus; desiring nothing but that God may be glorified in all thou art, all thou dost, all thou sufferest; seeking nothing but to know God, and his Son Jesus Christ, through the Eternal Spirit; pursuing nothing but to love him, to serve him, and to enjoy him, at this hour, and to all eternity!

Now unto God the Father, who hath made me and all the world; unto God the Son, who hath redeemed me and all mankind; unto God the Holy Ghost, who sanctifieth me and all the elect people of God: be honour, and praise, majesty, and dominion, for ever and ever! Amen.

29. THE USE OF MONEY

1760

An Introductory Comment

Wesley's social ethic, especially in terms of the use of money, was informed by his reading the works of the Puritan divine William Perkins and those of Richard Lucas, the prebend at Westminster Abbey, in particular the latter's *Enquiry After Happiness,* which was published in a modified form in *A Christian Library* (O, 2:264). Wesley preached on the text of this sermon, Luke 16:9, about two dozen times (from 1748 to 1759) before the sermon appeared in its present written form (WWS).

Sugden believed that Wesley's articulation of the three rules of "Gain all you can; Save all you can; and Give all you can," (O, 2:268, 273, 277) beyond celebrating the importance of prudent stewardship, held before the Methodists the universal love of God. As a result, such counsels would prove themselves "the best preventive and remedy of the distrust and hatred of the capitalists by the working classes" (S, 2:310). Accordingly, E. P. Thompson's criticism of Wesley's economic ethic is wide of the mark, for he failed to consider, among other things, the generous theological and ecclesiastical context of Wesley's reasoned judgments.

Pastorally adept, Wesley clearly recognized that the proper Christian faith, ironically enough, contains the seeds of its own destruction: "Wherever true Christianity spreads, it must cause diligence ("gain all you can") and frugality ("save all you can") (O, 4:95-96). Thus, unless the first two precepts issued in the third ("give all you can"), many of the Methodists would grow rich, a fact that was lamented in the Conference *Minutes* of 1766. Wesley's great fear was that the Methodists in becoming wealthy would have merely the form of religion without its power, and, as a result, would neglect both the temporal and the spiritual ministries to the poor.

Though Wesley regarded the excess accumulation of wealth, beyond one's needs, a grave danger, he nevertheless considered money itself a "most compendious instrument . . . of doing all manner of good" (O, 2:268).

The Use of Money

1.–2. An excellent branch of Christian wisdom is here offered by our Lord
   A. Namely, the right use of money
3. All the instructions which are necessary may be reduced to three rules

I. 1. The first rule is *gain all you can,* but not at the expense of life
2. We are to gain all we can without hurting our minds or our bodies
3. We are to gain all we can without hurting our neighbour
4. Neither may we gain by hurting our neighbours in their bodies
5.–8. Do not play with people's lives to enlarge your gain

II. 1. Having gained all you can by honest wisdom and unwearied diligence:
   A. The second rule of Christian prudence is *save all you can*
2. Do not waste money gratifying the desires of the flesh
3. Do not gratify the desire of the eye for expensive apparel or needless ornaments
4. Lay out nothing to gain the admiration of men
   A. Be content with the honor that comes from God
5. The more we indulge these desires, the more they increase
6. Do not throw away money upon your children
7.–8. Do not *leave it* to them, to throw away

III. 1. No one has done anything by going thus far
   A. All this is nothing if you do not go forward
2. God brought you into the world not as a proprietor, but as a steward
3. If you desire to be a faithful and wise steward:
   A. First, provide things needful for yourself: food and clothes
   B. Second, provide these for your wife, children, and servants
4. If then a doubt should arise, you have an easy way to remove it
   A. Inquire first, 'In expending this, am I acting according to my character?'
   B. Second, 'Am I doing this in obedience to [God's] Word?'
   C. Third, 'Can I offer up . . . this expense as a sacrifice to God?'
   D. Fourth, 'For this very work shall I have reward at the resurrection?'
5. If any doubt remains, farther examine yourself by prayer
6.–7. I entreat you, in the name of Jesus, act up to the dignity of your calling

Sermon 50: The Use of Money, 1760

Luke 16:9

I say unto you, Make unto yourselves friends of the mammon of unrighteousness, that when ye fail, they may receive you into the everlasting habitations.

1. Our Lord, having finished the beautiful parable of the Prodigal Son, which he had particularly addressed to those who murmured at his receiving publicans and sinners, adds another relation of a different kind, addressed rather to the children of God. 'He said unto his disciples'—not so much to the scribes and Pharisees to whom he had been speaking before—'There was a certain rich man, who had a steward, and he was accused to him of wasting his goods. And calling him he said, Give an account of thy stewardship, for thou canst be no longer steward' (Luke 16:1-2). After reciting the method which the bad steward used to provide against the day of necessity, our Saviour adds, 'His lord commended the unjust steward'—namely in this respect, that he used timely precaution—and subjoins this weighty reflection, 'The children of this world are wiser in their generation than the children of light' (Luke 16:8). Those who seek no other portion than 'this world are wiser' (not absolutely; for they are one and all the veriest fools, the most egregious madmen under heaven, but) 'in their generation', in their own way; they are more consistent with themselves, they are truer to their acknowledged principles, they more steadily pursue their end, 'than the children of light', than they who see 'the light of the glory of God in the face of Jesus Christ'. Then follow the words above recited: 'And I'—the only-begotten Son of God, the Creator, Lord and Possessor of heaven and earth, and all that is therein; the Judge of all, to whom ye are to 'give an account of your stewardship' when ye 'can be no longer stewards'—'I say unto you' (learn in this respect even of the unjust steward), 'make yourselves friends', by wise, timely precaution, 'of the mammon of unrighteousness.' 'Mammon' means riches or money. It is termed 'the mammon of unrighteousness' because of the unrighteous manner wherein it is frequently procured, and wherein even that which was honestly procured is generally employed. 'Make yourselves friends' of this by doing all possible good, particularly to the children of God; 'that when ye fail', when ye return to dust, when ye have no more place under the sun, those of them who are gone before 'may receive you', may welcome you 'into the everlasting habitations'.

2. An excellent branch of Christian wisdom is here inculcated by our Lord on all his followers, namely, the right use of money—a subject largely spoken of, after their manner, by men of the world, but not sufficiently considered by those whom God hath chosen out of the world. These generally do not consider as the importance of the subject requires the use of this excellent talent. Neither do they understand how to employ it to the greatest advantage; the introduction of which into the world is one admirable instance of the wise and gracious providence of God. It has indeed been the manner of poets, orators, and philosophers, in almost all ages and nations, to rail at this as the grand corrupter of the world, the bane of virtue, the pest of human society. Hence nothing so commonly heard as:

Ferrum, ferroque nocentius aurum—

'And gold, more mischievous than keenest steel'. Hence the lamentable complaint,

Effodiuntur opes, irritamenta malorum.

Nay, one celebrated writer gravely exhorts his countrymen, in order to banish all vice at once, to 'throw all their money into the sea':

. . . . in mare proximum[. . .]
Summi materiem mali!

But is not all this mere empty rant? Is there any solid reason therein? By no means. For let the world be as corrupt as it will, is gold or silver to blame? 'The love of money', we know, 'is the root of all evil;' but not the thing itself. The fault does not lie in the money, but in them that use it. It may be used ill; and what may not? But it may likewise be used well; it is full as applicable to the best as to the worst uses. It is of unspeakable service to all civilized nations in all the common affairs of life. It is a most compendious instrument of transacting all manner of business, and (if we use it according to Christian wisdom) of doing all manner of good. It is true, were man in a state of innocence, or were all men 'filled with the Holy Ghost', so that, like the infant church at Jerusalem, 'no man counted anything he had his own', but 'distribution was made to everyone as he had need,' the use of it would be superseded; as we cannot conceive there is anything of the kind among the inhabitants of heaven. But in the present state of mankind it is an excellent gift of God, answering the noblest ends. In the hands of his children it is food for the hungry, drink for the thirsty, raiment for the naked. It gives to the traveller and the stranger where to lay his head. By it we may supply the place of an husband to the widow, and of a father to the fatherless; we may be a defence for the oppressed, a means of health to the sick, of ease to them that are in pain. It may be as eyes to the blind, as feet to the lame; yea, a lifter up from the gates of death.

3. It is therefore of the highest concern that all who fear God know how to employ this valuable talent; that they be instructed how it may answer these glorious ends, and in the highest degree. And perhaps all the instructions which are necessary for this may be reduced to three plain rules, by the exact observance whereof we may approve ourselves faithful stewards of 'the mammon of unrighteousness'.

I.1. The first of these is (he that heareth let him understand!) *Gain all you can.* Here we may speak like the children of the world. We meet them on their own ground. And it is our bounden duty to do this. We ought to gain all we can gain without buying gold too dear, without paying more for it than it is worth. But this it is certain we ought not to do: we ought not to gain money at the expense of life; nor (which is in effect the same thing) at the expense of our health. Therefore no gain whatsoever should induce us to enter into, or to continue in, any employ which is of such a kind, or is attended with so hard or so long labour, as to impair our constitution. Neither should we begin or continue in any business which necessarily deprives us of proper seasons for food and sleep in such a proportion as our nature requires. Indeed there is a great difference here. Some employments are absolutely and totally unhealthy—as those which imply the dealing much with arsenic or other equally hurtful minerals, or the breathing an air tainted with steams of melting lead, which must at length destroy the firmest constitution. Others may not be absolutely unhealthy, but only to persons of a weak constitution. Such are those which require many hours to be spent in writing, especially if a person write sitting, and lean upon his stomach, or remain long in an uneasy posture. But whatever it is which reason or experience shows to be destructive of health or strength, that we may not submit to; seeing 'the life is more' valuable 'than meat, and the body than raiment.' And if we are already engaged in such an employ, we should exchange it as soon as possible for some which, if it lessen our gain, will however not lessen our health.

2. We are, secondly, to gain all we can without hurting our mind any more than our body. For neither may we hurt this. We must preserve, at all events, the spirit of an healthful mind. Therefore we may not engage or continue in any sinful trade, any that is contrary to the law of God, or of our country. Such are all that necessarily imply our robbing or defrauding the king of his lawful customs. For it is at least as sinful to defraud the king of his right as to rob our fellow subjects. And the king has full as much right to his customs as we have to our houses and apparel. Other businesses there are, which however innocent *in themselves*, cannot be followed with innocence *now* (at least, not in England): such, for instance, as will not afford a competent maintenance without cheating or lying, or conformity to some custom which is not consistent with a good conscience. These likewise are sacredly to be avoided, whatever gain they may be attended with provided we follow the custom of the trade; for to gain money we must not lose our souls. There are yet others which many pursue with perfect innocence without hurting either their body or mind. And yet perhaps *you* cannot: either they may entangle you in that company which would destroy your soul—and by repeated experiments it may appear that you cannot separate the one from the other—or there may be an idiosyncrasy, a peculiarity in your constitution of soul (as there is in the bodily constitution of many) by reason whereof that employment is deadly to *you* which another may safely follow. So I am convinced, from many experiments, I could not study to any degree of perfection either mathematics, arithmetic, or algebra, without being a deist, if not an atheist. And yet others may study them all their lives without sustaining any inconvenience. None therefore can here determine for another, but every man must judge for himself, and abstain from whatever he in particular finds to be hurtful to his soul.

3. We are, thirdly, to gain all we can without hurting our neighbour. But this we may not, cannot do, if we love our neighbour as ourselves. We cannot, if we love everyone as ourselves, hurt anyone *in his substance*. We cannot devour the increase of his lands, and perhaps the lands and houses themselves, by gaming, by overgrown bills (whether on account of physic, or law, or anything else), or by requiring or taking such interest as even the laws of our country forbid. Hereby all *pawnbroking* is excluded, seeing whatever good we might do thereby all unprejudiced men see with grief to be abundantly overbalanced by the evil. And if it were otherwise, yet we are not allowed to 'do evil that good may come'. We cannot, consistent with brotherly love, sell our goods below the market price.

We cannot study to ruin our neighbour's trade in order to advance our own. Much less can we entice away or receive any of his servants or workmen whom he has need of. None can gain by swallowing up his neighbour's substance, without gaining the damnation of hell.

4. Neither may we gain by hurting our neighbour *in his body*. Therefore we may not sell anything which tends to impair health. Such is, eminently, all that liquid fire commonly called 'drams' or 'spirituous liquor'. It is true, these may have a place in medicine; they may be of use in some bodily disorders (although there would rarely be occasion for them were it not for the unskillfulness of the practitioner). Therefore such as prepare and sell them *only for this end* may keep their conscience clear. But who are they? Who prepare and sell them *only for this end*? Do you know ten such distillers in England? Then excuse these. But all who sell them in the common way, to any that will buy, are poisoners-general. They murder his Majesty's subjects by wholesale, neither does their eye pity or spare. They drive them to hell like sheep. And what is their gain? Is it not the blood of these men? Who then would envy their large estates and sumptuous palaces? A curse is in the midst of them: the curse of God cleaves to the stones, the timber, the furniture of them. The curse of God is in their gardens, their walks, their groves; a fire that burns to the nethermost hell. Blood, blood is there—the foundation, the floor, the walls, the roof are stained with blood! And canst thou hope, O thou man of blood, though thou art 'clothed in scarlet and fine linen, and farest sumptuously every day', canst thou hope to deliver down thy 'fields of blood' to the third generation? Not so; for there is a God in heaven. Therefore thy name shall soon be rooted out. Like as those whom thou hast destroyed, body and soul, 'thy memorial shall perish with thee.'

5. And are not they partakers of the same guilt, though in a lower degree, whether surgeons, apothecaries, or physicians, who play with the lives or health of men to enlarge their own gain? Who purposely lengthen the pain or disease which they are able to remove speedily? Who protract the cure of their patient's body in order to plunder his substance? Can any man be clear before God who does not shorten every disorder *as much as he can*, and remove all sickness and pain *as soon as he can*. He cannot. For nothing can be more clear than that he does not 'love his neighbour as himself'; than that he does not 'do unto others as he would they should do unto himself'.

6. This is dear-bought gain. And so is whatever is procured by hurting our neighbour *in his soul*: by ministering, suppose either directly or indirectly, to his unchastity or intemperance, which certainly none can do who has any fear of God, or any real desire of pleasing him. It nearly concerns all those to consider this who have anything to do with taverns, victualling-houses, operahouses, playhouses, or any other places of public, fashionable diversion. If these profit the souls of men, you are clear; your employment is good, and your gain innocent. But if they are either sinful in themselves, or natural inlets to sin of various kinds, then it is to be feared you have a sad account to make. O beware lest God say in that day, 'These have perished in their iniquity, but their blood do I require at thy hands!'

7. These cautions and restrictions being observed, it is the bounden duty of all who are engaged in worldly business to observe that first and great rule of Christian wisdom with respect to money, 'Gain all you can.' Gain all you can by honest industry: use all

possible diligence in your calling. Lose no time. If you understand yourself and your relation to God and man, you know you have none to spare. If you understand your particular calling as you ought, you will have no time that hangs upon your hands. Every business will afford some employment sufficient for every day and every hour. That wherein *you* are placed, if you follow it in earnest, will leave you no leisure for silly, unprofitable diversions. You have always something better to do, something that will profit you, more or less. And 'whatsoever thy hand findeth to do, do it with thy might.' Do it *as soon* as possible. No delay! No putting off from day to day, or from hour to hour. Never leave anything till tomorrow which you can do today. And do it *as well* as possible. Do not sleep or yawn over it. Put your whole strength to the work. Spare no pains. Let nothing be done by halves, or in a slight and careless manner. Let nothing in your business be left undone if it can be done by labour or patience.

8. Gain *all* you can, by common sense, by using in your business all the understanding which God has given you. It is amazing to observe how few do this; how men run on in the same dull track with their forefathers. But whatever they do who know not God, this is no rule for *you*. It is a shame for a Christian not to improve upon *them* in whatever he takes in hand. *You* should be continually learning from the experience of others or from your own experience, reading, and reflection, to do everything you have to do better today than you did yesterday. And see that you practise whatever you learn, that you may make the best of all that is in your hands.

II.1. Having gained all you can, by honest wisdom and unwearied diligence, the second rule of Christian prudence is, *Save all you can.* Do not throw the precious talent into the sea: leave that folly to heathen philosophers. Do not throw it away in idle expenses, which is just the same as throwing it into the sea. Expend no part of it merely to gratify the desire of the flesh, the desire of the eye, or the pride of life.

2. Do not waste any part of so precious a talent merely in gratifying the desires of the flesh; in procuring the pleasures of sense of whatever kind; particularly, in enlarging the pleasure of tasting. I do not mean, avoid gluttony and drunkenness only: an honest heathen would condemn these. But there is a regular, reputable kind of sensuality, an elegant epicurism, which does not immediately disorder the stomach, nor (sensibly, at least) impair the understanding. And yet (to mention no other effects of it now) it cannot be maintained without considerable expense. Cut off all this expense. Despise delicacy and variety, and be content with what plain nature requires.

3. Do not waste any part of so precious a talent merely in gratifying the desire of the eye by superfluous or expensive apparel, or by needless ornaments. Waste no part of it in curiously adorning your houses in superfluous or expensive furniture; in costly pictures, painting, gilding, books; in elegant (rather than useful) gardens. Let your neighbours, who know nothing better, do this: 'Let the dead bury their dead.' But 'What is that to thee?' says our Lord: 'Follow thou me.' Are you willing? Then you are able so to do.

4. Lay out nothing to gratify the pride of life, to gain the admiration or praise of men. This motive of expense is frequently interwoven with one or both of the former. Men are

expensive in diet, or apparel, or furniture, not barely to please their appetite, or to gratify their eye, their imagination, but their vanity too. 'So long as thou dost well unto thyself, men will speak good of thee.' So long as thou art 'clothed in purple and fine linen, and farest sumptuously every day', no doubt many will applaud thy elegance of taste, thy generosity and hospitality. But do not buy their applause so dear. Rather be content with the honour that cometh from God.

5. Who would expend anything in gratifying these desires if he considered that to gratify them is to increase them? Nothing can be more certain than this: daily experience shows, the more they are indulged, they increase the more. Whenever therefore you expend anything to please your taste or other senses, you pay so much for sensuality. When you lay out money to please your eye, you give so much for an increase of curiosity, for a stronger attachment to these pleasures, which perish in the using. While you are purchasing anything which men use to applaud, you are purchasing more vanity. Had you not then enough of vanity, sensuality, curiosity before? Was there need of any addition? And would you pay for it, too? What manner of wisdom is this? Would not the literally throwing your money into the sea be a less mischievous folly?

6. And why should you throw away money upon your children, any more than upon yourself, in delicate food, in gay or costly apparel, in superfluities of any kind? Why should you purchase for them more pride or lust, more vanity, or foolish and hurtful desires? They do not want any more; they have enough already; nature has made ample provision for them. Why should you be at farther expense to increase their temptations and snares, and to 'pierce them through with more sorrows'?

7. Do not *leave it* to them, to throw away. If you have good reason to believe that they would waste what is now in your possession in gratifying and thereby increasing the desire of the flesh, the desire of the eye, or the pride of life (at the peril of theirs and your own soul), do not set these traps in their way. Do not offer your sons or your daughters unto Belial any more than unto Moloch. Have pity upon them, and remove out of their way what you may easily foresee would increase their sins, and consequently plunge them deeper into everlasting perdition. How amazing then is the infatuation of those parents who think they can never leave their children enough? What! cannot you leave them enough of arrows, firebrands, and death? Not enough of foolish and hurtful desires? Not enough of pride, lust, ambition, vanity? Not enough of everlasting burnings! Poor wretch! Thou fearest where no fear is. Surely both thou and they, when ye are lifting up your eyes in hell, will have enough both of the 'worm that never dieth', and of 'the fire that never shall be quenched'.

8. 'What then would you do if you was in my case? If you had a considerable fortune to leave?' Whether I *would* do it or no, I know what I *ought* to do: this will admit of no reasonable question. If I had one child, elder or younger, who knew the value of money, one who I believed would put it to the true use, I should think it my absolute, indispensable duty to leave that child the bulk of my fortune; and to the rest just so much as would enable them to live in the manner they had been accustomed to do. 'But what if all your children were equally ignorant of the true use of money?' I ought then (hard saying! Who can hear it?) to give each what would keep him above want, and to bestow all the rest in such a manner as I judged would be most for the glory of God.

III.1. But let not any man imagine that he has done anything barely by going thus far, by *gaining and saving all he can*, if he were to stop here. All this is nothing if a man go not forward, if he does not point all this at a farther end. Nor indeed can a man properly be said to *save* anything if he only *lays it up*. You may as well throw your money into the sea as bury it in the earth. And you may as well bury it in the earth as in your chest, or in the Bank of England. Not to use, is effectually to throw it away. If therefore you would indeed 'make yourselves friends of the mammon of unrighteousness', add the third rule to the two preceding. Having first gained all you can, and secondly saved all you can, then give all you can.

2. In order to see the ground and reason of this, consider: when the possessor of heaven and earth brought you into being and placed you in this world, he placed you here not as a proprietor, but a steward. As such he entrusted you for a season with goods of various kinds. But the sole property of these still rests in him, nor can ever be alienated from him. As you yourself are not your own, but his, such is likewise all that you enjoy. Such is your soul, and your body—not your own, but God's. And so is your substance in particular. And he has told you in the most clear and express terms how you are to employ it for him, in such a manner that it may be all an holy sacrifice, acceptable through Christ Jesus. And this light, easy service he has promised to reward with an eternal weight of glory.

3. The directions which God has given us touching the use of our worldly substance may be comprised in the following particulars. If you desire to be a faithful and a wise steward, out of that portion of your Lord's goods which he has for the present lodged in your hands, but with the right of resuming whenever it pleases him, first, provide things needful for yourself—food to eat, raiment to put on, whatever nature moderately requires for preserving the body in health and strength. Secondly, provide these for your wife, your children, your servants, or any others who pertain to your household. If when this is done there be an overplus left, then 'do good to them that are of the household of faith.' If there be an overplus still, 'as you have opportunity, do good unto all men.' In so doing, you *give all you can*; nay, in a sound sense, all you have. For all that is laid out in this manner is really given to God. You 'render unto God the things that are God's', not only by what you give to the poor, but also by that which you expend in providing things needful for yourself and your household.

4. If then a doubt should at any time arise in your mind concerning what you are going to expend, either on yourself or any part of your family, you have an easy way to remove it. Calmly and seriously inquire: (1). In expending this, am I acting according to my character? Am I acting herein, not as a proprietor, but as a steward of my Lord's goods? (2). Am I doing this in obedience to his Word? In what Scripture does he require me so to do? (3). Can I offer up this action, this expense, as a sacrifice to God through Jesus Christ? (4). Have I reason to believe that for this very work I shall have a reward at the resurrection of the just? You will seldom need anything more to remove any doubt which arises on this head; but by this fourfold consideration you will receive clear light as to the way wherein you should go.

5. If any doubt still remain, you may farther examine yourself by prayer according to those heads of inquiry. Try whether you can say to the Searcher of hearts, your conscience

not condemning you: 'Lord, thou seest I am going to expend this sum on that food, apparel, furniture. And thou knowest I act herein with a single eye as a steward of thy goods, expending this portion of them thus in pursuance of the design thou hadst in entrusting me with them. Thou knowest I do this in obedience to thy Word, as thou commandest, and because thou commandest it. Let this, I beseech thee, be an holy sacrifice, acceptable through Jesus Christ! And give me a witness in myself that for this labour of love I shall have a recompense when thou rewardest every man according to his works.' Now if your conscience bear you witness in the Holy Ghost that this prayer is well-pleasing to God, then have you no reason to doubt but that expense is right and good, and such as will never make you ashamed.

6. You see then what it is to 'make [to] yourselves friends of the mammon of unrighteousness', and by what means you may procure 'that when ye fail they may receive you into the everlasting habitations'. You see the nature and extent of truly Christian prudence so far as it relates to the use of that great talent—money. *Gain all you can*, without hurting either yourself or your neighbour, in soul or body, by applying hereto with unintermitted diligence, and with all the understanding which God has given you. *Save all you can*, by cutting off every expense which serves only to indulge foolish desire, to gratify either the desire of the flesh, the desire of the eye, or the pride of life. Waste nothing, living or dying, on sin or folly, whether for yourself or your children. And then, *Give all you can*, or in other words give all you have to God. Do not stint yourself, like a Jew rather than a Christian, to this or that proportion. 'Render unto God', not a tenth, not a third, not half, but 'all that is God's', be it more or less, by employing all on yourself, your household, the household of faith, and all mankind, in such a manner that you may give a good account of your stewardship when ye can be no longer stewards; in such a manner as the oracles of God direct, both by general and particular precepts; in such a manner that whatever ye do may be 'a sacrifice of a sweet-smelling savour to God', and that every act may be rewarded in that day when the Lord cometh with all his saints.

7. Brethren, can we be either wise or faithful stewards unless we thus manage our Lord's goods? We cannot, as not only the oracles of God, but our own conscience beareth witness. Then why should we delay? Why should we confer any longer with flesh and blood, or men of the world? Our kingdom, our wisdom 'is not of this world'. Heathen custom is nothing to us. We follow no men any farther than they are followers of Christ. Hear ye him. Yea, today, while it is called today, hear and obey his voice. At this hour and from this hour, do his will; fulfil his word in this and in all things. I entreat you, in the name of the Lord Jesus, act up to the dignity of your calling. No more sloth! Whatsoever your hand findeth to do, do it with your might. No more waste! Cut off every expense which fashion, caprice, or flesh and blood demand. No more covetousness! But employ whatever God has entrusted you with in doing good, all possible good, in every possible kind and degree, to the household of faith, to all men. This is no small part of 'the wisdom of the just'. Give all ye have, as well as all ye are, a spiritual sacrifice to him who withheld not from you his Son, his only Son; so 'laying up in store for yourselves a good foundation against the time to come, that ye may attain eternal life'.

30. THE DANGER OF RICHES

1781

An Introductory Comment

John Wesley continued his warnings about the perils of wealth in this present sermon that appeared in the January and February editions (vol. IV) of the *Arminian Magazine* in 1781 (O, 3:227). A couple of years later he preached on the text, 1 Timothy 6:9, with great effect while in Dublin. Later, in 1788, Wesley published "On Riches" and in 1790 "The Danger of Increasing Riches" to complete the series on this theme that had actually begun with the publication of "Upon our Lord's Sermon on the Mount, Discourse the Eighth," in 1748.

Wesley's basic definition of riches found here and elsewhere is "whatever is above the plain necessaries or (at most) conveniences of life" (O, 3:230). Matthew Henry, whom Wesley consulted in writing his own *Notes Upon the New Testament,* discerned the meaning of verse 9 in the distinction between those that are rich and those "that *will be* rich, that is, place their happiness in worldly wealth" (H, 1 Tim. 6:9). Reflecting prudent judgment, given the many circumstances of life, Wesley himself qualified his definition of riches in this sermon to make proper allowances for (1) providing for one's household, (2) ensuring sufficient resources are available to conduct business, (3) making ample provision for our children once we are gone, and (4) gathering sufficient funds to pay all our debts (O, 3:231).

Over time Wesley became increasingly concerned, especially during the 1780s, that the Methodists would become rich and as a consequence fall back into nominal Christianity. To be sure, he discerned a direct connection between laying up treasures on the earth and undermining the tempers and dispositions of the heart that constitute holiness. "Have they [riches] not so hurt you as to stab your religion to the heart?" (O, 3:242). Practicing what he preached, Wesley, according to Moore, his early biographer, gave away more than thirty thousand pounds over the course of fifty years (O, 3:238n59).

The Danger of Riches

I. 1. First, let us consider what it is to be rich

A. It is having more than the necessaries or conveniences of life

2.–3. 'They that will be rich' implies some desire more than food and coverings

4. Those that desire to be rich are laying up treasures on earth

5.–6. They are those who *possess* more of this world's goods than they use

7.–8. There is a more refined covetousness, a desire of having more

9. Those who desire to be rich fall into temptation

10. They fall into a snare, the snare of the devil

11. They fall into many foolish and hurtful desires

12. These desires may be summed up as desiring happiness outside of God

13. Many are ruled by a desire to enlarge the pleasure of *tasting*

14. The imagination is gratified chiefly by means of the eye

15. Seeking happiness in *learning* falls under the desire of the eyes

16. The pride of life implies chiefly the *desire of honour*

17. *Desire of ease* is another of these foolish and hurtful desires

18.–19. Riches, either desired or possessed, lead to these desires

II. 1. Second, let us apply what has been said

2.–4. Who of *you* desire to be rich?

5. Neither desire nor endeavour to lay up treasures on earth

6. I gain all I can; I also save and give all I can

7.–8. Having gained all you can and saved all you can, give all you can

9.–10. You lovers of money, hear the word of the Lord

11. You that desire to be rich, hear the word of the Lord

12. Have these desires not hurt you already?

13. Have they not cooled (if not quenched) your love of God?

14. Are you not hurt with regard to your *humility*?

15. Are you not equally hurt with regard to your *meekness*?

16. And are you not hurt in your *patience* too?

17. You no longer rejoice to endure hardship

18.–20. You have lost your zeal for works of mercy and piety

Sermon 87: The Danger of Riches, 1781

1 Timothy 6:9

They that will be rich fall into temptation, and a snare, and into many foolish and hurtful desires, which drown men in destruction and perdition.

1. How innumerable are the ill consequences which have followed from men's not knowing or not considering this great truth! And how few are there even in the Christian world that either know or duly consider it! Yea, how small is the number of those, even among real Christians, who understand and lay it to heart! Most of these too pass it very lightly over, scarce remembering there is such a text in the Bible. And many put such a construction upon it as makes it of no manner of effect. '"They that will be rich"', say they, 'that is, will be rich at all events, who will be rich right or wrong, that are resolved to carry their point, to compass this end, whatever means they use to attain it—"they fall into temptation," and into all the evils enumerated by the Apostle.' But truly if this were all the meaning of the text it might as well have been out of the Bible.

2. This is so far from being the whole meaning of the text that it is no part of its meaning. The Apostle does not here speak of gaining riches unjustly, but of quite another thing: his words are to be taken in their plain, obvious sense, without any restriction or qualification whatsoever. St. Paul does not say, 'They that will be rich *by evil means*', by theft, robbery, oppression, or extortion; they that will be rich by fraud, or dishonest art; but simply, 'they that will be rich'; these, allowing, supposing the means they use to be ever so innocent, 'fall into temptation, and a snare, and into many foolish and hurtful desires, which drown men in destruction and perdition.'

3. But who believes that? Who receives it as the truth of God? Who is deeply convinced of it? Who preaches this? Great is the company of preachers at this day, regular and irregular. But who of them all openly and explicitly preaches this strange doctrine? It is the keen observation of a great man, 'The pulpit is a fearful preacher's stronghold.' But who, even in his stronghold, has the courage to declare so unfashionable a truth? I do not remember that in threescore years I have heard one sermon preached upon this subject. And what author within the same term has declared it from the press? At least in the English tongue? I do not know one. I have neither seen nor heard of any such author. I have seen two or three who just touch upon it, but none that treats of it professedly. I have myself frequently touched upon it in preaching, and twice in what I have published to the world: once in explaining our Lord's Sermon on the Mount, and once in the discourse on the 'mammon of unrighteousness'. But I have never yet either published or preached any sermon expressly upon the subject. It is high time I should, that I should at length speak as strongly and explicitly as I can, in order to leave a full and clear testimony behind me whenever it pleases God to call me hence.

4. O that God would give me to speak *right* and *forcible* words! And you to receive them in honest and humble hearts! Let it not be said: 'They sit before thee as my people, and they hear thy words; but they will not do them. Thou art unto them as one that hath a pleasant voice, and can play well on an instrument; for they hear thy words, but they do them not!' O that ye may 'not be forgetful hearers, but doers of the word, that ye may be blessed in your deed'! In this hope I shall endeavour:

First, to explain the Apostle's words. And,

Secondly, to apply them.

But Oh! 'Who is sufficient for these things?' Who is able to stem the general torrent? To combat all the prejudices, not only of the vulgar, but of the learned and the religious world? Yet nothing is too hard for God! Still his grace is sufficient for us. In his name, then, and by his strength I will endeavour,

I. To explain the words of the Apostle.

1. And, first, let us consider what it is to 'be rich'. What does the Apostle mean by this expression?

The preceding verse fixes the meaning of this: 'Having food and raiment' (literally 'coverings', for the word includes *lodging* as well as *clothes*) 'let us be therewith content. But they that will be rich . . .'—that is, who will have more than these, more than 'food and coverings'. It plainly follows, whatever is more than these is, in the sense of the Apostle, *riches*—whatever is above the plain necessaries or (at most) conveniences of life. Whoever has sufficient food to eat and raiment to put on, with a place where to lay his head, and something over, is *rich.*

2. Let us consider, secondly, what is implied in that expression, 'they that will be rich'. And does not this imply, first, 'they that desire to be rich', to have more than 'food and coverings'; they that seriously and deliberately desire more than food to eat and raiment to put on, and a place where to lay their head; more than the plain necessaries and conveniences of life? All, at least, who allow themselves in this desire, who see no harm in it, 'desire to be rich'.

3. And so do, secondly, all those that calmly, deliberately, and of set purpose *endeavour* after more than 'food and coverings'; that aim at and endeavour after, not only so much worldly substance as will procure them the necessaries and conveniences of life, but more than this, whether to lay it up, or lay it out in superfluities. All these undeniably prove their 'desire to be rich' by their endeavours after it.

4. Must we not, thirdly, rank among those 'that desire to be rich' all that in fact 'lay up treasures on earth'—a thing as expressly and clearly forbidden by our Lord as either adultery or murder. It is allowed, (1), that we are to provide necessaries and conveniences for those of our own household; (2), that men in business are to lay up as much as is necessary for the carrying on of that business; (3), that we are to leave our children what will supply them with necessaries and conveniences after we have left the world; and (4), that we are to provide things honest in the sight of all men, so as to 'owe no man anything'. But to lay up any more, when this is done, is what our Lord has flatly forbidden. When it is calmly and deliberately done, it is a clear proof of our desiring to be rich. And thus to lay up money is no more consistent with good conscience than to throw it into the sea.

5. We must rank among them, fourthly, all who *possess* more of this world's goods than they use according to the will of the Donor—I should rather say of the Proprietor,

for he only *lends* them to us; or, to speak more strictly, *entrusts* them to us as stewards, reserving the property of them to himself. And indeed he cannot possibly do otherwise, seeing they are the work of his hands; he is and must be the Possessor of heaven and earth. This is his inalienable right, a right he cannot divest himself of. And together with that portion of his goods which he hath lodged in our hands he has delivered to us a writing, specifying the purposes for which he has entrusted us with them. If therefore we keep more of them in our hands than is necessary for the preceding purposes, we certainly fall under the charge of 'desiring to be rich'. Over and above that we are guilty of burying our Lord's talent in the earth, and on that account are liable to be pronounced 'wicked', because 'unprofitable servants'.

6. Under this imputation of 'desiring to be rich' fall, fifthly, all 'lovers of money'. The word properly means those that *delight in money*, those that take pleasure in it, those that seek their happiness therein, that brood over their gold and silver, bills or bonds. Such was the man described by the fine Roman painter, who broke out into that natural soliloquy,

. . . Populus me sibilat, at mihi plaudo
Ipse domi quoties nummos contemplor in arca.

If there are any vices which are not natural to man, I should imagine this is one; as money of itself does not seem to gratify any natural desire or appetite of the human mind; and as, during an observation of sixty years, I do not remember one instance of a man given up to the love of money till he had neglected to employ this precious talent according to the will of his master. After this, sin was punished by sin, and this evil spirit was permitted to enter into him.

7. But beside this gross sort of covetousness, 'the love of money', there is a more refined species of covetousness, termed by the great Apostle, πλεονεξία, which literally means 'a desire of having more'—more than we have already. And those also come under the denomination of 'they that will be rich'. It is true that this desire, under proper restrictions, is innocent; nay, commendable. But when it exceeds the bounds (and how difficult is it not to exceed them!) then it comes under the present censure.

8. But who is able to receive these hard sayings? Who can believe that they are the great truths of God? Not many wise, not many noble, not many famed for learning; none indeed who are not taught of God. And who are they whom God teaches? Let our Lord answer: 'If any man be willing to do his will, he shall know of the doctrine whether it be of God.' Those who are otherwise minded will be so far from receiving it that they will not be able to understand it. Two as sensible men as most in England sat down together, some time since, to read over and consider that plain discourse on, 'Lay not up for yourselves treasures upon earth.' After much deep consideration one of them broke out: 'Positively, I cannot understand it. Pray, do *you* understand it, Mr. L?' Mr. L. honestly replied: 'Indeed, not I. I cannot conceive what Mr. W[esley] means. I can make nothing at all of it.' So utterly blind is our natural understanding touching the truth of God!

9. Having explained the former part of the text, 'they that will be rich', and pointed

out in the clearest manner I could the persons spoken of, I will now endeavour, God being my helper, to explain what is spoken of them: 'They fall into temptation, and a snare, and into many foolish and hurtful desires, which drown men in destruction and perdition.'

'They fall into temptation.' This seems to mean much more than simply, 'they are tempted.' They 'enter into the temptation': they fall plump down into it. The waves of it compass them about, and cover them all over. Of those who thus enter into temptation very few escape out of it. And the few that do are sorely scorched by it, though not utterly consumed. If they escape at all it is with the skin of their teeth, and with deep wounds that are not easily healed.

10. They fall, secondly, 'into a snare', the snare of the devil, which he hath purposely set in their way. I believe the Greek word properly means a gin, a steel trap, which shows no appearance of danger. But as soon as any creature touches the spring it suddenly closes, and either crushes its bones in pieces or consigns it to inevitable ruin.

11. They fall, thirdly, 'into many foolish and hurtful desires': ἀνοήτους, silly, senseless, fantastic; as contrary to reason, to sound understanding, as they are to religion; 'hurtful', both to body and soul, tending to weaken, yea, destroy every gracious and heavenly temper; destructive of that faith which is of the operation of God; of that hope which is full of immortality; of love to God and to our neighbour, and of every good word and work.

12. But what desires are these? This is a most important question, and deserves the deepest consideration.

In general they may all be summed up in one—the desiring happiness out of God. This includes, directly or remotely, every foolish and hurtful desire. St. Paul expresses it by 'loving the creature more than the Creator'; and by being 'lovers of pleasure more than lovers of God'. In particular they are (to use the exact and beautiful enumeration of St. John) 'the desire of the flesh, the desire of the eyes, and the pride of life': all of which 'the desire of riches' naturally tends both to beget and to increase.

13. 'The desire of the flesh' is generally understood in far too narrow a meaning. It does not, as is commonly supposed, refer to one of the senses only, but takes in all the pleasures of sense, the gratification of any of the outward senses. It has reference to the *taste* in particular. How many thousands do we find at this day in whom the ruling principle is the desire to enlarge the pleasure of *tasting*? Perhaps they do not gratify this desire in a gross manner, so as to incur the imputation of intemperance; much less so as to violate health or impair their understanding by gluttony or drunkenness. But they live in a genteel, regular sensuality; in an elegant epicurism, which does not hurt the body, but only destroys the soul, keeping it at a distance from all true religion.

14. Experience shows that the imagination is gratified chiefly by means of the eye. Therefore 'the desire of the eyes', in its natural sense, is the desiring and seeking happiness in gratifying the imagination. Now the imagination is gratified either by grandeur, by beauty, or by novelty—chiefly by the last, for neither grand nor beautiful objects please any longer than they are new.

15. Seeking happiness in *learning*, of whatever kind, falls under 'the desire of the

eyes'; whether it be in history, languages, poetry, or any branch of natural or experimental philosophy; yea, we must include the several kinds of learning, such as geometry, algebra, and metaphysics. For if our supreme delight be in any of these, we are herein gratifying 'the desire of the eyes'.

16. 'The pride of life' (whatever else that very uncommon expression ἡ ἀλαζονεία τοῦ βίου may mean) seems to imply chiefly the *desire of honour*, of the esteem, admiration, and applause of men; as nothing more directly tends both to beget and cherish pride than the honour that cometh of men. And as *riches* attract much admiration, and occasion much applause, they proportionably minister food for pride, and so may also be referred to this head.

17. *Desire of ease* is another of these foolish and hurtful desires; desire of avoiding every cross, every degree of trouble, danger, difficulty; a desire of slumbering out of life, and going to heaven (as the vulgar say) upon a feather-bed. Everyone may observe how riches first beget and then confirm and increase this desire, making men more and more soft and delicate, more unwilling, and indeed more unable, to 'take up' their 'cross daily', to 'endure hardship as good soldiers of Jesus Christ', 'and to take the kingdom of heaven by violence'.

18. Riches, either desired or possessed, naturally lead to some or other of these foolish and hurtful desires; and by affording the means of gratifying them all, naturally tend to increase them. And there is a near connection between unholy desires and every other unholy passion and temper. We easily pass from these to pride, anger, bitterness, envy, malice, revengefulness; to an headstrong, unadvisable, unreprovable spirit—indeed to every temper that is earthly, sensual, or devilish. All these the desire or possession of riches naturally tends to create, strengthen, and increase.

19. And by so doing, in the same proportion as they prevail, they 'pierce men through with many sorrows'; sorrows from remorse, from a guilty conscience; sorrows flowing from all the evil tempers which they inspire or increase; sorrows inseparable from those desires themselves, as every unholy desire is an uneasy desire; and sorrows from the contrariety of those desires to each other, whence it is impossible to gratify them all. And in the end 'they drown' the body in pain, disease, 'destruction', and the soul in everlasting 'perdition'.

II.1. I am, in the second place, to apply what has been said. And this is the principal point. For what avails the clearest knowledge, even of the most excellent things, even of the things of God, if it go no farther than speculation, if it be not reduced to practice? He that hath ears to hear, let him hear! And what he hears, let him instantly put in practice. O that God would give me the thing which I long for—that before I go hence and am no more seen, I may see a people wholly devoted to God, crucified to the world, and the world crucified to them! A people truly given up to God, in body, soul, and substance! How cheerfully should I then say, 'Now lettest thou thy servant depart in peace!'

2. I ask, then, in the name of God, who of *you* 'desire to be rich'? Which of *you* (ask your own hearts in the sight of God) seriously and deliberately desire (and perhaps applaud yourselves for so doing, as no small instance of your *prudence*) to have more than

food to eat, and raiment to put on, and a house to cover you? Who of you desires to have more than the plain necessaries and conveniences of life? Stop! Consider! What are you doing? Evil is before you! Will you rush upon the point of a sword? By the grace of God, turn and live!

3. By the same authority I ask, who of you are *endeavouring* to be rich? To procure for yourselves more than the plain necessaries and conveniences of life? Lay, each of you, your hand to your heart, and seriously inquire, Am I of that number? Am I labouring, not only for what I want, but for more than I want? May the Spirit of God say to everyone whom it concerns, 'Thou art the man!'

4. I ask, thirdly, who of you are in fact 'laying up for yourselves treasures upon earth'? Increasing in goods? Adding, as fast as you can, house to house, and field to field? 'As long as thou' thus 'dost well unto thyself, men will speak good of thee.' They will call thee a 'wise', a 'prudent' man! A man that 'minds the main chance'. Such is, and always has been, the wisdom of the world. 'But God saith unto' thee, 'Thou fool!' Art thou not 'treasuring up to thyself wrath against the day of wrath', and 'revelation of the righteous judgment of God'?

5. Perhaps you will ask, 'But do not you yourself advise, To gain all we can, and to save all we can? And is it possible to do this without both "desiring" and "endeavouring to be rich"? Nay, suppose our endeavours are successful, without actually "laying up treasures upon earth"?'

I answer, it is possible. You may gain all you can without hurting either your soul or body; you may save all you can, by carefully avoiding every needless expense, and yet never 'lay up treasures on earth', nor either desire or endeavour so to do.

6. Permit me to speak as freely of myself as I would of another man. I 'gain all I can' (namely, by writing) without hurting either my soul or body. I 'save all I can', not willingly wasting anything, not a sheet of paper, not a cup of water. I do not lay out anything, not a shilling, unless as a sacrifice to God. Yet by 'giving all I can' I am effectually secured from 'laying up treasures upon earth'. Yea, and I am secured from either desiring or endeavouring it as long as I 'give all I can'. And that I do this I call all that know me, both friends and foes, to testify.

7. But some may say, 'Whether you endeavour it or no, you are undeniably *rich*. You have more than the necessaries of life.' I have. But the Apostle does not fix the charge barely on *possessing* any quantity of goods, but on possessing more than we employ according to the will of the Donor.

Two and forty years ago, having a desire to furnish poor people with cheaper, shorter, and plainer books than any I had seen, I wrote many small tracts, generally a penny apiece; and afterwards several larger. Some of these had such a sale as I never thought of; and by this means I unawares became rich. But I never desired or endeavoured after it. And now that it is come upon me unawares I lay up no treasures upon earth: I lay up nothing at all. My desire and endeavour in this respect is to 'wind my bottom round the year'. I cannot help leaving my books behind me whenever God calls me hence. But in every other respect my own hands will be my executors.

8. Herein, my brethren, let you that are rich be even as I am. Do you that possess more than food and raiment ask: 'What shall we do? Shall we throw into the sea what God hath given us?' God forbid that you should! It is an excellent talent: it may be employed much to the glory of God. Your way lies plain before your face; if you have courage, walk in it. Having 'gained' (in a right sense) 'all you can', and 'saved all you can'; in spite of nature, and custom, and worldly prudence, 'give all you can'. I do not say, 'Be a good Jew,' giving a tenth of all you possess. I do not say, 'Be a good Pharisee,' giving a fifth of all your substance. I dare not advise you to give half of what you have; no, nor three-quarters—but all! Lift up your hearts and you will see clearly in what sense this is to be done.

> If you desire to be a 'faithful and a wise steward', out of that portion of your Lord's goods which he has for the present lodged in your hands, but with the right of resumption whenever it pleaseth him, (1), provide things needful for yourself—food to eat, raiment to put on, whatever nature moderately requires for preserving you both in health and strength; (2), provide these for your wife, your children, your servants, or any others who pertain to your household. If when this is done there is an overplus left, then do good to 'them that are of the household of faith'. If there be an overplus still, 'as you have opportunity, do good unto all men'. In so doing, you *give all you can*; nay, in a sound sense, all you have. For all that is laid out in this manner is really given to God. You render unto God the things that are God's, not only by what you give to the poor, but also by that which you expend in providing things needful for yourself and your household. (*Works* [1771], Vol. 4, p. 56 [cf. Sermon 50, 'The Use of Money,' III.3])

9. O ye Methodists, hear the word of the Lord! I have a message from God to all men; but to *you* above all. For above forty years I have been a servant to you and to your fathers. And I have not been as a reed shaken with the wind: I have not varied in my testimony. I have testified to you the very same thing from the first day even until now. But 'who hath believed our report?' I fear, not many rich. I fear there is need to apply to some of *you* those terrible words of the Apostle: 'Go to, now, ye rich men! Weep and howl for the miseries which shall come upon you. Your gold and silver is cankered, and the rust of them shall witness against you, and shall eat your flesh, as it were fire.' Certainly it will, unless ye both save all you can and give all you can. But who of you hath considered this since you first heard the will of the Lord concerning it? Who is now determined to consider and practise it? By the grace of God begin today!

10. O ye 'lovers of money', hear the word of the Lord! Suppose ye that money, though multiplied as the sand of the sea, can give happiness? Then you are 'given up to a strong delusion, to believe a lie'; a palpable lie, confuted daily by a thousand experiments. Open your eyes! Look all around you! Are the richest men the happiest? Have those the largest share of content who have the largest possessions? Is not the very reverse true? Is it not a common observation that the richest of men are in general the most discontented, the most miserable? Had not the far greater part of them more content when they had less money? Look into your breasts. If you are increased in goods, are you proportionably increased in happiness? You have more substance; but have you more content? You know the contrary. You know that in seeking happiness from riches you are only striving to drink out of empty cups. And let them be painted and gilded ever so finely, they are empty still.

11. O ye that 'desire' or endeavour 'to be rich', hear ye the word of the Lord! Why should ye be stricken any more? Will not even experience teach you wisdom? Will ye leap into a pit with your eyes open? Why should you any more 'fall into temptation'? It cannot be but temptation will beset you as long as you are in the body. But though it should beset you on every side, why will you *enter into* it? There is no necessity for this; it is your own voluntary act and deed. Why should you any more plunge yourselves 'into a snare', into the trap Satan has laid for you, that is ready to break your bones in pieces, to crush your soul to death? After fair warning, why should you sink any more into 'foolish and hurtful desires'? Desires as foolish, as inconsistent with reason as they are with religion itself! Desires that have done you more hurt already than all the treasures upon earth can countervail.

12. Have they not hurt you already, have they not wounded you in the tenderest part, by slackening, if not utterly destroying your 'hunger and thirst after righteousness'? Have you now the same longing that you had once for the whole image of God? Have you the same vehement desire as you formerly had of 'going on unto perfection'? Have they not hurt you by weakening your *faith*? Have you now faith's 'abiding impression, realizing things to come'? Do you endure in all temptations from pleasure or pain, 'seeing him that is invisible'? Have you every day, and every hour, an uninterrupted sense of his presence? Have they not hurt you with regard to your *hope*? Have you now a hope full of immortality? Are you still big with earnest expectation of all the great and precious promises? Do you now 'taste the powers of the world to come'? Do you 'sit in heavenly places with Christ Jesus'?

13. Have they not so hurt you as to stab your religion to the heart? Have they not cooled (if not quenched) your *love of God*? This is easily determined. Have you the same delight in God which you once had? Can you now say,

> I nothing want beneath, above:
> Happy, happy in thy love!

I fear not. And if your love of God is in any wise decayed, so is also your love of your neighbour. You are then hurt in the very life and spirit of your religion! If you lose love, you lose all.

14. Are not you hurt with regard to your *humility*? If you are increased in goods, it cannot well be otherwise. Many will think you a better, because you are a richer man; and how can you help thinking so yourself? Especially considering the commendations which some will give you in simplicity, and many with a design to serve themselves of you.

If you are hurt in your humility it will appear by this token: you are not so teachable as you were, not so advisable; you are not so easy to be convinced, not so easy to be persuaded. You have a much better opinion of your own judgment, and are more attached to your own will. Formerly one might guide you with a thread; now one cannot turn you with a cart-rope. You were glad to be admonished or reproved; but that time is past. And you now account a man your enemy because he tells you the truth. O let each of you calmly consider this, and see if it be not your own picture!

15. Are you not equally hurt with regard to your *meekness*? You had once learned an excellent lesson of him that was meek as well as lowly in heart. When you were reviled, you reviled not again. You did not return railing for railing, but contrariwise, blessing. Your love was 'not provoked', but enabled you on all occasions to overcome evil with good. Is this your case now? I am afraid not. I fear you cannot 'bear all things'. Alas, it may rather be said you can bear nothing—no injury, nor even affront! How quickly are you ruffled! How readily does that occur: 'What! to use *me* so! What insolence is this! How did he dare to do it! I am not now what I was once. Let him know I am now able to defend myself.' You mean, to revenge yourself. And it is much if you are not willing as well as able; if you do not take your fellow servant by the throat.

16. And are you not hurt in your *patience* too? Does your love now 'endure all things'? Do you still 'in patience possess your soul', as when you first believed? O what a change is here! You have again learnt to be frequently out of humour. You are often fretful; you feel, nay, and give way to peevishness. You find abundance of things go so cross that you cannot tell how to bear them!

Many years ago I was sitting with a gentleman in London who feared God greatly, and generally gave away, year by year, nine-tenths of his yearly income. A servant came in and threw some coals on the fire. A puff of smoke came out. The baronet threw himself back in his chair and cried out, 'Oh! Mr. Wesley, these are the crosses I meet with daily!' Would he not have been less impatient if he had had fifty, instead of five thousand pounds a year?

17. But to return. Are not you who have been successful in your endeavours to increase in substance, insensibly sunk into softness of mind, if not of body too? You no longer rejoice to 'endure hardship, as good soldiers of Jesus Christ'. You no longer 'rush into the kingdom of heaven, and take it as by storm'. You do not cheerfully and gladly 'deny yourselves', and 'take up your cross daily'. You cannot deny yourself the poor pleasure of a little sleep, or of a soft bed, in order to hear the word that is able to save your souls! Indeed, you 'cannot go out so early in the morning; besides it is dark; nay, cold; perhaps rainy too. Cold, darkness, rain—all these together. I can never think of it.' You did not say so when you were a poor man. You then regarded none of these things. It is the change of circumstances which has occasioned this melancholy change in your body and mind; you are but the shadow of what you were. What have riches done for you?

'But it cannot be expected I should do as I have done; for I am now grown old.' Am not I grown old as well as you? Am not I in my seventy-eighth year? Yet by the grace of God I do not slack my pace yet. Neither would *you*, if you were a poor man still.

18. You are so deeply hurt that you have wellnigh lost your zeal for works of mercy, as well as of piety. You once pushed on, through cold or rain, or whatever cross lay in your way, to see the poor, the sick, the distressed. You went about doing good, and found out those who were not able to find you. You cheerfully crept down into their cellars, and climbed up into their garrets, to

Supply all their wants,
And spend and be spent in assisting his saints.

You found out every scene of human misery, and assisted according to your power:

Each form of woe your generous pity moved;
Your Saviour's face you saw, and seeing, loved.

Do you now tread in the same steps? What hinders? Do you fear spoiling your silken coat? Or is there another lion in the way? Are you afraid of catching vermin? And are you not afraid lest the roaring lion should catch *you*? Are you not afraid of him that hath said, 'Inasmuch as ye have not done it unto the least of these, ye have not done it unto me'? What will follow? 'Depart, ye cursed, into everlasting fire prepared for the devil and his angels.'

19. In time past how mindful were you of that word: 'Thou shalt not hate thy brother in thy heart. Thou shalt in any wise reprove thy brother, and not suffer sin upon him.' You *did* reprove, directly or indirectly, all those that sinned in your sight. And happy consequences quickly followed. How good was a word spoken in season! It was often as an arrow from the hand of a giant. Many a heart was pierced. Many of the stout-hearted, who scorned to hear a sermon,

Fell down before his cross subdued,
And felt his arrows dipped in blood.

But which of you now has that compassion for the ignorant, and for them that are out of the way? They may wander on for *you*, and plunge into the lake of fire without let or hindrance. Gold hath steeled your hearts. You have something else to do.

Unhelped, unpitied let the wretches fall.

20. Thus have I given you, O ye gainers, lovers, possessors of riches, one more (it may be the last) warning. O that it may not be in vain! May God write it upon all your hearts! Though 'it is easier for a camel to go through the eye of a needle, than for a rich man to enter into the kingdom of heaven,' yet the things impossible with men are possible with God. Lord, speak! And even the rich men that hear these words shall enter thy kingdom! Shall 'take the kingdom of heaven by violence'; shall 'sell all for the pearl of great price': Shall be 'crucified to the world', 'and count all things dung, that they may win Christ'!

31. THE GOOD STEWARD

May 14, 1768

An Introductory Comment

When one compares this present sermon to "The Use of Money," it is readily apparent that the former is more formal and makes a greater appeal to learning than does the latter (O, 2:281). Indeed, Outler has called "The Good Steward" an inaugural sermon since it was likely composed in the wake of Wesley's appointment as the chaplain to the Dowager Countess of Buchan through the good graces, in part, of the Countess of Huntingdon (O, 2:281) who had introduced the Dowager Countess to the circle of Wesley, Whitefield, and Fletcher (S, 2:462).

The specific text of Luke 16:2, which surfaces eleven times in the sermon register from 1741 to 1785 (WSS), appears not only in Wesley's sermon on economic ethics, that is, "The Use of Money," but also in his "Great Assize," which together treat the issues of stewardship and judgment that are united in this present sermon. The compass of stewardship in "The Good Steward" includes all of the following: soul, body, worldly goods, money, talents, time, and even the blessings of the Most High, specifically in the form of the graces that are showered on humanity.

Important clues as to Wesley's thinking on eschatology (the doctrine of last things) are found in this sermon, and two warrant special attention. First, Wesley clearly affirmed the immortality of the soul in a way similar to several of the early church fathers. Since souls are incorruptible and immortal, Wesley insisted, human memory, understanding, and volition will not only continue but will actually be "inconceivably strengthened" (O, 2:289–90). Second, Wesley specifically rejected the Roman Catholic teaching of two judgments, a particular one (at death) and a general one (later on), in his affirmation of the one general judgment when the Son of Man will come in his glory (O, 2:293). Wesley concluded the sermon on a very positive note in highlighting the sufficiency of God's grace throughout the fleeting time of stewardship.

The Good Steward

I. 1. We are to use all God entrusts to us not as we please but as God pleases

2. On this condition he entrusts us with our souls, bodies, goods, and talents

3. Of all these things we are only stewards

4. God also entrusts us with our bodies, with all the powers thereof

5. God imparts to us that most excellent talent of *speech*

6. We are equally accountable for all the *members* of our bodies

7. God also entrusts us with *worldly goods*

A. These are food, money, and the necessaries and conveniences of life

8. God entrusts us with several other talents, including learning and love

II. 1. In so many respects are we stewards of the Lord

2. Part of what God entrusts to us will end, including earthly possessions

3. The case is the same with regard to our bodies

4. Here end also strength, beauty, health, eloquence, honour, and power

5. The kind of speech we now use will be at an end

6. It is doubtful whether our senses will exist

7. How far the knowledge we have gained will remain we cannot tell

8. Our incorruptible and immortal souls will remain with all their faculties

9. Our understanding will doubtless be freed from present defects

10. Disembodied spirits are in a dead sleep from death to resurrection

11. As the soul will retain its understanding, the *will* will remain in its full vigour

12. Yet in this respect they are as though they were not;

A. We are no longer stewards of them

III. 1. We must now give an account of our stewardship

2. We will give this when the great white throne comes down from heaven

3. The Judge of all will inquire, 'How didst thou employ thy *soul*?'

4. Thy Lord will then inquire, 'How didst thou employ the *body* wherewith I entrusted thee?'

5. Thy Lord will next inquire, 'How didst thou employ the *worldly goods*?'

6. Then, 'Hast thou been a wise steward with the talents of a mixed nature?'

IV. 1. From these considerations we learn how important is this short day of life

2. We learn there is no action or conversation that is purely indifferent

3. We also learn that we can never do more than our duty

4. By faith, then, put on the Lord Jesus Christ; put on the full armour of God

A. And you shall be enabled to glorify him in all your words and works

Sermon51: The Good Steward, 1768

Luke 16:2

Give an account of thy stewardship; for thou canst be no longer steward.

1. The relation which man bears to God, the creature to his Creator, is exhibited to us in the oracles of God under various representations. Considered as a sinner, a fallen creature, he is there represented as a *debtor* to his Creator. He is also frequently represented as a *servant*, which indeed is essential to him as a creature, insomuch that this appellation is given to the Son of God when in his state of humiliation: he 'took upon him the form of a servant, being made in the likeness of men'.

2. But no character more exactly agrees with the present state of man than that of a *steward*. Our blessed Lord frequently represents him as such; and there is a peculiar propriety in the representation. It is only in one particular respect, namely, as he is a sinner, that he is styled a 'debtor'; and when he is styled a 'servant' the appellation is general and indeterminate. But a 'steward' is a servant of a particular kind; such a one as man is in all respects. This appellation is exactly expressive of his situation in the present world, specifying what kind of servant he is to God, and what kind of service his divine master expects from him.

It may be of use, then, to consider this point throughly, and to make our full improvement of it. In order to this let us, first, inquire in what respects we are now God's 'stewards'. Let us, secondly, observe that when he requires our souls of us we 'can be no longer stewards'. It will then only remain, as we may in the third place observe, to 'give an account of our stewardship'.

I.1. And, first, we are to inquire in what respects we are now God's stewards. We are now indebted to him for all we have; but although a debtor is obliged to return what he has received, yet until the time of payment comes he is at liberty to use it as he pleases. It is not so with a steward: he is not at liberty to use what is lodged in his hands as *he* pleases, but as his master pleases. He has no right to dispose of anything which is in his hands but according to the will of his lord. For he is not the proprietor of any of these things, but barely entrusted with them by another: and entrusted on this express condition, that he shall dispose of all as his master orders. Now this is exactly the case of every man with relation to God. We are not at liberty to use what he has lodged in our hands as *we* please, but as he pleases, who alone is the Possessor of heaven and earth, and the Lord of every creature. We have no right to dispose of anything we have but according to his will, seeing we are not proprietors of any of these things. They are all, as our Lord speaks, ἀλλότρια, 'belonging to another person'; nor is anything properly 'our own' in the land of our pilgrimage. We shall not receive τὰ ἴδια, 'our own things', till we come to our own country.

Eternal things only are our own: with all these temporal things we are barely entrusted by another—the Disposer and Lord of all. And he entrusts us with them on this express condition, that we use them only as our Master's goods, and according to the particular directions which he has given us in his Word.

2. On this condition he hath entrusted us with our souls, our bodies, our goods, and whatever other talents we have received: but in order to impress this weighty truth on our hearts it will be needful to come to particulars.

And first, God has entrusted us with our *soul*, an immortal spirit made in the image of God, together with all the powers and faculties thereof—understanding, imagination, memory; will, and a train of affections either included in it or closely dependent upon it; love and hatred, joy and sorrow, respecting present good and evil; desire and aversion, hope and fear, respecting that which is to come. All these St. Paul seems to include in two words when he says, 'The peace of God shall keep your *hearts* and *minds*.' Perhaps, indeed the latter word, νοήματα, might rather be rendered 'thoughts', provided we take that word in its most extensive sense, for every perception of the mind, whether active or passive.

3. Now of all these it is certain we are only stewards. God has entrusted us with these powers and faculties, not that we may employ them according to our own will, but according to the express orders which he has given us; although it is true that in doing his will we most effectually secure our own happiness, seeing it is herein only that we can be happy either in time or in eternity. Thus we are to use our understanding, our imagination, our memory, wholly to the glory of him that gave them. Thus our will is to be wholly given up to him, and all our affections to be regulated as he directs. We are to love and hate, to rejoice and grieve, to desire and shun, to hope and fear, according to the rule which he prescribes whose we are, and whom we are to serve in all things. Even our thoughts are not our own in this sense: they are not at our own disposal, but for every deliberate motion of our mind we are accountable to our great Master.

4. God has, secondly, entrusted us with our *bodies* (those exquisitely wrought machines, so 'fearfully and wonderfully made'), with all the powers and members thereof. He has entrusted us with the organs of *sense*, of sight, hearing, and the rest: but none of these are given us as our own, to be employed according to our own will. None of these are *lent* us in such a sense as to leave us at liberty to use them as we please for a season. No; we have received them on these very terms, that as long as they abide with us we should employ them all in that very manner, and no other, which he appoints.

5. It is on the same terms that he has imparted to us that most excellent talent of *speech*. 'Thou hast given me a tongue', says the ancient writer, 'that I may praise thee therewith.' For this purpose was it given to all the children of men, to be employed in glorifying God. Nothing therefore is more ungrateful, or more absurd, than to think or say, 'our tongues are our own.' That cannot be, unless we have created ourselves, and so are independent on the Most High. Nay, but 'it is he that hath made us, and not we ourselves.' The manifest consequence is that he is still *Lord over us*, in this as in all other respects. It follows that there is not a word of our tongue for which we are not accountable to him.

6. To him we are equally accountable for the use of our *hands* and *feet*, and all the *members* of our body. These are so many talents which are committed to our trust, until the time appointed by the Father. Until then we have the use of all these; but as stewards, not as proprietors: to the end we should 'render them, not as instruments of unrighteousness unto sin, but as instruments of righteousness unto God'.

7. God has entrusted us, thirdly, with a portion of *worldly goods*, with food to eat, raiment to put on, and a place where to lay our head, with not only the necessaries but the conveniences of life. Above all, he has committed to our charge that precious talent which contains all the rest, *money*. Indeed, it is unspeakably precious if we are 'wise and faithful stewards' of it; if we employ every part of it for such purposes as our blessed Lord has commanded us to do.

8. God has entrusted us, fourthly, with several talents which do not properly come under any of these heads: such is bodily *strength*; such are *health*, a pleasing *person*, an agreeable *address*; such are *learning* and *knowledge* in their various degrees, with all the other advantages of *education*. Such is the *influence* which we have over others, whether by their *love* and *esteem* of us, or by *power*—power to do them good or hurt, to help or hinder them in the circumstances of life. Add to these that invaluable talent of *time*, with which God entrusts us from moment to moment. Add, lastly, that on which all the rest depend, and without which they would all be curses, not blessings: namely, the *grace* of God, the power of his Holy Spirit, which alone worketh in us all that is acceptable in his sight.

II.1. In so many respects are the children of men stewards of the Lord, 'the possessor of heaven and earth'. So large a portion of his goods of various kinds hath he committed to their charge. But it is not for ever, nor indeed for any considerable time. We have this trust reposed in us only during the short, uncertain space that we sojourn here below; only so long as we remain on earth, as this fleeting breath is in our nostrils. The hour is swiftly approaching, it is just at hand, when we 'can be no longer stewards'. The moment the body 'returns to the dust as it was, and the spirit to God that gave it', we bear that character no more; the time of our stewardship is at an end. Part of those goods wherewith we were before entrusted are now come to an end; at least they are so with regard to *us*; nor are we longer entrusted with them—and that part which remains can no longer be employed or improved as it was before.

2. Part of what we were entrusted with before is at an end, at least with regard to us. What have we to do after this life with food, and raiment, and houses, and earthly possessions? The food of the dead is the dust of the earth: they are clothed only with worms and rottenness. They dwell in 'the house prepared for all flesh': their lands know them no more. All their worldly goods are delivered into other hands, and they have 'no more portion under the sun'.

3. The case is the same with regard to the *body*. The moment the spirit returns to God we are no longer stewards of this machine, which is then sown in corruption and dishonour. All the parts and members of which it was composed lie mouldering in the clay. The hands have no longer power to move; the feet have forgot their office; the flesh, the sinews, the bones are all hasting to be dissolved into common dust.

4. Here end also the talents of a *mixed* nature: our *strength*, our *health*, our *beauty*; our *eloquence* and *address*; our faculty of pleasing, of persuading or convincing others. Here end likewise all the *honours* we once enjoyed, all the *power* which was lodged in our hands, all the *influence* which we once had over others, either by the love or the esteem which they bore us. 'Our love, our hatred, our desire is perished:' none regard how we were once affected toward them. They look upon the dead as neither able to help nor hurt them; so that 'a living dog is better than a dead lion.'

5. Perhaps a doubt may remain concerning some of the other talents wherewith we are now entrusted, whether they will cease to exist when the body returns to dust, or only cease to be improvable. Indeed there is no doubt but the kind of *speech* which we now use, by means of these bodily organs, will then be entirely at an end, when those organs are destroyed. It is certain the tongue will no more occasion any vibrations in the air; neither will the ear convey these tremulous motions to the common sensory. Even the *sonus exilis*, the low, shrill voice which the poet supposes to belong to a separate spirit, we cannot allow to have a real being; it is a mere flight of imagination. Indeed it cannot be questioned but separate spirits have some way to communicate their sentiments to each other; but what inhabitant of flesh and blood can explain that way? What we term 'speech' they cannot have. So that we can no longer be stewards of this talent when we are numbered with the dead.

6. It may likewise admit of a doubt whether our *senses* will exist when the organs of sense are destroyed. Is it not probable that those of the lower kind will cease—the feeling, the smell, the taste—as they have a more immediate reference to the body, and are chiefly, if not wholly, intended for the preservation of it? But will not some kind of *sight* remain, although the eye be closed in death? And will there not be something in the soul equivalent to the present sense of *hearing*? Nay, is it not probable that these will not only exist in the separate state, but exist in a far greater degree, in a more eminent manner than now. When the soul, disentangled from its clay, is no longer

> A dying sparkle in a cloudy place;

when it no longer

> Looks through the windows of the eye and ear,

but rather is all eye, all ear, all sense, in a manner we cannot yet conceive. And have we not a clear proof of the possibility of this, of seeing without the use of the eye, and hearing without the use of the ear? Yea, and an earnest of it continually? For does not the soul see, in the clearest manner, when the eye is of no use, namely in dreams? Does she not then enjoy the faculty of hearing without any help from the ear? But however this be, certain it is that neither will our *senses*, any more than our *speech*, be entrusted to us in the manner they are now, when the body lies in the silent grave.

7. How far the *knowledge* or *learning* which we have gained by *education* will then remain, we cannot tell. Solomon indeed says, 'There is no work, nor device, nor knowledge,

nor wisdom, in the grave whither thou goest.' But it is evident, these words cannot be understood in an absolute sense; for it is so far from being true that there is *no knowledge* after we have quitted the body that the doubt lies on the other side, whether there be any such thing as real knowledge till then? Whether it be not a plain, sober truth, not a mere poetical fiction, that

> . . . all these shadows which for things we take,
> Are but the empty dreams which in death's sleep we make—

only excepting those things which God himself has been pleased to reveal to man? I will speak for one. After having sought for truth with some diligence for half a century I am at this day hardly sure of anything but what I learn from the Bible. Nay, I positively affirm I know nothing else so certainly that I would dare to stake my salvation upon it.

So much, however, we may learn from Solomon's words, that 'there is no' *such* 'knowledge or wisdom in the grave' as will be of any use to an unhappy spirit; there is 'no device' there whereby he can now improve those talents with which he was once entrusted. For *time* is no more: the time of our trial for everlasting happiness or misery is past. *Our day*, the day of man, is over; 'the day of salvation' is ended. Nothing now remains but the day of the Lord, ushering in wide, unchangeable eternity.

8. But still our souls, being incorruptible and immortal, of a nature 'little lower than the angels' (even if we are to understand that phrase of our original nature, which may well admit of a doubt), when our bodies are mouldered into earth, will remain with all their faculties. Our *memory*, our *understanding*, will be so far from being destroyed, yea, or impaired by the dissolution of the body, that on the contrary we have reason to believe they will be inconceivably strengthened. Have we not the clearest reason to believe that they will then be wholly freed from those defects which now naturally result from the union of the soul with the corruptible body? It is highly probable that from the time these are disunited our memory will let nothing slip; yea, that it will faithfully exhibit everything to our view which was ever committed to it. It is true that the invisible world is in Scripture termed 'the land of forgetfulness'; or, as it is still more strongly expressed in the old translation, 'the land where all things are forgotten'. They are forgotten; but by whom? Not by the inhabitants of that land, but by the inhabitants of the earth. It is with regard to them that the unseen world is 'the land of forgetfulness'. All things therein are too frequently forgotten by these; but not by disembodied spirits. From the time they have put off the earthly tabernacle we can hardly think they forget anything.

9. In like manner the *understanding* will doubtless be freed from the defects that are now inseparable from it. For many ages it has been an unquestioned maxim, *humanum est errare et nescire*—'ignorance and mistake are inseparable from human nature.' But the whole of this assertion is only true with regard to living men, and holds no longer than while 'the corruptible body presses down the soul'. Ignorance indeed belongs to every finite understanding (seeing there is none beside God that knoweth all things), but not mistake. When the body is laid aside, this also is laid aside for ever.

10. What then can we say to an ingenious man who has lately made a discovery that disembodied spirits have not only no senses (not even sight or hearing), but no memory or understanding, no thought or perception, not so much as a consciousness of their own existence! That they are in a dead sleep from death to the resurrection! *Consanguineus lethi sopor* indeed! Such a sleep we may well call 'a near kinsman of death', if it be not the same thing. What can we say but that ingenious men have strange dreams; and these they sometimes mistake for realities.

11. But to return. As the soul will retain its understanding and memory, notwithstanding the dissolution of the body, so undoubtedly the *will*, including all the *affections*, will remain in its full vigour. If our love or anger, our hope or desire, perish, it is only with regard to those whom we leave behind. To them it matters not whether they were the objects of our love or hate, of our desire or aversion. But in separate spirits themselves we have no reason to believe that any of these are extinguished. It is more probable that they work with far greater force than while the soul was clogged with flesh and blood.

12. But although all these, although both our knowledge and senses, our memory and understanding, together with our will, our love, hate, and all our affections, remain after the body is dropped off, yet in this respect they are as though they were not; we are no longer stewards of them. The things continue, but our stewardship does not; we no more act in that capacity. Even the *grace* which was formerly entrusted with us, in order to enable us to be faithful and wise stewards, is now no longer entrusted for that purpose. The days of our stewardship are ended.

III.1. It now remains that, being 'no longer stewards', we 'give an account of our stewardship'. Some have imagined, this is to be done immediately after death, as soon as we enter into the world of spirits. Nay, the Church of Rome does absolutely assert this; yea, makes it an article of faith. And thus much we may allow: the moment a soul drops the body, and stands naked before God, it cannot but know what its portion will be to all eternity. It will have full in its view either everlasting joy or everlasting torment, as it is no longer possible to be deceived in the judgment which we pass upon ourselves. But the Scripture gives us no reason to believe that God will then sit in judgment upon us. There is no passage in all the oracles of God which affirms any such thing. That which has been frequently alleged for this purpose seems rather to prove the contrary; namely, 'It is appointed for men once to die, and after this, the judgment' (Heb. 9:27). For in all reason, the word 'once' is here to be applied to judgment as well as death. So that the fair inference to be drawn from this very text is, not that there are two judgments, a particular and a general, but that we are to be judged, as well as to die, once only; not once immediately after death, and again after the general resurrection, but then only 'when the Son of Man shall come in his glory, and all his holy angels with him'. The imagination therefore of one judgment at death, and another at the end of the world, can have no place with those who make the written Word of God the whole and sole standard of their faith.

2. The time then when we are to give this account is when the 'great white throne comes down from heaven, and he that sitteth thereon, from whose face the heavens and

the earth flee away, and there is found no place for them'. It is then 'the dead, small, and great,' will 'stand before God; and the books' will be 'opened'—the book of Scripture, to them who were entrusted therewith, the book of conscience to all mankind. The 'book of remembrance' likewise (to use another scriptural expression), which had been writing from the foundation of the world, will then be laid open to the view of all the children of men. Before all these, even the whole human race, before the devil and his angels, before an innumerable company of holy angels, and before God the Judge of all; thou wilt appear without any shelter or covering, without any possibility of disguise, to give a particular account of the manner wherein thou hast employed all thy Lord's goods.

3. The Judge of all will then inquire: 'How didst thou employ thy *soul*? I entrusted thee with an immortal spirit, endowed with various powers and faculties, with understanding, imagination, memory, will, affections. I gave thee withal full and express directions how all these were to be employed. Didst thou employ thy *understanding*, as far as it was capable, according to those directions, namely, in the knowledge of thyself and me? My nature, my attributes? My works, whether of creation, of providence, or of grace? In acquainting thyself with my Word? In using every means to increase thy knowledge thereof? In meditating thereon day and night? Didst thou employ thy *memory* according to my will? In treasuring up whatever knowledge thou hadst acquired which might conduce to my glory, to thy own salvation, or the advantage of others? Didst thou store up therein, not things of no value, but whatever instructions thou hadst learned from my Word; and whatever experience thou hadst gained of my wisdom, truth, power, and mercy? Was thy *imagination* employed, not in painting vain images, much less such as nourished foolish and hurtful desires, but in representing to thee whatever would profit thy soul, and awaken thy pursuit of wisdom and holiness? Didst thou follow my directions with regard to thy *will*? Was it wholly given up to me? Was it swallowed up in mine, so as never to oppose, but always run parallel with it? Were thy *affections* placed and regulated in such a manner as I appointed in my Word? Didst thou give me thy heart? Didst thou not love the world, neither the things of the world? Was I the object of thy love? Was all thy desire unto me, and unto the remembrance of my name? Was I the joy of thy heart, the delight of thy soul, the chief among ten thousand? Didst thou sorrow for nothing but what grieved my spirit? Didst thou fear and hate nothing but sin? Did the whole stream of thy affections flow back to the ocean from whence they came? Were thy *thoughts* employed according to my will? Not in ranging to the ends of the earth, not on folly, or sin; but on "whatsoever things were pure, whatsoever things were holy", on whatsoever was conducive to my "glory", and to "peace and goodwill among men"?'

4. Thy Lord will then inquire, 'How didst thou employ the *body* wherewith I entrusted thee? I gave thee a *tongue* to praise me therewith. Didst thou use it to the end for which it was given? Didst thou employ it, not in evil-speaking or idle-speaking, not in uncharitable or unprofitable conversation; but in such as was good, as was necessary or useful, either to thyself or others? Such as always tended, directly or indirectly, to "minister grace to the hearers"? I gave thee, together with thy other senses, those grand avenues of knowledge, *sight*, and *hearing*. Were these employed to those excellent purposes for which they were bestowed upon thee? In bringing thee in more and more instruction in

righteousness and true holiness? I gave thee hands and feet and various *members* wherewith to perform the works which were prepared for thee. Were they employed, not in doing "the will of the flesh", of thy evil nature, or "the will of the mind", the things to which thy reason or fancy led thee, but "the will of him that sent" thee into the world, merely to work out thy own salvation? Didst thou present all thy members, not to sin, as instruments of unrighteousness, but to me alone, through the Son of my love, "as instruments of righteousness"?'

5. The Lord of all will next inquire, 'How didst thou employ the *worldly goods* which I lodged in thy hands? Didst thou use thy food, not so as to seek or place thy happiness therein, but so as to preserve thy body in health, in strength and vigour, a fit instrument for the soul? Didst thou use apparel, not to nourish pride or vanity, much less to tempt others to sin, but conveniently and decently to defend thyself from the injuries of the weather? Didst thou prepare and use thy house and all other conveniences with a single eye to my glory? In every point seeking not thy own honour, but mine; studying to please, not thyself, but me? Once more: in what manner didst thou employ that comprehensive talent, *money*? Not in gratifying the desire of the flesh, the desire of the eye, or the pride of life? Not squandering it away in vain expenses, the same as throwing it into the sea? Not hoarding it up to leave behind thee, the same as burying it in the earth? But first supplying thy own reasonable wants, together with those of thy family; then restoring the remainder to me, through the poor, whom I had appointed to receive it; looking upon thyself as only one of that number of poor whose wants were to be supplied out of that part of my substance which I had placed in thy hands for this purpose; leaving thee the right of being supplied first, and the blessedness of giving rather than receiving? Wast thou accordingly a general benefactor to mankind? Feeding the hungry, clothing the naked, comforting the sick, assisting the stranger, relieving the afflicted according to their various necessities? Wast thou eyes to the blind, and feet to the lame? A father to the fatherless, and an husband to the widow? And didst thou labour to improve all outward works of mercy, as means of saving souls from death?'

6. Thy Lord will farther inquire: 'Hast thou been a wise and faithful steward with regard to the talents of a mixed nature which I lent thee? Didst thou employ thy health and strength, not in folly or sin, not in pleasures which perished in the using, "not in making provision for the flesh, to fulfil the desires thereof", but in a vigorous pursuit of that better part which none could take away from thee? Didst thou employ whatever was pleasing in thy person or address, whatever advantages thou hadst by education, whatever share of learning, whatever knowledge of things or men was committed thee, for the promoting of virtue in the world, for the enlargement of my kingdom? Didst thou employ whatever share of power thou hadst, whatever influence over others, by the love or esteem of thee which they had conceived, for the increase of their wisdom and holiness? Didst thou employ that inestimable talent of time with wariness and circumspection, as duly weighing the value of every moment, and knowing that all were numbered in eternity? Above all, wast thou a good steward of my grace, preventing, accompanying, and following thee? Didst thou duly observe and carefully improve all the influences of my Spirit? Every good desire? Every measure of light? All his sharp or gentle reproofs? How didst thou profit by

"the spirit of bondage and fear" which was previous to "the Spirit of adoption"? And when thou wast made a partaker of this Spirit, "crying in thy heart, Abba, Father", didst thou stand fast in the glorious liberty wherewith I made thee free? Didst thou from thenceforth present thy soul and body, all thy thoughts, thy words, and actions, in one flame of love, as an holy sacrifice, glorifying me with thy body and thy spirit? Then "well done, good and faithful servant! [. . .] Enter thou into the joy of thy Lord!"' And what will remain either to the faithful or unfaithful steward? Nothing but the execution of that sentence which has been passed by the righteous Judge; fixing thee in a state which admits of no change, through everlasting ages. It remains only that thou be rewarded to all eternity according to thy works.

IV.1. From these plain considerations we may learn, first, how important is this short, uncertain day of life! How precious, above all utterance, above all conception, is every portion of it!

> The least of these a serious care demands;
> For though they are little, they are golden sands!

How deeply does it concern every child of man to let none of these run to waste; but to improve them all to the noblest purposes as long as the breath of God is in his nostrils!

2. We learn from hence, secondly, that there is no employment of our time, no action or conversation, that is purely *indifferent.* All is good or bad, because all our time, as everything we have, is *not our own.* All these are, as our Lord speaks, τὰ ἀλλότρια, the property of another—of God, our Creator. Now these either are or are not employed according to his will. If they are so employed, all is good; if they are not, all is evil. Again: it is his will that we should continually grow in grace and in the living knowledge of our Lord Jesus Christ. Consequently every thought, word, and work whereby this knowledge is increased, whereby we grow in grace, is good; and every one whereby this knowledge is not increased is truly and properly evil.

3. We learn from hence, thirdly, that there are no works of supererogation, that we can never do more than our duty; seeing all we have is not our own, but God's, all we can do is due to him. We have not received this or that, or many things only, but everything from him: therefore everything is his due. He that gives us all must needs have a right to all. So that if we pay him anything less than all we cannot be 'faithful stewards'. And considering 'every man shall receive his own reward, according to his own labour,' we cannot be 'wise stewards' unless we labour to the uttermost of our power; not leaving anything undone which we possibly can do, but putting forth all our strength.

4. Brethren, 'Who is an understanding man and endued with knowledge among you?' Let him show the wisdom from above by walking suitably to his character. If he so account of himself as a steward of the manifold gifts of God, let him see that all his thoughts, and words, and works be agreeable to the post God has assigned him. It is no

small thing to lay out for God all which you have received from God. It required all your wisdom, all your resolution, all your patience and constancy; for more than ever you had by nature, but not more than you may have by grace. For his grace is sufficient for you, and 'all things', you know, 'are possible to him that believeth.' By faith, then, 'put on the Lord Jesus Christ;' 'put on the whole armour of God,' and you shall be enabled to glorify him in all your words and works, yea, to bring every thought into captivity to the obedience of Christ.

Edinburgh

May 14, 1768

32. SELF-DENIAL

1760

An Introductory Comment

Growing up in the Epworth rectory, Wesley encountered the importance of self-denial in the disciplinary practices of Susanna, who insisted on "conquering the wills of children. . . [as] the only foundation for a religious education" (FB, 25:330–31). This same theme of self-denial was well developed in both Puritan and Anglican spiritual classics where Wesley would have encountered it in Richard Baxter's *Treatise of Self-Denyall* and in Jeremy Taylor's *The Rule and Exercises of Holy Living and Holy Dying* (O, 2:236). In his *Journal* for August 16, 1744, Wesley published a letter on self-denial he had received from Rev. Henry Piers, vicar of Bexley (WH, 20:35–36), and on February 17, 1745, he printed another one on the same topic from William Briggs, one of the first Methodist book stewards (WH, 20:52).

Wesley preached on the text of this sermon, Luke 9:23, on February 20, 1738, in London at Great St. Helen's shortly after he had returned from Georgia (WH, 18:226). The only other occurrences of the text in the sermon register are found on February 17 and March 24 of the year 1755 (WWS), though the text did emerge in the body of two important sermons late in Wesley's career: "On Riches" in 1788 and "Causes of the Inefficacy of Christianity" the following year. In the former, Wesley specifically linked the phrase "If any man will come after me" with being a real Christian (O, 3:527); in the latter he viewed abandoning self-denial and taking up the cross as two of the principal reasons why "Christianity [has] done so little good, even . . . among the Methodists" (O, 4:93).

Wesley carefully distinguished self-denial from taking up the cross in this present sermon by noting that the former entails the denying or refusing our own will for the sake of the will of God while the latter "goes a little farther than denying ourselves . . . it being more easy to forego pleasure than to endure pain" (O, 2:243).

Self-Denial

I. 1. Those who take nature, not grace, as their guide abhor 'denying themselves'
2. Self-denial is the denial or refusal to follow our own will
3. Our nature is altogether corrupt, in every power and faculty
4. God's will is a path leading to God; our will is contrary to it
5. By following our own will we strengthen its perverseness
6. To deny ourselves is to deny our will where it contradicts God's will
7. Everyone that would follow Christ must take up his cross
8.–9. This is not only not joyous, it is contrary to our will
10. The means to heal a sin-sick soul are often painful
11. The taking up differs a little from bearing his cross
12. Every disciple of Christ must take up as well as bear *his* cross
13.–14. In all this, our blessed Lord is the physician of our souls

II. 1. The great hindrance of receiving grace is the want of denying ourselves
2. A few instances will make this plain. People hear the word which can save
A. They are well pleased by it, yet remain dead in trespasses and sins
3. Suppose they begin to wake out of sleep and their eyes are a little opened
A. Why are they closed again? Because they again yield to sin
4. But this is not the case with all; many have been awakened and sleep no more
5. But this one received the heavenly gift and is now as weak as another
6. But perhaps she still has a measure of the Spirit of adoption
A. But she is not, as once, hungering and thirsting after righteousness
7. It follows that some who receive the heavenly gift do not retain it

III. 1. Those who oppose self-denial and the daily cross know little of Scripture
A. They also know little of the power of God
2. We may learn, secondly, the real cause why some have lost their light and heat
A. They neither valued nor practised the doctrine of self-denial
3. We may learn, thirdly, that it is not enough not to oppose self-denial
4. Lastly, see that you apply this, every one of you, to your own soul

Sermon 48: Self-denial, 1760

Luke 9:23

And he said to them all, If any man will come after me, let him deny himself, and take up his cross daily, and follow me.

1. It has been frequently imagined that the direction here given related chiefly, if not wholly, to the apostles; at least to the Christians of the first ages, or those in a state of persecution. But this is a grievous mistake; for although our blessed Lord is here directing his discourse more immediately to his apostles and those other disciples who attended him in the days of his flesh, yet in them he speaks to us, and to all mankind, without any exception or limitation. The very reason of the thing puts it beyond dispute that the duty which is here enjoined is not peculiar to them, or to the Christians of the early ages. It no more regards any particular order of men, or particular time, than any particular country. No; it is of the most universal nature, respecting all times and all persons. Yea, and all things—not meats and drinks only, and things pertaining to the senses. The meaning is, 'If any man', of whatever rank, station, circumstances, in any nation, in any age of the world, 'will' effectually 'come after me, let him deny himself in all things; let him take up his cross' of whatever kind, yea, and that 'daily, and follow me.'

2. The 'denying' ourselves and the 'taking up our cross', in the full extent of the expression, is not a thing of small concern. It is not expedient only, as are some of the circumstantials of religion; but it is absolutely, indispensably necessary, either to our becoming or continuing his disciples. It is absolutely necessary, in the very nature of the thing, to our 'coming after him' and 'following him', insomuch that as far as we do not practise it we are not his disciples. If we do not continually 'deny ourselves', we do not learn of him, but of other masters. If we do not 'take up our cross daily', we do not 'come after him', but after the world, or the prince of the world, or our own 'fleshly mind'. If we are not walking in the way of the cross, we are not following him; we are not treading in his steps, but going back from, or at least wide of, him.

3. It is for this reason that so many ministers of Christ in almost every age and nation, particularly since the Reformation of the Church from the innovations and corruptions gradually crept into it, have wrote and spoke so largely on this important duty, both in their public discourses and private exhortations. This induced them to disperse abroad many tracts upon the subject; and some in our own nation. They knew both from the oracles of God and from the testimony of their own experience how impossible it was not to deny our Master, unless we will deny ourselves; and how vainly we attempt to follow him that was crucified, unless we take up our cross daily.

4. But may not this very consideration make it reasonable to inquire, 'If so much has been said and wrote on the subject already, what need is there to say or write any more?' I answer, there are no inconsiderable numbers, even of people fearing God, who have not had the opportunity either of hearing what has been spoke, or reading what has been wrote upon it. And perhaps if they had read much of what has been written they would not have been much profited. Many who have wrote (some of them large volumes) do by no means appear to have understood the subject. Either they had imperfect views of

the very nature of it (and then they could never explain it to others) or they were unacquainted with the due extent of it; they did not see how *exceeding broad* this command is; or they were not sensible of the absolute, the indispensable necessity of it. Others speak of it in so dark, so perplexed, so intricate, so mystical a manner, as if they designed rather to conceal it from the vulgar than to explain it to common readers. Others speak admirably well, with great clearness and strength, on the necessity of self-denial; but then they deal in generals only, without coming to particular instances, and so are of little use to the bulk of mankind, to men of ordinary capacity and education. And if some of them do descend to particulars, it is to those particulars only which do not affect the generality of men, since they seldom, if ever, occur in common life: such as the enduring imprisonment or tortures; the giving up, in a literal sense, their houses or lands, their husbands or wives, children, or life itself—to none of which we are called, nor are likely to be, unless God should permit times of public persecution to return. In the meantime, I know of no writer in the English tongue who has described the nature of self-denial in plain and intelligible terms such as lie level with common understandings, and applied it to those little particulars which daily occur in common life. A discourse of this kind is wanted still. And it is wanted the more because in every stage of the spiritual life, although there is a variety of particular hindrances of our attaining grace or growing therein, yet are all resolvable into these general ones—either we do not deny ourselves, or we do not take up our cross.

In order to supply this defect in some degree, I shall endeavour to show, first, what it is for a man to deny himself, and what to take up his cross; and secondly, that if a man be not fully Christ's disciple, it is always owing to the want of this.

I.1. I shall, first, endeavour to show what it is for a man to 'deny himself and take up his cross daily'. This is a point which is of all others most necessary to be considered and throughly understood, even on this account, that it is of all others most opposed, by numerous and powerful enemies. All our nature must certainly rise up against this, even in its own defence. The world, consequently, the men who take nature, not grace, for their guide, abhor the very sound of it. And the great enemy of our souls, well knowing its importance, cannot but move every stone against it. But this is not all: even those who have in some measure shaken off the yoke of the devil, who have experienced, especially of late years, a real work of grace in their hearts, yet are no friends to this grand doctrine of Christianity, though it is so peculiarly insisted on by their Master. Some of them are as deeply and totally ignorant concerning it as if there was not one word about it in the Bible. Others are farther off still, having unawares imbibed strong prejudices against it. These they have received partly from outside Christians—men of a fair speech and behaviour who want nothing of godliness but the power, nothing of religion but the spirit—and partly from those who did once, if they do not now, 'taste of the powers of the world to come'. But are there any of these who do not both practise self-denial themselves and recommend it to others? You are little acquainted with mankind if you doubt of this. There are whole bodies of men who only do not declare war against it. To go no farther than London, look upon the whole body of predestinarians who by the free mercy of God have lately been called out of the darkness of nature into the light of faith. Are they patterns of self-denial? How few of them even profess to practise it at all! How few of them recommend it themselves, or are pleased with them that do! Rather do they not continually represent it in the most odious colours, as if it were seeking *salvation by works*, or 'seeking to establish our own righteousness'? And how readily do antinomians of all kinds, from the smooth Moravian to the boisterous foul-mouthed Ranter, join the cry with their silly unmeaning cant of 'legality', and 'preaching the law'! Therefore you are in constant danger of being wheedled, hectored, or ridiculed out of this important gospel doctrine either by false teachers or false brethren (more or less beguiled from the simplicity of the gospel) if you are not deeply grounded therein. Let fervent prayer then go before, accompany, and follow what you are now about to read, that it may be written in your heart by the finger of God, so as never to be erased.

2. But what is self-denial? Wherein are we to deny ourselves? And whence does the necessity of this arise? I answer, the will of God is the supreme, unalterable rule for every intelligent creature; equally binding every angel in heaven and every man upon earth. Nor can it be otherwise: this is the natural, necessary result of the relation between creatures and their Creator. But if the will of God be our one rule of action in everything, great and small, it follows by undeniable consequence that we are not to do our own will in anything. Here therefore we see at once the nature, with the ground and reason, of self-denial. We see the nature of self-denial: it is the denying or refusing to follow our own will, from a conviction that the will of God is the only rule of action to us. And we see the reason thereof, because we are creatures; because 'it is he that hath made us and not we ourselves.'

3. This reason for self-denial must hold even with regard to the angels of God in heaven; and with regard to man, innocent and holy, as he came out of the hands of his Creator. But a farther reason for it arises from the condition wherein all men are since the Fall. We are all now 'shapen in wickedness, and in sin did our mother conceive us'. Our nature is altogether corrupt, in every power and faculty. And our will, depraved equally with the rest, is wholly bent to indulge our natural corruption. On the other hand, it is the will of God that we resist and counteract that corruption, not at some times, or in some things only, but at all times, and in all things. Here therefore is a farther ground for constant and universal self-denial.

4. To illustrate this a little farther. The will of God is a path leading straight to God. The will of man which once ran parallel with it is now another path, not only different from it, but in our present state directly contrary to it. It leads from God; if therefore we walk in the one, we must necessarily quit the other. We cannot walk in both. Indeed a man of 'faint heart and feeble hands' may 'go in two ways', one after the other; but he cannot walk in two ways at the same time. He cannot at one and the same time follow his own will and follow the will of God; he must choose the one or the other—denying God's will to follow his own, or denying himself to follow the will of God.

5. Now it is undoubtedly pleasing for the time to follow our own will, by indulging, in any instance that offers, the corruption of our nature. But by following it in anything we so far strengthen the perverseness of our will; and by indulging it we continually increase the corruption of our nature. So by the food which is agreeable to the palate we

often increase a bodily disease. It gratifies the taste; but it inflames the disorder. It brings pleasure; but it also brings death.

6. On the whole, then, to deny ourselves is to deny our own will where it does not fall in with the will of God, and that however pleasing it may be. It is to deny ourselves any pleasure which does not spring from, and lead to, God; that is, in effect, to refuse going out of our way, though into a pleasant, flowery path; to refuse what we know to be deadly poison, though agreeable to the taste.

7. And everyone that would follow Christ, that would be his real disciple, must not only 'deny himself', but 'take up his cross' also. A cross is anything contrary to our will, anything displeasing to our nature. So that taking up our cross goes a little farther than denying ourselves; it rises a little higher, and is a more difficult task to flesh and blood, it being more easy to forego pleasure than to endure pain.

8. Now in 'running the race which is set before us' according to the will of God, there is often a cross lying in the way; that is, something which is not only not joyous, but grievous, something which is contrary to our will, which is displeasing to our nature. What then is to be done? The choice is plain: either we must 'take up our cross', or we must turn aside from the way of God, 'from the holy commandment delivered to us'—if we do not stop altogether, or turn back to everlasting perdition.

9. In order to the healing of that corruption, that evil disease which every man brings with him into the world, it is often needful to pluck out as it were a right eye, to cut off a right hand; so painful is either the thing itself which must be done, or the only means of doing it; the parting suppose with a foolish desire, with an inordinate affection; or a separation from the object of it, without which it can never be extinguished. In the former kind, the tearing away such a desire or affection when it is deeply rooted in the soul is often like the piercing of a sword, yea, like 'the dividing asunder of the soul and spirit, the joints and marrow'. The Lord then sits upon the soul 'as a refiner's fire', to burn up all the dross thereof. And this is a cross indeed; it is essentially painful; it must be so in the very nature of the thing. The soul cannot be thus torn asunder, it cannot pass through the fire, without pain.

10. In the latter kind, the means to heal a sin-sick soul, to cure a foolish desire, an inordinate affection, are often painful, not in the nature of the thing, but from the nature of the disease. So when our Lord said to the rich young man, 'Go sell that thou hast and give it to the poor' (as well knowing this was the only means of healing his covetousness), the very thought of it gave him so much pain that 'he went away sorrowful'; choosing rather to part with his hope of heaven than his possessions on earth. This was a burden he could not consent to lift, a cross he would not take up. And in the one kind or the other every follower of Christ will surely have need to 'take up his cross daily'.

11. The 'taking up' differs a little from 'bearing his cross'. We are then properly said to 'bear our cross' when we endure what is laid upon us without our choice, with meekness and resignation. Whereas we do not properly 'take up our cross' but when we voluntarily suffer what it is in our power to avoid; when we willingly embrace the will of God, though contrary to our own; when we choose what is painful because it is the will of our wise and gracious Creator.

12. And thus it behoves every disciple of Christ to 'take up' as well as to 'bear *his* cross'. Indeed in one sense it is not *his* alone: it is common to him and many others, seeing 'there is no temptation befalls any man', εἰ μὴ ἀνθρώπινος, 'but such as is common to men', such as is incident and adapted to their common nature and situation in the present world. But in another sense, as it is considered with all its circumstances, it is *his*; peculiar to himself. It is prepared of God for him; it is given by God to him, as a token of his love. And if he receives it as such, and (after using such means to remove the pressure as Christian wisdom directs) lies as clay in the potter's hand, it is disposed and ordered by God for his good, both with regard to the quality of it and in respect to its quantity and degree, its duration, and every other circumstance.

13. In all this we may easily conceive our blessed Lord to act as the physician of our souls, not merely 'for his own pleasure, but for our profit, that we may be partakers of his holiness'. If in searching our wounds he puts us to pain, it is only in order to heal them. He cuts away what is putrified or unsound in order to preserve the sound part. And if we freely choose the loss of a limb, rather than the whole body should perish, how much more should we choose, figuratively, to cut off a right hand, rather than the whole soul should be cast into hell!

14. We see plainly, then, both the nature and ground of 'taking up our cross'. It does not imply the 'disciplining ourselves' (as some speak), the literally tearing our own flesh: the wearing haircloth, or iron girdles, or anything else that would impair our bodily health (although we know not what allowance God may make for those who act thus through involuntary ignorance), but the embracing the will of God, though contrary to our own; the choosing wholesome, though bitter, medicines; the freely accepting temporary pain, of whatever kind, and in whatever degree, when it is either essentially or accidentally necessary to eternal pleasure.

II.1. I am, secondly, to show that it is always owing to the want either of self-denial or taking up his cross that any man does not throughly 'follow him', is not fully a 'disciple' of Christ.

It is true this may be partly owing, in some cases, to the want of the means of grace; of hearing the true word of God spoken with power; of the sacraments; or of Christian fellowship. But where none of these is wanting, the great hindrance of our receiving or growing in the grace of God is always the want of denying ourselves or taking up our cross.

2. A few instances will make this plain. A man hears the word which is able to save his soul. He is well pleased with what he hears, acknowledges the truth, and is a little affected by it. Yet he remains 'dead in trespasses and sins', senseless and unawakened. Why is this? Because he will not part with his bosom sin, though he now knows it is an abomination to the Lord. He came to hear, full of lust and unholy desires; and he will not part with them. Therefore no deep impression is made upon him, but his foolish heart is still hardened; that is, he is still senseless and unawakened, because he will not 'deny himself'.

3. Suppose he begins to awake out of sleep, and his eyes are a little opened, why are they so quickly closed again? Why does he again sink into the sleep of death? Because he

again yields to his bosom sin; he drinks again of the pleasing poison. Therefore it is impossible that any lasting impression should be made upon his heart; that is, he relapses into his fatal insensibility because he will not 'deny himself'.

4. But this is not the case with all. We have many instances of those who when once awakened sleep no more. The impressions once received do not wear away; they are not only deep, but lasting. And yet many of these have not found what they seek; they mourn, and yet are not comforted. Now why is this? It is because they do not 'bring forth fruits meet for repentance'; because they do not, according to the grace they have received, 'cease from evil and do good'. They do not cease from the easily besetting sin, the sin of their constitution, of their education, or of their profession. Or they omit doing the good they may, and know they ought to do, because of some disagreeable circumstance attending it; that is, they do not attain faith, because they will not 'deny themselves', or 'take up their cross'.

5. 'But this man did receive "the heavenly gift". He did "taste of the powers of the world to come". He saw "the light of the glory of God in the face of Jesus Christ". The "peace which passeth all understanding" did "rule his heart and mind"; and the love of God was shed abroad therein by the Holy Ghost which was given unto him. Yet he is now weak as another man. He again relishes the things of earth, and has more taste for the things which are seen than for those which are not seen. The eye of his understanding is closed again, so that he cannot "see him that is invisible". His love is waxed cold, and the peace of God no longer rules in his heart.' And no marvel: for he has again given place to the devil, and grieved the Holy Spirit of God. He has turned again unto folly, to some pleasing sin, if not in outward act, yet in heart. He has given place to pride, or anger, or desire; to self-will, or stubbornness. Or he did not stir up the gift of God which was in him; he gave way to spiritual sloth, and would not be at the pains of 'praying always, and watching thereunto with all perseverance'; that is, he made shipwreck of the faith for want of self-denial and 'taking up his cross daily'.

6. But perhaps he has not made shipwreck of the faith: he has still a measure of the Spirit of adoption, which continues to witness with his spirit that he is a child of God. However, he is not 'going on to perfection'; he is not, as once, hungering and thirsting after righteousness, panting after the whole image and full enjoyment of God, as the hart after the water-brook. Rather he is weary and faint in his mind, and as it were hovering between life and death. And why is he thus, but because he hath forgotten the word of God, 'By works is faith made perfect'? He does not use all diligence in working the works of God. He does not 'continue instant in prayer', private as well as public; in communicating, hearing, meditation, fasting, and religious conference. If he does not wholly neglect some of these means, at least he does not use them all, with his might. Or he is not zealous of works of charity, as well as works of piety. He is not merciful after his power, with the full ability which God giveth. He does not fervently serve the Lord by doing good to men, in every kind and in every degree he can, to their souls as well as their bodies. And why does he not continue in prayer? Because in times of dryness it is pain and grief unto him. He does not continue in hearing at all opportunities, because sleep is sweet; or it is cold, or dark, or rainy. But why does he not continue in works of mercy? Because he cannot feed

the hungry, or clothe the naked, unless he retrench the expense of his own apparel, or use cheaper and less pleasing food. Beside which the visiting the sick or those that are in prison is attended with many disagreeable circumstances. And so are most works of spiritual mercy—reproof, in particular. He *would* reprove his neighbour; but sometimes shame, sometimes fear, comes between. For he may expose himself not only to ridicule but to heavier inconveniences too. Upon these and the like considerations he omits one or more, if not all, works of mercy and piety. Therefore his faith is not made perfect, neither can he grow in grace; namely, because he will not 'deny himself, and take up his daily cross'.

7. It manifestly follows that it is always owing to the want either of self-denial or taking up his cross that a man does not throughly follow his Lord, that he is not fully a disciple of Christ. It is owing to this that he who is dead in sin does not awake, though the trumpet be blown; that he who begins to awake out of sleep yet has no deep or lasting conviction; that he who is deeply and lastingly convinced of sin does not attain remission of sins; that some who have received this heavenly gift retain it not, but make shipwreck of the faith; and that others, if they do not draw back to perdition, yet are weary and faint in their mind, and do not reach the mark of the prize of the high calling of God in Christ Jesus.

III.1. How easily may we learn hence that they know neither the Scripture nor the power of God who directly or indirectly, in public or in private, oppose the doctrine of self-denial and the daily cross! How totally ignorant are these men of an hundred particular texts, as well as of the general tenor of the whole oracles of God! And how entirely unacquainted must they be with true, genuine, Christian experience! Of the manner wherein the Holy Spirit ever did, and does at this day, work in the souls of men! They may talk indeed very loudly and confidently (a natural fruit of ignorance), as though they were the only men who understood either the Word of God, or the experience of his children. But their words are, in every sense, 'vain words': they are weighed in the balance and found wanting.

2. We may learn from hence, secondly, the real cause why not only many particular persons, but even bodies of men, who were once burning and shining lights, have now lost both their light and heat. If they did not hate and oppose, they at least lightly esteemed this precious gospel doctrine. If they did not boldly say, *Abnegationem omnem proculcamus, internecioni damus* ('We trample all self-denial under foot, we devote it to destruction'), yet they neither valued it according to its high importance, nor took any pains in practising it. *Hanc mystici docent*, said that great, bad man—'The mystic writers teach self-denial.' No; the inspired writers. And God teaches it to every soul who is willing to hear his voice.

3. We may learn from hence, thirdly, that it is not enough for a minister of the gospel not to oppose the doctrine of self-denial, to say nothing concerning it. Nay, he cannot satisfy his duty by saying a little in favour of it. If he would indeed be pure from the blood of all men he must speak of it frequently and largely; he must inculcate the necessity of it in the clearest and strongest manner; he must press it with his might on all persons, at

all times, and in all places; laying 'line upon line, line upon line, precept upon precept, precept upon precept'. So shall he have a conscience void of offence; so shall he save his own soul and those that hear him.

4. Lastly, see that you apply this, every one of you, to your own soul. Meditate upon it when you are in secret; ponder it in your heart. Take care not only to understand it throughly, but to remember it to your life's end. Cry unto the Strong for strength, that you may no sooner understand than enter upon the practice of it. Delay not the time, but practise it immediately, from this very hour. Practise it universally, on every one of the thousand occasions which will occur in all circumstances of life. Practise it daily, without intermission, from the hour you first set your hand to the plough; and perseveringly enduring therein to the end, till your spirit returns to God.

33. ON VISITING THE SICK

May 23, 1786

An Introductory Comment

Wesley composed this sermon as he was on a preaching tour in Scotland in 1786, and he finished the work in Aberdeen. The composition was published in two installments in the *Arminian Magazine* in September and October of that same year. The sermon register reveals that this was apparently the only time Wesley employed Matthew 25:36 as a text, though the verse itself emerged much earlier in the body of "Upon our Lord's Sermon on the Mount, Discourse the Eighth" (O, 3:384).

Likely building on Matthew Henry's insight that works of charity and beneficence are in some sense necessary to salvation (H, Matt. 25:36), Wesley clearly affirmed in this sermon that works of mercy, as with works of piety, are a "real means of grace" (O, 3:385). In light of this affirmation, he articulated the duty of visiting the sick and poor in a full-orbed way as embracing both their outward and their inward conditions (O, 3:390–91). In fact, Wesley stated repeatedly in this sermon, indicating the proper valuation, that after the temporal needs of the sick are met, ministers "may administer help of a more excellent kind, by supplying their spiritual wants" (O, 3:389). Again, "These little labours of love will pave your way to things of greater importance" (O, 3:391). Wesley maintained here, as elsewhere, that those who serve, in all their various labors, must ever "keep a higher end in view, even the saving of souls from death" (O, 3:393).

In Wesley's judgment the rich, defined as those who had more than "the conveniences of life" (O, 3:393), were especially called to this work, as were women who served in the early church in the office of deacon. Beyond this, Wesley insisted that such ministry, if it is to be a vital means of grace, cannot be done by proxy.

On Visiting the Sick

I. What is the nature of this duty? What is implied in it?
- 1. By the sick I do not mean only those that are sick in the strictest sense
  - A. Rather I would include all who are in a state of affliction
- 2. Must we visit the sick in person rather than at a distance?
  - A. The former ought to be done, but the latter not left undone
- 3.–4. The rich have little sympathy for the poor because they seldom visit them
- 5. You may administer a more excellent help by supplying spiritual wants

II. 1. How are we to visit the sick? In what manner?
  - A. First, be convinced that you are by no means sufficient for the work
  - B. You must turn to the Giver of every good gift for wisdom
- 2. As to particular methods, you need not tie yourself to any
- 3. You will easily discern what you can do for them
  - A. Most things can be done by those around them
  - B. But do not let delicacy or honour stand in your way
- 4. These little labours of love will pave your way to things of greater importance
  - A. Having shown regard for their bodies you may inquire about their souls
- 5. When you find any begin to fear God, it is proper to give them some tracts
  - A. At the next visit you may inquire about what they have read
- 6. It would be good to teach them industry and cleanliness

III. 1. By whom is this duty to be performed?
  - A. By all that desire to inherit the kingdom of their Father
- 2. All who desire to escape everlasting fire should perform this duty
- 3. But those who are rich in this world are peculiarly called to this work
- 4. But have *the poor* themselves any lot in this matter?
  - A. What can those who have hardly had the conveniences of life give?
- 5. You that are old may do a little more good before you depart
- 6. You that are young have several peculiar advantages
- 7. May women bear a part in this honorable service?
  - A. Undoubtedly they may and should; it is their duty
- 8. In the primitive church women were appointed for this kind of work
- 9. Let us from this day forward set about this work with general consent

Sermon 98: On Visiting the Sick, 1786

Matthew 25:36

I was sick, and ye visited me.

1. It is generally supposed that 'the means of grace' and 'the ordinances of God' are equivalent terms. We usually mean by that expression those that are usually termed 'works of piety', namely, hearing and reading the Scripture, receiving the Lord's Supper, public and private prayer, and fasting. And it is certain these are the ordinary channels which convey the grace of God to the souls of men. But are they the only means of grace? Are there no other means than these whereby God is pleased, frequently, yea, ordinarily to convey his grace to them that either love or fear him? Surely there are works of mercy, as well as works of piety, which are real means of grace. They are more especially such to those that perform them with a single eye. And those that neglect them do not receive the grace which otherwise they might. Yea, and they lose, by a continued neglect, the grace which they had received. Is it not hence that many who were once strong in faith are now weak and feeble-minded? And yet they are not sensible whence that weakness comes, as they neglect none of the ordinances of God. But they might see whence it comes were they seriously to consider St. Paul's account of all true believers. 'We are his workmanship, created anew in Christ Jesus unto good works, which God hath before prepared, that we might walk therein' (Eph. 2:10).

2. The walking herein is essentially necessary, as to the continuance of that faith whereby we 'are' already 'saved by grace', so to the attainment of everlasting salvation. Of this we cannot doubt, if we seriously consider that these are the very words of the great Judge himself: 'Come, ye blessed children of my Father, inherit the kingdom prepared for you from the foundation of the world. For I was hungry, and ye gave me meat, thirsty, and ye gave me drink. I was a stranger, and ye took me in; naked, and ye clothed me; I was sick, and ye visited me; I was in prison, and ye came unto me' (Matt. 25:34, etc.). 'Verily I say unto you, inasmuch as ye have done it unto one of the least of these my brethen, ye have done it unto me.' If this does not convince you that the continuance in works of mercy is necessary to salvation, consider what the Judge of all says to those on the left hand: 'Depart, ye cursed, into everlasting fire, prepared for the devil and his angels. For I was hungry, and ye gave me no meat: thirsty, and ye gave me no drink: I was a stranger, and ye took me not in: naked, and ye clothed me not: sick and in prison, and ye visited me not. Inasmuch as ye have not done it unto one of the least of these, neither have ye done it unto me.' You see, were it for this alone, they must 'depart' from God 'into everlasting punishment'.

3. Is it not strange that this important truth should be so little understood, or at least should so little influence the practice even of them that fear God? Suppose this representation be true, suppose the Judge of all the earth speaks right, those and those only that feed the hungry, give drink to the thirsty, clothe the naked, relieve the stranger, visit those that are sick and in prison, according to their power and opportunity, shall 'inherit the everlasting kingdom'. And those that do not shall 'depart into everlasting fire, prepared for the devil and his angels'.

4. I purpose at present to confine my discourse to one article of these, 'visiting the sick'; a plain duty, which all that are in health may practise in a higher or lower degree; and which nevertheless is almost universally neglected, even by those that profess to love God. And touching this I would inquire, first, what is implied in visiting the sick? Secondly, how is it to be performed? And thirdly, by whom?

I. First, I would inquire, What is the nature of this duty? What is implied in 'visiting the sick'?

1. By the sick I do not mean only those that keep their bed, or that are sick in the strictest sense. Rather I would include all such as are in a state of affliction, whether of mind or body; and that whether they are good or bad, whether they fear God or not.

[2.] 'But is there need of visiting them in person? May we not relieve them at a distance? Does it not answer the same purpose if we send them help as if we carry it ourselves?' Many are so circumstanced that they cannot attend the sick in person; and where this is the real case it is undoubtedly sufficient for them to send help, being the only expedient they can use. But this is not properly 'visiting the sick'; it is another thing. The word which we render 'visit' in its literal acceptation means to 'look upon'. And this, you well know, cannot be done unless you are present with them. To send them assistance is therefore entirely a different thing from visiting them. The former then ought to be done, but the latter not left undone.

'But I send a physician to those that are sick; and he can do them more good than I can.' He can in one respect: he can do them more good with regard to their bodily health. But he cannot do them more good with regard to their souls, which are of infinitely greater importance. And if he could, this would not excuse *you*: his going would not fulfil *your* duty. Neither would it do the same good to *you*, unless you saw them with your own eyes. If you do not, you lose a means of grace; you lose an excellent means of increasing your thankfulness to God, who saves you from this pain and sickness, and continues your health and strength; as well as of increasing your sympathy with the afflicted, your benevolence, and all social affections.

3. One great reason why the rich in general have so little sympathy for the poor is because they so seldom visit them. Hence it is that, according to the common observation, one part of the world does not know what the other suffers. Many of them do not know, because they do not care to know: they keep out of the way of knowing it—and then plead their voluntary ignorance as an excuse for their hardness of heart. 'Indeed, sir' (said a person of large substance), 'I am a very compassionate man. But to tell you the truth, I do not know anybody in the world that is in want.' How did this come to pass? Why, he took good care to keep out of their way. And if he fell upon any of them unawares, 'he passed over on the other side.'

4. How contrary to this is both the spirit and behaviour of even people of the highest rank in a neighbouring nation! In Paris ladies of the first quality—yea, princesses of the blood, of the royal family—constantly visit the sick, particularly the patients in the Grand Hospital. And they not only take care to relieve their wants (if they need anything more

than is provided for them) but attend on their sick-beds, dress their sores, and perform the meanest offices for them. Here is a pattern for the English, poor or rich, mean or honourable! For many years we have abundantly copied after the follies of the French. Let us for once copy after their wisdom and virtue, worthy the imitation of the whole Christian world. Let not the gentlewomen, or even the countesses in England, be ashamed to imitate those princesses of the blood! Here is a fashion that does honour to human nature. It began in France; but God forbid it should end there!

5. And if your delicacy will not permit you to imitate those truly honourable ladies, by abasing yourselves in the manner which they do, by performing the lowest offices for the sick, you may, however, without humbling yourselves so far, supply them with whatever they want. And you may administer help of a more excellent kind, by supplying their spiritual wants; instructing them (if they need such instruction) in the first principles of religion; endeavouring to show them the dangerous state they are in, under the wrath and curse of God through sin, and point them to the Lamb of God, who taketh away the sins of the world. Beside this general instruction, you might have abundant opportunities of comforting those that are in pain of body or distress of mind; you might find opportunities of strengthening the feeble-minded, quickening those that are faint and weary; and of building up those that have believed, and encouraging them to 'go on to perfection'. But these things you must do in your own person; you see, they cannot be done by proxy. Or suppose you could give the same relief to the sick by another, you could not reap the same advantage to yourself. You could not gain that increase in lowliness, in patience, in tenderness of spirit, in sympathy with the afflicted, which you might have gained if you had assisted them in person. Neither would you receive the same recompense in the resurrection of the just, when 'every man shall receive his own reward, according to his own labour.'

II.1. I proceed to inquire, in the second place, How are we to visit them? In what manner may this labour of love be most effectually performed? How may we do this most to the glory of God, and the benefit of our neighbour? But before ever you enter upon the work you should be deeply convinced that you are by no means sufficient for it; you have neither sufficient grace, nor sufficient understanding, to perform it in the most excellent manner. And this will convince you of the necessity of applying to the Strong for strength, and of flying to the Father of lights, the Giver of every good gift, for wisdom; ever remembering, 'there is a spirit in man that giveth wisdom, and the inspiration of the Holy One that giveth understanding.' Whenever therefore you are about to enter upon the work, seek his help by earnest prayer. Cry to him for the whole spirit of humility, lest if pride steal into your heart, if you ascribe anything to yourself, while you strive to save others you destroy your own soul. Before and through the work, from the beginning to the end, let your heart wait upon him for a continual supply of meekness and gentleness, of patience and long-suffering, that you may never be angry or discouraged, at whatever treatment, rough or smooth, kind or unkind, you may meet with. Be not moved with the deep ignorance of some, the dullness, the amazing stupidity of others; marvel not at their peevishness or stubbornness, at their non-improvement after all the pains that you have taken; yea, at some of them turning back to perdition, and being worse than they were before. Still your record is with the Lord, and your reward with the Most High.

2. As to the particular method of treating the sick, you need not tie yourself down to any; but may continually vary your manner of proceeding as various circumstances may require. But it may not be amiss usually to begin with inquiring into their outward condition. You may ask whether they have the necessaries of life. Whether they have sufficient food and raiment. If the weather be cold, whether they have fuel. Whether they have needful attendance. Whether they have proper advice with regard to their bodily disorder; especially if it be of a dangerous kind. In several of these respects you may be able to give them some assistance yourself: and you may move those that are more able than you to supply your lack of service. You might properly say in your own case, 'To beg I am ashamed;' but never be ashamed to beg for the poor; yea, in this case, be an importunate beggar—do not easily take a denial. Use all the address, all the understanding, all the influence you have; at the same time trusting in him that has the hearts of all men in his hands.

3. You will then easily discern whether there is any good office which you can do for them with your own hands. Indeed most of the things which are needful to be done, those about them can do better than you. But in some you may have more skill or more experience than them. And if you have, let not delicacy or honour stand in your way. Remember his word, 'Inasmuch as ye have done it unto the least of these, ye have done it unto me.' And think nothing too mean to do for him! Rejoice to be abased for his sake!

4. These little labours of love will pave your way to things of greater importance. Having shown that you have a regard for their bodies you may proceed to inquire concerning their souls. And here you have a large field before you; you have scope for exercising all the talents which God has given you. May you not begin with asking, Have you ever considered that God governs the world? That his providence is over all? And over *you* in particular? Does anything then befall you without his knowledge? Or without his designing it for your good? He knows all you suffer; he knows all your pains; he sees all your wants. He sees, not only your affliction in general, but every particular circumstance of it. Is he not looking down from heaven, and disposing all these things for your profit? You may then inquire whether he is acquainted with the general principles of religion. And afterwards lovingly and gently examine whether his life has been agreeable thereto. Whether he has been an outward, barefaced sinner, or has had a form of religion. See next whether he knows anything of the power [of godliness]; of worshipping God 'in spirit and in truth'. If he does not, endeavour to explain to him, 'Without holiness no man shall see the Lord;' and 'Except a man be born again, he cannot see the kingdom of God.' When he begins to understand the nature of holiness, and the necessity of the new birth, then you may press upon him 'repentance toward God, and faith in our Lord Jesus Christ'.

5. When you find any of them begin to fear God, it will be proper to give them one after another some plain tracts, as the *Instructions for Christians, Awake, thou that Sleepest,* and *The Nature and Design of Christianity.* At the next visit you may inquire what they have read; what they remember; and what they understand. And then will be the time to enforce what they understand, and if possible impress it on their hearts. Be

sure to conclude every meeting with prayer. If you cannot yet pray without a form you may use some of those composed by Mr. Spinckes, or any other pious writer. But the sooner you break through this backwardness the better. Ask of God, and he will soon open your mouth.

6. Together with the more important lessons which you endeavour to teach all the poor whom you visit, it would be a deed of charity to teach them two things more, which they are generally little acquainted with—industry and cleanliness. It was said by a pious man, 'Cleanliness is next to godliness.' Indeed the want of it is a scandal to all religion; causing the way of truth to be evil spoken of. And without industry we are neither fit for this world nor for the world to come. With regard to both, 'Whatsoever thy hand findeth to do, do it with thy might.'

III.1. The third point to be considered is, By whom is this duty to be performed? The answer is ready—by all that desire to 'inherit the kingdom' of their Father, which was prepared for them from the foundation of the world. For thus saith the Lord: 'Come, ye blessed . . . , inherit the kingdom. . . . For I was sick and ye visited me.' And to those on the left hand: 'Depart, ye cursed. . . . For I was sick, and ye visited me not.' Does not this plainly imply that as all who do this are 'blessed', and shall 'inherit the kingdom'; so all who do it not are 'cursed', and shall 'depart into everlasting fire'?

2. All therefore who desire to escape everlasting fire and to inherit the everlasting kingdom are equally concerned, according to their power, to practise this important duty. It is equally incumbent on young and old, rich and poor, men and women, according to their ability. None are so young, if they desire to save their own souls, as to be excused from assisting their neighbours. None are so poor (unless they want the necessaries of life) but they are called to do something, more or less, at whatever time they can spare, for the relief and comfort of their afflicted fellow-creatures.

3. But those who 'are rich in this world', who have more than the conveniences of life, are peculiarly called of God to this blessed work, and pointed out to it by his gracious providence. As you are not under a necessity of working for your bread, you have your time at your own disposal! You may therefore allot some part of it every day for this labour of love. If it be practicable it is far [the] best to have a fixed hour (for 'any time', we say, 'is no time'), and not to employ that time in any other business without urgent necessity. You have likewise a peculiar advantage over many, by your station in life. Being superior in rank to them, you have the more influence on that very account. Your inferiors of course look up to you with a kind of reverence. And the condescension which you show in visiting them gives them a prejudice in your favour which inclines them to hear you with attention, and willingly receive what you say. Improve this prejudice to the uttermost for the benefit of their souls, as well as their bodies. While you are as eyes to the blind and feet to the lame, a husband to the widow and a father to the fatherless, see that you still keep a higher end in view, even the saving of souls from death, and that you labour to make all you say and do subservient to that great end.

4. 'But have *the poor* themselves any part or lot in this matter? Are they any way concerned in visiting the sick?' What can they give to others who have hardly the conveniences, or perhaps necessaries, of life for themselves? If they have not, yet they need not be wholly excluded from the blessing which attends the practice of this duty. Even those may remember that excellent rule, 'Let our conveniences give way to our neighbour's necessities; and our necessities give way to our neighbour's extremities.' And few are so poor as not to be able sometimes to give 'two mites'; but if they are not, if they have no money to give, may they not give what is of more value? Yea, of more value than thousands of gold and silver? If you speak 'in the name of Jesus Christ of Nazareth', may not the words you speak be health to the soul, and marrow to the bones? Can you give them nothing? Nay, in administering to them the grace of God you give them more than all this world is worth! Go on! Go on! Thou poor disciple of a poor Master! Do as he did in the days of his flesh! Whenever thou hast an opportunity, go about doing good, and healing all that are oppressed of the devil; encouraging them to shake off his chains, and fly immediately to him

> Who sets the prisoners free, and breaks
> The iron bondage from their necks.

Above all, give them your prayers. Pray with them; pray for them! And who knows but you may save their souls alive?

5. You that are *old*, whose feet are ready to stumble upon the dark mountains, may not you do a little more good before you go hence and are no more seen! O remember,

> 'Tis time to live, if you grow old:
> Of little life the best to make,
> And manage wisely the last stake!

As you have lived many years, it may be hoped you have attained such knowledge as may be of use to others. You have certainly more knowledge of men, which is commonly learnt by dear-bought experience. With what strength you have left, employ the few moments you have to spare in ministering to those who are weaker than yourselves. Your grey hairs will not fail to give you authority, and add weight to what you speak. You may frequently urge, to increase their attention,

> Believe me, youth; for I am read in cares,
> And groan beneath the weight of more than threescore years.

You have frequently been a sufferer yourself; perhaps you are so still. So much the more give them all the assistance you can, both with regard to their souls and bodies, before they and you go to the place whence you will not return.

6. On the other hand, you that are *young* have several advantages that are almost peculiar to yourselves. You have generally a flow of spirits, and a liveliness of temper which,

by the grace of God, make you willing to undertake, and capable of performing, many good works at which others would be discouraged. And you have your health and strength of body, whereby you are eminently qualified to assist the sick and those that have no strength. You are able to take up and carry the crosses which may be expected to lie in the way. Employ then your whole vigour of body and mind in ministering to your afflicted brethren. And bless God that you have them to employ in so honourable a service; like those heavenly 'servants of his that do his pleasure' by continually ministering to the heirs of salvation.

7. 'But may not *women* as well as men bear a part in this honourable service?' Undoubtedly they may; nay, they ought—it is meet, right, and their bounden duty. Herein there is no difference: 'there is neither male nor female in Christ Jesus.' Indeed it has long passed for a maxim with many that 'women are only to be seen, not heard.' And accordingly many of them are brought up in such a manner as if they were only designed for agreeable playthings! But is this doing honour to the sex? Or is it a real kindness to them? No; it is the deepest unkindness; it is horrid cruelty; it is mere Turkish barbarity. And I know not how any woman of sense and spirit can submit to it. Let all you that have it in your power assert the right which the God of nature has given you. Yield not to that vile bondage any longer. You, as well as men, are rational creatures. You, like them, were made in the image of God: you are equally candidates for immortality. You too are called of God, as you have time, to 'do good unto all men'. Be 'not disobedient to the heavenly calling'. Whenever you have opportunity, do all the good you can, particularly to your poor sick neighbour. And every one of *you* likewise 'shall receive your own reward according to your own labour'.

8. It is well known that in the primitive church there were women particularly appointed for this work. Indeed there was one or more such in every Christian congregation under heaven. They were then termed 'deaconesses', that is, 'servants'—servants of the church and of its great Master. Such was Phebe (mentioned by St. Paul), 'a deaconess of the Church at Cenchrea' (Rom. 16:1). It is true most of these were women in years, and well experienced in the work of God. But were the young wholly excluded from that service? No; neither need they be, provided they know in whom they have believed, and show that they are holy of heart by being holy in all manner of conversation. Such a deaconess, if she answered her picture, was Mr. Law's Miranda. Would anyone object to her visiting and relieving the sick and poor because she was a woman? Nay, and a young one too? Do any of you that are young desire to tread in her steps? Have you a pleasing form? An agreeable address? So much the better, if you are wholly devoted to God. He will use these, if your eye be single, to make your words strike the deeper. And while you minister to others, how many blessings may redound into your own bosom! Hereby your natural levity may be destroyed, your fondness for trifles cured, your wrong tempers corrected, your evil habits weakened, until they are rooted out. And you will be prepared to adorn the doctrine of God our Saviour in every future scene of life. Only be very wary if you visit or converse with those of the other sex, lest your affections be entangled on one side or the other, and so you find a curse instead of a blessing.

9. Seeing then this is a duty to which we are called, rich and poor, young and old, male and female (and it would be well if parents would train up their children herein, as well as in saying their prayers and going to church), let the time past suffice that almost all of us have neglected it, as by general consent. O what need has every one of us to say, 'Lord, forgive me my sins of omission!' Well, in the name of God let us now from this day set about it with general consent. And, I pray, let it never go out of your mind that this is a duty which you cannot perform by proxy; unless in one only case—unless you are disabled by your own pain or weakness. In that only case it suffices to send the relief which you would otherwise give. Begin, my dear brethren, begin now: else the impression which you now feel will wear off; and possibly it may never return! What then will be the consequence? Instead of hearing that word, 'Come, ye blessed. . . . For I was sick and ye visited me,' you must hear that awful sentence, 'Depart, ye cursed! . . . For I was sick, and ye visited me not!'

Aberdeen, May 23, 1786

34. THE REFORMATION OF MANNERS

January 30, 1763

An Introductory Comment

Influenced by the preaching of Dr. Anthony Horneck, Dr. Richard Smithies, and Dr. William Beveridge, a few young men formed a religious society in England in 1677 in order to live out the Christian faith more earnestly (S, 2:481). The membership of this association increased significantly after the Act of Toleration was passed in 1689. By 1691, through the good graces of Archbishop Tillotson, the society received a letter from Queen Mary that allowed it to require magistrates to enforce the laws against public vice that included such things as swearing, drunkenness, prostitution, and Sabbath-breaking (S, 2:481).

One custom of this society was to have a yearly sermon preached before its membership, and Samuel Wesley Sr. took his turn on February 13, 1698, at St. James's, Westminster, and later in the day at St. Bride's, London (O, 2:300). By 1730 this reforming movement was no longer functioning, though it was revived in 1757 through the efforts of Mr. W. Welsh (S, 2:482). John Wesley was invited to preach the annual sermon in 1763, which he did at his own chapel in West Street, Seven Dials, and he employed the same text that his father had selected sixty-five years earlier (S, 2:482). Wesley published this sermon as a separate pamphlet and included it in the fourth volume of sermons produced in 1771 (S, 2:482).

The text of this sermon, Psalm 94:16, "Who will rise up with me against the wicked?" emerged earlier, once while Wesley was in Savannah in 1736 (FB, 25:472), and much later in 1760 as part of the body of the sermon "The Cure of Evil-speaking" (O, 2:261). Wesley insisted that such reforming activity must ever be undertaken with great care, especially with respect to the character of those involved who should evidence courage, steadiness, patience, love, and a right spirit (O, 2:313–16).

The Reformation of Manners

I. I will show the *nature* of the societies and the *steps* leading to them
- 1–2. On a Lord's Day in 1757 a small company met for prayer
- 3. They agreed to signify their design to persons of eminent rank
- 4. They printed and dispersed several thousand books of instruction
- 5. They attempted to prevent *tippling* on the Lord's Day
- 6. They restrained bakers from working on the Lord's Day
- 7.–8. They began to repress profane swearing and prostitutes
- 9.–10. God then prepared Magdalen Hospital for those in need of care
- 11. In admitting members no regard is given to any sect or party

II.
- 1.–2. These are the *steps* which have been taken
- 3. This design conduces to the establishing peace upon earth
- 4. It is not to individuals only that benefit rebounds
- 5.–11. This concerns all who fear God, love mankind, and wish well to their king

III.
- 1.–2. Who ought to engage in such a design?
- 3. Everyone engaging herein should be a person of faith
- 4. They will therefore also be persons of courage
- 5. To courage, patience is nearly allied
- 6. You also need *steadiness* to hold fast this profession of faith
- 7.–8. All should have the love of God shed abroad in their hearts
- 9.–10. Love is necessary; it produces not only courage and patience, but *humility*

IV.
- 1. Nothing is to be spoke or done with a view to any temporal advantage
- 2. Above all, take the shield of faith and let all things be done in love
- 3. Let everyone beware not to do evil that good may come
- 4. But let innocence be joined with *prudence*
- 5. Your manner of speaking should be deeply *serious*, *calm*, and *mild*

V.
- 1. Consider the nature of your undertaking
- 2. Do not be in haste to increase your number
- 3. Observe what motivates you
- 4. See that you do everything in a right *temper*
- 5.–6. Do everything with innocence and simplicity
- 7. Take up your cross and follow him

Sermon 52: The Reformation of Manners, 1763

Psalm 94:16

Who will rise up with me against the wicked?

1. In all ages men who neither feared God nor regarded man have combined together and formed confederacies to carry on the works of darkness. And herein they have shown themselves wise in their generation; for by this means they more effectually promoted the kingdom of their father the devil than otherwise they could have done. On the other hand, men who did fear God and desire the happiness of their fellow-creatures have in every age found it needful to join together in order to oppose the works of darkness, to spread the knowledge of God their Saviour, and to promote his kingdom upon earth. Indeed he himself has instructed them so to do. From the time that men were upon the earth he hath taught them to join together in his service, and has united them in one body by one spirit. And for this very end he has joined them together, 'that he might destroy the works of the devil', first in them that are already united, and by them in all that are round about them.

2. This is the original design of the church of Christ. It is a body of men compacted together in order, first, to save each his own soul, then to assist each other in working out their salvation, and afterwards, as far as in them lies, to save all men from present and future misery, to overturn the kingdom of Satan, and set up the kingdom of Christ. And this ought to be the continued care and endeavour of every member of his church. Otherwise he is not worthy to be called a member thereof, as he is not a living member of Christ.

3. Accordingly this ought to be the constant care and endeavour of all those who are united together in these kingdoms, and are commonly called 'the Church of England'. They are united together for this very end, to oppose the devil and all his works, and to wage war against the world and the flesh, his constant and faithful allies. But do they in fact answer the end of their union? Are all who style themselves 'members of the Church of England' heartily engaged in opposing the works of the devil and fighting against the world and the flesh? Alas, we cannot say this. So far from it that a great part—I fear, the greater part of them—are themselves 'the world', the people that know not God to any saving purpose; are indulging day by day instead of 'mortifying the flesh, with its affections and desires'; and doing themselves those works of the devil which they are peculiarly engaged to destroy.

4. There is therefore still need, even in this 'Christian country' (as we *courteously* style Great Britain) yea, in this 'Christian church' (if we may give that title to the bulk of our nation) of some to 'rise up against the wicked', and join together 'against the evil-doers'. Nay, there was never more need than there is at this day for 'them that fear the Lord' to 'speak often together' on this very head—how they may 'lift up a standard against' the iniquity which overflows the land. There is abundant cause for all the servants of God to join together against the works of the devil with united hearts and counsels and endeavours, to make a stand for God, and to repress, as much as in them lies, these 'floods of ungodliness'.

5. For this end a few persons in London, towards the close of the last century, united together, and after a while were termed 'The Society for Reformation of Manners'. And incredible good was done by them for near forty years. But then, most of the original members being gone to their reward, those who succeeded them grew faint in their mind, and departed from the work; so that a few years ago the Society ceased, nor did any of the kind remain in the kingdom.

6. It is a society of the same nature which has been lately formed. I purpose to show, first, the *nature* of their design, and the *steps* they have hitherto taken; (2), the *excellency* of it, with the various *objections* which have been raised against it; (3), *what manner of men* they ought to be who engage in such a design; and (4), with what *spirit* and in what *manner* they should proceed in the prosecution of it. I shall conclude with an *application* both to them and to all that fear God.

I.1. I am, first, to show the *nature* of their design, and the *steps* they have hitherto taken.

It was on a Lord's Day in August 1757 that in a small company who were met for prayer and religious conversation mention was made of the gross and open profanation of that sacred day, by persons buying and selling, keeping open shop, tippling in alehouses, and standing or sitting in the streets, roads, or fields, vending their wares as on common days; especially in Moorfields, which was then full of them every Sunday, from one end to the other. It was considered what method could be taken to redress these grievances. And it was agreed that six of them should in the morning wait upon Sir John Fielding for instruction. They did so. He approved of the design, and directed them how to carry it into execution.

2. They first delivered petitions to the right honourable the Lord Mayor and the Court of Aldermen, to the Justices sitting at Hicks's Hall, and those in Westminster Hall. And they received from all these honourable benches much encouragement to proceed.

3. It was next judged proper to signify their design to many persons of eminent rank, and to the body of the clergy, as well as the ministers of other denominations, belonging to the several churches and meetings in and about the cities of London and Westminster. And they had the satisfaction to meet with a hearty consent and universal approbation from them.

4. They then printed and dispersed, at their own expense, several thousand books of instruction to constables and other parish officers, explaining and enforcing their several duties. And to prevent as far as possible the necessity of proceeding to an actual execution of the laws, they likewise printed and dispersed in all parts of the town dissuasives from sabbath-breaking, extracts from Acts of Parliament against it, and notices to the offenders.

5. The way being paved by these precautions, it was in the beginning of the year 1758 that, after notices delivered again and again, which were as often set at naught, actual informations were made to magistrates against persons profaning the Lord's day. By this means they first cleared the streets and fields of those notorious offenders who,

without any regard either to God or the king, were selling their wares from morning to night. They proceeded to a more difficult attempt, the preventing *tippling* on the Lord's day, spending the time in alehouses which ought to be spent in the more immediate worship of God. Herein they were exposed to abundance of reproach, to insult and abuse of every kind; having not only the tipplers and those who entertained them, the alehouse keepers, to contend with, but rich and honourable men, partly the landlords of those alehouse keepers, partly those who furnished them with drink, and in general all who gained by their sins. Some of these were not only men of substance but men in authority; nay, in more instances than one they were the very persons before whom the delinquents were brought. And the treatment they gave those who laid the informations naturally encouraged 'the beasts of the people' to follow their example, and to use them as fellows not fit to live upon the earth. Hence they made no scruple, not only to treat them with the basest language, not only to throw at them mud or stones or whatever came to hand, but many times to beat them without mercy, and to drag them over the stones, or through the kennels. And that they did not murder them was not for want of will; but the bridle was in their teeth.

6. Having therefore received help from God, they went on to restrain *bakers* likewise from spending so great a part of the Lord's day in exercising the work of their calling. But many of these were more noble than the victuallers. They were so far from resenting this, or looking upon it as an affront, that several who had been hurried down the stream of custom to act contrary to their own conscience, sincerely thanked them for their labour, and acknowledged it as a real kindness.

7. In clearing the streets, fields, and alehouses of sabbath-breakers, they fell upon another sort of offenders as mischievous to society as any, namely, *gamesters* of various kinds. Some of these were of the lowest and vilest class, commonly called 'gamblers', who make a trade of seizing on young and unexperienced men, and tricking them out of all their money. And after they have beggared them, they frequently teach them the same mystery of iniquity. Several nests of these they have rooted out, and constrained not a few of them honestly to earn their bread by the sweat of their brow and the labour of their hands.

8. Increasing in number and strength, they extended their views, and began not only to repress *profane swearing*, but to remove out of our streets another public nuisance and scandal of the Christian name—*common prostitutes*. Many of these were stopped in their mid-career of audacious wickedness. And in order to go to the root of the disease, many of the *houses* that entertained them have been detected, prosecuted according to law, and totally suppressed. And some of the poor, desolate women themselves, though fallen to

> The lowest line of human infamy,

have acknowledged the gracious providence of God, and broke off their sins by lasting repentance. Several of these have been placed out, and several received into the Magdalen Hospital.

9. If a little digression may be allowed, who can sufficiently admire the wisdom of divine providence in the disposal of the times and seasons so as to suit one occurrence to another? For instance. Just at a time when many of these poor creatures, being stopped in their course of sin, found a desire of leading a better life, as it were in answer to that sad question, 'But if I quit the way I now am in, what can I do to live? For I am not mistress of any trade; and I have no friends that will receive me:' I say, just at this time, God has prepared the Magdalen Hospital. Here those who have no trade, nor any friends to receive them, are received with all tenderness. Here they may live, and that with comfort, being provided with all things that are needful 'for life and godliness'.

10. But to return. The number of persons brought to justice

From August 1757 to August 1762, is	9,596
From thence to the present time,	
For unlawful gaming, and profane swearing,	40
For sabbath-breaking,	400
Lewd women, and keepers of ill houses,	550
For offering to sale obscene prints,	2
In all,	10,588

11. In the admission of members into the society no regard is had to any particular sect or party. Whoever is found upon inquiry to be a good man is readily admitted. And none who has selfish or pecuniary views will long continue therein; not only because he can gain nothing thereby, but because he would quickly be a loser, inasmuch as he must commence subscriber as soon as he is a member. Indeed the vulgar cry is 'These are all *Whitfelites.*' But it is a great mistake. About twenty of the constantly subscribing members are all that are in connexion with Mr. Whitefield. About fifty are in connexion with Mr. Wesley. About twenty, who are of the established Church, have no connexion with either; and about seventy are Dissenters, who make in all an hundred and sixty. There are indeed many more who assist in the work by occasional subscriptions.

II.1. These are the *steps* which have been hitherto taken in prosecution of this design. I am, in the second place, to show the *excellency* thereof, notwithstanding the *objections* which have been raised against it. Now this may appear from several considerations. And, first, from hence—that the making an open stand against all the ungodliness and unrighteousness which overspread our land as a flood is one of the noblest ways of confessing Christ in the face of his enemies. It is giving glory to God, and showing mankind that even in these dregs of time,

> There are, who faith prefer,
> Though few, and piety to God.

And what more excellent than to render to God the honour due unto his name? To declare by a stronger proof than words, even by suffering, and running all hazards, 'Verily there is a reward for the righteous; doubtless there is a God that judgeth the earth.'

2. How excellent is the design to prevent in any degree the dishonour done to his glorious name, the contempt which is poured on his authority, and the scandal brought upon our holy religion by the gross, flagrant wickedness of those who are still called by the name of Christ! To stem in any degree the torrent of vice, to repress the floods of ungodliness, to remove in any measure those occasions of blaspheming the worthy name whereby we are called, is one of the noblest designs it can possibly enter into the heart of man to conceive.

3. And as this design thus evidently tends to bring 'glory to God in the highest', so it no less manifestly conduces to the establishing 'peace upon earth'. For as all sin directly tends both to destroy our peace with God by setting him at open defiance, to banish peace from our own breasts, and to set every man's sword against his neighbour; so whatever prevents or removes sin does in the same degree promote peace, both peace in our own soul, peace with God, and peace with one another. Such are the genuine fruits of this design, even in the present world. But why should we confine our views to the narrow bounds of time and space? Rather pass over these into eternity. And what fruit of it shall we find there? Let the Apostle speak: 'Brethren, if one of you err from the truth, and one convert him' (not to this or that opinion, but to God!) 'let him know that he who converteth a sinner from the error of his way shall save a soul from death, and hide a multitude of sins' (Jas. 5:19-20).

4. Nor is it to individuals only, whether those who betray others into sin or those that are liable to be betrayed and destroyed by them, that the benefit of this design redounds, but to the whole community whereof we are members. For is it not a sure observation, 'rightousness exalteth a nation'? And is it not as sure on the other hand that 'sin is a reproach to *any* people'? Yea, and bringeth down the curse of God upon them? So far therefore as righteousness in any branch is promoted, so far is the national interest advanced. So far as sin, especially open sin, is restrained, the curse and reproach are removed from us. Whoever therefore they are that labour herein, they are general benefactors. They are the truest friends of their king and country. And in the same proportion as their design takes place, there can be no doubt but God will give national prosperity, in accomplishment of his faithful word, 'Them that honour me, I will honour.'

5. But it is objected, 'However excellent a design this is, it does not concern *you.* For are there not persons to whom the repressing these offences and punishing the offenders properly belong? Are there not constables and other parish officers, who are bound by oath to this very thing?' There are. Constables and church wardens in particular are engaged by solemn oaths to give due information against profaners of the Lord's day, and all other scandalous sinners. But if they leave it undone, if notwithstanding their oaths they trouble not themselves about the matter, it concerns all that fear God, that love mankind, and that wish well to their king and country, to pursue this design with the very same vigour as if there were no such officers existing. It being just the same thing, if they are of no use, as if they had no being.

6. 'But this is only a pretence; their real design is to get money by giving informations.' So it has frequently and roundly been affirmed, but without the least shadow of truth. The contrary may be proved by a thousand instances: no member of the Society takes any part of the money which is by the law allotted to the informer. They never did from the beginning, nor does any of them ever receive anything to suppress or withdraw their information. This is another mistake, if not wilful slander, for which there is not the least foundation.

7. 'But the design is impracticable. Vice is risen to such an head that it is impossible to suppress it; especially by such means. For what can an handful of poor people do in opposition to all the world?' 'With men this is impossible, but not with God.' And they trust, not in themselves, but him. Be then the patrons of vice ever so strong, to him they are no more than grasshoppers. And all means are alike to him. It is the same thing with God 'to deliver by many or by few'. The small number therefore of those who are on the Lord's side is nothing, neither the great number of those that are against him. Still he doth whatever pleaseth him. And 'there is no counsel or strength against the Lord.'

8. 'But if the end you aim at be really to reform sinners, you choose the wrong means. It is the Word of God must effect this, and not human laws. And it is the work of ministers, not of magistrates. Therefore the applying to these can only produce an outward reformation. It makes no change in the heart.'

It is true the Word of God is the chief ordinary means whereby he changes both the hearts and lives of sinners; and he does this chiefly by the ministers of the gospel. But it is likewise true that the magistrate is 'the minister of God'; and that he is designed of God 'to be a terror to evil-doers', by executing human laws upon them. If this does not change the heart, yet to prevent outward sin is one valuable point gained. There is so much the less dishonour done to God, less scandal brought on our holy religion, less curse and reproach upon our nation, less temptation laid in the way of others. Yea, and less wrath heaped up by the sinners themselves against the day of wrath.

9. 'Nay, rather more; for it makes many of them hypocrites, pretending to be what they are not. Others, by exposing them to shame, and putting them to expense, are made impudent and desperate in wickedness; so that in reality none of them are any better, if they are not worse than they were before.'

This is a mistake all over. For (1), where are these hypocrites? We know none who have pretended to be what they were not. (2). The exposing obstinate offenders to shame, and putting them to expense, does not make them desperate in offending, but afraid to offend. (3). Some of them, far from being worse, are substantially better, the whole tenor of their lives being changed. Yea, (4), some are inwardly changed, even 'from darkness to light, and from the power of Satan unto God'.

10. 'But many are not convinced that buying or selling on the Lord's day is a sin.'

If they are not convinced, they ought to be: it is high time they should. The case is as plain as plain can be. For if an open, wilful breach both of the law of God and the law of the land is not sin, pray what is? And if such a breach both of divine and human laws is not to be punished because a man is not convinced it is a sin, there is an end of all execution of justice, and all men may live as they list.

11. 'But *mild* methods ought to be tried first.' They ought. And so they are. A mild admonition is given to every offender before the law is put in execution against him; nor is any man prosecuted till he has express notice that this will be the case unless he will prevent that prosecution by removing the cause of it. In every case the mildest method is used which the nature of the case will bear; nor are severer means ever applied but when they are absolutely necessary to the end.

12. 'Well, but after all this stir about reformation, what real good has been done?' Unspeakable good; and abundantly more than anyone could have expected in so short a time, considering the small number of the instruments, and the difficulties they had to encounter. Much evil has been already prevented, and much has been removed. Many sinners have been outwardly reformed; some have been inwardly changed. The honour of him whose name we bear, so openly affronted, has been openly defended. And it is not easy to determine how many and how great blessings even this little stand, made for God and his cause against his daring enemies, may already have derived upon our whole nation. On the whole, then, after all the objections that can be made, reasonable men may still conclude, a more excellent design could scarce ever enter into the heart of man.

III.1. But *what manner of men* ought they to be who engage in such a design? Some may imagine any that are willing to assist therein ought readily to be admitted; and that the greater the number of members, the greater will be their influence. But this is by no means true; matter of fact undeniably proves the contrary. While the former Society for Reformation of Manners consisted of chosen members only, though neither many, rich, nor powerful, they broke through all opposition, and were eminently successful in every branch of their undertaking. But when a number of men, less carefully chosen, were received into that Society, they grew less and less useful till, by insensible degrees, they dwindled into nothing.

2. The *number* therefore of the members is no more to be attended to than the riches or eminence. This is a work of God. It is undertaken in the name of God, and for his sake. It follows that men who neither love nor fear God have no part or lot in this matter. 'Why takest thou my covenant in thy mouth,' may God say to any of these, 'whereas thou' thyself 'hatest to be reformed, and have cast my words behind thee?' Whoever therefore lives in any known sin is not fit to engage in reforming sinners. More especially if he is guilty in any instance, or in the least degree, of profaning the name of God, of buying, selling, or doing any unnecessary work on the Lord's day, or offending in any other of those instances which this society is peculiarly designed to reform. No; let none who stands himself in need of this reformation presume to meddle with such an undertaking. First let him 'pull the beam out of his own eye'. Let him be himself *unblameable* in all things.

3. Not that this will suffice. Everyone engaging herein should be more than a harmless man. He should be a man of *faith*; having at least such a degree of that 'evidence of things not seen' as to 'aim not at the things that are seen, which are temporal, but at those that are not seen, which are eternal'; such a faith as produces a steady *fear of God*, with a lasting resolution by his grace to abstain from all that he has forbidden, and to do all that

he has commanded. He will more especially need that particular branch of faith, 'confidence in God'. It is this faith which 'removes mountains', which 'quenches the violence of fire', which breaks through all opposition, and enables 'one' to stand against and 'chase a thousand', knowing in whom his strength lies, and even when he has 'the sentence of death in himself, trusting in him who raiseth the dead'.

4. He that has faith and confidence in God will of consequence be a man of *courage.* And such it is highly needful every man should be who engages in this undertaking. For many things will occur in the prosecution thereof which are terrible to nature; indeed so terrible that all who 'confer with flesh and blood' will be afraid to encounter them. Here therefore true courage has its proper place, and is necessary in the highest degree. And this, faith only can supply. A believer can say,

> I fear no denial;
>   No danger I fear:
> Nor start from the trial;
>   For Jesus is near.

5. To courage, *patience* is nearly allied; the one regarding future, the other present evils. And whoever joins in carrying on a design of this nature will have great occasion for this. For notwithstanding all his unblameableness, he will find himself just in Ishmael's situation, 'his hand against every man, and every man's hand against him'. And no wonder. If it be true that 'all who will live godly shall suffer persecution,' how eminently must this be fulfilled in them who, not content to live godly themselves, compel the ungodly to do so too, or at least to refrain from notorious ungodliness! Is not this declaring war against all the world? Setting all the children of the devil at defiance? And will not Satan himself, 'the prince of this world', 'the ruler of the darkness' thereof, exert all his subtlety and all his force in support of his tottering kingdom? Who can expect the 'roaring lion' will tamely submit to have the prey plucked out of his teeth? 'Ye have,' therefore, 'need of patience, that when ye have done the will of God ye may receive the promise.'

6. And ye have need of *steadiness,* that ye may 'hold fast this profession of your faith without wavering'. This also should be found in all that unite in this society; which is not a task for a 'double-minded man', for one that 'is unstable in his ways'. He that is as a reed shaken with the wind is not fit for this warfare, which demands a firm purpose of soul, a constant, determined resolution. One that is wanting in this may 'set his hand to the plough'; but how soon will he 'look back'? He may indeed 'endure for a time; but when persecution or tribulation', public or private troubles, 'arise because of the work, immediately he is offended'.

7. Indeed it is hard for any to persevere in so unpleasing a work unless *love* overpowers both pain and fear. And therefore it is highly expedient that all engaged therein have 'the love of God shed abroad in their hearts'; that they should all be able to declare, 'we love him, because he first loved us.' The presence of him whom their soul loveth will then make their labour light. They can then say, not from the wildness of an heated imagination, but with the utmost truth and soberness,

With thee conversing, I forget
All time, and toil, and care;
Labour is rest, and pain is sweet,
While thou, my God, art here.

8. What adds a still greater sweetness even to labour and pain is the Christian *love of our neighbour.* When they 'love their neighbour', that is, every soul of man, 'as themselves', as their own souls; when 'the love of Christ constrains' them to love one another, 'even as he loved us'; when as he 'tasted death for every man', so they are 'ready to lay down their life for their brethren' (including in that number *every man,* every soul for which Christ died), what prospect of danger will then be able to fright them from their labour of love! What suffering will they not be ready to undergo to save one soul from everlasting burnings! What continuance of labour, disappointment, pain, will vanquish their fixed resolution! Will they not be

'Gainst all repulses steeled, nor ever tired
With toilsome day, or ill-succeeding night?

So love both 'hopeth and endureth all things'. So 'charity never faileth.'

9. Love is necessary for all the members of such a society on another account likewise; even because it 'is not puffed up'; it produces not only courage and patience, but *humility.* And Oh! how needful is this for all who are so employed! What can be of more importance than that they should be little, and mean, and base, and vile in their own eyes? For otherwise, should they think themselves anything, should they impute anything to themselves, should they admit anything of a pharisaic spirit, 'trusting in themselves that they were righteous, and despising others', nothing could more directly tend to overthrow the whole design. For then they would not only have all the world, but also God himself to contend with; seeing he 'resisteth the proud, and giveth grace' only 'to the humble'. Deeply conscious therefore should every member of this society be of his own foolishness, weakness, helplessness; continually hanging with his whole soul upon him who alone hath wisdom and strength, with an unspeakable conviction that 'the help which is done upon earth, God doth it himself;' and that it is he *alone* 'who worketh in us, both to will and to do of his good pleasure'.

10. One point more whoever engages in this design should have deeply impressed on his heart, namely, that 'the wrath of man worketh not the righteousness of God.' Let him therefore 'learn of' him 'who was meek' as well as lowly. And let him abide in meekness as well as humility: 'with all lowliness and meekness', let him 'walk worthy of the vocation wherewith he is called'. Let them be 'gentle toward all men', good or bad, for his own sake, for their sake, for Christ's sake. Are any 'ignorant and out of the way'? Let him 'have compassion' upon them. Do they even *oppose* the word and the work of God; yea, set themselves in battle array against it? So much the more hath he need 'in meekness to instruct those who' thus 'oppose themselves', if haply they may 'awake out of the snare of the devil', and no more be 'taken captive at his will'.

IV.1. From the qualifications of those who are proper to engage in such an undertaking as this I proceed to show, fourthly, with what *spirit* and in what *manner* it ought to be pursued. First, with what spirit. Now this first regards the *motive* which is to be preserved in every step that is taken. For 'if' at any time 'the light which is in thee be darkness, how great is that darkness!' But 'if thine eye be single, thy whole body shall be full of light.' This is therefore continually to be remembered, and carried into every word and action. Nothing is to be spoke or done, either great or small, with a view to any temporal advantage; nothing with a view to the favour or esteem, the love or the praise of men. But the intention, the eye of the mind, is always to be fixed on the glory of God and good of man.

2. But the spirit with which everything is to be done regards the *temper*, as well as the motive. And this is no other than that which has been described above. For the same courage, patience, steadiness, which qualify a man for the work, are to be exercised therein. 'Above all' let him 'take the shield of faith'; this will quench a thousand fiery darts. Let him exert all the faith which God has given him, in every trying hour. And 'let all his doings be done in love;' never let this be wrested from him. Neither must many waters quench this love, nor the floods of ingratitude drown it. 'Let' likewise that lowly 'mind be in him which was also in Christ Jesus'. Yea, and let him 'be clothed with humility', filling his heart, and adorning his whole behaviour. At the same time let him 'put on bowels of mercies, gentleness, long-suffering'; avoiding the least appearance of malice, bitterness, anger, or resentment; knowing it is our calling, not to be 'overcome of evil, but to overcome evil with good'. In order to preserve this humble, gentle love, it is needful to do all things with *recollection* of spirit, *watching* against all *hurry* or dissipation of thought, as well as against pride, wrath, or surliness. But this can be no otherwise preserved than by 'continuing instant in prayer', both before and after he comes into the field, and during the whole action; and by doing all in the *spirit of sacrifice*, offering all to God, through the Son of his love.

3. As to the outward *manner* of acting, a general rule is, let it be expressive of these inward tempers. But to be more particular. (1). Let every man beware not to 'do evil that good may come'. Therefore, 'putting away all lying', let 'every man speak the truth to his neighbour'. Use no *fraud* or *guile*, either in order to detect or to punish any man, but 'by simplicity and godly sincerity' 'commend yourself to men's consciences in the sight of God.' It is probable that by your adhering to these rules fewer offenders will be convicted. But so much the more will the blessing of God accompany the whole undertaking.

4. But let innocence be joined with *prudence*, properly so called. Not that offspring of hell which 'the world' calls prudence, which is mere craft, cunning dissimulation; but with that 'wisdom from above' which our Lord peculiarly recommends to all who would promote his kingdom upon earth. 'Be ye therefore wise as serpents', while ye are 'harmless as doves'. This wisdom will instruct you how to suit your words and whole behaviour to the persons with whom you have to do, to the time, place, and all other circumstances. It will teach you to cut off occasion of offence, even from those who seek occasion, and to do things of the most offensive nature in the least offensive manner that is possible.

5. Your *manner of speaking*, particularly to offenders, should be at all times deeply *serious* (lest it appear like insulting or triumphing over them), rather inclining to *sad*;

showing that you pity them for what they do, and sympathize with them in what they suffer. Let your *air* and *tone* of voice, as well as words, be *dispassionate, calm, mild*; yea, where it would not appear like dissimulation, even *kind* and *friendly*. In some cases, where it will probably be received as it is meant, you may *profess* the *goodwill* you bear them; but at the same time (that it may not be thought to proceed from fear, or any wrong inclination) professing your *intrepidity* and inflexible *resolution* to oppose and punish vice to the uttermost.

V.1. It remains only to make some application of what has been said, partly to you who are already engaged in this work, partly to all that fear God, and more especially to them that love as well as fear him.

With regard to you who are already engaged in this work, the first advice I would give you is calmly and deeply to consider the nature of your undertaking. Know what you are about; be throughly acquainted with what you have in hand. Consider the objections which are made to the whole of your undertaking. And before you proceed, be satisfied that those objections have no real weight. Then may every man act as he is fully persuaded in his own mind.

2. I advise you, secondly, be not in haste to increase your number. And in adding thereto regard not wealth, rank, or any outward circumstance. Only regard the qualifications above described. Inquire diligently whether the person proposed be of an *unblameable carriage*, and whether he be a man of *faith, courage, patience, steadiness*, whether he be a *lover* of God and man. If so, he will add to your strength as well as number. If not, you will lose by him more than you gain. For you will displease God. And be not afraid to purge out from among you any who do not answer the preceding character. By thus lessening your number you will increase your strength; you will be 'vessels meet for your master's use'.

3. I would, thirdly, advise you narrowly to observe from what *motive* you at any time act or speak. Beware that your intention be not stained with any regard either to profit or praise. Whatever you do, 'do it to the Lord,' as the servants of Christ. Do not aim at pleasing yourself in any point, but pleasing him whose you are, and whom you serve. Let your eye be single from first to last; eye God alone in every word and work.

4. I advise you, in the fourth place, see that you do everything in a right *temper*, with lowliness and meekness, with patience and gentleness, worthy the gospel of Christ. Take every step trusting in God, and in the most tender, loving spirit you are able. Meantime *watch always* against all hurry and dissipation of spirit, and *pray always* with all earnestness and perseverance that your faith fail not. And let nothing interrupt that *spirit of sacrifice* which you make of all you have and are, of all you suffer and do, that it may be an offering of a sweet smelling savour to God through Jesus Christ.

5. As to the *manner* of acting and speaking, I advise you to do it with all innocence and simplicity, prudence, and seriousness. Add to these all possible calmness and mildness; nay, all the tenderness which the case will bear. You are not to behave as butchers or hangmen, but as surgeons rather, who put the patient to no more pain than is necessary

in order to the cure. For this purpose each of *you* likewise has need of 'a lady's hand with a lion's heart'. So shall many even of them you are constrained to punish 'glorify God in the day of visitation'.

6. I exhort all of you who fear God, as ever you hope to find mercy at his hands, as you dread being found (though you knew it not) 'even to fight against God', do not on any account, reason, or pretence whatsoever, either directly or indirectly, oppose or hinder so merciful a design, and one so conducive to his glory. But this is not all. If you are lovers of mankind, if you long to lessen the sins and miseries of your fellow-creatures, can you satisfy yourselves, can you be clear before God, by barely not opposing it? Are not *you* also bound by the most sacred ties, 'as you have opportunity to do good to all men'? And is not here an opportunity of doing good to many, even good of the highest kind? In the name of God, then, embrace the opportunity. Assist in doing this good, if no otherwise, yet by your earnest prayers for them who are immediately employed therein. Assist them, according to your ability, to defray the expense which necessarily attends it, and which, without the assistance of charitable persons, would be a burden they could not bear. Assist them, if you can without inconvenience, by quarterly or yearly subscriptions. At least, assist them *now*: use the present hour, doing what God puts into your heart. Let it not be said that you saw your brethren labouring for God and would not help them with one of your fingers. In this way, however, 'come to the help of the Lord, to the help of the Lord against the mighty.'

7. I have an higher demand upon you who love, as well as fear, God. He whom you fear, whom you love, has qualified *you* for promoting his work in a more excellent way. Because you love God you love your brother also. You love not only your friends, but your enemies; not only the friends, but even the enemies of God. You have 'put on, as the elect of God', 'lowliness, gentleness, long-suffering'. You have faith in God, and in Jesus Christ whom he hath sent—faith which overcometh the world. And hereby you conquer both evil shame and that fear of man which 'bringeth a snare': so that you can 'stand with boldness before them that despise you and make no account of your labours'. Qualified then as you are, and armed for the fight, will *you* be 'like the children of Ephraim, who being harnessed, and carrying bows, turned back in the day of battle'? Will *you* leave a few of your brethren to stand alone against all the hosts of the aliens? O say not, 'This is too heavy a cross: I have not strength or courage to bear it.' True; not of yourself. But you that believe 'can do all things through Christ strengthening' you. 'If thou canst believe, all things are possible to him that believeth.' No cross is too heavy for *him* to bear, knowing that they that 'suffer with him, shall reign with him'. Say not, 'Nay, but I cannot bear to be *singular*.' Then you cannot enter into the kingdom of heaven. No one enters there but through the 'narrow way'. And all that walk in this are singular. Say not, 'But I cannot endure the reproach, the odious name of an *informer*.' And did any man ever save his soul that was not 'a by-word, and a proverb of reproach'? Neither canst thou ever save thine, unless thou art willing that men should 'say all manner of evil of thee'. Say not, 'But if I am active in this work I shall lose not only my reputation, but my friends, my customers, my business, my livelihood, so that I shall be brought to poverty.' Thou shalt not; thou canst not; it is absolutely impossible unless God himself chooseth it. For 'his kingdom

ruleth over all,' and 'the very hairs of thy head are all numbered.' But if the wise, the gracious God choose it for thee, wilt thou murmur or complain? Wilt thou not rather say, 'The cup which my Father hath given me, shall I not drink it?' If you 'suffer for Christ, happy are you; the spirit of glory and of Christ shall rest upon you.' Say not: 'I would suffer all things, but my wife will not consent to it. And certainly a man ought to "leave father and mother", and all, "and cleave to his wife".' True, all—but God; all—but Christ. But he ought not to leave *him* for his wife. He is not to 'leave any duty undone' for the dearest relative. Our Lord himself hath said in this very sense, 'If any man loveth father, or mother, or wife, or children, more than me, he is not worthy of me!' Say not: 'Well, I would forsake all for Christ. But one duty must not hinder another. And this would frequently hinder my attending public worship.' Sometimes it probably would. 'Go', then, 'and learn what that meaneth, I will have mercy and not sacrifice.' And whatever is lost by showing this mercy, God will repay sevenfold into thy bosom. Say not: 'But I shall hurt my own soul. I am a young man; and by taking up loose women I should expose myself to temptation.' Yes, if you did this in your own strength, or for your own pleasure. But that is not the case. You trust in God: and you aim at pleasing him only. And if he should call you even into the midst of a burning fiery furnace, 'though thou walkest through the fire thou shalt not be burnt, neither shall the flames kindle upon thee.' 'True; if *he called me* into the furnace. But I do not see that I am called to this.' Perhaps thou art not willing to see it. However, if thou wast not called before, I call thee *now*, in the name of Christ, 'Take up thy cross and follow him.' Reason no more with flesh and blood, but now resolve to cast in thy lot with the most despised, the most infamous of his followers, the filth and offscouring of the world. I call thee in particular who didst once strengthen their hands, but since art drawn back. Take courage! Be strong! Fulfil their joy by returning with heart and hand. Let it appear thou 'departedst for a season, that they might receive thee again for ever'. O be 'not disobedient to the heavenly calling'! And as for all of you who know whereunto ye are called, count ye all things loss, so ye may save one soul for which Christ died. And therein 'take no thought for the morrow', but 'cast all your care on him that careth for you.' 'Commit your souls', bodies, substance, all to him, 'as unto a merciful and faithful Creator'.

Appendix to the *Works*, edition of 1771:

N.B. After this Society had subsisted several years, and done unspeakable good, it was wholly destroyed by a verdict given against it in the King's Bench, with three hundred pounds damages. I doubt a severe account remains for the witnesses, the jury, and all who were concerned in that dreadful affair.

35. UPON OUR LORD'S SERMON ON THE MOUNT, DISCOURSE THE TENTH

1750

An Introductory Comment

The text of this sermon presents three major themes that Wesley developed: the first concerns a major obstacle to the Christian faith, namely, judging one's neighbor (vv. 1-5); the second considers the reception and proper use of gifts (vv. 6-11); and the third explores the Golden Rule itself (v. 12). In terms of actual preaching Wesley explored Matthew 7:1 with its counsel against judging while he was in London in 1763 and much later in 1788, and he exposited the text Matthew 7:7 ("Ask, and it shall be given you") before congregations at Wroot, Morvah, Taddington, Lewisham, Stoke, and Garth during the 1740s and later in 1761 at Southwark. What's so remarkable is that according to the sermon register, Wesley never made Matthew 7:12, the Golden Rule, the focus of his preaching (WWS). That is, this verse was always treated, as here, in light of other major texts.

As he wrote this sermon, Wesley was no doubt aware of Matthew Henry's observation that Christ's warning against judging does not preclude a proper place for reproving the wayward (H, Matt. 7:1). Moreover, Wesley was aware of the ignorance and misunderstanding that can easily lead to improper judging, especially with respect to different Christian traditions as evidenced in his "Letter to a Roman Catholic," in which he observed: ". . . it inclines us to think as hardly of you. Hence we are on both sides less willing to help one another, and more ready to hurt each other" (J, 10:80).

Beyond this, Wesley distinguished evil-speaking (the focus of a major sermon) from improper judging in two respects: first, the former concerns an absent person, but the latter may involve both those present and those absent; second, improper judging may not entail speaking at all but simply "*thinking evil* of another" (O, 1:654). A poem by Charles on Matthew 7:1 was published posthumously in the *Arminian Magazine* in June 1791.

Upon our Lord's Sermon on the Mount, Discourse the Tenth

1. Our blessed Lord here delivers the sum of true religion
    A. He gives rules touching right intention in outward actions
    B. He now points out the main hindrances of this religion
2. Jesus describes inward religion in its various branches
    A. He shows how our actions may be made holy by pure intention
3. He points out the most common hindrances to holiness
4. The first hindrance he cautions us against is judging
5. There is no station in life where this caution is not needful

6.–7. It does not appear that our Lord designed this only for Christians

8. The *judging* which is here forbidden is not the same as evil-speaking
9. It is thinking of another in a manner that is contrary to love
10. We may fall into the sin of judging by condemning the innocent
    A. Also by condemning the guilty in a higher degree than is deserved
11. All of this shows a want of that love which thinketh no evil

12.–13. We may also sin by condemning where there is not evidence

14. How rarely will we judge if we walk by the rule our Lord taught

15.–16. But if you cast the beam out of thine own eye
    A. And now clearly see the mote or beam in thy brother's eye
    B. Then beware you do not receive hurt by trying to help him

17. Be unwilling to pass judgment unless it is plain and undeniable
18. Do not despair of these who turn again and rend you

19.–20. Only remember always to pray, to seek, to knock, and not to faint

21. Confirm your love toward one another and toward all people
    A. And love them, not in word only, but in deed and in truth

22.–23. This is the royal law, the golden rule of mercy as well as justice

24. It may be understood either in a positive or a negative sense
25. In our conscience, we wish that others would not *judge* us
    A. We should not do to others what we do not want done to us
26. Let justice, mercy, and truth govern all our minds and actions
27. This is pure and genuine morality; do this and you will live

Sermon 30: Upon our Lord's Sermon on the Mount

Discourse the Tenth, 1750

Matthew 7:1-12

Judge not, that ye be not judged.

For with what judgment ye judge, ye shall be judged; and with what measure ye mete, it shall be measured to you again.

And why beholdest thou the mote that is in thy brother's eye, but considerest not the beam that is in thine own eye?

Or how wilt thou say to thy brother, Let me pull out the mote out of thine eye; and, behold, a beam is in thine own eye?

Thou hypocrite, first cast out the beam out of thine own eye; and then thou shalt see clearly to cast out the mote out of thy brother's eye.

Give not that which is holy unto dogs, neither cast your pearls before swine; lest they trample them under their feet, and turn again and rend you.

Ask, and it shall be given you; seek, and ye shall find; knock, and it shall be opened unto you.

For everyone that asketh, receiveth; and he that seeketh, findeth; and to him that knocketh, it shall be opened.

Or what man is there of you, who, if his son ask bread, will give him a stone? Or if he ask a fish, will give him a serpent?

If ye, then, being evil, know how to give good gifts unto your children, how much more shall your Father which is in heaven give good things to them that ask him!

Therefore all things whatsoever ye would that men should do to you, do ye even so to them; for this is the law and the prophets.

1. Our blessed Lord, having now finished his main design, having, first, delivered the sum of true religion, carefully guarded against those glosses of men whereby they would make the Word of God of none effect; and having, next, laid down rules touching that right intention which we are to preserve in all our outward actions, now proceeds to point out the main hindrances of this religion, and concludes all with a suitable application.

2. In the fifth chapter our great Teacher has fully described inward religion in its various branches. He has there laid before us those dispositions of soul which constitute real Christianity; the tempers contained in that holiness 'without which no man shall see the Lord'; the affections which, when flowing from their proper fountain, from a living faith in God through Christ Jesus, are intrinsically and essentially good, and acceptable to God. In the sixth he has shown how all our actions likewise, even those that are indifferent in their own nature, may be made holy, and good, and acceptable to God, by a pure and holy intention. Whatever is done without this he declares is of no value with God; whereas whatever outward works are thus consecrated to God are in his sight of great price.

3. In the former part of this chapter he points out the most common and most fatal hindrances of this holiness. In the latter he exhorts us by various motives to break through all and secure that prize of our high calling.

4. The first hindrance he cautions us against is judging: 'Judge not, that ye be not judged.' Judge not others, that ye be not judged of the Lord, that ye bring not vengeance on your own heads. 'For with what judgment ye judge, ye shall be judged; and with what measure ye mete, it shall be measured to you again'—a plain and equitable rule, whereby God permits you to determine for yourselves in what manner he shall deal with you in the judgment of the great day.

5. There is no station of life, nor any period of time, from the hour of our first repenting and believing the gospel till we are made perfect in love, wherein this caution is not needful for every child of God. For occasions of judging can never be wanting. And the temptations to it are innumerable; many whereof are so artfully disguised that we fall into the sin before we suspect any danger. And unspeakable are the mischiefs produced hereby: always to him that judges another, thus wounding his own soul, and exposing himself to the righteous judgment of God; and frequently to those who are judged, whose hands hang down, who are weakened and hindered in their course, if not wholly turned out of the way, and caused to draw back even to perdition. Yea, how often when this 'root of bitterness springs up', are 'many defiled thereby'; by reason whereof the way of truth itself is evil spoken of, and that worthy name blasphemed whereby we are called.

6. Yet it does not appear that our Lord designed this caution only or chiefly for the children of God; but rather for the children of the world, for the men who know not God. These cannot but hear of those who are not of the world; who follow after the religion above described; who endeavour to be humble, serious, gentle, merciful, and pure in heart; who earnestly desire such measures of these holy tempers as they have not yet attained, and wait for them in doing all good to all men, and patiently suffering evil. Whoever go but thus far cannot be hid, no more than 'a city set upon a hill'. And why do not those who 'see' their 'good works glorify their Father which is in heaven'? What excuse have they for not treading in their steps? For not imitating their example, and being followers of them, as they are also of Christ? Why, in order to provide an excuse for themselves, they condemn those whom they ought to imitate. They spend their time in finding out their neighbour's faults, instead of amending their own. They are so busied about others going out of the way, that themselves never come into it at all; at least, never get forward, never go beyond a poor dead form of godliness without the power.

7. It is to these more especially that our Lord says, 'Why beholdest thou the mote that is in thy brother's eye', the infirmities, the mistakes, the imprudence, the weakness of the children of God, 'but considerest not the beam that is in thine own eye?' Thou considerest not the damnable impenitence, the satanic pride, the accursed self-will, the idolatrous love of the world, which are in thyself, and which make thy whole life an abomination to the Lord. Above all, with what supine carelessness and indifference art thou dancing over the mouth of hell! And 'how', then, with what grace, with what decency or modesty, 'wilt thou say to thy brother, Let me pull out the mote out of thine eye'—the excess of zeal for God, the extreme of self-denial, the too great disengagement from worldly cares and

employments, the desire to be day and night in prayer, or hearing the words of eternal life—'And behold a beam is in thine own eye!' Not a mote, like one of these. 'Thou hypocrite!' who pretendest to care for others, and hast no care for thy own soul; who makest a show of zeal for the cause of God, when in truth thou neither lovest nor fearest him! 'First cast out the beam out of thine own eye.' Cast out the beam of impenitence. Know thyself. See and feel thyself a sinner. Feel that thy inward parts are very wickedness, that thou are altogether corrupt and abominable, and that the wrath of God abideth on thee. Cast out the beam of pride. Abhor thyself. Sink down as in dust and ashes. Be more and more little, and mean, and base, and vile in thine own eyes. Cast out the beam of self-will. Learn what that meaneth, 'If any man will come after me, let him renounce himself.' Deny thyself and take up thy cross daily. Let thy whole soul cry out, 'I came down from heaven' (for so thou didst, thou never-dying spirit, whether thou knowest it or no) 'not to do my own will, but the will of him that sent me.' Cast out the beam of love of the world. Love not the world, neither the things of the world. Be thou crucified unto the world, and the world crucified unto thee. Only *use* the world, but *enjoy* God. Seek all thy happiness in him. Above all cast out the grand beam, that supine carelessness and indifference. Deeply consider that 'one thing is needful', the one thing which thou hast scarce ever thought of. Know and feel that thou art a poor, vile, guilty worm, quivering over the great gulf! What art thou? A sinner born to die; a leaf driven before the wind; a vapour ready to vanish away, just appearing, and then scattered into air, to be no more seen! See this. 'And then shalt thou see clearly to cast out the mote out of thy brother's eye.' Then, if thou hast leisure from the concerns of thy own soul, thou shalt know how to correct thy brother also.

8. But what is properly the meaning of this word, 'judge not'? What is the *judging* which is here forbidden? It is not the same as evil-speaking, although it is frequently joined therewith. Evil-speaking is the relating anything that is evil concerning an absent person; whereas judging may indifferently refer either to the absent or the present. Neither does it necessarily imply the speaking at all, but only the *thinking evil* of another. Not that all kind of thinking evil of others is that judging which our Lord condemns. If I see one commit robbery or murder, or hear him blaspheme the name of God, I cannot refrain from thinking ill of the robber or murderer. Yet this is not evil judging: there is no sin in this, nor anything contrary to tender affection.

9. The thinking of another in a manner that is contrary to love is that judging which is here condemned; and this may be of various kinds. For, first, we may think another to blame when he is not. We may lay to his charge (at least in our own mind) the things of which he is not guilty—the words which he has never spoke, or the actions which he has never done. Or we may think his *manner* of acting was wrong, although in reality it was not. And even where nothing can justly be blamed, either in the thing itself or in the manner of doing it, we may suppose his *intention* was not good, and so condemn him on that ground, at the same time that he who searches the heart sees his simplicity and godly sincerity.

10. But we may not only fall into the sin of judging by condemning the innocent, but also, secondly, by condemning the guilty in a higher degree than he deserves. This species of judging is likewise an offence against justice as well as mercy; and yet such an offence

as nothing can secure us from but the strongest and tenderest affection. Without this we readily suppose one who is acknowledged to be in fault to be more in fault than he really is. We undervalue whatever good is found in him. Nay, we are not easily induced to believe that anything good can remain in him in whom we have found anything that is evil.

11. All this shows a manifest want of that love which οὐ λογίζεται κακόν, 'thinketh no evil'; which never draws an unjust or unkind conclusion from any premises whatsoever. Love will not infer from a person's falling once into an act of open sin that he is accustomed so to do, that he is habitually guilty of it. And if he was habitually guilty once, love does not conclude he is so still; much less that if he is now guilty of this, therefore he is guilty of other sins also. These evil reasonings all pertain to that sinful judging which our Lord here guards us against; and which we are in the highest degree concerned to avoid if we love either God or our own souls.

12. But supposing we do not condemn the innocent, neither the guilty any farther than they deserve; still we may not be altogether clear of the snare; for there is a third sort of sinful judging, which is the condemning any person at all where there is not sufficient evidence. And be the facts we suppose ever so true; yet that does not acquit us. For they ought not to have been supposed, but proved; and till they were we ought to have formed no judgment. I say, till they were; for neither are we excused; although the facts admit of ever so strong proof, unless that proof be produced before we pass sentence, and compared with the evidence on the other side. Nor can we be excused if ever we pass a full sentence before the accused has spoken for himself. Even a Jew might teach us this, as a mere lesson of justice abstracted from mercy and brotherly love. 'Doth our law', says Nicodemus, 'judge any man before it hear him, and know what he doth?' (John 7:51). Yea, a heathen could reply, when the chief of the Jewish nation desired to have judgment against his prisoner, 'It is not the manner of the Romans' to judge 'any man before he that is accused have the accusers face to face, and have licence to answer for himself concerning the crime laid against him.'

13. Indeed we could not easily fall into sinful judging were we only to observe that rule which another of those heathen Romans affirms to have been the measure of his own practice. 'I am so far', says he, 'from lightly believing every man's or any man's evidence against another, that I do not easily or immediately believe a man's evidence against himself. I always allow him second thoughts, and many times counsel too' (Seneca). Go, thou who art called a Christian, and do likewise, lest the heathen rise and condemn thee in that day.

14. But how rarely should we condemn or judge one another, at least how soon would that evil be remedied, were we to walk by that clear and express rule which our Lord himself has taught us! 'If thy brother shall trespass against thee' (or if thou hear, or believe that he hath) 'go and tell him of his fault, between him and thee alone.' This is the first step thou art to take. 'But if he will not hear, take with thee one or two more, that in the mouth of two or three witnesses every word may be established.' This is the second step. 'If he neglect to hear them, tell it unto the church;' either to the overseers thereof, or to the whole congregation. Thou hast then done thy part. Then think of it no more, but commend the whole to God.

15. But supposing thou hast, by the grace of God, 'cast the beam out of thine own eye', and dost now 'clearly see the mote or the beam which is in thy brother's eye'; yet beware thou dost not receive hurt thyself by endeavouring to help him. Still 'give not that which is holy unto dogs.' Do not lightly account any to be of this number. But if it evidently appear that they deserve the title, then cast ye not 'your pearls before swine'. Beware of that zeal which is not according to knowledge; for this is another great hindrance in their way who would be 'perfect as their heavenly Father is perfect'. They who desire this cannot but desire that all mankind should partake of the common blessing. And when we ourselves first partake of the heavenly gift, the divine 'evidence of things not seen', we wonder that all mankind do not see the things which we see so plainly; and make no doubt at all but we shall open the eyes of all we have any intercourse with. Hence we are for attacking all we meet without delay, and constraining them to see, whether they will or no. And by the ill success of this intemperate zeal, we often suffer in our own souls. To prevent this spending our strength in vain our Lord adds this needful caution (needful to all, but more especially to those who are now warm in their first love), 'Give not that which is holy unto the dogs, neither cast ye your pearls before swine; lest they trample them under foot, and turn again and rend you.'

16. 'Give not that which is holy unto the dogs.' Beware of thinking that any deserve this appellation till there is full and incontestable proof, such as you can no longer resist. But when it is clearly and indisputably proved that they are unholy and wicked men, not only strangers to, but enemies to God, to all righteousness and true holiness; 'give not that which is holy', τὸ ἅγιον, the holy thing, emphatically so called, unto these. The holy, the peculiar doctrines of the gospel, such as were 'hid from the ages and generations' of old, and are now made known to us only by the revelation of Jesus Christ and the inspiration of his Holy Spirit, are not to be prostituted unto these men who know not if there be any Holy Ghost. Not indeed that the ambassadors of Christ can refrain from declaring them in the great congregation, wherein some of these may probably be. We must speak, whether men will hear or whether they will forbear. But this is not the case with private Christians. They do not bear that awful character; nor are they under any manner of obligation to force these great and glorious truths on them who contradict and blaspheme, who have a rooted enmity against them. Nay, they ought not so to do, but rather to lead them as they are able to bear. Do not begin a discourse with these upon remission of sins and the gift of the Holy Ghost; but talk with them in their own manner, and upon their own principles. With the rational, honourable, unjust Epicure, 'reason of righteousness, temperance, and judgment to come'. This is the most probable way to make 'Felix tremble'. Reserve higher subjects for men of higher attainments.

17. 'Neither cast ye your pearls before swine.' Be very unwilling to pass this judgment on any man. But if the fact be plain and undeniable, if it is clear beyond all dispute, if the swine do not endeavour to disguise themselves, but rather glory in their shame, making no pretence to purity either of heart or life, but working all uncleanness with greediness; then 'cast' not 'ye your pearls before' them. Talk not to them of the mysteries of the kingdom; of the things which 'eye hath not seen, nor ear heard'; which of consequence, as they have no other inlets of knowledge, no spiritual senses, it cannot enter into their hearts to

conceive. Tell not them of the 'exceeding great and precious promises' which God hath given us in the Son of his love. What conception can they have of being made 'partakers of the divine nature' who do not even desire to 'escape the corruption that is in the world through lust'? Just as much knowledge as swine have of pearls, and as much relish as they have for them, so much relish have they for the deep things of God, so much knowledge of the mysteries of the gospel, who are immersed in the mire of this world, in worldly pleasures, desires, and cares. 'O cast not' those 'pearls before' these, 'lest they trample them under their feet', lest they utterly despise what they cannot understand, and speak evil of the things which they know not. Nay, 'tis probable this would not be the only inconvenience which would follow. It would not be strange if they were, according to their nature, to 'turn again, and rend you'; if they were to return you evil for good, cursing for blessing, and hatred for your goodwill. Such is the enmity of the carnal mind against God and all the things of God. Such the treatment you are to expect from these, if you offer them the unpardonable affront of endeavouring to save their souls from death, to pluck them as brands out of the burning!

18. And yet you need not utterly despair even of these, who for the present 'turn again and rend you'. For if all your arguments and persuasives fail, there is yet another remedy left; and one that is frequently found effectual when no other method avails. This is prayer. Therefore whatever you desire or want, either for others or for your own soul, 'Ask, and it shall be given you; seek, and ye shall find; knock, and it shall be opened unto you.' The neglect of this is a third grand hindrance of holiness. Still we 'have not, because we ask not'. O how meek and gentle, how lowly in heart, how full of love both to God and man, might ye have been at this day, if you had only asked! If you had 'continued instant in prayer'! Therefore now, at least, 'Ask, and it shall be given unto you.' 'Ask', that ye may throughly experience and perfectly practise the whole of that religion which our Lord has here so beautifully described. 'It shall' then 'be given you' to be holy as he is holy, both in heart and in all manner of conversation. 'Seek', in the way he hath ordained, in searching the Scriptures, in hearing his Word, in meditating thereon, in fasting, in partaking of the Supper of the Lord, and surely 'ye shall find.' Ye shall find that pearl of great price, that faith which overcometh the world, that peace which the world cannot give, that love which is the earnest of your inheritance. 'Knock': continue in prayer, and in every other way of the Lord. Be not weary or faint in your mind. Press on to the mark. Take no denial. Let him not go until he bless you. And the door of mercy, of holiness, of heaven 'shall be opened unto you'.

19. It is in compassion to the hardness of our hearts, so unready to believe the goodness of God, that our Lord is pleased to enlarge upon this head, and to repeat and confirm what he hath spoken. 'For everyone', saith he, 'that asketh, receiveth'; so that none need come short of the blessing; 'and he that seeketh', even everyone that seeketh, 'findeth' the love and the image of God; 'and to him that knocketh', to everyone that knocketh, the gate of righteousness shall be opened. So that here is no room for any to be discouraged, as though they might ask or seek or knock in vain. Only remember 'always to pray', to seek, to knock, 'and not to faint'. And then the promise standeth sure. It is firm as the pillars of heaven. Yea, more firm; for heaven and earth shall pass away; but his word shall not pass away.

20. To cut off every pretence for unbelief, our blessed Lord in the following verses illustrates yet farther what he had said, by an appeal to what passes in our own breasts. 'What man', saith he, 'is there of you, who, if his son ask bread, will give him a stone?' Will even natural affection permit you to refuse the reasonable request of one you love? 'Or if he ask a fish, will he give him a serpent?' Will he give him hurtful instead of profitable things? So that even from what you feel and do yourselves you may receive the fullest assurance, as on the one hand that no ill effect can possibly attend your asking, so on the other that it will be attended with that good effect, a full supply of all your wants. For 'if ye, being evil, know how to give good gifts unto your children, how much more shall your Father which is in heaven', who is pure, unmixed, essential goodness, 'give good things to them that ask him!' Or (as he expresses it on another occasion) 'give the Holy Ghost to them that ask him!' In him are included all good things; all wisdom, peace, joy, love; the whole treasures of holiness and happiness; all that God hath prepared for them that love him.

21. But that your prayer may have its full weight with God, see that ye be in charity with all men; for otherwise it is more likely to bring a curse than a blessing on your own head; nor can you expect to receive any blessing from God while you have not charity towards your neighbour. Therefore let this hindrance be removed without delay. Confirm your love towards one another and towards all men. And love them, not in word only, but in deed and in truth. 'Therefore all things whatsoever ye would that men should do to you, do ye even so unto them; for this is the law and the prophets.'

22. This is that royal law, that golden rule of mercy as well as justice, which even the heathen emperor caused to be written over the gate of his palace: a rule which many believe to be naturally engraved on the mind of everyone that comes into the world. And thus much is certain, that it commends itself, as soon as heard, to every man's conscience and understanding; insomuch that no man can knowingly offend against it without carrying his condemnation in his own breast.

23. 'This is the law and the prophets.' Whatsoever is written in that law which God of old revealed to mankind, and whatsoever precepts God has given by 'his holy prophets which have been since the world began', they are all summed up in these few words, they are all contained in this short direction. And this, rightly understood, comprises the whole of that religion which our Lord came to establish upon earth.

24. It may be understood either in a positive or negative sense. If understood in a negative sense the meaning is, 'Whatever ye would not that men should do to you, do not ye unto them.' Here is a plain rule, always ready at hand, always easy to be applied. In all cases relating to your neighbour, make his case your own. Suppose the circumstances to be changed, and yourself to be just as he is now. And then beware that you indulge no temper or thought, that no word pass out of your lips, that you take no step which you should have condemned in him, upon such a change of circumstances. If understood in a direct and positive sense, the plain meaning of it is, 'Whatsoever you could reasonably desire of him, supposing yourself to be in his circumstance, that do, to the uttermost of your power, to every child of man.'

25. To apply this in one or two obvious instances. It is clear to every man's own conscience, we would not that others should *judge* us, should causelessly or lightly think evil of us; much less would we that any should speak evil of us, should publish our real faults or infirmities. Apply this to yourself. Do not unto another what you would not he should do unto you; and you will never more judge your neighbour, never causelessly or lightly think evil of anyone; much less will you speak evil. You will never mention even the real fault of an absent person, unless so far as you are convinced it is absolutely needful for the good of other souls.

26. Again: we would that all men should love and esteem us, and behave towards us according to justice, mercy, and truth. And we may reasonably desire that they should do us all the good they can do without injuring themselves; yea, that in outward things (according to the known rule) their superfluities should give way to our conveniencies, their conveniencies to our necessities, and their necessities to our extremities. Now then, let us walk by the same rule: let us do unto all as we would they should do to us. Let us love and honour all men. Let justice, mercy, and truth govern all our minds and actions. Let our superfluities give way to our neighbour's conveniencies (and who then will have any superfluities left?); our conveniencies to our neighbour's necessities; our necessities to his extremities.

27. This is pure and genuine morality. This do, and thou shalt live. 'As many as walk by this rule, peace be to them, and mercy;' for they are 'the Israel of God'. But then be it observed, none can walk by this rule (nor ever did from the beginning of the world), none can love his neighbour as himself, unless he first love God. And none can love God unless he believe in Christ, unless he have redemption through his blood, and the Spirit of God bearing witness with his spirit that he is a child of God. Faith therefore is still the root of all, of present as well as future salvation. Still we must say to every sinner, Believe in the Lord Jesus Christ, and thou shalt be saved. Thou shalt be saved now, that thou mayst be saved for ever; saved on earth, that thou mayst be saved in heaven. Believe in him, and thy faith will work by love. Thou wilt love the Lord thy God because he hath loved thee; thou wilt love thy neighbour as thyself. And then it will be thy glory and joy to exert and increase this love, not barely by abstaining from what is contrary thereto—from every unkind thought, word, and action—but by showing all that kindness to every man which thou wouldst he should show unto thee.

36. UPON OUR LORD'S SERMON ON THE MOUNT, DISCOURSE THE ELEVENTH

1750

An Introductory Comment

So much of the early counsel of the Sermon on the Mount treats difficulties that "naturally arise from within" (O, 1:664), whereas this present sermon (Matt. 7:13-14) addresses those "hindrances from without, particularly ill example and ill advice" (O, 1:664), whose ongoing attraction is a function of the social and cultural pressures that celebrate a broad way in place of a narrow one.

Sugden was correct to call attention to the differences between the terms *strait* (used in Matt. 7:13, "Enter ye in at the strait gate") and *straight* employed elsewhere: the former signifies "strict, rigorous or narrow"; the latter means "free from curves, bends or angles." When these two senses are mixed, as in *Pilgrim's Progress*, confusion can only result (S, 1:532).

Wesley likely preached on the text Matthew 7:13 only once, that is, in January 1741 at Kingswood. However, he explored the verse Matthew 7:14 ("Because strait is the gate, and narrow is the way") in several pulpits during the 1770s ranging from Aberdeen, Scotland, to Chelsea and on to Brecon, Wales (WWS). The last use of this text occurred in London at the West Street Chapel not long before Wesley died.

In identifying the properties of the broad way with the path to perdition and the characteristics of the strait or narrow way with holiness and heaven (O, 1:664–65), Wesley interlaced the admonition of striving or agonizing "to enter in at the strait gate" in so many of his other sermons, such as "'Awake, Thou That Sleepeth,'" "The Circumcision of the Heart," "Sermon on the Mount, Discourse the Third," "Sermon on the Mount, Discourse theTwelfth," "The Wilderness State," "On Working Out Our Own Salvation," and "The More Excellent Way." Indeed, so emphatic was Wesley on this point that he reasoned in this present sermon: "This is an inseparable property of the way to heaven. . . . No sinner can pass through that gate until he is saved from all his sins" (O, 1:668).

Upon our Lord's Sermon on the Mount, Discourse the Eleventh

I. 1. We may observe, first, the inseparable properties of the way to hell
   - A. Wide is the gate and broad is the way that leads to destruction
   - B. And many there be that go in

2. Sin is the gate of hell and wickedness the way to destruction
3. How far do the parent sins extend, from which the rest derive their being
4. Who is able to reckon their accursed fruits, to count all the sins
5. The generality of every age and sex are walking in the way of destruction
6. This does not only concern the vulgar head, the poor, stupid part of mankind

II. 1. The reason many go on in the 'broad way' is because it is broad

2. Sinners cannot pass through that gate until they are saved from all their sins
   - A. Not only from outward sins; they must be inwardly changed
3. For narrow is the way that leads to life—the way of universal holiness
4. And few find it.

5.–6. There is a great danger that the torrent of example will bear us away

7. How can ignorant people maintain their cause against such opponents
   - A. There are many wise men in the way of destruction
8. Many rich are likewise in the broad way
9. The few who find the narrow way are not 'men of learning' or eloquence
10. Add to this that they are not noble, not honourable men

III. 1. Therefore it is that our Lord so earnestly exhorts:
   - A. Enter in at the strait gate, or elsewhere strive to enter in

2. 'Tis true he intimates what may seem another reason for this
3. It may be their delaying to seek that prevented them from entering
   - A. But it comes in effect to the same thing
   - B. They were to depart because they were workers of iniquity
4. Therefore strive now, in this your day, to enter in at the strait gate
5. Being penetrated with the deepest sense of the danger your soul is in
   - A. Strive by prayer without ceasing
6. Strive to enter in at the strait gate, not only by the agony of the soul
   - A. Or of conviction, sorrow, shame, desire, fear, or unceasing prayer
   - B. But by ordering thy conversation aright, walking in the ways of God

Sermon 31: Upon our Lord's Sermon on the Mount

Discourse the Eleventh, 1750

Matthew 7:13-14

Enter ye in at the strait gate: for wide is the gate, and broad is the way, which leadeth to destruction, and many there be which go in thereat:

Because strait is the gate, and narrow is the way, which leadeth unto life, and few there be that find it.

1. Our Lord, having warned us of the dangers which easily beset us at our first entrance upon real religion, the hindrances which naturally arise from within, from the wickedness of our own hearts, now proceeds to apprise us of the hindrances from without, particularly ill example and ill advice. By one or the other of these, thousands who once ran well have drawn back unto perdition; yea, many of those who were not novices in religion, who had made some progress in righteousness. His caution therefore against these he presses upon us with all possible earnestness, and repeats again and again, in variety of expressions, lest by any means we should let it slip. Thus, effectually to guard us against the former, 'Enter ye in', saith he, 'at the strait gate; for wide is the gate, and broad is the way, that leadeth to destruction, and many there be which go in thereat: because strait is the gate, and narrow is the way, which leadeth unto life, and few there be that find it.' To secure us from the latter, 'Beware', saith he, 'of false prophets.' We shall at present consider the former only.

2. 'Enter ye in', saith our blessed Lord, 'at the strait gate; for wide is the gate, and broad is the way, that leadeth to destruction, and many there be which go in thereat: because strait is the gate, and narrow is the way, which leadeth unto life, and few there be that find it.'

3. In these words we may observe, first, the inseparable properties of the way to hell: 'Wide is the gate, broad the way, that leadeth to destruction, and many there be that go in thereat;' secondly, the inseparable properties of the way to heaven: 'Strait is that gate, and narrow is the way, which leadeth unto life, and few there be that find it;' thirdly, a serious exhortation grounded thereon: 'Enter ye in at the strait gate.'

I.1. We may observe, first, the inseparable properties of the way to hell: 'Wide is the gate, and broad is the way, that leadeth to destruction, and many there be that go in thereat.'

2. Wide indeed is the gate, and broad the way, that leadeth to destruction. For sin is the gate of hell, and wickedness the way to destruction. And how wide a gate is that of sin! How broad is the way of wickedness! The 'commandment' of God 'is exceeding broad', as extending not only to all our actions, but to every word which goeth out of our lips, yea, every thought that rises in our heart. And sin is equally broad with the commandment, seeing any breach of the commandment is sin. Yea, rather, it is a thousand times broader, since there is only one way of keeping the commandment; for we do not properly keep it

unless both the thing done, the manner of doing it, and all the other circumstances, are right. But there are a thousand ways of breaking every commandment; so that this gate is wide indeed.

3. To consider this a little more particularly. How wide do those parent sins extend, from which all the rest derive their being: 'that carnal mind which is enmity against God', pride of heart, self-will, and love of the world! Can we fix any bounds to them? Do they not diffuse themselves through all our thoughts, and mingle with all our tempers? Are they not the leaven which leavens, more or less, the whole mass of our affections? May we not, on a close and faithful examination of ourselves, perceive these roots of bitterness continually springing up, infecting all our words, and tainting all our actions? And how innumerable an offspring do they bring forth, in every age and nation! Even enough to cover the whole earth with 'darkness and cruel habitations'.

4. O who is able to reckon up their accursed fruits! To count all the sins, whether against God or our neighbour, not which imagination might paint, but which may be matter of daily, melancholy experience! Nor need we range over all the earth to find them. Survey any one kingdom, any single country, or city, or town, and how plenteous is this harvest! And let it not be one of those which are still overspread with Mahometan or pagan darkness, but of those which name the name of Christ, which profess to see the light of his glorious gospel. Go no farther than the kingdom to which we belong, the city wherein we are now. We call ourselves Christians; yea, and that of the purest sort; we are Protestants, reformed Christians! But alas! who shall carry on the reformation of our opinions into our hearts and lives? Is there not a cause? For how innumerable are our sins! And those of the deepest dye! Do not the grossest abominations of every kind abound among us from day to day? Do not sins of every sort cover the land, as the waters cover the sea? Who can count them? Rather go and count the drops of rain, or the sands on the sea-shore. So 'wide is the gate', so 'broad is the way that leadeth to destruction'.

5. 'And many there be who go in at' that gate, many who walk in that way—almost as many as go in at the gate of death, as sink into the chambers of the grave. For it cannot be denied (though neither can we acknowledge it but with shame and sorrow of heart) that even in this which is called a Christian country the generality of every age and sex, of every profession and employment, of every rank and degree, high and low, rich and poor, are walking in the way of destruction. The far greater part of the inhabitants of this city to this day live in sin; in some palpable, habitual, known transgression of the law they profess to observe; yea, in some outward transgression, some gross, visible kind of ungodliness or unrighteousness; some open violation of their duty, either to God or man. These then, none can deny, are all in the way that leadeth to destruction. Add to these those who 'have a name, indeed, that they live', but were never yet alive to God; those that outwardly appear fair to men, but are inwardly full of all uncleanness; full of pride or vanity, of anger or revenge, of ambition or covetousness; lovers of themselves, lovers of the world, lovers of pleasure more than lovers of God. These indeed may be highly esteemed of men, but they are an abomination to the Lord. And how greatly will these saints of the world swell the number of the children of hell! Yea, add all—whatever they be in other respects, whether they have more or less of the form of godliness—who,

'being ignorant of God's righteousness, and seeking to establish their own righteousness' as the ground of their reconciliation to God and acceptance with him, of consequence have 'not submitted themselves unto the righteousness which is of God by faith.' Now all these things joined together in one, how terribly true is our Lord's assertion, 'Wide is the gate and broad is the way that leadeth to destruction, and many there be who go in thereat.'

6. Nor does this only concern the vulgar herd, the poor, base, stupid part of mankind. Nay; men of eminence in the world, men who have many fields and yoke of oxen, do not desire to be excused from this. On the contrary, 'many wise men after the flesh', according to the human methods of judging, 'many mighty' in power, in courage, in riches, many 'noble are called'; called into the broad way, by the world, the flesh, and the devil; and they are not disobedient to that calling. Yea, the higher they are raised in fortune and power, the deeper do they sink into wickedness. The more blessings they have received from God, the more sins do they commit; using their honour or riches, their learning or wisdom, not as means of working out their salvation, but rather of excelling in vice, and so ensuring their own destruction.

II.1. And the very reason why many of these go on so securely in the 'broad way' is because it is broad; not considering that this is the inseparable property of the way to destruction. 'Many there be', saith our Lord, 'who go in thereat'—for the very reason why they should flee from it, even 'because strait is the gate and narrow the way that leadeth unto life, and few there be that find it.'

2. This is an inseparable property of the way to heaven. So narrow is the way that leadeth unto life, unto life everlasting, so strait the gate, that nothing unclean, nothing unholy, can enter. No sinner can pass through that gate until he is saved from all his sins. Not only from his outward sins, from his evil 'conversation, received by tradition from his fathers'. It will not suffice that he hath 'ceased to do evil' and 'learned to do well'. He must not only be saved from all sinful actions and from all evil and useless discourse; but inwardly changed, throughly renewed in the spirit of his mind. Otherwise he cannot pass through the gate of life, he cannot enter into glory.

3. For 'narrow is the way that leadeth unto life'—the way of universal holiness. Narrow indeed is the way of poverty of spirit, the way of holy mourning, the way of meekness, and that of hungering and thirsting after righteousness. Narrow is the way of mercifulness, of love unfeigned; the way of purity of heart; of doing good unto all men, and of gladly suffering evil, all manner of evil, for righteousness' sake.

4. 'And few there be that find it.' Alas, how few find even the way of heathen honesty! How few are there that do nothing to another which they would not another should do unto them! How few that are clear before God from acts either of injustice or unkindness! How few that do not 'offend with their tongue'; that speak nothing unkind, nothing untrue! What a small proportion of mankind are innocent even of outward transgressions! And how much smaller a proportion have their hearts right before God, clean and holy in his sight! Where are they whom his all-searching eye discerns to be truly humble? To

abhor themselves in dust and ashes in the presence of God their Saviour? To be deeply and steadily serious, feeling their wants, and 'passing the time of their sojourning with fear'? Truly meek and gentle, never 'overcome of evil, but overcoming evil with good'? Throughly athirst for God, and continually panting after a renewal in his likeness? How thinly are they scattered over the earth, whose souls are enlarged in love to all mankind; and who love God with all their strength; who have given him their hearts, and desire nothing else in earth or heaven! How few are those lovers of God and man that spend their whole strength in doing good unto all men; and are ready to suffer all things, yea, death itself, to save one soul from eternal death!

5. But while so few are found in the way of life, and so many in the way of destruction, there is great danger lest the torrent of example should bear us away with them. Even a single example, if it be always in our sight, is apt to make much impression upon us; especially when it has nature on its side, when it falls in with our own inclinations. How great then must be the force of so numerous examples, continually before our eyes; and all conspiring together with our own hearts to carry us down the stream of nature! How difficult must it be to stem the tide, and to keep ourselves 'unspotted in the world'!

6. What heightens the difficulty still more is that they are not the rude and senseless part of mankind, at least not these alone, who set us the example, who throng the downward way; but the polite, the well-bred, the genteel, the wise, the men who understand the world; the men of knowledge, of deep and various learning, the rational, the eloquent! These are all, or nearly all, against us. And how shall we stand against these? Do not their tongues drop manna? And have they not learned all the arts of soft persuasion? And of reasoning too; for these are versed in all controversies and strife of words. It is therefore a small thing with them to prove that the way is *right* because it is *broad*; that he who follows a multitude cannot do evil, but only he who will not follow them; that your way must be *wrong* because it is *narrow* and because there are so few that find it. These will make it clear to a demonstration that evil is good, and good is evil; that the way of holiness is the way of destruction, and the way of the world the only way to heaven.

7. O how can unlearned and ignorant men maintain their cause against such opponents! And yet these are not all with whom they must contend, however unequal to the task; for there are many mighty and noble and powerful men, as well as wise, in the road that leadeth to destruction. And these have a shorter way of confuting than that of reason and argument. They usually apply, not to the understanding, but to the fears of any that oppose them—a method that seldom fails of success, even where argument profits nothing, as lying level to the capacities of all men: for all can fear, whether they can reason or no. And all who have not a firm trust in God, a sure reliance both on his power and love, cannot but fear to give any disgust to those who have the power of the world in their hands. What wonder, therefore, if the example of these is a law to all who know not God!

8. Many rich are likewise in the broad way. And these apply to the hopes of men, and to all their foolish desires, as strongly and effectually as the mighty and noble to their fears. So that hardly can you hold on in the way of the kingdom unless you are dead to all below, unless you are crucified to the world and the world crucified to you, unless you desire nothing more but God.

9. For how dark, how uncomfortable, how forbidding is the prospect on the opposite side! A strait gate! A narrow way! And few finding that gate! Few walking in the way. Besides, even those few are not wise men, not men of learning or eloquence. They are not able to reason either strongly or clearly; they cannot propose an argument to any advantage. They know not how to prove what they profess to believe; or to explain even what they say they experience. Surely such advocates as these will never recommend, but rather discredit the cause they have espoused.

10. Add to this that they are not noble, not honourable men: if they were, you might bear with their folly. They are men of no interest, no authority, of no account in the world. They are mean and base, low in life; and such as have no power, if they had the will, to hurt you. Therefore there is nothing at all to be feared from them; and there is nothing at all to hope: for the greater part of them may say, 'Silver and gold have I none'—at least a very moderate share. Nay, some of them have scarce food to eat or raiment to put on. For this reason, as well as because their ways are not like those of other men, they are everywhere spoken against, are despised, have their names cast out as evil, are variously persecuted, and treated as the filth and offscouring of the world. So that both your fears, your hopes, and all your desires (except those which you have immediately from God), yea, all your natural passions, continually incline you to return into the broad way.

III.1. Therefore it is that our Lord so earnestly exhorts, 'Enter ye in at the strait gate.' Or (as the same exhortation is elsewhere expressed) 'Strive to enter in': ἀγωνίζεσθε εἰσελθεῖν, strive as in an agony. 'For many', saith our Lord, 'shall seek to enter in'—indolently strive—'and shall not be able.'

2. 'Tis true he intimates what may seem another reason for this, for their 'not being able to enter in', in the words which immediately follow these. For after he had said, 'Many, I say unto you, will seek to enter in, and shall not be able,' he subjoins: 'When once the master of the house is risen up and hath shut to the door, and ye begin to stand without' (ἄρξησθε ἔξω ἑστάναι: rather, 'ye stand without', for ἄρξησθε seems to be only an elegant expletive) 'and to knock at the door, saying, Lord, Lord, open unto us; he shall answer and say unto you, I know you not. Depart from me, all ye workers of iniquity' (Luke 13:24-27).

3. It may appear, upon a transient view of these words, that their delaying to seek at all, rather than their manner of seeking, was the reason why they were not able to enter in. But it comes in effect to the same thing. They were therefore commanded to depart, because they had been 'workers of iniquity', because they had walked in the broad road; in other words, because they had not agonized to enter in at the strait gate. Probably they did *seek*, before the door was shut; but that did not suffice. And they did *strive*, after the door was shut; but then it was too late.

4. Therefore 'strive' ye now, in this your day, 'to enter in at the strait gate'. And in order hereto, settle it in your heart, and let it be ever uppermost in your thoughts, that if you are in a broad way, you are in the way that leadeth to destruction. If many go with you, as sure as God is true, both they and you are going to hell. If you are walking as the

generality of men walk, you are walking to the bottomless pit. Are many wise, many rich, many mighty or noble travelling with you in the same way? By this token, without going any farther, you know it does not lead to life. Here is a short, a plain, an infallible rule, before you enter into particulars. In whatever profession you are engaged, you must be singular or be damned. The way to hell has nothing singular in it; but the way to heaven is singularity all over. If you move but one step towards God you are not as other men are. But regard not this. 'Tis far better to stand alone than to fall into the pit. Run then with patience the race which is set before thee, though thy companions therein are but few. They will not always be so. Yet a little while and thou wilt 'come to an innumerable company of angels, to the general assembly and church of the first-born, and to the spirits of just men made perfect'.

5. Now, then, 'strive to enter in at the strait gate,' being penetrated with the deepest sense of the inexpressible danger your soul is in so long as you are in a broad way, so long as you are void of poverty of spirit and all that inward religion which the many, the rich, the wise, account madness. 'Strive to enter in,' being pierced with sorrow and shame for having so long run on with the unthinking crowd, utterly neglecting if not despising that 'holiness, without which no man can see the Lord'. *Strive* as in an agony of holy fear, lest 'a promise being made you of entering into his rest', even that 'rest which remaineth for the people of God', you should nevertheless 'come short of it'. Strive in all the fervour of desire, with 'groanings which cannot be uttered'. Strive by prayer without ceasing, at all times, in all places lifting up your heart to God, and giving him no rest till you 'awake up after his likeness' and are 'satisfied with it'.

6. To conclude: 'Strive to enter in at the strait gate,' not only by this agony of soul, of conviction, of sorrow, of shame, of desire, of fear, of unceasing prayer, but likewise by 'ordering thy conversation aright', by walking with all thy strength in all the ways of God, the way of innocence, of piety, and of mercy. Abstain from all appearance of evil; do all possible good to all men; deny thyself, thy own will, in all things, and take up thy cross daily. Be ready to cut off thy right hand, to pluck out thy right eye and cast it from thee; to suffer the loss of goods, friends, health, all things on earth, so thou mayst enter into the kingdom of heaven.

37. UPON OUR LORD'S SERMON ON THE MOUNT, DISCOURSE THE TWELFTH

1750

An Introductory Comment

On January 30, 1743, Wesley preached on Matthew 7:15 at Egham about five miles from Windsor with the hope of rescuing "the poor text out of so bad hands" (WH, 19:313). However, he much preferred to preach on verse 16 of this chapter as he did the following decade in Snowfields chapel at Southwark and on numerous occasions thereafter especially during the 1780s (WWS). Wesley's principal concern when he employed these texts, which raised the issue of false prophets, was to give the Methodists guidance about how they should receive the ministries, both in Word and in sacrament, of those Anglican priests who lived ungodly lives or were doctrinally perverse. Indeed, this present sermon was published separately in 1758 as "A Caution against False Prophets, particularly Recommended to the People called Methodists" (S, 2:10).

The chief characteristic of false prophets is that they have found a broader way, a wider gate, to heaven: one that not only receives the approval of so many people but also skirts the narrow path of holiness. As a result false prophets, though they appear to be religious, agreeable, useful, and even loving, do not lead sinners to repentance; they do not, as Wesley wrote, "save souls from sin" or direct them "to love and serve God" (O, 1:680–81).

Though Wesley did not repudiate the validity of the sacraments administered by aberrant clergy, thereby affirming the judgment of the ancient church with respect to the Donatist controversy, he nevertheless was willing to allow, at least by 1786, that Methodist services could compete with Anglican ones when "the minister is a notoriously wicked man, [and] when he preaches Arian, or equally pernicious doctrine" (J, 13:257). The key standard for ascertaining who are false prophets, of course, came from Jesus Christ himself, who taught, "By their fruits ye shall know them" (Matt. 7:20), a standard that Wesley took up in this present sermon as well.

Upon our Lord's Sermon on the Mount, Discourse the Twelfth

I. 1–2. False prophets are those who teach a false way to heaven
3. Every broad way is infallibly false; the way to heaven is narrow
4. They are false prophets who do not teach people to walk in *this way*
5. It does not matter what they call the other way—faith or good works
6.–7. Some teach the way of pride and worldly passions

II. 1. But do they come now in their own shape?
A. By no means. If it were so they could not destroy
2. They come to you in sheep's clothing, appearing harmless
3. They come, secondly, with the appearance of usefulness, to do good
4. They come, thirdly, with the appearance of religion
5. Above all, they come with the appearance of love

III. 1. But how may we know what they really are?
A. 'Ye shall know them by their fruits'
2. First, what are the fruits of their doctrine as to themselves?
A. What effect has it had upon their lives?
3. Second, what are the fruits of their doctrine for those who hear them?
4. Do they gather grapes of thorns, or figs of thistles?
5. Beware of these false prophets; they will not lead you to heaven
6.–7. Should we listen to false prophets at all?
8. False prophets are frequently those who administer the sacraments
A. If we do not hear them, we are cut off from God's ordinance
9. All I can say in any particular case is to wait upon God by humble prayer
10. To those whom we have now been speaking:
A. How long will you teach the way of death, and call it the way of life?
11. 'Woe unto you', you blind leaders of the blind
12. 'Where are your eyes? Where is your understanding?'
13. How can you possibly evade the force of our Lord's words?
14. My dear brethren, do not harden your hearts
A. You have too long shut your eyes against the light
B. Open them now, before it is too late and you are cast into darkness
C. Cry unto God that God may quicken your soul and give you faith

Sermon 32: Upon our Lord's Sermon on the Mount

Discourse the Twelfth, 1750

Matthew 7:15-20

Beware of false prophets, which come to you in sheep's clothing, but inwardly they are ravening wolves.

Ye shall know them by their fruits. Do men gather grapes of thorns, or figs of thistles?

Even so every good tree bringeth forth good fruit; but a corrupt tree bringeth forth evil fruit.

A good tree cannot bring forth evil fruit; neither can a corrupt tree bring forth good fruit.

Every tree that bringeth not forth good fruit is hewn down and cast into the fire.

Wherefore by their fruits ye shall know them.

1. It is scarce possible to express or conceive what multitudes of souls run on to destruction because they would not be persuaded to walk in a *narrow* way, even though it were the way to everlasting salvation. And the same thing we may still observe daily. Such is the folly and madness of mankind that thousands of men still rush on in the way to hell only because it is a broad way. They walk in it themselves because others do: because so many perish they will add to the number. Such is the amazing influence of example over the weak, miserable children of men! It continually peoples the regions of death, and drowns numberless souls in everlasting perdition.

2. To warn mankind of this, to guard as many as possible against this spreading contagion, God has commanded his watchmen to cry aloud, and show the people the danger they are in. For this end he has sent his servants, the prophets, in their succeeding generations, to point out the narrow path, and exhort all men not to be conformed to this world. But what if the watchmen themselves fall into the snare against which they should warn others? What if 'the prophets prophesy deceits'? If they 'cause the people to err from the way'? What shall be done if they point out, as the way to eternal life, what is in truth the way to eternal death? And exhort others to walk, as they do themselves, in the broad, not the narrow way?

3. Is this an unheard of, is it an uncommon thing? Nay, God knoweth it is not. The instances of it are almost innumerable. We may find them in every age and nation. But how terrible is this! When the ambassadors of God turn agents for the devil! When they who are commissioned to teach men the way to heaven do in fact teach them the way to hell! These are like the locusts of Egypt 'which eat up the residue that had escaped', that had 'remained after the hail'. They devour even the residue of men that had escaped, that were not destroyed by ill example. It is not therefore without cause that our wise and gracious master so solemnly cautions us against them: 'Beware', saith he, 'of false prophets, which come to you in sheep's clothing, but inwardly they are ravening wolves.'

4. A caution this of the utmost importance. That it may the more effectually sink into our hearts, let us inquire, first, who these false prophets are; secondly, what appearance

they put on; and, thirdly, how we may know what they really are, notwithstanding their fair appearance.

I.1. We are, first, to inquire who these false prophets are. And this it is needful to do the more diligently because these very men have so laboured to 'wrest this Scripture to their own (though not only their own) destruction'. In order therefore to cut off all dispute I shall raise no dust (as the manner of some is) neither use any loose, rhetorical exclamations to deceive the hearts of the simple, but speak rough, plain truths, such as none can deny who has either understanding or modesty left, and such truths as have the closest connection with the whole tenor of the preceding discourse; whereas too many have interpreted these words without any regard to all that went before, as if they bore no manner of relation to the sermon in the close of which they stand.

2. By 'prophets' here (as in many other passages of Scripture, particularly in the New Testament) are meant, not those who foretell things to come, but those who speak in the name of God; those men who profess to be sent of God to teach others the way to heaven.

Those are 'false prophets' who teach a false way to heaven, a way which does not lead thither; or (which comes in the end to the same point) who do not teach the true.

3. Every broad way is infallibly a false one. Therefore this is one plain, sure rule, 'They who teach men to walk in a broad way, a way that many walk in, are false prophets.'

Again, the true way to heaven is a narrow way. Therefore this is another plain, sure rule, 'They who do not teach men to walk in a narrow way, to be singular, are false prophets.'

4. To be more particular: the only true way to heaven is that pointed out in the preceding sermon. Therefore they are false prophets who do not teach men to walk in *this way*.

Now the way to heaven pointed out in the preceding sermon is the way of lowliness, mourning, meekness, and holy desire, love of God and of our neighbour, doing good, and suffering evil for Christ's sake. They are therefore false prophets who teach as the way to heaven any other way than *this.*

5. It matters not what they call that other way. They may call it 'faith', or 'good works'; or 'faith and works'; or 'repentance'; or 'repentance, faith, and new obedience'. All these are good words. But if under these, or any other terms whatever, they teach men any way distinct from *this,* they are properly false prophets.

6. How much more do they fall under that condemnation who speak evil of this good way! But above all they who teach the directly opposite way—the way of pride, of levity, of passion, of worldly desires, of loving pleasure more than God, of unkindness to our neighbour, of unconcern for good works, and suffering no evil, no persecution for righteousness' sake!

7. If it be asked, 'Why, who ever did teach this?' Or, 'Who does teach it as the way to heaven?' I answer, Ten thousand wise and honourable men; even all those, of whatever

denomination, who encourage the proud, the trifler, the passionate, the lover of the world, the man of pleasure, the unjust or unkind, the easy, careless, harmless, useless creature, the man who suffers no reproach for righteousness' sake, to imagine he is in the way to heaven. These are false prophets in the highest sense of the word. These are traitors both to God and man. These are no other than the first-born of Satan, the eldest sons of Apollyon, the destroyer. These are far above the rank of ordinary cut-throats; for they murder the souls of men. They are continually peopling the realms of night; and whenever they follow the poor souls whom they have destroyed, 'hell' shall be 'moved from beneath to meet them at their coming'.

II.1. But do they come now in their own shape? By no means. If it were so they could not destroy. You would take the alarm and flee for your life. Therefore they put on a quite contrary appearance, which was the second thing to be considered: 'they come to you in sheep's clothing,' although 'inwardly they are ravening wolves.'

2. 'They come to you in sheep's clothing'; that is, with an appearance of harmlessness. They come in the most mild, inoffensive manner, without any mark or token of enmity. Who can imagine that these quiet creatures would do any hurt to anyone? Perhaps they may not be so zealous and active in doing good as one would wish they were. However, you see no reason to suspect that they have even the desire to do any harm. But this is not all.

3. They come, secondly, with an appearance of usefulness. Indeed to this, to do good, they are particularly called. They are set apart for this very thing. They are particularly commissioned to watch over your soul, and to train you up to eternal life. 'Tis their whole business to 'go about doing good, and healing those that are oppressed of the devil'. And you have been always accustomed to look upon them in this light, as messengers of God sent to bring you a blessing.

4. They come, thirdly, with an appearance of religion. All they do is for conscience' sake! They assure you it is out of mere zeal for God that they are making God a liar. It is out of pure concern for religion that they would destroy it root and branch. All they speak is only from a love of truth, and a fear lest it should suffer. And, it may be, from a regard for the church, and a desire to defend her from all her enemies.

5. Above all, they come with an appearance of love. They take all these pains only for *your* good. They should not trouble themselves about you, but that they have a kindness for you. They will make large professions of their goodwill, of their concern for the danger you are in, and of their earnest desire to preserve you from error, from being entangled in new and mischievous doctrines. They should be very sorry to see one who *means* so well hurried into any extreme, perplexed with strange and unintelligible notions, or deluded into enthusiasm. Therefore it is that they advise you to keep still in the plain middle way; and to beware of 'being righteous overmuch', lest you should 'destroy yourself'.

III.1. But how may we know what they really are, notwithstanding their fair appearance? This was the third thing into which it was proposed to inquire.

Our blessed Lord saw how needful it was for all men to know false prophets, however disguised. He saw likewise how unable most men were to deduce a truth through a long train of consequences. He therefore gives us a short and plain rule, easy to be understood by men of the meanest capacities, and easy to be applied upon all occasions: 'Ye shall know them by their fruits.'

2. Upon all occasions you may easily apply this rule. In order to know whether any who speak in the name of God are false or true prophets it is easy to observe, first, What are the fruits of their doctrine as to themselves? What effect has it had upon their lives? Are they holy and unblameable in all things? What effect has it had upon their hearts? Does it appear by the general tenor of their conversation that their tempers are holy, heavenly, divine? That the mind is in them which was in Christ Jesus? That they are meek, lowly, patient lovers of God and man, and zealous of good works?

3. You may easily observe, secondly, what are the fruits of their doctrine as to those that hear them—in many, at least, though not in all; for the apostles themselves did not convert all that heard them. Have these the mind that was in Christ? And do they walk as he also walked? And was it by hearing these men that they began so to do? Were they inwardly and outwardly wicked till they heard them? If so, it is a manifest proof that those are true prophets, teachers sent of God. But if it is not so, if they do not effectually teach either themselves or others to love and serve God, it is a manifest proof that they are false prophets; that God hath not sent them.

4. An hard saying this! How few can bear it! This our Lord was sensible of, and therefore condescends to prove it at large by several clear and convincing arguments. 'Do men', says he, 'gather grapes of thorns, or figs of thistles?' (Matt. 7:16). Do you expect that these evil men should bring forth good fruit? As well might you expect that thorns should bring forth grapes, or that figs should grow upon thistles! 'Every good tree bringeth forth good fruit; but a corrupt tree bringeth forth evil fruit' (Matt. 7:17). Every true prophet, every teacher whom I have sent, bringeth forth the good fruit of holiness. But a false prophet, a teacher whom I have not sent, brings forth only sin and wickedness. 'A good tree cannot bring forth evil fruit; neither can a corrupt tree bring forth good fruit.' A true prophet, a teacher sent from God, does not bring forth good fruit sometimes only, but always; not accidentally, but by a kind of necessity. In like manner, a false prophet, one whom God hath not sent, does not bring forth evil fruit accidentally or sometimes only, but always, and of necessity. 'Every tree that bringeth not forth good fruit is hewn down and cast into the fire' (Matt. 7:19). Such infallibly will be the lot of those prophets who bring not forth good fruit, who do not save souls from sin, who do not bring sinners to repentance. 'Wherefore' let this stand as an eternal rule: 'By their fruits ye shall know them' (Matt. 7:20). They who in fact bring the proud, passionate, unmerciful lovers of the world to be lowly, gentle lovers of God and man—they are true prophets, they are sent from God, who therefore confirms their word. On the other hand they whose hearers, if unrighteous before, remain unrighteous still, or at least void of any righteousness which 'exceeds the righteousness of the scribes and Pharisees'—they are false prophets; they are not sent of

God; therefore their word falls to the ground. And without a miracle of grace they and their hearers together will fall into the bottomless pit.

5. O 'beware of' these 'false prophets'! For though they 'come in sheep's clothing, yet inwardly they are ravening wolves'. They only destroy and devour the flock: they tear them in pieces if there is none to help them. They will not, cannot lead you in the way to heaven. How should they, when they know it not themselves? O beware they do not turn you out of the way, and cause you to 'lose what you have wrought'.

6. But perhaps you will ask, 'If there is such danger in hearing them, ought I to hear them at all?' It is a weighty question, such as deserves the deepest consideration, and ought not to be answered but upon the calmest thought, the most deliberate reflection. For many years I have been almost afraid to speak at all concerning it; being unable to determine one way or the other, or to give any judgment upon it. Many reasons there are which readily occur, and incline me to say, 'Hear them not.' And yet what our Lord speaks concerning the false prophets of his own times seems to imply the contrary. 'Then spake Jesus unto the multitude, and to his disciples, saying, The scribes and the Pharisees sit in Moses' seat,' are the ordinary, stated teachers in your church: 'All therefore whatsoever they bid you observe, that observe and do. But do not ye after their works; for they say and do not.' Now that these were false prophets in the highest sense our Lord had shown during the whole course of his ministry, as indeed he does in those very words, 'they say and do not.' Therefore by their fruits his disciples could not but know them, seeing they were open to the view of all men. Accordingly he warns them again and again to 'beware of' these 'false prophets'. And yet he does not forbid them to hear even these. Nay, he in effect commands them so to do in those words: 'All therefore whatsoever they bid you observe, that observe and do.' For unless they heard them they could not know, much less 'observe, whatsoever they bade them do'. Here then our Lord himself gives a plain direction, both to his apostles and the whole multitude, in some circumstances to hear even false prophets, known and acknowledged so to be.

7. But perhaps it will be said, he only directed to hear them when they read the Scripture to the congregation. I answer, at the same time that they thus read the Scripture they generally expounded it too. And here is no kind of intimation that they were to hear the one and not the other also. Nay, the very terms, 'All things whatsoever they bid you observe', exclude any such limitation.

8. Again, unto them, unto false prophets, undeniably such, is frequently committed (O grief to speak! for surely these things ought not so to be) the administration of the sacraments also. To direct men, therefore, not to hear them would be in effect to cut them off from the ordinance of God. But this we dare not do, considering the validity of the ordinance doth not depend on the goodness of him that administers, but on the faithfulness of him that ordained it; who will and doth meet us in his appointed ways. Therefore on this account likewise I scruple to say, 'Hear not even the false prophets.' Even by these who are under a curse themselves God can and doth give us his blessing. For the bread which they break we have experimentally known to be 'the communion of the body of Christ'; and the cup which God blessed, even by their unhallowed lips, was to us the communion of the blood of Christ.

9. All, therefore, which I can say is this: in any particular case wait upon God by humble and earnest prayer, and then act according to the best light you have. Act according to what you are persuaded upon the whole will be most for your spiritual advantage. Take great care that you do not judge rashly; that you do not lightly think any to be false prophets. And when you have full proof, see that no anger or contempt have any place in your heart. After this, in the presence and in the fear of God, determine for yourself. I can only say, if by experience you find that the hearing them hurts your soul, then hear them not; then quietly refrain, and hear those that profit you. If on the other hand you find it does not hurt your soul, you then may hear them still. Only 'take heed how you hear.' Beware of them and of their doctrine. Hear with fear and trembling, lest *you* should be deceived, and given up like them to a strong delusion. As they continually mingle truth and lies, how easily may you take in both together! Hear with fervent and continual prayer to him who alone teacheth man wisdom. And see that you bring whatever you hear 'to the law and to the testimony'. Receive nothing untried, nothing till it is weighed in 'the balance of the sanctuary'. Believe nothing they say unless it is clearly confirmed by plain passages of Holy Writ. Wholly reject whatsoever differs therefrom, whatever is not confirmed thereby. And in particular reject with the utmost abhorrence whatsoever is described as the way of salvation that is either different from, or short of, the way our Lord has marked out in the foregoing discourse.

10. I cannot conclude without addressing a few plain words to those of whom we have now been speaking. O ye false prophets, O ye dry bones, hear ye for once the word of the Lord. How long will ye lie in the name of God, saying God hath spoken, and God hath not spoken by you? How long will ye pervert the right ways of the Lord, putting darkness for light, and light for darkness? How long will ye teach the way of death, and call it the way of life? How long will ye deliver to Satan the souls whom you profess to bring unto God?

11. 'Woe unto you, ye blind leaders of the blind!' 'For ye shut the kingdom of heaven against men: ye neither go in yourselves, neither suffer ye them that are entering to go in.' Them that would strive to enter in at the strait gate ye call back into the broad way. Them that have scarce gone one step in the ways of God you devilishly caution against 'going too far'. Them that just begin to hunger and thirst after righteousness you warn not to be 'righteous overmuch'. Thus you cause them to stumble at the very threshold; yea, to fall and rise no more. O wherefore do ye this? What profit is there in their blood when they go down to the pit? Miserable profit to *you*. They 'shall perish in their iniquity; but their blood will God require at *your* hands'!

12. Where are your eyes? Where is your understanding? Have ye deceived others till you have deceived yourselves also? Who hath required this at your hands, to *teach* a way which ye never *knew*? Are you 'given up to' so 'strong a delusion' that ye not only teach but 'believe a lie'? And can you possibly believe that God hath sent you? That ye are *his* messengers? Nay, if the Lord had sent you, the 'work of the Lord', would 'prosper in your hands'. As the Lord liveth, if ye were messengers of God he would 'confirm the word of his messengers'. But the work of the Lord doth not prosper in your hand: you bring no sinners to repentance. The Lord doth not confirm your word, for you save no souls from death.

13. How can you possibly evade the force of our Lord's words—so full, so strong, so express? How can ye evade 'knowing yourselves by your fruits'? Evil fruits of evil trees! And how should it be otherwise? 'Do men gather grapes of thorns, or figs of thistles?' Take this to yourselves, ye to whom it belongs. O ye barren trees, why cumber ye the ground? 'Every good tree bringeth forth good fruit.' See ye not that here is no exception? Take knowledge, then, ye are not good trees; for ye do not bring forth good fruit. 'But a corrupt tree bringeth forth evil fruit.' And so have ye done from the beginning. Your speaking as from God has only confirmed them that heard you in the tempers, if not works, of the devil. O take warning of him in whose name ye speak, before the sentence he hath pronounced take place. 'Every tree which bringeth not forth good fruit is hewn down, and cast into the fire.'

14. My dear brethren, harden not your hearts. You have too long shut your eyes against the light. Open them now, before it is too late; before you are cast into outer darkness. Let not any temporal consideration weigh with you; for eternity is at stake. Ye have run before ye were sent. O go no farther. Do not persist to damn yourselves and them that hear you! You have no fruit of your labours. And why is this? Even because the Lord is not with you. But can you go this warfare at your own cost? It cannot be. Then humble yourselves before him. Cry unto him out of the dust, that he may first quicken *thy* soul, give *thee* the faith that worketh by love; that is lowly and meek, pure and merciful, zealous of good works; rejoicing in tribulation, in reproach, in distress, in persecution for righteousness' sake. So shall 'the Spirit of glory and of Christ rest upon thee', and it shall appear that God hath sent thee. So shalt thou indeed 'do the work of an evangelist, and make full proof of thy ministry.' So shall the word of God in thy mouth be 'an hammer that breaketh the rocks in pieces'. It shall then be known by thy fruits that thou art a prophet of the Lord, even by the children whom God hath given thee. And having 'turned many to righteousness, thou shalt shine as the stars for ever and ever'!

38. UPON OUR LORD'S SERMON ON THE MOUNT, DISCOURSE THE THIRTEENTH

1750

An Introductory Comment

Wesley preached on Matthew 7:21 ("Not everyone that saith unto me, Lord, Lord") at Bexley, York, and Pembroke. Of his preaching at St. Saviour-gate Church in York Wesley recorded in his *Journal* on July 20, 1766: "I did not see one person laugh or smile, though we had an elegant congregation" (WH, 22:51). And of the congregation at St. Daniel's in Pembroke Wesley remarked on July 20, 1777: "Many were cut to the heart; and at the Lord's Supper, many were wounded and many healed" (WH, 23:62).

In terms of the larger passage of this sermon (Matt. 7:21-27), Wesley employed verse 24 ("I will liken him unto a wise man, which built his house upon a rock") in the pulpit far more often than verse 21, or any other for that matter in this pericope, with numerous examples in the sermon ledger ranging from Bristol in 1774 to Stratford in 1786 and on to Hinxworth in 1789. Of his pulpit exposition in Bristol, Miss J. C. Marsh remarked in a letter: "[it] was the prettiest and most simple discourse I ever heard on the text" (WH, 22:424 n68).

Wesley developed the distinction of building a house upon a rock (v. 24) as opposed to sand (v. 26) in order to underscore the futility of (1) doing no harm, (2) being zealous of good works, and (3) attending all the ordinances of God (the very substance of the General Rules of the United Societies) if such elements did not result in "the religion of the heart" (O, 1:698). Indeed, on this point Wesley was emphatic: "Let nothing satisfy thee but the power of godliness, but a religion that is spirit and life; the dwelling in God and God in thee; the being an inhabitant of eternity; the entering in by the blood of sprinkling 'within the veil', and 'sitting in heavenly places with Christ Jesus'" (O, 1:697).

Upon our Lord's Sermon on the Mount, Discourse the Thirteenth

I. 1. First, consider the case of the one who builds a house upon sand
   A. Not everyone who calls, 'Lord, Lord!' will enter the kingdom
   B. This implies some try to get to heaven another way than through Christ
   C. This is whom Jesus is addressing
   D. It first implies those who try to reach the kingdom through good words
2.–3. Saying, 'Lord, Lord!' may also imply doing no harm
4.–6. Those who marvel at this are strangers to the religion of Christ

II. 1. Second, consider the wisdom of the one who builds a house upon rock
2. He was sent not to do his will, but the will of the one who sent him
3. He is a wise man, even in God's account; he builds his house upon rock
4. Let no one think he shall not see war anymore
   A. He is not out of the reach of temptation
   B. It still remains for God to prove the grace he has given him
      i. He shall be tried as gold in the fire

III. 1. Diligently examine what foundation you build upon, rock or sand
2. Upon what will you build your salvation?
   A. Upon your innocence? Upon your doing no harm?
   B. In grounding your hope of salvation on this you are building on sand
3. Do you go farther yet? Do you add attending all the ordinances of God?
4. Over and above all this, are you zealous of good works?
5. Faith which does not produce holiness is not Christian
6. Build upon rock. By the grace of God, know yourself
   A. Know and feel that you are shapen in wickedness
7. Weep for your sins; mourn until God turns your heaviness into joy
8. Add to your seriousness, meekness of wisdom
   A. Learn in every state to be content
9. Hunger and thirst not for the meat that perisheth
   A. But for that which endureth unto everlasting life
10. Be merciful as your Father in heaven is merciful
11. Be pure in heart, purified through faith from every unholy affection
12. In a word: let your religion be the religion of the heart

Sermon 33: Upon our Lord's Sermon on the Mount

Discourse the Thirteenth, 1750

Matthew 7:21-27

Not everyone that saith unto me, Lord, Lord, shall enter into the kingdom of heaven; but he that doeth the will of my Father which is in heaven.

Many will say to me in that day, Lord, Lord, have we not prophesied in thy name? And in thy name have cast out devils? And in thy name done many wonderful works?

And then will I profess unto them, I never knew you: depart from me, ye that work iniquity.

Therefore whosoever heareth these sayings of mine, and doeth them, I will liken him unto a wise man, which built his house upon a rock;

And the rain descended, and the floods came, and the winds blew, and beat upon that house; and it fell not; for it was founded upon a rock.

And everyone that heareth these sayings of mine, and doeth them not, shall be likened unto a foolish man, which built his house upon the sand;

And the rain descended, and the floods came, and the winds blew, and beat upon that house; and it fell: and great was the fall of it.

1. Our divine Teacher, having declared the whole counsel of God with regard to the way of salvation, and observed the chief hindrance of those who desire to walk therein, now closes the whole with these weighty words; thereby, as it were, setting his seal to his prophecy, and impressing his whole authority on what he had delivered, that it might stand firm to all generations.

2. For thus saith the Lord, that none may ever conceive there is any other way than this: 'Not everyone that saith unto me, Lord, Lord, shall enter into the kingdom of heaven, but he that doeth the will of my Father which is in heaven. Many will say to me in that day, Lord, Lord, have we not prophesied in thy name? And in thy name have cast out devils? And in thy name done many wonderful works? And then will I profess unto them, I never knew you: depart from me, ye that work iniquity. [. . .] Therefore everyone that heareth these sayings of mine and doeth them not, shall be likened unto a foolish man which built his house upon the sand. And the rain descended, and the floods came, and the winds blew, and beat upon that house; and it fell: and great was the fall of it.'

3. I design in the following discourse, first, to consider the case of him who thus builds his house upon the sand; secondly, to show the wisdom of him who builds upon a rock; and thirdly, to conclude with a practical application.

I.1. And, first, I am to consider the case of him who builds his house upon the sand. It is concerning him our Lord saith, 'Not everyone that saith unto me, Lord, Lord! shall enter into the kingdom of heaven.' And this is a decree which cannot pass; which standeth fast for ever and ever. It therefore imports us in the highest degree throughly to understand the force of these words. Now what are we to understand by that expression, 'that saith unto me, Lord, Lord'? It undoubtedly means, 'that thinks of going to heaven by any other way than that which I have now described'. It therefore implies (to begin at the lowest point) all good words, all verbal religion. It includes whatever creeds we may rehearse; whatever professions of faith we make; whatever number of prayers we may repeat, whatever thanksgivings we read or say to God. We may speak good of his name; and declare his loving-kindness to the children of men. We may be talking of all his mighty acts, and telling of his salvation from day to day. By comparing spiritual things with spiritual, we may show the meaning of the oracles of God. We may explain the mysteries of his kingdom, which have been hid from the beginning of the world. We may speak with the tongue of angels rather than men concerning the deep things of God. We may proclaim to sinners, 'Behold the Lamb of God, who taketh away the sin of the world.' Yea, we may do this with such a measure of the power of God, and such demonstration of his Spirit, as to save many souls from death, and hide a multitude of sins. And yet 'tis very possible all this may be no more than 'saying, Lord, Lord!' After I have thus successfully preached to others, still I myself may be a castaway. I may in the hand of God snatch many souls from hell, and yet drop into it when I have done. I may bring many others to the kingdom of heaven, and yet myself never enter there. Reader, if God hath ever blessed my word to *thy* soul, pray that he may be merciful to *me* a sinner.

2. The 'saying, Lord, Lord!' may, secondly, imply the doing no harm. We may abstain from every presumptuous sin, from every kind of outward wickedness. We may refrain from all those ways of acting or speaking which are forbidden in Holy Writ. We may be able to say to all those among whom we live, Which of you convinceth me of sin? We may have a conscience void of any external offence towards God and towards man. We may be clear of all uncleanness, ungodliness, and unrighteousness as to the outward act, or (as the Apostle testifies concerning himself) 'touching the righteousness of the law', i.e. outward righteousness, 'blameless'; but yet we are not hereby justified. Still this is no more than 'saying, Lord, Lord!' And if we go no farther than this we shall never 'enter into the kingdom of heaven'.

3. The 'saying, Lord, Lord!' may imply, thirdly, many of what are usually styled good works. A man may attend the Supper of the Lord, may hear abundance of excellent sermons, and omit no opportunity of partaking all the other ordinances of God. I may do good to my neighbour, deal my bread to the hungry, and cover the naked with a garment. I may be so zealous of good works as even to 'give all my goods to feed the poor'. Yea, and I may do all this with a desire to please God and a real belief that I do please him thereby (which is undeniably the case of those our Lord introduces, 'saying unto him, Lord, Lord!'); and still I may have no part in the glory which shall be revealed.

4. If any man marvels at this, let him acknowledge he is a stranger to the whole religion of Jesus Christ; and in particular to that perfect portraiture thereof which he has set before us in this discourse. For how far short is all this of that righteousness and true holiness which he has described therein! How widely distant from that inward kingdom of heaven which is now opened in the believing soul! Which is first sown in the heart as a grain of mustard seed, but afterwards putteth forth great branches, on which grow all the fruits of righteousness, every good temper and word and work.

5. Yet as clearly as he had declared this, as frequently as he had repeated that none who have not this kingdom of God within them shall enter into the kingdom of heaven, our Lord well knew that many would not receive this saying, and therefore confirms it yet again. 'Many' (saith he; not one; not a few only; it is not a rare or an uncommon case) 'shall say unto me in that day'. Not only, we have said many prayers; we have spoken thy praise; we have refrained from evil; we have exercised ourselves in doing good; but what is abundantly more than this—'We have prophesied in thy name. In thy name have we cast out devils; in thy name done many wonderful works.' 'We have prophesied': we have declared thy will to mankind; we have showed sinners the way to peace and glory. And we have done this 'in thy name', according to the truth of thy gospel. Yea, and by thy authority, who didst confirm the Word with the Holy Ghost sent down from heaven. For 'in' (or *by*) 'thy name', by the power of thy Word and of thy Spirit, 'have we cast out devils;' out of the souls which they had long claimed as their own, and whereof they had full and quiet possession. 'And in thy name', by thy power, not our own, 'have we done many wonderful works'; insomuch that even 'the dead heard the voice of the Son of God' speaking by us, and lived. 'And then will I profess' even 'unto them, I never knew you:' no, not then, when you were 'casting out devils in my name'. Even then I did not know you as my own; for your heart was not right toward God. Ye were not yourselves meek and lowly; ye were not lovers of God and of all mankind; ye were not renewed in the image of God. Ye were not holy as I am holy. 'Depart from me, ye' who, notwithstanding all this, are 'workers of iniquity' (ἀνομία). Ye are transgressors of my law—my law of holy and perfect love.

6. It is to put this beyond all possibility of contradiction that our Lord confirms it by that apposite comparison. 'Everyone', saith he, 'who heareth these sayings of mine and doeth them not, shall be likened unto a foolish man which built his house upon the sand. And the rain descended, and the floods came, and the winds blew, and beat upon that house:' as they will surely do, sooner or later, upon every soul of man; even the floods of outward affliction, or inward temptation; the storms of pride, anger, fear, or desire. 'And it fell: and great was the fall of it;' so that it perished for ever and ever. Such must be the portion of all who rest in anything short of that religion which is above described. And the *greater* will their fall be because they 'heard those sayings, and yet did them not'.

II.1. I am, secondly, to show the wisdom of him that doth them, that 'buildeth his house upon a rock'. He indeed is wise who 'doeth the will of my Father which is in heaven'. He is truly wise whose 'righteousness exceeds the righteousness of the scribes and Pharisees'. He is poor in spirit; knowing himself even as also he is known. He sees and feels all his sin, and all his guilt, till it is washed away by the atoning blood. He is conscious of his lost estate, of the wrath of God abiding on him, and of his utter inability to help himself till he is filled with peace and joy in the Holy Ghost. He is meek and gentle, patient toward all men, never 'returning evil for evil, or railing for railing, but contrariwise blessing', till he overcomes evil with good. His soul is athirst for nothing on earth, but only for God, the living God. He has bowels of love for all mankind, and is ready to lay down his life for his enemies. He loves the Lord his God with all his heart, and with all his mind and soul and strength. He alone shall enter into the kingdom of heaven who in this spirit doth good unto all men; and who, being for this cause despised and rejected of men, being hated, reproached, and persecuted, 'rejoices and is exceeding glad', knowing in whom he hath believed; and being assured these light, momentary afflictions will 'work out for him an eternal weight of glory'.

2. How truly wise is this man! He knows himself: an everlasting spirit which came forth from God, and was sent down into an house of clay, not to do his own will, but the will of him that sent him. He knows the world: the place in which he is to pass a few days or years, not as an inhabitant, but as a stranger and sojourner in his way to the everlasting habitations; and accordingly he uses the world, as not abusing it, and as knowing the fashion of it passes away. He knows God: his Father and his friend, the parent of all good, the centre of the spirits of all flesh, the sole happiness of all intelligent beings. He sees, clearer than the light of the noonday sun, that this is the end of man: to glorify him who made him for himself, and to love and enjoy him for ever. And with equal clearness he sees the means to that end, to the enjoyment of God in glory; even now to know, to love, to imitate God, and to believe in Jesus Christ whom he hath sent.

3. He is a wise man, even in God's account; for 'he buildeth his house upon a rock;' upon the Rock of Ages, the everlasting Rock, the Lord Jesus Christ. Fitly is he so called; for he changeth not. He is 'the same yesterday, today, and for ever'. To him both the man of God of old, and the Apostle citing his words, bear witness: 'Thou, Lord, in the beginning hast laid the foundation of the earth, and the heavens are the works of thine hands. They shall perish, but thou remainest; they all shall wax old as doth a garment: and as a vesture shalt thou fold them up, and they shall be changed: but thou art the same, and thy years shall not fail' (Heb. 1:10-12). Wise therefore is the man who buildeth on him; who layeth him for his only foundation; who builds only upon his blood and righteousness, upon what he hath done and suffered for us. On this corner-stone he fixes his faith, and rests the whole weight of his soul upon it. He is taught of God to say, Lord I have sinned; I deserve the nethermost hell. But I am 'justified freely by thy grace, through the redemption that is in Jesus Christ'. 'And the life I now live I live by faith in him who loved me and gave himself for me.' 'The life I now live': namely, a divine, heavenly life, a life which is 'hid with Christ in God'. I now live, even in the flesh, a life of love, of pure love both to God and man; a life of holiness and happiness, praising God and doing all things to his glory.

4. Yet let not such an one think that he shall not see war any more, that he is now out of the reach of temptation. It still remains for God to prove the grace he hath given: he shall be tried as gold in the fire. He shall be tempted not less than they who know not God; perhaps abundantly more. For Satan will not fail to try to the uttermost those whom he is not able to destroy. Accordingly 'the rain' will impetuously 'descend'; only at such times and in such a manner as seems good, not to the prince of the power of the air, but to him whose 'kingdom ruleth over all'. 'The floods', or torrents, 'will come;' they will lift up their waves and rage horribly. But to them also the Lord that sitteth above the waterfloods, that remaineth a King for ever, will say, 'Hitherto shall ye come and no farther: here shall your proud waves be stayed.' 'The winds will blow, and beat upon that house,' as though they would tear it up from the foundation. But they cannot prevail: it falleth

not; for it is founded upon a rock. He buildeth on Christ by faith and love; therefore he shall not be cast down. 'He shall not fear, though the earth be moved, and though the hills be carried into the midst of the sea. Though the waters thereof rage and swell, and the mountains shake at the tempest of the same;' still he 'dwelleth under the defence of the Most High, and is safe under the shadow of the Almighty'.

III.1. How nearly then does it concern every child of man practically to apply these things to himself! Diligently to examine on what foundation he builds, whether on a rock or on the sand! How deeply are *you* concerned to inquire, What is the foundation of *my* hope? Whereon do I build my expectation of entering into the kingdom of heaven? Is it not built on the sand? Upon my *orthodoxy* or right opinions (which by a gross abuse of words I have called *faith*); upon my having a set of notions—suppose more rational or scriptural than many others have? Alas! What madness is this? Surely this is building on the sand; or rather, on the froth of the sea! Say I am convinced of this. Am I not again building my hope on what is equally unable to support it? Perhaps on my belonging to 'so excellent a church; reformed after the true Scripture model; blessed with the purest doctrine, the most primitive liturgy, the most apostolical form of government'. These are doubtless so many reasons for praising God, as they may be so many helps to holiness. But they are not holiness itself. And if they are separate from it they will profit me nothing. Nay, they will leave me the more without excuse, and exposed to the greater damnation. Therefore, if I build my hope upon this foundation I am still building upon the sand.

2. You cannot, you dare not, rest here. Upon what next will you build your hope of salvation? Upon your innocence? Upon your doing no harm? Your not wronging or hurting anyone? Well; allow this plea to be true. You are just in all your dealings; you are a downright honest man; you pay every man his own; you neither cheat nor extort; you act fairly with all mankind. And you have a conscience towards God; you do not live in any known sin. Thus far is well. But still it is not the thing. You may go thus far and yet never come to heaven. When all this harmlessness flows from a right principle it is the *least part* of the religion of Christ. But in you it does not flow from a right principle, and therefore is no part at all of religion. So that in grounding your hope of salvation on this you are still building upon the sand.

3. Do you go farther yet? Do you add to the doing no harm the attending all the ordinances of God? Do you at all opportunities partake of the Lord's Supper? Use public and private prayer? Fast often? Hear and search the Scriptures, and meditate thereon? These things likewise ought you to have done, from the time you first set your face towards heaven. Yet these things also are nothing, being alone. They are nothing without the weightier matters of the law. And those you have forgotten. At least you experience them not: faith, mercy, and love of God; holiness of heart; heaven opened in the soul. Still therefore you build upon the sand.

4. Over and above all this, are you zealous of good works? Do you, as you have time, do good to all men? Do you feed the hungry and clothe the naked, and visit the fatherless and widow in their affliction? Do you visit those that are sick? Relieve them that are in

prison? Is any a stranger and you take him in? Friend, come up higher. Do you 'prophesy in the name' of Christ? Do you preach the truth as it is in Jesus? And does the influence of his Spirit attend your word, and make it the power of God unto salvation? Does he enable you to bring sinners from darkness to light, from the power of Satan unto God? Then go and learn what thou hast so often taught, 'By grace ye are saved, through faith.' 'Not by works of righteousness which we have done, but of his own mercy he saveth us.' Learn to hang naked upon the cross of Christ, counting all thou hast done but dung and dross. Apply to him just in the spirit of the dying thief, of the harlot with her seven devils; else thou art still on the sand, and after saving others thou wilt lose thy own soul.

5. Lord! Increase my faith, if I now believe! Else, give me faith, though but as a grain of mustard seed! But 'what doth it profit if a man say he hath faith, and have not works? Can' *that* 'faith save him?' O no! That faith which hath not works, which doth not produce both inward and outward holiness, which does not stamp the whole image of God on the heart, and purify us as he is pure; that faith which does not produce the whole of the religion described in the foregoing chapters, is not the faith of the gospel, not the Christian faith, not the faith which leads to glory. O beware of this, above all other snares of the devil, of resting on unholy, unsaving faith! If thou layest stress on this thou art lost for ever: thou still buildest thy house upon the sand. When 'the rain descends and the floods come it' will surely 'fall; and great' will be 'the fall of it.'

6. Now, therefore, build thou upon a rock. By the grace of God, know thyself. Know and feel that thou wast shapen in wickedness, and in sin did thy mother conceive thee; and that thou thyself hast been heaping sin upon sin ever since thou couldst discern good from evil. Own thyself guilty of eternal death; and renounce all hope of ever being able to save thyself. Be it all thy hope to be washed in his blood and purified by his Spirit 'who himself bore all thy sins in his own body upon the tree'. And if thou knowest he hath taken away thy sins, so much the more abase thyself before him in a continued sense of thy total dependence on him for every good thought and word and work, and of thy utter inability to all good unless he 'water thee every moment'.

7. Now weep for your sins, and mourn after God till he turns your heaviness into joy. And even then weep with them that weep; and for them that weep not for themselves. Mourn for the sins and miseries of mankind. And see, but just before your eyes, the immense ocean of eternity, without a bottom or a shore; which has already swallowed up millions of millions of men, and is gaping to devour them that yet remain. See here the house of God, eternal in the heavens; there, hell and destruction without a covering. And thence learn the importance of every moment, which just appears, and is gone for ever!

8. Now add to your seriousness, meekness of wisdom. Hold an even scale as to all your passions, but in particular as to anger, sorrow, and fear. Calmly acquiesce in whatsoever is the will of God. Learn in every state wherein you are, therewith to be content. Be mild to the good; be gentle toward all men, but especially toward the evil and the unthankful. Beware not only of outward expressions of anger, such as calling thy brother 'Raca', or 'Thou fool' but of every inward emotion contrary to love, though it go no farther than the heart. Be angry at sin, as an affront offered to the majesty of heaven; but love the sinner still, like our Lord who 'looked round about upon' the Pharisees 'with anger,

being grieved for the hardness of their hearts'. He was grieved at the sinners, angry at the sin. Thus 'be thou angry and sin not.'

9. Now do thou hunger and thirst, not for 'the meat that perisheth, but for that which endureth unto everlasting life'. Trample under foot the world and the things of the world—all these riches, honours, pleasures. What is the world to thee? Let the dead bury their dead: but follow thou after the image of God. And beware of quenching that blessed thirst, if it is already excited in thy soul, by what is vulgarly called religion—a poor, dull farce, a religion of form, of outside show—which leaves the heart still cleaving to the dust, as earthly and sensual as ever. Let nothing satisfy thee but the power of godliness, but a religion that is spirit and life; the dwelling in God and God in thee; the being an inhabitant of eternity; the entering in by the blood of sprinkling 'within the veil', and 'sitting in heavenly places with Christ Jesus'.

10. Now, seeing thou canst do all things through Christ strengthening thee, be merciful as thy Father in heaven is merciful. Love thy neighbour as thyself. Love friends and enemies as thy own soul. And let thy love be *long-suffering*, and patient towards all men. Let it be *kind*, soft, benign: inspiring thee with the most amiable sweetness, and the most fervent and tender affection. Let it 'rejoice in the truth', wheresoever it is found, the truth that is after godliness. Enjoy whatsoever brings glory to God, and promotes peace and goodwill among men. In love 'cover all things', of the dead and the absent speaking nothing but good; 'believe all things' which may any way tend to clear your neighbour's character; 'hope all things' in his favour; and 'endure all things', triumphing over all opposition. For true 'love never faileth', in time or in eternity.

11. Now be thou 'pure in heart'; purified through faith from every unholy affection, 'cleansing thyself from all filthiness of flesh and spirit, and perfecting holiness in the fear of God'. Being through the power of his grace purified from pride by deep poverty of spirit; from anger, from every unkind or turbulent passion by meekness and mercifulness; from every desire but to please and enjoy God by hunger and thirst after righteousness; now love the Lord thy God with all thy heart and with all thy strength.

12. In a word: let thy religion be the religion of the heart. Let it lie deep in thy inmost soul. Be thou little and base, and mean and vile (beyond what words can express) in thy own eyes; amazed and humbled to the dust by the love of God which is in Christ Jesus. Be serious. Let the whole stream of thy thoughts, words, and actions flow from the deepest conviction that thou standest on the edge of the great gulf, thou and all the children of men, just ready to drop in, either into everlasting glory or everlasting burnings. Let thy soul be filled with mildness, gentleness, patience, long-suffering towards all men, at the same time that all which is in thee is athirst for God, the living God; longing to awake up after his likeness, and to be satisfied with it. Be thou a lover of God and of all mankind. In this spirit do and suffer all things. Thus show thy faith by thy works: thus 'do the will of thy Father which is in heaven.' And as sure as thou now walkest with God on earth, thou shalt also reign with him in glory.

39. A CAUTION AGAINST BIGOTRY

1750

An Introductory Comment

Wesley's doctrine of prevenient grace allowed him to acknowledge what good was accomplished by the Spirit of God even outside the church. In terms of casting out devils, which is the spiritual gift celebrated in the text of this sermon (Mark 9:38-39), Wesley rightly noted that Jesus taught that such a practice ought not to be forbidden. In a real sense, the exercise of this particular gift is the work of God, "But he is generally pleased to do this by man" (O, 2:68). Eighteenth-century England, caught up in the Enlightenment, balked at the reality of evil spirit, the demonic, and considered it to be a species of superstition. Wesley's letter to Conyers Middleton on January 4, 1749, however, affirmed that the spiritual gift of casting out devils was a part of the apostolic church and was clearly expressed in the writings of both Justin Martyr and Theophilus of Antioch (T, 2:332).

Defining *bigotry* as a strong attachment to "our own party, opinion, church, and religion" (O, 2:62), Wesley developed the argument of this sermon specifically in terms of the relation of the infrastructure of Methodism, lay preaching in particular, to the polity of the broader Anglican church. "But what if he be only a *layman* who casts out devils? Ought I not to forbid him then?" Wesley asked. To which he replied, "forbid him not" (O, 2:73). Wesley substantiated this judgment, and therefore his own practice, by noting not only can no person do these works "unless God is with him" (O, 2:73) but also that an outward call (by bishops, for example) is not absolutely required for such ministry. That is, the inward, divine call that results in a *charism* or gift may itself be sufficient. Indeed, Wesley contended that this approach to ministry had been the practice of the apostolic age (O, 2:74). No record exists that Wesley ever preached this sermon (WWS).

A Caution against Bigotry

I. 1. I will first show in what sense we may and may not cast out devils

2.–3. The devil dwells in the wicked and rules the darkness of the world

4. There are countries where the devil works openly

5. He reigns as absolute in one land as in the other

6. He works with energy in them; he binds their understanding

7.–8. In Rome there were gluttony and lewdness, injustice and crime

9.–11. As gross and palpable are the works of the devil today

12. He works less openly in liars, slanderers, in oppressors and extortioners

13. It is in this sense that we cast out devils

14. God alone can cast out Satan, but God does this through people

II. 1. I will now consider the meaning of 'he followeth not us'

2. One meaning of this expression may be, 'He is *not of our party*'

3. It may also mean, 'He differs from us in our *religious opinions*'

4. He may differ from us not only in opinion, but also in practice

5.–6. He may be of a church that we regard as antiscriptual and antichristian

7. I do not think that the person of whom the Apostle speaks went this far

III. 1. Of the one who is not of our party Jesus said, 'Forbid him not'

2. Some are unwilling to see any good in those who disagree with them

3.–4. If someone was a sinner quit sinning, then forbid him not

5. If he is only a *layman*, do not forbid him, so long as there is proof

6.'If this man were not of God, he could do nothing

7. A preacher should have an outward as well as an inward call

8. In Acts, a multitude of lay preachers were only sent of God

9. Paul *proved* a man before he was ordained, trying whether he had gifts

10. I do not forbid someone from casting out devils if she has gifts

11.–12. Whosoever fears God, forbid him not, directly or indirectly

IV. 1. If we willingly fail in any of these points, then we are bigots

2. Take care that you do not convict yourself of bigotry

3. I cannot be sorry that God blesses some who hold erroneous opinions

4. Search me, O Lord, and prove me

5.–6. Do not return evil for evil, but labor to love he who is a bigot

Sermon 38: A Caution against Bigotry, 1750

Mark 9:38-39

And John answered him, saying, Master, we saw one casting out devils in thy name, and we forbade him, because he followeth not us.

And Jesus said, Forbid him not.

1. In the preceding verses we read that after the twelve had been disputing 'which of them should be the greatest', Jesus 'took a little child, and set him in the midst of them, and taking him in his arms said unto them, Whosoever shall receive one of these little children in my name receiveth me; and whosoever receiveth me receiveth not me (only), but him that sent me.' Then 'John answered' (that is, said with reference to what our Lord had spoken just before), 'Master, we saw one casting out devils in thy name, and we forbade him, because he followeth not us.' As if he had said: 'Ought we to have received him? In receiving him, should we have received thee? Ought we not rather to have forbidden him? Did not we do well therein?' 'But Jesus said, Forbid him not.'

2. The same passage is recited by St. Luke, and almost in the same words. But it may be asked: 'What is this to us? Seeing no man now "casts out devils". Has not the power of doing this been withdrawn from the church for twelve or fourteen hundred years? How then are *we* concerned in the case here proposed, or in our Lord's decision of it?'

3. Perhaps more nearly than is commonly imagined, the case proposed being no uncommon case. That we may reap our full advantage from it I design to show, first, in what sense men may, and do now, 'cast out devils'; secondly, what we may understand by, 'He followeth not us.' I shall, thirdly, explain our Lord's direction, 'Forbid him not,' and conclude with an inference from the whole.

I.1. I am, in the first place, to show in what sense men may, and do now, 'cast out devils'.

In order to have the clearest view of this we should remember that (according to the scriptural account) as God dwells and works in the children of light, so the devil dwells and works in the children of darkness. As the Holy Spirit possesses the souls of good men, so the evil spirit possesses the souls of the wicked. Hence it is that the Apostle terms him 'the god of this world'—from the uncontrolled power he has over worldly men. Hence our blessed Lord styles him 'the prince of this world'—so absolute is his dominion over it. And hence St. John, 'We know that we are of God,' and all who are not of God, 'the whole world', ἐν τῷ πονηρῷ κεῖται—not, lieth in wickedness, but 'lieth in the wicked one'—lives and moves in him, as they who are not of the world do in God.

2. For the devil is not to be considered only as 'a roaring lion, going about seeking whom he may devour'; nor barely as a subtle enemy who cometh unawares upon poor souls and 'leads them captive at his will'; but as he who dwelleth in them and walketh in them; who 'ruleth the darkness' or wickedness 'of this world', of worldly men and all

their dark designs and actions, by keeping possession of their hearts, setting up his throne there, and bringing every thought into obedience to himself. Thus the 'strong one armed keepeth his house'; and if this 'unclean spirit' sometime 'go out of a man', yet he often returns with 'seven spirits worse than himself; and they enter in and dwell there.' Nor can he be idle in his dwelling. He is continually 'working in' these 'children of disobedience'. He works in them with power, with mighty energy, transforming them into his own likeness, effacing all the remains of the image of God, and preparing them for every evil word and work.

3. It is therefore an unquestionable truth that the god and prince of this world still possesses all who know not God. Only the manner wherein he possesses them now differs from that wherein he did it of old time. Then he frequently tormented their bodies as well as souls, and that openly, without any disguise; now he torments their souls only (unless in some rare cases) and that as covertly as possible. The reason of this difference is plain. It was then his aim to drive mankind into superstition. Therefore he wrought as openly as he could. But 'tis his aim to drive *us* into infidelity. Therefore he works as privately as he can; for the more secret he is, the more he prevails.

4. Yet if we may credit historians there are countries even now where he works as openly as aforetime. 'But why in savage and barbarous countries only? Why not in Italy, France, or England?' For a very plain reason: he knows his men. And he knows what he hath to do with each. To Laplanders he appears barefaced; because he is to fix them in superstition and gross idolatry. But with you he is pursuing a different point. He is to make you idolize yourselves, to make you wiser in your own eyes than God himself, than all the oracles of God. Now in order to this he must not appear in his own shape. That would frustrate his design. No; he uses all his art to make you deny his being, till he has you safe in his own place.

5. He reigns, therefore, although in a different way, yet as absolute in one land as in the other. He has the gay Italian infidel in his teeth as sure as the wild Tartar. But he is fast asleep in the mouth of the lion, who is too wise to wake him out of sleep. So he only plays with him for the present, and when he pleases swallows him up.

The god of this world holds his English worshippers full as fast as those in Lapland. But it is not his business to affright them, lest they should fly to the God of heaven. The prince of darkness therefore does not appear while he rules over these his willing subjects. The conqueror holds his captives so much the safer because they imagine themselves at liberty. Thus the 'strong one armed keepeth his house, and his goods are in peace': neither the deist nor nominal Christian suspects he is there; so he and they are perfectly at peace with each other.

6. All this while he works with energy in them. He blinds the eyes of their understanding so that the light of the glorious gospel of Christ cannot shine upon them. He chains their souls down to earth and hell with the chains of their own vile affections. He binds them down to the earth by love of the world, love of money, of pleasure, of praise. And by pride, envy, anger, hate, revenge, he causes their souls to draw nigh unto hell; acting the more secure and uncontrolled because they know not that he acts at all.

7. But how easily may we know the cause from its effects! These are sometimes gross and palpable. So they were in the most refined of the heathen nations. Go no farther than the admired, the virtuous Romans. And you will find these, when at the height of their learning and glory, 'filled with all unrighteousness, fornication, wickedness, covetousness, maliciousness; full of envy, murder, debate, deceit, malignity; whisperers, backbiters, despiteful, proud, boasters, disobedient to parents, covenant-breakers, without natural affection, implacable, unmerciful'.

8. The strongest parts of this description are confirmed by one whom some may think a more unexceptionable witness. I mean their brother heathen, Dion Cassius, who observes that before Caesar's return from Gaul not only gluttony and lewdness of every kind were open and barefaced; not only falsehood, injustice, and unmercifulness abounded in public courts as well as private families; but the most outrageous robberies, rapine, and murders were so frequent in all parts of Rome that few men went out of doors without making their wills, as not knowing if they should return alive.

9. As gross and palpable are the works of the devil among many (if not all) the modern heathens. The *natural religion* of the Creeks, Cherokees, Chicasaws, and all other Indians bordering on our southern settlements (not of a few single men, but of entire nations) is to torture all their prisoners from morning to night, till at length they roast them to death; and upon the slightest undesigned provocation to come behind and shoot any of their own countrymen. Yea, it is a common thing among them for the son, if he thinks his father lives too long, to knock out his brains; and for a mother, if she is tired of her children, to fasten stones about their necks, and throw three or four of them into the river one after another.

10. It were to be wished that none but heathens had practised such gross, palpable works of the devil. But we dare not say so. Even in cruelty and bloodshed, how little have the Christians come behind them! And not the Spaniards or Portuguese alone, butchering thousands in South America. Not the Dutch only in the East Indies, or the French in North America, following the Spaniards step by step. Our own countrymen, too, have wantoned in blood, and exterminated whole nations: plainly proving thereby what spirit it is that dwells and works in the children of disobedience.

11. These monsters might almost make us overlook the works of the devil that are wrought in our own country. But, alas! We cannot open our eyes even here without seeing them on every side. Is it a small proof of his power that common swearers, drunkards, whoremongers, adulterers, thieves, robbers, sodomites, murderers, are still found in every part of our land? How triumphant does the prince of this world reign in all these children of disobedience!

12. He less openly but no less effectually works in dissemblers, talebearers, liars, slanderers; in oppressors and extortioners; in the perjured, the seller of his friend, his honour, his conscience, his country. And yet these may talk of religion or conscience still! Of honour, virtue, and public spirit. But they can no more deceive Satan than they can God. He likewise knows those that are his: and a great multitude they are, out of every nation and people, of whom he has full possession at this day.

13. If you consider this you cannot but see in what sense men may now also 'cast out devils'; yea, and every minister of Christ does cast them out, if his Lord's work prosper in his hand.

By the power of God attending his Word he brings these sinners to repentance: an entire inward as well as outward change, from all evil to all good. And this is in a sound sense to 'cast out devils', out of the souls wherein they had hitherto dwelt. The strong one can no longer keep his house. A stronger than he is come upon him, and hath cast him out, and taken possession for himself, and made it an habitation of God through his Spirit. Here then the energy of Satan ends, and the Son of God 'destroys the works of the devil'. The understanding of the sinner is now enlightened, and his heart sweetly drawn to God. His desires are refined, his affections purified; and being filled with the Holy Ghost he grows in grace till he is not only holy in heart, but in all manner of conversation.

14. All this is indeed the work of God. It is God alone who can cast out Satan. But he is generally pleased to do this by man, as an instrument in his hand, who is then said to 'cast out devils in his name'—by his power and authority. And he sends whom he will send upon this great work; but usually such as man would never have thought of. For 'his ways are not as our ways, neither his thoughts as our thoughts.' Accordingly he chooses the weak to confound the mighty; the foolish to confound the wise: for this plain reason, that he may secure the glory to himself, that 'no flesh may glory in his sight'.

II.1. But shall we not *forbid* one who thus 'casteth out devils', if 'he followeth not us'? This it seems was both the judgment and practice of the Apostle, till he referred the case to his Master. 'We forbade him', saith he, 'because he followeth not us,' which he supposed to be a very sufficient reason. What we may understand by this expression, 'He followeth not us,' is the next point to be considered.

The lowest circumstance we can understand thereby is, 'He has no outward connection with us. We do not labour in conjunction with each other. He is not our fellow-helper in the gospel.' And indeed whensoever our Lord is pleased to send many labourers into his harvest, they cannot all act in subordination to, or connection with, each other. Nay, they cannot all have personal acquaintance with, nor be so much as known to, one another. Many there will necessarily be in different parts of the harvest, so far from having any mutual intercourse that they will be as absolute strangers to each other, as if they had lived in different ages. And concerning any of these whom we know not we may doubtless say, 'He followeth not us.'

2. A second meaning of this expression may be, 'He is *not of our party.*' It has long been matter of melancholy consideration to all who pray for the peace of Jerusalem that so many several parties are still subsisting among those who are all styled Christians. This has been particularly observable in our own countrymen, who have been continually dividing from each other upon points of no moment, and many times such as religion had no concern in. The most trifling circumstances have given rise to different parties, which have continued for many generations. And each of these would be ready to object to one who was on the other side, 'He followeth not us.'

3. That expression may mean, thirdly, 'He differs from us in our *religious opinions.*' There was a time when all Christians were of one mind, as well as of one heart. So great grace was upon them all when they were first filled with the Holy Ghost. But how short a space did this blessing continue! How soon was that unanimity lost, and difference of opinion sprang up again, even in the church of Christ! And that not in nominal but in real Christians; nay, in the very chief of them, the apostles themselves! Nor does it appear that the difference which then began was ever entirely removed. We do not find that even those pillars in the temple of God, so long as they remained upon earth, were ever brought to think alike, to be of one mind, particularly with regard to the ceremonial law. 'Tis therefore no way surprising that infinite varieties of opinion should now be found in the Christian church. A very probable consequence of this is that whenever we see any 'casting out devils' he will be one that in this sense 'followeth not us'—that is not of our opinion. 'Tis scarce to be imagined he will be of our mind in all points, even of religion. He may very probably think in a different manner from us even on several subjects of importance, such as the nature and use of the moral law, the eternal decrees of God, the sufficiency and efficacy of his grace, and the perseverance of his children.

4. He may differ from us, fourthly, not only in opinion, but likewise in some points of practice. He may not approve of that manner of worshipping God which is practised in our congregation, and may judge that to be more profitable for his soul which took its rise from Calvin, or Martin Luther. He may have many objections to that liturgy which we approve of beyond all others, many doubts concerning that form of church government which we esteem both apostolical and scriptural. Perhaps he may go farther from us yet: he may, from a principle of conscience, refrain from several of those which we believe to be the ordinances of Christ. Or if we both agree that they are ordained of God, there may still remain a difference between us either as to the manner of administering those ordinances or the persons to whom they should be administered. Now the unavoidable consequence of any of these differences will be that he who thus differs from us must separate himself with regard to those points from our society. In this respect therefore 'he followeth not us'; he is 'not (as we phrase it) of our church'.

5. But in a far stronger sense 'he followeth not us' who is not only of a different church, but of such a church as we account to be in many respects antiscriptural and antichristian: a church which we believe to be utterly false and erroneous in her doctrines, as well as very dangerously wrong in her practice, guilty of gross superstition as well as idolatry; a church that has added many articles to the faith which was once delivered to the saints; that has dropped one whole commandment of God, and made void several of the rest by her traditions; and that pretending the highest veneration for, and strictest conformity to, the ancient church, has nevertheless brought in numberless innovations without any warrant either from antiquity or Scripture. Now most certainly 'he followeth not us' who stands at so great a distance from us.

6. And yet there may be a still wider difference than this. He who differs from us in judgment or practice may possibly stand at a greater distance from us in affection than in judgment. And this indeed is a very natural and a very common effect of the other. The differences which begin in points of opinion seldom terminate there. They generally

spread into the affections, and then separate chief friends. Nor are any animosities so deep and irreconcilable as those that spring from disagreement in religion. For this cause the bitterest enemies of a man are those of his own household. For this the father rises against his own children, and the children against the father; and perhaps persecute each other even to the death, thinking all the time they are doing God service. It is therefore nothing more than we may expect if those who differ from us either in religious opinions or practice soon contract a sharpness, yea, bitterness toward us; if they are more and more prejudiced against us, till they conceive as ill an opinion of our persons as of our principles. An almost necessary consequence of this will be, they will speak in the same manner as they think of us. They will set themselves in opposition to us, and, as far as they are able hinder our work, seeing it does not appear to them to be the work of God, but either of man or of the devil. He that thinks, speaks, and acts in such a manner as this, in the highest sense 'followeth not us'.

7. I do not indeed conceive that the person of whom the Apostle speaks in the text (although we have no particular account of him either in the context or in any other part of Holy Writ) went so far as this. We have no ground to suppose that there was any material difference between him and the apostles; much less that he had any prejudice either against them or their Master. It seems we may gather thus much from our Lord's own words which immediately follow the text, 'There is no man which shall do a miracle in my name that can lightly speak evil of me.' But I purposely put the case in the strongest light, adding all the circumstances which can well be conceived; that being forewarned of the temptation in its full strength we may in no case yield to it and fight against God.

III.1. Suppose then a man have no intercourse with us, suppose he be not of our party, suppose he separate from our Church, yea, and widely differ from us both in judgment, practice, and affection; yet if we see even this man 'casting out devils' Jesus saith, 'Forbid him not.' This important direction of our Lord, I am, in the third place, to explain.

2. If we see this man casting out devils—but 'tis well if in such a case we would believe even what we saw with our eyes, if we did not give the lie to our own senses. He must be little acquainted with human nature who does not immediately perceive how extremely unready we should be to believe that any man does cast out devils who 'followeth not us' in all or most of the senses above recited. I had almost said, in any of them; seeing we may easily learn even from what passes in our own breasts how unwilling men are to allow anything good in those who do not in all things agree with themselves.

3. 'But what is a sufficient, reasonable proof that a man does (in the sense above) cast out devils?' The answer is easy. Is there full proof, first, that a person before us was a gross, open sinner? Secondly, that he is not so now; that he has broke off his sins, and lives a Christian life? And thirdly, that his change was wrought by his hearing this man preach? If these three points be plain and undeniable, then you have sufficient, reasonable proof, such as you cannot resist without wilful sin, that this man casts out devils.

4. Then 'forbid him not.' Beware how you attempt to hinder him, either by your authority or arguments or persuasions. Do not in any wise strive to prevent his using all the

power which God has given him. If you have *authority* with him, do not use that authority to stop the work of God. Do not furnish him with *reasons* why he ought not any more to speak in the name of Jesus. Satan will not fail to supply him with these if you do not second him therein. *Persuade* him not to depart from the work. If he should give place to the devil and you, many souls might perish in their iniquity, but their blood would God require at *your* hands.

5. 'But what if he be only a *layman* who casts out devils? Ought I not to forbid him then?'

Is the fact allowed? Is there reasonable proof that this man has or does 'cast out devils'? If there is, forbid him not; no, not at the peril of your soul. Shall not God work by whom he will work? 'No man can do these works unless God is with him'—unless God hath sent him for this very thing. But if God hath sent him, will you call him back? Will you forbid him to go?

6. 'But I do not know that he is sent of God.' 'Now herein is a marvellous thing' (may any of the seals of his mission say, any whom he hath brought from Satan to God) 'that ye know not whence this man is, and behold he hath opened mine eyes! If this man were not of God, he could do nothing.' If you doubt the fact, send for the parents of the man; send for his brethren, friends, acquaintance. But if you cannot doubt this, if you must needs acknowledge that 'a notable miracle hath been wrought', then with what conscience, with what face can you charge him whom God hath sent 'not to speak any more in his name'?

7. I allow that it is *highly expedient*, whoever preaches in his name should have an outward as well as an inward call; but that it is *absolutely necessary* I deny.

'Nay, is not the Scripture express? "No man taketh this honour unto himself, but he that is called of God, as was Aaron"' (Heb. 5:4).

Numberless times has this text been quoted on the occasion, as containing the very strength of the cause. But surely never was so unhappy a quotation. For, first, Aaron was not called to preach at all. He was called to 'offer gifts and sacrifice for sin'. That was his peculiar employment. Secondly, these men do not offer sacrifice at all, but only preach, which Aaron did not. Therefore it is not possible to find one text in all the Bible which is more wide of the point than this.

8. 'But what was the practice of the apostolic age?' You may easily see in the Acts of the Apostles. In the eighth chapter we read: 'There was a great persecution against the church which was at Jerusalem; and they were all scattered abroad throughout the regions of Judea and Samaria, except the apostles' (Acts 8:1). 'Therefore they that were scattered abroad went everywhere preaching the word' (Acts 8:4). Now, were all these outwardly called to preach? No man in his senses can think so. Here then is an undeniable proof what was the practice of the apostolic age. Here you see not one but a multitude of 'lay preachers', men that were only sent of God.

9. Indeed so far is the practice of the apostolic age from inclining us to think it was *unlawful* for a man to preach before he was ordained, that we have reason to think it was

then accounted *necessary*. Certainly the practice and the direction of the Apostle Paul was to *prove* a man before he was ordained at all. 'Let these' (the deacons), says he, 'first be proved; then let them use the office of a deacon' (1 Tim. 3:10). Proved? How? By setting them to construe a sentence of Greek? And asking them a few commonplace questions? O amazing proof of a minister of Christ! Nay; but by making a clear, open trial (as is still done by most of the Protestant Churches in Europe) not only whether their lives be holy and unblameable, but whether they have such gifts as are absolutely and indispensably necessary in order to edify the church of Christ.

10. 'But what if a man has these? And has brought sinners to repentance? And yet the bishop will not ordain him?' Then the bishop does 'forbid him to cast out devils'. But I dare not forbid him. I have published my reasons to all the world. Yet 'tis still insisted I ought to do it. You who insist upon it, answer those reasons. I know not that any have done this yet, or even made a feint of doing it. Only some have spoken of them as very weak and trifling. And this was prudent enough. For 'tis far easier to despise—at least, seem to despise—an argument than to answer it. Yet till this is done I must say, when I have reasonable proof that any man does cast out devils, whatever others do I dare not forbid him, lest I be found even to fight against God.

11. And whosoever thou art that fearest God, 'forbid him not,' either directly or indirectly. There are many ways of doing this. You indirectly forbid him if you either wholly deny, or despise and make little account of the work which God has wrought by his hands. You indirectly forbid him when you discourage him in his work by drawing him into disputes concerning it, by raising objections against it, or frighting him with consequences which very possibly will never be. You forbid him when you show any unkindness toward him either in language or behaviour; and much more when you speak of him to others either in an unkind or a contemptuous manner, when you endeavour to represent him to any either in an odious or a despicable light. You are forbidding him all the time you are speaking evil of him or making no account of his labours. O forbid him not in any of these ways; nor by forbidding others to hear him, by discouraging sinners from hearing that word which is able to save their souls.

12. Yea, if you would observe our Lord's direction in its full meaning and extent, then remember his word, 'He that is not for us is against us, and he that gathereth not with me, scattereth.' He that gathereth not men into the kingdom of God assuredly scatters them from it. For there can be no neuter in this war: everyone is either on God's side or on Satan's. Are you on God's side? Then you will not only not forbid any man that 'casts out devils', but you will labour to the uttermost of your power to forward him in the work. You will readily acknowledge the work of God, and confess the greatness of it. You will remove all difficulties and objections, as far as may be, out of his way. You will strengthen his hands by speaking honourably of him before all men, and avowing the things which you have seen and heard. You will encourage others to attend upon his word, to hear him whom God hath sent. And you will omit no actual proof of tender love which God gives you an opportunity of showing him.

IV.1. If we willingly fail in any of these points, if we either directly or indirectly forbid him 'because he followeth not us', then we are 'bigots'. This is the inference I draw from what has been said. But the term 'bigotry', I fear, as frequently as it is used, is almost as little understood as 'enthusiasm'. It is too strong an attachment to, or fondness for, our own party, opinion, Church, and religion. Therefore he is a bigot who is so fond of any of these, so strongly attached to them, as to forbid any who casts out devils, because he differs from himself in any or all these particulars.

2. Do *you* beware of this. Take care, first, that you do not convict yourself of bigotry by your unreadiness to believe that any man does cast out devils who differs from you. And if you are clear thus far, if you acknowledge the fact, then examine yourself, secondly: 'Am I not convicted of bigotry in this, in forbidding him directly or indirectly? Do I not directly forbid him on this ground, because he is not of my *party*? Because he does not fall in with my *opinions*? Or because he does not worship God according to that scheme of religion which I have received from my fathers?'

3. Examine yourself: 'Do I not indirectly, at least, forbid him on any of these grounds? Am I not sorry that God should thus own and bless a man that holds such erroneous opinions? Do I not discourage him because he is not of my Church? By disputing with him concerning it, by raising objections, and by perplexing his mind with distant consequences? Do I show no anger, contempt, or unkindness of any sort, either in my words or actions? Do I not mention behind his back his (real or supposed) faults? His defects or infirmities? Do not I hinder sinners from hearing his word?' If you do any of these things you are a bigot to this day.

4. 'Search me, O Lord, and prove me. Try out my reins and my heart.' 'Look well if there be any way of *bigotry* in me, and lead me in the way everlasting.' In order to examine ourselves throughly let the case be proposed in the strongest manner. What if I were to see a Papist, an Arian, a Socinian casting out devils? If I did, I could not forbid even him without convicting myself of bigotry. Yea, if it could be supposed that I should see a Jew, a deist, or a Turk doing the same, were I to forbid him either directly or indirectly I should be no better than a bigot still.

5. O stand clear of this. But be not content with not forbidding any that casts out devils. 'Tis well to go thus far; but do not stop here. If you will avoid all bigotry, go on. In every instance of this kind, whatever the instrument be, acknowledge the finger of God. And not only acknowledge but rejoice in his work, and praise his name with thanksgiving. Encourage whomsoever God is pleased to employ, to give himself wholly up thereto. Speak well of him wheresoever you are; defend his character and his mission. Enlarge as far as you can his sphere of action. Show him all kindness in word and deed. And cease not to cry to God in his behalf, that he may save both himself and them that hear him.

6. I need add but one caution. Think not the bigotry of another is any excuse for your own. 'Tis not impossible that one who casts out devils himself may yet forbid you so to do. You may observe this is the very case mentioned in the text. The apostles forbade another to do what they did themselves. But beware of retorting. It is not your part to return evil for evil. Another's not observing the direction of our Lord is no reason why

you should neglect it. Nay, but let him have all the bigotry to himself. If he forbids *you*, do not you forbid *him*. Rather labour and watch and pray the more, to confirm your love toward him. If he speaks all manner of evil of *you*, speak all manner of good (that is true) of *him*. Imitate herein that glorious saying of a great man (O that he had always breathed the same spirit!) 'Let Luther call me an hundred devils; I will still reverence him as a messenger of God.'

40. CATHOLIC SPIRIT

1750

An Introductory Comment

Wesley produced this sermon in 1750 and sent a copy of it to Rev. Mr. Clark of Hollymount, who claimed that the content of this work actually had little to do with the text, 2 Kings 10:15 (S, 2:127). At any rate, Wesley published this sermon separately in 1755 and again in 1770 since in many ways it epitomized his basic theological posture that highlighted the essentials of the Christian faith (O, 2:79–80), though there is no record of this text in the sermon register (WWS).

Considering the two grand hindrances that stand in the way of those who genuinely love God, namely, that they can't all think or walk alike, Wesley proposed that fellowship should remain, even thrive, since all may love alike. In other words, here as in his sermon "On Zeal," Wesley focused on the holy love that is at the heart of it all as the goal, the telos, of all true religion. Put another way, right tempers or dispositions of the heart are crucial to real, proper, scriptural Christianity. With this reality in place, brought about by the ministrations of the Holy Spirit, Wesley was willing to extend the hand of Christian fellowship though differences remain in terms of such things as opinions, polity, modes of worship, the sacraments, and extemporaneous prayer (O, 2:90). Such generosity of spirit, however, does not represent speculative latitudinarianism (indifference to all opinions), practical latitudinarianism (indifference to modes of worship), or indifference to all congregations, that is, that one ought not to be well grounded in a particular theological tradition (O, 2:92–94).

Rejecting the principle of *cuius regio, eius religio* (loosely translated, "the place of our birth fixes the church"; O, 2:86), Wesley made generous allowances for the roles of conscience and the right of private judgment, "on which [the] whole Reformation stands" (O, 2:86).

Catholic Spirit

I. 1–2. First, let us consider the question proposed by Jehu to Jehonadab

A. Is thine heart right, as my heart is with thy heart?

3. All people will not see all things alike

4.–5. None can be assured that all their opinions are true

6. A wise person will allow others the same liberty of thinking she desires

7.–8. Among those with upright hearts, there will be various ways of worshipping

9. But how shall we choose?

10.–11. But I dare not presume to impose my mode of worship on another

A. My only question: Is thine heart right?

12. But what is properly implied in the question?

A. The first thing implied is this: Is your heart right with God?

13. Have you submitted yourself to the righteousness of God?

14. Is your faith filled with the energy of love? Do you love God?

15. Are you doing the will of the one who sent you?

16. Does the love of God constrain you to serve God with fear?

17. Is your heart right toward your neighbour?

18. Do you show your love by your works? Do you do good to all men?

II. 1.–2. If it be, give me thine hand. I do not mean, 'Be of my opinion'

3. I mean, first, love me. Love me as a friend that is closer than a brother

4. Love me with the love that is long-suffering and kind

5. I mean, secondly, commend me to God in all your prayers

6. I mean, thirdly, provoke me to love and to good works

7.–8. I mean, lastly, love me not in word only, but in deed and in truth

III. 1. We may learn from this what is a catholic spirit

A. First, we may learn that it is not *speculative latitudinarianism*

B. It is not indifference to all opinions. This is the spawn of hell

2. We may learn, secondly, that it is not any kind of *practical latitudinarianism*

A. It is not indifference as to public worship or the manner of performance

3. Thirdly, we may learn that it is not indifference to congregations

4. While we are fixed in religious principles, our hearts are enlarged to all

5.–6. The one of catholic spirit gives his hand to all whose hearts are right

Sermon 39: Catholic Spirit, 1750

2 Kings 10:15

And when he was departed thence, he lighted on Jehonadab the son of Rechab coming to meet him. And he saluted him and said, Is thine heart right, as my heart is with thy heart? And Jehonadab answered, It is. If it be, give me thine hand.

1. It is allowed even by those who do not pay this great debt that love is due to all mankind, the royal law, 'Thou shalt love thy neighbour as thyself,' carrying its own evidence to all that hear it. And that, not according to the miserable construction put upon it by the zealots of old times, 'Thou shalt love thy neighbour', thy relation, acquaintance, friend, 'and hate thine enemy.' Not so. 'I say unto you', said our Lord, 'Love your enemies, bless them that curse you, do good to them that hate you, and pray for them that despitefully use you and persecute you; that ye may be the children'—may appear so to all mankind—'of your Father which is in heaven, who maketh his sun to rise on the evil and on the good, and sendeth rain on the just and on the unjust.'

2. But it is sure, there is a peculiar love which we owe to those that love God. So David: 'All my delight is upon the saints that are in the earth, and upon such as excel in virtue.' And so a greater than he: 'A new commandment I give unto you, that ye love one another: as I have loved you, that ye also love one another. By this shall all men know that ye are my disciples, if ye have love one to another' (John 13:34-35). This is that love on which the Apostle John so frequently and strongly insists. 'This', said he, 'is the message that ye heard from the beginning, that we should love one another' (1 John 3:11). 'Hereby perceive we the love of God, because he laid down his life for us. And we ought', if love should call us thereto, 'to lay down our lives for the brethren' (1 John 3:16). And again, 'Beloved, let us love one another; for love is of God. He that loveth not, knoweth not God; for God is love' (1 John 4:7-8). 'Not that we loved God, but that he loved us, and sent his Son to be the propitiation for our sins. Beloved, if God so loved us, we ought also to love one another' (1 John 4:10-11).

3. All men approve of this. But do all men practise it? Daily experience shows the contrary. Where are even the Christians who 'love one another, as he hath given us commandment'? How many hindrances lie in the way! The two grand, general hindrances are, first, that they can't all think alike; and in consequence of this, secondly, they can't all walk alike; but in several smaller points their practice must differ in proportion to the difference of their sentiments.

4. But although a difference in opinions or modes of worship may prevent an entire external union, yet need it prevent our union in affection? Though we can't think alike, may we not love alike? May we not be of one heart, though we are not of one opinion? Without all doubt we may. Herein all the children of God may unite, notwithstanding these smaller differences. These remaining as they are, they may forward one another in love and in good works.

5. Surely in this respect the example of Jehu himself, as mixed a character as he was of, is well worthy both the attention and imitation of every serious Christian. 'And when

he was departed thence, he lighted on Jehonadab the son of Rechab coming to meet him. And he saluted him and said, Is thine heart right, as my heart is with thy heart? And Jehonadab answered, It is. If it be, give me thine hand.'

The text naturally divides itself into two parts. First a question proposed by Jehu to Jehonadab, 'Is thine heart right, as my heart is with thy heart?' Secondly, an offer made on Jehonadab's answering, 'It is.'—'If it be, give me thine hand.'

I.1. And, first, let us consider the question proposed by Jehu to Jehonadab, 'Is thine heart right, as my heart is with thy heart?'

The very first thing we may observe in these words is that here is no inquiry concerning Jehonadab's opinions. And yet 'tis certain he held some which were very uncommon, indeed quite peculiar to himself; and some which had a close influence upon practice, on which likewise he laid so great a stress as to entail them upon his children's children, to their latest posterity. This is evident from the account given by Jeremiah, many years after his death. 'I took Jaazaniah and his brethren, and all his sons, and the whole house of the Rechabites; . . . and set before them pots full of wine, and cups, and said unto them, Drink ye wine. But they said, We will drink no wine; for Jonadab (or Jehonadab) the son of Rechab our father' (it would be less ambiguous if the words were placed thus: Jehonadab 'our father the son of Rechab', out of love and reverence to whom he probably desired his descendants might be called by his name) 'commanded us, saying, Ye shall drink no wine, neither ye nor your sons for ever. Neither shall ye build house, nor sow seed, nor plant vineyard, nor have any; but all your days ye shall dwell in tents. . . . And we have obeyed, and done according to all that Jonadab our father commanded us' (Jer. 35:3-10).

2. And yet Jehu (although it seems to have been his manner, both in things secular and religious, to 'drive furiously') does not concern himself at all with any of these things, but lets Jehonadab abound in his own sense. And neither of them appears to have given the other the least disturbance touching the opinions which he maintained.

3. 'Tis very possible that many good men now also may entertain peculiar opinions; and some of them may be as singular herein as even Jehonadab was. And 'tis certain, so long as 'we know' but 'in part', that all men will not see all things alike. It is an unavoidable consequence of the present weakness and shortness of human understanding that several men will be of several minds, in religion as well as in common life. So it has been from the beginning of the world, and so it will be 'till the restitution of all things'.

4. Nay farther: although every man necessarily believes that every particular opinion which he holds is true (for to believe any opinion is not true is the same thing as not to hold it) yet can no man be assured that all his own opinions taken together are true. Nay, every thinking man is assured they are not, seeing *humanum est errare et nescire*—to be ignorant of many things, and to mistake in some, is the necessary condition of humanity. This therefore, he is sensible, is his own case. He knows in the general that he himself is mistaken; although in what particulars he mistakes he does not, perhaps cannot, know.

5. I say, perhaps he cannot know. For who can tell how far invincible ignorance may

extend? Or (what comes to the same thing) invincible prejudice; which is often so fixed in tender minds that it is afterwards impossible to tear up what has taken so deep a root. And who can say, unless he knew every circumstance attending it, how far any mistake is culpable? Seeing all guilt must suppose some concurrence of the will—of which he only can judge who searcheth the heart.

6. Every wise man therefore will allow others the same liberty of thinking which he desires they should allow him; and will no more insist on their embracing his opinions than he would have them to insist on his embracing theirs. He bears with those who differ from him, and only asks him with whom he desires to unite in love that single question. 'Is thine heart right, as my heart is with thy heart?'

7. We may, secondly, observe that here is no inquiry made concerning Jehonadab's mode of worship, although 'tis highly probable there was in this respect also a very wide difference between them. For we may well believe Jehonadab, as well as all his posterity, worshipped God at Jerusalem, whereas Jehu did not; he had more regard to state policy than religion. And therefore although he slew the worshippers of Baal, and 'destroyed Baal out of Israel', yet 'from the' convenient 'sin of Jeroboam', the worship of 'the golden calves, he departed not' (2 Kgs. 10:28-29).

8. But even among men of an upright heart, men who desire 'to have a conscience void of offence', it must needs be that as long as there are various opinions there will be various ways of worshipping God; seeing a variety of opinion necessarily implies a variety of practice. And as in all ages men have differed in nothing more than in their opinions concerning the Supreme Being, so in nothing have they more differed from each other than in the manner of worshipping him. Had this been only in the heathen world it would not have been at all surprising, for we know these 'by their wisdom knew not God'; nor therefore could they know how to worship him. But is it not strange that even in the Christian world, although they all agree in the general, 'God is a Spirit, and they that worship him must worship him in spirit and in truth,' yet the particular modes of worshipping God are almost as various as among the heathens?

9. And how shall we choose among so much variety? No man can choose for or prescribe to another. But everyone must follow the dictates of his own conscience in simplicity and godly sincerity. He must be fully persuaded in his own mind, and then act according to the best light he has. Nor has any creature power to constrain another to walk by his own rule. God has given no right to any of the children of men thus to lord it over the conscience of his brethren. But every man must judge for himself, as every man must give an account of himself to God.

10. Although therefore every follower of Christ is obliged by the very nature of the Christian institution to be a member of some particular congregation or other, some church, as it is usually termed (which implies a particular manner of worshipping God; for 'two cannot walk together unless they be agreed'); yet none can be obliged by any power on earth but that of his own conscience to prefer this or that congregation to another, this or that particular manner of worship. I know it is commonly supposed that the place of our birth fixes the church to which we ought to belong; that one, for instance, who is

born in England ought to be a member of that which is styled 'the Church of England', and consequently to worship God in the particular manner which is prescribed by that church. I was once a zealous maintainer of this, but I find many reasons to abate of this zeal. I fear it is attended with such difficulties as no reasonable man can get over. Not the least of which is that if this rule had took place, there could have been no Reformation from popery, seeing it entirely destroys the right of private judgment on which that whole Reformation stands.

11. I dare not therefore presume to impose my mode of worship on any other. I believe it is truly primitive and apostolical. But my belief is no rule for another. I ask not therefore of him with whom I would unite in love, 'Are you of my Church? Of my congregation? Do you receive the same form of church government and allow the same church officers with me? Do you join in the same form of prayer wherein I worship God?' I inquire not, 'Do you receive the Supper of the Lord in the same posture and manner that I do?' Nor whether, in the administration of baptism, you agree with me in admitting sureties for the baptized, in the manner of administering it, or the age of those to whom it should be administered. Nay, I ask not of you (as clear as I am in my own mind) whether you allow baptism and the Lord's Supper at all. Let all these things stand by: we will talk of them, if need be, at a more convenient season. My only question at present is this, 'Is thine heart right, as my heart is with thy heart?'

12. But what is properly implied in the question? I do not mean what did Jehu imply therein, but what should a follower of Christ understand thereby when he proposes it to any of his brethren?

The first thing implied is this: Is thy heart right with God? Dost thou believe his being, and his perfections? His eternity, immensity, wisdom, power; his justice, mercy, and truth? Dost thou believe that he now 'upholdeth all things by the word of his power'? And that he governs even the most minute, even the most noxious, to his own glory, and the good of them that love him? Hast thou a divine evidence, a supernatural conviction, of the things of God? Dost thou 'walk by faith, not by sight'? 'Looking not at temporal things, but things eternal'?

13. Dost thou believe in the Lord Jesus Christ, 'God over all, blessed for ever'? Is he 'revealed in' thy soul? Dost thou 'know Jesus Christ and him crucified'? Does he 'dwell in thee, and thou in him'? Is he 'formed in thy heart by faith'? Having absolutely disclaimed all thy own works, thy own righteousness, hast thou 'submitted thyself unto the righteousness of God', 'which is by faith in Christ Jesus'? Art thou 'found in him, not having thy own righteousness, but the righteousness which is by faith'? And art thou, through him, 'fighting the good fight of faith, and laying hold of eternal life'?

14. Is thy faith ἐνεργουμένη δἰ ἀγάπης—filled with the energy of love? Dost thou love God? I do not say 'above all things', for it is both an unscriptural and an ambiguous expression, but 'with all thy heart, and with all thy mind, and with all thy soul, and with all thy strength'? Dost thou seek all thy happiness in him alone? And dost thou find what thou seekest? Does thy soul continually 'magnify the Lord, and thy spirit rejoice in God thy Saviour'? Having learned 'in everything to give thanks', dost thou find it is 'a joyful

and a pleasant thing to be thankful'? Is God the centre of thy soul? The sum of all thy desires? Art thou accordingly 'laying up' thy 'treasure in heaven', and 'counting all things else dung and dross'? Hath the love of God cast the love of the world out of thy soul? Then thou art 'crucified to the world'. 'Thou art dead' to all below, 'and thy life is hid with Christ in God.'

15. Art thou employed in doing 'not thy own will, but the will of him that sent thee'? Of him that sent thee down to sojourn here a while, to spend a few days in a strange land, till having finished the work he hath given thee to do thou return to thy Father's house? Is it thy meat and drink 'to do the will of thy Father which is in heaven'? Is 'thine eye single' in all things? Always fixed on him? Always 'looking unto Jesus'? Dost thou point at him in whatsoever thou dost? In all thy labour, thy business, thy conversation? Aiming only at the glory of God in all? 'Whatsoever' thou dost, either 'in word or deed, doing it all in the name of the Lord Jesus, giving thanks unto God, even the Father, through him'?

16. Does the love of God constrain thee to 'serve' him 'with fear'? To 'rejoice unto him with reverence'? Art thou more afraid of displeasing God than either of death or hell? Is nothing so terrible to thee as the thought of 'offending the eyes of his glory'? Upon this ground dost thou 'hate all evil ways', every transgression of his holy and perfect law? And herein 'exercise' thyself 'to have a conscience void of offence toward God and toward man'?

17. Is thy heart right toward thy neighbour? Dost thou 'love as thyself' all mankind without exception? 'If you love those only that love you, what thank have you?' Do you 'love your enemies'? Is your soul full of goodwill, of tender affection toward them? Do you love even the enemies of God? The unthankful and unholy? Do your bowels yearn over them? Could you 'wish yourself (temporally) accursed' for their sake? And do you show this by 'blessing them that curse you, and praying for those that despitefully use you and persecute you'?

18. Do you show your love by your works? While you have time, as you have opportunity, do you in fact 'do good to all men'—neighbours or strangers, friends or enemies, good or bad? Do you do them all the good you can? Endeavouring to supply all their wants, assisting them both in body and soul to the uttermost of your power? If thou art thus minded, may every Christian say—yea, if thou art but sincerely desirous of it, and following on till thou attain—then 'thy heart is right, as my heart is with thy heart.'

II.1. 'If it be, give me thine hand.' I do not mean, 'Be of my opinion.' You need not. I do not expect nor desire it. Neither do I mean, 'I will be of your opinion.' I cannot. It does not depend on my choice. I can no more think than I can see or hear as I will. Keep you your opinion, I mine; and that as steadily as ever. You need not even endeavour to come over to me, or bring me over to you. I do not desire you to dispute those points, or to hear or speak one word concerning them. Let all opinions alone on one side and the other. Only 'give me thine hand.'

2. I do not mean, 'Embrace my modes of worship,' or, 'I will embrace yours.' This also is a thing which does not depend either on your choice or mine. We must both act as each is fully persuaded in his own mind. Hold you fast that which you believe is most

acceptable to God, and I will do the same. I believe the episcopal form of church government to be scriptural and apostolical. If you think the presbyterian or independent is better, think so still, and act accordingly. I believe infants ought to be baptized, and that this may be done either by dipping or sprinkling. If you are otherwise persuaded, be so still, and follow your own persuasion. It appears to me that forms of prayer are of excellent use, particularly in the great congregation. If you judge extemporary prayer to be of more use, act suitably to your own judgment. My sentiment is that I ought not to forbid water wherein persons may be baptized, and that I ought to eat bread and drink wine as a memorial of my dying Master. However, if you are not convinced of this, act according to the light you have. I have no desire to dispute with you one moment upon any of the preceding heads. Let all these smaller points stand aside. Let them never come into sight. 'If thine heart is as my heart', if thou lovest God and all mankind, I ask no more: 'Give me thine hand.'

3. I mean, first, love me. And that not only as thou lovest all mankind; not only as thou lovest thine enemies or the enemies of God, those that hate thee, that 'despitefully use thee and persecute thee'; not only as a stranger, as one of whom thou knowest neither good nor evil. I am not satisfied with this. No; 'If thine heart be right, as mine with thy heart', then love me with a very tender affection, as a friend that is closer than a brother; as a brother in Christ, a fellow-citizen of the new Jerusalem, a fellow-soldier engaged in the same warfare, under the same Captain of our salvation. Love me as a companion in the kingdom and patience of Jesus, and a joint-heir of his glory.

4. Love me (but in an higher degree than thou dost the bulk of mankind) with the love that is 'long-suffering and kind'; that is patient if I am ignorant or out of the way, bearing and not increasing my burden; and is tender, soft, and compassionate still; that 'envieth not' if at any time it please God to prosper me in his work even more than thee. Love me with the love that 'is not provoked' either at my follies or infirmities, or even at my acting (if it should sometimes so appear to thee) not according to the will of God. Love me so as to 'think no evil' of me, to put away all jealousy and evil surmising. Love me with the love that 'covereth all things', that never reveals either my faults or infirmities; that 'believeth all things', is always willing to think the best, to put the fairest construction on all my words and actions; that 'hopeth all things', either that the thing related was never done, or not done with such circumstances as are related, or, at least, that it was done with a good intention, or in sudden stress of temptation. And hope to the end that whatever is amiss will, by the grace of God, be corrected, and whatever is wanting supplied, through the riches of his mercy in Christ Jesus.

5. I mean, secondly, commend me to God in all thy prayers; wrestle with him in my behalf, that he would speedily correct what he sees amiss and supply what is wanting in me. In thy nearest access to the throne of grace beg of him who is then very present with thee that my heart may be more as thy heart, more right both toward God and toward man; that I may have a fuller conviction of things not seen, and a stronger view of the love of God in Christ Jesus; may more steadily walk by faith, not by sight, and more earnestly grasp eternal life. Pray that the love of God and of all mankind may be more largely poured into my heart; that I may be more fervent and active in doing the will of

my Father which is in heaven, more zealous of good works, and more careful to abstain from all appearance of evil.

6. I mean, thirdly, provoke me to love and to good works. Second thy prayer as thou hast opportunity by speaking to me in love whatsoever thou believest to be for my soul's health. Quicken me in the work which God has given me to do, and instruct me how to do it more perfectly. Yea, 'smite me friendly and reprove me' whereinsoever I appear to thee to be doing rather my own will than the will of him that sent me. O speak and spare not, whatever thou believest may conduce either to the amending my faults, the strengthening my weakness, the building me up in love, or the making me more fit in any kind for the Master's use.

7. I mean, lastly, love me not in word only, but in deed and in truth. So far as in conscience thou canst (retaining still thy own opinions and thy own manner of worshipping God), join with me in the work of God, and let us go on hand in hand. And thus far, it is certain, thou mayst go. Speak honourably, wherever thou art, of the work of God, by whomsoever he works, and kindly of his messengers. And if it be in thy power, not only sympathize with them when they are in any difficulty or distress, but give them a cheerful and effectual assistance, that they may glorify God on thy behalf.

8. Two things should be observed with regard to what has been spoken under this last head. The one, that whatsoever love, whatsoever offices of love, whatsoever spiritual or temporal assistance, I claim from him whose heart is right, as my heart is with his, the same I am ready, by the grace of God, according to my measure, to give him. The other, that I have not made this claim in behalf of myself only, but of all whose heart is right toward God and man, that we may all love one another as Christ hath loved us.

III.1. One inference we may make from what has been said. We may learn from hence what is a 'catholic spirit'.

There is scarce any expression which has been more grossly misunderstood and more dangerously misapplied than this. But it will be easy for any who calmly consider the preceding observations to correct any such misapprehensions of it, and to prevent any such misapplication.

For from hence we may learn, first, that a catholic spirit is not *speculative latitudinarianism.* It is not an indifference to all opinions. This is the spawn of hell, not the offspring of heaven. This unsettledness of thought, this being 'driven to and fro, and tossed about with every wind of doctrine', is a great curse, not a blessing; an irreconcilable enemy, not a friend, to true catholicism. A man of a truly catholic spirit has not now his religion to seek. He is fixed as the sun in his judgment concerning the main branches of Christian doctrine. 'Tis true he is always ready to hear and weigh whatsoever can be offered against his principles. But as this does not show any wavering in his own mind, so neither does it occasion any. He does not halt between two opinions, nor vainly endeavour to blend them into one. Observe this, you who know not what spirit ye are of, who call yourselves men of a catholic spirit only because you are of a muddy understanding; because your mind is all in a mist; because you have no settled, consistent principles, but are for jumbling all opinions together. Be convinced that you have quite missed your way: you know not where you are. You think you are got into the very spirit of Christ, when in truth you are nearer the spirit of antichrist. Go first and learn the first elements of the gospel of Christ, and then shall you learn to be of a truly catholic spirit.

2. From what has been said we may learn, secondly, that a catholic spirit is not any kind of *practical latitudinarianism.* It is not indifference as to public worship or as to the outward manner of performing it. This likewise would not be a blessing but a curse. Far from being an help thereto it would, so long as it remained, be an unspeakable hindrance to the worshipping of God in spirit and in truth. But the man of a truly catholic spirit, having weighed all things in the balance of the sanctuary, has no doubt, no scruple at all concerning that particular mode of worship wherein he joins. He is clearly convinced that *this* manner of worshipping God is both scriptural and rational. He knows none in the world which is more scriptural, none which is more rational. Therefore without rambling hither and thither he cleaves close thereto, and praises God for the opportunity of so doing.

3. Hence we may, thirdly, learn that a catholic spirit is not indifference to all congregations. This is another sort of latitudinarianism, no less absurd and unscriptural than the former. But it is far from a man of a truly catholic spirit. He is fixed in his congregation as well as his principles. He is united to one, not only in spirit, but by all the outward ties of Christian fellowship. There he partakes of all the ordinances of God. There he receives the Supper of the Lord. There he pours out his soul in public prayer, and joins in public praise and thanksgiving. There he rejoices to hear the word of reconciliation, the gospel of the grace of God. With these his nearest, his best beloved brethren, on solemn occasions he seeks God by fasting. These particularly he watches over in love, as they do over his soul, admonishing, exhorting, comforting, reproving, and every way building up each other in the faith. These he regards as his own household, and therefore according to the ability God has given him naturally cares for them, and provides that they may have all the things that are needful for life and godliness.

4. But while he is steadily fixed in his religious principles, in what he believes to be the truth as it is in Jesus; while he firmly adheres to that worship of God which he judges to be most acceptable in his sight; and while he is united by the tenderest and closest ties to one particular congregation; his heart is enlarged toward all mankind, those he knows and those he does not; he embraces with strong and cordial affection neighbours and strangers, friends and enemies. This is catholic or universal love. And he that has this is of a catholic spirit. For love alone gives the title to this character—catholic love is a catholic spirit.

5. If then we take this word in the strictest sense, a man of a catholic spirit is one who in the manner above mentioned 'gives his hand' to all whose 'hearts are right with his heart'. One who knows how to value and praise God for all the advantages he enjoys: with regard to the knowledge of the things of God, the true, scriptural manner of worshipping him; and above all his union with a congregation fearing God and working righteousness. One who, retaining these blessings with the strictest care, keeping them as the apple of his eye, at the same time loves as friends, as brethren in the Lord, as members of Christ and

children of God, as joint partakers now of the present kingdom of God, and fellow-heirs of his eternal Kingdom, all of whatever opinion or worship or congregation who believe in the Lord Jesus Christ; who love God and man; who, rejoicing to please and fearing to offend God, are careful to abstain from evil and zealous of good works. He is the man of a truly catholic spirit who bears all these continually upon his heart, who having an unspeakable tenderness for their persons, and longing for their welfare, does not cease to commend them to God in prayer, as well as to plead their cause before men; who speaks comfortably to them, and labours by all his words to strengthen their hands in God. He assists them to the uttermost of his power in all things, spiritual and temporal. He is ready 'to spend and be spent for them'; yea, 'to lay down his life for' their sake.

6. Thou, O man of God, think on these things. If thou art already in this way, go on. If thou hast heretofore mistook the path, bless God who hath brought thee back. And now run the race which is set before thee, in the royal way of universal love. Take heed lest thou be either wavering in thy judgment or straitened in thy bowels. But keep an even pace, rooted in the faith once delivered to the saints and grounded in love, in true, catholic love, till thou art swallowed up in love for ever and ever.

41. THE CURE OF EVIL-SPEAKING

1760

An Introductory Comment

Concerned about avoiding unnecessary conflict and division among their preachers, John and Charles Wesley drafted a letter on January 29, 1752 that became widely known. Its contents formed the heart of the counsels offered in this present sermon against the disruptive practice of evil-speaking as revealed in the following:

> *1. That we will not listen, or willingly inquire after any ill concerning each other.*
> *2. That if we do hear any ill of each other, we will not be forward to believe it.*
> *3. That as soon as possible we will communicate what we hear, by speaking or writing to the person concerned.*
> *4. That till we have done this we will not write or speak a syllable of it to any other person whatsoever.*
> *5. That neither will we mention it after we have done this to any other person.*
> *6. That we will not make any exception to any of these rules, unless we think ourselves absolutely obliged in conscience so to do. (FB, 26:490)*

So concerned was John Wesley about this matter that he preached nine times against evil-speaking in 1752 in such places as London, Bristol, Manchester, Newcastle, Athlone, Limerick, Dublin, and Kingswood. The following year he took up the same theme at Bradford-on-Avon and then once more in London in 1758 (WWS).

Recognizing that so many sinned in this area, Wesley took great pains to state clearly the viciousness of this practice, which is "neither more nor less than speaking evil of an absent person; relating something evil which was really done or said by one that is not present when it is related" (O, 2:252). This fault was so common "among all orders and degrees of men" (O, 2:253) because it gratified pride that took an odd sort of satisfaction in pointing out the evils of others that supposedly were not one's own. "We commit sin," Wesley observed, "from mere hatred of sin!" (O, 2:254).

The Cure of Evil-speaking

1. 'Speak evil of no man,' says the great Apostle
2. How extremely common is this sin among all people
3. The commonness of this sin makes it difficult to avoid
4. It is the more difficult to avoid because it frequently attacks us
5. But there is a way to avoid the snare

I. 1. First, if your brother sins against you, go and tell him of his fault
2. See that you speak according to the gospel of Christ
    A. Avoid anything that savours of *pride, contempt, anger*, or *hate*
3. Speaking in your own person is far better than through someone else
4.–5. If you can neither speak in person nor find a messenger, then write
6.–7. Do not think to excuse yourself for taking a different step by saying:
    A. I did not speak to anyone until I was *so burdened* I could not refrain

II. 1. But what if they will not hear?
    A. In this case, our Lord gives us a clear and full direction:
    B. Take with you one or two more: this is the second step
2. Love will dictate the manner wherein they should proceed
3. In order to do this, they may:
    A. Briefly repeat what you spoke, and what the accused answered
    B. Enlarge upon, open, and confirm the reasons which the accused gives
    C. Give weight to your reproof, showing how just, kind, and sensible it was
    D. Enforce the advices and persuasions which you had annexed to it
4. Our Lord directs us to take this step after the first and before the third

III. 1. Our Lord gives us a third step
    A. If he will not hear them, tell it to the church
2. Also let it be observed that this, and no other, is the third step we are to take
3. When you have done this you have delivered your own soul
4. Who will take God's part against the evil-speakers?
    A. From this hour walk by this rule, speaking evil of no man
5. Let this be the distinguishing mark of the Methodists:
    A. They do not censure people behind their backs

Sermon 49: The Cure of Evil-speaking, 1760

Matthew 18:15-17

If thy brother shall sin against thee, go and tell him his fault between thee and him alone: if he will hear thee, thou hast gained thy brother.

But if he will not hear, take with thee one or two more, that by the mouth of two or three witnesses every word may be established.

And if he will not hear them, tell it to the church: but if he will not hear the church, let him be to thee as an heathen man and a publican.

1. 'Speak evil of no man,' says the great Apostle—as plain a command as 'Thou shalt do no murder.' But who even among Christians regards this command? Yea, how few are there that so much as understand it? What is 'evil-speaking'? It is not (as some suppose) the same with lying or slandering. All a man says may be as true as the Bible; and yet the saying of it is evil-speaking. For evil-speaking is neither more nor less than speaking evil of an absent person; relating something evil which was really done or said by one that is not present when it is related. Suppose, having seen a man drunk, or heard him curse or swear, I tell this when he is absent, it is evil-speaking. In our language this is also by an extremely proper name termed 'backbiting'. Nor is there any material difference between this and what we usually style 'talebearing'. If the tale be delivered in a soft and quiet manner (perhaps with expressions of goodwill to the person, and of hope that things may not be quite so bad) then we call it 'whispering'. But in whatever manner it be done the thing is the same—the same in substance if not in circumstance. Still it is evil-speaking; still this command, 'Speak evil of no man,' is trampled under foot if we relate to another the fault of a third person when he is not present to answer for himself.

2. And how extremely common is this sin among all orders and degrees of men! How do high and low, rich and poor, wise and foolish, learned and unlearned, run into it continually! Persons who differ from each other in all things else, nevertheless agree in this. How few are there that can testify before God, 'I am clear in this matter: I have always set a watch before my mouth, and kept the door of my lips!' What conversation do you hear of any considerable length whereof evil-speaking is not one ingredient? And that even among persons who in the general have the fear of God before their eyes, and do really desire to have a conscience void of offence toward God and toward man.

3. And the very commonness of this sin makes it difficult to be avoided. As we are encompassed with it on every side, so if we are not deeply sensible of the danger, and continually guarding against it, we are liable to be carried away by the torrent. In this instance almost the whole of mankind is, as it were, in a conspiracy against us. And their example steals upon us we know not how, so that we insensibly slide into the imitation of it. Besides, it is recommended from within as well as from without. There is scarce any wrong temper in the mind of man which may not be occasionally gratified by it, and consequently incline us to it. It gratifies our *pride* to relate those faults of others whereof we think ourselves not to be guilty. *Anger*, resentment, and all unkind tempers are indulged by speaking against those with whom we are displeased. And in

many cases, by reciting the sins of their neighbours, men indulge their own 'foolish and hurtful desires'.

4. Evil-speaking is the more difficult to be avoided because it frequently attacks us in disguise. We speak thus out of a noble, generous ('tis well if we do not say, 'holy') 'indignation' against these vile creatures! We commit sin from mere hatred of sin! We serve the devil out of pure zeal for God! It is merely in order to punish the wicked that we run into this wickedness. So do 'the passions' (as one speaks) 'all justify themselves', and palm sin upon us under the veil of holiness!

5. But is there no way to avoid the snare? Unquestionably there is. Our blessed Lord has marked out a plain way for his followers in the words above recited. None who warily and steadily walks in this path will ever fall into evil-speaking. This rule is either an infallible preventive or a certain cure of it. In the preceding verses our Lord had said, 'Woe to the world because of offences!' Unspeakable misery will arise in the world from this baleful fountain. ('Offences' are all things whereby anyone is turned out of, or hindered in, the ways of God.) 'For it must be that offences come.' Such is the nature of things; such the weakness, folly, and wickedness of mankind. 'But woe to that man', miserable is that man, 'by whom the offence cometh. Wherefore if thy hand, thy foot, thine eye cause thee to offend'—if the most dear enjoyment, the most beloved and useful person, turn thee out of or hinder thee in the way—'pluck it out, cut them off, and cast them from thee.' But how can we avoid giving offence to some, and being offended at others? Especially suppose they are quite in the wrong, and we see it with our own eyes? Our Lord here teaches us how: he lays down a sure method of avoiding offences and evil-speaking together. 'If thy brother shall sin against thee, go and tell him of his fault, between thee and him alone: if he will hear thee, thou hast gained thy brother. But if he will not hear thee, take with thee one or two more, that by the mouth of two or three witnesses every word may be established. And if he will not hear them, tell it to the church: but if he will not hear the church, let him be to thee as an heathen man and a publican.'

I.1. First, 'if thy brother shall sin against thee, go and tell him of his fault, between thee and him alone.' The most literal way of following this first rule, where it is practicable, is the best. Therefore, if thou seest with thine own eyes a brother, a fellow-Christian, commit undeniable sin, or hearest it with thine own ears, so that it is impossible for thee to doubt the fact, then thy part is plain: take the very first opportunity of going to him; and if thou canst have access, 'tell him of his fault between thee and him alone.' Indeed great care is to be taken that this is done in a right *spirit*, and in a right *manner*. The success of a reproof greatly depends on the spirit wherein it is given. Be not therefore wanting in earnest prayer to God that it may be given in a lowly spirit; with a deep, piercing conviction that it is God alone who maketh thee to differ, and that if any good be done by what is now spoken, God doth it himself. Pray that he would guard thy heart, enlighten thy mind, and direct thy tongue to such words as he may please to bless. See that thou speak in a meek as well as a lowly spirit; 'for the wrath of man worketh not the righteousness of God.' If he 'be overtaken in a fault', he can no otherwise be 'restored' than 'in the spirit of meekness'. If he 'opposes' the truth, yet he cannot be 'brought to the knowledge' thereof but by 'gentleness'. Still speak in a spirit of tender love, 'which many waters cannot quench'. If love is not conquered, it conquers all things. Who can tell the force of love?

> Love can bow down the stubborn neck,
>   The stone to flesh convert;
> Soften and melt and pierce and break
>   An adamantine heart.

Confirm then your love toward him, and you will thereby 'heap coals of fire upon his head'.

2. But see that the *manner* also wherein you speak be according to the gospel of Christ. Avoid everything in look, gesture, word, and tone of voice that savours of *pride* or self-sufficiency. Studiously avoid everything magisterial or dogmatical; everything that looks like arrogance or assuming. Beware of the most distant approach to disdain, overbearing, or *contempt*. With equal care avoid all appearance of *anger*, and though you use great plainness of speech, yet let there be no reproach, no railing accusation, no token of any warmth but that of love. Above all, let there be no shadow of *hate* or ill will, no bitterness or sourness of expression; but use the air and language of sweetness, as well as gentleness, that all may appear to flow from love in the heart. And yet this sweetness need not hinder your speaking in the most serious and solemn manner, as far as may be in the very words of the oracles of God (for there are none like them), and as under the eye of him who is coming to judge the quick and [the] dead.

3. If you have not an opportunity of speaking to him in person, or cannot have access, you may do it by a messenger, by a common friend in whose prudence as well as uprightness you can throughly confide. Such a person, speaking in your name, and in the spirit and manner above described, may answer the same end, and in a good degree supply your lack of service. Only beware you do not feign want of opportunity in order to shun the cross; neither take it for granted that you cannot have access without ever making the trial. Whenever you can speak in your own person it is far better. But you should rather do it by another than not at all: this way is better than none.

4. But what if you can neither speak yourself, nor find such a messenger as you can confide in? If this is really the case, it then only remains to write. And there may be some circumstances which make this the most advisable way of speaking. One of these circumstances is when the person with whom we have to do is of so warm and impetuous a temper as does not easily bear reproof, especially from an equal or inferior. But it may be so introduced and softened in writing as to make it far more tolerable. Besides, many will read the very same words which they could not bear to hear. It does not give so violent a shock to their pride, nor so sensibly touch their honour. And suppose it makes little impression at first, they will perhaps give it a second reading, and upon farther consideration lay to heart what before they disregarded. If you add your name, this is nearly the same thing as going to him and speaking in person. And this should always be done, unless it be rendered improper by some very particular reason.

5. It should be well observed, not only that this is a step which our Lord absolutely commands us to take, but that he commands us to take this step first, before we attempt any other. No alternative is allowed, no choice of anything else; this is the way; walk thou in it. It is true he enjoins us, if need require, to take two other steps. But they are to be taken successively *after* this step, and neither of them *before* it. Much less are we to take any other step either before or beside this. To do anything else, or not to do this, is therefore equally inexcusable.

6. Do not think to excuse yourself for taking an entirely different step by saying, 'Why, I did not speak to anyone till I was so *burdened* that I could not refrain.' You was burdened! It was no wonder you should, unless your conscience was seared; for you was under the guilt of sin, of disobeying a plain commandment of God. You ought immediately to have gone and 'told your brother of his fault between you and him alone'. If you did not, how should you be other than burdened (unless your heart was utterly hardened) while you was trampling the command of God under foot, and 'hating your brother in your heart'? And what a way have you found to *unburden* yourself? God reproves you for a sin of omission, for not telling your brother of his fault; and you comfort yourself under his reproof by a sin of commission, by telling your brother's fault to another person! Ease bought by sin is a dear purchase: I trust in God you will have no ease, but will be burdened so much the more till you 'go to your brother and tell him', and no one else.

7. I know but of one exception to this rule. There may be a peculiar case wherein it is necessary to accuse the guilty, though absent, in order to preserve the innocent. For instance: you are acquainted with the design which a man has against the property or life of his neighbour. Now the case may be so circumstanced that there is no other way of hindering that design from taking effect but the making it known without delay to him against whom it is laid. In this case therefore this rule is set aside, as is that of the Apostle, 'Speak evil of no man,' and it is lawful, yea, it is our bounden duty to speak evil of an absent person, in order to prevent his doing evil to others and himself at the same time. But remember meanwhile that all evil-speaking is in its own nature deadly poison. Therefore if you are sometimes constrained to use it as a medicine, yet use it with fear and trembling, seeing it is so dangerous a medicine that nothing but absolute necessity can excuse your using it at all. Accordingly use it as seldom as possible; never but when there is such a necessity. And even then use as little of it as is possible; only so much as is necessary for the end proposed. At all other times, 'go and tell him of his fault, between thee and him alone.'

II.1. But what 'if he will not hear'? If he repay evil for good? If he be enraged rather than convinced? What if he hear to no purpose, and go on still in the evil of his way? We must expect this will frequently be the case; the mildest and tenderest reproof will have no effect, but the blessing we wished for another will return into our own bosom. And what are we to do then? Our Lord has given us a clear and full direction. Then 'take with thee one or two more:' this is the second step. Take one or two whom you know to be of a loving spirit, lovers of God and of their neighbour. See likewise that they be of a lowly spirit, and 'clothed with humility'. Let them also be such as are meek and gentle, patient and longsuffering; not apt to 'return evil for evil, or railing for railing, but contrariwise blessing'. Let them be men of understanding, such as are endued with wisdom from above; and men unbiased, free from partiality, free from prejudice of any kind. Care should likewise be taken that both the persons and their characters be well known to him. And let those that are acceptable to him be chosen preferable to any others.

2. Love will dictate the manner wherein they should proceed, according to the nature of the case. Nor can any one particular manner be prescribed for all cases. But perhaps in general one might advise, before they enter upon the thing itself, let them mildly and affectionately declare that they have no anger or prejudice toward him, and that it is merely from a principle of goodwill that they now come, or at all concern themselves with his affairs. To make this the more apparent, they might then calmly attend to your repetition of your former conversation with him, and to what he said in his own defence, before they attempted to determine anything. After this they would be better able to judge in what manner to proceed, 'that by the mouth of two or three witnesses, every word might be established'; that whatever you have said may have its full force by the additional weight of their authority.

3. In order to this, may they not, (1). Briefly repeat what you spoke, and what he answered? (2). Enlarge upon, open, and confirm the reasons which you had given? (3). Give weight to your reproof, showing how just, how kind, and how seasonable it was? And, lastly, enforce the advices and persuasions which you had annexed to it? And these may likewise hereafter, if need should require, bear witness of what was spoken.

4. With regard to this, as well as the preceding rule, we may observe that our Lord gives us no choice, leaves us no alternative, but expressly commands us to do this, and nothing else in the place of it. He likewise directs us when to do this. Neither sooner, nor later: namely, *after* we have taken the first, and *before* we have taken the third step. It is then only that we are authorized to relate the evil another has done to those whom we desire to bear a part with us in this great instance of brotherly love. But let us have a care how we relate it to any other person till both these steps have been taken. If we neglect to take these, or if we take any others, what wonder if we are burdened still! For we are sinners against God and against our neighbour. And how fairly soever we may colour it, yet if we have any conscience our sin will find us out, and bring a burden upon our soul.

III.1. That we may be throughly instructed in this weighty affair our Lord has given us a still farther direction. 'If he will not hear them'—then and not till then—'tell it to the church.' This is the third step. All the question is how this word, 'the church', is here to be understood. But the very nature of the thing will determine this beyond all reasonable doubt. You cannot tell it to the national church, the whole body of men termed 'the Church of England'. Neither would it answer any Christian end if you could: this therefore is not the meaning of the word. Neither can you tell it to that whole body of people in England with whom you have a more immediate connexion. Nor indeed would this answer any good end: the word therefore is not to be understood thus. It would not answer any valuable end to tell the faults of every particular member to 'the church' (if you would so term it), the congregation or *society* united together in London. It remains that you tell it to the elder or elders of the church, to those who are overseers of that flock of Christ to which you both belong, who watch over yours and his soul 'as they that must give account'. And this should be done, if it conveniently can, in the presence of the person concerned, and, though plainly, yet with all the tenderness and love which the nature of the thing will admit. It properly belongs to their office to determine concerning the behaviour of those under their care, and to 'rebuke', according to the demerit of the offence, 'with all authority'. When therefore you have done this, you have done all which the Word of God or the law of love requireth of you. You are not now partaker of his sin, but if he perish his blood is on his own head.

2. Here also let it be observed that this, and no other, is the third step which we are to take; and that we are to take it in its order, after the other two; not before the second, much less the first, unless in some very particular circumstance. Indeed in one case the second step may coincide with this: they may be, in a manner, one and the same. The elder or elders of the church may be so connected with the offending brother that they may set aside the necessity, and supply the place of the 'one or two' witnesses. So that it may suffice to tell it to them after you have told it to your brother, 'between you and him alone'.

3. When you have done this you have delivered your own soul. 'If he will not hear the church', if he persist in his sin, 'let him be to thee as an heathen man and a publican.' You are under no obligation to think of him any more—only when you commend him to God in prayer. You need not speak of him any more, but leave him to his own Master. Indeed you still owe to him, as to all other heathens, earnest, tender goodwill. You owe him courtesy, and as occasion offers all the offices of humanity. But have no friendship, no familiarity with him; no other intercourse than with an open heathen.

4. But if this be the rule by which Christians walk, which is the land where the Christians live? A few you may possibly find scattered up and down who make a conscience of observing it. But how very few! How thinly scattered upon the face of the earth! And where is there any body of men that universally walk thereby? Can we find them in Europe? Or, to go no farther, in Great Britain or Ireland? I fear not: I fear we may search these kingdoms throughout, and yet search in vain. Alas for the Christian world! Alas for Protestants, for Reformed Christians! 'O who will rise up with me against the wicked? Who will take God's part against the evil-speakers?' 'Art thou the man?' By the grace of God wilt thou be one who art not carried away by the torrent? Art thou fully determined, God being thy helper, from this very hour to set a watch, a continual 'watch before thy mouth, and keep the door of thy lips'? From this hour wilt thou walk by this rule, 'speaking evil of no man'? If thou seest thy brother do evil, wilt thou 'tell him of his fault between thee and him alone'? Afterwards 'take one or two witnesses', and then only 'tell it to the church'? If this be the full purpose of thy heart, then learn one lesson well: *Hear evil of no man.* If there were no hearers, there would be no speakers of evil. And is not (according to the vulgar proverb) the receiver as bad as the thief? If then any begin to speak evil in thy hearing, check him immediately. Refuse to hear the voice of the charmer, charm he never so sweetly: let him use ever so soft a manner, so mild an accent, ever so many professions of goodwill for him whom he is stabbing in the dark, whom he smiteth under the fifth rib.

Resolutely refuse to hear, though the whisperer complain of being 'burdened' till he speak. Burdened! thou fool, dost thou 'travail with' thy cursed *secret*, 'as a woman travaileth with child'? Go then and be delivered of thy burden, in the way the Lord hath ordained. First, 'go and tell thy brother of his fault, between thee and him alone.' Next, 'take with thee one or two' common friends, and tell him in their presence. If neither of these steps take effect, then 'tell it to the church.' But at the peril of thy soul tell it to no one else, either before or after, unless in that one exempt case, when it is absolutely needful to preserve the innocent. Why shouldst thou burden another as well as thyself by making him partaker of thy sin?

5. O that all you who bear the reproach of Christ, who are in derision called 'Methodists', would set an example to the Christian world, so called, at least in this one instance! Put ye away evil-speaking, talebearing, whispering: let none of them proceed out of your mouth. See that you 'speak evil of no man;' of the absent nothing but good. If ye must be distinguished, whether ye will or no, let this be the distinguishing mark of a Methodist: 'He censures no man behind his back: by this fruit ye may know him.' What a blessed effect of this self-denial should we quickly feel in our hearts! How would our 'peace flow as a river', when we thus 'followed peace with all men'! How would the love of God abound in our own souls while we thus confirmed our love to our brethren! And what an effect would it have on all that were united together in the name of the Lord Jesus! How would brotherly love continually increase when this grand hindrance of it was removed! All the members of Christ's mystical body would then *naturally care for* each other: 'If one member suffered, all would suffer with it; if one was honoured, all would rejoice with it;' and everyone would love his brother 'with a pure heart fervently'. Nor is this all: but what an effect might this have even on the wild unthinking world! How soon would they descry in us what they could not find among all the thousands of their brethren, and cry (as Julian the Apostate to his heathen courtiers), 'See how these Christians love one another!' By this chiefly would God convince the world, and prepare them also for his kingdom, as we may easily learn from those remarkable words in our Lord's last, solemn prayer: 'I pray for them who will believe in me, that they all may be one, as thou, Father, art in me, and I in thee; that the world may believe that thou hast sent me!' The Lord hasten the time! The Lord enable *us* thus to love one another, not only 'in word and in tongue, but in deed and in truth', even as Christ hath loved us.

42. THE WILDERNESS STATE

1760

An Introductory Comment

These next two sermons, "The Wilderness State" and "Heaviness through Manifold Temptations," should be read together since they treat the difficulties that may emerge in Christian formation. In this first sermon, Wesley employed the allegory of the wilderness that recalls the wanderings of the ancient Hebrews in the desert and that was utilized so ably by the Puritans (O, 2:202). Making a sharp distinction between the wilderness state and heaviness through temptations, Wesley insisted in his *Notes Upon the New Testament* that believers need not ever enter the wilderness state, which is one of spiritual darkness. Accordingly, its causes are often found in sins of commission or omission and yielding to some kind of inward sin, among other things (O, 2:208–10).

As with other mystical writers, William Law maintained that it may be beneficial for the soul to lose its sense of the love of God (B, 457), a notion that Wesley clearly repudiated. This present sermon, then, may in part be a response to and entail criticism of Law's earlier work, *The Spirit of Prayer,* that was published in 1749 (S, 2:244). Indeed, the first Methodist Conference in 1744 (in *Q.* 10) affirmed that a believer "need not come into a state of doubt, or fear, or darkness," though it quickly added that the "first joy" is "commonly followed by doubts and fears [but not darkness]" (R, 10:128).

The language of this sermon emerged in Wesley's pastoral counsel on at least two occasions: the first, in a letter to Mrs. Marston on August 11, 1770, in which he cautioned her "to beware of supposing darkness, that is unbelief, to be better than the light of faith" (T, 5:196); the second, in a letter to Rebecca Yeoman on February 5, 1772, in which Wesley urged her to read this sermon and "examine yourself thereby" (T, 5:303). The sermon register reveals that Wesley preached on this text (John 16:22) more than thirty-five times (WWS).

The Wilderness State

I. 1. What is the disease into which so many fall after believing?
  A. First, it consists in the loss of faith
 2. Second, a loss of love accompanies the loss of faith
 3. Third, there is a loss of joy in the Holy Ghost
 4.–5. Fourth, there are the loss of peace and the loss of power

II. What is the cause of the wilderness state?
 1.–3. The most usual cause is *sin* of one kind or another
  A. First, there are sins of *commission*
  B. Second, there are sins of *omission*
 4. No sin of omission occasions this more than neglect of private prayer
 5.–8. Third, there are *inward* sins such as anger and sinful desires
 9. If we give way to *spiritual sloth* this will effectually darken the soul
 10. The cause of darkness is not always nigh at hand
  A. Ignorance of the work of God in the soul also occasions darkness

III. What is the cure of this darkness?
 1. The cure is not the same in all cases
  A. The cure must correspond with the cause
 2. For instance: is it sin which occasions darkness? If so, then what sin?
 3. If no sin of commission causes it, inquire if there is a sin of omission
 4. Perhaps you are not conscious of any *sin of omission*
 5.–6. Perhaps this very thing keeps your soul in darkness
  A. This is the want of striving, or *spiritual sloth*
 7.–11. The cure will be different if the cause is *ignorance*
 12.–13. But is not darkness much more profitable for the soul than light?
  A. So the *mystics* teach, but not *the oracles of God*
 14. Lastly, if temptation is the cause of darkness, the way to remove this is:
  A. Teach believers to expect temptation, seeing they dwell in an evil world

Sermon 46: The Wilderness State, 1760

John 16:22

Ye now have sorrow; but I will see you again, and your heart shall rejoice, and your joy no man taketh from you.

1. After God had wrought a great deliverance for Israel by bringing them out of the house of bondage, they did not immediately enter into the land which he had promised to their fathers, but 'wandered out of the way in the wilderness', and were variously tempted and distressed. In like manner after God has delivered them that fear him from the bondage of sin and Satan; after they are 'justified freely by his grace, through the redemption that is in Jesus', yet not many of them immediately enter into 'the rest' which 'remaineth for the people of God'. The greater part of them wander more or less out of the good way into which he hath brought them. They come as it were into a 'waste and howling desert', where they are variously tempted and tormented. And this some, in allusion to the case of the Israelites, have termed 'a wilderness state'.

2. Certain it is that the condition wherein these are has a right to the tenderest compassion. They labour under an evil and sore disease, though one that is not commonly understood. And for this very reason it is the more difficult for them to find a remedy. Being in darkness themselves, they cannot be supposed to understand the nature of their own disorder; and few of their brethren—nay, perhaps of their teachers—know either what their sickness is, or how to heal it. So much the more need there is to inquire, first, what is the nature of this disease; secondly, what is the cause; and thirdly, what is the cure of it.

I.1. And, first, what is the nature of this disease into which so many fall after they have believed? Wherein does it properly consist? And what are the genuine symptoms of it? It properly consists in the loss of that faith which God once wrought in their heart. They that are 'in the wilderness' have not now that divine 'evidence', that satisfactory 'conviction of things not seen', which they once enjoyed. They have not now that inward demonstration of the Spirit which before enabled each of them to say, 'The life I live, I live by faith in the Son of God, who loved *me* and gave himself for *me*.' The light of heaven does not now 'shine in their hearts', neither do they 'see him that is invisible'; but darkness is again on the face of their souls, and blindness on the eyes of their understanding. The Spirit no longer 'witnesses with their spirits that they are the children of God'; neither does he continue as the Spirit of adoption, 'crying in their hearts, Abba, Father'. They have not now a sure trust in his love, and a liberty of approaching him with holy boldness. 'Though he slay me, yet will I trust in him' is no more the language of their heart. But they are shorn of their strength, and become weak and feeble-minded, even as other men.

2. Hence, secondly, proceeds the loss of love, which cannot but rise or fall at the same time, and in the same proportion, with true, living faith. Accordingly they that are deprived of their faith are deprived of the love of God also. They cannot now say, 'Lord, thou knowest all things; thou knowest that I love thee.' They are not now happy in God, as everyone is that truly loves him. They do not delight in him as in time past,

and 'smell the odour of his ointments'. Once all their 'desire was unto him, and to the remembrance of his name'. But now even their desires are cold and dead, if not utterly extinguished. And as their love of God is 'waxed cold', so is also their love of their neighbour. They have not now that zeal for the souls of men, that longing after their welfare, that fervent, restless, active desire of their being reconciled to God. They do not feel those 'bowels of mercies' for the sheep that are lost, that tender 'compassion for the ignorant, and them that are out of the way'. Once they were 'gentle toward all men', meekly 'instructing' such as 'opposed' the truth, and 'if any was overtaken in a fault, restoring such an one in the spirit of meekness'. But after a suspense perhaps of many days, anger begins to regain its power. Yea, peevishness and impatience thrust sore at them, that they may fall. And it is well if they are not sometimes driven even to 'render evil for evil and railing for railing'.

3. In consequence of the loss of faith and love follows, thirdly, loss of joy in the Holy Ghost. For if the loving consciousness of pardon be no more, the joy resulting therefrom cannot remain. If the Spirit does not witness with our spirit that we are the children of God, the joy that flowed from that inward witness must also be at an end. And in like manner they who once 'rejoiced with joy unspeakable in hope of the glory' of God, now they are deprived of that 'hope full of immortality', are deprived of the joy it occasioned; as also of that which resulted from a consciousness of 'the love of God' then 'shed abroad in their hearts'. For the cause being removed, so is the effect: the fountain being dammed up, those living waters spring no more to refresh the thirsty soul.

4. With loss of faith and love and joy there is also joined, fourthly, the loss of that peace which once passed all understanding. That sweet tranquillity of mind, that composure of spirit, is gone. Painful doubt returns: doubt whether we ever did, and perhaps whether we ever shall, believe. We begin to doubt whether we ever did find in our hearts the real testimony of the Spirit. Whether we did not rather deceive our own souls, and mistake the voice of nature for the voice of God. Nay, and perhaps whether we shall ever hear his voice and find favour in his sight. And these doubts are again joined with servile fear, with that 'fear' which 'hath torment'. We fear the wrath of God, even as before we believed; we fear lest we should be cast out of his presence; and thence sink again into that fear of death from which we were before wholly delivered.

5. But even this is not all. For loss of peace is accompanied with loss of power. We know everyone who has peace with God through Jesus Christ has power over all sin. But whenever he loses the peace of God he loses also the power over sin. While that peace remained, power also remained, even over the besetting sin, whether it were the sin of his nature, his constitution, the sin of his education, or that of his profession; yea, and over those evil tempers and desires which till then he could not conquer. 'Sin' had then 'no more dominion over him'; but he hath now no more dominion over sin. He may struggle indeed, but he cannot overcome; the crown is fallen from his head. His enemies again prevail over him, and more or less bring him into bondage. The glory is departed from him, even the kingdom of God which was in his heart. He is dispossessed of righteousness, as well as of peace and joy in the Holy Ghost.

II.1. Such is the nature of what many have termed, and not improperly, 'the wilderness state'. But the nature of it may be more fully understood by inquiring, secondly, What are the causes of it? These indeed are various. But I dare not rank among these the bare, arbitrary, sovereign will of God. He rejoiceth 'in the prosperity of his servants'. He delighteth not to 'afflict or grieve the children of men'. His invariable 'will is our sanctification', attended with 'peace and joy in the Holy Ghost'. These are his own free gifts; and we are assured 'the gifts of God are' on his part 'without repentance.' He never repenteth of what he hath given, or desires to withdraw them from us. Therefore he never *deserts* us, as some speak: it is we only that *desert* him.

2. [(I).] The most usual cause of inward darkness is *sin* of one kind or another. This it is which generally occasions what is often a complication of sin and misery. And, first, sin of *commission.* This may frequently be observed to darken the soul in a moment; especially if it be a known, a wilful, or presumptuous sin. If, for instance, a person who is now walking in the clear light of God's countenance should be any way prevailed on to commit a single act of drunkenness or uncleanness, it would be no wonder if in that very hour he fell into utter darkness. It is true, there have been some very rare cases wherein God has prevented this by an extraordinary display of his pardoning mercy, almost in the very instant. But in general such an abuse of the goodness of God, so gross an insult on his love, occasions an immediate estrangement from God, and a 'darkness that may be felt'.

3. But it may be hoped this case is not very frequent; that there are not many who so despise the riches of his goodness as, while they walk in his light, so grossly and presumptuously to rebel against him. That light is much more frequently lost by giving way to sins of *omission.* This indeed does not immediately quench the Spirit, but gradually and slowly. The former may be compared to pouring water upon a fire; the latter to withdrawing the fuel from it. And many times will that loving Spirit reprove our neglect before he departs from us. Many are the inward checks, the secret notices, he gives before his influences are withdrawn. So that only a train of omissions wilfully persisted in can bring us into utter darkness.

4. Perhaps no sin of omission more frequently occasions this than the neglect of private prayer; the want whereof cannot be supplied by any other ordinance whatever. Nothing can be more plain than that the life of God in the soul does not continue, much less increase, unless we use all opportunities of communing with God, and pouring out our hearts before him. If therefore we are negligent of this, if we suffer business, company, or any avocation whatever, to prevent these secret exercises of the soul (or which comes to the same thing, to make us hurry them over in a slight and careless manner) that life will surely decay. And if we long or frequently intermit them, it will gradually die away.

5. Another sin of omission which frequently brings the soul of a believer into darkness is the neglect of what was so strongly enjoined even under the Jewish dispensation: 'Thou shalt in any wise rebuke thy neighbour, and not suffer sin upon him:' 'Thou shalt not hate thy brother in thy heart.' Now if we do 'hate our brother in our heart', if we do not 'rebuke' him when we see him in a fault, but 'suffer sin upon him', this will soon bring leanness into our own soul; seeing hereby we are 'partakers of his sin'. By neglecting to reprove our neighbour we make his sin our own. We become accountable for it to God:

we saw his danger, and gave him no warning. So 'if he perish in his iniquity' God may justly 'require his blood at our hands'. No wonder then if by thus grieving the Spirit we lose the light of his countenance.

6. A third cause of our losing this is the giving way to some kind of *inward sin*. For example: we know 'everyone that is proud in heart is an abomination to the Lord;' and that although this pride of heart should not appear in the outward conversation. Now how easily may a soul filled with peace and joy fall into this snare of the devil! How natural is it for him to imagine that he has more grace, more wisdom or strength, than he really has! 'To think more highly of himself than he ought to think!' How natural to glory in something he has received as if he had not received it! But seeing God continually 'resisteth the proud, and giveth grace' only 'to the humble', this must certainly obscure, if not wholly destroy, the light which before shone on his heart.

7. The same effect may be produced by giving place to anger, whatever the provocation or occasion be; yea, though it were coloured over with the name of *zeal* for the truth, or for the glory of God. Indeed all zeal which is any other than the flame of love is 'earthly, animal, devilish'. It is the flame of wrath. It is flat, sinful anger, neither better nor worse. And nothing is a greater enemy to the mild, gentle love of God than this. They never did, they never can, subsist together in one breast. In the same proportion as this prevails, love and joy in the Holy Ghost decrease. This is particularly observable in the case of *offence*, I mean, anger at any of our brethren, at any of those who are united with us either by civil or religious ties. If we give way to the spirit of offence but one hour we lose the sweet influences of the Holy Spirit; so that instead of amending them we destroy ourselves, and become an easy prey to any enemy that assaults us.

8. But suppose we are aware of this snare of the devil, we may be attacked from another quarter. When fierceness and anger are asleep, and love alone is waking, we may be no less endangered by *desire*, which equally tends to darken the soul. This is the sure effect of any 'foolish desire', any vain or inordinate affection. If we 'set our affection on things of the earth', on any person or thing under the sun, if we desire anything but God and what tends to God, if we seek happiness in any creature, the jealous God will surely contend with us; for he can admit of no rival. And 'if' we 'will' not 'hear' his warning 'voice', and return to him with our whole soul; if we continue to grieve him with our idols, and running after other gods, we shall soon be cold, barren, and dry, and 'the god of this world' will 'blind' and darken 'our hearts'.

9. But this he frequently does, even when we do not give way to any positive sin. It is enough, it gives him sufficient advantage, if we do not 'stir up the gift of God which is in us'; if we do not 'agonize' continually 'to enter in at the strait gate'; if we do not earnestly 'strive for the mastery', and 'take the kingdom of heaven by violence'. There needs no more than not to fight, and we are sure to be conquered. Let us only be careless or 'faint in our mind', let us be easy and indolent, and our natural darkness will soon return, and overspread our soul. It is enough, therefore, if we give way to *spiritual sloth*: this will effectually darken the soul. It will as surely destroy the light of God, if not so swiftly, as murder or adultery.

10. But it is well to be observed that the cause of our darkness (whatsoever it be, whether omission or commission, whether inward or outward sin) is not always nigh at hand. Sometimes the sin which occasioned the present distress may lie at a considerable distance. It might be committed days or weeks or months before. And that God now withdraws his light and peace on account of what was done so long ago is not (as one might at first imagine) an instance of his severity, but rather a proof of his long-suffering and tender mercy. He waited all this time if haply we would see, acknowledge, and correct what was amiss. And in default of this he at length shows his displeasure, if thus, at last, he may bring us to repentance.

(II). 1. Another general cause of this darkness is *ignorance*; which is likewise of various kinds. If men know not the Scriptures, if they imagine there are passages either in the Old or New Testament which assert that all believers without exception *must* sometimes be in darkness, this ignorance will naturally bring upon them the darkness which they expect. And how common a case has this been among us! How few are there that do not expect it! And no wonder, seeing they are taught to expect it; seeing their guides lead them into this way. Not only the mystic writers of the Romish Church, but many of the most spiritual and experimental in our own (very few of the last century excepted), lay it down with all assurance as a plain, unquestionable Scripture doctrine, and cite many texts to prove it.

2. Ignorance also of the work of God in the soul frequently occasions this darkness. Men imagine (because so they have been taught, particularly by writers of the Romish communion, whose plausible assertions too many Protestants have received without due examination) that they are not always to walk in 'luminous faith'; that this is only a 'lower dispensation'; that as they rise higher they are to leave those 'sensible comforts', and to live by 'naked faith' (*naked* indeed, if it be stripped both of love and peace and joy in the Holy Ghost!); that a state of light and joy is good, but a state of 'darkness' and 'dryness' is better, that it is by these alone we can be 'purified' from pride, love of the world, and inordinate self-love; and that therefore we ought neither to expect nor desire to 'walk in the light' always. Hence it is (though other reasons may concur) that the main body of pious men in the Romish Church generally walk in a dark uncomfortable way, and if ever they receive, soon lose the light of God.

(III). 1. A third general cause of this darkness is *temptation*. When the candle of the Lord first shines on our head, temptation frequently flees away, and totally disappears. All is calm within: perhaps without, too, while God makes our enemies to be at peace with us. It is then very natural to suppose that we shall not see war any more. And there are instances wherein this calm has continued, not only for weeks, but for months or years. But commonly it is otherwise: in a short time 'the winds blow, the rains descend, and the floods arise' anew. They who 'know not either the Son or the Father', and consequently hate his children, when God slackens the bridle which is in their teeth, will show that hatred in various instances. As of old 'he that was born after the flesh persecuted him that was born after the Spirit, even so it is now;' the same cause still producing the same effect.

The evil which yet remains in the heart will then also move afresh; anger and many other 'roots of bitterness' will endeavour to spring up. At the same time Satan will not be wanting to cast in his fiery darts; and the soul will have to 'wrestle', not only with the world, not only 'with flesh and blood, but with principalities and powers, with the rulers of the darkness of this world, with wicked spirits in high places'. Now when so various assaults are made at once, and perhaps with the utmost violence, it is not strange if it should occasion not only heaviness, but even darkness in a weak believer. More especially if he was not watching, if these assaults are made in an hour when he looked not for them; if he expected nothing less, but had fondly told himself,

The day of evil would return no more.

2. The force of those temptations which arise from within will be exceedingly heightened if we before thought too highly of ourselves, as if we had been cleansed from all sin. And how naturally do we imagine this during the warmth of our first love! How ready are we to believe that God has 'fulfilled' in us the whole 'work of faith with power'! That because we *feel* no sin, we *have* none in us, but the soul is all love! And well may a sharp attack from an enemy whom we supposed to be not only conquered but slain, throw us into much heaviness of soul, yea, sometimes into utter darkness; particularly when we *reason* with this enemy, instead of instantly calling upon God, and casting ourselves upon him by simple faith who *alone* 'knoweth how to deliver' his [own] 'out of temptation'.

III. These are the usual causes of this second darkness. Inquire we, thirdly, what is the cure of it?

1. To suppose that this is one and the same in all cases is a great and fatal mistake; and yet extremely common even among many who pass for experienced Christians; yea, perhaps take upon them to be 'teachers in Israel', to be the guides of other souls. Accordingly they know and use but one medicine, whatever be the cause of the distemper. They begin immediately to apply the promises, to 'preach the gospel', as they call it. To give comfort is the single point at which they aim, in order to which they say many soft and tender things concerning the love of God to poor, helpless sinners, and the efficacy of the blood of Christ. Now this is 'quackery' indeed, and that of the worse sort, as it tends, if not to kill men's bodies, yet without the peculiar mercy of God to 'destroy both' their 'bodies and souls in hell'. It is hard to speak of these 'daubers with untempered mortar', these promise-mongers, as they deserve. They well deserve the title which has been ignorantly given to others: they are 'spiritual mountebanks'. They do, in effect, make 'the blood of the covenant an unholy thing'. They vilely prostitute the promises of God by thus applying them to all without distinction. Whereas indeed the cure of spiritual, as of bodily diseases, must be as various as are the causes of them. The first thing, therefore, is to find out the cause, and this will naturally point out the cure.

2. For instance: is it sin which occasions darkness? What sin? Is it outward sin of any kind? Does your conscience accuse you of committing any sin whereby you grieve the

Holy Spirit of God? Is it on this account that he is departed from you, and that joy and peace are departed with him? And how can you expect they should return till you put away the accursed thing? 'Let the wicked forsake his way;' 'cleanse your hands, ye sinners;' 'put away the evil of your doings.' So shall your 'light break out of obscurity': 'the Lord will return and abundantly pardon.'

3. If upon the closest search you can find no sin of commission which causes the cloud upon your soul, inquire next if there be not some sin of omission which separates between God and you. Do you 'not suffer sin upon your brother'? Do you reprove them that sin in your sight? Do you walk in all the ordinances of God? In public, family, private prayer? If not, if you habitually neglect any one of these known duties, how can you expect that the light of his countenance should continue to shine upon you? Make haste to 'strengthen the things that remain'; then your soul shall live. 'Today, if ye will hear his voice', by his grace supply what is lacking. When you 'hear a voice behind you, saying, This is the way; walk thou in it,' 'harden not your heart.' Be no more 'disobedient to the heavenly calling'. Till the sin, whether of omission or commission, be removed, all comfort is false and deceitful. It is only skinning the wound over, which still festers and rankles beneath. Look for no peace within till you are at peace with God; which cannot be without 'fruits meet for repentance'.

4. But perhaps you are not conscious of even any *sin of omission* which impairs your peace and joy in the Holy Ghost. Is there not then some *inward sin*, which as a 'root of bitterness springs up' in your heart to 'trouble you'? Is not your dryness and barrenness of soul occasioned by your heart's 'departing from the living God'? Has not 'the foot of pride come against' you? Have you not 'thought' of yourself 'more highly than you ought to think'? Have you not in any respect 'sacrificed to your own net, and burnt incense to your own drag'? Have you not ascribed your success in any undertaking to your own courage, or strength, or wisdom? Have you not boasted of something 'you have received, as though you had not received it'? Have you not gloried 'in anything save the cross of our Lord Jesus Christ'? Have you not sought after or desired the praise of men? Have you not taken pleasure in it? If so, you see the way you are to take. If you have fallen by pride, 'humble yourself under the mighty hand of God, and he will exalt you in due time.' Have you not forced him to depart from you by giving place to anger? Have you not 'fretted yourself because of the ungodly' or 'been envious against the evil-doers'? Have you not been offended at any of your brethren? Looking at their (real or imagined) sin, so as to sin yourself against the great law of love by estranging your heart from them? Then look unto the Lord, that you may renew your strength, that all this sharpness and coldness may be done away, that love and peace and joy may return together, and you may be invariably 'kind to each other, and tender-hearted; forgiving one another, even as God for Christ's sake hath forgiven you'. Have not you given way to any foolish desire? To any kind or degree of inordinate affection? How then can the love of God have place in your heart, till you put away your idols? 'Be not deceived; God is not mocked:' he will not dwell in a divided heart. As long therefore as you cherish Delilah in your bosom he has no place there. It is vain to hope for a recovery of his light till you pluck out the right eye and cast it from you. O let there be no longer delay. Cry to him that he may enable you so to do!

Bewail your own impotence and helplessness; and the Lord being your helper, enter in at the strait gate: take the kingdom of heaven by violence! Cast out every idol from his sanctuary, and the glory of the Lord shall soon appear.

5. Perhaps it is this very thing, the want of striving, *spiritual sloth*, which keeps your soul in darkness. You dwell at ease in the land: there is no war in your coasts, and so you are quiet and unconcerned. You go on in the same even track of outward duties, and are content there to abide. And do you wonder meantime that your soul is dead? O stir yourself up before the Lord! Arise, and shake yourself from the dust: wrestle with God for the mighty blessing. Pour out your soul unto God in prayer, and continue therein with all perseverance. Watch! Awake out of sleep, and keep awake! Otherwise there is nothing to be expected but that you will be alienated more and more from the light and life of God.

6. If upon the fullest and most impartial examination of yourself you cannot discern that you at present give way either to spiritual sloth or any other inward or outward sin, then call to mind the time that is past. Consider your former tempers, words, and actions. Have these been right before the Lord? 'Commune with him in your chamber, and be still,' and desire of him to try the ground of your heart, and bring to your remembrance whatever has at any time offended the eyes of his glory. If the guilt of any unrepented sin remain on our soul it cannot be but you will remain in darkness, till, having been 'renewed by repentance', you are again washed by faith in the 'fountain opened for sin and uncleanness'.

7. Entirely different will be the manner of the cure if the cause of the disease be not sin, but *ignorance*. It may be ignorance of the meaning of Scripture; perhaps occasioned by ignorant commentators—ignorant at least in this respect, however knowing or learned they may be in other particulars. And in this case that ignorance must be removed before we can remove the darkness arising from it. We must show the true meaning of those texts which have been misunderstood. My design does not permit me to consider all the passages of Scripture which have been pressed into this service. I shall just mention two or three which are frequently brought to prove that all believers must, sooner or later, 'walk in darkness'.

8. One of these is Isaiah 50:10: 'Who is among you that feareth the Lord, and obeyeth the voice of his servant, that walketh in darkness and hath no light? Let him trust in the name of the Lord, and stay upon his God.' But how does it appear either from the text or context that the person here spoken of ever had light? One who is 'convinced of sin' 'feareth the Lord and obeyeth the voice of his servant'. And him we should advise, though he was still dark of soul, and had never seen the light of God's countenance, yet to 'trust in the name of the Lord, and stay upon his God.' This text therefore proves nothing less than that a believer in Christ 'must sometimes "walk in darkness"'.

9. Another text which has been supposed to speak the same doctrine is Hosea 2:14: 'I will allure her, and bring her into the wilderness, and speak comfortably unto her.' Hence it has been inferred that God will bring every believer 'into the wilderness', into a state of deadness and darkness. But it is certain the text speaks no such thing. For it does not appear that it speaks of particular believers at all. It manifestly refers to the Jewish nation;

and perhaps to that only. But if it be applicable to particular persons, the plain meaning of it is this: I will draw him by love; I will next convince him of sin, and then comfort him by my pardoning mercy.

10. A third Scripture from whence the same inference has been drawn is that above-recited: 'Ye now have sorrow; but I will see you again, and your heart shall rejoice, and your joy no man taketh from you.' This has been supposed to imply that God would after a time withdraw himself from all believers; and that they could not, till after they had thus sorrowed, have the joy which no man could take from them. But the whole context shows that our Lord is here speaking personally to the apostles, and no others; and that he is speaking concerning those particular events—his own death and resurrection. 'A little while', says he, 'and ye shall not see me;' namely, while I am in the grave. 'And again a little while, and ye shall see me,' when I am risen from the dead. 'Ye will weep and lament, and the world will rejoice: but your sorrow shall be turned into joy. . . . Ye now have sorrow,' because I am about to be taken from your head; 'but I will see you again,' after my resurrection, 'and your heart shall rejoice. And your joy', which I will then give you, 'no man taketh from you.' All this we know was literally fulfilled in the particular case of the apostles. But no inference can be drawn from hence with regard to God's dealings with believers in general.

11. A fourth text (to mention no more) which has been frequently cited in proof of the same doctrine is 1 Peter 4:12: 'Beloved, think it not strange concerning the fiery trial which is to try you.' But this is full as foreign to the point as the preceding. The text, literally rendered, runs thus: 'Beloved, wonder not at the burning which is among you, which is for your trial.' Now however this may be accommodated to inward trials, in a secondary sense, yet primarily it doubtless refers to martyrdom and the sufferings connected with it. Neither therefore is this text anything at all to the purpose for which it is cited. And we may challenge all men to bring one text, either from the Old or New Testament, which is any more to the purpose than this.

12. 'But is not darkness much more profitable for the soul than light? Is not the work of God in the heart most swiftly and effectually carried on during a state of inward suffering? Is not a believer more swiftly and throughly purified by sorrow than by joy? By anguish and pain and distress and spiritual martyrdoms than by continual peace?' So the *mystics* teach; so it is written in their books—but not in *the oracles of God.* The Scripture nowhere says that the absence of God best perfects his work in the heart! Rather his presence, and a clear communion with the Father and the Son. A strong consciousness of this will do more in an hour than his absence in an age. Joy in the Holy Ghost will far more effectually purify the soul than the want of that joy; and the peace of God is the best means of refining the soul from the dross of earthly affections. Away then with the idle conceit that the kingdom of God is divided against itself; that the peace of God and joy in the Holy Ghost are obstructive of righteousness; and that 'we are saved', not 'by faith', but by unbelief; not by hope, but by despair!

13. So long as men dream thus they may well 'walk in darkness'. Nor can the effect cease till the cause is removed. But yet we must not imagine it will immediately cease, even when the cause is no more. When either ignorance or sin has caused darkness, one or the

other may be removed, and yet the light which was obstructed thereby may not immediately return. As it is the free gift of God, he may restore it sooner or later, as it pleases him. In the case of sin we cannot reasonably expect that it should immediately return. The sin began before the punishment, which may therefore justly remain after the sin is at an end. And even in the natural course of things, though a wound cannot be healed while the dart is sticking in the flesh, yet neither is it healed as soon as that is drawn out, but soreness and pain may remain long after.

14. Lastly, if darkness be occasioned by manifold, heavy, and unexpected temptations, the best way for removing and preventing this is—teach believers always to expect temptation; seeing they dwell in an evil world, among wicked, subtle, malicious spirits, and have an heart capable of all evil. Convince them that the whole work of sanctification is not (as they imagined) wrought at once; that when they first believe they are but as new-born babes, who are gradually to grow up, and may expect many storms before they come to the full stature of Christ. Above all let them be instructed, when the storm is upon them, not to reason with the devil, but to pray; to pour out their souls before God, and show him of their trouble. And these are the persons unto whom chiefly we are to apply the great and precious promises—not to the ignorant, till the ignorance is removed; much less to the impenitent sinner. To these we may largely and affectionately declare the loving-kindness of God our Saviour, and expatiate upon his tender mercies, which have been ever of old. Here we may dwell upon the faithfulness of God, whose 'word is tried to the uttermost', and upon the virtue of that blood which was shed for us, to 'cleanse us from all sin'. And God will then bear witness to his word, and bring their souls out of trouble. He will say, 'Arise, shine; for thy light is come, and the glory of the Lord is risen upon thee.' Yea, and that light, if thou walk humbly and closely with God, will 'shine more and more unto the perfect day'.

43. HEAVINESS THROUGH MANIFOLD TEMPTATIONS

1760

An Introductory Comment

"Heaviness through Manifold Temptations" was the natural sequel to the preceding sermon, "The Wilderness State." Wesley published the former in order to distinguish carefully the spiritual darkness and sin typical of the wilderness state from the heaviness of soul that may characterize even the lives of believers, that is, those marked by the gracious theological virtues. For example, in his notes on 1 Peter 1:6, the text of this sermon, Wesley wrote, "Ye are in heaviness . . . but not darkness; for they still retained both faith . . . hope and love" (NT). And Matthew Henry observed in his commentary that Wesley surely read, "The best of Christians, those who have reason greatly to rejoice, may yet be in great heaviness through manifold temptations" (H, 1 Pet. 1:6).

Given such concerns, the phrase "manifold temptations" not surprisingly surfaced numerous times in Wesley's writings as revealed in the following: in a *Journal* entry concerning a certain Mrs. Plat who was saved in "the midst of heaviness, through manifold temptations, without raiment, or food, or health, or friends" (WH, 19:127); in a letter to Bishop Gibson in 1747 in which Wesley affirmed, "I believe 'there is no such perfection in this life as implies an entire deliverance from manifold temptations'" (T, 2:280); and in a letter to Mrs. Barton much later in 1781 in which he cautioned, "You have met, and undoubtedly will meet, with manifold temptations" (T, 7:87).

Reflecting on the experience of the Methodists across the years, Wesley observed that the causes of heaviness are often found in poverty, the deaths of dear friends, the "apostasy of those who were united to us in the closest ties," and through "our great adversary . . . [who is] 'walking about seeking whom he may devour'" (O, 2:228–29). This pastoral sermon, with an eye on the challenges of the Christian life, appeared sixteen times in the register from 1754 to 1757 and was preached in London, Newcastle, Dublin, and Manchester, among other settings (WWS).

Heaviness through Manifold Temptations

I. 1. Those whom the Apostle addresses in heaviness were believers
A. However, their heaviness did not destroy their faith
2. Nor did their heaviness destroy their peace
3. The believers to whom the Apostle speaks were full of a living hope
4. They were filled with joy in the Holy Ghost
5. In the midst of their heaviness they still enjoyed the love of God
6. Though they were heavy, they retained power over sin

II. 1. The believers spoken of here were grieved
2. Translators rendered it 'heaviness' to denote two things
A. First, the degree; and next, the continuance of it
3. This heaviness may sometimes be so deep as to overshadow the whole soul
A. It may likewise have an influence over the whole body
B. Yet all this may consist with faith which still worketh by love
4. The Spirit of glory rests on those in heaviness

III. 1. What are the causes of such heaviness and sorrow in believers?
2. All diseases of long continuance are apt to produce heaviness
3. Calamity and poverty also give rise to heaviness
4. Next to this we place the death of those who are dear to us
5.–9. A still deeper sorrow we may feel for those who are dead while they live

IV. 1. For what ends does God permit heaviness to befall so many believers?
2. The first great end is the trial of our faith, through which it is purified
3. Heaviness serves to try, to purify, to confirm and increase living hope
4. The trials which increase our faith and hope increase our love also
5.–6. Yet another is their advance in holiness of heart and conversation
7. Add the advantage others receive seeing our behavior under affliction

V. 1. There is a great difference between *darkness* of soul and *heaviness*
2. There may be need of heaviness, but not darkness
3. Even heaviness is not *always* needful
4. We ought therefore to watch and pray

Sermon 47: Heaviness through Manifold Temptations, 1760

1 Peter 1:6

Now for a season, if need be, ye are in

heaviness through manifold temptations.

1. In the preceding discourse I have particularly spoken of that *darkness* of mind into which those are often observed to fall who once walked in the light of God's countenance. Nearly related to this is the *heaviness* of soul which is still more common, even among believers; indeed almost all the children of God experience this in an higher or lower degree. And so great is the resemblance between one and the other that they are frequently confounded together; and we are apt to say indifferently, 'Such an one is in *darkness*, or such an one is in *heaviness*,' as if they were equivalent terms, one of which implied no more than the other. But they are far, very far from it. Darkness is one thing; heaviness is another. There is a difference, yea a wide, an essential difference, between the former and the latter. And such a difference it is as all the children of God are deeply concerned to understand; otherwise nothing will be more easy than for them to slide out of heaviness into darkness. In order to prevent this I will endeavour to show,

I. What manner of persons those were to whom the Apostle says, 'Ye are in heaviness.'

II. What kind of 'heaviness' they were in.

III. What were the causes, and

IV. What were the ends of it.

I shall conclude with some inferences.

I.1. I am in the first place to show what manner of persons those were to whom the Apostle says, 'Ye are in heaviness.' And, first, it is beyond all dispute that they were believers at the time the Apostle thus addressed them. For so he expressly says, verse five: Ye 'who are kept through the power of God by *faith* unto salvation'. Again, verse seven, he mentions 'the trial of their *faith*, much more precious than that of gold which perisheth'. And yet again, verse nine, he speaks of their 'receiving the end of their *faith*, the salvation of their souls'. At the same time, therefore, that they were 'in heaviness', they were possessed of living faith. Their heaviness did not destroy their faith; they still 'endured, [as] seeing him that is invisible'.

2. Neither did their heaviness destroy their peace, the peace that passeth all understanding, which is inseparable from true, living faith. This we may easily gather from the second verse, wherein the Apostle prays, not that 'grace and peace' may be given them, but only that it may 'be multiplied unto them'; that the blessing which they already enjoyed might be more abundantly bestowed upon them.

3. The persons to whom the Apostle here speaks were also full of a living hope. For thus he speaks, verse three: 'Blessed be the God and Father of our Lord Jesus Christ, who according to his abundant mercy hath begotten us again'—me and you, all of us who are

'sanctified by the Spirit', and enjoy the 'sprinkling of the blood of Jesus Christ'—'unto a living hope, unto an inheritance', that is, unto a living hope of an inheritance, 'incorruptible, undefiled, and that fadeth not away.' So that notwithstanding their heaviness they still retained an hope full of immortality.

4. And they still 'rejoiced in hope of the glory of God'. They were filled with joy in the Holy Ghost. So, verse eight, the Apostle having just mentioned the final 'revelation of Jesus Christ' (namely, when he cometh to judge the world), immediately adds, 'In whom, though now ye see him not (not with your bodily eyes), yet believing, ye rejoice with joy unspeakable and full of glory.' Their heaviness therefore was not only consistent with living hope, but also with 'joy unspeakable'. At the same time they were thus heavy they nevertheless rejoiced with 'joy full of glory'.

5. In the midst of their heaviness they likewise still enjoyed the love of God which had been shed abroad in their hearts. 'Whom', says the Apostle, 'having not seen, ye love.' Though ye have not yet seen him face to face, yet knowing him by faith ye have obeyed his word, 'My son, give me thy heart.' He is your God, and your love, the desire of your eyes, and your 'exceeding great reward'. Ye have sought and found happiness in him; ye 'delight in the Lord, and he hath given you your heart's desire'.

6. Once more. Though they were heavy, yet were they holy. They retained the same power over sin. They were still 'kept' from this 'by the power of God'. They were 'obedient children, not fashioned according to their former desires', but 'as he that had called them is holy', so were they 'holy in all manner of conversation. . . . Knowing they were redeemed by the precious blood of Christ, a Lamb without spot and without blemish', they had, through the 'faith and hope which they had in God', 'purified their souls by the Spirit'. So that upon the whole their heaviness well consisted with faith, with hope, with love of God and man; with the peace of God, with joy in the Holy Ghost, with inward and outward holiness. It did no way impair, much less destroy, any part of the work of God in their hearts. It did not at all interfere with that 'sanctification of the Spirit' which is the root of all true 'obedience'; neither with the happiness which must needs result from 'grace and peace' reigning in the heart.

II.1. Hence we may easily learn what kind of heaviness they were in—the second thing which I shall endeavour to show. The word in the original is λυπηθέντες, 'made sorry', 'grieved', from λύπη, 'grief' or 'sorrow'. This is the constant, literal meaning of the word: and this being observed, there is no ambiguity in the expression, nor any difficulty in understanding it. The persons spoken of here were *grieved*: the heaviness they were in was neither more nor less than *sorrow* or *grief*—a passion which every child of man is well acquainted with.

2. It is probable our translators rendered it 'heaviness' (though a less common word) to denote two things: first, the degree; and next, the continuance of it. It does indeed seem that it is not a slight or inconsiderable degree of grief which is here spoken of, but such as makes a strong impression upon and sinks deep into the soul. Neither does this appear to be a transient sorrow, such as passes away in an hour; but rather such as having

taken fast hold of the heart is not presently shaken off, but continues for some time, as a settled temper, rather than a passion—even in them that have living faith in Christ, and the genuine love of God in their hearts.

3. Even in these this heaviness may sometimes be so deep as to overshadow the whole soul, to give a colour, as it were, to all the affections, such as will appear in the whole behaviour. It may likewise have an influence over the body; particularly in those that are either of a naturally weak constitution, or weakened by some accidental disorder, especially of the nervous kind. In many cases we find 'the corruptible body presses down the soul.' In this the soul rather presses down the body, and weakens it more and more. Nay, I will not say that deep and lasting sorrow of heart may not sometimes weaken a strong constitution, and lay the foundation of such bodily disorders as are not easily removed. And yet all this may consist with a measure of that 'faith which' still 'worketh by love'.

4. This may well be termed a 'fiery trial': and though it is not the same with that the Apostle speaks of in the fourth chapter, yet many of the expressions there used concerning outward sufferings may be accommodated to this inward affliction. They cannot indeed with any propriety be applied to them that are *in darkness*: these do not, cannot, *rejoice*; neither is it true that 'the Spirit of glory and of God resteth upon' them. But he frequently doth on those that are 'in heaviness', so that though 'sorrowful, yet' are they 'always rejoicing'.

III.1. But to proceed to the third point. What are the causes of such sorrow or heaviness in a true believer? The Apostle tells us clearly: 'Ye are in heaviness', says he, 'through manifold temptations'—ποικίλοις, 'manifold'; not only many in number, but of many kinds. They may be varied and diversified a thousand ways by the change or addition of numberless circumstances. And this very diversity and variety makes it more difficult to guard against them. Among these we may rank all bodily disorders; particularly acute diseases, and violent pain of every kind, whether affecting the whole body or the smallest part of it. It is true, some who have enjoyed uninterrupted health, and have felt none of these, may make light of them, and wonder that sickness or pain of body should bring heaviness upon the mind. And perhaps one in a thousand is of so peculiar a constitution as not to feel pain like other men. So hath it pleased God to show his almighty power by producing some of these prodigies of nature who have seemed not to regard pain at all, though of the severest kind; if that contempt of pain was not owing partly to the force of education, partly to a preternatural cause—to the power either of good or evil spirits who raised those men above the state of mere nature. But abstracting from these particular cases, it is in general a just observation, that

> . . . pain is perfect misery, and extreme
> Quite overturns all patience.

And even where this is prevented by the grace of God, where men do 'possess their souls in patience', it may nevertheless occasion much inward heaviness, the soul sympathizing with the body.

2. All diseases of long continuance, though less painful, are apt to produce the same effect. When God 'appoints over us consumption' or 'the chilling and burning ague', if it be not speedily removed it will not only 'consume the eyes', but 'cause sorrow of heart'. This is eminently the case with regard to all those which are termed 'nervous disorders'. And faith does not overturn the course of nature: natural causes still produce natural effects. Faith no more hinders the 'sinking of the spirits' (as it is called) in an hysteric illness, than the rising of the pulse in a fever.

3. Again, when 'calamity cometh as a whirlwind,' and poverty 'as an armed man', is this a little temptation? Is it strange if it occasion sorrow and heaviness? Although this also may appear but a small thing to those who stand at a distance, or who look and 'pass by on the other side', yet it is otherwise to them who feel it. 'Having food and raiment' (indeed the latter word, σκεπάσματα, implies lodging as well as apparel) we may, if the love of God is in our hearts, 'be therewith content'. But what shall they do who have none of these? Who as it were 'embrace the rock for a shelter'? Who have only the earth to lie upon, and only the sky to cover them? Who have not a dry, or warm, much less a clean abode for themselves and their little ones? No, nor clothing to keep themselves, or those they love next themselves, from pinching cold, either by day or night? I laugh at the stupid heathen, crying out,

Nil habet infelix paupertas durius in se
Quam quod ridiculos homines facit!

Has poverty nothing worse in it than this, that it 'makes men liable to be laughed at'? 'Tis a sign this idle poet talked by rote of the things which he knew not. Is not want of food something worse than this? God pronounced it as a curse upon man that he should earn it by 'the sweat of his brow'. But how many are there in this Christian country that toil and labour, and sweat, and have it not at last, but struggle with weariness and hunger together? Is it not worse for one after an hard day's labour to come back to a poor, cold, dirty, uncomfortable lodging, and to find there not even the food which is needful to repair his wasted strength? You that live at ease in the earth, that want nothing but eyes to see, ears to hear, and hearts to understand how well God has dealt with you—is it not worse to seek bread day by day, and find none? Perhaps to find the comfort also of five or six children, crying for what he has not to give. Were it not that he is restrained by an unseen hand, would he not soon 'curse God and die'? O want of bread! Want of bread! Who can tell what this means unless he hath felt it himself? I am astonished it occasions no more than heaviness even in them that believe!

4. Perhaps next to this we may place the death of those who were near and dear unto us; of a tender parent, and one not much declined into the vale of years; of a beloved child just rising into life, and clasping about our heart; of a friend that was as our own soul—next the grace of God the last, best gift of heaven. And a thousand circumstances may enhance the distress: perhaps the child, the friend, died in our embrace! Perhaps was snatched away when we looked not for it! Flourishing, cut down like a flower! In all these

cases we not only may, but ought to be affected: it is the design of God that we should. He would not have us stocks and stones. He would have our affections regulated, not extinguished. Therefore

> . . . nature unreproved may drop a tear:

There may be sorrow without sin.

5. A still deeper sorrow we may feel for those who are dead while they live, on account of the unkindness, ingratitude, apostasy of those who were united to us in the closest ties. Who can express what a lover of souls may feel for a friend, a brother dead to God? For an husband, a wife, a parent, a child, rushing into sin as an horse into the battle, and in spite of all arguments and persuasions hasting to work out his own damnation? And this anguish of spirit may be heightened to an inconceivable degree by the consideration that he who is now posting to destruction once ran well in the way of life. Whatever he was in time past serves now to no other purpose than to make our reflections on what he is more piercing and afflictive.

6. In all these circumstances we may be assured our great adversary will not be wanting to improve his opportunity. He who is always 'walking about seeking whom he may devour' will then especially use all his power, all his skill, if haply he may gain any advantage over the soul that is already cast down. He will not be sparing of his fiery darts, such as are most likely to find an entrance, and to fix most deeply in the heart, by their suitableness to the temptation that assaults it. He will labour to inject unbelieving, or blasphemous, or repining thoughts. He will suggest that God does not regard, does not govern the earth; or at least that he does not govern it aright, not by the rules of justice and mercy. He will endeavour to stir up the heart against God, to renew our natural enmity against him. And if we attempt to fight him with his own weapons, if we begin to *reason* with him, more and more heaviness will undoubtedly ensue, if not utter darkness.

7. It has been frequently supposed that there is another cause (if not of darkness, at least) of heaviness, namely, God's withdrawing himself from the soul because it is his sovereign will. Certainly he will do this if we grieve his Holy Spirit, either by outward or inward sin; either by doing evil or neglecting to do good; by giving way either to pride or anger, to spiritual sloth, to foolish desire or inordinate affection. But that he ever withdraws himself because he *will,* merely because it is his good pleasure, I absolutely deny: there is no text in all the Bible which gives any colour for such a supposition. Nay, it is a supposition contrary not only to many particular texts, but to the whole tenor of Scripture. It is repugnant to the very nature of God; it is utterly beneath his majesty and wisdom (as an eminent writer strongly expresses it) 'to play at *bo-peep* with his creatures'. It is inconsistent both with his justice and mercy, and with the sound experience of all his children.

8. One more cause of heaviness is mentioned by many of those who are termed mystic authors. And the notion has crept in, I know not how, even among plain people who have no acquaintance with them. I cannot better explain this than in the words of a late

writer, who relates this as her own experience: 'I continued so happy in my Beloved, that although I should have been forced to live a vagabond in a desert, I should have found no difficulty in it. This state had not lasted long when in effect I found myself led into a desert. . . . I found myself in a forlorn condition, altogether poor, wretched, and miserable. . . . The proper source of this grief is the knowledge of ourselves, by which we find that there is an extreme unlikeness between God and us. We see ourselves most opposite to him, and that our inmost soul is entirely corrupted, depraved and full of all kind of evil and malignity, of the world and the flesh and all sorts of abominations.' From hence it has been inferred that the knowledge of ourselves, without which we should perish everlastingly, *must*, even after we have attained justifying faith, occasion the deepest heaviness.

9. But upon this I would observe, (1). In the preceding paragraph this writer says, 'Hearing I had not a true faith in Christ, I offered myself up to God, and immediately felt his love.' It may be so; and yet it does not appear that this was justification. 'Tis more probable it was no more than what are usually termed the 'drawings of the Father'. And if so, the heaviness and darkness which followed was no other than conviction of sin, which in the nature of things must precede that faith whereby we are justified. (2). Suppose she was justified almost the same moment she was convinced of wanting faith, there was then no time for that gradually increasing self-knowledge which uses to precede justification. In this case therefore it came after, and was probably the more severe the less it was expected. (3). It is allowed there will be a far deeper, a far clearer and fuller knowledge of our inbred sin, of our total corruption by nature, after justification, than ever there was before it. But this need not occasion darkness of soul. I will not say that it *must* bring us into heaviness. Were it so the Apostle would not have used that expression, 'if need be'; for there would be an absolute, indispensable need of it, for all that would know themselves; that is, in effect, for all that would know the perfect love of God, and be thereby 'made meet to be partakers of the inheritance of the saints in light'. But this is by no means the case. On the contrary, God may increase the knowledge of ourselves to any degree, and increase in the same proportion the knowledge of himself and the experience of his love. And in this case there would be no desert, no misery, no forlorn condition; but love and peace and joy, gradually springing up into everlasting life.

IV.1. For what ends, then (which was the fourth thing to be considered), does God permit heaviness to befall so many of his children? The Apostle gives us a plain and direct answer to this important question: 'That the trial of their faith, which is much more precious than gold that perisheth though it be tried by fire, may be found unto praise and honour and glory, at the revelation of Jesus Christ' (1 Pet. 1:7). There may be an allusion to this in that well-known passage of the fourth chapter (although it primarily relates to quite another thing, as has been already observed): 'Think it not strange concerning the fiery trial which is to try you', 'but rejoice that ye are partakers of the sufferings of Christ; that when his glory shall be revealed ye may likewise rejoice with exceeding great joy' (1 Pet. 1:12, etc.).

2. Hence we learn that the first and great end of God's permitting the temptations which bring heaviness on his children is the trial of their faith, which is tried by these, even

as gold by the fire. Now we know gold tried in the fire is purified thereby, is separated from its dross. And so is faith in the fire of temptation; the more it is tried, the more it is purified. Yea, and not only purified, but also strengthened, confirmed, increased abundantly, by so many more proofs of the wisdom and power, the love and faithfulness of God. This then—to increase our faith—is one gracious end of God's permitting those manifold temptations.

3. They serve to try, to purify, to confirm and increase that living hope also, whereunto 'the God and Father of our Lord Jesus Christ hath begotten us again of his abundant mercy'. Indeed our hope cannot but increase in the same proportion with our faith. On this foundation it stands: believing in his name, living by faith in the Son of God, we hope for, we have a confident expectation of, the glory which shall be revealed. And consequently, whatever strengthens our faith increases our hope also. At the same time it increases our joy in the Lord, which cannot but attend an hope full of immortality. In this view the Apostle exhorts believers in the other chapter, 'Rejoice that ye are partakers of the sufferings of Christ.' On this very account, 'Happy are you; for the Spirit of glory and of God resteth upon you.' And hereby ye are enabled, even in the midst of sufferings, to 'rejoice with joy unspeakable and full of glory'.

4. They rejoice the more because the trials which increase their faith and hope increase their love also; both their gratitude to God for all his mercies, and their goodwill to all mankind. Accordingly the more deeply sensible they are of the loving-kindness of God their Saviour, the more is their heart inflamed with love to him who 'first loved us'. The clearer and stronger evidence they have of the glory that shall be revealed, the more do they love him who hath purchased it for them, and 'given them the earnest' thereof 'in their hearts'. And this, the increase of their love, is another end of the temptations permitted to come upon them.

5. Yet another is their advance in holiness, holiness of heart and holiness of conversation; the latter naturally resulting from the former; for a good tree will bring forth good fruit. And all inward holiness is the immediate fruit of the faith that worketh by love. By this the blessed Spirit purifies the heart from pride, self-will, passion; from love of the world, from foolish and hurtful desires, from vile and vain affections. Beside that, sanctified afflictions have (through the grace of God) an immediate and direct tendency to holiness. Through the operation of his Spirit they humble more and more, and abase the soul before God. They calm and meeken our turbulent spirit, tame the fierceness of our nature, soften our obstinacy and self-will, crucify us to the world, and bring us to expect all our strength from, and to seek all our happiness in, God.

6. And all these terminate in that great end, that our faith, hope, love, and holiness, 'may be found' (if it doth not yet appear) 'unto praise' from God himself, 'and honour' from men and angels, 'and glory' assigned by the great Judge to all that have endured to the end. And this will be assigned in that awful day to every man 'according to his works', according to the work which God had wrought in his heart, and the outward works which he has wrought for God; and likewise according to what he had suffered; so that all these trials are unspeakable gain. So many ways do these 'light afflictions, which are but for a moment, work out for us a far more exceeding and eternal weight of glory'!

7. Add to this the advantage which others may receive by seeing our behaviour under affliction. We find by experience, example frequently makes a deeper impression upon us than precept. And what examples have a stronger influence, not only on those who are partakers of like precious faith, but even on them who have not known God, than that of a soul calm and serene in the midst of storms, sorrowful, yet always rejoicing; meekly accepting whatever is the will of God, however grievous it may be to nature; saying, in sickness and pain, 'The cup which my Father hath given me, shall I not drink it?' In loss or want, 'The Lord gave; the Lord hath taken away; blessed be the name of the Lord!'

V.1. I am to conclude with some inferences. And, first, how wide is the difference between *darkness* of soul and *heaviness*! Which nevertheless are so generally confounded with each other, even by experienced Christians! Darkness, or the wilderness state, implies a total loss of joy in the Holy Ghost; heaviness does not; in the midst of this we may 'rejoice with joy unspeakable'. They that are in darkness have lost the peace of God; they that are in heaviness have not. So far from it that at the very time 'peace' as well as 'grace' may 'be multiplied unto' them. In the former the love of God is waxed cold, if it be not utterly extinguished; in the latter it retains its full force, or rather increases daily. In these faith itself, if not totally lost, is however grievously decayed. Their evidence and conviction of things not seen, particularly of the pardoning love of God, is not so clear or strong as in time past; and their trust in him is proportionably weakened. Those, though they see him not, yet have a clear, unshaken confidence in God, and an abiding evidence of that love whereby all their sins are blotted out. So that as long as we can distinguish faith from unbelief, hope from despair, peace from war, the love of God from the love of the world, we may infallibly distinguish *heaviness* from *darkness*.

2. We may learn from hence, secondly, that there may be need of *heaviness*, but there can be no need of *darkness*. There may be need of our being in 'heaviness for a season', in order to the ends above recited; at least in this sense, as it is a natural result of those 'manifold temptations' which are needful to try and increase our faith, to confirm and enlarge our hope, to purify our heart from all unholy tempers, and to perfect us in love. And by consequence they are needful in order to brighten our crown, and add to our eternal weight of glory. But we cannot say that darkness is needful in order to any of these ends. It is no way conducive to them: the loss of faith, hope, love, is surely neither conducive to holiness nor to the increase of that reward in heaven which will be in proportion to our holiness on earth.

3. From the Apostle's manner of speaking we may gather, thirdly, that even heaviness is not *always* needful. 'Now, for a season, if need be'; so it is not needful for *all persons*; nor for any person at *all times*. God is able, he has both power and wisdom, to work when he pleases the same work of grace, in any soul, by other means. And in some instances he does so: he causes those whom it pleaseth him to go on from strength to strength, even till they 'perfect holiness in his fear', with scarce any heaviness at all; as having an absolute power over the heart of man, and moving all the springs of it at his pleasure. But these cases are rare: God generally sees good to try 'acceptable men in the furnace of affliction'; so that manifold temptations and heaviness, more or less, are usually the portion of his dearest children.

4. We ought therefore, lastly, to watch and pray, and use our utmost endeavours to avoid falling into darkness. But we need not be solicitous how to avoid, so much as how to improve by heaviness. Our great care should be so to behave ourselves under it, so to wait upon the Lord therein, that it may fully answer all the design of his love in permitting it to come upon us; that it may be a means of increasing our faith, of confirming our hope, of perfecting us in all holiness. Whenever it comes, let us have an eye to these gracious ends for which it is permitted, and use all diligence that we may not 'make void the counsel of' God 'against ourselves'. Let us earnestly 'work together with him', by the grace which he is continually giving us, in 'purifying ourselves from all pollution both of flesh and spirit', and daily 'growing in the grace of our Lord Jesus Christ', till we are received into his everlasting kingdom!

44. SATAN'S DEVICES

1750

An Introductory Comment

The Methodist Conference on June 17, 1747, raised twenty-two questions pertaining to the topic of sanctification that form the context for the proper understanding of this present sermon, which appeared three years later (R, 10:195). Wesley employed the text, 2 Corinthians 2:11, at Baptist Hills, Kingswood, Bristol, Birstall, Brentford, and London according to the sermon register (WWS).

The actual phrase "Satan's devices" emerged elsewhere in Wesley's writings in which he associated it with the antinomianism (lawlessness) that results from teaching that "Christ has fulfilled the Law for you" (WH, 20:101); the perplexity and loss of peace left in the wake of a particular Anabaptist teacher (WH, 21:335); and the assault of numerous temptations with respect to believers as expressed in a letter to Elizabeth Ritchie on June 3, 1774 (T, 6:89).

Though Satan's devices are as numerous as "the stars of heaven or the sand upon the sea-shore" (O, 2:139), in this sermon Wesley focused on how the *joy* of believers is dampened and their *peace* shaken by a consideration of "our own vileness, sinfulness, [and] unworthiness" (O, 2:140–41). Viewed in yet another way, the chief obstacle that constitutes the device of Satan is "to think lightly of the present gifts of God, and to undervalue what we have already received because of what we have not received" (O, 2:141). Such an approach, marked by a spirit of ingratitude, is often expressed in the depreciation of the nature of the new birth, not recognizing the glorious work that it actually is, in order to highlight the graces not yet received in entire sanctification. Interestingly enough, the first work of God in the soul is undermined or even destroyed "by our expectation of that greater work" (O, 2:140).

The way forward out of this malaise is to "admire more and more the free grace of God" and to remember "I am 'justified freely by his grace, through the redemption that is in Jesus Christ'" (O, 2:148).

Satan's Devices

I. 1. The god of this world works to dampen our joy by our unworthiness
   2. If he can prevail in this, he will soon attack our peace also
   3. He will not cease to urge the tree is known by its fruits
      A. He will ask, 'Have you the fruits of justification?'
   4. He will press, 'Without holiness no man shall see God'
   5. Not content to strike your peace and joy, he will go even farther
      A. He will assault your righteousness also
   6.–8. Above all, our adversary endeavours to weaken, if not destroy, our faith
   9. It is no marvel that he put forth all his strength on this front
   10. Here is another snare laid for our feet:
      A. We pant for the part of the promise to be accomplished here
      B. But we may be led unaware of the glory which will be revealed
   11. While we are reaching to this, we may fall into another snare
      A. We may take too much thought for tomorrow, neglecting today
   12. Thus he makes that blessed hope an occasion of unholy tempers
   13. He labors to excite fretfulness or impatience
   14. From here he hopes to reap another advantage
      A. He sees how few distinguish between abuse and tendency of a doctrine
      B. These he will continually blend together regarding Christian perfection
      C. Let us next observe how we may resist these fiery darts

II. 1. First, Satan endeavours to steal your joy by pointing out your sinfulness
      A. To cast back this dart, rejoice with hope that all this will pass
   2. Second, he assaults peace with the suggestion: 'God is holy, you are unholy'
      A. Value the truth that by grace we are saved through faith
   3. Hold fast to the faith which you have attained
   4. In the same power of faith press on to glory
   5. If you taste of the good word you will not murmur against God
      A. You will praise God for delivering you; you will magnify God
   6. If you see any who appear made perfect in love let it comfort your heart
   7. Redeem the time; improve the present moment
   8. Lastly, if you have abused this hope, do not cast it away
      A. Press on unto perfection, growing in the knowledge of Jesus

Sermon 42: Satan's Devices, 1750

2 Corinthians 2:11

We are not ignorant of his devices.

1. The devices whereby the subtle 'god of this world' labours to destroy the children of God, or at least to torment whom he cannot destroy, to perplex and hinder them in running the race which is set before them, are numberless as the stars of heaven or the sand upon the sea-shore. But it is of one of them only that I now propose to speak (although exerted in various ways), whereby he endeavours to divide the gospel against itself, and by one part of it to overthrow the other.

2. The inward kingdom of heaven, which is set up in the heart of all that 'repent and believe the gospel', is no other than 'righteousness and peace and joy in the Holy Ghost'. Every babe in Christ knows we are made partakers of these the very hour that we believe in Jesus. But these are only the first-fruits of his Spirit; the harvest is not yet. Although these blessings are inconceivably great, yet we trust to see greater than these. We trust to 'love the Lord our God' not only as we do now, with a weak though sincere affection, but 'with all our heart, with all our mind, with all our soul, and with all our strength'. We look for power to 'rejoice evermore', to 'pray without ceasing', and 'in everything to give thanks'; knowing 'this is the will of God concerning' us 'in Christ Jesus'.

3. We expect to be 'made perfect in love', in that love which 'casts out' all painful 'fear', and all desire but that of glorifying him we love, and of loving and serving him more and more. We look for such an increase in the experimental knowledge and love of God our Saviour as will enable us always to 'walk in the light, as he is in the light'. We believe the whole 'mind' will be in us 'which was also in Christ Jesus'; that we shall love every man so as to be ready 'to lay down our life for his sake', so as by this love to be freed from anger and pride, and from every unkind affection. We expect to be 'cleansed' from all our idols, 'from all filthiness', whether 'of flesh or spirit'; to be 'saved from all our uncleannesses', inward or outward; to be 'purified as he is pure'.

4. We trust in his promise who cannot lie, that the time will surely come when in every word and work we shall 'do his' blessed 'will on earth, as it is done in heaven'; when all our conversation shall be 'seasoned with salt', all meet to 'minister grace to the hearers'; when 'whether we eat or drink, or whatever we do', it shall be done 'to the glory of God'; when all our words and deeds shall be 'in the name of the Lord Jesus, giving thanks unto God, even the Father, through him'.

5. Now this is the grand device of Satan: to destroy the first work of God in the soul, or at least to hinder its increase by our expectation of that greater work. It is therefore my present design, first, to point out the several ways whereby he endeavours this; and, secondly, to observe how we may retort these fiery darts of the wicked one—how we may rise the higher by what he intends for an occasion of our falling.

I.1. I am, first, to point out the several ways whereby Satan endeavours to destroy the first work of God in the soul, or at least to hinder its increase by our expectation of that greater work. And, (1), he endeavours to damp our joy in the Lord by the consideration of our own vileness, sinfulness, unworthiness; added to this, that there *must* be a far greater change than is yet, or we cannot see the Lord. If we knew we *must* remain as we are, even to the day of our death, we might possibly draw a kind of comfort, poor as it was, from that necessity. But as we know, we need not remain in this state, as we are assured, there is a greater change to come—and that unless sin be all done away in this life we cannot see God in glory—that subtle adversary often damps the joy we should otherwise feel in what we have already attained, by a perverse representation of what we have not attained, and the absolute necessity of attaining it. So that we cannot rejoice in what we have, because there is more which we have not. We cannot rightly taste the goodness of God, who hath done so great things for us, because there are so much greater things which as yet he hath not done. Likewise the deeper conviction God works in us of our present unholiness, and the more vehement desire we feel in our heart of the entire holiness he hath promised, the more are we tempted to think lightly of the present gifts of God, and to undervalue what we have already received because of what we have not received.

2. If he can prevail thus far, if he can damp our joy, he will soon attack our peace also. He will suggest, 'Are you fit to see God? He is of purer eyes than to behold iniquity. How then can you flatter yourself so as to imagine he beholds *you* with approbation? God is holy; you are unholy. What communion hath light with darkness? How is it possible that *you*, unclean as you are, should be in a state of acceptance with God? You see indeed the mark, the prize of your high calling. But do you not see it is afar off? How can you presume then to think that all your sins are already blotted out? How can this be until you are brought nearer to God, until you bear more resemblance to him?' Thus will he endeavour, not only to shake your peace, but even to overturn the very foundation of it; to bring you back by insensible degrees to the point from whence you set out first: even to seek for justification by works, or by your own righteousness; to make something in *you* the ground of your acceptance, or at least necessarily previous to it.

3. Or if we hold fast—'other foundation can no man lay than that which is laid, even Jesus Christ;' and I am 'justified freely by God's grace, through the redemption which is in Jesus'—yet he will not cease to urge, 'But "the tree is known by its fruits." And have you the fruits of justification? Is "that mind in you which was in Christ Jesus"? Are you "dead unto sin and alive unto" righteousness? Are you made conformable to the death of Christ, and do you know the power of his resurrection?' And then, comparing the small fruits we feel in our souls with the fullness of the promises, we shall be ready to conclude: 'Surely God hath not said that my sins are forgiven me! Surely I have not received the remission of my sins; for what lot have I among them that are sanctified?'

4. More especially in the time of sickness and pain he will press this with all his might: 'Is it not the word of him that cannot lie, "Without holiness no man shall see the Lord"? But you are not holy. You know it well; you know holiness is the full image of God. And how far is this above, out of your sight? You cannot attain unto it. Therefore all your labour has been in vain. All these things you have suffered in vain. You have spent your strength for nought. You are yet in your sins and must therefore perish at the last.' And thus, if your eye be not steadily fixed on him who hath borne all your sins, he will bring

you again under that 'fear of death' whereby you was so long 'subject unto bondage'; and by this means impair, if not wholly destroy, your peace as well as joy in the Lord.

5. But his masterpiece of subtlety is still behind. Not content to strike at your peace and joy, he will carry his attempts farther yet: he will level his assault against your righteousness also. He will endeavour to shake, yea, if it be possible, to destroy the holiness you have already received by your very expectation of receiving more, of attaining all the image of God.

6. The manner wherein he attempts this may partly appear from what has been already observed. For, first, by striking at our joy in the Lord he strikes likewise at our holiness: seeing joy in the Holy Ghost is a precious means of promoting every holy temper; a choice instrument of God whereby he carries on much of his work in a believing soul. And it is a considerable help not only to inward but also to outward holiness. It strengthens our hands to go on in the work of faith and in the labour of love; manfully to 'fight the good fight of faith,' and to 'lay hold on eternal life.' It is peculiarly designed of God to be a balance both against inward and outward sufferings; to 'lift up the hands that hang down' and confirm 'the feeble knees'. Consequently, whatever damps our joy in the Lord proportionably obstructs our holiness. And therefore so far as Satan shakes our joy he hinders our holiness also.

7. The same effect will ensue if he can by any means either destroy or shake our peace. For the peace of God is another precious means of advancing the image of God in us. There is scarce a greater help to holiness than this: a continual tranquility of spirit, the evenness of a mind stayed upon God, a calm repose in the blood of Jesus. And without this it is scarce possible to grow in grace, and in the vital knowledge of our Lord Jesus Christ. For all fear (unless the tender, filial fear) freezes and benumbs the soul. It binds up all the springs of spiritual life, and stops all motion of the heart toward God. And doubt, as it were, bemires the soul, so that it sticks fast in the deep clay. Therefore in the same proportion as either of these prevail, our growth in holiness is hindered.

8. At the same time that our wise adversary endeavours to make our conviction of the necessity of perfect love an occasion of shaking our peace by doubts and fears, he endeavours to weaken, if not destroy, our faith. Indeed these are inseparably connected, so that they must stand or fall together. So long as faith subsists we remain in peace; our heart stands fast while it believes in the Lord. But if we let go our faith, our filial confidence in a loving, pardoning God, our peace is at an end, the very foundation on which it stood being overthrown. And this is the only foundation of holiness as well as of peace. Consequently whatever strikes at this strikes at the very root of all holiness. For without this faith, without an abiding sense that Christ loved me and gave himself for me, without a continuing conviction that God for Christ's sake is merciful to me a sinner, it is impossible that I should love God. 'We love him because he first loved us;' and in proportion to the strength and clearness of our conviction that he hath loved us and accepted us in his Son. And unless we love God it is not possible that we should love our neighbour as ourselves; nor, consequently, that we should have any right affections either toward God or toward man. It evidently follows that whatever weakens our faith must in the same degree obstruct our holiness. And this is not only the most effectual but also the most

compendious way of destroying all holiness; seeing it does not affect any one Christian temper, any single grace or fruit of the Spirit, but, so far as it succeeds, tears up the very root of the whole work of God.

9. No marvel, therefore, that the ruler of the darkness of this world should here put forth all his strength. And so we find by experience. For it is far easier to conceive than it is to express the unspeakable violence wherewith this temptation is frequently urged on them who hunger and thirst after righteousness. When they see in a strong and clear light, on the one hand the desperate wickedness of their own hearts, on the other hand the unspotted holiness to which they are called in Christ Jesus; on the one hand the depth of their own corruption, of their total alienation from God; on the other the height of the glory of God, that image of the Holy One wherein they are to be renewed; there is many times no spirit left in them; they could almost cry out, 'With God this is impossible.' They are ready to give up both faith and hope, to cast away that very confidence whereby they are to overcome all things, and do all things, through Christ strengthening them; whereby, 'after' they 'have done the will of God', they are to 'receive the promise'.

10. And if they 'hold fast the beginning of their confidence steadfast unto the end', they shall undoubtedly receive the promise of God, reaching through both time and eternity. But here is another snare laid for our feet. While we earnestly pant for that part of the promise which is to be accomplished here, for 'the glorious liberty of the children of God', we may be led unawares from the consideration of the glory which shall hereafter be revealed. Our eye may be insensibly turned aside from that 'crown which the righteous Judge' hath promised to 'give at that day to all that love his appearing'; and we may be drawn away from the view of that incorruptible inheritance which is reserved in heaven for us. But this also would be a loss to our souls, and an obstruction to our holiness. For to walk in the continual sight of our goal is a needful help in our running the race that is set before us. This it was, the having 'respect unto the recompense of reward', which of old time encouraged Moses rather 'to suffer affliction with the people of God than to enjoy the pleasures of sin for a season; esteeming the reproach of Christ greater riches than the treasures of Egypt'. Nay, it is expressly said of a greater than him, that 'for the joy that was set before him, he endured the cross, and despised the shame,' till he 'sat down at the right hand of the throne of God'. Whence we may easily infer how much more needful for us is the view of that joy set before us, that we may endure whatever cross the wisdom of God lays upon us, and press on through holiness to glory.

11. But while we are reaching to this, as well as to that glorious liberty which is preparatory to it, we may be in danger of falling into another snare of the devil, whereby he labours to entangle the children of God. We may take too much 'thought for tomorrow', so as to neglect the improvement of today. We may so expect 'perfect love' as not to use that which is already 'shed abroad in our hearts'. There have not been wanting instances of those who have greatly suffered hereby. They were so taken up with what they were to receive hereafter as utterly to neglect what they had already received. In expectation of having five talents more, they buried their one talent in the earth. At least they did not improve it as they might have done to the glory of God and the good of their own souls.

12. Thus does the subtle adversary of God and man endeavour to make void the

counsel of God by dividing the gospel against itself, and making one part of it overthrow the other—while the first work of God in the soul is destroyed by the expectation of his perfect work. We have seen several of the ways wherein he attempts this by cutting off, as it were, the springs of holiness; but this he likewise does more directly by making that blessed hope an occasion of unholy tempers.

13. Thus, whenever our heart is eagerly athirst for all the great and precious promises, when we pant after the fullness of God, as the hart after the water brook, when our soul breaketh out in fervent desire, 'Why are his chariot wheels so long a-coming?' he will not neglect the opportunity of tempting us to murmur against God. He will use all his wisdom and all his strength if haply, in an unguarded hour, we may be influenced to repine at our Lord for thus delaying his coming. At least he will labour to excite some degree of fretfulness or impatience; and perhaps of envy at those whom we believe to have already attained the prize of our high calling. He well knows that by giving way to any of these tempers we are pulling down the very thing we would build up. By *thus* following after perfect holiness we become more unholy than before. Yea, there is great danger that our last state should be worse than the first; like them of whom the Apostle speaks in those dreadful words, 'It had been better they had never known the way of righteousness, than after they had known it to turn back from the holy commandment delivered to them.'

14. And from hence he hopes to reap another advantage, even to bring up an evil report of the good way. He is sensible how few are able to distinguish (and too many are not willing so to do) between the accidental abuse and the natural tendency of a doctrine. These, therefore, will he continually blend together with regard to the doctrine of Christian perfection, in order to prejudice the minds of unwary men against the glorious promises of God. And how frequently, how generally—I had almost said, how universally—has he prevailed herein! For who is there that observes any of these accidental ill effects of this doctrine, and does not immediately conclude, 'This is its natural tendency'? And does not readily cry out, 'See, these are the fruits (meaning the natural, necessary fruits) of such doctrine!' Not so. They are fruits which may accidentally spring from the abuse of a great and precious truth. But the abuse of this, or any other scriptural doctrine, does by no means destroy its use. Neither can the unfaithfulness of man, perverting his right way, 'make the promise of God of none effect'. No; let God be true and every man a liar. The word of the Lord, it shall stand. 'Faithful is he that hath promised;' 'he also will do it.' Let not us then be 'removed from the hope of the gospel'. Rather let us observe—which was the second thing proposed—how we may retort these fiery darts of the wicked one; how we may rise the higher by what he intends for an occasion of our falling.

II.1. And, first, does Satan endeavour to damp your joy in the Lord by the consideration of your sinfulness, added to this, that without entire, universal 'holiness no man can see the Lord'? You may cast back this dart upon his own head while, through the grace of God, the more you feel of your own vileness the more you rejoice in confident hope that all this shall be done away. While you hold fast this hope, every evil temper you feel, though you hate it with a perfect hatred, may be a means, not of lessening your humble joy, but rather of increasing it. 'This and this', may you say, 'shall likewise perish from the presence of the Lord. Like as the wax melteth at the fire, so shall this melt away before his face.' By this means the greater that change is which remains to be wrought in your soul, the more may you triumph in the Lord and rejoice in the God of your salvation—who hath done so great things for you already, and will do so much greater things than these.

2. Secondly, the more vehemently he assaults your peace with that suggestion: 'God is holy; you are unholy. You are immensely distant from that holiness without which you cannot see God. How then can you be in the favour of God? How can you fancy you are justified?'—take the more earnest heed to hold fast that, 'not by works of righteousness which I have done' I am 'found in him'. I am 'accepted in the Beloved', 'not having my own righteousness' (as the cause either in whole or in part of our justification before God), 'but that which is by faith in Christ, the righteousness which is of God by faith'. O bind this about your neck; write it upon the table of thy heart; wear it as a bracelet upon thy arm, as frontlets between thine eyes: I am 'justified freely by his grace, through the redemption that is in Jesus Christ'. Value and esteem more and more that precious truth, 'By grace we are saved through faith.' Admire more and more the free grace of God in so loving the world as to give 'his only Son, that whosoever believeth on him might not perish but have everlasting life'. So shall the sense of the sinfulness you feel on the one hand, and of the holiness you expect on the other, both contribute to establish your peace, and to make it flow as a river. So shall that peace flow on with an even stream, in spite of all those mountains of ungodliness, which shall become a plain in the day when the Lord cometh to take full possession of your heart. Neither will sickness or pain, or the approach of death, occasion any doubt or fear. You know a day, an hour, a moment with God is as a thousand years. He cannot be straitened for time wherein to work whatever remains to be done in your soul. And God's time is always the best time. Therefore be thou 'careful for nothing'. Only 'make thy request known unto him,' and that, not with doubt or fear, but 'thanksgiving'; as being previously assured, he cannot withhold from thee any manner of thing that is good.

3. Thirdly, the more you are tempted to give up your shield, to cast away your faith, your confidence in his love, so much the more take heed that you hold fast that whereunto you have attained. So much the more labour to 'stir up the gift of God which is in you.' Never let that slip: I have 'an advocate with the Father, Jesus Christ the righteous'; and 'the life I now live, I live by faith in the Son of God, who loved me and gave himself for me.' Be this thy glory and crown of rejoicing. And see that no one take thy crown. Hold that fast: 'I know that my Redeemer liveth, and shall stand at the latter day upon the earth.' And I now 'have redemption in his blood, even the forgiveness of sins'. Thus, being filled with all peace and joy in believing, press on in the peace and joy of faith to the renewal of thy whole soul in the image of him that created thee. Meanwhile, cry continually to God that thou mayst see that prize of thy high calling, not as Satan represents it, in a horrid dreadful shape, but in its genuine native beauty; not as something that *must* be, or thou wilt go to hell, but as what *may* be, to lead thee to heaven. Look upon it as the most *desirable* gift which is in all the stores of the rich mercies of God. Beholding it in this true point of light, thou wilt hunger after it more and more: thy whole soul will be athirst for God, and for this glorious conformity to his likeness. And having received a good hope of this, and

strong consolation through grace, thou wilt no more be weary or faint in thy mind, but wilt follow on till thou attainest.

4. In the same power of faith press on to glory. Indeed this is the same prospect still. God hath joined from the beginning pardon, holiness, heaven. And why should man put them asunder? O beware of this. Let not one link of the golden chain be broken. God for Christ's sake hath forgiven me. He is now renewing me in his own image. Shortly he will make me meet for himself, and take me to stand before his face. I, whom he hath justified through the blood of his Son, being thoroughly sanctified by his Spirit, shall quickly ascend to the 'New Jerusalem, the city of the living God'. Yet a little while and I shall 'come to the general assembly and church of the first-born, and to God the judge of all, and to Jesus the Mediator of the new covenant'. How soon will these shadows flee away, and the day of eternity dawn upon me! How soon shall I drink of 'the river of the water of life, going out of the throne of God and of the Lamb! There all his servants shall praise him, and shall see his face, and his name shall be upon their foreheads. And no night shall be there; and they have no need of a candle or the light of the sun. For the Lord God enlighteneth them, and they shall reign for ever and ever.'

5. And if you thus 'taste of the good word, and of the powers of the world to come', you will not murmur against God, because you are not yet 'meet for the inheritance of the saints in light'. Instead of repining at your not being wholly delivered, you will praise God for thus far delivering you. You will magnify God for what he hath done, and take it as an earnest of what he will do. You will not fret against him because you are not yet renewed, but bless him because you shall be; and because 'now is your salvation' from all sin 'nearer than when you' first 'believed'. Instead of uselessly tormenting yourself because the time is not fully come you will calmly and quietly wait for it, knowing that it 'will come and will not tarry'. You may therefore the more cheerfully endure as yet the burden of sin that still remains in you, because it will not always remain. Yet a little while and it shall be clean gone. Only 'tarry thou the Lord's leisure: be strong, and he shall comfort thy heart; and put thou thy trust in the Lord.'

6. And if you see any who appear (so far as man can judge, but God alone searcheth the hearts) to be already partakers of their hope, already 'made perfect in love'; far from envying the grace of God in them, let it rejoice and comfort your heart. Glorify God for their sake. 'If one member is honoured', shall not 'all the members rejoice with it'? Instead of jealousy or evil surmising concerning them, praise God for the consolation. Rejoice in having a fresh proof of the faithfulness of God in fulfilling all his promises. And stir yourself up the more to 'apprehend that for which you also are apprehended of Christ Jesus'.

7. In order to this, redeem the time. Improve the present moment. Buy up every opportunity of growing in grace, or of doing good. Let not the thought of receiving more grace tomorrow make you negligent of today. You have one talent now. If you expect five more, so much the rather improve that you have. And the more you expect to receive hereafter, the more labour for God now. Sufficient for the day is the grace thereof. God is now pouring his benefits upon you. Now approve yourself a faithful steward of the present grace of God. Whatever may be tomorrow, give all diligence today to 'add to your faith courage, temperance, patience, brotherly kindness, and the fear of God,' till you attain

that pure and perfect love. Let 'these things be' now 'in you and abound'. Be not now slothful or unfruitful. So shall an entrance be ministered 'into the everlasting kingdom of our Lord Jesus Christ'.

[8]. Lastly, if in time past you have abused this blessed hope of being holy as he is holy, yet do not therefore cast it away. Let the abuse cease, the use remain. Use it now to the more abundant glory of God and profit of your own soul. In steadfast faith, in calm tranquility of spirit, in full assurance of hope, rejoicing evermore for what God hath done, 'press' ye 'on unto perfection.' Daily growing in the knowledge of our Lord Jesus Christ, and going on from strength to strength, in resignation, in patience, in humble thankfulness for what ye have attained and for what ye shall, run the race set before you, 'looking unto Jesus', till through perfect love ye enter into his glory.

45. UPON OUR LORD'S SERMON ON THE MOUNT, DISCOURSE THE FIRST

1748

An Introductory Comment

En route to Georgia aboard the *Simmonds* (1735–36), Wesley went over the Lord's Sermon on the Mount for the edification of his fellow travelers (S, 1:313). Years later while in Bristol on April 1, 1739, Wesley began to expound upon the Sermon on the Mount once more, an endeavor that he referred to as "one pretty remarkable precedent of field-preaching" (WH, 19:46). In all Wesley preached more than one hundred sermons drawn from the texts of the Sermon on the Mount. He preached specifically on Matthew 5:1-4, the text of this sermon, at Bowling Green in 1739, at Bexley in 1740, at Oxford in 1771, and at Edinburgh the following year (WWS).

The first discourse of the series of thirteen sermons is similar in several respects to the earlier "Way to the Kingdom," written in 1746, in that it not only sees the goal or telos of the Christian life in terms of happiness and holiness, the staples of what Wesley called "the inward kingdom of God" (WH, 19:198), but it also charts the way along the lines of repentance specifically in the form of poverty of spirit. Indeed, though "the rich, the wise" account such a spirit as madness (O, 1:673), Wesley affirmed in this present sermon that "real Christianity always begins in poverty of spirit" (O, 1:475). So understood, such poverty does not refer to an economic condition or to "outward circumstances" (O, 1:475–76); instead, it highlights the penitence, "the deep sense of sinfulness, guiltiness and helplessness" (NT, Matt. 5:3) that marks the hearts of sinners who know their need of the Savior.

With the proper groundwork in place, Wesley then shifted his attention in this sermon to the inward kingdom, which he explored in terms of having not only "righteousness, and peace, and joy in the Holy Ghost" (O, 1:481) but also the "mind which was in Christ Jesus" (O, 1:481).

Upon our Lord's Sermon on the Mount, Discourse the First

1. Seeing the multitudes, he went to a mountain where there was room
2. It is the Lord of heaven and earth, Creator of all, who speaks
3. He is showing us the way to heaven
4.–6. He is teaching the whole human race
7. He speaks as the Creator of the universe
8–10. With what amazing love does the Son reveal his Father's will

I. 1. Our Lord lays down the sum of all true religion in eight particulars
2. The foundation of all is poverty of spirit
3. It is not those in poverty to which Jesus refers
4. They are the humble, who know themselves and are convinced of sin
5. They know the punishment they deserve
6. The sinner can only cry out, 'Lord, save, or I perish'
7.–8. Poverty of spirit is a sense of our inward and outward sins
9. Christianity begins with poverty of spirit, a conviction of sin
10. Sinner awake! Know thyself! Know that you were shapen in wickedness
11. This is the kingdom of heaven which is within us
12. About the poor in spirit, God says, 'Theirs is the kingdom of heaven'
13. This is true Christian humility, which flows from the love of God

II. 1. Sin is so bruised that believers can scarce believe it remains in them
   A. But our Lord well knew that this state does not often last long
   B. Therefore, blessed are they that mourn; for they shall be comforted
2. Not that this promise belongs to those who mourn on worldly account
3. The mourners spoken of are those that mourn after God
4. This affliction is not joyous, but grievous
5. This process seems shadowed by what he spoke on the night before his death
6. Although this mourning is at an end, there is yet another mourning
   A. This occurs by the return of the Comforter; a blessed mourning it is
7. But all this wisdom of God is foolishness with the world
8. Let not the children of God be troubled by those who walk on in darkness

Sermon 21: Upon our Lord's Sermon on the Mount

Discourse the First, 1748

Matthew 5:1-4

And seeing the multitudes, he went up into a mountain, and when he was set, his disciples came unto him:

And he opened his mouth and taught them, saying,

Blessed are the poor in spirit; for theirs is the kingdom of heaven.

Blessed are they that mourn; for they shall be comforted.

1. Our Lord had now 'gone about all Galilee' (Matt. 4:23), beginning at the time 'when John was cast into prison' (Matt. 4:12), not only 'teaching in their synagogues, and preaching the gospel of the kingdom', but likewise 'healing all manner of sickness, and all manner of disease among the people'. It was a natural consequence of this that 'there followed him great multitudes from Galilee and from Decapolis, and from Jerusalem and from Judea, and from the region beyond Jordan' (Matt. 4:25). 'And seeing the multitudes', whom no synagogue could contain, even had there been any at hand, 'he went up into a mountain' (Matt. 5:1, etc.), where there was room for all that 'came unto him from every quarter'. 'And when he was set', as the manner of the Jews was, 'his disciples came unto him. And he opened his mouth' (an expression denoting the beginning of a solemn discourse) 'and taught them, saying. . . .'

2. Let us observe who it is that is here speaking, that we may 'take heed how we hear'. It is the Lord of heaven and earth, the Creator of all, who, as such, has a right to dispose of all his creatures; the Lord our Governor, whose kingdom is from everlasting, and ruleth over all; the great Lawgiver, who can well enforce all his laws, 'being able to save and to destroy'; yea, to punish with everlasting destruction from his presence and from the glory of his power. It is the eternal Wisdom of the Father, who knoweth whereof we are made, and understands our inmost frame: who knows how we stand related to God, to one another, to every creature which God hath made; and consequently, how to adapt every law he prescribes to all the circumstances wherein he hath placed us. It is he who is 'loving unto every man, whose mercy is over all his works:' the God of love, who, having emptied himself of his eternal glory, is come forth from his Father to declare his will to the children of men, and then goeth again to the Father; who is sent to God to 'open the eyes of the blind', 'to give light to them that sit in darkness'. It is the great Prophet of the Lord, concerning whom God had solemnly declared long ago, 'Whosoever will not hearken unto my words, which he shall speak in my name, I will require it of him' (Deut. 18:19); or, as the Apostle expresses it, 'Every soul which will not hear that prophet shall be destroyed from among the people' (Acts 3:23).

3. And what is it which he is teaching? The Son of God, who came from heaven, is here showing us the way to heaven, to the place which he hath prepared for us, the glory he had before the world began. He is teaching us the true way to life everlasting, the royal way which leads to the kingdom. And the only true way; for there is none besides—all other paths lead to destruction. From the character of the speaker we are well assured that

he hath declared the full and perfect will of God. He hath uttered not one tittle too much: nothing more than he had received of the Father. Nor too little: he hath not shunned to declare the whole counsel of God. Much less hath he uttered anything wrong, anything contrary to the will of him that sent him. All his words are true and right concerning all things, and shall stand fast for ever and ever.

And we may easily remark that in explaining and confirming these faithful and true sayings he takes care to refute not only the mistakes of the scribes and Pharisees which then were, the false comments whereby the Jewish teachers of that age had perverted the Word of God, but all the practical mistakes that are inconsistent with salvation which should ever arise in the Christian Church; all the comments whereby the Christian teachers (so called) of any age or nation should pervert the Word of God, and teach unwary souls to seek death in the error of their life.

4. And hence we are naturally led to observe whom it is that he is here teaching. Not the apostles alone; if so, he had no need to have gone 'up into the mountain'. A room in the house of Matthew, or any of his disciples, would have contained the Twelve. Nor does it in any wise appear that the 'disciples who came unto him' were the Twelve only. Οἱ μαθηταὶ αὐτοῦ, without any force put upon the expression, may be understood of all who desired to 'learn of him'. But to put this out of all question, to make it undeniably plain that where it is said, 'He opened his mouth and taught them,' the word 'them' includes all the multitudes who went up with him into the mountain, we need only observe the concluding verses of the seventh chapter: 'And it came to pass, when Jesus had ended these sayings, the multitudes, οἱ ὄχλοι, were astonished at his doctrine (or teaching). For he taught *them* (the multitudes) as one having authority, and not as the scribes.'

Nor was it only those multitudes who were with him on the mount to whom he now taught the way of salvation, but all the children of men, the whole race of mankind, the children that were yet unborn—all the generations to come even to the end of the world who should ever hear the words of this life.

5. And this all men allow with regard to some parts of the ensuing discourse. No man, for instance, denies that what is said of 'poverty of spirit' relates to all mankind. But many have supposed that other parts concerned only the apostles, or the first Christians, or the ministers of Christ; and were never designed for the generality of men, who consequently have nothing at all to do with them.

But may we not justly inquire who told them this—that some parts of this discourse concerned only the apostles, or the Christians of the apostolic age, or the ministers of Christ? Bare assertions are not a sufficient proof to establish a point of so great importance. Has then our Lord himself taught us that some parts of his discourse do not concern all mankind? Without doubt had it been so he would have told us; he could not have omitted so necessary an information. But has he told us so? Where? In the discourse itself? No: here is not the least intimation of it. Has he said so elsewhere? In any other of his discourses? Not one word so much as glancing this way can we find in anything he ever spoke, either to the multitudes or to his disciples. Has any of the apostles, or other inspired writers, left such an instruction upon record? No such thing. No assertion of this kind is to be found in all the oracles of God. Who then are the men who are so much wiser than God? Wise so far above that [which] is written?

6. Perhaps they will say that the reason of the thing requires such a restriction to be made. If it does, it must be on one of these two accounts: because without such a restriction the discourse would either be apparently absurd, or would contradict some other Scripture. But this is not the case. It will plainly appear, when we come to examine the several particulars, that there is no absurdity at all in applying all which our Lord hath here delivered to all mankind. Neither will it infer any contradiction to anything else he has delivered, nor to any other Scripture whatever. Nay, it will farther appear that either all the parts of this discourse are to be applied to men in general or no part; seeing they are all connected together, all joined as the stones in an arch, of which you cannot take one away without destroying the whole fabric.

7. We may, lastly, observe how our Lord teaches here. And surely, as at all times, so particularly at this, he speaks 'as never man spake'. Not as the holy men of old; although they also spoke 'as they were moved by the Holy Ghost'. Not as Peter, or James, or John, or Paul. They were indeed wise masterbuilders in his church. But still in this, in the degrees of heavenly wisdom, the servant is not as his Lord. No, nor even as himself at any other time, or on any other occasion. It does not appear that it was ever his design, at any other time or place, to lay down at once the whole plan of his religion, to give us a full prospect of Christianity, to describe at large the nature of that holiness without which no man shall see the Lord. Particular branches of this he has indeed described on a thousand different occasions. But never besides here did he give, of set purpose, a general view of the whole. Nay, we have nothing else of this kind in all the Bible; unless one should except that short sketch of holiness delivered by God in those ten words or commandments to Moses on Mount Sinai. But even here how wide a difference is there between one and the other! 'Even that which was made glorious had no glory in this respect, by reason of the glory that excelleth' (2 Cor. 3:10).

8. Above all, with what amazing love does the Son of God here reveal his Father's will to man! He does not bring us again 'to the mount that [. . .] burned with fire, nor unto blackness, and darkness, and tempest'. He does not speak as when he 'thundered out of heaven, when the highest gave his thunder, hailstones, and coals of fire'. He now addresses us with his still, small voice. 'Blessed (or happy) are the poor in spirit.' Happy are the mourners, the meek; those that hunger after righteousness; the merciful, the pure in heart: happy in the end and in the way; happy in this life and in life everlasting! As if he had said, 'Who is he that lusteth to live, and would fain see good days? Behold, I show you the thing which your soul longeth for; see the way you have below and heaven above!'

9. At the same time with what authority does he teach! Well might they say, 'not as the scribes'. Observe the manner (but it cannot be expressed in words), the air with which he speaks! Not as Moses, the servant of God; not as Abraham, his friend; not as any of the prophets; nor as any of the sons of men. It is something more than human; more than can agree to any created being. It speaks the Creator of all—a God, a God appears! Yea, ὁ ὤν, the being of beings, Jehovah, the self-existent, the supreme, the God who is over all, blessed for ever!

10. This divine discourse, delivered in the most excellent method, every subsequent part illustrating those that precede, is commonly, and not improperly, divided into three principal branches: the first contained in the fifth, the second in the sixth, and the third in the seventh chapter. In the first the sum of all true religion is laid down in eight particulars, which are explained and guarded against the false glosses of man in the following parts of the fifth chapter. In the second are rules for that right intention which we are to preserve in all our outward actions, unmixed with worldly desires, or anxious cares for even the necessaries of life. In the third are cautions against the main hindrances of religion, closed with an application of the whole.

I.1. Our Lord, first, lays down the sum of all true religion in eight particulars, which he explains and guards against the false glosses of men, to the end of the fifth chapter.

Some have supposed that he designed in these to point out the several stages of the Christian course, the steps which a Christian successively takes in his journey to the promised land; others, that all the particulars here set down belong at all times to every Christian. And why may we not allow both the one and the other? What inconsistency is there between them? It is undoubtedly true that both 'poverty of spirit' and every other temper which is here mentioned are at all times found in a greater or less degree in every real Christian. And it is equally true that real Christianity always begins in poverty of spirit, and goes on in the order here set down till the 'man of God' is made 'perfect'. We begin at the lowest of these gifts of God; yet so as not to relinquish this when we are called of God to come up higher: but 'whereunto we have already attained' we 'hold fast', while we 'press on' to what is yet before, to the highest blessings of God in Christ Jesus.

2. The foundation of all is 'poverty of spirit'. Here therefore our Lord begins: 'Blessed (saith he) are the poor in spirit, for theirs is the kingdom of heaven.'

It may not improbably be supposed that our Lord, looking on those who were round about him, and observing that not many rich were there, but rather the poor of the world, took occasion from thence to make a transition from temporal to spiritual things. 'Blessed', saith he (or *happy*: so the word should be rendered both in this and the following verses) 'are the poor in spirit.' He does not say they that are poor as to *outward circumstances* (it being not impossible that some of these may be as far from happiness as a monarch upon his throne) but 'the poor in spirit'; they who, whatever their outward circumstances are, have that disposition of heart which is the first step to all real, substantial happiness, either in this world or that which is to come.

3. Some have judged that by the 'poor in spirit' here are meant those who love poverty; those who are free from covetousness, from the love of money; who fear rather than desire riches. Perhaps they have been induced so to judge by wholly confining their thought to the very term, or by considering that weighty observation of St. Paul, that 'the love of money is the root of all evil.' And hence many have wholly divested themselves, not only of riches, but of all worldly goods. Hence also the vows of voluntary poverty seem to have arisen in the Romish Church; it being supposed that so eminent a degree of this fundamental grace must be a large step toward the kingdom of heaven.

But these do not seem to have observed, first, that the expression of St. Paul must be understood with some restriction; otherwise it is not true. For the love of money is not 'the root'—the sole root—'of all evil'. There are a thousand other roots of evil in the world, as sad experience daily shows. His meaning can only be, it is the root of very many evils; perhaps of more than any single vice besides. Secondly, that this sense of the expression 'poor in spirit' will by no means suit our Lord's present design, which is to lay a general foundation whereon the whole fabric of Christianity may be built; a design which would be in no wise answered by guarding against one particular vice: so that even if this were supposed to be one part of his meaning, it could not possibly be the whole. Thirdly, that it cannot be supposed to be any part of his meaning unless we charge him with manifest tautology: seeing if 'poverty of spirit' were only freedom from covetousness, from the love of money, or the desire of riches, it would coincide with what he afterwards mentions; it would be only a branch of 'purity of heart'.

4. Who then are the 'poor in spirit'? Without question, the humble; they who know themselves, who are convinced of sin; those to whom God hath given that first repentance which is previous to faith in Christ.

One of these can no longer say, 'I am rich, and increased in goods, and have need of nothing': as now knowing that he is 'wretched, and poor, and miserable, and blind, and naked'. He is convinced that he is spiritually poor indeed; having no spiritual good abiding in him. 'In me (saith he) dwelleth no good thing;' but whatsoever is evil and abominable. He has a deep sense of the loathsome leprosy of sin, which he brought with him from his mother's womb, which overspreads his whole soul, and totally corrupts every power and faculty thereof. He sees more and more of the evil tempers which spring from that evil root: the pride and haughtiness of spirit, the constant bias to think of himself more highly than he ought to think; the vanity, the thirst after the esteem or honour that cometh from men; the hatred or envy, the jealousy or revenge, the anger, malice, or bitterness; the inbred enmity both against God and man which appears in ten thousand shapes; the love of the world, the self-will, the foolish and hurtful desires which cleave to his inmost soul. He is conscious how deeply he has offended by his tongue; if not by profane, immodest, untrue, or unkind words, yet by discourse which was not 'good to the use of edifying', not 'meet to minister grace to the hearers'; which consequently was all *corrupt* in God's account, and grievous to his Holy Spirit. His evil works are now likewise ever in his sight; if he tell them 'they are more than he is able to express'. He may as well think to number the 'drops of rain, the sands of the sea, or the days of eternity'.

5. His guilt is now also before his face: he knows the punishment he has deserved, were it only on account of his 'carnal mind', the entire, universal corruption of his nature; how much more on account of all his evil desires and thoughts, of all his sinful words and actions! He cannot doubt for a moment but the least of these deserves the damnation of hell, 'the worm that dieth not', and 'the fire that never shall be quenched'. Above all, the guilt of 'not believing on the name of the only-begotten Son of God' lies heavy upon him. 'How (saith he) shall I escape, who neglect so great salvation!' 'He that believeth not is condemned already', and 'the wrath of God abideth on him.'

6. But what shall he give in exchange for his soul, which is forfeit to the just vengeance of God? 'Wherewithal shall he come before the Lord?' How shall he pay him that he oweth? Were he from this moment to perform the most perfect obedience to every command of God, this would make no amends for a single sin, for any one act of past disobedience: seeing he owes God all the service he is able to perform from this moment to all eternity, could he pay this it would make no manner of amends for what he ought to have done before. He sees himself therefore utterly helpless with regard to atoning for his past sins; utterly unable to make any amends to God, to pay any ransom for his own soul.

But if God would forgive him all that is past, on this one condition, that he should sin no more, that for the time to come he should entirely and constantly obey all his commands: he well knows that this would profit him nothing, being a condition he could never perform. He knows and feels that he is not able to obey even the outward commands of God; seeing these cannot be obeyed while his heart remains in its natural sinfulness and corruption—inasmuch as an evil tree cannot bring forth good fruit. But he cannot cleanse a sinful heart: with men this is impossible. So that he is utterly at a loss even how to begin walking in the path of God's commandments. He knows not how to get one step forward in the way. Encompassed with sin and sorrow and fear, and finding no way to escape, he can only cry out, 'Lord, save, or I perish!'

7. 'Poverty of spirit', then, as it implies the first step we take in running the race which is set before us, is a just sense of our inward and outward sins, and of our guilt and helplessness. This some have monstrously styled the 'virtue of humility'; thus teaching us to be proud of knowing we deserve damnation. But our Lord's expression is quite of another kind; conveying no idea to the hearer but that of mere want, of naked sin, of helpless guilt and misery.

8. The great Apostle, where he endeavours to bring sinners to God, speaks in a manner just answerable to this. 'The wrath of God (saith he) is revealed from heaven against all ungodliness and unrighteousness of men' (Rom. 1:18)—a charge which he immediately fixes on the heathen world, and thereby proves they were under the wrath of God. He next shows that the Jews were no better than they, and were therefore under the same condemnation: and all this not in order to their attaining 'the noble virtue of humility', 'but that every mouth might be stopped, and all the world become guilty before God'.

He proceeds to show that they were helpless as well as guilty; which is the plain purport of all those expressions—'Therefore by the deeds of the law there shall no flesh be justified'—'But now the righteousness of God, which is by faith of Jesus Christ, without the law is manifested'—'We conclude that a man is justified by faith, without the deeds of the law'—expressions all tending to the same point, even to 'hide pride from man'; to humble him to the dust, without teaching him to reflect upon his humility as a virtue; to inspire him with that full piercing conviction of his utter sinfulness, guilt, and helplessness, which casts the sinner, stripped of all, lost, and undone, on his strong helper, 'Jesus Christ the righteous'.

9. One cannot but observe here that Christianity begins just where heathen morality ends: 'poverty of spirit', 'conviction of sin', the 'renouncing ourselves', the 'not having our

own righteousness', the very first point in the religion of Jesus Christ, leaving all pagan religion behind. This was ever hid from the wise men of this world; insomuch that the whole Roman language, even with all the improvements of the Augustan age, does not afford so much as a name for *humility* (the word from which we borrow this, as is well known, bearing in Latin a quite different meaning): no, nor was one found in all the copious language of Greece till it was *made* by the great Apostle.

10. O that we may feel what they were not able to express! Sinner, awake! Know thyself! Know and feel that thou 'wert shapen in wickedness, and that in sin did thy mother conceive thee', and that thou thyself hast been heaping sin upon sin ever since thou couldst discern good from evil. Sink under the mighty hand of God, as guilty of death eternal; and cast off, renounce, abhor all imagination of ever being able to help thyself ! Be it all thy hope to be washed in his blood and renewed by his almighty Spirit 'who himself bare all our sins in his own body on the tree'. So shalt thou witness, 'Happy are the poor in spirit; for theirs is the kingdom of heaven.'

11. This is that kingdom of heaven or of God which is 'within' us, even 'righteousness, and peace, and joy in the Holy Ghost'. And what is righteousness but the life of God in the soul, the mind which was in Christ Jesus, the image of God stamped upon the heart, now renewed after the likeness of him that created it? What is it but the love of God because he first loved us, and the love of all mankind for his sake?

And what is this peace, the peace of God, but that calm serenity of soul, that sweet repose in the blood of Jesus, which leaves no doubt of our acceptance in him? Which excludes all fear but the loving, filial fear of offending our Father which is in heaven?

This inward kingdom implies also 'joy in the Holy Ghost', who seals upon our hearts 'the redemption which is in Jesus', the righteousness of Christ, imputed to us for 'the remission of the sins that are past': who giveth us now 'the earnest of our inheritance' of the crown which the Lord, the righteous Judge, will give at that day. And well may this be termed 'the kingdom of heaven'; seeing it is heaven already opened in the soul, the first springing up of those rivers of pleasure which flow at God's right hand for evermore.

12. 'Theirs is the kingdom of heaven.' Whosoever thou art to whom God hath given to be 'poor in spirit', to feel thyself lost, thou hast a right thereto, through the gracious promise of him who cannot lie. It is purchased for thee by the blood of the Lamb. It is very nigh: thou art on the brink of heaven. Another step, and thou enterest into the kingdom of righteousness, and peace, and joy. Art thou all sin? 'Behold the Lamb of God who taketh away the sin of the world.' All unholy? See thy 'advocate with the Father, Jesus Christ the righteous'. Art thou unable to atone for the least of thy sins? 'He is the propitiation for' all thy 'sins.' Now believe on the Lord Jesus Christ, and all thy sins are blotted out. Art thou totally unclean in soul and in body? Here is the 'fountain for sin and uncleanness'. 'Arise, [. . .] and wash away thy sins': stagger no more at the promise through unbelief. Give glory to God. Dare to believe! Now cry out, from the ground of thy heart:

Yes, I yield, I yield at last,
Listen to thy speaking blood;

Me with all my sins I cast
On my atoning God!

13. Then thou learnest of him to be 'lowly of heart'. And this is the true, genuine, Christian humility, which flows from a sense of the love of God, reconciled to us in Christ Jesus. 'Poverty of spirit', in this meaning of the word, begins where a sense of guilt and of the wrath of God ends; and is a continual sense of our total dependence on him for every good thought or word or work; of our utter inability to all good unless he 'water us every moment': and an abhorrence of the praise of men, knowing that all praise is due unto God only. With this is joined a loving shame, a tender humiliation before God, even for the sins which we know he hath forgiven us, and for the sin which still remaineth in our hearts, although we know it is not imputed to our condemnation. Nevertheless the conviction we feel of inbred sin is deeper and deeper every day. The more we grow in grace the more do we see of the desperate wickedness of our heart. The more we advance in the knowledge and love of God, through our Lord Jesus Christ (as great a mystery as this may appear to those who know not the power of God unto salvation), the more do we discern of our alienation from God, of the enmity that is in our carnal mind, and the necessity of our being entirely renewed in righteousness and true holiness.

II.1. It is true, he has scarce any conception of this who now begins to know the inward kingdom of heaven. 'In his prosperity he saith, I shall never be moved; Thou, Lord, hast made my hill so strong.' Sin is so utterly bruised beneath his feet that he can scarce believe it remaineth in him. Even temptation is silenced and speaks not again; it cannot approach, but stands afar off. He is borne aloft on the chariots of joy and love; he soars 'as upon the wings of an eagle'. But our Lord well knew that this triumphant state does not often continue long. He therefore presently subjoins, 'Blessed are they that mourn; for they shall be comforted.'

2. Not that we can imagine this promise belongs to those who mourn only on some worldly account; who are in sorrow and heaviness merely on account of some worldly trouble or disappointment, such as the loss of their reputation, or friends, or the impairing of their fortune. As little title to it have they who are afflicting themselves, through fear of some temporal evil; or who pine away with anxious care, or that desire of earthly things which 'maketh the heart sick'. Let us not think these 'shall receive any thing from the Lord': he is not in all their thoughts. Therefore it is that they thus 'walk in a vain shadow, and disquiet themselves in vain'. And 'This shall ye have of mine hand;' saith the Lord, 'ye shall lie down in sorrow.'

3. The mourners of whom our Lord here speaks are those that mourn on quite another account: they that mourn after God, after him in whom they did 'rejoice with joy unspeakable' when he gave them to 'taste the good', the pardoning 'word, and the powers of the world to come'. But he now 'hides his face, and they are troubled'; they cannot see him through the dark cloud. But they see temptation and sin—which they fondly supposed were gone never to return—arising again, following after them amain, and holding

them in on every side. It is not strange if their soul is now disquieted within them, if trouble and heaviness take hold upon them. Nor will their great enemy fail to improve the occasion; to ask, 'Where is now thy God? Where is now the blessedness whereof thou spakest? The beginning of the kingdom of heaven? Yea, hath God said, "Thy sins are forgiven thee"? Surely God hath not said it. It was only a dream, a mere delusion, a creature of thy own imagination. If thy sins are forgiven, why art thou thus? Can a pardoned sinner be thus unholy?' And if then, instead of immediately crying to God, they reason with him that is wiser than they, they will be in heaviness indeed, in sorrow of heart, in anguish not to be expressed. Nay, even when God shines again upon the soul, and takes away all doubt of his past mercy, still he that is 'weak in faith' may be tempted and troubled on account of what is to come; especially when inward sin revives, and thrusts sore at him that he may fall. Then may he again cry out:

> I have a sin of fear, that when I've spun
> My last thread, I shall perish on the shore!—

lest I should make shipwreck of the faith, and my last state be worse than the first—

> Lest all my bread of life should fail,
> And I sink down unchanged to hell.

4. Sure it is that this affliction 'for the present is not joyous, but grievous. Nevertheless afterward it bringeth forth peaceable fruit unto them that are exercised thereby.' 'Blessed' therefore 'are they that' thus 'mourn,' if they 'tarry the Lord's leisure', and suffer not themselves to be turned out of the way by the miserable comforters of the world; if they resolutely reject all the comforts of sin, of folly, and vanity; all the idle diversions and amusements of the world, all the pleasures which 'perish in the using', and which only tend to benumb and stupefy the soul, that it may neither be sensible of itself nor God. Blessed are they who 'follow on to know the Lord', and steadily refuse all other comfort. They shall be comforted by the consolations of his Spirit, by a fresh manifestation of his love: by such a witness of his accepting them in the Beloved as shall never more be taken away from them. This 'full assurance of faith' swallows up all doubt, as well as all tormenting fear, God now giving them a sure hope of an enduring substance and 'strong consolation through grace'. Without disputing whether it be possible for any of those to 'fall away' 'who were once enlightened and [. . .] made partakers of the Holy Ghost', it suffices them to say, by the power now resting upon them, 'Who shall separate us from the love of Christ? [. . .] I am persuaded, that neither death nor life, [. . .] nor things present, nor things to come; nor height nor depth . . . , shall be able to separate us from the love of God, which is in Christ Jesus our Lord!' (Rom. 8:35, 38-39).

5. This whole process, both of mourning for an absent God and recovering the joy of his countenance, seems to be shadowed out in what our Lord spoke to his apostles the night before his Passion: 'Do ye inquire of that I said, a little while and ye shall not see me,

and again a little while and ye shall see me? Verily, verily, I say unto you, that ye shall weep and lament,' namely, when ye do not see me; 'but the world shall rejoice,' shall triumph over you, as though your hope were now come to an end. 'And ye shall be sorrowful,' through doubt, through fear, through temptation, through vehement desire; 'but your sorrow shall be turned into joy,' by the return of him whom your soul loveth. 'A woman when she is in travail hath sorrow because her hour is come. But as soon as she is delivered of the child, she remembereth no more the anguish, for joy that a man is born into the world. And ye now have sorrow:' ye mourn and cannot be comforted. 'But I will see you again; and your heart shall rejoice' with calm, inward joy, 'and your joy no man taketh from you' (John 16:19-22).

6. But although this mourning is at an end, is lost in holy joy, by the return of the Comforter, yet is there another, and a blessed mourning it is, which abides in the children of God. They still mourn for the sins and miseries of mankind: they 'weep with them that weep'. They weep for them that weep not for themselves, for the sinners against their own souls. They mourn for the weakness and unfaithfulness of those that are in some measure saved from their sins. 'Who is weak and they are not weak? Who is offended, and they burn not?' They are grieved for the dishonour continually done to the Majesty of heaven and earth. At all times they have an awful sense of this, which brings a deep seriousness upon their spirit; a seriousness which is not a little increased since the eyes of their understanding were opened by their continually seeing the vast ocean of eternity, without a bottom or a shore, which has already swallowed up millions of millions of men, and is gaping to devour them that yet remain. They see here the house of God eternal in the heavens; there, hell and destruction without a covering; and thence feel the importance of every moment, which just appears, and is gone for ever.

7. But all this wisdom of God is foolishness with the world. The whole affair of 'mourning' and 'poverty of spirit' is with them stupidity and dullness. Nay, 'tis well if they pass so favourable a judgment upon it, if they do not vote it to be mere moping and melancholy, if not downright lunacy and distraction. And it is no wonder at all that this judgment should be passed by those who know not God. Suppose as two persons were walking together one should suddenly stop, and with the strongest signs of fear and amazement cry out: 'On what a precipice do we stand! See, we are on the point of being dashed in pieces! Another step and we fall into that huge abyss. Stop! I will not go on for all the world.' When the other, who seemed to himself at least equally sharp-sighted, looked forward and saw nothing of all this, what would he think of his companion but that 'he was beside himself', that his head was out of order, that much religion (if he was not guilty of much learning) had certainly 'made him mad'?

8. But let not the children of God, 'the mourners in Zion', be moved by any of these things. Ye whose eyes are enlightened, be not troubled by those who walk on still in darkness. Ye do not walk on in a vain shadow: God and eternity are real things. Heaven and hell are in very deed open before you: and ye are on the edge of the great gulf. It has already swallowed up more than words can express, nations and kindreds and peoples and tongues, and still yawns to devour, whether they see it or no, the giddy, miserable children of men. O cry aloud! Spare not! Lift up your voice to him who grasps both time

and eternity, both for yourselves and your brethren, that ye may be counted worthy to escape the destruction that cometh as a whirlwind! That ye may be brought safe, through all the waves and storms, into the haven where you would be. Weep for yourselves, till he wipes away the tears from your eyes. And even then weep for the miseries that come upon the earth, till the Lord of all shall put a period to misery and sin, shall wipe away the tears from all faces, and 'the knowledge of the Lord shall cover the earth, as the waters cover the sea.'

46. UPON OUR LORD'S SERMON ON THE MOUNT, DISCOURSE THE SECOND

1748

An Introductory Comment

Wesley considered the third through the fifth Beatitudes (Matt. 5:5-7) as part of what constituted "the sum of all true religion" (B, 199). Indeed, those whom Christ called blessed want a "religion of a nobler kind" (O, 1:497), greater than simply doing no harm, doing good, and employing the means of grace. They *hunger* and *thirst* for righteousness (v. 6). Wesley likely drew from Bishop Offspring Blackall, John Norris, John Cardinal Bona, and Henry Hammond in crafting this sermon (O, 1:466–67), and he preached on this text at least nine times (WWS). While he was at Shire Hall in Cardiff, Wales, for example, on October 19, 1739, he noted in his *Journal*: "I explained the six last Beatitudes, but my heart was so enlarged I know not how to give over, so that we continued three hours" (WH, 19:108).

In his *Notes Upon the New Testament* with respect to this text Wesley described the meek as those who "hold all their passions and affections evenly balanced." Moreover, in this present sermon he remarked that such a grace "poises the mind aright" with the result that those who are so blessed preserve "the mean in every circumstance of life" (O, 1:489), though they are deemed by the "wise of the world" (O, 1:494) as foolish.

Toward the end of the sermon Wesley identified the merciful (v. 7) as those who are tender-hearted, a quality that finds its expression in loving all people as themselves. With this identification in place, Wesley concluded the sermon in delineating several characteristics of holy love that mark scriptural Christianity, such as long-suffering, not envying or being puffed up, not behaving unseemly or being rude, not being easily provoked or rejoicing in iniquity, forsaking all evil-speaking, and continually overflowing with love (O, 1:499–505), traits that taken together constitute nothing less than the mind of Christ.

Upon our Lord's Sermon on the Mount, Discourse the Second

I. 1. Blessed are the meek; for they shall inherit the earth
2. Who are the meek? Not those who grieve at nothing
3. Nor does Christian meekness imply being without zeal for God
4.–5. Meekness may be referred either to God or our neighbor
6. The meek are gentle toward all persons
7. Nor does meekness restrain only the outward act
8. Our Lord ranks anger which goes no farther than the heart as murder
9.–11. Whoever utters a contemptuous word will be subject to judgment
12.–13. God secures the meek in spite of the force, fraud, or malice of men

II. 1. Blessed are those who hunger and thirst after righteousness
2. Righteousness is the image of God, the mind which was in Jesus Christ
3. Hunger and thirst are the strongest of bodily functions
4. It is impossible to satisfy a soul that is thirsty for God
5. They will be filled with the thing which they long for, true holiness
6. Let nothing satisfy you but the power of godliness

III. 1. As they are filled, their concern for those without God increases
2. Because of this love, we discern who are the merciful
3. *Charity*, or love, the love of our neighbour, is patient toward all
4. In every step toward this desirable end they are soft, mild, benign
5. Consequently, love envieth not
6. Love is not rash or hasty in judging
7. We should not think more highly of ourselves than we ought
8. Love is not rude or willingly offensive to any
9. In becoming all things to all people, love seeketh not her own
10.–11. Love does not yield to provocation
12. Love rejoiceth not in iniquity
13. Love rejoiceth in the truth, wherever it is found
14. This love covereth all things
15. Love believeth all things; it is always willing to think the best
16. And when it can no longer believe, then love hopeth all things
17. Lastly, it endureth all things; this completes the merciful
18. May your soul continually overflow with love till God calls you

Sermon 22: Upon our Lord's Sermon on the Mount

Discourse the Second, 1748

Matthew 5:5-7

Blessed are the meek; for they shall inherit the earth.

Blessed are they which do hunger and thirst after righteousness; for they shall be filled.

Blessed are the merciful; for they shall obtain mercy.

I. 1. When 'the winter is past', when 'the time of singing is come, and the voice of the turtle is heard in the land'; when he that comforts the mourners is now returned, 'that he may abide with them for ever'; when at the brightness of his presence the clouds disperse, the dark clouds of doubt and uncertainty, the storms of fear flee away, the waves of sorrow subside, and their spirit again 'rejoiceth in God their Saviour': then is it that this word is eminently fulfilled; then those whom he hath comforted can bear witness, 'Blessed (or happy) are the meek; for they shall inherit the earth.'

2. But who are the meek? Not those who grieve at nothing because they know nothing, who are not discomposed at the evils that occur because they discern not evil from good. Not those who are sheltered from the shocks of life by a stupid insensibility; who have either by nature or art the virtue of stocks and stones, and resent nothing because they feel nothing. Brute philosophers are wholly unconcerned in this matter. Apathy is as far from meekness as from humanity. So that one would not easily conceive how any Christians of the purer ages, especially any of the Fathers of the Church, could confound these, and mistake one of the foulest errors of heathenism for a branch of true Christianity.

3. Nor does Christian meekness imply the being without zeal for God, any more than it does ignorance or insensibility. No; it keeps clear of every extreme, whether in excess or defect. It does not destroy but balance the affections, which the God of nature never designed should be rooted out by grace, but only brought and kept under due regulations. It poises the mind aright. It holds an even scale with regard to anger and sorrow and fear; preserving the mean in every circumstance of life, and not declining either to the right hand or the left.

4. Meekness therefore seems properly to relate to ourselves. But it may be referred either to God or our neighbour. When this due composure of mind has reference to God it is usually termed resignation—a calm acquiescence in whatsoever is his will concerning us, even though it may not be pleasing to nature, saying continually, 'It is the Lord; let him do what seemeth him good.' When we consider it more strictly with regard to ourselves we style it patience or contentedness. When it is exerted toward other men then it is mildness to the good and gentleness to the evil.

5. They who are truly meek can clearly discern what is evil; and they can also suffer it. They are *sensible* of everything of this kind; but still meekness holds the reins. They are exceeding 'zealous for the Lord of hosts'; but their zeal is always guided by knowledge, and tempered in every thought and word and work with the love of man as well as the love of

God. They do not desire to extinguish any of the passions which God has for wise ends implanted in their nature. But they have the mastery of all; they hold them all in subjection, and employ them only in subservience to those ends. And thus even the harsher and more unpleasing passions are applicable to the noblest purposes. Even hate and anger and fear, when engaged against sin, and regulated by faith and love, are as walls and bulwarks to the soul, so that the wicked one cannot approach to hurt it.

6.'Tis evident this divine temper is not only to abide but to increase in us day by day. Occasions of exercising, and thereby increasing it, will never be wanting while we remain upon earth. We 'have need of patience, that after we have done' and suffered 'the will of God, we may receive the promise'. We have need of resignation, that we may in all circumstances say, 'Not as I will, but as thou wilt.' And we have need of 'gentleness toward all men'; but especially toward the evil and the unthankful; otherwise we shall be overcome of evil, instead of overcoming evil with good.

7. Nor does meekness restrain only the outward act, as the scribes and Pharisees taught of old, and the miserable teachers who are not taught of God will not fail to do in all ages. Our Lord guards us against this, and shows the true extent of it, in the following words: 'Ye have heard that it was said by them of old time, Thou shalt not kill; and whosoever shall kill shall be in danger of the judgment. But I say unto you, that whosoever shall be angry with his brother without a cause shall be in danger of the judgment; and whosoever shall say to his brother, Raca, shall be in danger of the council; but whosoever shall say, Thou fool, shall be in danger of hell-fire' (Matt. 5:21-22).

8. Our Lord here ranks under the head of murder even that anger which goes no farther than the heart; which does not show itself by an outward unkindness, no, not so much as a passionate word.

'Whosoever is angry with his brother'—with any man living, seeing we are all brethren; whosoever feels any unkindness in his heart, any temper contrary to love; whosoever is angry 'without a cause'—without a sufficient cause, or farther than that cause requires—'shall be in danger of the judgment', ἔνοχος ἔσται, 'shall' in that moment 'be obnoxious to' the righteous judgment of God.

But would not one be inclined to prefer the reading of those copies which omit the word εἰκῇ, 'without a cause'? Is it not entirely superfluous? For if *anger at persons* be a temper contrary to love, how can there be a cause, a sufficient cause for it? Any that will justify it in the sight of God?

Anger at sin we allow. In this sense we may 'be angry and' yet we 'sin not'. In this sense our Lord himself is once recorded to have been angry: 'He looked round about upon them with anger, being grieved for the hardness of their hearts.' He was grieved at the sinners, and angry at the sin. And this is undoubtedly right before God.

9. 'And whosoever shall say to his brother, Raca.' Whosoever shall give way to anger, so as to utter any contemptuous word. It is observed by commentators that *Raca* is a Syriac word which properly signifies empty, vain, foolish: so that it is as inoffensive an expression as can well be used toward one at whom we are displeased. And yet whosoever shall use this, as our Lord assures us, 'shall be in danger of the council'—rather, 'shall be

obnoxious thereto'. He shall be liable to a severer sentence from the Judge of all the earth.

'But whosoever shall say, Thou fool'—whosoever shall so give place to the devil as to break out into reviling, into designedly reproachful and contumelious language, 'shall be obnoxious to hell-fire'—shall in that instant be liable to the highest condemnation. It should be observed that our Lord describes all these as obnoxious to capital punishment: the first to strangling, usually inflicted on those who were condemned in one of the inferior courts; the second to stoning, which was frequently inflicted on those who were condemned by the Great Council at Jerusalem; the third to burning alive, inflicted only on the highest offenders, in the 'valley of the sons of Hinnom', Γῆ Ἐννών, from which that word is evidently taken which we translate hell.

10. And whereas men naturally imagine that God will excuse their defect in some duties for their exactness in others, our Lord next takes care to cut off that vain though common imagination. He shows that it is impossible for any sinner to *commute* with God, who will not accept one duty for another, nor take a part of obedience for the whole. He warns us that the performing our duty to God will not excuse us from our duty to our neighbour; that works of piety, as they are called, will be so far from commending us to God if we are wanting in charity, that on the contrary that want of charity will make all those works an abomination to the Lord.

'Therefore, if thou bring thy gift to the altar, and there rememberest that thy brother hath ought against thee'—on account of thy unkind behaviour toward him, of thy calling him 'Raca', or 'Thou fool'—think not that thy gift will atone for thy anger, or that it will find any acceptance with God so long as thy conscience is defiled with the guilt of unrepented sin. 'Leave there thy gift before the altar, and go thy way; first be reconciled to thy brother' (at least do all that in thee lies toward being reconciled) 'and then come and offer thy gift' (Matt. 5:23-24).

11. And let there be no delay in what so nearly concerneth thy soul. 'Agree with thine adversary quickly'—now; upon the spot—'while thou art in the way with him'—if it be possible, before he go out of thy sight—'lest at any time the adversary deliver thee to the judge'—lest he appeal to God, the Judge of all—'and the judge deliver thee to the officer'—to Satan, the executioner of the wrath of God—'and thou be cast into prison'—into hell, there to be reserved to the judgment of the great day. 'Verily I say unto thee, thou shalt by no means come out thence till thou hast paid the uttermost farthing.' But this it is impossible for thee ever to do; seeing thou hast nothing [with which] to pay. Therefore if thou art once in that prison the smoke of thy torment must 'ascend up for ever and ever'.

12. Meantime, 'the meek shall inherit the earth.' Such is the foolishness of worldly wisdom! The wise of the world had warned them again and again that if they did not resent such treatment, if they would tamely suffer themselves to be thus abused, there would be no living for them upon earth; that they would never be able to procure the common necessaries of life, nor to keep even what they had; that they could expect no peace, no quiet possession, no enjoyment of anything. Most true—suppose there were no God in the world; or suppose he did not concern himself with the children of men. But 'when God ariseth to judgment, and to help all the meek upon earth', how doth he laugh

all this heathen wisdom to scorn, and turn the 'fierceness of man to his praise'! He takes a peculiar care to provide them with all things needful for life and godliness. He secures to them the provision he hath made, in spite of the force, fraud, or malice of men. And what he secures he 'gives them richly to enjoy'. It is sweet to them, be it little or much. As 'in patience they possess their souls', so they truly possess whatever God hath given them. They are always content, always pleased with what they have. It pleases them because it pleases God; so that while their heart, their desire, their joy is in heaven, they may truly be said to 'inherit the earth'.

13. But there seems to be a yet farther meaning in these words, even that they shall have a more eminent part in the 'new earth, wherein dwelleth righteousness', in that inheritance, a general description of which (and the particulars we shall know hereafter) St. John has given in the twentieth chapter of the Revelation. 'And I saw an angel come down from heaven. . . . And he laid hold on the dragon, that old serpent, . . . and bound him a thousand years. . . . And I saw the souls of them that were beheaded for the witness of Jesus, and for the Word of God, and of them which had not worshipped the beast, neither his image, neither had received his mark upon their foreheads or in their hands; and they lived and reigned with Christ a thousand years. But the rest of the dead lived not again until the thousand years were expired. This is the first resurrection. Blessed and holy is he that hath part in the first resurrection: on such the second death hath no power; but they shall be priests of God and of Christ, and shall reign with him a thousand years.'

II.1. Our Lord has hitherto been more immediately employed in removing the hindrances of true religion: such is pride, the first, grand hindrance of all religion, which is taken away by 'poverty of spirit'; levity and thoughtlessness, which prevent any religion from taking root in the soul till they are removed by holy *mourning*; such are anger, impatience, discontent, which are all healed by Christian *meekness*. And when once these hindrances are removed—these evil diseases of the soul which were continually raising false cravings therein, and filling it with sickly appetites—the native appetite of a heaven-born spirit returns; it hungers and thirsts after righteousness. And 'blessed are they which do hunger and thirst after righteousness; for they shall be filled.'

2. Righteousness (as was observed before) is the image of God, the mind which was in Christ Jesus. It is every holy and heavenly temper in one; springing from as well as terminating in the love of God as our Father and Redeemer, and the love of all men for his sake.

3. 'Blessed are they which do hunger and thirst after' this; in order fully to understand which expression we should observe, first, that hunger and thirst are the strongest of all our bodily appetites. In like manner this hunger in the soul, this thirst after the image of God, is the strongest of all our spiritual appetites when it is once awakened in the heart; yea, it swallows up all the rest in that one great desire to be renewed after the likeness of him that created us. We should, secondly, observe that from the time we begin to hunger and thirst those appetites do not cease, but are more and more craving and importunate till we either eat and drink, or die. And even so, from the time that we begin to hunger and thirst after the whole mind which was in Christ these spiritual appetites do not cease,

but cry after their food with more and more importunity. Nor can they possibly cease before they are satisfied, while there is any spiritual life remaining. We may, thirdly, observe that hunger and thirst are satisfied with nothing but meat and drink. If you would give to him that is hungry all the world beside, all the elegance of apparel, all the trappings of state, all the treasure upon earth, yea thousands of gold and silver; if you would pay him ever so much honour, he regards it not; all these things are then of no account with him. He would still say, 'These are not the things I want; give me food, or else I die.' The very same is the case with every soul that truly hungers and thirsts after righteousness. He can find no comfort in anything but this: he can be satisfied with nothing else. Whatever you offer beside, it is lightly esteemed; whether it be riches, or honour, or pleasure, he still says, 'This is not the thing which I want. Give me love or else I die!'

4. And it is as impossible to satisfy such a soul, a soul that is athirst for God, the living God, with what the world accounts religion, as with what they account happiness. The religion of the world implies three things: first, the doing no harm, the abstaining from outward sin—at least from such as is scandalous, as robbery, theft, common swearing, drunkenness; secondly, the doing good—the relieving the poor, the being charitable, as it is called; thirdly, the using the means of grace—at least the going to church and to the Lord's Supper. He in whom these three marks are found is termed by the world a religious man. But will this satisfy him who hungers after God? No. It is not food for his soul. He wants a religion of a nobler kind, a religion higher and deeper than this. He can no more feed on this poor, shallow, formal thing, than he can 'fill his belly with the east wind'. True, he is careful to abstain from the very appearance of evil. He is zealous of good works. He attends all the ordinances of God. But all this is not what he longs for. This is only the outside of that religion which he insatiably hungers after. The knowledge of God in Christ Jesus; 'the life that is hid with Christ in God'; the being 'joined unto the Lord in one Spirit'; the having 'fellowship with the Father and the Son'; the 'walking in the light as God is in the light'; the being 'purified even as he is pure'—this is the religion, the righteousness he thirsts after. Nor can he rest till he thus rests in God.

5. 'Blessed are they who' thus 'hunger and thirst after righteousness; for they shall be filled.' They shall be filled with the thing which they long for, even with righteousness and true holiness. God shall satisfy them with the blessings of his goodness, with the felicity of his chosen. He shall feed them with the bread of heaven, with the manna of his love. He shall give them to drink of his pleasures, as out of the river which he that drinketh of shall never thirst—only for more and more of the water of life. This thirst shall endure for ever.

> The painful thirst, the fond desire,
> Thy joyous presence shall remove;
> But my full soul shall still require
> A whole eternity of love.

6. Whosoever then thou art to whom God hath given to 'hunger and thirst after righteousness', cry unto him that thou mayst never lose that inestimable gift, that this

divine appetite may never cease. If many rebuke thee, and bid thee hold thy peace, regard them not; yea, cry so much the more, '"Jesus, Master, have mercy on me!" Let me not live but to be holy as thou art holy!' No more 'spend thy money for that which is not bread', nor thy 'labour for that which satisfieth not'. Canst thou hope to dig happiness out of the earth? To find it in the things of the world? O trample under foot all its pleasures, despise its honours, count its riches as dung and dross—yea, and all the things which are beneath the sun—'for the excellency of the knowledge of Christ Jesus'; for the entire renewal of thy soul in that image of God wherein it was originally created. Beware of quenching that blessed hunger and thirst by what the world calls religion—a religion of form, of outward show, which leaves the heart as earthly and sensual as ever. Let nothing satisfy thee but the power of godliness, but a religion that is spirit and life; the dwelling in God and God in thee, the being an inhabitant of eternity; the entering in by the blood of sprinkling 'within the veil', and 'sitting in heavenly places with Christ Jesus'.

III.1. And the more they are filled with the life of God, the more tenderly will they be concerned for those who are still without God in the world, still dead in trespasses and sins. Nor shall this concern for others lose its reward. 'Blessed are the merciful; for they shall obtain mercy.'

The word used by our Lord more immediately implies the compassionate, the tender-hearted; those who, far from despising, earnestly grieve for those that do not hunger after God. This eminent part of brotherly love is here (by a common figure) put for the whole; so that 'the merciful', in the full sense of the term, are they who 'love their neighbours as themselves'.

2. Because of the vast importance of this love—without which, 'though we spake with the tongues of men and angels, though we had the gift of prophecy and understood all mysteries and all knowledge, though we had all faith so as to remove mountains; yea, though we gave all our goods to feed the poor, and our very bodies to be burned, it would profit us nothing'—the wisdom of God has given us by the Apostle Paul a full and particular account of it, by considering which we shall most clearly discern who are 'the merciful that shall obtain mercy'.

3. *Charity*, or love (as it were to be wished it had been rendered throughout, being a far plainer and less ambiguous word), the love of our neighbour as Christ hath loved us, 'suffereth long', is patient toward all men. It suffers all the weakness, ignorance, errors, infirmities, all the frowardness and littleness of faith in the children of God; all the malice and wickedness of the children of the world. And it suffers all this, not only for a time, for a short season, but to the end: still feeding our enemy when he hungers; if he thirst, still giving him drink; thus continually 'heaping coals of fire', of melting love, 'upon his head'.

4. And in every step toward this desirable end, the 'overcoming evil with good', 'love is kind' (χρηστεύεται, a word not easily translated)—it is soft, mild, benign. It stands at the utmost distance from moroseness, from all harshness or sourness of spirit; and inspires the sufferer at once with the most amiable sweetness and the most fervent and tender affection.

5. Consequently, 'Love envieth not.' It is impossible it should; it is directly opposite to that baneful temper. It cannot be that he who has this tender affection to all, who earnestly wishes all temporal and spiritual blessings, all good things in this world and the world to come, to every soul that God hath made, should be pained at his bestowing any good gift on any child of man. If he has himself received the same he does not grieve but rejoice that another partakes of the common benefit. If he has not he blesses God that his brother at least has, and is herein happier than himself. And the greater his love, the more does he rejoice in the blessings of all mankind, the farther is he removed from every kind and degree of envy toward any creature.

6. Love οὐ περπερεύεται: not 'vaunteth not itself', which coincides with the very next words, but rather (as the word likewise properly imports) 'is not rash' or 'hasty' in judging. It will not hastily condemn anyone. It does not pass a severe sentence on a slight or sudden view of things. It first weighs all the evidence, particularly that which is brought in favour of the accused. A true lover of his neighbour is not like the generality of men, who, even in cases of the nicest nature, 'see a little, presume a great deal, and so jump to the conclusion'. No; he proceeds with wariness and circumspection, taking heed to every step; willingly subscribing to that rule of the ancient heathen (O where will the modern Christian appear!): 'I am so far from lightly believing what one man says against another that I will not easily believe what a man says against himself. I will always allow him second thoughts, and many times counsel too.'

7. It follows, love 'is not puffed up'. It does not incline or suffer any man 'to think more highly of himself than he ought to think', but rather 'to think soberly'. Yea, it humbles the soul unto the dust. It destroys all high conceits engendering pride, and makes us rejoice to be as nothing, to be little and vile, the lowest of all, the servant of all. They who are 'kindly affectioned one to another with brotherly love' cannot but 'in honour prefer one another'. Those who, 'having the same love, are of one accord', do 'in lowliness of mind each esteem other better than themselves'.

8. It 'doth not behave itself unseemly'. It is not rude or willingly offensive to any. It 'renders to all their due: fear to whom fear, honour to whom honour'; courtesy, civility, humanity to all the world, in their several degrees 'honouring all men'. A late writer defines good breeding, nay, the highest degree of it, politeness: 'A continual desire to please, appearing in all the behaviour.' But if so, there is none so well-bred as a Christian, a lover of all mankind; for he cannot but desire to 'please all men', 'for their good to edification'. And this desire cannot be hid: it will necessarily appear in all his intercourse with men. For his 'love is without dissimulation'; it will appear in all his actions and conversation. Yea, and will constrain him, though without guile, to 'become all things to all men, if by any means he may save some'.

9. And in becoming all things to all men 'love seeketh not her own.' In striving to please all men the lover of mankind has no eye at all to his own temporal advantage. He covets no man's silver, or gold, or apparel: he desires nothing but the salvation of their souls. Yea, in some sense he may be said 'not to seek his own' spiritual, any more than temporal advantage. For while he is on the full stretch to save their souls from death he as it were forgets himself. He does not think of himself so long as that zeal for the glory

of God swallows him up. Nay, at some times he may almost seem, through an excess of love, to give up himself, both his soul and his body; while he cries out with Moses, 'Oh! this people have sinned a great sin[. . .]! Yet now, if thou wilt, forgive their sin. And if not, blot me out of the book which thou hast written' (Exod. 32:31-32). Or with St. Paul, 'I could wish that myself were accursed from Christ for my brethren, my kinsmen according to the flesh!' (Rom. 9:3).

10. No marvel that 'such love is not provoked,' οὐ παροξύνεται. Let it be observed, the word 'easily', strangely inserted in the translation, is not in the original. St. Paul's words are absolute: 'Love is not provoked'—it is not provoked to unkindness toward anyone. Occasions indeed will frequently occur, outward provocations of various kinds. But love does not yield to provocation. It triumphs over all. In all trials it looketh unto Jesus, and is more than conqueror in his love.

'Tis not improbable that our translators inserted that word as it were to *excuse* the Apostle, who, as they supposed, might otherwise appear to be wanting in the very love which he so beautifully describes. They seem to have supposed this from a phrase in the Acts of the Apostles, which is likewise very inaccurately translated. When Paul and Barnabas disagreed concerning John, the translation runs thus: 'And the contention was so sharp between them that they departed asunder' (Acts 15:39). This naturally induces the reader to suppose that they were equally sharp therein; that St. Paul, who was undoubtedly right with regard to the point in question (it being quite improper to take John with them again, who had deserted them before) was as much provoked as Barnabas, who gave such a proof of his anger as to leave 'the work' for which he had been 'set apart by the Holy Ghost'. But the original imports no such thing; nor does it affirm that St. Paul was provoked at all. It simply says, καὶ ἐγένετο παροξυσμός, 'And there was a sharpness, a paroxysm' of anger; in consequence of which Barnabas left St. Paul, took John, and went his own way. 'Paul' then 'chose Silas and departed, being recommended by the brethren to the grace of God' (which is not said concerning Barnabas), 'and he went through Syria and Cilicia', as he had proposed, 'confirming the churches'. But to return.

11. Love prevents a thousand provocations which would otherwise arise, because it 'thinketh no evil'. Indeed the merciful man cannot avoid knowing many things that are evil, he cannot but see them with his own eyes and hear them with his own ears. For love does not put out his eyes, so that it is impossible for him not to see that such things are done. Neither does it take away his understanding, any more than his senses, so that he cannot but know that they are evil. For instance: when he sees a man strike his neighbour, or hears him blaspheme God, he cannot either question the thing done or the words spoken, or doubt of their being evil. Yet οὐ λογίζεται τὸ κακόν. The word λογίζεται ('thinketh') does not refer either to our seeing and hearing, or to the first and involuntary acts of our understanding; but to our willingly thinking what we need not; our *inferring* evil where it does not appear: to our *reasoning* concerning things which we do not see, our *supposing* what we have neither seen nor heard. This is what true love absolutely destroys. It tears up, root and branch, all *imagining* what we have not known. It casts out all jealousies, all evil surmisings, all readiness to believe evil. It is frank, open, unsuspicious; and as it cannot design, so neither does it fear, evil.

12. It 'rejoiceth not in iniquity', common as this is, even among those who bear the name of Christ; who scruple not to rejoice over their enemy when he falleth either into affliction, or error, or sin. Indeed, how hardly can they avoid this who are zealously attached to any party! How difficult is it for them not to be pleased with any fault which they discover in those of the opposite party! With any real or supposed blemish, either in their principles or practice! What warm defender of any cause is clear of these? Yea, who is so calm as to be altogether free? Who does not rejoice when his adversary makes a false step which he thinks will advantage his own cause? Only a man of love. He alone weeps over either the sin or folly of his enemy, takes no pleasure in hearing or in repeating it, but rather desires that it may be forgotten for ever.

13. But he 'rejoiceth in the truth', wheresoever it is found, in the 'truth which is after godliness', bringing forth its proper fruit, holiness of heart and holiness of conversation. He rejoices to find that even those who oppose him, whether with regard to opinions or some points of practice, are nevertheless lovers of God, and in other respects unreprovable. He is glad to hear good of them, and to speak all he can, consistently with truth and justice. Indeed, good in general is his glory and joy, wherever diffused throughout the race of mankind. As a citizen of the world he claims a share in the happiness of all the inhabitants of it. Because he is a man he is not unconcerned in the welfare of any man; but enjoys whatsoever brings glory to God and promotes peace and goodwill among men.

14. This love 'covereth all things'. (So without all doubt πάντα στέγει should be translated; for otherwise it would be the very same with πάντα ὑπομένει, 'endureth all things'.) Because the merciful man 'rejoiceth not in iniquity', neither does he willingly make mention of it. Whatever evil he sees, hears, or knows, he nevertheless conceals so far as he can without making himself 'partaker of other men's sins'. Wheresoever or with whomsoever he is, if he sees anything which he approves not it goes not out of his lips unless to the person concerned, if haply he may gain his brother. So far is he from making the faults or failures of others the matter of his conversation, that of the absent he never does speak at all unless he can speak well. A talebearer, a backbiter, a whisperer, an evil-speaker, is to him all one as a murderer. He would just as soon cut his neighbour's throat as thus murder his reputation. Just as soon would he think of diverting himself by setting fire to his neighbour's house as of thus 'scattering abroad arrows, firebrands, and death, and saying, Am I not in sport?'

He makes one only exception. Sometimes he is convinced that it is for the glory of God or (which comes to the same) the good of his neighbour that an evil should not be covered. In this case, for the benefit of the innocent he is constrained to declare the guilty. But even here: (1). He will not speak at all till love, superior love, constrains him; (2). He cannot do it from a general confused view of doing good or of promoting the glory of God, but from a clear sight of some particular end, some determinate good which he pursues; (3). Still he cannot speak unless he be fully convinced that this very means is necessary to that end—that the end cannot be answered, at least not so effectually, by any other way; (4). He then doth it with the utmost sorrow and reluctance, using it as the last and worst medicine, a desperate remedy in a desperate case, a kind of poison never to be used but to expel poison; consequently, (5). He uses it as sparingly as possible. And this he does with fear and trembling, lest he should transgress the law of love by speaking too much, more than he would have done by not speaking at all.

15. Love 'believeth all things'. It is always willing to think the best, to put the most favourable construction on everything. It is ever ready to believe whatever may tend to the advantage of anyone's character. It is easily convinced of (what it earnestly desires) the innocence or integrity of any man; or, at least, of the sincerity of his repentance, if he had once erred from the way. It is glad to excuse whatever is amiss, to condemn the offender as little as possible, and to make all the allowance for human weakness which can be done without betraying the truth of God.

16. And when it can no longer believe, then love 'hopeth all things'. Is any evil related of any man? Love hopes that the relation is not true, that the thing related was never done. Is it certain it was?—'But perhaps it was not done with such circumstances as are related; so that, allowing the fact, there is room to hope it was not so ill as it is represented.' Was the action apparently, undeniably evil? Love hopes the intention was not so. Is it clear the design was evil too?—'Yet might it not spring, [not] from the settled temper of the heart, but from a start of passion, or from some vehement temptation, which hurried the man beyond himself?' And even when it cannot be doubted but all the actions, designs, and tempers are equally evil; still love hopes that God will at last make bare his arm, and get himself the victory; and that there shall be 'joy in heaven over this one sinner that repenteth, more than over ninety and nine just persons that need no repentance.'

17. Lastly, it 'endureth all things'. This completes the character of him that is truly merciful. He endureth not some, not many things only, not most, but absolutely 'all things'. Whatever the injustice, the malice, the cruelty of men can inflict, he is able to suffer. He calls nothing intolerable; he never says of anything, 'This is not to be borne.' No; he can not only do but suffer all things through Christ which strengtheneth him. And all he suffers does not destroy his love, nor impair it in the least. It is proof against all. It is a flame that burns even in the midst of the great deep. 'Many waters cannot quench his love, neither can the floods drown it.' It triumphs over all. It 'never faileth', either in time or in eternity.

> In obedience to what heaven decrees,
> Knowledge shall fail and prophecy shall cease.
> But lasting charity's more ample sway,
> Nor bound by time, nor subject to decay,
> In happy triumph shall for ever live,
> And endless good diffuse, and endless praise receive.

So shall 'the merciful obtain mercy'; not only by the blessing of God upon all their ways, by his now repaying the love they bear to their brethren a thousandfold into their own bosom, but likewise by an 'exceeding and eternal weight of glory' in the 'kingdom prepared for them from the beginning of the world'.

18. For a little while you may say, 'Woe is me, that I am constrained to dwell with Mesech, and to have my habitation among the tents of Kedar!' You may pour out your soul, and bemoan the loss of true genuine love in the earth. Lost indeed! You may well say (but not in the ancient sense), 'See how *these* Christians love one another!' These Christian kingdoms that are tearing out each other's bowels, desolating one another with fire and sword! These Christian armies that are sending each other by thousands, by ten thousands, quick into hell! These Christian nations that are all on fire with intestine broils, party against party, faction against faction! These Christian cities where deceit and fraud, oppression and wrong, yea, robbery and murder, go not out of their streets! These Christian families, torn asunder with envy, jealousy, anger, domestic jars—without number, without end! Yea, what is most dreadful, most to be lamented of all, these Christian churches!—churches ('Tell it not in Gath'; but alas, how can we hide it, either from Jews, Turks, or pagans?) that bear the name of Christ, 'the Prince of Peace', and wage continual war with each other! That convert sinners by burning them alive: that are 'drunk with the blood of the saints'! Does this praise belong only to 'Babylon the great, the mother of harlots and abominations of the earth'? Nay, verily; but Reformed churches (so called) have fairly learned to tread in her steps. Protestant churches, too, know to persecute, when they have power in their hands, even unto blood. And meanwhile, how do they also anathematize each other! Devote each other to the nethermost hell! What wrath, what contention, what malice, what bitterness is everywhere found among them! Even when they agree in essentials, and only differ in opinions, or in the circumstantials of religion. Who 'follows after' only 'the things that make for peace, and things wherewith one may edify another'? O God! How long? Shall thy promise fail? Fear it not, ye little flock. Against hope believe in hope. It is your Father's good pleasure yet to renew the face of the earth. Surely all these things shall come to an end, and the inhabitants of the earth shall learn righteousness. 'Nation shall not lift up sword against nation, neither shall they know war any more.' 'The mountain of the Lord's house shall be established in the top of the mountains;' and all the kingdoms of the world shall become the kingdoms of our God. 'They shall not' then 'hurt or destroy in all his holy mountain;' but 'they shall call their walls salvation and their gates praise.' They shall all be without spot or blemish, loving one another, even as Christ hath loved us. Be thou part of the first-fruits, if the harvest is not yet. Do thou love thy neighbour as thyself. The Lord God fill thy heart with such a love to every soul that thou mayst be ready to lay down thy life for his sake! May thy soul continually overflow with love, swallowing up every unkind and unholy temper, till he calleth thee up into the region of love, there to reign with him for ever and ever!

47. UPON OUR LORD'S SERMON ON THE MOUNT, DISCOURSE THE THIRD

1748

An Introductory Comment

This third discourse completes a discussion of the eight Beatitudes, and it was published in volume II of the sermons in 1748. Wesley preached on Matthew 5:8-12, the text of this sermon, at least two times: once in Bristol on August 19, 1739, and the other in Hanham Mount the same day (WWS). And Charles Wesley, for his part, published a number of poems on this particular chapter in Matthew as found in the *Arminian Magazine.* The strong ethical force of these discourses on the Sermon on the Mount proved that Wesley's energetic articulation of justification by faith in no way resulted in the antinomianism or lawlessness that many Anglicans feared (S, 1:313).

Much of this present sermon is taken up with a description of the pure in heart, whom Wesley described as "they whose hearts God hath 'purified even as he is pure'" (O, 1:510). Those marked by the tempers or dispositions of heart purity evidence a gracious simplicity since the love of God is ever before their eyes, and they not surprisingly "see all things full of God" (O, 1:513). As peacemakers, marked by holy affections, the pure in heart do good to their neighbors in terms of their temporal needs. And how much more do they rejoice, Wesley observed, "if [they] can do any good to the soul of any man!" (O, 1:519).

In this context as well as in his *Explanatory Notes Upon the New Testament* Wesley made clear that the pure in heart will inevitably be persecuted precisely because they seek the righteousness that comes from God alone. The world will therefore blacken the saints in order to excuse itself, not willing to acknowledge the light of holy love. Wesley concluded the sermon with an exhortation to be "perfect as our Father which is in heaven is perfect" (O, 1:530).

Upon our Lord's Sermon on the Mount, Discourse the Third

I. 1. Blessed are the pure in heart: for they will see God
2. The pure in heart are they whose hearts God has purified through faith
3. But how little has this purity of heart been regarded by false teachers
4. God admits no excuse for retaining any occasion of impurity
5. Marriage itself should not be a pretense for being loose in our desires
6. The pure in heart see all things full of God in heaven
7. In all God's providences the pure in heart see God
8. In a more special way, they see God in prayer, worship, or the Lord's Supper
9. But how far were they from seeing God who were given to swearing
10. Our Lord does not forbid swearing oaths when required by a magistrate
11. The great lesson which our Lord teaches here is that God is in all things

II. 1. Blessed are the peacemakers; they will be called children of God
2. Peace in sacred writings implies all manner of good
3. Peacemakers are those lovers of God and people who abhor strife
4. They are those who do good unto all people
5. They do good, to their uttermost power, even to the bodies of all people
6. How much more do they rejoice if they can do any good to the soul
7. Blessed are they who are employed in the work of faith and the labor of love

III. 1. One would imagine that such a person would be the darling of humankind
2. But the Scriptures show that the righteous will be persecuted
3. Secondly, they show that they are persecuted because they are not of the world
4. Thirdly, they show that it is he that is born after the flesh that persecutes
5. They are persecuted in the manner that brings glory to the Disposer of all
6. God seldom suffers the storm to rise to torture or death or imprisonment
7. Jesus says they will be reviled, persecuted, and have evil said against them
8. The scandal of the cross is not yet ceased
9. How are the children of God to act with regard to persecution?
   A. First, they ought not knowingly bring it upon themselves
10. Yet do not think that you can always avoid it
11. Rejoice and be glad when people persecute you for Jesus' sake
12. Let no persecution turn you out of the way of lowliness and meekness
13. The Lord describes the lowliness and meekness we are to feel

IV. Behold Christianity in its native form, as delivered by its great Author!

Sermon 23: Upon our Lord's Sermon on the Mount

Discourse the Third, 1748

Matthew 5:8-12

Blessed are the pure in heart: for they shall see God.

Blessed are the peacemakers: for they shall be called the children of God.

Blessed are they which are persecuted for righteousness' sake: for theirs is the kingdom of heaven.

Blessed are ye when men shall revile you, and persecute you, and shall say all manner of evil against you falsely for my sake.

Rejoice, and be exceeding glad; for great is your reward in heaven: for so persecuted they the prophets which were before you.

I. 1. How excellent things are spoken of the love of our neighbour! It is 'the fulfilling of the law', 'the end of the commandment'. Without this all we have, all we do, all we suffer, is of no value in the sight of God. But it is that love of our neighbour which springs from the love of God; otherwise itself is nothing worth. It behoves us therefore to examine well upon what foundation our love of our neighbour stands: whether it is really built upon the love of God; whether 'we' do 'love him because he first loved us;' whether we are 'pure in heart'. For this is the foundation which shall never be moved: 'Blessed are the pure in heart: for they shall see God.'

2. 'The pure in heart' are they whose hearts God hath 'purified even as he is pure'; who are purified through faith in the blood of Jesus from every unholy affection; who, being 'cleansed from all filthiness of flesh and spirit, perfect holiness in the' loving 'fear of God'. They are, through the power of his grace, purified from pride by the deepest poverty of spirit; from anger, from every unkind or turbulent passion, by meekness and gentleness; from every desire but to please and enjoy God, to know and love him more and more, by that hunger and thirst after righteousness which now engrosses their whole soul: so that now they love the Lord their God with all their heart, and with all their soul, and mind, and strength.

3. But how little has this 'purity of heart' been regarded by the false teachers of all ages! They have taught men barely to abstain from such outward impurities as God hath forbidden by name. But they did not strike at the heart; and by not guarding against, they in effect countenanced inward corruptions.

A remarkable instance of this our Lord has given us in the following words: 'Ye have heard that it was said by them of old time, Thou shalt not commit adultery' (Matt. 5:27). And in explaining this those blind leaders of the blind only insist on men's abstaining from the outward act. 'But I say unto you, whosoever looketh on a woman to lust after her hath committed adultery with her already in his heart' (Matt. 5:28). For God requireth truth in the inward parts. He searcheth the heart and trieth the reins. And 'if thou incline unto iniquity with thy heart, the Lord will not hear thee.'

4. And God admits no excuse for retaining anything which is an occasion of impurity. Therefore 'if thy right eye offend thee, pluck it out and cast it from thee; for it is profitable for thee that one of thy members should perish, and not that thy whole body should be cast into hell' (Matt. 5:29). If persons as dear to thee as thy right eye be an occasion of thy thus offending God, a means of exciting unholy desire in thy soul, delay not—forcibly separate from them. 'And if thy right hand offend thee, cut it off, and cast it from thee; for it is profitable for thee that one of thy members should perish, and not that thy whole body should be cast into hell' (Matt. 5:30). If any who seem as necessary to thee as thy right hand be an occasion of sin, of impure desire, even though it were never to go beyond the heart, never to break out in word or action, constrain thyself to an entire and final parting: cut them off at a stroke; give them up to God. Any loss, whether of pleasure, or substance, or friends, is preferable to the loss of thy soul.

Two steps only it may not be improper to take before such an absolute and final separation. First, try whether the unclean spirit may not be driven out by fasting and prayer, and by carefully abstaining from every action and word and look which thou hast found to be an occasion of evil. Secondly, if thou art not by this means delivered, ask counsel of him that watcheth over thy soul, or at least of some who have experience in the ways of God, touching the time and manner of that separation. But confer not with flesh and blood, lest thou be 'given up to a strong delusion to believe a lie'.

5. Nor may marriage itself, holy and honourable as it is, be used as a pretence for giving a loose to our desires. Indeed 'It hath been said, Whosoever will put away his wife, let him give her a writing of divorcement.' And then all was well, though he alleged no cause but that he did not like her, or liked another better. 'But I say unto you, That whosoever shall put away his wife, saving for the case of fornication' (that is adultery, the word πορνεία signifying unchastity in general, either in the married or unmarried state) 'causeth her to commit adultery' if she marry again; 'and whosoever shall marry her that is put away committeth adultery' (Matt. 5:31-32).

All polygamy is clearly forbidden in these words, wherein our Lord expressly declares that for any woman who has a husband alive, to marry again is adultery. By parity of reason it is adultery for any man to marry again so long as he has a wife alive. Yea, although they were divorced—unless that divorce had been for the cause of adultery. In that only case there is no Scripture which forbids to marry again.

6. Such is the purity of heart which God requires, and works in those who believe on the Son of his love. And 'blessed' are they who are thus 'pure in heart; for they shall see God'. He will 'manifest himself unto them', not only 'as he doth not unto the world', but as he doth not always to his own children. He will bless them with the clearest communications of his Spirit, the most intimate 'fellowship with the Father and with the Son'. He will cause his presence to go continually before them, and the light of his countenance to shine upon them. It is the ceaseless prayer of their heart, 'I beseech thee, show me thy glory:' and they have the petition they ask of him. They now see him by faith (the veil of the flesh being made, as it were, transparent) even in these his lowest works, in all that surrounds them, in all that God has created and made. They see him in the height above, and in the depth beneath; they see him filling all in all.

The pure in heart see all things full of God. They see him in the firmament of heaven, in the moon walking in brightness, in the sun when he rejoiceth as a giant to run his course. They see him 'making the clouds his chariots, and walking upon the wings of the wind'. They see him 'preparing rain for the earth', 'and blessing the increase of it'; 'giving grass for the cattle, and green herb for the use of man'. They see the Creator of all wisely governing all, and 'upholding all things by the word of his power'. 'O Lord, our Governor, how excellent is thy name in all the world!'

7. In all his providences relating to themselves, to their souls or bodies, the pure in heart do more particularly see God. They see his hand ever over them for good; giving them all things in weight, and measure, numbering the hairs of their head, making a hedge round about them and all that they have, and disposing all the circumstances of their life according to the depth both of his wisdom and mercy.

8. But in a more especial manner they see God in his ordinances. Whether they appear in the great congregation to 'pay him the honour due unto his name, and worship him in the beauty of holiness'; or 'enter into their closets' and there pour out their souls before their 'Father which is in secret'; whether they search the oracles of God, or hear the ambassadors of Christ proclaiming glad tidings of salvation; or by eating of that bread and drinking of that cup 'show forth his death till he come' in the clouds of heaven. In all these his appointed ways they find such a near approach as cannot be expressed. They see him, as it were, face to face, and 'talk with him as a man talking with his friend'—a fit preparation for those mansions above wherein they shall 'see him as he is'.

9. But how far were they from seeing God, who having 'heard that it had been said by them of old time, Thou shalt not forswear thyself, but shalt perform unto the Lord thine oaths' (Matt. 5:33), interpreted it thus: thou shalt not forswear thyself when thou swearest by the Lord Jehovah; thou 'shalt perform unto the Lord *these* thine oaths'—but as to other oaths, he regardeth them not.

So the Pharisees taught. They not only allowed all manner of swearing in common conversation; but accounted even forswearing a little thing, so they had not sworn by the peculiar name of God.

But our Lord here absolutely forbids all common swearing as well as all false swearing; and shows the heinousness of both by the same awful consideration, that every creature is God's, and he is everywhere present, in all, and over all.

'I say unto you, Swear not at all; neither by heaven, for it is God's throne'(Matt. 5:34)—and therefore this is the same as to swear by him who sitteth upon the circle of the heavens—'nor by the earth, for it is his footstool,' and he is as intimately present in earth as heaven; 'neither by Jerusalem, for it is the city of the great King' (Matt. 5:35), and 'God is well known in her palaces.' 'Neither shalt thou swear by thy head, because thou canst not make one hair white or black' (Matt. 5:36); because even this, it is plain, is not thine but God's, the sole disposer of all in heaven and earth. 'But let your communication'—your conversation, your discourse with each other—'be, Yea, yea; Nay, nay'—a bare serious affirming or denying—'for whatsoever is more than these cometh of evil'

(Matt. 5:37)—ἐκ τοῦ πονηροῦ ἐστιν, ('is the evil one', proceedeth from the devil and is a mark of his children).

10. That our Lord does not here forbid the 'swearing in judgment and truth' when we are required so to do by a magistrate may appear: (1). From the occasion of this part of his discourse, the abuse he was here reproving, which was false swearing and common swearing, the swearing before a magistrate being quite out of the question. (2) From the very words wherein he forms the general conclusion, 'Let your communication', or discourse, 'be, Yea, yea; Nay, nay.' (3). From his own example; for he answered himself upon oath when required by a magistrate. When 'the High Priest said unto him, I adjure thee by the living God that thou tell us whether thou be the Christ, the Son of God,' Jesus immediately answered in the affirmative, 'Thou hast said' (i.e., the truth). 'Nevertheless' (or rather, 'Moreover') 'I say unto you, Hereafter shall ye see the Son of man sitting on the right hand of power, and coming in the clouds of heaven' (Matt. 26:63-64). (4). From the example of God, even the Father, who 'willing the more abundantly to show unto the heirs of promise the immutability of his counsel, confirmed it by an oath' (Heb. 6:17). (5). From the example of St. Paul, who we 'think had the Spirit of God', and well understood the mind of his Master. 'God is my witness', saith he to the Romans, 'that without ceasing I make mention of you always in my prayers' (Rom. 1:9); to the Corinthians, 'I call God to record upon my soul, that to spare you I came not as yet unto Corinth' (2 Cor. 1:23); and to the Philippians, 'God is my record, how greatly I long after you in the bowels of Jesus Christ' (Phil. 1:8). (Hence it undeniably appears that if the Apostle knew the meaning of his Lord's words, they do not forbid swearing on weighty occasions, even to one another—how much less before a magistrate!) And lastly, from that assertion of the great Apostle concerning solemn swearing in general (which it is impossible he could have mentioned without any touch of blame if his Lord had totally forbidden it): 'Men verily swear by the greater' (by one greater than themselves), 'and an oath for confirmation is to them the end of all strife' (Heb. 6:16).

11. But the great lesson which our blessed Lord inculcates here, and which he illustrates by this example, is that God is in all things, and that we are to see the Creator in the glass of every creature; that we should use and look upon nothing as separate from God, which indeed is a kind of practical atheism; but with a true magnificence of thought survey heaven and earth and all that is therein as contained by God in the hollow of his hand, who by his intimate presence holds them all in being, who pervades and actuates the whole created frame, and is in a true sense the soul of the universe.

II.1. Thus far our Lord has been more directly employed in teaching the religion of the heart. He has shown what Christians are to be. He proceeds to show what they are to do also: how inward holiness is to exert itself in our outward conversation. 'Blessed', saith he, 'are the peacemakers; for they shall be called the children of God.'

2. 'The peacemakers'—the word in the original is οἱ εἰρηνοποιοί. It is well known that εἰρήνη in the sacred writings implies all manner of good—every blessing that relates either to the soul or the body, to time or eternity. Accordingly, when St. Paul in the titles

of his epistles wishes 'grace and peace' to the Romans or the Corinthians it is as if he had said, 'As a fruit of the free, undeserved love and favour of God, may you enjoy all blessings, spiritual and temporal, all the good things "which God hath prepared for them that love him."'

3. Hence we may easily learn in how wide a sense the term 'peacemakers' is to be understood. In its literal meaning it implies those lovers of God and man who utterly detest and abhor all strife and debate, all variance and contention; and accordingly labour with all their might either to prevent this fire of hell from being kindled, or when it is kindled from breaking out, or when it is broke out from spreading any farther. They endeavour to calm the stormy spirits of men, to quiet their turbulent passions, to soften the minds of contending parties, and if possible reconcile them to each other. They use all innocent arts, and employ all their strength, all the talents which God has given them, as well to preserve peace where it is as to restore it where it is not. It is the joy of their heart to promote, to confirm, to increase mutual goodwill among men, but more especially among the children of God, however distinguished by things of smaller importance; that as they have all 'one Lord, one faith', as they are all 'called in one hope of their calling', so they may all 'walk worthy of the vocation wherewith they are called': 'with all lowliness and meekness, with long-suffering, forbearing one another in love; endeavouring to keep the unity of the Spirit in the bond of peace.'

4. But in the full extent of the word a 'peacemaker' is one that as he hath opportunity 'doth good unto all men'; one that being filled with the love of God and of all mankind cannot confine the expressions of it to his own family, or friends, or acquaintance, or party; or to those of his own opinions; no, nor those who are partakers of like precious faith; but steps over all these narrow bounds that he may do good to every man; that he may some way or other manifest his love to neighbours and strangers, friends and enemies. He doth good to them all as he hath opportunity, that is, on every possible occasion; 'redeeming the time' in order thereto, 'buying up every opportunity', improving every hour, losing no moment wherein he may profit another. He does good, not of one particular kind, but good in general: in every possible way, employing herein all his talents of every kind, all his powers and faculties of body and soul, all his fortune, his interest, his reputation; desiring only that when his Lord cometh he may say, 'Well done, good and faithful servant!'

5. He doth good, to the uttermost of his power, even to the bodies of all men. He rejoices to 'deal his bread to the hungry', and to 'cover the naked with a garment'. Is any a stranger? He takes him in, and relieves him according to his necessities. Are any sick or in prison? He visits them, and administers such help as they stand most in need of. And all this he does, not as unto man, but remembering him that hath said, 'Inasmuch as ye have done it unto one of the least of these my brethren, ye have done it unto me.'

6. How much more does he rejoice if he can do any good to the soul of any man! This power indeed belongeth unto God. It is he only that changes the heart, without which every other change is lighter than vanity. Nevertheless it pleases him who worketh all in all to help man chiefly by man; to convey his own power and blessing and love through one man to another. Therefore, although it be certain that 'the help which is done upon earth, God doth it himself,' yet has no man need on this account to stand idle in his vineyard.

The peacemaker cannot: he is ever labouring therein, and as an instrument in God's hand preparing the ground for his Master's use, or sowing the seed of the kingdom, or watering what is already sown, if haply God may give the increase. According to the measure of grace which he has received he uses all diligence either to reprove the gross sinner, to reclaim those who run on headlong in the broad way of destruction, or 'to give light to them that sit in darkness' and are ready to 'perish for lack of knowledge'; or to 'support the weak', to 'lift up the hands that hang down, and the feeble knees'; or to bring back and heal that which was 'lame and turned out of the way'. Nor is he less zealous to confirm those who are already striving to enter in at the strait gate; to strengthen those that stand, that they may 'run with patience the race which is set before them'; to 'build up in their most holy faith' those that know in whom they have believed; to exhort them to stir up the gift of God which is in them, that daily 'growing in grace', 'an entrance may be ministered unto them abundantly into the everlasting kingdom of our Lord and Saviour Jesus Christ'.

7. Blessed are they who are thus continually employed in the work of faith and the labour of love; 'for they shall be called'—that is 'shall be' (a common Hebraism)—'the children of God.' God shall continue unto them the Spirit of adoption, yea, shall pour it more abundantly into their hearts. He shall bless them with all the blessings of his children. He shall acknowledge them as sons before angels and men; 'and if sons, then heirs; heirs of God, and joint heirs with Christ.'

III.1. One would imagine such a person as has been above described, so full of genuine humility, so unaffectedly serious, so mild and gentle, so free from all selfish design, so devoted to God, and such an active lover of men, should be the darling of mankind. But our Lord was better acquainted with human nature in its present state. He therefore closes the character of this man of God with showing him the treatment he is to expect in the world. 'Blessed', saith he, 'are they which are persecuted for righteousness' sake; for theirs is the kingdom of heaven.'

2. In order to understand this throughly, let us first inquire who are they that are persecuted. And this we may easily learn from St. Paul: 'As of old he that was born after the flesh persecuted him that was born after the Spirit, even so it is now' (Gal. 4:29). 'Yea', saith the Apostle, 'and all that will live godly in Christ Jesus shall suffer persecution' (2 Tim. 3:12). The same we are taught by St. John: 'Marvel not, my brethren, if the world hate you. We know that we have passed from death unto life, because we love the brethren' (1 John 3:13-14). As if he had said, The brethren, the Christians, cannot be loved but by them who have passed from death unto life. And most expressly by our Lord: 'If the world hate you, ye know that it hated me before it hated you. If ye were of the world, the world would love its own; but because ye are not of the world, . . . therefore the world hateth you. Remember the word that I said unto you, The servant is not greater than the Lord. If they have persecuted me, they will also persecute you' (John 15:18-20).

By all these Scriptures it manifestly appears who they are that are persecuted, namely the righteous: 'he that is born after the Spirit'; 'all that will live godly in Christ Jesus'; they that are 'passed from death unto life'; those who 'are not of the world'; all those who are meek and lowly in heart, that mourn for God, that hunger after his likeness; all that love God and their neighbour, and therefore as they have opportunity do good unto all men.

3. If it be, secondly, inquired why they are persecuted, the answer is equally plain and obvious. It is 'for righteousness' sake': because they are righteous; because they are 'born after the Spirit'; because they 'will live godly in Christ Jesus'; because they 'are not of the world'. Whatever may be pretended, this is the real cause; be their infirmities more or less, still if it were not for this they would be borne with, and the world would love its own. They are persecuted because they are 'poor in spirit': that is, say the world, 'poor-spirited, mean, dastardly souls, good for nothing, not fit to live in the world'; because they 'mourn': 'They are such dull, heavy, lumpish creatures, enough to sink anyone's spirits that sees them! They are mere death's-heads; they kill innocent mirth, and spoil company wherever they come;' because they are *meek*: 'Tame, passive fools, just fit to be trampled upon;' because they 'hunger and thirst after righteousness': 'A parcel of hot-brained enthusiasts, gaping after they know not what, not content with rational religion, but running mad after raptures and inward feelings;' because they are 'merciful', lovers of all, lovers of the evil and unthankful: 'Encouraging all manner of wickedness; nay, tempting people to do mischief by impunity; and men who, it is to be feared, have their own religion still to seek; very loose in their principles;' because they are 'pure in heart': 'Uncharitable creatures that damn all the world but those that are of their own sort! Blasphemous wretches that pretend to make God a liar, to live without sin!' Above all because they are 'peacemakers', because they take all opportunities of doing good to all men. This is the grand reason why they have been persecuted in all ages, and will be till the restitution of all things.

'If they would but keep their religion to themselves it would be tolerable. But it is this spreading their errors, this infecting so many others, which is not to be endured. They do so much mischief in the world that they ought to be tolerated no longer. It is true the men do some things well enough; they relieve some of the poor. But this, too, is only done to gain the more to their party; and so in effect to do the more mischief.' Thus the men of the world sincerely think and speak. And the more the kingdom of God prevails, the more the peacemakers are enabled to propagate lowliness, meekness, and all other divine tempers, the more mischief is done—in their account. Consequently the more are they enraged against the authors of this, and the more vehemently will they persecute them.

4. Let us, thirdly, inquire who are they that persecute them. St. Paul answers, 'He that is born after the flesh'; everyone who is not 'born of the Spirit', or at least desirous so to be; all that do not at least labour to 'live godly in Christ Jesus'; all that are not 'passed from death unto life', and consequently cannot 'love the brethren'; 'the world', that is, according to our Saviour's account, 'they who know not him that sent me'; they who know not God, even the loving, pardoning God, by the teaching of his own Spirit.

The reason is plain. The spirit which is in the world is directly opposite to the Spirit which is of God. It must therefore needs be that those who are of the world will be opposite to those who are of God. There is the utmost contrariety between them in all their opinions, their desires, designs, and tempers. And hitherto 'the leopard and the kid' cannot 'lie down in peace together.' The proud, because he is proud, cannot but persecute the lowly; the light and airy, those that mourn: and so in every other kind, the unlikeness of disposition (were there no other) being a perpetual ground of enmity. Therefore (were it only on this account) all the servants of the devil will persecute the children of God.

5. Should it be inquired, fourthly, how they will persecute them, it may be answered in general, just in that manner and measure which the wise Disposer of all sees will be most for his glory, will tend most to his children's growth in grace and the enlargement of his own kingdom. There is no one branch of God's government of the world which is more to be admired than this. His ear is never heavy to the threatenings of the persecutor or the cry of the persecuted. His eye is ever open and his hand stretched out to direct every the minutest circumstance. When the storm shall begin, how high it shall rise, which way it shall point its course, when and how it shall end, are all determined by his unerring wisdom. The ungodly are only a sword of his; an instrument which he uses as it pleaseth him, and which itself, when the gracious ends of his providence are answered, is cast into the fire.

At some rare times, as when Christianity was planted first, and while it was taking root in the earth, as also when the pure doctrine of Christ began to be planted again in our nation, God permitted the storm to rise high, and his children were called to resist unto blood. There was a peculiar reason why he suffered this with regard to the apostles—that their evidence might be the more unexceptionable. But from the annals of the church we learn another and a far different reason why he suffered the heavy persecutions which rose in the second and third centuries: namely, because the mystery of iniquity did so strongly work, because of the monstrous corruptions which even then reigned in the church; these God chastised, and at the same time strove to heal, by those severe but necessary visitations.

Perhaps the same observation may be made with regard to the grand persecution in our own land. God had dealt very graciously with our nation; he had poured out various blessings upon us. He had given us peace abroad and at home; and a king wise and good beyond his years. And above all he had caused the pure light of his gospel to arise and shine amongst us. But what return did he find? 'He looked for righteousness; but behold a cry!' A cry of oppression and wrong, of ambition and injustice, of malice and fraud and covetousness. Yea, the cry of those who even then expired in the flames entered into the ears of the Lord of sabaoth. It was then God arose to maintain his own cause against those that held the truth in unrighteousness. Then he sold them into the hands of their persecutors, by a judgment mixed with mercy, an affliction to punish and yet a medicine to heal the grievous backslidings of his people.

6. But it is seldom God suffers the storm to rise so high as torture or death or bonds or imprisonment. Whereas his children are frequently called to endure those lighter kinds of persecution: they frequently suffer the estrangement of kinsfolk, the loss of the friends that were as their own soul. They find the truth of their Lord's word (concerning the event, though not the design of his coming): 'Suppose ye that I am come to give peace on earth? I tell you, Nay, but rather division' (Luke 12:51). And hence will naturally follow loss of business or employment, and consequently of substance. But all these circumstances likewise are under the wise direction of God, who allots to everyone what is most expedient for him.

7. But the persecution which attends all the children of God is that our Lord describes in the following words: 'Blessed are ye, when men shall revile you, and persecute you (shall persecute by reviling you), and say all manner of evil against you falsely, for my sake.' This cannot fail: it is the very badge of our discipleship; it is one of the seals of our calling. It is a sure portion entailed on all the children of God; if we have it not we are bastards and not sons. Straight through 'evil report' as well as 'good report' lies the only way to the kingdom. The meek, serious, humble, zealous lovers of God and man are of good report among their brethren; but of evil report with the world, who count and treat them 'as the filth [. . .] and offscouring of all things'.

8. Indeed some have supposed that before the fullness of the Gentiles shall come in the scandal of the cross will cease; that God will cause Christians to be esteemed and loved, even by those who are as yet in their sins. Yea, and sure it is that even now he at some times suspends the contempt as well as the fierceness of men. 'He makes a man's enemies to be at peace with him' for a season, and gives him favour with his bitterest persecutors. But setting aside this exempt case, 'the scandal of the cross is' not yet 'ceased': but a man may say still, 'If I please men, I am not the servant of Christ.' Let no man therefore regard that pleasing suggestion (pleasing doubtless to flesh and blood), that 'Bad men only *pretend* to hate and despise them that are good, but do indeed love and esteem them in their hearts.' Not so: they may employ them sometimes, but it is for their own profit. They may put confidence in them, for they know their ways are not like other men's. But still they love them not, unless so far as the Spirit of God may be striving with them. Our Saviour's words are express: 'If ye were of the world, the world would love its own: but because ye are not of the world, [. . .] therefore the world hateth you.' Yea (setting aside what exceptions may be made by the preventing grace or the peculiar providence of God) it hateth them as cordially and sincerely as ever it did their Master.

9. It remains only to inquire, 'How are the children of God to behave with regard to persecution?' And first, they ought not knowingly or designedly to bring it upon themselves. This is contrary both to the example and advice of our Lord and all his apostles, who teach us not only not to seek, but to avoid it as far as we can without injuring our conscience, without giving up any part of that righteousness which we are to prefer before life itself. So our Lord expressly saith, 'When they persecute you in this city, flee ye into another'—which is indeed, when it can be taken, the most unexceptionable way of avoiding persecution.

10. Yet think not that you can always avoid it, either by this or any other means. If ever that idle imagination steals into your heart, put it to flight by that earnest caution: 'Remember the word that I said unto you, The servant is not greater than his Lord. If they have persecuted me, they will also persecute you.' 'Be ye wise as serpents, and harmless as doves.' But will this screen you from persecution? Not unless you have more wisdom than your Master, or more innocence than the Lamb of God.

Neither desire to avoid it, to escape it wholly; for if you do, you are none of his. If you escape the persecution you escape the blessing, the blessing of those who are persecuted for righteousness' sake. If you are not persecuted for righteousness' sake you cannot enter into the kingdom of heaven. 'If we suffer with him we shall also reign with him. But if we deny him he will also deny us.'

11. Nay, rather, 'rejoice and be exceeding glad' when men persecute you for his sake, when 'they persecute you by reviling' you, and by 'saying all manner of evil against you falsely' (which they will not fail to mix with every kind of persecution; they must blacken you to excuse themselves): 'for so persecuted they the prophets which were before you,' those who were most eminently holy in heart and life; yea, and all the righteous which ever have been from the beginning of the world. Rejoice, because by his mark also ye know unto whom ye belong. And because 'great is your reward in heaven,' the reward purchased by the blood of the covenant, and freely bestowed in proportion to your sufferings, as well as to your holiness of heart and life. 'Be exceeding glad,' knowing that 'these light afflictions, which are but for a moment, work out for you a far more exceeding and eternal weight of glory.'

12. Meantime, let no persecution turn you out of the way of lowliness and meekness, of love and beneficence. 'Ye have heard' indeed 'that it hath been said, An eye for an eye and a tooth for a tooth' (Matt. 5:38). And your miserable teachers have hence allowed you to avenge yourselves, to return evil for evil.

'But I say unto you, that ye resist not evil'—not thus: not by returning it in kind. 'But' (rather than do this) 'whosoever smiteth thee on thy right cheek, turn to him the other also. And if any man will sue thee at the law, and take away thy coat, let him have thy cloak also. And whosoever shall compel thee to go a mile, go with him twain.'

So invincible let thy meekness be. And be thy love suitable thereto. 'Give to him that asketh thee, and from him that would borrow of thee turn not thou away.' Only give not away that which is another man's, that which is not thine own. Therefore, (1). Take care to owe no man anything. For what thou owest is not thy own, but another man's. (2). Provide for those of thine own household. This also God hath required of thee: and what is necessary to sustain them in life and godliness is also not thine own. Then, (3), give or lend all that remains from day to day, or from year to year: only first, seeing thou canst not give or lend to all, remember the household of faith.

13. The meekness and love we are to feel, the kindness we are to show to them which persecute us for righteousness' sake, our blessed Lord describes farther in the following verses. O that they were graven upon our hearts!

'Ye have heard that it hath been said, Thou shalt love thy neighbour, and hate thy enemy' (Matt. 5:43, etc.). (God indeed had said only the former part, 'Thou shalt love thy neighbour;' the children of the devil had added the latter, 'and hate thy enemy.') 'But I say unto you': (1). 'Love your enemies.' See that you bear a tender goodwill to those who are most bitter of spirit against you, who wish you all manner of evil. (2). 'Bless them that curse you.' Are there any whose bitterness of spirit breaks forth in bitter words? Who are continually cursing and reproaching you when you are present, and 'saying all evil against you' when absent? So much the rather do you bless. In conversing with them use all mildness and softness of language. Reprove them by repeating a better lesson before them, by showing them how they ought to have spoken. And in speaking of them say all the good you can without violating the rules of truth and justice. (3). 'Do good to them that hate you.' Let your actions show that you are as real in love as they in hatred. Return good for evil. 'Be not overcome of evil, but overcome evil with good.' (4). If you can do nothing more, at least 'pray for them that despitefully use you and persecute you.' You can never be disabled from doing this; nor can all their malice or violence hinder you. Pour out your souls to God, not only for those who did this once but now repent. This is a little thing. 'If thy brother seven times a day turn and say unto thee, I repent'—that is, if after ever so many relapses he give thee reason to believe that he is really and throughly changed—then 'thou shalt forgive him' (Luke 17:3-4), so as to trust him, to put him in thy bosom, as if he had never sinned against thee at all. But pray for, wrestle with God for those that do not repent, that now despitefully use thee and persecute thee. Thus far forgive them, 'not until seven times only, but until seventy times seven' (Matt. 18:22). Whether they repent or no, yea, though they appear farther and farther from it, yet show them this instance of kindness: 'that ye may be the children', that ye may approve yourselves the genuine children, 'of your Father which is in heaven', who shows his goodness by giving such blessings as they are capable of even to his stubbornest enemies; who 'maketh his sun to rise on the evil and on the good, and sendeth rain on the just and on the unjust.' 'For if ye love them which love you, what reward have ye? Do not even the publicans the same?' (Matt. 5:46)—who pretend to no religion, whom ye yourselves acknowledge to be without God in the world. 'And if ye salute', show kindness in word or deed to 'your brethren', your friends or kinsfolk, 'only, what do ye more than others?' Than those who have no religion at all? 'Do not even the publicans so?' (Matt. 5:47). Nay, but follow ye a better pattern than them. In patience, in longsuffering, in mercy, in beneficence of every kind, to all, even to your bitterest persecutors: 'Be ye' Christians 'perfect' (in kind though not in degree) even 'as your Father which is in heaven is perfect' (Matt. 5:48).

IV. Behold Christianity in its native form, as delivered by its great Author! This is the genuine religion of Jesus Christ. Such he presents it to him whose eyes are opened. See a picture of God, so far as he is imitable by man! A picture drawn by God's own hand! 'Behold, ye despisers, and wonder and perish!' Or rather, wonder and adore! Rather cry out, 'Is this the religion of Jesus of Nazareth? The religion which I persecuted! Let me no more be found even to fight against God. Lord, what wouldst thou have me to do?' What beauty appears in the whole! How just a symmetry! What exact proportion in every part! How desirable is the happiness here described! How venerable, how lovely the holiness! This is the *spirit* of religion; the quintessence of it. These are indeed the *fundamentals* of Christianity. O that we may not be hearers of it only! 'Like a man beholding his own face in a glass, who goeth his way, and straightway forgetteth what manner of man he was.' Nay, but let us steadily 'look into this perfect law of liberty, and continue therein'. Let us not rest until every line thereof is transcribed into our own hearts. Let us watch and pray and believe and love, and 'strive for the mastery', till every part of it shall appear in our soul, graven there by the finger of God; till we are 'holy as he which hath called us is holy', 'perfect as our Father which is in heaven is perfect'!

48. UPON OUR LORD'S SERMON ON THE MOUNT, DISCOURSE THE FOURTH

1748

An Introductory Comment

Wesley preached on the text of this sermon, Matthew 5:13-16, at West Street in London on February 3, 1747. In 1740 he had exposited these same verses at Bexley and the Foundery (WWS), underscoring the theme of faith active in love. Such preaching demonstrated the conjunctive balance (both/and; not either/or) and the good sense of Wesley's practical theology in that inward religion, the religion of the heart, must have an outward, public expression. And Charles Wesley, for his part, published a poem on verse 14 ("Ye are the light of the world") much later, in June 1790 to be exact, in the *Arminian Magazine.*

Criticizing the mystic preference for withdrawal, and well aware of William Law's mystical turn that was evident by 1733 (S, 1:378), Wesley maintained in this sermon that Christianity is "a social religion, and that to turn it into a solitary one is to destroy it" (O, 1:533). Christianity cannot subsist without society, and believers must have "some intercourse even with ungodly and unholy men," Wesley wrote, for "the full exertion of every temper which he [Christ] has described as the way of the kingdom" (O, 1:536). Moreover, precisely because Christians are both the salt of the earth and the light of the world, their witness necessarily entails serving those beyond the walls of the church. On this point Wesley was emphatic: "a secret, unobserved religion cannot be the religion of Jesus Christ" (O, 1:540).

The sermon concludes by answering several objections to the balance of inward and outward religion, ranging from "We used outward things many years; and yet they profited nothing (O, 1:545), to "What does it avail to feed or clothe men's bodies if they are just dropping into everlasting fire?" (O, 1:545). In the face of such criticisms, these "plausible pretenses," Wesley counseled, "Let your light so shine" (O, 1:547).

Upon our Lord's Sermon on the Mount, Discourse the Fourth

I. 1. First, I will show that Christianity is essentially a social religion
  A. It cannot exist without society, without conversing with others
 2. Several branches of Christianity require conversation with the world
 3. For instance, no disposition is more essential to Christianity than meekness
  A. Yet meekness has no being without intercourse with others
 4. Another branch of Christianity is peacemaking
  A. Peacemaking cannot subsist without conversing with the world
 5. But is it not expedient to converse with only good people?
 6. Without having commerce with the world we cannot be Christians
 7. This is the great reason why Christ has mingled you together with others
 8. If the salt loses its savour, where will it be salted?
 9. For those who have not tasted of the good word, God is merciful

II. 1.–2. I will now show that true religion is impossible to conceal
 3. Those who love darkness will work to prove that the light in you is darkness
 4. It is impossible to keep our religion invisible
 5.–7. People do not light a candle to put it under a bushel

III. 1. Some object that religion does not lie in outward things
 2. Others object that love is all in all: it is the fulfilling of the law
 3. The Apostle directs us to follow after charity, but not after that alone
 4. Does not attending to outward things clog the soul and distract the mind?
 5. Giving ourselves entirely to this would destroy other branches of worship
 6. But the grand objection is this: we appeal to experience
  A. We used outward things many years; and they profited nothing
  B. You have mistaken the means for the ends
 7. They affirm: experience shows that trying to do good is lost labor
 8. We have tried. We have laboured to reform sinners. And what did it avail?
  A. Is a servant above the master? How often did he strive to save sinners?

IV. 1. Let your light so shine before men that they may see your good works
 2. Only do not seek your own praise, and do not desire any honor
 3. May this be your one ultimate end in all things
 4. With this one design, that people glorify God in you

Sermon 24: Upon our Lord's Sermon on the Mount

Discourse the Fourth, 1748

Matthew 5:13-16

Ye are the salt of the earth. But if the salt hath lost its savour, wherewith shall it be salted? It is thenceforth good for nothing but to be cast out, and trodden under foot of men.

Ye are the light of the world. A city that is set on an hill cannot be hid.

Neither do men light a candle and put it under a bushel, but on a candlestick; and it giveth light to all that are in the house.

Let your light so shine before men that they may see your good works, and glorify your Father which is in heaven.

1. The beauty of holiness, of that inward man of the heart which is renewed after the image of God, cannot but strike every eye which God hath opened, every enlightened understanding. The ornament of a meek, humble, loving spirit will at least excite the approbation of all those who are capable in any degree of discerning spiritual good and evil. From the hour men begin to emerge out of the darkness which covers the giddy, unthinking world, they cannot but perceive how desirable a thing it is to be thus transformed into the likeness of him that created us. This inward religion bears the shape of God so visibly impressed upon it that a soul must be wholly immersed in flesh and blood when he can doubt of its divine original. We may say of this, in a secondary sense, even as of the Son of God himself, that it is 'the brightness of his glory, the express image of his person': ἀπαύγασμα τῆς δόξης [...] αὐτοῦ, 'the beaming forth of his' eternal 'glory'; and yet so tempered and softened that even the children of men may herein see God and live: χαρακτὴρ τῆς ὑποστάσεως αὐτοῦ, 'the character, the stamp, the living impression, of his person' who is the fountain of beauty and love, the original source of all excellency and perfection.

2. If religion therefore were carried no farther than this they could have no doubt concerning it—they should have no objection against pursuing it with the whole ardour of their souls. But why, say they, is it clogged with other things? What need of loading it with *doing* and *suffering*? These are what damps the vigour of the soul and sinks it down to earth again. Is it not enough to 'follow after charity'? To soar upon the wings of love? Will it not suffice to worship God, who is a Spirit, with the spirit of our minds, without encumbering ourselves with outward things, or even thinking of them at all? Is it not better that the whole extent of our thought should be taken up with high and heavenly contemplation? And that instead of busying ourselves at all about externals, we should only commune with God in our hearts?

3. Many eminent men have spoken thus: have advised us 'to cease from all outward actions'; wholly to withdraw from the world; to leave the body behind us; to abstract ourselves from all sensible things—to have no concern at all about outward religion, but to 'work all virtues in the will', as the far more excellent way, more perfective of the soul, as well as more acceptable to God.

4. It needed not that any should tell our Lord of this masterpiece of the wisdom from beneath, this fairest of all the devices wherewith Satan hath ever perverted the right ways of the Lord! And Oh! what instruments hath he found from time to time to employ in this his service! To wield this grand engine of hell against some of the most important truths of God! Men that 'would deceive, if it were possible, the very elect', the men of faith and love. Yea, that have for a season deceived and led away no inconsiderable number of them who have fallen in all ages into the gilded snare, and hardly escaped with the skin of their teeth.

5. But has our Lord been wanting on his part? Has he not sufficiently guarded us against this pleasing delusion? Has he not armed us here with armour of proof against Satan 'transformed into an angel of light'? Yea, verily. He here defends, in the clearest and strongest manner, the active, patient religion he had just described. What can be fuller and plainer than the words he immediately subjoins to what he had said of doing and suffering? 'Ye are the salt of the earth. But if the salt have lost its savour, wherewith shall it be salted? It is thenceforth good for nothing but to be cast out and trodden under foot of men. Ye are the light of the world. A city that is set on an hill cannot be hid. Neither do men light a candle and put it under a bushel, but on a candlestick; and it giveth light to all that are in the house. Let your light so shine before men that they may see your good works, and glorify your Father which is in heaven.'

In order fully to explain and enforce these important words I shall endeavour to show, first, that Christianity is essentially a social religion, and that to turn it into a solitary one is to destroy it; secondly, that to conceal this religion is impossible, as well as utterly contrary to the design of its author. I shall, thirdly, answer some objections; and conclude the whole with a practical application.

I.1. First, I shall endeavour to show that Christianity is essentially a social religion, and that to turn it into a solitary religion is indeed to destroy it.

By Christianity I mean that method of worshipping God which is here revealed to man by Jesus Christ. When I say this is essentially a social religion, I mean not only that it cannot subsist so well, but that it cannot subsist at all without society, without living and conversing with other men. And in showing this I shall confine myself to those considerations which will arise from the very discourse before us. But if this be shown, then doubtless to turn this religion into a solitary one is to destroy it.

Not that we can in any wise condemn the intermixing solitude or retirement with society. This is not only allowable but expedient; nay, it is necessary, as daily experience shows, for everyone that either already is or desires to be a real Christian. It can hardly be that we should spend one entire day in a continued intercourse with men without suffering loss in our soul, and in some measure grieving the Holy Spirit of God. We have need daily to retire from the world, at least morning and evening, to converse with God, to commune more freely with our Father which is in secret. Nor indeed can a man of experience condemn even longer seasons of religious retirement, so they do not imply any neglect of the worldly employ wherein the providence of God has placed us.

2. Yet such retirement must not swallow up all our time; this would be to destroy, not advance, true religion. For that the religion described by our Lord in the foregoing words cannot subsist without society, without our living and conversing with other men, is manifest from hence, that several of the most essential branches thereof can have no place if we have no intercourse with the world.

3. There is no disposition, for instance, which is more essential to Christianity than meekness. Now although this, as it implies resignation to God, or patience in pain and sickness, may subsist in a desert, in a hermit's cell, in total solitude; yet as it implies (which it no less necessarily does) mildness, gentleness, and long-suffering, it cannot possibly have a being, it has no place under heaven, without an intercourse with other men. So that to attempt turning this into a solitary virtue is to destroy it from the face of the earth.

4. Another necessary branch of true Christianity is peacemaking, or doing of good. That this is equally essential with any of the other parts of the religion of Jesus Christ there can be no stronger argument to evince (and therefore it would be absurd to allege any other) than that it is here inserted in the original plan he has laid down of the fundamentals of his religion. Therefore to set aside this is the same daring insult on the authority of our great Master as to set aside mercifulness, purity of heart, or any other branch of his institution. But this is apparently set aside by all who call us to the wilderness, who recommend entire solitude either to the babes, or the young men, or the fathers in Christ. For will any man affirm that a solitary Christian (so called, though it is little less than a contradiction in terms) can be a merciful man—that is, one that takes every opportunity of doing all good to all men? What can be more plain than that this fundamental branch of the religion of Jesus Christ cannot possibly subsist without society, without our living and conversing with other men?

5. But is it not expedient, however (one might naturally ask), to converse only with good men? Only with those whom we know to be meek and merciful, holy of heart and holy of life? Is it not expedient to refrain from any conversation or intercourse with men of the opposite character? Men who do not obey, perhaps do not believe, the gospel of our Lord Jesus Christ? The advice of St. Paul to the Christians at Corinth may seem to favour this: 'I wrote unto you in an epistle not to company with fornicators' (1 Cor. 5:9). And it is certainly not advisable so to company with them, or with any of the workers of iniquity, as to have any particular familiarity, or any strictness of friendship with them. To contract or continue an intimacy with any such is no way expedient for a Christian. It must necessarily expose him to abundance of dangers and snares, out of which he can have no reasonable hope of deliverance.

But the Apostle does not forbid us to have any intercourse at all, even with the men that know not God. For then, says he, 'ye must needs go out of the world,' which he could never advise them to do. But, he subjoins, 'If any man that is called a brother', that professes himself a Christian, 'be a fornicator, or covetous, or an idolator, or a railer, or a drunkard, or an extortioner', 'now I have written unto you not to keep company' with him; 'with such an one, no, not to eat' (1 Cor. 5:11). This must necessarily imply that we break off all familiarity, all intimacy of acquaintance with him. 'Yet count him not', saith the Apostle elsewhere, 'as an enemy, but admonish him as a brother' (2 Thess. 3:15):

plainly showing that even in such a case as this we are not to renounce all fellowship with him; so that here is no advice to separate wholly, even from wicked men. Yea, these very words teach us quite the contrary.

6. Much more the words of our Lord, who is so far from directing us to break off all commerce with the world that without it, according to his account of Christianity, we cannot be Christians at all. It would be easy to show that some intercourse even with ungodly and unholy men is absolutely needful in order to the full exertion of every temper which he has described as the way of the kingdom; that it is indispensably necessary in order to the complete exercise of poverty of spirit, of mourning, and of every other disposition which has a place here in the genuine religion of Jesus Christ. Yea, it is necessary to the very being of several of them; of that meekness, for example, which instead of demanding 'an eye for an eye, or a tooth for a tooth', doth 'not resist evil', but causes us rather, when smitten 'on the right cheek, to turn the other also'; of that mercifulness whereby 'we love our enemies, bless them that curse us, do good to them that hate us, and pray for them which despitefully use us and persecute us;' and of that complication of love and all holy tempers which is exercised in suffering for righteousness' sake. Now all these, it is clear, could have no being were we to have no commerce with any but real Christians.

7. Indeed, were we wholly to separate ourselves from sinners, how could we possibly answer that character which our Lord gives us in these very words: 'Ye' (Christians, ye that are lowly, serious and meek; ye that hunger after righteousness, that love God and man, that do good to all, and therefore suffer evil: Ye) 'are the salt of the earth.' It is your very nature to season whatever is round about you. It is the nature of the divine savour which is in you to spread to whatsoever you touch; to diffuse itself on every side, to all those among whom you are. This is the great reason why the providence of God has so mingled you together with other men, that whatever grace you have received of God may through you be communicated to others; that every holy temper, and word, and work of yours, may have an influence on them also. By this means a check will in some measure be given to the corruption which is in the world; and a small part, at least, saved from the general infection, and rendered holy and pure before God.

8. That we may the more diligently labour to season all we can with every holy and heavenly temper, our Lord proceeds to show the desperate state of those who do not impart the religion they have received; which indeed they cannot possibly fail to do, so long as it remains in their own hearts. 'If the salt have lost its savour, wherewith shall it be salted? It is thenceforth good for nothing but to be cast out, and trodden under foot of men.' If ye who were holy and heavenly-minded, and consequently zealous of good works, have no longer that savour in yourselves, and do therefore no longer season others; if you are grown flat, insipid, dead, both careless of your own soul and useless to the souls of other men, 'wherewith shall' ye 'be salted?' How shall ye be recovered? What help? What hope? Can tasteless salt be restored to its savour? No; 'it is thenceforth good for nothing but to be cast out', even as the mire in the streets, 'and to be trodden under foot of men,' to be overwhelmed with everlasting contempt. If ye had never known the Lord there might have been hope—if ye had never been 'found in him'. But what can you now say to that his solemn declaration, just parallel to what he hath here spoken? 'Every branch

in me that beareth not fruit, he (the Father) taketh away. . . . He that abideth in me, and I in him, bringeth forth much fruit. . . . If a man abide not in me' (or, do not bring forth fruit) 'he is cast out as a branch, and withered; and men gather them' (not to plant them again, but) 'to cast them into the fire' (John 15:2, 5-6).

9. Toward those who have never tasted of the good word God is indeed pitiful and of tender mercy. But justice takes place with regard to those who have tasted that the Lord is gracious, and have afterwards 'turned back from the holy commandment then delivered to them'. 'For it is impossible for those who were once enlightened', in whose hearts God had once shined, to enlighten them with the knowledge of the glory of God in the face of Jesus Christ; who 'have tasted of the heavenly gift' of redemption in his blood, the forgiveness of sins; 'and were made partakers of the Holy Ghost'—of lowliness, of meekness, and of the love of God and man shed abroad in their hearts by the Holy Ghost which was given unto them—'and have fallen away', *καὶ παραπεσόντας* (here is not a supposition, but a flat declaration of matter of fact), 'to renew them again unto repentance; seeing they crucify to themselves the Son of God afresh, and put him to an open shame' (Heb. 6:4, etc.).

But that none may misunderstand these awful words it should be carefully observed, (1), who they are that are here spoken of; namely they, and they only, who 'were once' thus 'enlightened'; they only 'who did taste of that heavenly gift, and were' thus 'made partakers of the Holy Ghost'. So that all who have not experienced these things are wholly unconcerned in this Scripture. (2). What that falling away is which is here spoken of. It is an absolute, total apostasy. A believer may fall, and not fall away. He may fall and rise again. And if he should fall, even into sin, yet this case, dreadful as it is, is not desperate. For 'we have an advocate with the Father, Jesus Christ the righteous; and he is the propitiation for our sins.' But let him above all things beware lest his 'heart be hardened by the deceitfulness of sin'; lest he should sink lower and lower till he wholly fall away, till he become as 'salt that hath lost its savour': 'For if we thus sin wilfully, after we have received the' experimental 'knowledge of the truth, there remaineth no more sacrifice for sins; but a certain, fearful looking for of fiery indignation, which shall devour the adversaries.'

II.1. 'But although we may not wholly separate ourselves from mankind; although it be granted we ought to season them with the religion which God has wrought in our hearts; yet may not this be done insensibly? May we not convey this into others in a secret and almost imperceptible manner? So that scarce anyone shall be able to observe how or when it is done? Even as salt conveys its own savour into that which is seasoned thereby, without any noise, and without being liable to any outward observation. And if so, although we do not go out of the world, yet we may lie hid in it. We may thus far keep our religion to ourselves, and not offend those whom we cannot help.'

2. Of this plausible reasoning of flesh and blood our Lord was well aware also. And he has given a full answer to it in those words which come now to be considered: in explaining which I shall endeavour to show, as I proposed to do in the second place, that so long as true religion abides in our hearts it is impossible to conceal it, as well as absolutely contrary to the design of its great author.

And, first, it is impossible for any that have it to conceal the religion of Jesus Christ. This our Lord makes plain beyond all contradiction by a twofold comparison: 'Ye are the light of the world. A city set upon an hill cannot be hid.'

'Ye' Christians 'are the light of the world,' with regard both to your tempers and actions. Your holiness makes you as conspicuous as the sun in the midst of heaven. As ye cannot go out of the world, so neither can ye stay in it without appearing to all mankind. Ye may not flee from men, and while ye are among them it is impossible to hide your lowliness and meekness and those other dispositions whereby ye aspire to be perfect, as your Father which is in heaven is perfect. Love cannot be hid any more than light; and least of all when it shines forth in action, when ye exercise yourselves in the labour of love, in beneficence of every kind. As well may men think to hide a city as to hide a Christian: yea, as well may they conceal a city set upon a hill as a holy, zealous, active lover of God and man.

3. It is true, men who love darkness rather than light, because their deeds are evil, will take all possible pains to prove that the light which is in you is darkness. They will say evil, all manner of evil, falsely, of the good which is in you: they will lay to your charge that which is farthest from your thoughts, which is the very reverse of all you are and all you do. And your patient continuance in well-doing, your meek suffering all things for the Lord's sake, your calm, humble joy in the midst of persecution, your unwearied labour to overcome evil with good, will make you still more visible and conspicuous than ye were before.

4. So impossible it is to keep our religion from being seen, unless we cast it away; so vain is the thought of hiding the light, unless by putting it out. Sure it is that a secret, unobserved religion cannot be the religion of Jesus Christ. Whatever religion can be concealed is not Christianity. If a Christian could be hid, he could not be compared to a city set upon an hill; to the light of the world, the sun shining from heaven and seen by all the world below. Never therefore let it enter into the heart of him whom God hath renewed in the spirit of his mind to hide that light, to keep his religion to himself; especially considering it is not only impossible to conceal true Christianity, but likewise absolutely contrary to the design of the great Author of it.

5. This plainly appears from the following words: 'Neither do men light a candle, to put it under a bushel.' As if he had said, 'As men do not light a candle only to cover or conceal it, so neither does God enlighten any soul with his glorious knowledge and love to have it covered or concealed, either by prudence, falsely so called, or shame, or voluntary humility; to have it hid either in a desert, or in the world; either by avoiding men, or in conversing with them. "But they put it on a candlestick, and it giveth light to all that are in the house."' In like manner it is the design of God that every Christian should be in an open point of view; that he may give light to all around; that he may visibly express the religion of Jesus Christ.

6. Thus hath God in all ages spoken to the world, not only by precept but by example also. He hath 'not left himself without witness' in any nation where the sound of the gospel hath gone forth, without a few who testified his truth by their lives as well as their words. These have been 'as lights shining in a dark place'. And from time to time they have been the means of enlightening some, of preserving a remnant, a little seed, which

was 'counted unto the Lord for a generation'. They have led a few poor sheep out of the darkness of the world, and guided their feet into the way of peace.

7. One might imagine that where both Scripture and the reason of things speak so clearly and expressly there could not be much advanced on the other side, at least not with any appearance of truth. But they who imagine thus know little of the depths of Satan. After all that Scripture and reason have said, so exceeding plausible are the pretences for solitary religion, for a Christian's going out of the world, or at least hiding himself in it, that we need all the wisdom of God to see through the snare, and all the power of God to escape it—so many and strong are the objections which have been brought against being social, open, active Christians.

III.1. To answer these was the third thing which I proposed. And, first, it has been often objected that religion does not lie in outward things but in the heart, the inmost soul; that it is the union of the soul with God, the life of God in the soul of man; that outside religion is nothing worth; seeing God 'delighteth not in burnt offerings', in outward services, but a pure and holy heart is 'the sacrifice he will not despise'.

I answer, it is most true that the root of religion lies in the heart, in the inmost soul; that this is the union of the soul with God, the life of God in the soul of man. But if this root be really in the heart it cannot but put forth branches. And these are the several instances of outward obedience, which partake of the same nature with the root, and consequently are not only marks or signs, but substantial parts of religion.

It is also true that bare, outside religion, which has no root in the heart, is nothing worth; that God delighteth not in *such* outward services, no more than in Jewish burnt offerings, and that a pure and holy heart is a sacrifice with which he is always well pleased. But he is also well pleased with all that outward service which arises from the heart; with the sacrifice of our prayers (whether public or private), of our praises and thanksgivings; with the sacrifice of our goods, humbly devoted to him, and employed wholly to his glory; and with that of our bodies, which he peculiarly claims; which the Apostle 'beseeches us, by the mercies of God, to present unto him, a living sacrifice, holy, acceptable to God'.

2. A second objection, nearly related to this, is that love is all in all: that it is 'the fulfilling of the law', 'the end of the commandment', of every commandment of God; that all we do and all we suffer, if we have not charity or love, profiteth us nothing; and therefore the Apostle directs us to 'follow after charity', and terms this, the 'more excellent way'.

I answer, it is granted that the love of God and man arising from 'faith unfeigned' is all in all 'the fulfilling of the law', the end of every commandment of God. It is true that without this whatever we do, whatever we suffer, profits us nothing. But it does not follow that love is all [in all] in such a sense as to supersede either faith or good works. It is 'the fulfilling of the law', not by releasing us from but by constraining us to obey it. It is 'the end of the commandment' as every commandment leads to and centres in it. It is allowed that whatever we do or suffer, without love, profits us nothing. But withal whatever we do or suffer in love, though it were only the suffering reproach for Christ, or the giving a cup of cold water in his name, it shall in no wise lose its reward.

3. 'But does not the Apostle direct us to "follow after charity"? And does he not term it "a more excellent way"?' He does direct us to 'follow after charity;' but not after that alone. His words are, 'Follow after charity; and desire spiritual gifts' (1 Cor. 14:1). Yea, 'follow after charity,' and desire to spend and to be spent for your brethren. 'Follow after charity;' and as you have opportunity do good to all men.

In the same verse also wherein he terms this, the way of love, 'a more excellent way', he directs the Corinthians to desire other gifts besides it; yea, to desire them earnestly. 'Covet earnestly', saith he, 'the best gifts: and yet I show unto you a more excellent way' (1 Cor. 12:31). More excellent than what? Than the gifts of 'healing', of 'speaking with tongues', and of 'interpreting', mentioned in the preceding verse. But not more excellent than the way of obedience. Of this the Apostle is not speaking; neither is he speaking of outward religion at all. So that this text is quite wide of the present question.

But suppose the Apostle had been speaking of outward as well as inward religion, and comparing them together; suppose in the comparison he had given the preference ever so much to the latter; suppose he had preferred (as he justly might) a loving heart before all outward works whatever. Yet it would not follow that we were to reject either one or the other. No; God hath joined them together from the beginning of the world. And let not man put them asunder.

4. 'But "God is a Spirit, and they that worship him must worship him in spirit and in truth". And is not this enough? Nay, ought we not to employ the whole strength of our mind herein? Does not attending to outward things clog the soul, that it cannot soar aloft in holy contemplation? Does it not damp the vigour of our thought? Has it not a natural tendency to encumber and distract the mind? Whereas St. Paul would have us "to be without carefulness", and to "wait upon the Lord without distraction".'

I answer, 'God is a Spirit, and they that worship him must worship him in spirit and in truth.' Yea, and this is enough: we ought to employ the whole strength of our mind therein. But then I would ask, 'What is it to worship God, a Spirit, in spirit and in truth?' Why, it is to worship him with our spirit; to worship him in that manner which none but spirits are capable of. It is to believe in him as a wise, just, holy being, of purer eyes than to behold iniquity; and yet merciful, gracious, and longsuffering; forgiving iniquity and transgression and sin; casting all our sins behind his back, and accepting us in the beloved. It is to love him, to delight in him, to desire him, with all our heart and mind and soul and strength; to imitate him we love by purifying ourselves, even as he is pure; and to obey him whom we love, and in whom we believe, both in thought and word and work. Consequently one branch of the worshipping God in spirit and in truth is the keeping his outward commandments. To glorify him therefore with our bodies as well as with our spirits, to go through outward work with hearts lifted up to him, to make our daily employment a sacrifice to God, to buy and sell, to eat and drink to his glory: this is worshipping God in spirit and in truth as much as the praying to him in a wilderness.

5. But if so, then contemplation is only one way of worshipping God in spirit and in truth. Therefore to give ourselves up entirely to this would be to destroy many branches

of spiritual worship, all equally acceptable to God, and equally profitable, not hurtful, to the soul. For it is a great mistake to suppose that an attention to those outward things whereto the providence of God hath called us is any clog to a Christian, or any hindrance at all to his always seeing him that is invisible. It does not at all damp the ardour of his thought; it does not encumber or distract his mind; it gives him no uneasy or hurtful care who does it all as unto the Lord: who hath learned whatsoever he doth, in word or deed, to do all in the name of the Lord Jesus; having only one eye of the soul which moves round on outward things, and one immovably fixed on God. Learn what this meaneth, ye poor recluses, that you may clearly discern your own littleness of faith. Yea, that you may no longer judge others by yourselves, go and learn what that meaneth:

Thou, O Lord, in tender love
Dost all my burdens bear;
Lift my heart to things above,
And fix it ever there.
Calm on tumult's wheel I sit,
Midst busy multitudes alone,
Sweetly waiting at thy feet,
Till all thy will be done.

6. But the grand objection is still behind. 'We appeal', say they, 'to experience. Our light did shine: we used outward things many years; and yet they profited nothing. We attended on all the ordinances; but we were no better for it—nor indeed anyone else. Nay, we were the worse. For we fancied ourselves Christians for so doing, when we knew not what Christianity meant.'

I allow the fact. I allow that you and ten thousand more have thus abused the ordinances of God, mistaking the means for the end, supposing that the doing these or some other outward works either was the religion of Jesus Christ or would be accepted in the place of it. But let the abuse be taken away and the use remain. Now use all outward things; but use them with a constant eye to the renewal of your soul in righteousness and true holiness.

7. But this is not all. They affirm: 'Experience likewise shows that the trying to do good is but lost labour. What does it avail to feed or clothe men's bodies if they are just dropping into everlasting fire? And what good can any man do to their souls? If these are changed, God doth it himself. Besides, all men are either good, at least desirous so to be, or obstinately evil. Now the former have no need of us. Let them ask help of God, and it shall be given them. And the latter will receive no help from us. Nay, and our Lord forbids to "cast our pearls before swine".'

I answer, (1), whether they will finally be lost or saved, you are expressly commanded to feed the hungry and clothe the naked. If you can and do not, whatever becomes of them, you shall go away into everlasting fire. (2). Though it is God only changes hearts, yet he generally doth it by man. It is our part to do all that in us lies as diligently as if we could change them ourselves, and then to leave the event to him. (3). God, in answer to their prayers, builds up his children by each other in every good gift, nourishing and strengthening the whole 'body by that which every joint supplieth'. So that 'the eye cannot say to the hand, I have no need of thee'; no, nor even 'the head to the feet, I have no need of you'. Lastly, how are you assured that the persons before you are dogs or swine? Judge them not until you have tried. 'How knowest thou, O man, but thou mayst gain thy brother,' but thou mayst, under God, save his soul from death? When he spurns thy love and blasphemes the good word, then it is time to give him up to God.

8. 'We have tried. We have laboured to reform sinners. And what did it avail? On many we could make no impression at all. And if some were changed for a while, yet their goodness was but as the morning dew, and they were soon as bad, nay worse than ever. So that we only hurt them—and ourselves too; for our minds were hurried and discomposed; perhaps filled with anger instead of love. Therefore we had better have kept our religion to ourselves.'

It is very possible this fact also may be true, that you have tried to do good and have not succeeded; yea, that those who seemed reformed relapsed into sin, and their last state was worse than the first. And what marvel? Is the servant above his master? But how often did he strive to save sinners! And they would not hear; or when they had followed him awhile they turned back as a dog to his vomit. But he did not therefore desist from striving to do good. No more should you, whatever your success be. It is your part to do as you are commanded: the event is in the hand of God. You are not accountable for this: leave it to him who orders all things well. 'In the morning sow thy seed, and in the evening withhold not thy hand; for thou knowest not whether shall prosper' (Eccles. 11:6).

'But the trial hurries and frets your own soul.' Perhaps it did so for this very reason, because you thought you was accountable for the event—which no man is, nor indeed can be. Or perhaps because you was off your guard; you was not watchful over your own spirit. But this is no reason for disobeying God. Try again; but try more warily than before. Do good (as you forgive) 'not seven times only; but until seventy times seven.' Only be wiser by experience: attempt it every time more cautiously than before. Be more humbled before God, more deeply convinced that of yourself you can do nothing. Be more jealous over your own spirit, more gentle and watchful unto prayer. Thus 'cast your bread upon the waters, and you shall find it again after many days.'

IV.1. Notwithstanding all these plausible pretences for hiding it, 'Let your light so shine before men that they may see your good works, and glorify your Father which is in heaven.' This is the practical application which our Lord himself makes of the foregoing considerations.

'Let your light so shine'—your lowliness of heart, your gentleness and meekness of wisdom; your serious, weighty concern for the things of eternity, and sorrow for the sins and miseries of men; your earnest desire of universal holiness and full happiness in God; your tender goodwill to all mankind, and fervent love to your supreme benefactor. Endeavour not to conceal this light wherewith God hath enlightened your soul, but let it 'shine before men', before all with whom you are, in the whole tenor of your conversation.

Let it shine still more eminently in your actions, in your doing all possible good to all men; and in your suffering for righteousness' sake, while you 'rejoice and are exceeding glad, knowing that great is your reward in heaven'.

2. 'Let your light so shine before men that they may see your good works:' so far let a Christian be from ever designing or desiring to conceal his religion. On the contrary let it be your desire not to conceal it, not to put the 'light under a bushel'. Let it be your care to place it 'on a candlestick, that it may give light to all that are in the house'. Only take heed not to seek your own praise herein, not to desire any honour to yourselves. But let it be your sole aim that all who see your good works may 'glorify your Father which is in heaven'.

3. Be this your one ultimate end in all things. With this view be plain, open, undisguised. Let your love be without dissimulation. Why should you hide fair, disinterested love? Let there be no guile found in your mouth: let your words be the genuine picture of your heart. Let there be no darkness or reservedness in your conversation, no disguise in your behaviour. Leave this to those who have other designs in view—designs which will not bear the light. Be ye artless and simple to all mankind, that all may see the grace of God which is in you. And although some will harden their hearts, yet others will take knowledge that ye have been with Jesus, and by returning themselves 'to the great Bishop of their souls', 'glorify your Father which is in heaven'.

4. With this one design, that men may 'glorify God in you', go on in his name and in the power of his might. Be not ashamed even to stand alone, so it be in the ways of God. Let the light which is in your heart shine in all good works, both works of piety and works of mercy. And in order to enlarge your ability of doing good, renounce all superfluities. Cut off all unnecessary expense, in food, in furniture, in apparel. Be a good steward of every gift of God, even of these his lowest gifts. Cut off all unnecessary expense of time, all needless or useless employments. And 'whatsoever thy hand findeth to do, do it with thy might.' In a word, be thou full of faith and love; do good; suffer evil. And herein be thou 'steadfast, unmovable'; yea, 'always abounding in the work of the Lord; forasmuch as thou knowest that thy labour is not in vain in the Lord.'

49. UPON OUR LORD'S SERMON ON THE MOUNT, DISCOURSE THE FIFTH

1748

An Introductory Comment

One of the more important conjunctions in Wesley's theology that can be seen as a particularization of the ongoing orienting concern of holiness and grace is none other than law and gospel, a conjunction developed earlier by Martin Luther, though in a much different way. In exploring the text of this present sermon, Matthew 5:17-20, Wesley carefully balanced law and gospel and underscored the prophetic role of Christ as a Lawgiver (B, 199) in a manner that highlighted the continuity of the two gracious covenants, both Old and New.

Wesley preached on the text of this sermon with good effect at the Back Lane Society in Bristol on May 15, 1739 (WH, 19:57–58). He took Matthew 5:20 in particular as his text about twenty more times over the course of his career (WWS), and Charles, for his part, wrote two hymns, one on Matthew 5:17 and the other on Matthew 5:18, for publication in the *Arminian Magazine* in 1790.

Throughout this sermon Wesley took issue with the notion that Christ abolished the moral law in the name of grace and that the only duty of the Christian therefore is to believe. Paraphrases from such well-known antinomians (who made the law void through faith) such as Tobias Crisp, James Saltmarsh, James Wheatley, and William Cudworth emerged in this context (O, 1:559). Distinguishing the moral law from both the ceremonial and the ritual law, Wesley affirmed as a corrective to the teaching that would set aside obedience in the name of faith that there is, after all, no contradiction between the law, properly understood, and the gospel. Indeed, the gospel is none other than "the commands of the law proposed by way of promises" (O, 1:554). Put another way, the law points to the promises of the gospel; the gospel leads us "to a more exact fulfilling of the law" (O, 1:554) as an emblem of vital holiness.

Upon our Lord's Sermon on the Mount, Discourse the Fifth

1. Among the reproaches that fell on Jesus was that he introduced a *new religion*
2. But the Lord plainly refutes this charge in these words

I. 1. First, 'think not that I am come to destroy the law or the prophets'
2.–4. He did not come to take away the moral law, only the ceremonial law

II. 1. He adds that no part of the law will pass away until all is fulfilled
2. From this we see there is no contrariety between the law and the gospel
3. The law points to the gospel; the gospel leads to the fulfilling of the law
4. Christianity is designed to be the last of God's dispensations

III. 1. Whosoever breaks one of these commandments will be least in the kingdom
2. 'These commandments' is a term used by the Lord to mean the law
3. Whosoever openly breaks a commandment teaches others to do the same
4. For whom does our Lord intend these words?
5. These are several audiences; the first are those who live in willful sin
6. Next to these are good-natured people who live easy, harmless lives
7. But above all are those who openly speak evil of the law
   A. They are in the highest rank of enemies of the gospel of Christ
   B. They teach that the Lord abolished the law
8. They who preach this believe they honour Christ, but they do not
9. It is impossible to have too high an esteem of the faith of God's elect

IV. 1. Other ways to the kingdom are in truth ways to destruction
2. The Pharisees and the scribes are the wisest and holiest of men
3. Their righteousness is first their belief that they are not like other men
4.–5. Their righteousness also includes fasting and tithing
6. They trusted in themselves that they were righteous, and despised others
7. Yet, except your righteousness exceeds them you will not enter the kingdom
8. Pharisees used means of grace, like fasting, praying, or Scripture reading
9. Pharisees paid tithes and gave alms
10. Christian righteousness exceeds theirs, first, in the extent of it
11. It exceeds theirs by fulfilling the spirit as well as the letter of the law
12. See that your righteousness does not fall short of theirs
13. Then you will be called great in the kingdom of heaven

Sermon 25: Upon our Lord's Sermon on the Mount

Discourse the Fifth, 1748

Matthew 5:17-20

Think not that I am come to destroy the law or the prophets: I am not come to destroy, but to fulfil.

For verily I say unto you, Till heaven and earth pass, one jot or one tittle shall in no wise pass from the law, till all be fulfilled.

Whosoever therefore shall break one of these least commandments, and shall teach men so, he shall be called the least in the kingdom of heaven; but whosoever shall do and teach them, the same shall be called great in the kingdom of heaven.

For verily I say unto you, That except your righteousness shall exceed the righteousness of the scribes and Pharisees, ye shall in no case enter into the kingdom of heaven.

1. Among the multitude of reproaches which fell upon him who was 'despised and rejected of men', it could not fail to be one that he was a teacher of novelties, an introducer of a *new religion.* This might be affirmed with the more colour because many of the expressions he had used were not common among the Jews: either they did not use them at all, or not in the same sense, not in so full and strong a meaning. Add to this that the worshipping God 'in spirit and in truth' must always appear a new religion to those who have hitherto known nothing but outside worship, nothing but the 'form of godliness'.

2. And 'tis not improbable some might hope it was so, that he was abolishing the old religion and bringing in another, one which they might flatter themselves would be an easier way to heaven. But our Lord refutes in these words both the vain hopes of the one and the groundless calumnies of the other.

I shall consider them in the same order as they lie, taking each verse for a distinct head of discourse.

I.1. And, first, 'think not that I am come to destroy the law or the prophets. I am not come to destroy, but to fulfil.'

The ritual or ceremonial law delivered by Moses to the children of Israel, containing all the injunctions and ordinances which related to the old sacrifices and service of the temple, our Lord indeed did come to destroy, to dissolve and utterly abolish. To this bear all the apostles witness: not only Barnabas and Paul, who vehemently withstood those who taught that Christians ought 'to keep the law of Moses' (Acts 15:5); not only St. Peter, who termed the insisting on this, on the observance of the ritual law, a[s] 'tempting God, and putting a yoke upon the neck of the disciples which neither our fathers (saith he) nor we were able to bear' (Acts 15:10); but 'all the apostles, elders, and brethren,[. . .] being assembled with one accord', declared that to command them to keep this law was to 'subvert their souls'; and that 'it seemed good to the Holy Ghost and to them to lay no such burden upon them' (Acts 15:24, etc.). This 'handwriting of ordinances our Lord did blot out, take away, and nail to his cross.'

2. But the moral law, contained in the Ten Commandments, and enforced by the prophets, he did not take away. It was not the design of his coming to revoke any part of this. This is a law which never can be broken, which 'stands fast as the faithful witness in heaven'. The moral stands on an entirely different foundation from the ceremonial or ritual law, which was only designed for a temporary restraint upon a disobedient and stiff-necked people; whereas this was from the beginning of the world, being 'written not on tables of stone' but on the hearts of all the children of men when they came out of the hands of the Creator. And however the letters once wrote by the finger of God are now in a great measure defaced by sin, yet can they not wholly be blotted out while we have any consciousness of good and evil. Every part of this law must remain in force, upon all mankind, and in all ages; as not depending either on time or place, or any other circumstances liable to change, but on the nature of God and the nature of man, and their unchangeable relation to each other.

3. 'I am not come to destroy, but to fulfil.' Some have conceived our Lord to mean, I am come to fulfil this by my entire and perfect obedience to it. And it cannot be doubted but he did in this sense fulfil every part of it. But this does not appear to be what he intends here, being foreign to the scope of his present discourse. Without question his meaning in this place is (consistently with all that goes before and follows after): I am come to establish it in its fullness, in spite of all the glosses of men; I am come to place in a full and clear view whatsoever was dark or obscure therein; I am come to declare the true and full import of every part of it; to show the length and breadth, the entire extent of every commandment contained therein, and the height and depth, the inconceivable purity and spirituality of it in all its branches.

4. And this our Lord has abundantly performed in the preceding and subsequent parts of the discourse before us, in which he has not introduced a new religion into the world, but the same which was from the beginning: a religion the substance of which is, without question, 'as old as the creation'; being coeval with man, and having proceeded from God at the very time when 'man became a living soul'. (The substance, I say, for some circumstances of it now relate to man as a fallen creature); a religion witnessed to both by the law and by the prophets in all succeeding generations. Yet was it never so fully explained nor so throughly understood till the great Author of it himself condescended to give mankind this authentic comment on all the essential branches of it; at the same time declaring it should never be changed, but remain in force to the end of the world.

II.1. 'For verily I say unto you' (a solemn preface, which denotes both the importance and certainty of what is spoken), 'Till heaven and earth pass, one jot or one tittle shall in no wise pass from the law till all be fulfilled.'

'One jot'—it is literally, *not one iota*, not the most inconsiderable vowel; 'or one tittle', *μία κεραία*, one corner, or point of a consonant. It is a proverbial expression which signifies that no one commandment contained in the moral law, nor the least part of one, however inconsiderable it might seem, should ever be disannulled.

'Shall in no wise pass from the law;' οὐ μὴ παρέλθῃ ἀπὸ τοῦ νόμου. The double negative here used strengthens the sense so as to admit of no contradiction. And the word παρέλθῃ, it may be observed, is not barely *future*, declaring what *will* be; but has likewise the force of an *imperative*, ordering what *shall* be. It is a word of authority, expressing the sovereign will and power of him that spake, of him whose word is the law of heaven and earth, and stands fast for ever and ever.

'One jot or one tittle shall in no wise pass till heaven and earth pass'; or as it is expressed immediately after, ἕως ἂν πάντα γένηται, 'till all' (or rather, *all things*) 'be fulfilled', till the consummation of all things. Here is therefore no room for that poor evasion (with which some have delighted themselves greatly) that 'no part of the law was to pass away till *all the law* was fulfilled; but it has been fulfilled by Christ, and therefore now must pass, for the gospel to be established.' Not so; the word 'all' does not mean all the law, but all things in the universe; as neither has the term 'fulfilled' any reference to the law, but to all things in heaven and earth.

2. From all this we may learn that there is no contrariety at all between the law and the gospel; that there is no need for the law to pass away in order to the establishing of the gospel. Indeed neither of them supersedes the other, but they agree perfectly well together. Yea, the very same words, considered in different respects, are parts both of the law and of the gospel. If they are considered as commandments, they are parts of the law: if as promises, of the gospel. Thus, 'Thou shalt love the Lord thy God with all thy heart,' when considered as a commandment, is a branch of the law; when regarded as a promise, is an essential part of the gospel—the gospel being no other than the commands of the law proposed by way of promises. Accordingly poverty of spirit, purity of heart, and whatever else is enjoined in the holy law of God, are no other, when viewed in a gospel light, than so many great and precious promises.

3. There is therefore the closest connection that can be conceived between the law and the gospel. On the one hand the law continually makes way for and points us to the gospel; on the other the gospel continually leads us to a more exact fulfilling of the law. The law, for instance, requires us to love God, to love our neighbour, to be meek, humble, or holy. We feel that we are not sufficient for these things, yea, that 'with man this is impossible.' But we see a promise of God to give us that love, and to make us humble, meek, and holy. We lay hold of this gospel, of these glad tidings: it is done unto us according to our faith, and 'the righteousness of the law is fulfilled in us' through faith which is in Christ Jesus.

We may yet farther observe that every command in Holy Writ is only a covered promise. For by that solemn declaration, 'This is the covenant I will make after those days, saith the Lord; I will put my laws in your minds, and write them in your hearts,' God hath engaged to give whatsoever he commands. Does he command us then to 'pray without ceasing'? To 'rejoice evermore'? To be 'holy as he is holy'? It is enough. He will work in us this very thing. It shall be unto us according to his word.

4. But if these things are so, we cannot be at a loss what to think of those who in all ages of the church have undertaken to change or supersede some commands of God, as

they professed, by the peculiar direction of his Spirit. Christ has here given us an infallible rule whereby to judge of all such pretentions. Christianity, as it includes the whole moral law of God, both by way of injunction and of promise, if we will hear him, is designed of God to be the last of all his dispensations. There is no other to come after this. This is to endure till the consummation of all things. Of consequence all such new revelations are of Satan, and not of God; and all pretences to another more perfect dispensation fall to the ground of course. 'Heaven and earth shall pass away; but this word shall not pass away.'

III.1. 'Whosoever therefore shall break one of these least commandments, and shall teach men so, he shall be called the least in the kingdom of heaven; but whosoever shall do and teach them, the same shall be called great in the kingdom of heaven.'

Who, what are they that make 'the preaching of the law' a character of reproach? Do they not see on whom their reproach must fall? On whose head it must light at last? Whosoever on this ground despiseth us, despiseth him that sent us. For did ever any man preach the law like him? Even when he 'came not to condemn but to save the world'; when he came purposely to bring 'life and immortality to light through the gospel'. Can any 'preach the law' more expressly, more rigorously, than Christ does in these words? And who is he that shall amend them? Who is he that shall instruct the Son of God how to preach? Who will teach him a better way of delivering the message which he hath received of the Father?

2. 'Whosoever shall break one of these least commandments', or one of the least of these commandments. 'These commandments', we may observe, is a term used by our Lord as equivalent with 'the law', or the 'law and the prophets', which is the same thing, seeing the prophets added nothing to the law, but only declared, explained, or enforced it, as they were moved by the Holy Ghost.

'Whosoever shall break one of these least commandments', especially if it be done wilfully or presumptuously. *One*—for 'he that keepeth the whole law and' thus 'offends in one point, is guilty of all:' the wrath of God abideth on him as surely as if he had broken every one. So that no allowance is made for one darling lust; no reserve for one idol; no excuse for refraining from all besides, and only giving way to one bosom sin. What God demands is an entire obedience; we are to have an eye to all his commandments; otherwise we lose all the labour we take in keeping some, and our poor souls for ever and ever.

'One of these least', or one of the least of these 'commandments'. Here is another excuse cut off, whereby many, who cannot deceive God, miserably deceive their own souls. 'This sin, saith the sinner, is it not a little one? Will not the Lord spare me in this thing? Surely he will not be extreme to mark this, since I do not offend in the greater matters of the law.' Vain hope! Speaking after the manner of men we may term these great, and those little commandments. But in reality they are not so. If we use propriety of speech there is no such thing as a little sin, every sin being a transgression of the holy and perfect law, and an affront of the great majesty of heaven.

3. 'And shall teach men so'—In some sense it may be said that whosoever openly breaks any commandment teaches others to do the same; for example speaks, and many

times louder than precept. In this sense it is apparent every open drunkard is a teacher of drunkenness; every sabbath-breaker is constantly teaching his neighbour to profane the day of the Lord. But this is not all; an habitual breaker of the law is seldom content to stop here. He generally teaches other men to do so too, by word as well as example; especially when he hardens his neck, and hateth to be reproved. Such a sinner soon commences an advocate for sin: he defends what he is resolved not to forsake. He excuses the sin which he will not leave, and thus directly teaches every sin which he commits.

'He shall be called least in the kingdom of heaven'—that is, shall have no part therein. He is a stranger to the kingdom of heaven which is on earth; he hath no portion in that inheritance; no share of that righteousness and peace and joy in the Holy Ghost. Nor by consequence can he have any part in the glory which shall be revealed.

4. But if those who even thus break and teach others to break one of the least of these commandments shall be called least in the kingdom of heaven, shall have no part in the kingdom of Christ and of God; if even these 'shall be cast into outer darkness', where is 'wailing and gnashing of teeth', then where will they appear whom our Lord chiefly and primarily intends in these words? They who, bearing the character of teachers sent from God, do nevertheless themselves break his commandments, yea and openly teach others so to do, being corrupt both in life and doctrine?

5. These are of several sorts. Of the first sort are they who live in some wilful, habitual sin. Now if an ordinary sinner teaches by his example, how much more a sinful minister, even if he does not attempt to defend, excuse, or extenuate his sin! If he does he is a murderer indeed, yea, the murderer-general of his congregation! He peoples the regions of death. He is the choicest instrument of the prince of darkness. When he goes hence 'hell from beneath is moved to meet him at his coming.' Nor can he sink into the bottomless pit without dragging a multitude after him.

6. Next to these are the good-natured, good sort of men: who live an easy, harmless life, neither troubling themselves with outward sin, nor with inward holiness; men who are remarkable neither one way nor the other, neither for religion nor irreligion; who are very regular both in public and private, but don't pretend to be any stricter than their neighbours. A minister of this kind breaks not one, or a few only, of the least commandments of God, but all the great and weighty branches of his law which relate to the power of godliness, and all that require us to 'pass the time of our sojourning in fear'; to 'work out our salvation with fear and trembling'; to have our 'loins always girt and our lights burning'; to 'strive or "agonize" to enter in at the strait gate'. And he 'teaches men so', by the whole form of his life and the general tenor of his preaching, which uniformly tends to soothe those in their pleasing dream who imagine themselves Christians and are not; to persuade all who attend upon his ministry to sleep on and take their rest. No marvel, therefore, if both he and they that follow him wake together in everlasting burnings.

7. But above all these, in the highest rank of the enemies of the gospel of Christ are they who openly and explicitly 'judge the law' itself, and 'speak evil of the law'; who teach men to break (λῦσαι, to dissolve, to loose, to untie the obligation of) not one only—whether of the least or of the greatest—but all the commandments at a stroke; who teach,

without any cover, in so many words: 'What did our Lord do with the law? He abolished it.' 'There is but one duty, which is that of believing.' 'All commands are unfit for our times.' 'From any demand of the law no man is obliged now to go one step, to give away one farthing, to eat or omit one morsel.' This is indeed carrying matters with a high hand. This is withstanding our Lord to the face, and telling him that he understood not how to deliver the message on which he was sent. 'O Lord, lay not this sin to their charge!' 'Father, forgive them; for they know not what they do!'

8. The most surprising of all the circumstances that attend this strong delusion is that they who are given up to it really believe that they honour Christ by overthrowing his law, and that they are magnifying his office while they are destroying his doctrine! Yea, they honour him just as Judas did when he 'said, Hail, Master, and kissed him'. And he may as justly say to every one of them, 'Betrayest thou the Son of man with a kiss?' It is no other than betraying him with a kiss to talk of his blood and take away his crown; to set light by any part of his law under pretence of advancing his gospel. Nor indeed can anyone escape this charge who preaches faith in any such manner as either directly or indirectly tends to set aside any branch of obedience; who preaches Christ so as to disannul or weaken in any wise the least of the commandments of God.

9. It is impossible indeed to have too high an esteem for 'the faith of God's elect'. And we must all declare, 'By grace ye are saved through faith: . . . not of works, lest any man should boast.' We must cry aloud to every penitent sinner, 'Believe in the Lord Jesus Christ, and thou shalt be saved.' But at the same time we must take care to let all men know we esteem no faith but that 'which worketh by love'; and that we are not 'saved by faith' unless so far as we are delivered from the power as well as the guilt of sin. And when we say, 'Believe, and thou shalt be saved,' we do not mean, 'Believe, and thou shalt step from sin to heaven, without any holiness coming between, faith supplying the place of holiness;' but, believe and thou shalt be holy; believe in the Lord Jesus, and thou shalt have peace and power together. Thou shalt have power from him in whom thou believest to trample sin under thy feet; power to love the Lord thy God with all thy heart, and to serve him with all thy strength. Thou shalt have power 'by patient continuance in well-doing' to 'seek for glory and honour and immortality'. Thou shalt both 'do and teach' all the commandments of God, from the least even to the greatest. Thou shalt teach them by thy life as well as thy words, and so 'be called great in the kingdom of heaven'.

IV.1. Whatever other way we teach to the kingdom of heaven, to glory, honour, and immortality, be it called 'the way of faith' or by any other name, it is in truth the way to destruction. It will not bring a man peace at the last. For thus saith the Lord, 'Verily I say unto you, except your righteousness shall exceed the righteousness of the scribes and Pharisees, ye shall in no case enter into the kingdom of heaven.'

The *scribes*, mentioned so often in the New Testament as some of the most constant and vehement opposers of our Lord, were not secretaries, or men employed in writing only, as that term might incline us to believe. Neither were they *lawyers*, in our common sense of the word (although the word νομικοί is so rendered in our translation). Their employment had no affinity at all to that of a lawyer among us. They were conversant with the laws of God, and not with the laws of man. These were their study: it was their proper and peculiar business to read and expound the law and the prophets, particularly in the synagogues. They were the ordinary, stated preachers among the Jews; so that if the sense of the original word was attended to we might render it, the divines. For these were the men who made divinity their profession; and they were generally (as their name literally imports) men of letters; men of the greatest account for learning that were then in the Jewish nation.

2. The Pharisees were a very ancient sect or body of men among the Jews: originally so called from the Hebrew word פרש, which signifies to 'separate' or 'divide'. Not that they made any formal separation from or division in the national church. They were only distinguished from others by greater strictness of life, by more exactness of conversation. For they were zealous of the law in the minutest points, paying tithes of mint, anise, and cummin. And hence they were had in honour of all the people and generally esteemed the holiest of men.

Many of the scribes were of the sect of the Pharisees. Thus St. Paul himself, who was educated for a scribe, first at the university of Tarsus, and after that in Jerusalem at the feet of Gamaliel (one of the most learned scribes or doctors of the law that were then in the nation), declares of himself before the council, 'I am a Pharisee, the son of a Pharisee' (Acts 23:6); and before King Agrippa, 'after the straitest sect of our religion I lived a Pharisee' (Acts 26:5). And the whole body of the scribes generally esteemed and acted in concert with the Pharisees. Hence we find our Saviour so frequently coupling them together, as coming in many respects under the same consideration. In this place they seem to be mentioned together as the most eminent professors of religion: the former of whom were accounted the wisest, the latter the holiest of men.

3. What 'the righteousness of the scribes and Pharisees' really was it is not difficult to determine. Our Lord has preserved an authentic account which one of them gave of himself. And he is clear and full in describing his own righteousness, and cannot be supposed to have omitted any part of it. He 'went up' indeed 'into the temple to pray', but was so intent upon his own virtues that he forgot the design upon which he came. For 'tis remarkable he does not properly pray at all. He only tells God how wise and good he was. 'God, I thank thee that I am not as other men are, extortioners, unjust, adulterers; or even as this publican. I fast twice in the week: I give tithes of all that I possess.' His righteousness therefore consisted of three parts: first, saith he, 'I am not as other men are.' I am not an 'extortioner', not 'unjust', not an 'adulterer'; not 'even as this publican'. Secondly, 'I fast twice in the week;' and thirdly, 'give tithes of all that I possess.'

'I am not as other men are.' This is not a small point. It is not every man that can say this. It is as if he had said, I do not suffer myself to be carried away by that great torrent, custom. I live not by custom but by reason; not by the examples of men but the word of God. 'I am not an extortioner, not unjust, not an adulterer;' however common these sins are, even among those who are called the people of God (extortion, in particular, a kind of legal injustice, not punishable by any human law, the making gain of another's ignorance or necessity, having filled every corner of the land); 'nor even as this publican', not guilty of any open or presumptuous sin, not an outward sinner, but a fair, honest man, of blameless life and conversation.

4. 'I fast twice in the week.' There is more implied in this than we may at first be sensible of. All the stricter Pharisees observed the weekly fasts, namely, every Monday and Thursday. On the former day they fasted in memory of Moses receiving on that day (as their tradition taught) the two tables of stone written by the finger of God; on the latter in memory of his casting them out of his hand when he saw the people dancing round the golden calf. On these days they took no sustenance at all till three in the afternoon, the hour at which they began to offer up the evening sacrifice in the temple. Till that hour it was their custom to remain in the temple—in some of the corners, apartments, or courts thereof—that they might be ready to assist at all the sacrifices and to join in all the public prayers. The time between they were accustomed to employ partly in private addresses to God, partly in searching the Scriptures, in reading the law and the prophets, and in meditating thereon. Thus much is implied in, 'I fast twice in the week', the second branch of the righteousness of a Pharisee.

5. 'I give tithes of all that I possess.' This the Pharisees did with the utmost exactness. They would not except the most inconsiderable thing, no, not mint, anise, or cummin. They would not keep back the least part of what they believed properly to belong to God, but gave a full tenth of their whole substance yearly, and of all their increase, whatsoever it was.

Yea, the stricter Pharisees (as has been often observed by those who are versed in the ancient Jewish writings), not content with giving one tenth of their substance to God in his priests and Levites, gave another tenth to God in the poor, and that continually. They gave the same proportion of all they had in alms as they were accustomed to give in tithes. And this likewise they adjusted with the utmost exactness, that they might not keep back any part, but might fully render unto God the things which were God's, as they accounted this to be. So that upon the whole they gave away from year to year an entire fifth of all that they possessed.

6. This was 'the righteousness of the scribes and Pharisees': a righteousness which in many respects went far beyond the conception which many have been accustomed to entertain concerning it. But perhaps it will be said it was all false and feigned; for they were all a company of hypocrites. Some of them doubtless were; men who had really no religion at all, no fear of God, or desire to please him; who had no concern for the honour that cometh of God, but only for the praise of men. And these are they whom our Lord so severely condemns, so sharply reproves, on many occasions. But we must not suppose, because many Pharisees were hypocrites, therefore all were so. Nor indeed is hypocrisy by any means essential to the character of a Pharisee. This is not the distinguishing mark of their sect. It is rather this (according to our Lord's account)—they 'trusted in themselves that they were righteous, and despised others'. This is their genuine badge. But the Pharisee of this kind cannot be a hypocrite. He must be, in the common sense, sincere; otherwise he could not 'trust in himself that he is righteous'. The man who was here commending himself to God unquestionably thought himself righteous. Consequently, he was no hypocrite—he was not conscious to himself of any insincerity. He now spoke to God just what he thought, namely, that he was abundantly better than other men.

But the example of St. Paul, were there no other, is sufficient to put this out of all question. He could not only say, when he was a Christian, 'Herein do I exercise myself, to have always a conscience void of offence toward God and toward men' (Acts 24:16); but even concerning the time when he was a Pharisee, 'Men and brethren, I have lived in all good conscience before God until this day' (Acts 23:1). He was therefore sincere when he was a Pharisee, as well as when he was a Christian. He was no more an hypocrite when he persecuted the church than when he preached the faith which once he persecuted. Let this then be added to 'the righteousness of the scribes and Pharisees'—a sincere belief that they are righteous, and in all things 'doing God service'.

7. And yet, 'Except your righteousness', saith our Lord, 'shall exceed the righteousness of the scribes and Pharisees, ye shall in no case enter into the kingdom of heaven.' A solemn and weighty declaration! And which it behoves all who are called by the name of Christ seriously and deeply to consider. But before we inquire how our righteousness may exceed theirs, let us examine whether at present we come up to it.

First, a Pharisee was 'not as other men are'. In externals he was singularly good. Are we so? Do we dare to be singular at all? Do we not rather swim with the stream? Do we not many times dispense with religion and reason together because we would not 'look particular'? Are we not often more afraid of being out of the fashion than of being out of the way of salvation? Have we courage to stem the tide? To run counter to the world? 'To obey God rather than man'? Otherwise the Pharisee leaves us behind at the very first step. 'Tis well if we overtake him any more.

But to come closer. Can we use his first plea with God, which is in substance, 'I do no harm. I live in no outward sin. I do nothing for which my own heart condemns me.' Do you not? Are you sure of that? Do you live in no practice for which your own heart condemns you? If you are not an adulterer, if you are not unchaste either in word or deed, are you not unjust? The grand measure of justice, as well as of mercy, is, Do unto others as thou wouldst they should do unto thee. Do you walk by this rule? Do you never do unto any what you would not they should do unto you? Nay, are you not grossly unjust? Are you not an extortioner? Do you not make a gain of anyone's ignorance or necessity? Neither in buying nor selling? Suppose you are engaged in trade, do you demand, do you receive, no more than the real value of what you sell? Do you demand, do you receive, no more of the ignorant than of the knowing; of a little child than of an experienced trader? If you do, why does not your heart condemn you? You are a barefaced extortioner. Do you demand no more than the usual price of the goods of any who is in pressing want? Who must have, and that without delay, the things which you only can furnish him with? If you do, this also is flat extortion. Indeed you do not come up to the righteousness of a Pharisee.

8. A Pharisee, secondly (to express his sense in our common way), used all the means of grace. As he fasted *often* and *much*, 'twice in every week', so he attended all the sacrifices. He was constant in public and private prayer, and in reading and hearing the Scriptures. Do you go as far as this? Do you fast *much* and *often*? Twice in the week? I fear not! Once, at least: 'On all Fridays in the year.' (So our church clearly and peremptorily enjoins all her members to do, to observe all these as well as the vigils and the forty days of Lent as

'days of fasting, or abstinence'.) Do you fast twice in the year? I am afraid some among us cannot plead even this! Do you neglect no opportunity of attending and partaking of the Christian sacrifice? How many are they who call themselves Christians and yet are utterly regardless of it; yet do not eat of that bread or drink of that cup for months, perhaps years together? Do you every day either hear the Scriptures or read them and meditate thereon? Do you join in prayer with the great congregation? Daily, if you have opportunity? If not, whenever you can, particularly on that day which you 'remember to keep it holy'? Do you strive to *make* opportunities? Are you 'glad when they say unto you, we will go into the house of the Lord'? Are you zealous of, and diligent in, private prayer? Do you suffer no day to pass without it? Rather are not some of you so far from spending therein (with the Pharisee) several hours in one day that you think one hour full enough, if not too much? Do you spend an hour in a day, or in a week, in praying to your Father which is in secret? Yea, an hour in a month? Have you spent one hour together in private prayer ever since you was born? Ah, poor Christian! Shall not the Pharisee rise up in the judgment against thee and condemn thee? His righteousness is as far above thine as the heaven is above the earth.

9. The Pharisee, thirdly, 'paid tithes' and gave alms 'of all that he possessed'. And in how ample a manner! So that he was (as we phrase it) 'a man that did much good'. Do we come up to him here? Which of us is so abundant as he was in good works? Which of us gives a fifth of all his substance to God? Both of the principal and of the increase? Who of us out of (suppose) an hundred pounds a year, gives twenty to God and the poor; out of fifty, ten: and so in a larger or a smaller proportion? When shall our righteousness, in using all the means of grace, in attending all the ordinances of God, in avoiding evil and doing good, equal at least the righteousness of the scribes and Pharisees?

10. Although if it only equalled theirs what would that profit? 'For verily I say unto you, except your righteousness shall exceed the righteousness of the scribes and Pharisees, ye shall in no case enter into the kingdom of heaven.' But how can it exceed theirs? Wherein does the righteousness of a Christian exceed that of a scribe or Pharisee?

Christian righteousness exceeds theirs, first, in the extent of it. Most of the Pharisees, though they were rigorously exact in many things, yet were emboldened by the traditions of the elders to dispense with others of equal importance. Thus they were extremely punctual in keeping the fourth commandment—they would not even 'rub an ear of corn' on the sabbath day—but not at all in keeping the third, making little account of light, or even false swearing. So that their righteousness was partial—whereas the righteousness of a real Christian is universal. He does not observe one, or some parts, of the law of God, and neglect the rest; but keeps all his commandments, loves them all, values them above gold or precious stones.

11. It may be indeed that some of the scribes and Pharisees endeavoured to keep all the commandments, and consequently were, as touching the righteousness of the law, that is, according to the letter of it, blameless. But still the righteousness of a Christian exceeds all this righteousness of a scribe or Pharisee by fulfilling the spirit as well as the letter of the law, by inward as well as outward obedience. In this, in the spirituality of it, it admits of no comparison. This is the point which our Lord has so largely proved in the whole tenor

of this discourse. Their righteousness was external only; Christian righteousness is in the inner man. The Pharisee 'cleansed the outside of the cup and the platter'; the Christian is clean within. The Pharisee laboured to present God with a good life; the Christian with a holy heart. The one shook off the leaves, perhaps the fruits of sin; the other 'lays the axe to the root', as not being content with the outward form of godliness, how exact soever it be, unless the life, the spirit, the power of God unto salvation, be felt in the inmost soul.

Thus to do no harm, to do good, to attend the ordinances of God (the righteousness of a Pharisee) are all external; whereas, on the contrary, poverty of spirit, mourning, meekness, hunger and thirst after righteousness, the love of our neighbour, and purity of heart (the righteousness of a Christian) are all internal. And even peacemaking (or doing good) and suffering for righteousness' sake, stand entitled to the blessings annexed to them only as they imply these inward dispositions, as they spring from, exercise, and confirm them. So that whereas the righteousness of the scribes and Pharisees was external only, it may be said in some sense that the righteousness of a Christian is internal only—all his actions and sufferings being as nothing in themselves, being estimated before God only by the tempers from which they spring.

12. Whosoever therefore thou art who bearest the holy and venerable name of a Christian, see, first, that thy righteousness fall not short of the righteousness of the scribes and Pharisees. Be not thou 'as other men are'. Dare to stand alone, to be

Against example, singularly good!

If thou 'follow a multitude' at all it must be 'to do evil'. Let not custom or fashion be thy guide, but reason and religion. The practice of others is nothing to thee: 'Every man must give an account of himself to God.' Indeed if thou canst save the soul of another, do; but at least save one, thy own. Walk not in the path of death because it is broad, and many walk therein. Nay, by this very token thou mayst know it. Is the way wherein thou now walkest a broad, well-frequented, fashionable way? Then it infallibly leads to destruction. O be not thou 'damned for company'—'cease from evil'; fly from sin as from the face of a serpent. At least, do no harm. 'He that committeth sin is of the devil.' Be not thou found in that number. Touching outward sins, surely the grace of God is even now sufficient for thee. 'Herein' at least 'exercise thyself to have a conscience void of offence toward God and toward men.'

Secondly, let not thy righteousness fall short of theirs with regard to the ordinances of God. If thy labour or bodily strength will not allow of thy fasting 'twice in the week', however, deal faithfully with thy own soul, and fast as often as thy strength will permit. Omit no public, no private opportunity of pouring out thy soul in prayer. Neglect no occasion of eating that bread and drinking that cup which is the communion of the body and blood of Christ. Be diligent in searching the Scriptures: read as thou mayst, and meditate therein day and night. Rejoice to embrace every opportunity of hearing 'the word of reconciliation' declared by the 'ambassadors of Christ, the stewards of the mysteries of God'. In using all the means of grace, in a constant and careful attendance on every ordinance of God, live up to (at least, till thou canst go beyond) 'the righteousness of the scribes and Pharisees'.

Thirdly, fall not short of a Pharisee in doing good. Give alms of all thou dost possess. Is any hungry? Feed him. Is he athirst? Give him drink. Naked? Cover him with a garment. If thou hast this world's goods, do not limit thy beneficence to a scanty proportion. Be merciful to the uttermost of thy power. Why not, even as this Pharisee? 'Now make thyself friends', while the time is, 'of the mammon of unrighteousness, that when thou failest', when this earthly tabernacle is dissolved, 'they may receive thee into everlasting habitations.'

13. But rest not here. Let thy 'righteousness exceed the righteousness of the scribes and Pharisees'. Be not thou content to 'keep the whole law, and offend in one point'. 'Hold thou fast all his commandments, and all false ways do thou utterly abhor.' Do all the things whatsoever he hath commanded, and that with all thy might. Thou canst do all things through Christ strengthening thee, though without him thou canst do nothing.

Above all, let thy righteousness exceed theirs in the purity and spirituality of it. What is the exactest form of religion to thee? The most perfect outside righteousness? Go thou higher and deeper than all this. Let thy religion be the religion of the heart. Be thou poor in spirit; little and base and mean and vile in thy own eyes; amazed and humbled to the dust at the love of God which is in Christ Jesus thy Lord. Be serious: let the whole stream of thy thoughts, words, and works, be such as flows from the deepest conviction that thou standest on the edge of the great gulf, thou and all the children of men, just ready to drop in, either into everlasting glory, or everlasting burnings. Be meek: let thy soul be filled with mildness, gentleness, patience, long-suffering toward all men; at the same time that all which is in thee is athirst for God, the living God, longing to awake up after his likeness, and to be satisfied with it. Be thou a lover of God and of all mankind. In this spirit do and suffer all things. Thus 'exceed the righteousness of the scribes and Pharisees', and thou shalt be 'called great in the kingdom of heaven'.

50. THE LAW ESTABLISHED THROUGH FAITH, DISCOURSE I

1750

An Introductory Comment

Evidencing remarkable balance in his practical theology, Wesley affirmed law *and* grace in his pastoral counsel to the Methodists. Indeed, in his first four volumes of sermons published in the eighteenth century, sermons particularly devoted to the moral law emerged at least four times. This present sermon and the one that follows make up a single discourse on the moral law, which is divided into two parts (O, 2:3).

Part of Wesley's purpose in publishing this first discourse in volume III of his sermons was to address the potential moral and spiritual evil that could be left in the wake of antinomian teaching in the form that Christ utterly abolished the moral law. Carefully distinguishing the moral law (a law that the Apostle Paul in Romans 7:12 calls "holy, and just, and good") from the ceremonial and from the Mosaic institution, Wesley took exception in particular to some of the theological teaching of the Moravian leaders, Molther and Spangenberg, and to that of the Reverend William Cudworth, a minister of the Independent Chapel in Margaret Street, London (S, 2:37). In 1745 the Methodist Conference at Bristol questioned what more could be done to stop the spread of antinomianism, and the work *A Second Dialogue Between an Antinomian and His Friend* was the result. Interestingly enough, this *Dialogue*, along with these two present discourses, took Romans 3:31 as the text.

The usual ways of making void the law through faith consist in the following: (1) not preaching it at all, as if preaching the gospel answered all the ends of the law; (2) teaching that faith supersedes the necessity of holiness; and (3) doing it practically, that is, living as if "faith was designed to excuse us from holiness" (O, 2:22–29). Wesley concluded this first discourse with a pointed, challenging question: "Shall we be less obedient to God from filial love than we were from servile fear?" (O, 2:30).

The Law Established through Faith, Discourse I

1. Paul shows that a person can be saved only through Christ
2. Some think that faith in Christ abolishes the law
3.–6. He makes void the *ceremonial* law, not the *moral* law

I. 1. What are the usual ways of making void the law through faith?
  A. Preachers void the law by not preaching it at all
2. This proceeds from ignorance of the nature, properties, and use of the law
3.–9. Their grand plea is that preaching Christ answers all the ends of the law
10. From this it is plain that they do not know what it is to preach Christ
11.–12. To preach Christ is to preach all things that Christ has spoken

II. 1. A second way to make void the law is to teach that faith supersedes the necessity of holiness
2. This supposes that holiness is less necessary than it was before Christ came
  A. Or it supposes that a less degree of it is necessary
  B. Or it supposes that it is less necessary to believers than to others
3. Some teach that we are under the covenant of grace, not works
4. The covenant of grace gives you no ground to set aside any part of holiness
5. We are justified by faith, without the works of the ceremonial or moral law
6. But works are an immediate fruit of that faith whereby we are justified
7. The Apostle does not say that faith is counted for *subsequent righteousness*

III. 1.–2. There is yet another way of making void the law through faith
  A. This is the *living* as if faith was designed to excuse us from holiness
3. A believer is not without law to God, but under the law to Christ
4. This evangelical principle of action should not be less powerful than the legal
5. When you were under conviction, you did not indulge in lust
6. You were once scrupulous, too, of commending any to their face
7. Remember how strong a conviction you had concerning these things
8. I cannot conclude this without exhorting to you to avoid sins of omission

Sermon 35: The Law Established through Faith, Discourse I, 1750

Romans 3:31

Do we then make void the law through faith?

God forbid! Yea, we establish the law.

1. St. Paul having in the beginning of this Epistle laid down his general proposition, namely, that 'the gospel of Christ is the power of God unto salvation to everyone that believeth'—the powerful means whereby God makes every believer a partaker of present and eternal salvation—goes on to show that there is no other way under heaven whereby men can be saved. He speaks particularly of salvation from the guilt of sin, which he commonly terms justification. And that all men stood in need of this, that none could plead their own innocence, he proves at large by various arguments addressed to the Jews as well as the heathens. Hence he infers (in the nineteenth verse of this chapter) 'that every mouth', whether of Jew or heathen, must 'be stopped' from excusing or justifying himself, 'and all the world become guilty before God. Therefore', saith he, by his own obedience, 'by the works of the law, shall no flesh be justified in his sight' (Rom. 3:20). 'But now the righteousness of God without the law', without our previous obedience thereto, 'is manifested (Rom. 3:21); even the righteousness of God which is by faith of Jesus Christ unto all and upon all that believe; for there is no difference' (Rom. 3:22) as to their need of justification, or the manner wherein they attain it. 'For all have sinned, and come short of the glory of God' (Rom. 3:23), the glorious image of God wherein they were created: and all (who attain) 'are justified freely by his grace, through the redemption that is in Jesus Christ (Rom. 3:24); whom God hath set forth to be a propitiation through faith in his blood (Rom. 3:25); . . . that he might be just, and yet the justifier of him which believeth in Jesus' (Rom. 3:26); that without any impeachment to his justice he might show him mercy for the sake of that propitiation. 'Therefore we conclude' (which was the grand position he had undertaken to establish) 'that a man is justified by faith, without the works of the law' (Rom. 3:28).

2. It was easy to foresee an objection which might be made, and which has in fact been made in all ages; namely, that to say 'we are justified without the works of the law' is to abolish the law. The Apostle, without entering into a formal dispute, simply denies the charge. 'Do we then', says he, 'make void the law through faith? God forbid! Yea, we establish the law.'

3. The strange imagination of some that St. Paul, when he says, 'A man is justified without the works of the law,' means only the *ceremonial* law, is abundantly confuted by these very words. For did St. Paul 'establish' the *ceremonial* law? It is evident he did not. He did 'make void' that law through faith, and openly avowed his doing so. It was the *moral* law only of which he might truly say, we do not make void but 'establish' this 'through faith'.

4. But all men are not herein of his mind. Many there are who will not agree to this. Many in all ages of the church, even among those who bore the name of Christians, have contended that 'the faith once delivered to the saints' was designed to make void the whole

law. They would no more spare the moral than the ceremonial law, but were for 'hewing', as it were, 'both in pieces before the Lord': vehemently maintaining, 'If you establish any law, "Christ shall profit you nothing. [. . .] Christ is become of no effect to you; . . .] ye are fallen from grace."'

5. But is the zeal of these men according to knowledge? Have they observed the connection between the law and faith? And that, considering the close connection between them, to destroy one is indeed to destroy both? That to abolish the moral law is, in truth, to abolish faith and the law together, as leaving no proper means either of bringing us to faith or of 'stirring up that gift of God' in our soul?

6. It therefore behoves all who desire either to come to Christ, or to 'walk in him whom they have received', to take heed how they 'make void the law through faith'; to secure us effectually against which let us inquire, first, which are the most usual ways of 'making void the law through faith'; and, secondly, how we may follow the Apostle, and by faith 'establish the law'.

I.1. Let us, first, inquire which are the most usual ways of 'making void the law through faith'. Now the way for a preacher to make it all void at a stroke is not to preach it at all. This is just the same thing as to blot it out of the oracles of God. More especially when it is done with design; when it is made a rule, 'not to preach the law'—and the very phrase, 'a preacher of the law', is used as a term of reproach, as though it meant little less than 'an enemy to the gospel'.

2. All this proceeds from the deepest ignorance of the nature, properties, and use of the law; and proves that those who act thus either know not Christ, are utter strangers to the living faith, or at least that they are but babes in Christ, and as such 'unskilled in the word of righteousness'.

3. Their grand plea is this, that preaching the gospel (that is, according to their judgment, the speaking of nothing but the sufferings and merits of Christ) answers all the ends of the law. But this we utterly deny. It does not answer the very first end of the law, namely, the convincing men of sin, the awakening those who are still asleep on the brink of hell. There may have been here and there an exempt case. One in a thousand may have been awakened by the gospel. But this is no general rule. The ordinary method of God is to convict sinners by the law, and that only. The gospel is not the means which God hath ordained, or which our Lord himself used, for this end. We have no authority in Scripture for applying it thus, nor any ground to think it will prove effectual. Nor have we any more ground to expect this from the nature of the thing. 'They that be whole', as our Lord himself observes, 'need not a physician, but they that be sick.' It is absurd therefore to offer a physician to them that are whole, or that at least imagine themselves so to be. You are first to convince them that they are sick; otherwise they will not thank you for your labour. It is equally absurd to offer Christ to them whose heart is whole, having never yet been broken. It is, in the proper sense, 'casting pearls before swine'. Doubtless 'they will trample them under foot'; and it is no more than you have reason to expect if they also 'turn again and rend you'.

4. 'But although there is no command in Scripture to offer Christ to the careless sinner, yet are there not scriptural precedents for it?' I think not: I know not any. I believe you can't produce one, either from the four evangelists, or the Acts of the Apostles. Neither can you prove this to have been the practice of any of the apostles from any passage in all their writings.

5. 'Nay, does not the Apostle Paul say, in his former Epistle to the Corinthians, "We preach Christ crucified"? (1 Cor. 1:23) and in his latter, "We preach not ourselves, but Christ Jesus the Lord"?' (2 Cor. 4:5).

We consent to rest the cause on this issue: to tread in his steps, to follow his example. Only preach you just as St. Paul preached, and the dispute is at an end.

For although we are certain he *preached Christ* in as perfect a manner as the very chief of the apostles, yet who *preached the law* more than St. Paul? Therefore he did not think the gospel answered the same end.

6. The very first sermon of St. Paul's which is recorded concludes in these words: 'By him all that believe are justified from all things, from which ye could not be justified by the law of Moses. Beware therefore lest that come upon you which is spoken of in the Prophets: Behold, ye despisers, and wonder and perish; for I work a work in your days, a work which you will in no wise believe, though a man declare it unto you' (Acts 13:39-45). Now it is manifest, all this is 'preaching the law', in the sense wherein you understand the term; even although great part of, if not all, his hearers were either 'Jews or religious proselytes' (Acts 13:43), and therefore probably many of them, in some degree at least, convinced of sin already. He first reminds them that they could not be justified by the law of Moses, but only by faith in Christ; and then severely threatens them with the judgments of God, which is, in the strongest sense, 'preaching the law'.

7. In his next discourse, that to the heathens at Lystra (Acts 14:15, etc.), we do not find so much as the name of Christ. The whole purport of it is that they should 'turn from those vain idols unto the living God'. Now confess the truth. Do not you think if you had been there you could have preached much better than he? I should not wonder if you thought too that his *preaching so ill* occasioned his being *so ill treated*; and that his being *stoned* was a just judgment upon him for not *preaching Christ*!

8. To the jailor indeed, when he 'sprang in and came trembling, and fell down before Paul and Silas, [. . .] and said, Sirs, What must I do to be saved?', he immediately 'said, Believe in the Lord Jesus Christ' (Acts 16:29-31). And in the case of one so deeply convinced of sin, who would not have said the same? But to the men of Athens you find him speaking in a quite different manner, reproving their superstition, ignorance, and idolatry, and strongly moving them to repent, from the consideration of a future judgment, and of the resurrection from the dead (Acts 17:22-31). Likewise 'when Felix sent for Paul', on purpose that he might 'hear him concerning the faith in Christ'; instead of preaching Christ in *your* sense (which would probably have caused the governor either to mock or to contradict and blaspheme) 'he reasoned of righteousness, temperance, and judgment to come', till 'Felix' (hardened as he was) 'trembled' (Acts 24:24-25). Go thou and tread in

his steps. *Preach* Christ to the careless sinner by 'reasoning of righteousness, temperance, and judgment to come'!

9. If you say, 'But he *preached Christ* in a different manner in his epistles,' I answer, [(1),] he did not there preach at all, not in that sense wherein we speak; for 'preaching' in our present question means speaking before a congregation. But waiving this I answer, (2), his epistles are directed, not to unbelievers, such as those we are now speaking of, but to 'the saints of God' in Rome, Corinth, Philippi, and other places. Now unquestionably he would speak more of Christ to these than to those who were without God in the world. And yet, (3), every one of these is full of the law, even the Epistles to the Romans and the Galatians, in both of which he does what you term preaching the law, and that to believers as well as unbelievers.

10. From hence 'tis plain you know not what it is to 'preach Christ', in the sense of the Apostle. For doubtless St. Paul judged himself to be preaching Christ both to Felix, and at Antioch, Lystra, and Athens: from whose example every thinking man must infer that not only the declaring the love of Christ to sinners, but also the declaring that he will come from heaven in flaming fire, is, in the Apostle's sense, 'preaching Christ'. Yea, in the full scriptural meaning of the word. To preach Christ is to preach what he hath revealed, either in the Old or New Testament; so that you are then as really preaching Christ when you are saying, 'The wicked shall be turned into hell, and all the people that forget God,' as when you are saying, 'Behold the Lamb of God, which taketh away the sin of the world!'

11. Consider this well: that to 'preach Christ' is to preach all things that Christ hath spoken: all his promises; all his threatenings and commands; all that is written in his Book. And then you will know how to preach Christ without making void the law.

12. 'But does not the greatest blessing attend those discourses wherein we peculiarly preach the merits and sufferings of Christ?'

Probably, when we preach to a congregation of mourners or of believers, these will be attended with the greatest blessing; because such discourses are peculiarly suited to their state. At least these will usually convey the most comfort. But this is not always the greatest blessing. I may sometimes receive a far greater by a discourse that cuts me to the heart and humbles me to the dust. Neither should I receive that comfort if I were to preach or to hear no discourses but on the sufferings of Christ. These by constant repetition would lose their force, and grow more and more flat and dead, till at length they would become a dull round of words, without any spirit or life or virtue. So that thus to 'preach Christ' must, in process of time, make void the gospel as well as the law.

II.1. A second way of 'making void the law through faith' is the teaching that faith supersedes the necessity of holiness. This divides itself into a thousand smaller paths—and many there are that walk therein. Indeed there are few that wholly escape it; few who are convinced we 'are saved by faith' but are sooner or later, more or less, drawn aside into this by-way.

2. All those are drawn into this by-way who, if it be not their settled judgment that faith in Christ entirely sets aside the necessity of keeping his law, yet suppose either, (1), that holiness is less necessary now than it was before Christ came; or, (2), that a less degree of it is necessary; or, (3), that it is less necessary to believers than to others. Yea, and so are all those who, although their judgment be right in the general, yet think they may take more liberty in particular cases than they could have done before they believed. Indeed the using the term *liberty* in such a manner for 'liberty from obedience or holiness' shows at once that their judgment is perverted, and that they are guilty of what they imagined to be far from them; namely, of 'making void the law through faith', by supposing faith to supersede holiness.

3. The first plea of those who teach this expressly is that we are now under the covenant of grace, not works; and therefore we are no longer under the necessity of performing the works of the law.

And who ever was under the covenant of works? None but Adam before the fall. He was fully and properly under that covenant, which required perfect, universal obedience, as the one condition of acceptance, and left no place for pardon, upon the very least transgression. But no man else was ever under this, neither Jew nor Gentile, neither before Christ nor since. All his sons were and are under the covenant of grace. The manner of their acceptance is this: the free grace of God, through the merits of Christ, gives pardon to them that believe, that believe with such a faith as, working by love, produces all obedience and holiness.

4. The case is not therefore, as you suppose, that men were *once* more obliged to obey God, or to work the works of his law, than they are *now*. This is a supposition you cannot make good. But we should have been obliged, if we had been under the covenant of works, to have done those works antecedent to our acceptance. Whereas now all good works, though as necessary as ever, are not antecedent to our acceptance, but consequent upon it. Therefore the nature of the covenant of grace gives you no ground, no encouragement at all, to set aside any instance or degree of obedience, any part or measure of holiness.

5. 'But are we not "justified by faith, without the works of the law"?' Undoubtedly we are, without the works either of the ceremonial or the moral law. And would to God all men were convinced of this! It would prevent innumerable evils: antinomianism in particular—for, generally speaking, they are the Pharisees who make the antinomians. Running into an extreme so palpably contrary to Scripture, they occasion others to run into the opposite one. These, seeking to be justified by works, affright those from allowing any place for them.

6. But the truth lies between both. We are, doubtless, 'justified by faith'. This is the corner-stone of the whole Christian building. 'We are justified without the works of the law' as any previous condition of justification. But they are an immediate fruit of that faith whereby we are justified. So that if good works do not follow our faith, even all inward and outward holiness, it is plain our faith is nothing worth; we are yet in our sins. Therefore that we are 'justified by faith', even by 'faith without works', is no ground for 'making

void the law through faith'; or for imagining that faith is a dispensation from any kind or degree of holiness.

7. 'Nay, but does not St. Paul expressly say, "Unto him that worketh not, but believeth on him that justifieth the ungodly, his faith is counted for righteousness"? And does it not follow from hence that faith is to a believer in the room, in the place, of righteousness? But if faith is in the room of righteousness or holiness, what need is there of this too?'

This, it must be acknowledged, comes home to the point, and is indeed the main pillar of antinomianism. And yet it needs not a long or laboured answer. We allow, (1), that God 'justifies the ungodly', him that till that hour is totally ungodly, full of all evil, void of all good; (2), that he justifies 'the ungodly that worketh not', that till that moment worketh no good work—neither can he: for an evil tree cannot bring forth good fruit; (3), that he justifies him 'by faith alone', without any goodness or righteousness preceding; and (4), that 'faith is' then 'counted to him for righteousness', namely, for *preceding righteousness*; i.e. God, through the merits of Christ, accepts him that believes as if he had already fulfilled all righteousness. But what is all this to your point? The Apostle does not say either here or elsewhere that this faith is counted to him for *subsequent righteousness*. He does teach that there is no righteousness *before* faith; but where does he teach that there is none *after* it? He does assert holiness cannot *precede* justification; but not that it need not *follow* it. St. Paul therefore gives you no colour for 'making void the law' by teaching that faith supersedes the necessity of holiness.

III.1. There is yet another way of 'making void the law through faith', which is more common than either of the former. And that is, the doing it practically; the making it void in *fact*, though not in *principle*; the *living* as if faith was designed to excuse us from holiness.

How earnestly does the Apostle guard us against this, in those well-known words: 'What then? Shall we sin, because we are not under the law, but under grace? God forbid!' (Rom. 6:15). A caution which it is needful thoroughly to consider, because it is of the last importance.

2. The being 'under the law' may here mean, (1), the being obliged to observe the ceremonial laws; (2), the being obliged to conform to the whole Mosaic institution; (3), the being obliged to keep the whole moral law as the condition of our acceptance with God; and, (4), the being under the wrath and curse of God, under sentence of eternal death; under a sense of guilt and condemnation, full of horror and slavish fear.

3. Now although a believer is 'not without law to God, but under the law to Christ', yet from the moment he believes he is not 'under the law', in any of the preceding senses. On the contrary, he is 'under grace', under a more benign, gracious dispensation. As he is no longer under the ceremonial law, nor under the Mosaic institution; as he is not obliged to keep even the moral law as the condition of his acceptance, so he is delivered from the wrath and the curse of God, from all sense of guilt and condemnation, and from all that horror and fear of death and hell whereby he was 'all his life' before 'subject to bondage'. And he now performs (which while 'under the law' he could not do) a willing and uni-

versal obedience. He obeys, not from the motive of slavish fear, but on a nobler principle, namely, the grace of God ruling in his heart, and causing all his works to be wrought in love.

4. What then? Shall this evangelical principle of action be less powerful than the legal? Shall we be less obedient to God from filial love than we were from servile fear?

'Tis well if this is not a common case; if this practical antinomianism, this unobserved way of 'making void the law through faith', has not infected thousands of believers.

Has it not infected you? Examine yourself honestly and closely. Do you not do now what you durst not have done when you was 'under the law', or (as we commonly call it) 'under conviction'? For instance: you durst not then indulge yourself in food. You took just what was needful, and that of the cheapest kind. Do you not allow yourself more latitude now? Do you not indulge yourself a *little* more than you did? O beware lest you 'sin because you are not under the law, but under grace'!

5. When you was under conviction, you durst not indulge the lust of the eye in any degree. You would not do anything, great or small, merely to gratify your curiosity. You regarded only cleanliness and necessity, or at most very moderate convenience, either in furniture or apparel; superfluity and finery of whatever kind, as well as fashionable elegance, were both a terror and an abomination to you.

Are they so still? Is your conscience as tender now in these things as it was then? Do you still follow the same rule both in furniture and apparel, trampling all finery, all superfluity, everything useless, everything merely ornamental, however fashionable, under foot? Rather, have you not resumed what you had once laid aside, and what you could not then use without wounding your conscience? And have you not learned to say, 'Oh, I am not *so scrupulous* now.' I would to God you were! Then you would not sin thus 'because you are not under the law, but under grace'.

6. You was once scrupulous, too, of commending any to their face; and still more of suffering any to commend *you*. It was a stab to your heart; you could not bear it; you sought the honour that cometh of God only. You could not endure such conversation, nor any conversation which was not good to the use of edifying. All idle talk, all trifling discourse, you abhorred; you hated as well as feared it, being deeply sensible of the value of time, of every precious fleeting moment. In like manner you dreaded and abhorred idle expense; valuing your money only less than your time, and trembling lest you should be found an unfaithful steward even of the mammon of unrighteousness.

Do you now look upon praise as deadly poison, which you can neither give nor receive but at the peril of your soul? Do you still dread and abhor all conversation which does not tend to the use of edifying, and labour to improve every moment that it may not pass without leaving you better than it found you? Are not you less careful as to the expense both of money and time? Cannot you now lay out either as you could not have done once? Alas! How has that 'which should have been for your health proved to you an occasion of falling'! How have you 'sinned, because you was not under the law, but under grace'!

7. God forbid you should any longer continue thus to 'turn the grace of God into lasciviousness'! O remember how clear and strong a conviction you once had concerning all these things! And at the same time you was fully satisfied from whom that conviction came. The world told you you was in a delusion; but you knew it was the voice of God. In these things you was not *too scrupulous* then; but you are not now *scrupulous enough.* God kept you longer in that painful school that you might learn those great lessons the more perfectly. And have you forgot them already? O recollect them, before it is too late. Have you suffered so many things in vain? I trust it is not yet in vain. Now use the conviction without the pain. Practise the lesson without the rod. Let not the mercy of God weigh less with you now than his fiery indignation did before. Is love a less powerful motive than fear? If not, let it be an invariable rule, 'I will do nothing now I am *under grace* which I durst not have done when *under the law*'.

8. I cannot conclude this head without exhorting you to examine yourself, likewise, touching sins of omission. Are you as clear of these, now you are 'under grace', as you was when 'under the law'? How diligent was you then in hearing the Word of God! Did you neglect any opportunity? Did you not attend thereon day and night? Would a small hindrance have kept you away? A little business? A visitant? A slight indisposition? A soft bed? A dark or cold morning? Did not you then fast often? Or use abstinence to the uttermost of your power? Was not you much in prayer (cold and heavy as you was) while you was hanging over the mouth of hell? Did you not speak and not spare, even for an unknown God? Did you not boldly plead his cause? Reprove sinners? And avow the truth before an adulterous generation? And are you now a believer in Christ? Have you the 'faith that overcometh the world'? What! and are less zealous for your Master now than you was when you knew him not? Less diligent in fasting, in prayer, in hearing his Word, in calling sinners to God? O repent! See and feel your grievous loss! Remember from whence you are fallen! Bewail your unfaithfulness! Now be zealous and do the first works; lest, if you continue to 'make void the law through faith', God cut you off, and 'appoint' you your 'portion with the unbelievers'!

51. THE LAW ESTABLISHED THROUGH FAITH, DISCOURSE II

1750

An Introductory Comment

This second installment on the theme of the establishment of the moral law, like the first one, may be considered a "tract for the times" and not "the distillate of oral preaching," as Outler puts it (O, 2:3), though the sermon register lists the text Romans 3:31 first for Portarlington, Ireland, on June 22, 1750, and then for Poppleton, England, in April 1752 (WWS). Beyond this, the substance of the text of this sermon, "Do we then make void the law through faith?" was employed in London on June 27, 1741 (WH, 19:203) and at Horton and Bradford on April 25, 1745 (WH, 20:63).

Whereas in the earlier sermon, Wesley explored the several ways in which the moral law is made void through faith, in this present context he took up the practical task, in order that "we may follow a better pattern" (O, 2:33), of articulating just how the law may rightly be established by faith. Arguing in a way very similar to John Calvin, Wesley upheld a third use of the law (*tertius usus*) in that he explored the prescriptive, guiding value of the moral law in the ongoing Christian life. That is, the moral law is "divine virtue and wisdom assuming a visible form" (O, 2:9); it is the express will of God. It therefore should be established, first of all, through the doctrinal life of the church by declaring it openly to all people (O, 2:34–35); second, by preaching in such a way that it is clearly understood that faith does not supersede holiness; and third, by "establishing it in our own hearts and lives" (O, 2:41).

This sermon is also notable in that it offers the key to what Wesley understood as the end or goal of religion as far back as 1725, namely, holy love: "It [faith] is the grand means of restoring that holy love wherein man was originally created" (O, 2:40).

The Law Established through Faith, Discourse II

I. 1. We establish the law first by our doctrine
   A. By endeavouring to preach it to the whole extent
 2. We establish it when we openly declare it to all people
   A. Not only in its literal sense, but also in its spiritual meaning
 3. We do this diligently because these things are so little understood
   A. The full spiritual meaning of the law was hid from heathens
   B. It was almost equally hid from the bulk of the Jewish nation
 4. But the spiritual meaning of the law is also hid from the Christian world
   A. At least from a vast majority of Christians
 5. We also proclaim all the blessings and privileges God has prepared
 6. It is our part to preach Christ by preaching all that he has revealed

II. 1. We establish it secondly, by preaching that faith does not supersede holiness
   A. Faith in Christ does not supersede but produces holiness
   B. It produces all manner of holiness of heart and life
 2. Very excellent things are spoken of faith
   A. Yet it still loses its excellence when brought into comparison with love
 3. As love will exist after faith, so it did exist long before it
   A. Love existed from eternity, in God, the great ocean of love
 4.–5. It is probable that, before he rebelled, Adam walked by sight, not faith
   A. Faith necessarily presupposes sin
 6. Faith, then, was originally designed by God to re-establish the law of love

III. 1. We establish the law, third, in our hearts and lives
 2. This can only be done by faith
 3. By faith we establish God's law in our own hearts in a more effectual manner
   A. It incites us to do good, fulfilling the positive and negative law of God
 4. Nor does faith fulfil the law in external things alone
   A. It works inwardly by love, purifying the heart
 5. Let us endeavour to establish the law in ourselves
 6. Use all of the knowledge, love, life, and power you have attained
   A. Continually go on from faith to faith, increasing in holy love

Sermon 36: The Law Established through Faith, Discourse II, 1750

Romans 3:31

Do we then make void the law through faith?

God forbid! Yea, we establish the law.

1. It has been shown in the preceding discourse which are the most usual ways of 'making void the law through faith'. Namely, first, the not preaching it at all, which effectually makes it all void at a stroke, and this under colour of 'preaching Christ' and magnifying the gospel—though it be, in truth, destroying both the one and the other. Secondly, the teaching (whether directly or indirectly) that faith supersedes the necessity of holiness, that this is less necessary now, or a less degree of it necessary, than before Christ came; that it is less necessary to us because we believe than otherwise it would have been; or that Christian liberty is a liberty from any kind or degree of holiness—so perverting those great truths that we are now under the *covenant of grace* and not of *works*; that 'a man is justified by faith, without the works of the law'; and that 'to him that worketh not, but believeth, his faith is counted for righteousness'. Or, thirdly, the doing this practically: the making void the law in practice though not in principle; the living or acting as if faith was designed to excuse us from holiness; the allowing ourselves in sin 'because we are not under the law, but under grace'. It remains to inquire how we may follow a better pattern, how we may be able to say with the Apostle, 'Do we then make void the law through faith? God forbid! Yea, we establish the law.'

2. We do not indeed establish the old ceremonial law: we know that is abolished for ever. Much less do we establish the whole Mosaic dispensation—this, we know, our Lord has 'nailed to his cross'. Nor yet do we so establish the moral law (which, it is to be feared, too many do) as if the fulfilling it, the keeping all the commandments, were the condition of our justification. If it were so, surely 'in his sight should no man living be justified'. But all this being allowed, we still, in the Apostle's sense, 'establish the law', the moral law.

I.1. We 'establish the law', first, by our doctrine: by endeavouring to preach it in its whole extent, to explain and enforce every part of it in the same manner as our great Teacher did while upon earth. We establish it by following St. Peter's advice, 'If any man speak, let him speak as the oracles of God;' as the holy men of old, moved by the Holy Ghost, spoke and wrote for our instruction; and as the apostles of our blessed Lord, by the direction of the same Spirit. We establish it whenever we speak in his name, by keeping back nothing from them that hear; by declaring to them without any limitation or reserve the whole counsel of God. And in order the more effectually to establish it we use herein great plainness of speech. 'We are not as many that corrupt the word of God', καπηλεύουσι (as artful men their bad wines); we do not cauponize, mix, adulterate, or soften it to make it suit the taste of the hearers. 'But as of sincerity, but as of God, in the sight of God speak we in Christ,' as having no other aim than by 'manifestation of the truth to commend ourselves to every man's conscience in the sight of God'.

2. We then, by our doctrine, establish the law when we thus openly declare it to all men, and that in the fullness wherein it is delivered by our blessed Lord and his apostles; when we publish it in the height and depth and length and breadth thereof. We then establish the law when we declare every part of it, every commandment contained therein, not only in its full, literal sense, but likewise in its spiritual meaning; not only with regard to the outward actions which it either forbids or enjoins, but also with respect to the inward principle, to the thoughts, desires, and intents of the heart.

3. And indeed this we do the more diligently, not only because it is of the deepest importance—inasmuch as all the fruit, every word and work, must be only evil continually if the tree be evil, if the dispositions and tempers of the heart be not right before God—but likewise because, as important as these things are, they are little considered or understood; so little that we may truly say of the law, too, when taken in its full spiritual meaning, it is 'a mystery which was hid from ages and generations since the world began'. It was utterly hid from the heathen world. They, with all their boasted wisdom, neither 'found out God' nor the law of God, not in the letter, much less in the spirit of it. 'Their foolish hearts were' more and more 'darkened'; while 'professing themselves wise, they became fools'. And it was almost equally hid, as to its spiritual meaning, from the bulk of the Jewish nation. Even these, who were so ready to declare concerning others, 'this people that know not the law is accursed', pronounced their own sentence therein, as being under the same curse, the same dreadful ignorance. Witness our Lord's continual reproof of the wisest among them for their gross misinterpretations of it. Witness the supposition, almost universally received among them, that they needed only to make clean the outside of the cup, that the paying tithe of mint, anise, and cummin, outward exactness, would atone for inward unholiness, for the total neglect both of justice and mercy, of faith and the love of God. Yea, so absolutely was the spiritual meaning of the law hidden from the wisest of them, that one of their most eminent rabbis comments thus on those words of the Psalmist, 'If I incline unto iniquity with my heart, the Lord will not hear me.' 'That is', saith he, 'if it be only in my heart, if I do not commit outward wickedness, the Lord will not regard it; he will not punish me unless I proceed to the outward act!'

4. But alas! the law of God, as to its inward spiritual meaning, is not hid from the Jews or heathens only, but even from what is called the Christian world; at least, from a vast majority of them. The spiritual sense of the commandments of God is still a mystery to these also. Nor is this observable only in those lands which are overspread with Romish darkness and ignorance. But this is too sure, that the far greater part, even of those who are called 'Reformed Christians', are utter strangers at this day to the law of Christ, in the purity and spirituality of it.

5. Hence it is that to this day 'the scribes and Pharisees'—the men who have the form but not the power of religion, and who are generally wise in their own eyes, and righteous in their own conceits—'hearing these things are offended', are deeply offended when we speak of the religion of the heart, and particularly when we show that without this, were we to 'give all our goods to feed the poor', it would profit us nothing. But offended they must be, for we cannot but speak the truth as it is in Jesus. It is our part, whether they will hear or whether they will forbear, to deliver our own soul. All that is written in the Book

of God we are to declare, not as pleasing men, but the Lord. We are to declare not only all the promises but all the threatenings, too, which we find therein. At the same time that we proclaim all the blessings and privileges which God had prepared for his children, we are likewise to 'teach all the things whatsoever he hath commanded'. And we know that all these have their use; either for the awakening those that sleep, the instructing the ignorant, the comforting the feeble-minded, or the building up and perfecting of the saints. We know that 'all Scripture given by inspiration of God is profitable' either 'for doctrine' or 'for reproof', either 'for correction' or 'for instruction in righteousness'; and 'that the man of God', in the process of the work of God in his soul, has need of every part thereof, that he 'may' at length 'be perfect, throughly furnished unto all good works'.

6. It is our part thus to 'preach Christ' by preaching all things whatsoever he hath revealed. We may indeed, without blame, yea, and with a peculiar blessing from God, declare the love of our Lord Jesus Christ. We may speak in a more especial manner of 'the Lord our righteousness'. We may expatiate upon the grace of 'God in Christ, reconciling the world unto himself'. We may, at proper opportunities, dwell upon his praise, as bearing 'the iniquities of us all', as 'wounded for our transgressions' and 'bruised for our iniquities', that 'by his stripes we might be healed'. But still we should not 'preach Christ' according to his word if we were wholly to confine ourselves to this. We are not ourselves clear before God unless we proclaim him in all his offices. To preach Christ as a workman that needeth not to be ashamed is to preach him not only as our great 'High Priest, taken from among men, and ordained for men, in things pertaining to God'; as such, 'reconciling us to God by his blood', and 'ever living to make intercession for us'; but likewise as the Prophet of the Lord, 'who of God is made unto us wisdom', who by his word and his Spirit 'is with us always', 'guiding us into all truth'; yea, and as remaining a King for ever; as giving laws to all whom he has bought with his blood; as restoring those to the image of God whom he had first reinstated in his favour; as reigning in all believing hearts until he has 'subdued all things to himself'; until he hath utterly cast out all sin, and 'brought in everlasting righteousness.'

II.1. 'We establish the law', secondly, when we so preach faith in Christ as not to supersede but produce holiness: to produce all manner of holiness, negative and positive, of the heart and of the life.

In order to this we continually declare (what should be frequently and deeply considered by all who would not 'make void the law through faith') that faith itself, even Christian faith, the faith of God's elect, the faith of the operation of God, still is only the handmaid of love. As glorious and honourable as it is, it is not the end of the commandment. God hath given this honour to love alone. Love is the end of all the commandments of God. Love is the end, the sole end, of every dispensation of God, from the beginning of the world to the consummation of all things. And it will endure when heaven and earth flee away; for 'love' alone 'never faileth'. Faith will totally fail; it will be swallowed up in sight, in the everlasting vision of God. But even then love,

Its nature and its office still the same,
Lasting its lamp and unconsumed its flame,
In deathless triumph shall for ever live,
And endless good diffuse, and endless praise receive.

2. Very excellent things are spoken of faith, and whosoever is a partaker thereof may well say with the Apostle, 'Thanks be to God for his unspeakable gift.' Yet still it loses all its excellence when brought into a comparison with love. What St. Paul observes concerning the superior glory of the gospel above that of the law may with great propriety be spoken of the superior glory of love above that of faith: 'Even that which was made glorious hath no glory in this respect, by reason of the glory that excelleth. For if that which is done away is glorious, much more doth that which remaineth exceed in glory.' Yea, all the glory of faith before it is done away arises hence, that it ministers to love. It is the great temporary means which God has ordained to promote that eternal end.

3. Let those who magnify faith beyond all proportion, so as to swallow up all things else, and who so totally misapprehend the nature of it as to imagine it stands in the place of love, consider farther that as love will exist after faith, so it did exist long before it. The angels, who from the moment of their creation beheld the face of their Father that is in heaven, had no occasion for faith in its general notion, as it is the evidence of things not seen. Neither had they need of faith in its more particular acceptation, faith in the blood of Jesus; for he took not upon him the nature of angels, but only the seed of Abraham. There was therefore no place before the foundation of the world for faith either in the general or particular sense. But there was for love. Love existed from eternity, in God, the great ocean of love. Love had a place in all the children of God, from the moment of their creation. They received at once from their gracious Creator to exist, and to love.

4. Nor is it certain (as ingeniously and plausibly as many have descanted upon this) that faith, even in the general sense of the word, had any place in paradise. It is highly probable, from that short and uncircumstantial account which we have in Holy Writ, that Adam, before he rebelled against God, walked with him by sight and not by faith.

For then his reason's eye was strong and clear,
And as an eagle can behold the sun,
Might have beheld his Maker's face as near,
As th' intellectual angels could have done.

He was then able to talk with him face to face, whose face we cannot now see and live; and consequently had no need of that faith whose office it is to supply the want of sight.

5. On the other hand, it is absolutely certain, faith, in its particular sense, had then no place. For in that sense it necessarily presupposes sin, and the wrath of God declared against the sinner; without which there is no need of an atonement for sin in order to the sinner's reconciliation with God. Consequently, as there was no need of an atonement before the fall, so there was no place for faith in that atonement; man being then pure from every stain of sin, holy as God is holy. But love even then filled his heart. It reigned in him

without a rival. And it was only when love was lost by sin that faith was added, not for its own sake, nor with any design that it should exist any longer than until it had answered the end for which it was ordained—namely, to restore man to the love from which he was fallen. At the fall therefore was added this evidence of things unseen, which before was utterly needless; this confidence in redeeming love, which could not possibly have any place till the promise was made that the seed of the woman should bruise the serpent's head.

6. Faith then was originally designed of God to re-establish the law of love. Therefore, in speaking thus, we are not undervaluing it, or robbing it of its due praise, but on the contrary showing its real worth, exalting it in its just proportion, and giving it that very place which the wisdom of God assigned it from the beginning. It is the grand means of restoring that holy love wherein man was originally created. It follows, that although faith is of no value in itself (as neither is any other means whatsoever) yet as it leads to that end—the establishing anew the law of love in our hearts—and as in the present state of things it is the only means under heaven for effecting it, it is on that account an unspeakable blessing to man, and of unspeakable value before God.

III.1. And this naturally brings us to observe, thirdly, the most important way of 'establishing the law'; namely, the establishing it in our own hearts and lives. Indeed, without this, what would all the rest avail? We might establish it by our doctrine; we might preach it in its whole extent; might explain and enforce every part of it. We might open it in its most spiritual meaning, and declare the mysteries of the kingdom; we might preach Christ in all his offices, and faith in Christ as opening all the treasures of his love. And yet, all this time, if the law we preached were not established in our hearts we should be of no more account before God than 'sounding brass or tinkling cymbals'. All our preaching would be so far from profiting ourselves that it would only increase our damnation.

2. This is therefore the main point to be considered: How may we establish the law in our own hearts so that it may have its full influence on our lives? And this can only be done by faith.

Faith alone it is which effectually answers this end, as we learn from daily experience. For so long as we walk by faith, not by sight, we go swiftly on in the way of holiness. While we steadily look, not at the things which are seen, but at those which are not seen, we are more and more crucified to the world and the world crucified to us. Let but the eye of the soul be constantly fixed, not on the things which are temporal, but on those which are eternal, and our affections are more and more loosened from earth and fixed on things above. So that faith in general is the most direct and effectual means of promoting all righteousness and true holiness; of establishing the holy and spiritual law in the hearts of them that believe.

3. And by faith, taken in its more particular meaning for a confidence in a pardoning God, we establish his law in our own hearts in a still more effectual manner. For there is no motive which so powerfully inclines us to love God as the sense of the love of God in Christ. Nothing enables us like a piercing conviction of this to give our hearts to him who was given for us. And from this principle of grateful love to God arises love to our brother

also. Neither can we avoid loving our neighbour, if we truly believe the love wherewith God hath loved us. Now this love to man, grounded on faith and love to God, 'worketh no ill to our neighbour'. Consequently it is, as the Apostle observes, 'the fulfilling of the' whole negative 'law'. 'For this, Thou shalt not commit adultery, Thou shalt not kill, Thou shalt not steal, Thou shalt not bear false witness, Thou shalt not covet; and if there be any other commandment, it is briefly comprehended in this saying, Thou shalt love thy neighbour as thyself.' Neither is love content with barely working no evil to our neighbour. It continually incites us to do good: as we have time and opportunity, to do good in every possible kind and in every possible degree to all men. It is therefore the fulfilling of the positive, likewise, as well as of the negative law of God.

4. Nor does faith fulfil either the negative or positive law as to the external part only; but it works inwardly by love to the purifying of the heart, the cleansing it from all vile affections. 'Everyone that hath this' faith 'in him purifieth himself, even as he is pure'—purifieth himself from every earthly, sensual desire, from all vile and inordinate affections; yea, from the whole of that carnal mind which is enmity against God. At the same time, if it have its perfect work, it fills him with all goodness, righteousness, and truth. It brings all heaven into his soul, and causes him to walk in the light, even as God is in the light.

5. Let us thus endeavour to establish the law in ourselves; not sinning 'because we are under grace', but rather using all the power we receive thereby 'to fulfil all righteousness'. Calling to mind what light we received from God while his Spirit was convincing us of sin, let us beware we do not put out that light. What we had then attained let us hold fast. Let nothing induce us to build again what we have destroyed; to resume anything, small or great, which we then clearly saw was not for the glory of God or the profit of our own soul; or to neglect anything, small or great, which we could not then neglect without a check from our own conscience. To increase and perfect the light which we had before, let us now add the light of faith. Confirm we the former gift of God by a deeper sense of whatever he had then shown us, by a greater tenderness of conscience, and a more exquisite sensibility of sin. Walking now with joy and not with fear, in a clear, steady sight of things eternal, we shall look on pleasure, wealth, praise—all the things of earth—as on bubbles upon the water; counting nothing important, nothing desirable, nothing worth a deliberate thought, but only what is 'within the veil', where 'Jesus sitteth at the right hand of God'.

6. Can *you* say, 'Thou art merciful to my unrighteousness; my sins thou rememberest no more'? Then for the time to come see that you fly from sin, as from the face of a serpent. For how exceeding sinful does it appear to you now! How heinous above all expression! On the other hand, in how amiable a light do you now see the holy and perfect will of God! Now, therefore, labour that it may be fulfilled, both in you, by you, and upon you. Now watch and pray that you may sin no more, that you may see and shun the least transgression of his law. You see the motes which you could not see before when the sun shines into a dark place. In like manner you see the sins which you could not see before, now the sun of righteousness shines in your heart. Now, then, do all diligence to walk in every respect according to the light you have received. Now be zealous to receive more

light daily, more of the knowledge and love of God, more of the Spirit of Christ, more of his life, and of the power of his resurrection. Now use all the knowledge and love and life and power you have already attained. So shall you continually go on from faith to faith. So shall you daily increase in holy love, till faith is swallowed up in sight, and the law of love established to all eternity.

52. ON SIN IN BELIEVERS

March 28, 1763

An Introductory Comment

There are more than twenty references to the text of this sermon (2 Cor. 5:17) in the sermon register, though Wesley did not relate the specific Pauline phrase "if any man be in Christ, he is a new creature" to the theme at hand in printed form until 1763. Retiring to Lewisham in March of that year, likely at the home of his good friend Ebenezer Blackwell, Wesley composed this sermon to put aside the erroneous notion that the children of God are utterly holy, free from the carnal nature itself.

In 1741 at Gray's Inn Walks, Wesley held a conversation with Count von Zinzendorf (in Latin!) in which the Moravian leader contended that the moment believers are justified, they are sanctified wholly (WH, 19:213). While Wesley was willing to affirm the conjoined nature of justification and the new birth in the lives of Christian believers ("everyone that 'believes' is both 'justified' and 'born of God'"; O, 1:319–20), he nevertheless rejected the teaching that such babes in Christ were pure in heart. To be sure, in August 1738 while he was at Herrnhut, Wesley had become aware of the distinction that Christian David had made in the following observation: "though it [sin] did not reign, it did remain in me" (WH, 18:274). Wesley developed this important distinction throughout this sermon in this form: "The *guilt* is one thing, the *power* another, and the *being* yet another. That believers are delivered from the *guilt* and *power* of sin we allow; that they are delivered from the *being* of it we deny" (O, 1:328).

Wesley supported his doctrinal corrective in this sermon by pointing out that the universal church (Roman, Greek, and Reformed) has affirmed that the carnal nature remains in a child of God and that the opposite teaching, in his own judgment, "was never heard of for seventeen hundred years, never till it was discovered by Count Zinzendorf" (O, 1:324).

On Sin in Believers

I. 1.–2. Is there sin in those who are in Christ? Does sin *remain* in a believer?

3. Our own church affirms the corruption of the nature of every man

4. The same testimony is given by all churches, not only the Greek or Romish

5. Many affirm that believers are saved from the *dominion* and the *being* of sin

6.–7. The Germans allow that sin remains *in the flesh*, but not *in the heart*

II. 1. 'Regenerate' denotes an inward, *actual* change; 'justified', a *relative* one

2. By 'sin' I understand inward sin, any temper contrary to the mind of Christ

3. This question is not about *outward sin*, whether a child of God *commits sin*

4. A justified person has the power over both outward and inward sin

III. 1.–6. In Paul's Epistles, there are two contrary principles in believers

7. The proposition 'there is no sin a believer' is contrary to the Word of God

8. But can Christ be in the same heart where sin is?

A. Undoubtedly he can; otherwise people could not be saved therefrom

9.–10. That there is no sin in believers is quite *new* in the church of Christ

IV. 1. Some observe that Scripture says believers are holy or sanctified

2.–3. The Bible says, if anyone is a believer in Christ, he is a new creature

A. A person cannot be a *new creature* and an *old creature* at once

B. I answer: Yes he may; he may be *partly renewed*

4.–9. But, they say, the Spirit of God dwells in believers

A. They are therefore delivered from the guilt and the power of sin

B. These are coupled together as if the same; they are not

10.–11. Can people have pride and not be proud?

A. Pride may be in the same heart with humility and meekness

12. But no one who is justified is a slave to sin

13. This doctrine encourages people to remain in sin

A. Understand the proposition right, and no such consequence follows

V. 1. Even after justification, two contrary principles remain in every person

2. Let us hold fast to the sound doctrine once delivered to the saints

Sermon 13: On Sin in Believers, 1763

2 Corinthians 5:17

If any man be in Christ, he is a new creature.

I. 1. Is there then sin in him that is in Christ? Does sin *remain* in one that 'believes in him'? Is there any sin in them that are 'born of God', or are they wholly delivered from it? Let no one imagine this to be a question of mere curiosity, or that it is of little importance whether it be determined one way or the other. Rather it is a point of the utmost moment to every serious Christian, the resolving of which very nearly concerns both his present and eternal happiness.

2. And yet I do not know that ever it was controverted in the primitive Church. Indeed there was no room for disputing concerning it, as all Christians were agreed. And so far as I have observed, the whole body of ancient Christians who have left us anything in writing declare with one voice that even believers in Christ, till they are 'strong in the Lord, and in the power of his might', have need to 'wrestle with flesh and blood', with an evil nature, as well as 'with principalities and powers'.

3. And herein our own Church (as indeed in most points) exactly copies after the primitive; declaring (in her Ninth Article), 'Original sin [. . .] is the corruption of the nature of every man, [. . .] whereby man is [. . .] in his own nature inclined to evil, so that the flesh lusteth contrary to the Spirit. [. . .] And this infection of nature doth remain, yea, in them that are regenerated; whereby the lust of the flesh, called in Greek φρόνημα σαρκός, [. . .] is not subject to the law of God. And although there is no condemnation for them that believe [. . .], yet this lust hath of itself the nature of sin.'

4. The same testimony is given by all other churches; not only by the Greek and Romish Church, but by every Reformed Church in Europe, of whatever denomination. Indeed some of these seem to carry the thing too far; so describing the corruption of heart in a believer as scarce to allow that he has dominion over it, but rather is in bondage thereto. And by this means they leave hardly any distinction between a believer and an unbeliever.

5. To avoid this extreme many well-meaning men, particularly those under the direction of the late Count Zinzendorf, ran into another, affirming that 'all true believers are not only saved from the *dominion* of sin but from the *being* of inward as well as outward sin, so that it no longer *remains* in them.' And from them, about twenty years ago, many of our countrymen imbibed the same opinion, that even the corruption of nature *is no more* in those who believe in Christ.

6. It is true that when the Germans were pressed upon this head they soon allowed (many of them at least) that sin did still remain *in the flesh*, but not *in the heart* of a believer. And after a time, when the absurdity of this was shown, they fairly gave up the point; allowing that sin did still *remain*, though not *reign*, in him that is born of God.

7. But the English who had received it from them (some directly, some at second or third hand) were not so easily prevailed upon to part with a favourite opinion. And even when the generality of them were convinced it was utterly indefensible, a few could not be persuaded to give it up, but maintain it to this day.

II.1. For the sake of these who really fear God and desire to know 'the truth as it is in Jesus', it may not be amiss to consider the point with calmness and impartiality. In doing this I use indifferently the words 'regenerate', 'justified', or 'believers'; since, though they have not precisely the same meaning (the first implying an inward, *actual* change; the second a *relative* one; and the third the means whereby both the one and the other are wrought) yet they come to one and the same thing, as everyone that 'believes' is both 'justified' and 'born of God'.

2. By 'sin' I here understand inward sin: any sinful temper, passion, or affection; such as pride, self-will, love of the world, in any kind or degree; such as lust, anger, peevishness; any disposition contrary to the mind which was in Christ.

3. The question is not concerning *outward sin*, whether a child of God *commits sin* or no. We all agree and earnestly maintain, 'He that committeth sin is of the devil.' We agree, 'Whosoever is born of God doth not commit sin.' Neither do we now inquire whether inward sin will *always* remain in the children of God; whether sin will continue in the soul *as long as* it continues in the body. Nor yet do we inquire whether a justified person may *relapse* either into inward or outward sin. But simply this: is a justified or regenerate man freed from *all sin* as soon as he is justified? Is there then no sin in his heart? Nor ever after, unless he fall from grace?

4. We allow that the state of a justified person is inexpressibly great and glorious. He is 'born again, not of blood, nor of the flesh, nor of the will of man, but of God'. He is a child of God, a member of Christ, an heir of the kingdom of heaven. 'The peace of God which passeth all understanding keepeth his heart and mind in Christ Jesus.' His very 'body is a temple of the Holy Ghost', and 'an habitation of God through the Spirit'. He is 'created anew in Christ Jesus'; he is *washed*; he is *sanctified.* His 'heart is purified by faith'; he is cleansed from 'the corruption that is in the world'. 'The love of God is shed abroad in his heart by the Holy Ghost which is given unto him.' And so long as he 'walketh in love' (which he may always do) he 'worships God in spirit and in truth'. He 'keepeth the commandments of God, and doth those things that are pleasing in his sight': so 'exercising himself as to have a conscience void of offence toward God and toward man'. And he has power both over outward and inward sin, even from the moment he is justified.

III.1. 'But was he not then "freed from all sin", so that there is no sin in his heart?' I cannot say this: I cannot believe it, because St. Paul says the contrary. He is speaking to believers, and describing the state of believers in general, when he says, 'The flesh lusteth against the spirit, and the spirit against the flesh: these are contrary the one to the other' (Gal. 5:17). Nothing can be more express. The Apostle here directly affirms that 'the flesh', evil nature, opposes 'the spirit', even in believers; that even in the regenerate there are two principles 'contrary the one to the other'.

2. Again: when he writes to the believers at Corinth, to those who were 'sanctified in Christ Jesus' (1 Cor. 1:2), he says: 'I, brethren, could not speak unto you as unto spiritual, but as unto carnal, as unto babes in Christ. . . . Ye are yet carnal: for whereas there is among you envying and strife, [. . .] are ye not carnal?' (1 Cor. 3:1, 3). Now here the

Apostle speaks unto those who were unquestionably believers, whom in the same breath he styles his 'brethren in Christ', as being still in a measure *carnal.* He affirms there was 'envying' (an evil temper) occasioning 'strife' among them, and yet does not give the least intimation that they had lost their faith. Nay, he manifestly declares they had not; for then they would not have been 'babes in Christ'. And (what is most remarkable of all) he speaks of being 'carnal' and 'babes in Christ' as one and the same thing; plainly showing that every believer is (in a degree) 'carnal' while he is only a 'babe in Christ'.

3. Indeed this grand point, that there are two contrary principles in believers—nature and grace, the flesh and the spirit—runs through all the epistles of St. Paul, yea, through all the Holy Scriptures. Almost all the directions and exhortations therein are founded on this supposition, pointing at wrong tempers or practices in those who are, notwithstanding, acknowledged by the inspired writers to be believers. And they are continually exhorted to fight with and conquer these, by the power of the faith which was in them.

4. And who can doubt but there was faith in the angel of the church of Ephesus when our Lord said to him: 'I know thy works, and thy labour, and thy patience. . . . Thou hast patience, and for my name's sake hast laboured and hast not fainted.' But was there meantime no sin in his heart? Yea, or Christ would not have added, 'Nevertheless I have somewhat against thee, because thou hast left thy first love' (Rev. 2:2-4). This was real sin which God saw in his heart, of which accordingly he is exhorted to *repent.* And yet we have no authority to say that even then he had no faith.

5. Nay, the angel of the church at Pergamos also is exhorted to 'repent', which implies sin, though our Lord expressly says, 'Thou hast not denied my faith' (Rev. 2:13, 16). And to the angel of the church in Sardis he says, 'Strengthen the things which remain that are ready to die' (Rev. 3:2). The good which remained was 'ready to die', but was not actually dead. So there was still a spark of faith even in him; which he is accordingly commanded to 'hold fast' (Rev. 3:3).

6. Once more: when the Apostle exhorts believers to 'cleanse' themselves 'from all filthiness of flesh and spirit' (2 Cor. 7:1), he plainly teaches that those believers were not yet cleansed therefrom. Will you answer, 'He that "abstains from all appearance of evil" does *ipso facto* cleanse himself from all filthiness'? Not in any wise. For instance, a man reviles me; I feel resentment, which is 'filthiness of spirit'; yet I say not a word. Here I 'abstain from all appearance of evil', but this does not cleanse me from that filthiness of spirit, as I experience to my sorrow.

7. And as this position, 'there is no sin in a believer, no carnal mind, no bent to backsliding,' is thus contrary to the Word of God, so it is to the *experience* of his children. These continually feel an heart bent to backsliding, a natural tendency to evil, a proneness to depart from God, and cleave to the things of earth. They are daily sensible of sin remaining in their heart, pride, self-will, unbelief, and of sin cleaving to all they speak and do, even their best actions and holiest duties. Yet at the same time they 'know that they are of God'; they cannot doubt of it for a moment. They feel 'his Spirit clearly witnessing with their spirit that they are the children of God'. They 'rejoice in God through Christ

Jesus, by whom they have now received the atonement'. So that they are equally assured that sin is in them and that 'Christ is in them, the hope of glory.'

8. 'But can Christ be in the same heart where sin is?' Undoubtedly he can; otherwise it never could be saved therefrom. Where the sickness is, there is the physician,

> Carrying on his work within,
> Striving till he cast out sin.

Christ indeed cannot *reign* where sin *reigns*; neither will he *dwell* where any sin is *allowed*. But he *is* and *dwells* in the heart of every believer who is fighting against all sin; although it be 'not' yet 'purified according to the purification of the sanctuary'.

9. It has been observed before, that the opposite doctrine, 'that there is no sin in believers', is quite *new* in the church of Christ; that it was never heard of for seventeen hundred years, never till it was discovered by Count Zinzendorf. I do not remember to have seen the least intimation of it either in any ancient or modern writer, unless perhaps in some of the wild, ranting antinomians. And these likewise say and unsay, acknowledging there is sin 'in their flesh', although no sin 'in their heart'. But whatever doctrine is *new* must be *wrong*; for the *old* religion is the only *true* one; and no doctrine can be right unless it is the very same 'which was from the beginning'.

10. One argument more against this new, unscriptural doctrine may be drawn from the dreadful consequences of it. One says, 'I felt anger today.' Must I reply, 'Then you have no faith'? Another says, 'I know what you advise is good; but my will is quite averse to it.' Must I tell him, 'Then you are an unbeliever, under the wrath and the curse of God'? What will be the natural consequence of this? Why, if he believe what I say, his soul will not only be grieved and wounded but perhaps utterly destroyed; inasmuch as he will 'cast away that confidence which hath great recompense of reward'. And having cast away his shield, how shall he 'quench the fiery darts of the wicked one'? How shall he overcome the world? Seeing 'this is the victory that overcometh the world, even our faith.' He stands disarmed in the midst of his enemies, open to all their assaults. What wonder then if he be utterly overthrown, if they take him captive at their will; yea, if he fall from one wickedness to another, and never see good any more? I cannot therefore by any means receive this assertion 'that there is no sin in a believer from the moment he is justified'. First, because it is contrary to the whole tenor of Scripture; secondly, because it is contrary to the experience of the children of God; thirdly, because it is absolutely new, never heard of in the world till yesterday; and lastly, because it is naturally attended with the most fatal consequences, not only grieving those whom God hath not grieved, but perhaps dragging them into everlasting perdition.

IV.1. However, let us give a fair hearing to the chief arguments of those who endeavour to support it. And it is, first, from Scripture they attempt to prove that there is no sin in a believer. They argue thus: 'The Scripture says every believer is "born of God", is "clean", is "holy", is "sanctified"; is "pure in heart", has a new heart, is a temple of the Holy Ghost. Now, as "that which is born of the flesh is flesh", is altogether evil, so "that which is born of the Spirit is spirit", is altogether good. Again: a man cannot be clean, sanctified, holy, and at the same time unclean, unsanctified, unholy. He cannot be pure and impure, or have a new and an old heart together. Neither can his soul be unholy while it is a temple of the Holy Ghost.'

I have put this objection as strong as possible, that its full weight may appear. Let us now examine it, part by part. And (1). '"That which is born of the Spirit is spirit," is altogether good.' I allow the text, but not the comment; for the text affirms this, and no more, that every man who is 'born of the Spirit' is a *spiritual man*. He is so. But so he may be, and yet not be *altogether* spiritual. The Christians at *Corinth* were *spiritual* men; else they had been no Christians at all. And yet they were not *altogether* spiritual: they were still (in part) *carnal*. 'But they were fallen from grace.' St. Paul says, 'No: they were even then "babes in Christ".' (2). 'But a man cannot be clean, sanctified, holy, and at the same time unclean, unsanctified, unholy.' Indeed he may. So the Corinthians were. 'Ye are washed,' says the Apostle, 'ye are sanctified'; namely cleansed from 'fornication, idolatry, drunkenness', and all other outward sin (1 Cor. 6:9, 10, 11). And yet at the same time, in another sense of the word, they were *unsanctified*: they were not *washed*, not inwardly *cleansed* from envy, evil surmising, partiality. 'But sure they had not a new heart and an old heart together.' It is most sure they had; for at that very time their hearts were *truly*, yet not *entirely*, renewed. Their carnal mind was nailed to the cross; yet it was not wholly destroyed. 'But could they be *unholy* while they were "temples of the Holy Ghost"?' (1 Cor. 6:19). Yes, that they were 'temples of the Holy Ghost' is certain. And it is equally certain they were, in some degree, *carnal*, that is, *unholy*.

2. 'However, there is one Scripture more which will put the matter out of question: "If any man be (a believer) in Christ, he is a new creature. Old things are passed away; behold all things are become new" (2 Cor. 5:17). Now certainly a man cannot be a *new creature* and an *old creature* at once.' Yes, he may: he may be *partly renewed*, which was the very case with those at Corinth. They were doubtless 'renewed in the spirit of their mind', or they could not have been so much as 'babes in Christ'. Yet they had not the whole mind which was in Christ, for they *envied* one another. 'But it is said expressly, "Old things are passed away: all things are become new."' But we must not so interpret the Apostle's words as to make him contradict himself. And if we will make him consistent with himself the plain meaning of the words is this: his *old judgment* (concerning justification, holiness, happiness, indeed concerning the things of God in general) is now 'passed away'; so are his *old desires, designs, affections, tempers,* and *conversation*. All these are undeniably 'become new', greatly changed from what they were. And yet, though they are *new*, they are not *wholly* new. Still he feels, to his sorrow and shame, remains of the 'old man', too manifest taints of his former tempers and affections, a law in his members which frequently *fights* against that law of his mind, though it cannot 'gain any advantage' over him as long as he 'watches unto prayer'.

3. This whole argument, 'If he is clean, he is clean,' 'if he is holy, he is holy' (and twenty more expressions of the same kind may easily be heaped together) is really no

better than playing upon words: it is the fallacy of arguing from a *particular* to a *general*, of inferring a general conclusion from particular premises. Propose the sentence entire, and it runs thus: 'If he is holy *at all*, he is holy *altogether*.' That does not follow: every babe in Christ is holy, and yet not altogether so. He is saved from sin; yet not entirely: it *remains*, though it does not *reign*. If you think it does not *remain* (in *babes* at least, whatever be the case with *young men*, or *fathers*) you certainly have not considered the height and depth and length and breadth of the law of God (even the law of love laid down by St. Paul in the thirteenth of Corinthians); and that 'every ἀνομία', disconformity to, or deviation from this law, 'is sin.' Now, is there no disconformity to this in the heart or life of a believer? What may be in an adult Christian is another question. But what a stranger must he be to human nature who can possibly imagine that this is the case with every babe in Christ!

4.[1] 'But believers "walk after the Spirit" (Rom. 8:1), and the Spirit of God *dwells* in them. Consequently they are delivered from the guilt, the power, *or, in one word*, the being of sin.'

These are coupled together as if they were the same thing. But they are not the same thing. The *guilt* is one thing, the *power* another, and the *being* yet another. That believers are delivered from the *guilt* and *power* of sin we allow; that they are delivered from the *being* of it we deny. Nor does it in any wise follow from these texts. A man may have the Spirit of God *dwelling in* him, and may 'walk after the Spirit', though he still feels 'the flesh lusting against the Spirit'.

5. 'But the "church is the body of Christ" (Col. 1:24). This implies that its members are washed from all filthiness; otherwise it will follow that Christ and Belial are incorporated with each other.'

Nay, it will not follow from hence—'Those who are the mystical body of Christ still feel the flesh lusting against the Spirit'—that Christ has any fellowship with the devil, or with that sin which he enables them to resist and overcome.

6. 'But are not Christians "come to the heavenly Jerusalem", where "nothing defiled can enter"?' Yes; 'and to an innumerable company of angels', 'and to the spirits of just men made perfect' (Heb. 12:22-23): that is,

> Earth and heaven all agree,
> All his one great family.

And they are likewise holy and *undefiled* while they 'walk after the Spirit'; although sensible there is another principle in them, and that 'these are contrary to each other'.

7. 'But Christians are "reconciled to God". Now this could not be if any of the "carnal mind" remained; for this "is enmity against God". Consequently no reconciliation can be effected but by its total destruction.'

We 'are reconciled to God through the blood of the cross'. And in that moment, the φρόνημα σαρκός, the corruption of nature which is 'enmity with God', is put under our feet. The flesh has 'no more dominion over us'. But it still *exists*; and it is still in its nature enmity with God, lusting against his Spirit.

8. 'But "they that are Christ's have crucified the flesh, with its affections and lusts"' (Gal. 5:24). They have so; yet it remains in them still, and often struggles to break from the cross. 'Nay, but they have "put off the old man with his deeds"' (Col. 3:9). They have; and in the sense above-described, 'old things are passed away; all things are become new.' An hundred texts may be cited to the same effect. And they will all admit of the same answer. 'But, to say all in one word, "Christ gave himself for the church, that . . . it might be holy and without blemish"' (Eph. 5:25, 27). And so it will be in the end: but it never was yet, from the beginning to this day.

9. 'But let *experience* speak: all who are justified do at that time find an absolute freedom from all sin.' That I doubt; but if they do, do they find it ever after? Else you gain nothing. 'If they do not, it is their own fault.' That remains to be proved.

10. 'But, in the very nature of things, can a man have pride in him, and not be proud? Anger, and yet not be angry?'

A man may have *pride* in him, may think of himself in *some particulars* above what he ought to think (and so be *proud* in that particular) and yet not be a proud man in his *general* character. He may have *anger* in him, yea, and a strong propensity to furious anger, without *giving way* to it. 'But can anger and pride be in that heart where *only* meekness and humility are felt?' No; but *some* pride and anger may be in that heart where there is *much* humility and meekness.

'It avails not to say these tempers *are* there, but they do not *reign*; for sin cannot in any kind or degree *exist* where it does not *reign*; for *guilt* and *power* are essential properties of sin. Therefore where one of them is, all must be.'

Strange indeed! 'Sin cannot in any kind or degree *exist* where it does not *reign*'? Absolutely contrary this to all experience, all Scripture, all common sense. Resentment of an affront is sin. It is ἀνομία, disconformity to the law of love. This has existed in me a thousand times. Yet it did not, and does not, *reign*. But '*guilt* and *power* are essential properties of sin; therefore where one is, all must be.' No; in the instance before us, if the resentment I feel is not yielded to, even for a moment, there is no *guilt* at all, no condemnation from God upon that account. And in this case it has no *power*: though it 'lusteth against the Spirit' it cannot prevail. Here, therefore, as in ten thousand instances, there is *sin* without either *guilt* or *power*.

11. 'But the supposing sin in a believer is pregnant with everything frightful and discouraging. It implies the contending with a power that has the possession of our strength, maintains his usurpation of our hearts, and there prosecutes the war in defiance of our Redeemer.' Not so. The supposing sin is *in* us does not imply that it has the possession of our strength; no more than a man crucified has the possession of those that crucify him. As little does it imply that sin 'maintains its usurpation of our hearts'. The usurper is dethroned. He *remains* indeed where he once reigned; but remains *in chains*. So that he does in some sense 'prosecute the war', yet he grows weaker and weaker, while the believer goes on from strength to strength, conquering and to conquer.

12. 'I am not satisfied yet. He that has sin in him is a slave to sin. Therefore you suppose a man to be justified while he is a slave to sin. Now if you allow men may be justified while they have pride, anger, or unbelief in them—nay if you aver these are (at least for a time) in all that are justified—what wonder that we have so many proud, angry, unbelieving believers!'

I do not suppose any man who is justified is a slave to sin. Yet I do suppose sin remains (at least for a time) in all that are justified. 'But if sin remains in a believer he is a sinful man: if pride, for instance, then he is proud; if self-will, then he is self-willed; if unbelief, then he is an unbeliever—consequently, no believer at all. How then does he differ from unbelievers, from unregenerate men?'

This is still mere playing upon words. It means no more than, 'If there is sin, pride, self-will in him, then—there is sin, pride, self-will.' And this nobody can deny. In *that sense*, then, he is proud or self-willed. But he is not proud or self-willed in the same sense that unbelievers are, that is, *governed* by pride or self-will. Herein he differs from unregenerate men. They *obey* sin; he does not. Flesh is in them both. But they 'walk after the flesh'; he 'walks after the Spirit'.

'But how can *unbelief* be in a *believer*?' That word has two meanings. It means either *no faith*, or *little faith*; either the *absence* of faith, or the *weakness* of it. In the former sense, unbelief is not in a believer; in the latter, it is in all babes. Their faith is commonly mixed with doubt or fear, that is (in the latter sense) with unbelief. 'Why are ye fearful,' says our Lord, 'O ye of little faith?' Again, 'O thou of little faith, wherefore didst thou doubt?' You see, here was *unbelief* in *believers*: little faith and much unbelief.

13. 'But this doctrine—that sin remains in a believer, that a man may be in the favour of God while he has sin in his heart—certainly tends to encourage men in sin.' Understand the proposition right, and no such consequence follows. A man may be in God's favour though he *feel* sin; but not if he *yields* to it. *Having sin* does not forfeit the favour of God; *giving way to sin* does. Though the flesh in *you* 'lust against the Spirit', you may still be a child of God. But if you 'walk after the flesh', you are a child of the devil. Now, this doctrine does not encourage to *obey* sin, but to *resist* it with all our might.

V.1. The sum of all is this: there are in every person, even after he is justified, two contrary principles, nature and grace, termed by St. Paul the 'flesh' and the 'spirit'. Hence although even babes in Christ are *sanctified*, yet it is only *in part*. In a degree, according to the measure of their faith, they are *spiritual*; yet in a degree they are *carnal*. Accordingly, believers are continually exhorted to watch against the flesh, as well as the world and the devil. And to this agrees the constant experience of the children of God. While they feel this witness in themselves they feel a will not wholly resigned to the will of God. They know they are in him, and yet find an heart ready to depart from him, a proneness to evil in many instances, and a backwardness to that which is good. The contrary doctrine is wholly *new*; never heard of in the church of Christ from the time of his coming into the world till the time of Count Zinzendorf. And it is attended with the most fatal consequences. It cuts off all watching against our evil nature, against the Delilah which we are told is gone, though she is still lying in our bosom. It tears away the shield of weak believers, deprives them of their faith, and so leaves them exposed to all the assaults of the world, the flesh, and the devil.

2. Let us therefore hold fast the sound doctrine 'once delivered to the saints', and delivered down by them with the written word to all succeeding generations: that although we are renewed, cleansed, purified, sanctified, the moment we truly believe in Christ, yet we are not then renewed, cleansed, purified altogether; but the flesh, the evil nature, still remains (though subdued) and wars against the Spirit. So much the more let us use all diligence in 'fighting the good fight of faith'. So much the more earnestly let us 'watch and pray' against the enemy within. The more carefully let us 'take to' ourselves and 'put on the whole armour of God'; that although 'we wrestle' both with 'flesh and blood, and with principalities and powers, and wicked spirits in high places, we may be able to withstand in the evil day, and having done all, to stand'.

53. THE REPENTANCE OF BELIEVERS

April 24, 1767

An Introductory Comment

This sermon, which was written at Londonberry and published the following year in London in 1768 (S, 2:379), should be read in light of the earlier composition "On Sin in Believers." Together they display Wesley's mature understanding of sin in a twofold way as both act (actual sins) and being (inbred sin). This duplex nature of sin is reflected in the two foci of the Wesleyan *ordo salutis* in terms of justification and entire sanctification. And John Wesley himself, not the nineteenth-century holiness movement, repeatedly employed the language of "second blessing" (in letters to Thomas Olivers, March 24, 1757 [T, 3:212–13]; Samuel Bardsley, April 3, 1772 [T, 5:315], and Jane Salkeld, August 9, 1772 [T, 5:333], for example) to express the nature of entire sanctification as a separate, distinct work of grace. Indeed, the evangelical repentance referred to in this present sermon is different from the earlier legal repentance in that it is now the carnal nature or inbred sin of which the *believer* repents on the way to heart purity.

This sermon is also an important window on Wesley's overall practical theology in two important respects. First, in this work Wesley specifically rejected a gradualist understanding of salvation as if redemption were simply an incremental process of changes by degree: "if there be no instantaneous deliverance after justification, if there be none but a gradual work of God (that there is a gradual work none denies) then we must be content, as well as we can, to remain full of sin till death" (O, 1:346). Second, in exploring the substance of a second repentance Wesley highlighted the "utter helplessness" (O, 1:345) of believers to deliver themselves from the carnal nature. Entire sanctification, then, is a gift of God's free grace and as a consequence can be received *now*: "He is willing to save you *now* . . . Only believe; and you also will immediately find, 'All things are possible to him that believeth'" (O, 1:348).

The Repentance of Believers

I. 1. Repentance means an inward change of mind from sin to holiness

2. Some say that when we first find redemption we are no longer sinners

A. Sin does not *reign*, but it does *remain*

3. Not long after we imagine all sin is gone, we feel *pride* in our hearts

4. Nor is it long before we feel *self-will* in our hearts

5. Self-will, as well as pride, is a species of idolatry

6. We must keep ourselves every moment

7. And how hard is it to conquer the desire of love and praise

8. Do we never feel jealousy, resentment, or revenge?

9. *Covetousness* in every kind and degree is contrary to the love of God

10. A conviction of this sin *remaining* is the repentance of the justified

11.–12. Many of our words are sinful, such as *uncharitable conversation*

13. And how much sin may we find cleaving to our actions also?

14. How many *sins of omission* are we chargeable with?

15. Besides outward omission, may we not find *inward defects*?

16.–18. A conviction of guilt also belongs to the children of God

19. If anyone is not satisfied of this, make the experiment

A. See whether you can expel pride, self-will, or inbred sin

20. We may *weaken* our enemies day by day, yet we cannot *drive them out*

II. 1. In this sense we are to *repent* after we are justified

2.–3. This is different from the repentance that led to justification

4. By faith in Christ, we are renewed moment by moment

5. As long as we retain faith, we 'draw water out of the wells of salvation'

6. Thus it is that in the children of God repentance and faith answer each other

III. 1. From what has been said we may easily learn:

A. We should not think we are *wholly* sanctified when we are justified

2. A conviction that we are not yet whole reveals the necessity of further change

3. A conviction of our *demerit* after we are accepted is necessary

4. So too is a deep conviction of our utter *helplessness*

Sermon 14: The Repentance of Believers, 1767

Mark 1:15

Repent and believe the gospel.

1. It is generally supposed that repentance and faith are only the gate of religion; that they are necessary only at the beginning of our Christian course, when we are setting out in the way of the kingdom. And this may seem to be confirmed by the great Apostle, where exhorting the Hebrew Christians to 'go on to perfection' he teaches them to 'leave' these first 'principles of the doctrine of Christ: not laying again the foundation of repentance from dead works and faith toward God'; which must at least mean that they should comparatively leave these, that at first took up all their thoughts, in order to 'press forward toward the prize of the high calling of God in Christ Jesus'.

2. And this is undoubtedly true, that there is a repentance and a faith which are more especially necessary at the beginning: a repentance which is a conviction of our utter sinfulness and guiltiness and helplessness, and which precedes our receiving that kingdom of God which our Lord observes 'is within us'; and a faith whereby we receive that kingdom, even 'righteousness, and peace, and joy in the Holy Ghost'.

3. But notwithstanding this, there is also a repentance and a faith (taking the words in another sense, a sense not quite the same, nor yet entirely different) which are requisite after we have 'believed the gospel'; yea, and in every subsequent stage of our Christian course, or we cannot 'run the race which is set before us'. And this repentance and faith are full as necessary, in order to our continuance and growth in grace, as the former faith and repentance were in order to our entering into the kingdom of God.

But in what sense are we to repent and believe, after we are justified? This is an important question, and worthy of being considered with the utmost attention.

I. And first, in what sense are we to repent?

1. Repentance frequently means an inward change, a change of mind from sin to holiness. But we now speak of it in a quite different sense, as it is one kind of self-knowledge—the knowing ourselves sinners, yea, guilty, helpless sinners, even though we know we are children of God.

2. Indeed when we first know this, when we first find redemption in the blood of Jesus, when the love of God is first shed abroad in our hearts and his kingdom set up therein, it is natural to suppose that we are no longer sinners, that all our sins are not only covered but destroyed. As we do not then feel any evil in our hearts, we readily imagine none is there. Nay, some well-meaning men have imagined this, not only at that time, but ever after; having persuaded themselves that when they were justified they were entirely sanctified. Yea, they have laid it down as a general rule, in spite of Scripture, reason, and experience. These sincerely believe and earnestly maintain that all sin is destroyed when we are justified, and that there is no sin in the heart of a believer, but that it is altogether clean from that moment. But though we readily acknowledge, 'he that believeth is born

of God,' and 'he that is born of God doth not commit sin,' yet we cannot allow that he does not *feel* it within: it does not *reign*, but it does *remain*. And a conviction of the sin which *remains* in our heart is one great branch of the repentance we are now speaking of.

3. For it is seldom long before he who imagined all sin was gone feels there is still *pride* in his heart. He is convinced, both that in many respects he has thought of himself more highly than he ought to think, and that he has taken to himself the praise of something he had received, and gloried in it as though he had not received it. And yet he knows he is in the favour of God. He cannot and ought not to 'cast away his confidence'. 'The Spirit still witnesses with his spirit, that he is a child of God.'

4. Nor is it long before he feels *self-will* in his heart, even a will contrary to the will of God. A will every man must inevitably have, as long as he has an understanding. This is an essential part of human nature, indeed of the nature of every intelligent being. Our blessed Lord himself had a will as a man; otherwise he had not been a man. But his human will was invariably subject to the will of his Father. At all times, and on all occasions, even in the deepest affliction, he could say, 'Not as I will, but as thou wilt.' But this is not the case at all times, even with a true believer in Christ. He frequently finds his will more or less exalting itself against the will of God. He wills something, because it is pleasing to nature, which is not pleasing to God. And he nills (is averse from) something because it is painful to nature, which is the will of God concerning him. Indeed (suppose he continues in the faith) he fights against it with all his might. But this very thing implies that it really exists, and that he is conscious of it.

5. Now self-will, as well as pride, is a species of idolatry; and both are directly contrary to the love of God. The same observation may be made concerning *the love of the world*. But this likewise even true believers are liable to feel in themselves; and every one of them does feel it, more or less, sooner or later, in one branch or another. It is true, when he first passes from death unto life he desires nothing more but God. He can truly say, 'All my desire is unto thee,' 'and unto the remembrance of thy name.' 'Whom have I in heaven but thee? And there is none upon earth that I desire besides thee?' But it is not so always. In process of time he will feel again (though perhaps only for a few moments) either 'the desire of the flesh, or the desire of the eye, or the pride of life'. Nay, if he does not continually watch and pray he may find *lust* reviving, yea, and thrusting sore at him that he may fall, till he has scarce any strength left in him. He may feel the assaults of *inordinate affection*, yea, a strong propensity to 'love the creature more than the Creator'—whether it be a child, a parent, an husband or wife, or 'the friend that is as his own soul'. He may feel in a thousand various ways a desire of earthly things or pleasures. In the same proportion he will forget God, not seeking his happiness in him, and consequently being a 'lover of pleasure more than a lover of God'.

6. If he does not keep himself every moment he will again feel 'the desire of the eye', the desire of gratifying his imagination with something great, or beautiful, or uncommon. In how many ways does this desire assault the soul! Perhaps with regard to the poorest trifles, such as dress, or furniture—things never designed to satisfy the appetite of an immortal spirit. Yet how natural it is for us, even after we 'have tasted of the powers of the world to come', to sink again into these foolish, low desires of things that perish in the

using! How hard is it, even for those who know in whom they have believed, to conquer but one branch of the desire of the eye, curiosity; constantly to trample it under their feet, to desire nothing merely because it is new!

7. And how hard is it even for the children of God wholly to conquer 'the pride of life'! St. John seems to mean by this nearly the same with what the world terms 'the sense of honour'. This is no other than a desire of and delight in 'the honour that cometh of men'—a desire and love of praise, and (which is always joined with it) a proportionable *fear of dispraise.* Nearly allied to this is *evil shame,* the being ashamed of that wherein we ought to glory. And this is seldom divided from 'the fear of man', which brings a thousand snares upon the soul. Now where is he, even among those that seem strong in faith, who does not find in himself a degree of all these evil tempers? So that even these are but in part 'crucified to the world;' for the evil root remains in their heart.

8. And do we not feel other tempers, which are as contrary to the love of our neighbour as these are to the love of God? The love of our neighbour 'thinketh no evil'. Do not we find anything of the kind? Do we never find any *jealousies,* any evil surmisings, any groundless or unreasonable suspicions? He that is clear in these respects, let him cast the first stone at his neighbour. Who does not sometimes feel other tempers or inward motions which he knows are contrary to brotherly love? If nothing of malice, hatred, or bitterness, is there no touch of envy? Particularly toward those who enjoy some (real or supposed) good which we desire but cannot attain? Do we never find any degree of *resentment* when we are injured or affronted? Especially by those whom we peculiarly loved, and whom we had most laboured to help or oblige. Does injustice or ingratitude never excite in us any desire of *revenge*; any desire of returning evil for evil, instead of 'overcoming evil with good'? This also shows how much is still in our heart which is contrary to the love of our neighbour.

9. *Covetousness* in every kind and degree is certainly as contrary to this as to the love of God. Whether φιλαργυρία, 'the love of money' which is too frequently 'the root of all evils', or πλεονεξία, literally, a desire of *having more,* or increasing in substance. And how few even of the real children of God are entirely free from both! Indeed one great man, Martin Luther, used to say he 'never had any covetousness in him (not only in his converted state, but) ever since he was born'. But if so, I would not scruple to say he was the only man born of a woman (except him that was God as well as man) who had not, who was born without it. Nay, I believe, never was anyone born of God, that lived any considerable time after, who did not feel more or less of it many times, especially in the latter sense. We may therefore set it down as an undoubted truth that *covetousness,* together with pride, and self-will, and anger, *remain* in the hearts even of them that are justified.

10. It is their experiencing this which has inclined so many serious persons to understand the latter part of the seventh chapter to the Romans, not of them that 'are under the law'—that are convinced of sin, which is undoubtedly the meaning of the Apostle—but of them that 'are under grace', that are 'justified freely, through the redemption that is in Jesus Christ'. And it is most certain they are thus far right; there does still *remain,* even in them that are justified, a 'mind' which is in some measure 'carnal' (so the Apostle tells even the believers at Corinth, 'Ye are carnal'); an heart 'bent to backsliding', still ever ready

to 'depart from the living God'; a propensity to pride, self-will, anger, revenge, love of the world, yea, and all evil: a root of bitterness which, if the restraint were taken off for a moment, would instantly spring up; yea, such a depth of corruption as without clear light from God we cannot possibly conceive. And a conviction of all this sin *remaining* in their hearts is the repentance which belongs to them that are justified.

11. But we should likewise be convinced that as sin remains in our hearts, so it *cleaves* to our words and actions. Indeed it is to be feared that many of our words are more than mixed with sin, that they are sinful altogether. For such undoubtedly is all *uncharitable conversation*, all which does not spring from brotherly love, all which does not agree with that golden rule, 'What ye would that others should do to you, even so do unto them.' Of this kind is all backbiting, all talebearing, all whispering, all evil-speaking; that is, repeating the faults of absent persons—for none would have others repeat his faults when he is absent. Now how few are there, even among believers, who are in no degree guilty of this? Who steadily observe the good old rule, 'Of the dead and the absent—nothing but good.' And suppose they do, do they likewise abstain from *unprofitable conversation*? Yet all this is unquestionably sinful, and 'grieves the Holy Spirit of God'. Yea, and for 'every idle word that men shall speak they shall give an account in the day of judgment'.

12. But let it be supposed that they continually 'watch and pray', and so do 'not enter into this temptation'; that they constantly set a watch before their mouth, and keep the door of their lips: suppose they exercise themselves herein, that *all* their 'conversation may be in grace seasoned with salt', and meet 'to minister grace to the hearers'; yet do they not daily slide into useless discourse, notwithstanding all their caution? And even when they endeavour to speak for God, are their words pure, free from unholy mixtures? Do they find nothing wrong in their very *intention*? Do they speak merely to please God, and not partly to please themselves? Is it wholly to do the will of God, and not their own will also? Or, if they begin with a single eye, do they go on 'looking unto Jesus', and talking with him all the time they are with their neighbour? When they are reproving sin do they feel no anger or unkind temper to the sinner? When they are instructing the ignorant do they not find any pride, any self-preference? When they are comforting the afflicted, or provoking one another to love and to good works, do they never perceive any inward self-commendation—'Now you have spoken well'? Or any vanity, a desire that others should think so, and esteem them on the account? In some or all of these respects how much sin *cleaves* to the best conversation even of believers! The conviction of which is another branch of the repentance which belongs to them that are justified.

13. And how much sin, if their conscience is throughly awake, may they find *cleaving to their actions* also? Nay, are there not many of these which, though they are such as the world would not condemn, yet cannot be commended, no, nor excused, if we judge by the Word of God? Are there not many of their actions which they themselves know are not 'to the glory of God'? Many wherein they did not even aim at this, which were not undertaken with an eye to God? And of those that were, are there not many wherein their eye is not singly fixed on God? Wherein they are doing their own will at least as much as his, and seeking to please themselves as much if not more than to please God? And while they are endeavouring to do good to their neighbour, do they not feel wrong tempers of

various kinds? Hence their good actions, so called, are far from being strictly such, being polluted with such a mixture of evil! Such are their works of *mercy*! And is there not the same mixture in their works of *piety*? While they are hearing the word which is able to save their souls, do they not frequently find such thoughts as make them afraid lest it should turn to their condemnation rather than their salvation? Is it not often the same case while they are endeavouring to offer up their prayers to God, whether in public, or private? Nay, while they are engaged in the most solemn service. Even while they are at the table of the Lord, what manner of thoughts arise in them? Are not their hearts sometimes wandering to the ends of the earth, sometimes filled with such imaginations as make them fear lest all their sacrifice should be an abomination to the Lord? So that they are more ashamed of their best duties than they were once of their worst sins.

14. Again: how many *sins of omission* are they chargeable with? We know the words of the Apostle, 'To him that knoweth to do good, and doth it not, to him it is sin.' But do they not know a thousand instances wherein they might have done good, to enemies, to strangers, to their brethren, either with regard to their bodies or their souls, and they did it not? How many omissions have they been guilty of in their duty toward God? How many opportunities of communicating, of hearing his word, of public or private prayer have they neglected? So great reason had even that holy man Archbishop Ussher, after all his labours for God, to cry out, almost with his dying breath, 'Lord, forgive me my sins of omission.'

15. But besides these outward omissions, may they not find in themselves *inward defects* without number? Defects of every kind: they have not the love, the fear, the confidence they ought to have toward God. They have not the love which is due to their neighbour, to every child of man; no, nor even that which is due to their brethren, to every child of God, whether those that are at a distance from them, or those with whom they are immediately connected. They have no holy temper in the degree they ought; they are defective in everything: in a deep consciousness of which they are ready to cry out with Mr. de Renty, 'I am a ground all overrun with thorns;' or with Job, 'I am vile;' 'I abhor myself, and repent as in dust and ashes.'

16. A conviction of their *guiltiness* is another branch of that repentance which belongs to the children of God. But this is cautiously to be understood, and in a peculiar sense. For it is certain, 'there is no condemnation for them that are in Christ Jesus', that believe in him, and in the power of that faith 'walk not after the flesh, but after the Spirit'. Yet can they no more bear the *strict justice* of God now than before they believed. This pronounces them to be still *worthy of death* on all the preceding accounts. And it would absolutely condemn them thereto, were it not for the atoning blood. Therefore, they are throughly convinced that they still *deserve* punishment, although it is hereby turned aside from them. But here there are extremes on one hand and on the other, and few steer clear of them. Most men strike on one or the other, either thinking themselves condemned when they are not, or thinking they *deserve* to be acquitted. Nay, the truth lies between: they still *deserve*, strictly speaking, only the damnation of hell. But what they deserve does not come upon them because they 'have an advocate with the Father'. His life and death and intercession still interpose between them and condemnation.

17. A conviction of their *utter helplessness* is yet another branch of this repentance. I mean hereby two things: (1). That they are no more able now *of themselves* to think one good thought, to form one good desire, to speak one good word, or do one good work, than before they were justified; that they have still no kind or degree of strength *of their own*, no power either to do good or resist evil; no ability to conquer or even withstand the world, the devil, or their own evil nature. They 'can', it is certain, 'do all these things'; but it is not by *their own strength*. They have power to overcome all these enemies; 'for sin hath no dominion over' them. But it is not from nature, either in whole or in part; 'it is the *mere* gift of God.' Nor is it given all at once, as if they had a stock laid up for many years, but from moment to moment.

18. By this helplessness I mean, secondly, an absolute inability to deliver ourselves from that guiltiness or desert of punishment whereof we are still conscious; yea, and an inability to remove by all the grace we have (to say nothing of our natural powers) either the pride, self-will, love of the world, anger, and general proneness to *depart from God* which we experimentally know to *remain* in the heart, even of them that are regenerate; or the evil which, in spite of all our endeavours, *cleaves* to all our words and actions. Add to this an utter inability wholly to avoid *uncharitable* and, much more, *unprofitable conversation*. Add an inability to avoid *sins of omission*, or to supply the numberless *defects* we are convinced of, especially the want of love and other right tempers both to God and man.

19. If any man is not satisfied of this, if any believes that whoever is justified is able to remove these sins out of his heart and life, let him make the experiment. Let him try whether, by the grace he has already received, he can expel pride, self-will, or inbred sin in general. Let him try whether he can cleanse his words and actions from all mixture of evil; whether he can avoid all uncharitable and unprofitable conversation, with all sins of omission; and lastly, whether he can supply the numberless defects which he still finds in himself. Let him not be discouraged by one or two experiments, but repeat the trial again and again. And the longer he tries the more deeply will he be convinced of his utter helplessness in all these respects.

20. Indeed this is so evident a truth that wellnigh all the children of God scattered abroad, however they differ in other points, yet generally agree in this, that although we may 'by the Spirit mortify the deeds of the body', resist and conquer both outward and inward sin, although we may *weaken* our enemies day by day, yet we cannot *drive them out*. By all the grace which is given at justification we cannot extirpate them. Though we watch and pray ever so much, we cannot wholly cleanse either our hearts or hands. Most sure we cannot, till it shall please our Lord to speak to our hearts again, to 'speak the second time, "Be clean"'. And then only 'the leprosy is cleansed.' Then only the evil root, the carnal mind, is destroyed, and inbred sin subsists no more. But if there be no such second change, if there be no instantaneous deliverance after justification, if there be none but a gradual work of God (that there is a gradual work none denies) then we must be content, as well as we can, to remain full of sin till death. And if so, we must remain *guilty* till death, continually *deserving* punishment. For it is impossible the guilt or desert of punishment should be removed from us as long as all this sin remains in our heart, and

cleaves to our words and actions. Nay, in rigorous justice, all we think, and speak, and act, continually increases it.

II.1. In this sense we are to *repent* after we are justified. And till we do so we can go no farther. For till we are sensible of our disease it admits of no cure. But supposing we do thus repent, then are we called to 'believe the gospel'.

2. And this also is to be understood in a peculiar sense, different from that wherein we believed in order to justification. Believe the 'glad tidings of great salvation' which God hath prepared for all people. Believe that he who is 'the brightness of his Father's glory, the express image of his person', 'is able to save unto the uttermost all that come unto God through him'. He is able to save you from all the sin that still remains in your heart. He is able to save you from all the sin that cleaves to all your words and actions. He is able to save you from sins of omission, and to supply whatever is wanting in you. It is true, 'This is impossible with man; but with [the] God-man all things are possible.' For what can be too hard for him who hath 'all power in heaven and in earth'? Indeed his bare power to do this is not a sufficient foundation for our faith that he *will* do it, that he will thus exert his power, unless he hath promised it. But this he has done: he has promised it over and over, in the strongest terms. He has given us these 'exceeding great and precious promises', both in the Old and the New Testament. So we read in the law, in the most ancient part of the oracles of God, 'The Lord thy God will circumcise thy heart, and the heart of thy seed, to love the Lord thy God with all thy heart and all thy soul' (Deut. 30:6). So in the Psalms: 'He shall redeem Israel (the Israel of God) from all his sins.' So in the Prophet: 'Then will I sprinkle clean water upon you, and ye shall be clean; from all your filthiness, and from all your idols, will I cleanse you. . . . And I will put my Spirit within you, [. . .] and ye shall keep my judgments and do them. [. . .] I will also save you from all your uncleannesses' (Ezek. 36:25, 27, 29). So likewise in the New Testament: 'Blessed be the Lord God of Israel; for he hath visited and redeemed his people, and hath raised up an horn of salvation for us. . . . To perform [. . .] the oath which he swore to our father Abraham, that he would grant unto us that we, being delivered out of the hands of our enemies, should serve him without fear, in holiness and righteousness before him, all the days of our life' (Luke 1:68-69, 72-75).

3. You have therefore good reason to believe he is not only able but *willing* to do this—to 'cleanse you from all your filthiness of flesh and spirit', to 'save you from all your uncleannesses'. This is the thing which you now long for: this is the faith which you now particularly need, namely, that the great physician, the lover of my soul, is willing to 'make me clean'. But is he willing to do this tomorrow or today? Let him answer for himself: 'Today, if ye will hear my voice, harden not your hearts.' If you put it off till tomorrow, you 'harden your hearts'; you refuse to 'hear his voice'. Believe therefore that he is willing to save you *today*. He is willing to save you *now*. 'Behold, now is the accepted time.' He now saith, 'Be thou clean!' Only believe; and you also will immediately find, 'All things are possible to him that believeth.'

4. Continue to believe in him 'that loved thee, and gave himself for thee', that 'bore all thy sins in his own body on the tree'; and he saveth thee from all condemnation, by his blood continually applied. Thus it is that we continue in a justified state. And when we go 'from faith to faith', when we have a faith to be cleansed from indwelling sin, to be saved from all our uncleannesses, we are likewise saved from all that *guilt*, that *desert* of punishment, which we felt before. So that then we may say, not only,

Every moment, Lord, I want
The merit of thy death:

but likewise, in the full assurance of faith,

Every moment, Lord, I have
The merit of thy death.

For by that faith in his life, death, and intercession for us, renewed from moment to moment, we are every whit clean, and there is not only now no condemnation for us, but no such desert of punishment as was before, the Lord cleansing both our hearts and lives.

5. By the same faith we feel the power of Christ every moment resting upon us, whereby alone we are what we are, whereby we are enabled to continue in spiritual life, and without which, notwithstanding all our present holiness, we should be devils the next moment. But as long as we retain our faith in him we 'draw water out of the wells of salvation'. Leaning on our Beloved, even Christ in us the hope of glory, who dwelleth in our hearts by faith, who likewise is ever interceding for us at the right hand of God, we receive help from him to think and speak and act what is acceptable in his sight. Thus does he 'prevent them that believe in all their doings, and further them with his continual help', so that all their designs, conversations, and actions are 'begun, continued, and ended in him'. Thus doth he 'cleanse the thoughts of their hearts, by the inspiration of his Holy Spirit, that they may perfectly love him, and worthily magnify his holy name'.

6. Thus it is that in the children of God repentance and faith exactly answer each other. By repentance we feel the sin remaining in our hearts, and cleaving to our words and actions. By faith we receive the power of God in Christ, purifying our hearts and cleansing our hands. By repentance we are still sensible that we deserve punishment for all our tempers and words and actions. By faith we are conscious that our advocate with the Father is continually pleading for us, and thereby continually turning aside all condemnation and punishment from us. By repentance we have an abiding conviction that there is no help in us. By faith we receive not only mercy, but 'grace to help in *every* time of need'. Repentance disclaims the very possibility of any other help. Faith accepts all the help we stand in need of from him that hath all power in heaven and earth. Repentance says, 'Without him I can do nothing:' faith says, 'I can do all things through Christ strength-

ening me.' Through him I cannot only overcome, but expel all the enemies of my soul. Through him I can 'love the Lord my God with all my heart, mind, soul, and strength'; yea, and walk in holiness and righteousness before him all the days of my life.

III.1. From what has been said we may easily learn the mischievousness of that opinion that we are *wholly* sanctified when we are justified; that our hearts are then cleansed from all sin. It is true we are then delivered (as was observed before) from the dominion of outward sin: and at the same time the power of inward sin is so broken that we need no longer follow or be led by it. But it is by no means true that inward sin is then totally destroyed, that the root of pride, self-will, anger, love of the world, is then taken out of the heart, or that the carnal mind and the heart bent to backsliding are entirely extirpated. And to suppose the contrary is not, as some may think, an innocent, harmless mistake. No: it does immense harm; it entirely blocks up the way to any farther change. For it is manifest, 'They that are whole do not need a physician, but they that are sick.' If therefore we think we are quite made whole already, there is no room to seek any farther healing. On this supposition it is absurd to expect a farther deliverance from sin, whether gradual or instantaneous.

2. On the contrary, a deep conviction that we are not yet whole, that our hearts are not fully purified, that there is yet in us 'a carnal mind' which is still in its nature 'enmity against God'; that a whole body of sin remains in our heart, weakened indeed, but not destroyed, shows beyond all possibility of doubt the absolute necessity of a farther change. We allow that at the very moment of justification we are 'born again': in that instant we experience that inward change from 'darkness into marvellous light'; from the image of the brute and the devil into the image of God, from the earthly, sensual, devilish mind, to the mind which was in Christ Jesus. But are we then *entirely* changed? Are we *wholly* transformed into the image of him that created us? Far from it: we still retain a depth of sin; and it is the consciousness of this which constrains us to groan for a full deliverance to him that is mighty to save. Hence it is that those believers who are not convinced of the deep corruption of their hearts, or but slightly and as it were notionally convinced, have little concern about *entire sanctification.* They may possibly hold the opinion that such a thing is to be, either at death, or some time (they know not when) before it. But they have no great uneasiness for the want of it, and no great hunger or thirst after it. They cannot, until they know themselves better, until they repent in the sense above described, until God unveils the inbred monster's face, and shows them the real state of their souls. Then only, when they feel the burden, will they groan for deliverance from it. Then and not till then will they cry out, in the agony of their soul,

Break off the yoke of inbred sin,
  And fully set my spirit free!
I cannot rest till pure within,
  Till I am wholly lost in thee!

3. We may learn from hence, secondly, that a deep conviction of our *demerit* after we are accepted (which in one sense may be termed *guilt*) is absolutely necessary in order to our seeing the true value of the atoning blood; in order to our feeling that we need this as much after we are justified as ever we did before. Without this conviction we cannot but account the blood of the covenant *as a common thing*, something of which we have not now any great need, seeing all our past sins are blotted out. Yea, but if both our hearts and lives are thus unclean, there is a kind of guilt which we are contracting every moment, and which of consequence would every moment expose us to fresh condemnation, but that

He ever lives above,
For us to intercede,
His all-atoning love,
His precious blood to plead.

It is this repentance, and the faith intimately connected with it, which are expressed in those strong lines:

I sin in every breath I draw,
Nor do thy will, nor keep thy law
On earth as angels do above:
But still the Fountain open stands,
Washes my feet, my heart, my hands,
Till I am perfected in love.

4. We may observe, thirdly, a deep conviction of our utter *helplessness*—of our total inability to retain anything we have received, much more to deliver ourselves from the world of iniquity remaining both in our hearts and lives—teaches us truly to live upon Christ by faith, not only as our Priest, but as our King. Hereby we are brought to 'magnify him', indeed, to 'give him all the glory of his grace', to 'make him a whole Christ, an entire Saviour', and truly to 'set the crown upon his head'. These excellent words, as they have frequently been used, have little or no meaning. But they are fulfilled in a strong and a deep sense when we thus, as it were, go out of ourselves, in order to be swallowed up in him; when we sink into nothing that he may be all in all. Then, his almighty grace having abolished 'every high thing which exalted itself against' him, every temper, and thought, and word, and work is 'brought to the obedience of Christ'.

Londonderry, April 24, 1767

54. THE SCRIPTURE WAY OF SALVATION

1765

An Introductory Comment

This sermon was apparently produced to counter the error of the Glasites or Sandemanians who contended that salvation simply entails an assent to the truth of the gospel, a limited view of redemption that was likely embraced by Thomas Maxfield and George Bell (S, 2:442). The sermon appeared in 1765 and was published in volume III of Wesley's collected *Works* of 1771 (S, 2:442).

Taking Ephesians 2:8 as his text for both sermons, Wesley drew a parallel between "The Scripture Way of Salvation" and "Salvation by Faith," which he had preached much earlier before Oxford University on June 11, 1738. Remarkably, both sermons raise the very same questions: "What is salvation?" and "What is that faith whereby we are saved?" though the one delivered before St. Mary's reverses this order. The third question of the two sermons, however, does indeed differ: the earlier sermon queries "how we may answer objections," while the later one asks, "How are we saved by it [faith]?"

The twenty-seven-year interim between the two sermons informs Wesley's mature theological judgment reflected in the "Scripture Way," in that in it he gave prevenient grace a distinct role; he distinguished between justification and sanctification (S, 2:443); he underscored the twofold nature of sin in terms of act and being (requiring a twofold work of grace); he stressed the necessity of entire sanctification (S, 2:443); he carefully nuanced the whole matter of repentance, works, and faith in his important distinctions "not in the same sense," "not in the same degree"; and finally Wesley once again affirmed in parallel language that entire sanctification, just like justification, is an utter gift of God and therefore can be received by grace through faith *now* (O, 2:169). Not surprisingly, Albert Outler referred to "The Scripture Way of Salvation" as "the most successful summary of the Wesleyan vision of the *ordo salutis* in the entire sermon corpus" (O, 2:154).

The Scripture Way of Salvation

1. Nothing is more complex than religion as it is often described
2. Faith and salvation comprise the substance of Scripture

I. 1. The salvation spoken about is not going to heaven; it is a present thing
2. It will include that wrought in the soul by natural conscience
3. Salvation consists of two parts: justification and sanctification
4. At the same moment we are justified, sanctification begins
5. Those experiencing such a change imagine that all sin is gone
6. But it is seldom long before they are undeceived
7. How exactly did Macarius describe the experience of God's children
8. From the time of our being born again the work of sanctification takes place
9. We wait for entire sanctification, from full salvation from our sins

II. But what is that faith through which we are saved?
1. Faith is a divine evidence and conviction of things not yet seen
2. In a more particular sense, it is a divine evidence that God was in Christ
3. This faith necessarily implies *assurance*
4. It is by this faith that we are justified and sanctified

III. 1. Faith is the only condition of justification
2. God undoubtedly commands us to *repent* and bring forth fruits
3. We are sanctified, as well as justified, by faith
4. Is there no repentance consequent on justification?
5. I do allow this and continually maintain it as the truth of God
6. Repentance consequent upon justification is different from the prior repentance
7.–8. There is clear conviction of the sin *remaining* in our hearts and lives
9. Necessary for sanctification are works of piety, such as prayer or Bible study
10. Also necessary are works of mercy, such as feeding the hungry
11. Some believe that there is no sin in believers
12. There is therefore also no danger in expecting full salvation
13. Repentance and fruits are necessary, but not in the same *degree* as faith
14. This faith is a conviction of what God has promised in Scripture
15. It is a faith that what God has promised he is *able* to perform
16. It is a faith that God is able and willing to do it *now*
17. To this confidence is added one more thing, a faith that *God does it*
18. Look for it, therefore, at every moment

Sermon 43: The Scripture Way of Salvation, 1765

Ephesians 2:8

Ye are saved through faith.

1. Nothing can be more intricate, complex, and hard to be understood, than religion as it has been often described. And this is not only true concerning the religion of the heathens, even many of the wisest of them, but concerning the religion of those also who were in some sense Christians; yea, and men of great name in the Christian world, men 'who seemed to be pillars' thereof. Yet how easy to be understood, how plain and simple a thing, is the genuine religion of Jesus Christ! Provided only that we take it in its native form, just as it is described in the oracles of God. It is exactly suited by the wise Creator and Governor of the world to the weak understanding and narrow capacity of man in his present state. How observable is this both with regard to the end it proposes and the means to attain that end! The end is, in one word, salvation: the means to attain it, faith.

2. It is easily discerned that these two little words—I mean faith and salvation—include the substance of all the Bible, the marrow, as it were, of the whole Scripture. So much the more should we take all possible care to avoid all mistake concerning them, and to form a true and accurate judgment concerning both the one and the other.

Let us then seriously inquire,

I. What is salvation?

II. What is that faith whereby we are saved? And

III. How we are saved by it.

I.1. And first let us inquire, What is *salvation*? The salvation which is here spoken of is not what is frequently understood by that word, the going to heaven, eternal happiness. It is not the soul's going to paradise, termed by our Lord 'Abraham's bosom'. It is not a blessing which lies on the other side death, or (as we usually speak) in the other world. The very words of the text itself put this beyond all question. 'Ye *are* saved.' It is not something at a distance: it is a present thing, a blessing which, through the free mercy of God, ye are now in possession of. Nay, the words may be rendered, and that with equal propriety, 'Ye *have been* saved.' So that the salvation which is here spoken of might be extended to the entire work of God, from the first dawning of grace in the soul till it is consummated in glory.

2. If we take this in its utmost extent it will include all that is wrought in the soul by what is frequently termed 'natural conscience', but more properly, 'preventing grace'; all the 'drawings' of 'the Father', the desires after God, which, if we yield to them, increase more and more; all that 'light' wherewith the Son of God 'enlighteneth everyone that cometh into the world', *showing* every man 'to do justly, to love mercy, and to walk humbly with his God'; all the *convictions* which his Spirit from time to time works in every child of man. Although it is true the generality of men stifle them as soon as possible, and after a while forget, or at least deny, that ever they had them at all.

3. But we are at present concerned only with that salvation which the Apostle is directly speaking of. And this consists of two general parts, justification and sanctification.

Justification is another word for pardon. It is the forgiveness of all our sins, and (what is necessarily implied therein) our acceptance with God. The price whereby this hath been procured for us (commonly termed the 'meritorious cause' of our justification) is the blood and righteousness of Christ, or (to express it a little more clearly) all that Christ hath done and suffered for us till 'he poured out his soul for the transgressors.' The immediate effects of justification are, the peace of God, a 'peace that passeth all understanding', and a 'rejoicing in *hope* of the glory of God', with *joy* unspeakable and full of glory'.

4. And at the same time that we are justified, yea, in that very moment, *sanctification* begins. In that instant we are 'born again', 'born from above', born of the Spirit'. There is a *real* as well as a *relative* change. We are inwardly renewed by the power of God. We feel the 'love of God shed abroad in our heart by the Holy Ghost which is given unto us', producing love to all mankind, and more especially to the children of God; expelling the love of the world, the love of pleasure, of ease, of honour, of money; together with pride, anger, self-will, and every other evil temper—in a word, changing the 'earthly, sensual, devilish' mind into 'the mind which was in Christ Jesus'.

5. How naturally do those who experience such a change imagine that all sin is gone! That it is utterly rooted out of their heart, and has no more any place therein! How easily do they draw that inference, 'I *feel* no sin; therefore I *have* none.' It does not *stir*; therefore it does not *exist*: it has no *motion*; therefore it has no *being*.

6. But it is seldom long before they are undeceived, finding sin was only suspended, not destroyed. Temptations return and sin revives, showing it was but stunned before, not dead. They now feel two principles in themselves, plainly contrary to each other: 'the flesh lusting against the spirit', nature opposing the grace of God. They cannot deny that although they still feel power to believe in Christ and to love God, and although his 'Spirit' still 'witnesses with' their 'spirits that' they 'are the children of God'; yet they feel in themselves, sometimes pride or self-will, sometimes anger or unbelief. They find one or more of these frequently *stirring* in their heart, though not *conquering*; yea, perhaps 'thrusting sore at them, that they' may 'fall; but the Lord is' their 'help'.

7. How exactly did Macarius, fourteen hundred years ago, describe the present experience of the children of God! 'The unskilful (or unexperienced), when grace operates, presently imagine they have no more sin. Whereas they that have discretion cannot deny that even we who have the grace of God may be molested again. . . . For we have often had instances of some among the brethren who have experienced such grace as to affirm that they had no sin in them. And yet after all, when they thought themselves entirely freed from it, the corruption that lurked within was stirred up anew, and they were wellnigh burnt up.'

8. From the time of our being 'born again' the gradual work of sanctification takes place. We are enabled 'by the Spirit' to 'mortify the deeds of the body', of our evil nature. And as we are more and more dead to sin, we are more and more alive to God. We go on from grace to grace, while we are careful to 'abstain from all appearance of evil', and are

'zealous of good works', 'as we have opportunity, doing good to all men'; while we walk in all his ordinances blameless, therein worshipping him in spirit and in truth; while we take up our cross and deny ourselves every pleasure that does not lead us to God.

9. It is thus that we wait for entire sanctification, for a full salvation from all our sins, from pride, self-will, anger, unbelief, or, as the Apostle expresses it, 'Go on to perfection.' But what is perfection? The word has various senses: here it means perfect love. It is love excluding sin; love filling the heart, taking up the whole capacity of the soul. It is love 'rejoicing evermore, praying without ceasing, in everything giving thanks'.

II. But what is that 'faith through which we are saved'? This is the second point to be considered.

1. Faith in general is defined by the Apostle, ἔλεγκος πραγμάτων οὐ βλεπομένων—'an evidence', a divine 'evidence and conviction' (the word means both), 'of things not seen'—not visible, not perceivable either by sight or by any other of the external senses. It implies both a supernatural *evidence* of God and of the things of God, a kind of spiritual *light* exhibited to the soul, and a supernatural *sight* or perception thereof. Accordingly the Scripture speaks sometimes of God's giving light, sometimes a power of discerning it. So St. Paul: 'God, who commanded light to shine out of darkness, hath shined in our hearts, to give us the light of the knowledge of the glory of God in the face of Jesus Christ.' And elsewhere the same Apostle speaks 'of the eyes of' our 'understanding being opened'. By this twofold operation of the Holy Spirit—having the eyes of our soul both *opened* and *enlightened*—we see the things which the natural 'eye hath not seen, neither the ear heard'. We have a prospect of the invisible things of God. We see the *spiritual world*, which is all round about us, and yet no more discerned by our natural faculties than if it had no being; and we see the *eternal world*, piercing through the veil which hangs between time and eternity. Clouds and darkness then rest upon it no more, but we already see the glory which shall be revealed.

2. Taking the word in a more particular sense, faith is a divine evidence and conviction, not only that 'God was in Christ, reconciling the world unto himself', but also that Christ 'loved *me*, and gave himself for *me*'. It is by this faith (whether we term it the *essence*, or rather a *property* thereof) that we 'receive Christ'; that we receive him in all his offices, as our Prophet, Priest, and King. It is by this that he 'is made of God unto us wisdom, and righteousness, and sanctification, and redemption'.

3. 'But is this the "faith of assurance" or "faith of adherence"?' The Scripture mentions no such distinction. The Apostle says: 'There is one faith, and one hope of our calling,' one Christian, saving faith, as 'there is one Lord' in whom we believe, and 'one God and Father of us all.' And it is certain this faith necessarily implies an *assurance* (which is here only another word for *evidence*, it being hard to tell the difference between them) that 'Christ loved *me*, and gave himself for *me*.' For 'he that believeth' with the true, living faith, 'hath the witness in himself.' 'The Spirit witnesseth with his spirit that he is a child of God.' 'Because he is a son, God hath sent forth the Spirit of his Son into his heart, crying, Abba, Father;' giving him an assurance that he is so, and a childlike confidence in

him. But let it be observed that, in the very nature of the thing, the assurance goes before the confidence. For a man cannot have a childlike confidence in God till he knows he is a child of God. Therefore confidence, trust, reliance, adherence, or whatever else it be called, is not the first, as some have supposed, but the second branch or act of faith.

4. It is by this faith we 'are saved', justified and sanctified, taking that word in its highest sense. But how are we justified and sanctified by faith? This is our third head of inquiry. And this being the main point in question, and a point of no ordinary importance, it will not be improper to give it a more distinct and particular consideration.

III.1. And first, how are we justified by faith? In what sense is this to be understood? I answer, faith is the condition, and the only condition, of justification. It is the condition: none is justified but he that believes; without faith no man is justified. And it is the only condition: this alone is sufficient for justification. Everyone that believes is justified, whatever else he has or has not. In other words: no man is justified till he believes; every man when he believes is justified.

2. 'But does not God command us to *repent* also? Yea, and to "bring forth fruits meet for repentance"? To "cease", for instance, "from doing evil", and "learn to do well"? And is not both the one and the other of the utmost necessity? Insomuch that if we willingly neglect either we cannot reasonably expect to be justified at all? But if this be so, how can it be said that faith is the only condition of justification?'

God does undoubtedly command us both to repent and to bring forth fruits meet for repentance; which if we willingly neglect we cannot reasonably expect to be justified at all. Therefore both repentance and fruits meet for repentance are in some sense necessary to justification. But they are not necessary in the *same sense* with faith, nor in the *same degree.* Not in the *same degree*; for those fruits are only necessary *conditionally*, if there be time and opportunity for them. Otherwise a man may be justified without them, as was the 'thief' upon the cross (if we may call him so; for a late writer has discovered that he was no thief, but a very honest and respectable person!). But he cannot be justified without faith: this is impossible. Likewise let a man have ever so much repentance, or ever so many of the fruits meet for repentance, yet all this does not at all avail: he is not justified till he believes. But the moment he believes, with or without those fruits, yea, with more or less repentance, he is justified. Not in the *same sense*: for repentance and its fruits are only *remotely* necessary, necessary in order to faith; whereas faith is *immediately* and *directly* necessary to justification. It remains that faith is the only condition which is *immediately* and *proximately* necessary to justification.

3. 'But do you believe we are sanctified by faith? We know you believe that we are justified by faith; but do not you believe, and accordingly teach, that we are sanctified by our works?'

So it has been roundly and vehemently affirmed for these five and twenty years. But I have constantly declared just the contrary, and that in all manner of ways. I have continually testified in private and in public that we are sanctified, as well as justified, by faith. And indeed the one of these great truths does exceedingly illustrate the other. Exactly as we are justified by faith, so are we sanctified by faith. Faith is the condition, and the only condition of sanctification, exactly as it is of justification. It is the condition: none is sanctified but he that believes; without faith no man is sanctified. And it is the only condition: this alone is sufficient for sanctification. Everyone that believes is sanctified, whatever else he has or has not. In other words: no man is sanctified till he believes; every man when he believes is sanctified.

4. 'But is there not a repentance consequent upon, as well as a repentance previous to, justification? And is it not incumbent on all that are justified to be "zealous of good works"? Yea, are not these so necessary that if a man willingly neglect them he cannot reasonably expect that he shall ever be sanctified in the full sense, that is, "perfected in love"? Nay, can he "grow" at all "in grace, in the" loving "knowledge of our Lord Jesus Christ"? Yea, can he retain the grace which God has already given him? Can he continue in the faith which he has received, or in the favour of God? Do not you yourself allow all this, and continually assert it? But if this be so, how can it be said that faith is the only condition of sanctification?'

5. I do allow all this, and continually maintain it as the truth of God. I allow there is a repentance consequent upon, as well as a repentance previous to, justification. It is incumbent on all that are justified to be zealous of good works. And these are so necessary that if a man willingly neglect them, he cannot reasonably expect that he shall ever be sanctified. He cannot 'grow in grace', in the image of God, the mind which was in Christ Jesus; nay, he cannot retain the grace he has received, he cannot continue in faith, or in the favour of God.

What is the inference we must draw herefrom? Why, that both repentance, rightly understood, and the practice of all good works, works of piety, as well as works of mercy (now properly so called, since they spring from faith) are in some sense necessary to sanctification.

6. I say 'repentance rightly understood'; for this must not be confounded with the former repentance. The repentance consequent upon justification is widely different from that which is antecedent to it. This implies no guilt, no sense of condemnation, no consciousness of the wrath of God. It does not suppose any doubt of the favour of God, or any 'fear that hath torment'. It is properly a conviction wrought by the Holy Ghost of the 'sin' which still 'remains' in our heart, of the φρόνημα σαρκός, 'the carnal mind', which 'does still *remain*', as our Church speaks, 'even in them that are regenerate'—although it does no longer *reign*, it has not now dominion over them. It is a conviction of our proneness to evil, of an heart 'bent to backsliding', of the still continuing tendency of the 'flesh' to 'lust against the Spirit'. Sometimes, unless we continually watch and pray, it lusteth to pride, sometimes to anger, sometimes to love of the world, love of ease, love of honour, or love of pleasure more than of God. It is a conviction of the tendency of our heart to self-will, to atheism, or idolatry; and above all to unbelief, whereby in a thousand ways, and under a thousand pretences, we are ever 'departing' more or less 'from the living God'.

7. With this conviction of the sin *remaining* in our hearts there is joined a clear conviction of the sin remaining in our lives, still *cleaving* to all our words and actions. In

the best of these we now discern a mixture of evil, either in the spirit, the matter, or the manner of them; something that could not endure the righteous judgment of God, were he 'extreme to mark what is done amiss'. Where we least suspected it we find a taint of pride of self-will, of unbelief or idolatry; so that we are now more ashamed of our best duties than formerly of our worst sins. And hence we cannot but feel that these are so far from having anything meritorious in them, yea, so far from being able to stand in sight of the divine justice, that for those also we should be guilty before God were it not for the blood of the covenant.

8. Experience shows that together with this conviction of sin *remaining* in our hearts and *cleaving* to all our words and actions, as well as the guilt which on account thereof we should incur were we not continually sprinkled with the atoning blood, one thing more is implied in this repentance, namely, a conviction of our helplessness, of our utter inability to think one good thought, or to form one good desire; and much more to speak one word aright, or to perform one good action but through his free, almighty grace, first preventing us, and then accompanying us every moment.

9. 'But what good works are those, the practice of which you affirm to be necessary to sanctification?' First, all works of piety, such as public prayer, family prayer, and praying in our closet; receiving the Supper of the Lord; searching the Scriptures by hearing, reading, meditating; and using such a measure of fasting or abstinence as our bodily health allows.

10. Secondly, all works of mercy, whether they relate to the bodies or souls of men; such as feeding the hungry, clothing the naked, entertaining the stranger, visiting those that are in prison, or sick, or variously afflicted; such as the endeavouring to instruct the ignorant, to awaken the stupid sinner, to quicken the lukewarm, to confirm the wavering, to comfort the feebleminded, to succour the tempted, or contribute in any manner to the saving of souls from death. This is the repentance, and these the fruits meet for repentance, which are necessary to full sanctification. This is the way wherein God hath appointed his children to wait for complete salvation.

11. Hence may appear the extreme mischievousness of that seemingly innocent opinion that 'there is no sin in a believer; that all sin is destroyed, root and branch, the moment a man is justified.' By totally preventing that repentance it quite blocks up the way to sanctification. There is no place for repentance in him who believes there is no sin either in his life or heart. Consequently there is no place for his being 'perfected in love', to which that repentance is indispensably necessary.

12. Hence it may likewise appear that there is no possible danger in *thus* expecting full salvation. For suppose we were mistaken, suppose no such blessing ever was or can be attained, yet we lose nothing. Nay, that very expectation quickens us in using all the talents which God has given us; yea, in improving them all, so that when our Lord cometh he will 'receive his own with increase'.

13. But to return. Though it be allowed that both this repentance and its fruits are necessary to full salvation, yet they are not necessary either in the *same sense* with faith or in the *same degree.* Not in the same degree; for these fruits are only necessary *conditionally,* if there be time and opportunity for them. Otherwise a man may be sanctified without

them. But he cannot be sanctified without faith. Likewise let a man have ever so much of this repentance, or ever so many good works, yet all this does not at all avail: he is not sanctified till he believes. But the moment he believes, with or without those fruits, yea, with more or less of this repentance, he is sanctified. Not in the *same sense*; for this repentance and these fruits are only *remotely* necessary, necessary in order to the continuance of his faith, as well as the increase of it; whereas faith is *immediately* and *directly* necessary to sanctification. It remains that faith is the only condition which is *immediately* and *proximately* necessary to sanctification.

14. 'But what is that faith whereby we are sanctified, saved from sin and perfected in love?' It is a divine evidence and conviction, first, that God hath promised it in the Holy Scripture. Till we are thoroughly satisfied of this there is no moving one step farther. And one would imagine there needed not one word more to satisfy a reasonable man of this than the ancient promise, 'Then will I circumcise thy heart, and the heart of thy seed, to love the Lord your God with all your heart, and with all your soul.' How clearly does this express the being perfected in love! How strongly imply the being saved from all sin! For as long as love takes up the whole heart, what room is there for sin therein?

15. It is a divine evidence and conviction, secondly, that what God hath promised he is *able* to perform. Admitting therefore that 'with men it is impossible' to bring a clean thing out of an unclean, to purify the heart from all sin, and to fill it with all holiness, yet this creates no difficulty in the case, seeing 'with God all things are possible.' And surely no one ever imagined it was possible to any power less than that of the Almighty! But if God speaks, it shall be done. God saith, 'Let there be light: and there is light.'

16. It is, thirdly, a divine evidence and conviction that he is able and willing to do it *now*. And why not? Is not a moment to him the same as a thousand years? He cannot want more time to accomplish whatever is his will. And he cannot want or stay for any more *worthiness* of *fitness* in the persons he is pleased to honour. We may therefore boldly say, at any point of time, 'Now is the day of salvation.' '*Today* if ye will hear his voice, harden not your hearts.' 'Behold! all things are now ready! Come unto the marriage!'

17. To this confidence, that God is both able and willing to sanctify us *now*, there needs to be added one thing more, a divine evidence and conviction that *he doth it*. In that hour it is done. God says to the inmost soul, 'According to thy faith be it unto thee!' Then the soul is pure from every spot of sin; 'it is clean from all unrighteousness.' The believer then experiences the deep meaning of those solemn words, 'If we walk in the light, as he is in the light, we have fellowship one with another, and the blood of Jesus Christ his Son cleanseth us from all sin.'

18. 'But does God work this great work in the soul *gradually* or *instantaneously*?' Perhaps it may be gradually wrought in some. I mean in this sense—they do not advert to the particular moment wherein sin ceases to be. But it is infinitely desirable, were it the will of God, that it should be done instantaneously; that the Lord should destroy sin 'by the breath of his mouth' in a moment, in the twinkling of an eye. And so he generally does, a plain fact of which there is evidence enough to satisfy any unprejudiced person. *Thou* therefore look for it every moment. Look for it in the way above described; in all

those 'good works' whereunto thou art 'created anew in Christ Jesus'. There is then no danger. You can be no worse, if you are no better for that expectation. For were you to be disappointed of your hope, still you lose nothing. But you shall not be disappointed of your hope: it will come, and will not tarry. Look for it then every day, every hour, every moment. Why not this hour, this moment? Certainly you may look for it *now*, if you believe it is by faith. And by this token may you surely know whether you seek it by faith or by works. If by works, you want something to be done *first, before* you are sanctified. You think, 'I must first *be* or *do* thus or thus.' Then you are seeking it by works unto this day. If you seek it by faith, you may expect it *as you are*: and if as you are, then expect it *now*. It is of importance to observe that there is an inseparable connection between these three points—expect it *by faith*, expect it *as you are*, and expect it *now*! To deny one of them is to deny them all: to allow one is to allow them all. Do *you* believe we are sanctified by faith? Be true then to your principle, and look for this blessing just as you are, neither better, nor worse; as a poor sinner that has still nothing to pay, nothing to plead but 'Christ died.' And if you look for it as you are, then expect it *now*. Stay for nothing. Why should you? Christ is ready. And he is all you want. He is waiting for you. He is at the door! Let your inmost soul cry out,

Come in, come in, thou heavenly Guest!
Nor hence again remove:
But sup with me, and let the feast
Be everlasting love.

55. THE CIRCUMCISION OF THE HEART

January 1, 1733

An Introductory Comment

This is one of the early sermons in this present collection, preached at St. Mary's, Oxford, in 1733, and it represents Wesley's careful reflections on the topic of holiness that went back to the time of 1725 to 1729 when he read the writings of the triumvirate of Jeremy Taylor, Thomas à Kempis, and William Law (T, 4:299). The text of the sermon (Rom, 2:29) was suggested by the January date with the celebration of the Feast of the Circumcision. Wesley did not publish this sermon, however, until several years later when he placed it at the head of the second volume of *Sermons on Several Occasions* in 1748. In the interim between 1733 and 1748, Wesley had come to understand both the nature and the fruits of justifying faith (in the Christian sense) more clearly, and these insights are reflected in the material added to section I.7 of the sermon (S, 1:265).

Developing the scriptural metaphor of circumcision expressed in Deuteronomy 30:6, while maintaining that sin depicts a perverted relation, Wesley remarked to Thomas Olivers in a letter drafted on March 24, 1757, "In the two sermons on this subject ['The Circumcision of the Heart' and 'Christian Perfection'], the *Minutes* of the Conference, the preface to the second and third volumes of Hymns, and some of our controversial writings, you have a full account of Christian Perfection" (T, 3:212–13). Two years later, in correspondence to John Downes on November 11, 1759, Wesley observed that "The Circumcision of the Heart" contains the "model of religion with which the Methodists set out" (T, 4:330). And finally, Wesley pointed out to John Newton on May 14, 1765, that this sermon "contains all that I now teach concerning salvation from all sin and loving God with an undivided heart" (T, 4:299).

After 1733, Wesley employed the text of Romans 2:29 four more times: thrice during the 1780s and once more not long before his death in 1791 (WWS).

The Circumcision of the Heart

I. 1. What is the circumcision of the heart?
- A. It is the disposition of the soul called 'holiness'
- B. It directly implies being cleansed from sin
- C. It also involves being endued with the virtues of Christ

2. It implies humility, faith, hope, and charity

3.–4. Without the Spirit of God we can do nothing but add sin to sin

5. It is lowliness of mind brought about by *faith*

6. The best guide of the blind is faith

7. All things are possible to those who believe

8. Such a faith reveals the power of the One who inspires it

9. Those who by faith are born of God have *hope*
- A. This is the next thing which the circumcision of the heart implies

10. By this discipline Christians are to endure hardships

11. If you are to be perfect, then add to all these things *love*
- A. Love is the fulfilling of the law, the end of the commandment

12. Not that this forbids us to love anything besides God
- A. It implies that we love our brother also
- B. Not yet does it forbid us to take pleasure in anything but God

13. Yet have no end, no ultimate end, but God

II. 1. Consider some additional reflections that naturally arise:
- A. We do not merit the praise of God unless our hearts are circumcised

2. We shall not obtain honor from God unless our hearts are circumcised by faith

3. Some spend much of their time laying another foundation
- A. They ground religion on the intrinsic *excellence* of virtue

4. But our gospel knows no other foundation of good works than faith
- A. We are not his disciples if we deny his Spirit to be the author of faith

5. We are not truly led unless the Spirit bears witness that we are children of God

6. If these things are so, then it is time for them to deal with their own souls

7. These blasphemers almost persuade some to imagine themselves guiltless

8. What less than this can we infer from the words of St. Paul

9. We may infer that his heart is circumcised by love

10. Here is the sum of the perfect law: this is true circumcision of the heart

Sermon 17: The Circumcision of the Heart

A Sermon preached at St. Mary's, Oxford, before the University, on January 1, 1733.

Romans 2:29

Circumcision is that of the heart, in the spirit and not in the letter.

1.'Tis the melancholy remark of an excellent man that 'he who now preaches the most essential duties of Christianity runs the hazard of being esteemed by a great part of his hearers "a setter forth of new doctrines".' Most men have so *lived away* the substance of that religion, the profession whereof they still retain, that no sooner are any of those truths proposed which difference the Spirit of Christ from the spirit of the world than they cry out, 'Thou bringest strange things to our ears; we would know what these things mean'—though he is only preaching to them 'Jesus, and the resurrection', with the necessary consequence of it. If Christ be risen, ye ought then to die unto the world, and to live wholly unto God.

2. A hard saying this to the 'natural man' who is alive unto the world, and dead unto God, and one that he will not readily be persuaded to receive as the truth of God, unless it be so qualified in the interpretation as to have neither use nor significancy left. He 'receiveth not the' words 'of the Spirit of God', taken in their plain and obvious meaning. 'They are foolishness unto him; neither' indeed 'can he know them, because they are spiritually discerned:' they are perceivable only by that spiritual sense which in him was never yet awakened, for want of which he must reject as idle fancies of men what are both the 'wisdom' and the 'power of God'.

3. That 'circumcision is that of the heart, in the spirit, and not in the letter', that the distinguishing mark of a true follower of Christ, of one who is in a state of acceptance with God, is not either outward circumcision or baptism, or any other outward form, but a right state of soul—a mind and spirit renewed after the image of him that created it—is one of those important truths that can only be 'spiritually discerned'. And this the Apostle himself intimates in the next words: 'Whose praise is not of men, but of God.' As if he had said, 'Expect not, whoever thou art who thus followest thy great Master, that the world, the men who follow him not, will say, "Well done, good and faithful servant!" Know that the "circumcision of the heart", the seal of thy calling, is "foolishness with the world". Be content to wait for thy applause till the day of thy Lord's appearing. In that day shalt thou "have praise of God" in the great assembly of men and angels.'

I design, first, particularly to inquire wherein this circumcision of the heart consists; and secondly to mention some reflections that naturally arise from such an inquiry.

I.1. I am first to inquire wherein that circumcision of the heart consists which will receive the praise of God. In general we may observe it is that habitual disposition of soul which in the Sacred Writings is termed 'holiness', and which directly implies the being cleansed from sin, 'from all filthiness both of flesh and spirit', and by consequence the being endued with those virtues which were also in Christ Jesus, the being so 'renewed in the image of our mind' as to be 'perfect, as our Father in heaven is perfect'.

2. To be more particular, circumcision of heart implies humility, faith, hope, and charity. Humility, a right judgment of ourselves, cleanses our minds from those high conceits of our own perfections, from the undue opinions of our own abilities and attainments which are the genuine fruit of a corrupted nature. This entirely cuts off that vain thought, 'I am rich, and wise, and have need of nothing;' and convinces us that we are by nature 'wretched, and poor, and miserable, and blind, and naked'. It convinces us that in our best estate we are of ourselves all sin and vanity; that confusion, and ignorance, and error, reign over our understanding; that unreasonable, earthly, sensual, devilish passions usurp authority over our will: in a word, that there is no whole part in our soul, that all the foundations of our nature are out of course.

3. At the same time we are convinced that we are not sufficient of ourselves to help ourselves; that without the Spirit of God we can do nothing but add sin to sin; that it is he alone 'who worketh in us' by his almighty power, either 'to will or do' that which is good—it being as impossible for us even to think a good thought without the supernatural assistance of his Spirit as to create ourselves, or to renew our whole souls in righteousness and true holiness.

4. A sure effect of our having formed this right judgment of the sinfulness and helplessness of our nature is a disregard of that 'honour which cometh of man' which is usually paid to some supposed excellency in us. He who knows himself neither desires nor values the applause which he knows he deserves not. It is therefore 'a very small thing with him to be judged by man's judgment'. He has all reason to think, by comparing what it has said either for or against him with what he feels in his own breast, that the world, as well as the god of this world, was 'a liar from the beginning'. And even as to those who are not of the world, though he would choose (if it were the will of God) that they should account of him as of one desirous to be found a faithful steward of his Lord's goods, if haply this might be a means of enabling him to be of more use to his fellow-servants, yet as this is the one end of his wishing for their approbation, so he does not at all rest upon it. For he is assured that whatever God wills he can never want instruments to perform; since he is able, even of these stones, to raise up servants to do his pleasure.

5. This is that lowliness of mind which they have learned of Christ who follow his example and tread in his steps. And this knowledge of their disease, whereby they are more and more cleansed from one part of it, pride and vanity, disposes them to embrace with a willing mind the second thing implied in 'circumcision of heart'—that faith which alone is able to make them whole, which is the one medicine given under heaven to heal their sickness.

6. The best guide of the blind, the surest light of them that are in darkness, the most perfect instructor of the foolish, is faith. But it must be such a faith as is 'mighty through God, to the pulling down of strongholds', to the overturning all the prejudices of corrupt reason, all the false maxims revered among men, all evil customs and habits, all that 'wisdom of the world' which 'is foolishness with God'; as 'casteth down imaginations'

(reasonings) 'and every high thing that exalteth itself against the knowledge of God, and bringeth into captivity every thought to the obedience of Christ'.

7. 'All things are possible to him that' thus 'believeth:' 'the eyes of his understanding being enlightened,' he *sees* what is his calling, even to 'glorify God, who hath bought him with' so high 'a price, in his body and in his spirit, which now are God's' by redemption, as well as by creation. He feels what is 'the exceeding greatness of his power' who, as he raised up Christ from the dead, so is able to quicken us—'dead in sin'—'by his Spirit which dwelleth in us'. 'This is the victory which overcometh the world, even our faith:' that faith which is not only an unshaken assent to all that God hath revealed in Scripture, and in particular to those important truths, 'Jesus Christ came into the world to save sinners;' he 'bare our sins in his own body on the tree'; 'he is the propitiation for our sins; and not for ours only, but also for the sins of the whole world' (N.B. The following part of this paragraph is now added [in 1748] to the sermon formerly preached [in 1733].); but likewise the revelation of Christ in our hearts: a divine evidence or conviction of his love, his free, unmerited love to me a sinner; a sure confidence in his pardoning mercy, wrought in us by the Holy Ghost—a confidence whereby every true believer is enabled to bear witness, 'I know that my Redeemer liveth;' that *I* 'have an advocate with the Father', that 'Jesus Christ the righteous is' *my* Lord, and 'the propitiation for *my* sins.' I know he 'hath loved *me*, and given himself for *me*'. He 'hath reconciled *me*, even *me* to God'; and *I* 'have redemption through his blood, even the forgiveness of sins'.

8. Such a faith as this cannot fail to show evidently the power of him that inspires it, by delivering his children from the yoke of sin, and 'purging their consciences from dead works'; by strengthening them so that they are no longer constrained to 'obey sin in the desires thereof'; but instead of 'yielding their members unto' it, 'as instruments of unrighteousness', they now 'yield' themselves entirely 'unto God, as those that are alive from the dead'.

9. Those who are thus by faith 'born of God' have also 'strong consolation through hope'. This is the next thing which the 'circumcision of the heart' implies—even the testimony of their own spirit with the Spirit which witnesses in their hearts, that they are the children of God. Indeed it is the same Spirit who works in them that clear and cheerful confidence that their heart is upright toward God; that good assurance that they now do, through his grace, the things which are acceptable in his sight; that they are now in the path which leadeth to life, and shall, by the mercy of God, endure therein to the end. It is he who giveth them a lively expectation of receiving all good things at God's hand—a joyous prospect of that 'crown of glory' which is 'reserved in heaven' for them. By this anchor a Christian is kept steady in the midst of the waves of this troublesome world, and preserved from striking upon either of those fatal rocks, presumption or despair. He is neither discouraged by the misconceived severity of his Lord, nor does he 'despise the richness of his goodness'. He neither apprehends the difficulties of the race set before him to be greater than he has strength to conquer, nor expects them to be so little as to yield him the conquest till he has put forth all his strength. The experience he already has in the Christian warfare, as it assures him his 'labour is not in vain' if 'whatever his hand findeth to do, he doth it with his might,' so it forbids his entertaining so vain a thought as that he

can otherwise gain any advantage, as that any virtue can be shown, any praise attained, by 'faint hearts and feeble hands'—or indeed by any but those who pursue the same course with the great Apostle of the Gentiles: 'I (says he) so run, not as uncertainly; so fight I, not as one that beateth the air. But I keep under my body, and bring it into subjection; lest by any means when I have preached to others, I myself should be a castaway.'

10. By the same discipline is every good soldier of Christ to 'inure himself to endure hardships'. Confirmed and strengthened by this, he will be able not only to renounce 'the works of darkness', but every appetite, too, and every affection which is not subject to the law of God. For 'everyone', saith St. John, 'who hath this hope purifieth himself, even as he is pure.' It is his daily care, by the grace of God in Christ, and through the blood of the covenant, to purge the inmost recesses of his soul from the lusts that before possessed and defiled it: from uncleanness, and envy, and malice, and wrath, from every passion and temper that is 'after the flesh', that either springs from or cherishes his native corruption; as well knowing that he whose very 'body is the temple of God' ought to admit into it nothing common or unclean; and that 'holiness becometh' that 'house for ever' where the Spirit of holiness vouchsafes to dwell.

11. Yet lackest thou one thing, whosoever thou art, that to a deep humility and a steadfast faith hast joined a lively hope, and thereby in a good measure cleansed thy heart from its inbred pollution. If thou wilt be perfect, add to all these charity: add love, and thou hast the 'circumcision of the heart'. 'Love is the fulfilling of the law,' 'the end of the commandment'. Very excellent things are spoken of love; it is the essence, the spirit, the life of all virtue. It is not only the first and great command, but it is all the commandments in one. Whatsoever things are just, whatsoever things are pure, whatsoever things are amiable or honourable; if there be any virtue, if there be any praise, they are all comprised in this one word—love. In this is perfection and glory and happiness. The royal law of heaven and earth is this, 'Thou shalt love the Lord thy God with all thy heart, and with all thy soul, and with all thy mind, and with all thy strength.'

12. Not that this forbids us to love anything besides God: it implies that we 'love our brother also'. Nor yet does it forbid us (as some have strangely imagined) to take pleasure in anything but God. To suppose this is to suppose the fountain of holiness is directly the author of sin, since he has inseparably annexed pleasure to the use of those creatures which are necessary to sustain the life he has given us. This therefore can never be the meaning of his command. What the real sense of it is both our blessed Lord and his apostles tell us too frequently and too plainly to be misunderstood. They all with one mouth bear witness that the true meaning of those several declarations—'The Lord thy God is one Lord; thou shalt have no other gods but me,' 'Thou shalt love the Lord thy God with all thy strength,' 'Thou shalt cleave unto him;' 'The desire of thy soul shall be to his name'—is no other than this. The one perfect good shall be your ultimate end. One thing shall ye desire for its own sake—the fruition of him that is all in all. One happiness shall ye propose to your souls, even an union with him that made them, the having 'fellowship with the Father and the Son', the being 'joined to the Lord in one Spirit'. One design ye are to pursue to the end of time—the enjoyment of God in time and in eternity. Desire other things so far as they tend to this. Love the creature—as it leads to the Creator. But in every step you take

be this the glorious point that terminates your view. Let every affection, and thought, and word, and work, be subordinate to this. Whatever ye desire or fear, whatever ye seek or shun, whatever ye think, speak, or do, be it in order to your happiness in God, the sole end as well as source of your being.

13. Have no end, no ultimate end, but God. Thus our Lord: 'One thing is needful.' And if thine eye be singly fixed on this one thing, 'thy whole body shall be full of light.' Thus St. Paul: 'This one thing I do; [. . .] I press toward the mark, for the prize of the high calling in Christ Jesus.' Thus St. James: 'Cleanse your hands, ye sinners, and purify your hearts, ye double-minded.' Thus St. John: 'Love not the world, neither the things that are in the world. [. . .] For all that is in the world, the lust of the flesh, the lust of the eye, and the pride of life, is not of the Father, but is of the world.' The seeking happiness in what gratifies either the desire of the flesh, by agreeably striking upon the outward senses; the desire of the eye, of the imagination, by its novelty, greatness, or beauty; or the pride of life, whether by pomp, grandeur, power, or the usual consequence of them, applause and admiration: 'is not of the Father'—cometh not from, neither is approved by, the Father of spirits—'but of the world'—it is the distinguishing mark of those who will not have him reign over them.

II.1. Thus have I particularly inquired what that 'circumcision of the heart' is which will obtain the praise of God. I am in the second place to mention some reflections that naturally arise from such an inquiry, as a plain rule whereby every man may judge himself whether he be of the world or of God.

And, first, it is clear from what has been said that no man has a title to the praise of God unless his heart is circumcised by humility, unless he is little, and base, and vile in his own eyes; unless he is deeply convinced of that inbred 'corruption of his nature, whereby he is very far gone from original righteousness', being prone to all evil, averse to all good, corrupt and abominable; having a 'carnal mind', which 'is enmity against God, and is not subject to the Law of God, nor indeed can be'; unless he continually feels in his inmost soul that without the Spirit of God resting upon him he can neither think, nor desire, nor speak, nor act, anything good or well-pleasing in his sight.

No man, I say, has a title to the praise of God till he feels his want of God: nor indeed till he seeketh that 'honour, which cometh of God only', and neither desires nor pursues that which cometh of man, unless so far only as it tends to this.

2. Another truth which naturally follows from what has been said is that none shall obtain the honour that cometh of God unless his heart be circumcised by faith, even a 'faith of the operation of God'; unless, refusing to be any longer led by his senses, appetites, or passions, or even by that blind leader of the blind, so idolized by the world, natural reason, he lives and 'walks by faith', directs every step as 'seeing him that is invisible', 'looks not at the things that are seen, which are temporal, but at the things that are not seen, which are eternal'; and governs all his desires, designs, and thoughts, all his actions and conversations, as one who is entered in within the veil, where Jesus sits at the right hand of God.

3. It were to be wished that they were better acquainted with this faith who employ much of their time and pains in laying another foundation, in grounding religion on 'the eternal *fitness* of things', on 'the intrinsic *excellence* of virtue', and the *beauty* of actions flowing from it—on the *reasons*, as they term them, of good and evil, and the *relations* of beings to each other. Either these accounts of the grounds of Christian duty coincide with the scriptural or not. If they do, why are well-meaning men perplexed, and drawn from the weightier matters of the law by a cloud of terms whereby the easiest truths are explained into obscurity? If they are not, then it behoves them to consider who is the author of this new doctrine, whether he is likely to be 'an angel from heaven' who 'preacheth another gospel' than that of Christ Jesus—though if he were, God, not we, hath pronounced his sentence: 'Let him be accursed!'

4. Our gospel, as it knows no other foundation of good works than faith, or of faith than Christ, so it clearly informs us we are not his disciples while we either deny him to be the author or his Spirit to be the inspirer and perfecter both of our faith and works. 'If any man have not the Spirit of Christ, he is none of his.' He alone can quicken those who are dead unto God, can breathe into them the breath of Christian life, and so prevent, accompany, and follow them with his grace as to bring their good desires to good effect. And 'as many as are thus led by the Spirit of God, they are the sons of God.' This is God's short and plain account of true religion and virtue; and 'other foundation can no man lay.'

5. From what has been said we may, thirdly, learn that none is truly 'led by the Spirit' unless that 'Spirit bear witness with his spirit, that he is a child of God'; unless he see the prize and the crown before him, and 'rejoice in hope of the glory of God': so greatly have they erred who have taught that in serving God we ought not to have a view to our own happiness. Nay, but we are often and expressly taught of God to have 'respect unto the recompense of reward', to balance the toil with the 'joy set before us', these 'light afflictions' with that 'exceeding weight of glory'. Yea, we are 'aliens to the covenant of promise', we are 'without God in the world', until God of 'his abundant mercy hath begotten us again unto a living hope' of the 'inheritance incorruptible, undefiled, and that fadeth not away'.

6. But if these things are so, 'tis high time for those persons to deal faithfully with their own souls—who are so far from finding in themselves this joyful assurance, that they fulfil the terms and shall obtain the promises of that covenant, as to quarrel with the covenant itself, and blaspheme the terms of it, to complain they are too severe, and that no man ever did or shall live up to them! What is this but to reproach God, as if he were an hard master requiring of his servants more than he enables them to perform; as if he had mocked the helpless works of his hands by binding them to impossibilities, by commanding them to overcome where neither their own strength nor his grace was sufficient for them?

7. These blasphemers might almost persuade those to imagine themselves guiltless who, in the contrary extreme, hope to fulfil the commands of God without taking any pains at all. Vain hope! that a child of Adam should ever expect to see the kingdom of Christ and of God without striving, without '*agonizing*' first 'to enter in at the strait gate'! That one who was 'conceived and born in sin', and whose 'inward parts are very wickedness', should once entertain a thought of being 'purified as his Lord is pure' unless

he 'tread in his steps', and 'take up his cross daily'; unless he 'cut off the right hand', and 'pluck out the right eye and cast it from him'; that he should ever dream of shaking off his old opinions, passions, tempers, of being 'sanctified throughout in spirit, soul, and body', without a constant and continued course of general self-denial!

8. What less than this can we possibly infer from the above cited words of St. Paul, who, 'living in "infirmities, in reproaches, in necessities, in persecutions, in distresses" for Christ's sake, who being full of "signs, and wonders, and mighty deeds", who having been "caught up into the third heaven", yet reckoned' (as a late author strongly expresses it) that 'all his virtues' would be 'insecure, and' even 'his salvation in danger, without this constant self-denial. [. . .] "So run I", says he, "not as uncertainly; so fight I, not as one that beateth the air." By which he plainly teaches us that he who does not thus run, who does not thus' deny himself daily, does 'run uncertainly, and fighteth to as little purpose as he that "beateth the air".'

9. To as little purpose does he talk of 'fighting the fight of faith', as vainly hope to attain the crown of incorruption (as we may, lastly, infer from the preceding observations), whose heart is not circumcised by love. Cutting off both the lust of the flesh, the lust of the eye, and the pride of life, engaging the whole man, body, soul, and spirit, in the ardent pursuit of that one object, is so essential to a child of God that 'without it whosoever liveth is counted dead before him.' 'Though I speak with the tongues of men and angels, and have not love, I am as sounding brass, or a tinkling cymbal. Though I have the gift of prophecy, and understand all mysteries, and all knowledge, and though I have all faith so as to remove mountains, and have not love, I am nothing. Nay, though I give all my goods to feed the poor, and my body to be burned, and have not love, it profiteth me nothing.'

10. Here then is the sum of the perfect law: this is the true 'circumcision of the heart'. Let the spirit return to God that gave it, with the whole train of its affections. 'Unto the place from whence all the rivers came, thither' let them flow again. Other sacrifices from us he would not; but the living sacrifice of the heart he hath chosen. Let it be continually offered up to God through Christ, in flames of holy love. And let no creature be suffered to share with him: for he is a jealous God. His throne will he not divide with another: he will reign without a rival. Be no design, no desire admitted there but what has him for its ultimate object. This is the way wherein those children of God once walked, who being dead still speak to us: 'Desire not to live but to praise his name; let all your thoughts, words, and works tend to his glory. Set your heart firm on him, and on other things only as they are in and from him.' 'Let your soul be filled with so entire a love of him that you may love nothing but for his sake.' 'Have a pure intention of heart, a steadfast regard to his glory in all your actions.' 'Fix your eye upon the blessed hope of your calling, and make all the things of the world minister unto it.' For then, and not till then, is that 'mind in us which was also in Christ Jesus', when in every motion of our heart, in every word of our tongue, in every work of our hands, we 'pursue nothing but in relation to him, and in subordination to his pleasure'; when we, too, neither think, nor speak, nor act, to fulfil our 'own will, but the will of him that sent us'; when whether we 'eat, or drink, or whatever we do, we do all to the glory of God'.

56. WANDERING THOUGHTS

1762

An Introductory Comment

Though Wesley began to explore the topic of wandering thoughts in 1757, in order to clear up some misunderstanding in terms of the doctrine of Christian perfection, he did not preach on this theme until three years later at Spitalfields, London, and then the following year at West Street Chapel (WWS). The sermon was published in 1762 by Elizabeth Farley, and it appeared the next year as William Pine brought forth a second edition of *Sermons on Several Occasions* (O, 2:125).

Wesley had been criticized for making the path to heaven much too difficult. Indeed, Rev. James Clark, a presbyter in the diocese of Tuam, Ireland, accused Wesley and the Methodists (who were known in Ireland as "Swaddlers") of reviving the ancient heresy of Montanism in their discipline and rigor. This present sermon, then, is in some sense a response to Clark's sermon preached on 1 John 4:1 in the parish church at Hollymount in 1756 and published in Dublin in 1760 as *Montanus Redivivus; or Montanism Revived, in the Principles and Discipline of the Methodists.*

No doubt with his critics in mind, Wesley made a distinction between the wandering thoughts from which the pure in heart can expect to be delivered and those thoughts from which they will not be set free. The former consist of those ideas and reflections that depart from the living God, which arise therefore out of sinful tempers, and are expressed in such things as murmuring or repining; angry, malicious, or revengeful thoughts; or pride, vanity, lust, and covetousness (O, 2:127–29). The latter, by way of contrast, are made up of those thoughts that "wander from the particular point we have in hand," and the sanctity of the soul, however lofty, will by no means deliver from these. Wesley concluded the sermon, which has 2 Corinthians 10:5 as its text, with a prayer that the Methodists may be "cleansed from all pollution of flesh and spirit" to the glory of God (O, 2:137).

Wandering Thoughts

I. 1. What are the several sorts of wandering thoughts?
   A. First, there are thoughts that wander from God
   B. Second, there are thoughts that wander from the point at hand
 2. With regard to the former, all our thoughts are naturally of this kind
 3. Often we are not only without God in the world but are fighting against him
 4. The latter thoughts occur when my mind runs from one circumstance to another

II. What are the general occasions of wandering thoughts?
 1.–2. The occasions of the former sort are sinful tempers: pride, anger, lust, etc.
 3.–7. The occasions of the latter sort are exceedingly various
   A. Multitudes are occasioned by the union of soul and body
   B. How deeply is the understanding affected by a diseased body
 8. The latter sort will also arise from the impulses of outward objects
 9. Evil spirits make use of all these occasions to hurry and distract our minds

III. What kind of thoughts are sinful?
 1. All thoughts which wander from God are undoubtedly sinful
 2. All thoughts which spring from sinful tempers are undoubtedly sinful
 3. And so must those be which either produce or feed any sinful temper
 4. Even thoughts occasioned by sickness but producing sinful tempers are sinful
 5. But thoughts wherein our understanding wanders from the point in view are not
 6. If they wander by means of other things affecting our senses they are innocent
 7. None of these types of wandering thoughts are inconsistent with perfect love

IV. What kind of thoughts may we expect and pray to be delivered from?
 1. From thoughts that wander from God, those perfect in love are delivered
 2. Those that wander from the point of view in mind are widely different
 3.–4. Suppose a soul, however holy, dwells in a distempered body
   A. Will not all the thoughts be wild, as long as that disorder continues?
 5. Only when we lie down in the dust shall we be delivered from such thoughts
 6. As long as evil spirits roam a disordered world they shall attack its inhabitants
 7. Do not expect deliverance from wandering caused by spirits, men, or sickness
 8. Let us pray that all these things may work together for our good

Sermon 41: Wandering Thoughts, 1762

2 Corinthians 10:5

Bringing into captivity every thought
to the obedience of Christ

1. But will God so 'bring every thought into captivity to the obedience of Christ' that no wandering thought will find a place in the mind, even while we remain in the body? So some have vehemently maintained; yea, have affirmed that none are perfected in love unless they are so far perfected in understanding that all wandering thoughts are done away; unless not only every affection and temper be holy, and just, and good, but every individual thought which arises in the mind be wise and regular.

2. This is a question of no small importance. For how many of those who fear God, yea, and love him, perhaps with all their heart, have been greatly distressed on this account! How many, by not understanding it right, have not only been distressed, but greatly hurt in their souls! Cast into unprofitable, yea, mischievous reasonings, such as slackened their motion towards God, and weakened them in running the race set before them. Nay, many, through misapprehensions of this very thing, have cast away the precious gift of God. They have been induced first to doubt of, and then to deny, the work God had wrought in their souls; and hereby have grieved the Spirit of God, till he withdrew and left them in utter darkness.

3. How is it, then, that amidst the abundance of books which have been lately published almost on all subjects, we should have none upon 'wandering thoughts'? At least none that will at all satisfy a calm and serious mind? In order to do this in some degree I purpose to inquire,

I. What are the several sorts of wandering thoughts?

II. What are the general occasions of them?

III. Which of them are sinful, and which not?

IV. Which of them we may expect and pray to be delivered from?

I.1. I purpose to inquire, first, What are the several sorts of wandering thoughts? The particular sorts are innumerable; but in general they are of two sorts—thoughts that wander from God, and thoughts that wander from the particular point we have in hand.

2. With regard to the former, all our thoughts are naturally of this kind. For they are continually wandering from God: we think nothing about him. God is not in all our thoughts: we are one and all, as the Apostle observes, 'without God in the world'. We think of what we love; but we do not love God; therefore we think not of him. Or if we are now and then constrained to think of him for a time, yet as we have no pleasure therein, nay, rather, as these thoughts are not only insipid, but distasteful and irksome to us, we drive them out as soon as we can, and return to what we love to think of. So that the world and the things of the world—what we shall eat, what we shall drink, what we

shall put on, what we shall see, what we shall hear, what we shall gain, how we shall please our senses or our imagination—takes up all our time, and engrosses all our thoughts. So long therefore as we love the world, that is, so long as we are in our natural state, all our thoughts from morning to evening, and from evening to morning, are no other than wandering thoughts.

3. But many times we are not only 'without God in the world', but also 'fighting against him', as there is in every man by nature 'a carnal mind which is enmity against God'. No wonder, therefore, that men abound with *unbelieving* thoughts, either saying in their hearts, There is no God, or questioning, if not denying, his power or wisdom, his mercy, or justice, or holiness. No wonder that they so often doubt of his providence, at least of its extending to all events; or that, even though they allow it, they still entertain *murmuring* or *repining* thoughts. Nearly related to these, and frequently connected with them, are *proud* and *vain* imaginations. Again: sometimes they are taken up with *angry, malicious,* or *revengeful* thoughts; at other times with airy scenes of pleasure, whether of sense or imagination; whereby the earthy sensual mind becomes more *earthy* and *sensual* still. Now by all these they make flat war with God; these are wandering thoughts of the highest kind.

4. Widely different from these are the other sort of wandering thoughts, in which the heart does not wander from God, but the understanding wanders from the particular point it had then in view. For instance: I sit down to consider those words in the verse preceding the text, 'The weapons of our warfare are not carnal, but mighty through God.' I think, 'This ought to be the case with all that are called Christians. But how far is it otherwise! Look round into almost every part of what is termed the Christian world! What manner of weapons are these using? In what kind of warfare are they engaged,

> While men, like fiends, each other tear
> In all the hellish rage of war?

See how *these* Christians love one another. Wherein are they preferable to Turks and pagans? What abomination can be found among Mahometans or heathens which is not found among Christians also?' And thus my mind runs off, before I am aware, from one circumstance to another. Now all these are in some sense wandering thoughts; for although they do not wander from God, much less fight against him, yet they do wander from the particular point I had in view.

II. Such is the nature, such are the sorts (to speak rather usefully than philosophically) of wandering thoughts. But what are the general occasions of them? This we are in the second place to consider.

1. And it is easy to observe that the occasion of the former sort of thoughts which oppose or wander from God are, in general, sinful tempers. For instance: why 'is not God in all the thoughts', in any of the thoughts, of a natural man? For a plain reason: be he rich

or poor, learned or unlearned, he is an atheist (though not vulgarly so called)—he neither knows nor loves God. Why are his thoughts continually wandering after the world? Because he is an idolater. He does not indeed worship an image, or bow down to the stock of a tree; yet is he sunk into equally damnable idolatry: he loves, that is, worships the world. He seeks happiness in the things that are seen, in the pleasures that perish in the using. Why is it that his thoughts are perpetually wandering from the very end of his being, the knowledge of God in Christ? Because he is an unbeliever; because he has no faith, or at least no more than a devil. So all these wandering thoughts easily and naturally spring from that evil root of unbelief.

2. The case is the same in other instances: pride, anger, revenge, vanity, lust, covetousness—every one of them occasion[s] thoughts suitable to their own nature. And so does every sinful temper of which the human kind is capable. The particulars it is hardly possible, nor is it needful, to enumerate. It suffices to observe that as many evil tempers as find a place in any soul, so many ways that soul will depart from God, by the worst kind of wandering thoughts.

3. The occasions of the latter kind of wandering thoughts are exceeding various. Multitudes of them are occasioned by the natural union between the soul and body. How immediately and how deeply is the understanding affected by a diseased body! Let but the blood move irregularly in the brain, and all regular thinking is at an end. Raging madness ensues, and then farewell to all evenness of thought. Yea, let only the spirits be hurried or agitated to a certain degree, and a temporary madness, a delirium, prevents all settled thought. And is not the same irregularity of thought in a measure occasioned by every nervous disorder? So does 'the corruptible body press down the soul, and cause it to muse about many things'.

4. But does it only cause this in the time of sickness or preternatural disorder? Nay, but more or less at all times, even in a state of perfect health. Let a man be ever so healthy, he will be more or less delirious every four and twenty hours. For does he not sleep? And while he sleeps is he not liable to dream? And who then is master of his own thoughts, or able to preserve the order and consistency of them? Who can then keep them fixed to any one point, or prevent their wandering from pole to pole?

5. But suppose we are awake, are we always so awake that we can steadily govern our thoughts? Are we not unavoidably exposed to contrary extremes by the very nature of this machine, the body? Sometimes we are too heavy, too dull and languid, to pursue any chain of thought. Sometimes, on the other hand, we are too lively. The imagination, without leave, starts to and fro, and carries us away, hither and thither, whether we will or no; and all this from the merely natural motion of the spirits, or vibration of the nerves.

6. Farther: how many wanderings of thought may arise from those various associations of our ideas which are made entirely without our knowledge and independently on our choice! How these connections are formed we cannot tell; but they are formed in a thousand different manners. Nor is it in the power of the wisest or holiest of men to break those associations, or to prevent what is the necessary consequence of them, and matter

of daily observation. Let the fire but touch one end of the train, and it immediately runs on to the other.

7. Once more: let us fix our attention as studiously as we are able on any subject, yet let either pleasure or pain arise, especially if it be intense, and it will demand our immediate attention, and attach our thought to itself. It will interrupt the steadiest contemplation, and divert the mind from its favourite subject.

8. These occasions of wandering thoughts lie within, are wrought into our very nature. But they will likewise naturally and necessarily arise from the various impulse[s] of outward objects. Whatever strikes upon the organ of sense, the eye or ear, will raise a perception in the mind. And accordingly, whatever we see or hear will break in upon our former train of thought. Every man, therefore, that does anything in our sight, or speaks anything in our hearing, occasions our mind to wander more or less from the point it was thinking of before.

9. And there is no question but those evil spirits who are continually 'seeking whom they may devour' make use of all the foregoing occasions to hurry and distract our minds. Sometimes by one, sometimes by another of these means, they will harass and perplex us, and, so far as God permits, interrupt our thoughts, particularly when they are engaged on the best subjects. Nor is this at all strange: they well understand the very springs of thought, and know on which of the bodily organs the imagination, the understanding, and every other faculty of the mind, more immediately depends. And hereby they know how, by affecting those organs, to affect the operations dependent on them. Add to this that they can inject a thousand thoughts without any of the preceding means; it being as natural for spirit to act upon spirit as for matter to act upon matter. These things being considered, we cannot wonder that our thought so often wanders from any point which we have in view.

III.1. What kind of wandering thoughts are sinful, and what not, is the third thing to be inquired into. And, first, all those thoughts which wander from God, which leave him no room in our minds, are undoubtedly sinful. For all these imply practical atheism, and by these we are without God in the world. And so much more are all those which are contrary to God, which imply opposition or enmity to him. Such are all murmuring, discontented thoughts, which say, in effect, 'We will not have thee to rule over us;' all unbelieving thoughts, whether with regard to his being, his attributes, or his providence. I mean his particular providence over all things as well as all persons in the universe: that without which 'not a sparrow falls to the ground', by which 'the hairs of our head are all numbered'. For as to a general providence (vulgarly so called) contradistinguished from a particular, it is only a decent, well-sounding word, which means just nothing.

2. Again: all thoughts which spring from sinful tempers are undoubtedly sinful. Such, for instance are those that spring from a revengeful temper, from pride, or lust, or vanity. 'An evil tree cannot bring forth good fruit;' therefore if the tree be evil, so must the fruit be also.

3. And so must those be which either produce or feed any sinful temper; those which either give rise to pride or vanity, to anger or love of the world, or confirm and increase these or any other unholy temper, passion, or affection. For not only whatever flows from evil is evil, but also whatever leads to it; whatever tends to alienate the soul from God, and to make or keep it 'earthly, sensual, and devilish'.

4. Hence even those thoughts which are occasioned by weakness or disease, by the natural mechanism of the body, or by the laws of vital union, however innocent they may be in themselves, do nevertheless become sinful when they either produce or cherish and increase in us any sinful temper—suppose the desire of the flesh, the desire of the eye, or the pride of life. In like manner the wandering thoughts which are occasioned by the words or actions of other men, if they cause or feed any wrong disposition, then commence sinful. And the same we may observe of those which are suggested or injected by the devil. When they minister to any earthly or devilish temper (which they do whenever we give place to them, and thereby make them our own) then they are equally sinful with the tempers to which they minister.

5. But abstracting from these cases, wandering thoughts in the latter sense of the word—that is, thoughts wherein our understanding wanders from the point it has in view—are no more sinful than the motion of the blood in our veins, or of the spirits in our brain. If they arise from an infirm constitution or from some accidental weakness or distemper they are as innocent as it is to have a weak constitution or a distempered body. And surely no one doubts but a bad state of nerves, a fever of any kind, and either a transient or a lasting delirium, may consist with perfect innocence. And if they should arise in a soul which is united to a healthful body, either from the natural union between the body and soul, or from any of ten thousand changes which may occur in those organs of the body that minister to thought—in any of these cases they are as perfectly innocent as the causes from which they spring. And so they are when they spring from the casual, involuntary associations of our ideas.

6. If our thoughts wander from the point we had in view by means of other men variously affecting our senses, they are equally innocent still: for it is no more a sin to understand what I see and hear, and in many cases cannot help seeing, hearing, and understanding, than it is to have eyes and ears. 'But if the devil injects wandering thoughts, are not those thoughts evil?' They are troublesome, and in that sense evil; but they are not sinful. I do not know that he spoke to our Lord with an audible voice; perhaps he spoke to his heart only when he said, 'All these things will I give thee, if thou wilt fall down and worship me.' But whether he spoke inwardly or outwardly, our Lord doubtless understood what he said. He had therefore a thought correspondent to those words. But was it a sinful thought? We know it was not. 'In him was no sin,' either in action, or word, or thought. Nor is there any sin in a thousand thoughts of the same kind which Satan may inject into any of our Lord's followers.

7. It follows that none of these wandering thoughts (whatever unwary persons have affirmed, thereby grieving whom the Lord had not grieved) are inconsistent with perfect love. Indeed if they were, then not only sharp pain, but sleep itself would be inconsistent with it. Sharp pain; for whenever this supervenes, whatever we were before thinking of, it

will interrupt our thinking, and of course draw our thoughts into another channel. Yea, and sleep itself, as it is a state of insensibility and stupidity; and such as is generally mixed with thoughts wandering over the earth, loose, wild, and incoherent. Yet certainly these are consistent with perfect love: so then are all wandering thoughts of this kind.

IV.1. From what has been observed it is easy to give a clear answer to the last question—what kind of wandering thoughts we may expect and pray to be delivered from.

From the former sort of wandering thoughts, those wherein the heart wanders from God; from all that are contrary to his will, or that leave us without God in the world, everyone that is perfected in love is unquestionably delivered. This deliverance therefore we may expect; this we may, we ought to pray for. Wandering thoughts of this kind imply unbelief, if not enmity against God. But both of these he will destroy, will bring utterly to an end. And, indeed, from all sinful wandering thoughts we shall be absolutely delivered. All that are perfected in love are delivered from these; else they were not saved from sin. Men and devils will tempt them all manner of ways; but they cannot prevail over them.

2. With regard to the latter sort of wandering thoughts the case is widely different. Till the cause is removed we cannot in reason expect the effect should cease. But the causes or occasions of these will remain as long as we remain in the body. So long therefore we have all reason to believe the effects will remain also.

3. To be more particular. Suppose a soul, however holy, to dwell in a distempered body; suppose the brain be so throughly disordered as that raging madness follows; will not all the thoughts be wild and unconnected, as long as that disorder continues? Suppose a fever occasions that temporary madness which we term a delirium, can there be any just connection of thought till that delirium is removed? Yea, suppose what is called a nervous disorder to rise to so high a degree as occasions at least a partial madness, will there not be a thousand wandering thoughts? And must not these irregular thoughts continue as long as the disorder which occasions them?

4. Will not the case be the same with regard to those thoughts that necessarily arise from violent pain? They will more or less continue while that pain continues, by the inviolable order of nature. This order likewise will obtain where the thoughts are disturbed, broken, or interrupted, by any defect of the apprehension, judgment, or imagination, flowing from the natural constitution of the body. And how many interruptions may spring from the unaccountable and involuntary associations of our ideas! Now all these are directly or indirectly caused by the corruptible body pressing down the mind. Nor therefore can we expect them to be removed till 'this corruptible shall put on incorruption.'

5. And then only, when we lie down in the dust, shall we be delivered from those wandering thoughts which are occasioned by what we see and hear among those by whom we are now surrounded. To avoid these we must go out of the world. For as long as we remain therein, as long as there are men and women round about us, and we have eyes to see and ears to hear, the things which we daily see and hear will certainly affect our mind, and will more or less break in upon and interrupt our preceding thoughts.

6. And as long as evil spirits roam to and fro in a miserable, disordered world, so long they will assault (whether they can prevail or no) every inhabitant of flesh and blood. They will trouble even those whom they cannot destroy: they will attack, if they cannot conquer. And from these attacks of our restless, unwearied enemies, we must not look for an entire deliverance till we are lodged 'where the wicked cease from troubling, and where the weary are at rest'.

7. To sum up the whole: to expect deliverance from those wandering thoughts which are occasioned by evil spirits is to expect that the devil should die or fall asleep; or at least should no more go about as a roaring lion. To expect deliverance from those which are occasioned by other men is to expect either that men should cease from the earth, or that *we* should be absolutely secluded from them, and have no intercourse with them; or that having eyes we should not see, neither hear with our ears, but be as senseless as stocks or stones. And to pray for deliverance from those which are occasioned by the body is in effect to pray that we may leave the body. Otherwise it is praying for impossibilities and absurdities; praying that God would reconcile contradictions by continuing our union with a corruptible body without the natural, necessary consequences of that union. It is as if we should pray to be angels and men, mortal and immortal, at the same time. Nay, but when that which is immortal is come, mortality is done away.

8. Rather let us pray, both with the spirit and with the understanding, that 'all' these 'things may work together for our good'; that we may suffer all infirmities of our nature, all the interruptions of men, all the assaults and suggestions of evil spirits, and in all be 'more than conquerors'. Let us pray that we may be delivered from all sin; that both root and branch may be destroyed; that we may be 'cleansed from all pollution of flesh and spirit', from every evil temper and word and work; that we may 'love the Lord our God with all our heart, with all our mind, with all our soul, and with all our strength'; that all 'the fruit of the Spirit' may be found in us—not only 'love, joy, peace'; but also 'long-suffering, gentleness, goodness; fidelity, meekness, temperance.' Pray that all 'these things may flourish and abound', may increase in you more and more, till an abundant 'entrance be ministered unto you into the everlasting kingdom of our Lord Jesus Christ'!

57. CHRISTIAN PERFECTION

1741

An Introductory Comment

Some eight years after the publication of "The Circumcision of the Heart," Wesley composed this present sermon, once again on the topic of entire sanctification. The sermon register indicates that it was likely preached only once during Wesley's career, in 1741 to be exact (WWS), with the result that the contents of this sermon were communicated to the Methodists principally in a printed form. A second edition appeared in 1743, which was published by Gooding of Newcastle (S, 2:147). Wesley, however, had already employed the text of this sermon, Philippians 3:12, as he described the perfect Christian—informed by Clement of Alexandria's depiction in his *Stromateis* (O, 2:98)—in his own work *The Character of a Methodist* produced in 1739. Much later, in 1784, Wesley took up this same theme once more in his "On Perfection," a sermon that took Hebrews 6:1 as its text and one that Wesley employed numerous times.

One of the more remarkable characteristics of this sermon, given its purpose, is that Wesley spent considerable time displaying what are the gifts and graces of a *child of God* on the way to perfection: "even babes in Christ are in such a sense perfect, or 'born of God' . . . as, first not to commit sin" (O, 2:105). Again, the lowest sense of those who are justified and born of God, as Wesley put it, is that they "do not 'continue in sin'" (O, 2:106). And to those who would take exception to his basic gospel truth by citing 1 John 1:8, "If we say that we have no sin, we deceive ourselves" (O, 2:115), Wesley pointed out that "the tenth verse ['If we say we have not sinned'] fixes the sense of the eighth" (O, 2:115). Wesley marked the distinction between freedom from the *guilt* of sin (justification), the *power* of sin (regeneration), and the *being* of sin (Christian perfection) in his sermons "On Sin in Believers," and "The Repentance of Believers."

Christian Perfection

I. 1. First, I will show in what sense Christians are *not* perfect

A. Scripture and experience show they are not perfect in knowledge

2.–3. Innumerable are the things which they do not know

4. They are not free from mistake; it is an unavoidable consequence

5.–6. With regard to the Holy Scriptures, even the best are liable to mistake

A. We no more expect anyone to be *infallible* than *omniscient*

7. To ignorance and error we may add infirmities

8.–9. Lastly, we are not free from temptation

II. 1. Second, I will show in what sense Christians are perfect

2. Babes in Christ are in some sense perfect; but I speak of mature Christians

3. The Word of God declares that those born again do not continue in sin

4.–9. The least which can be implied is that we are made free from outward sin

10. But does not Solomon declare, 'There is no man that sinneth not'?

A. I answer: so it was in the days of Solomon

11. We should note the difference between the Jewish and Christian dispensation

12. Peter testifies that salvation from sin was not given until Jesus was glorified

13.–18. The Holy Ghost is now given; the salvation of God is given through Jesus

19.–20. If we confess our sins, God cleanses us from all unrighteousness

21. Those strong in the Lord are perfect, first, in being freed from evil thoughts

22.–23. Why should evil thoughts proceed in the servant who is as his master?

A. If his heart is no longer evil, then evil thoughts cannot proceed from it

24. As Christians are freed from evil thoughts, they are freed from evil tempers

25. Every real Christian can say with St. Paul, 'I am crucified with Christ'

A. This verse describes deliverance from inward as well as outward sin

26. He who lives in true believers has purified their hearts by faith

27. Jesus saves his people from their sins, both outward and inward

28. Christians are saved in the world from all sin and from all unrighteousness

29. Thus the Lord fulfills the things which he spoke by his holy prophets

30. Let us press forward toward the mark for the prize of the high calling of God

Sermon 40: Christian Perfection, 1741

Philippians 3:12

Not as though I had already attained,

either were already perfect.

1. There is scarce any expression in Holy Writ which has given more offence than this. The word 'perfect' is what many cannot bear. The very sound of it is an abomination to them. And whosoever 'preaches perfection' (as the phrase is), i.e. asserts that it is attainable in this life, runs great hazard of being accounted by them worse than a heathen man or a publican.

2. And hence some have advised, wholly to lay aside the use of those expressions, 'because they have given so great offence'. But are they not found in the oracles of God? If so, by what authority can any messenger of God lay them aside, even though all men should be offended? We have not so learned Christ; neither may we thus give place to the devil. Whatsoever God hath spoken, that will we speak, whether men will hear or whether they will forbear: knowing that then alone can any minister of Christ be 'pure from the blood of all men', when he hath 'not shunned to declare unto them all the counsel of God'.

3. We may not therefore lay these expressions aside, seeing they are the words of God, and not of man. But we may and ought to explain the meaning of them, that those who are sincere of heart may not err to the right hand or to the left from the mark of the prize of their high calling. And this is the more needful to be done because in the verse already repeated the Apostle speaks of himself as not perfect: 'Not', saith he, 'as though I were already perfect.' And yet immediately after, in the fifteenth verse, he speaks of himself, yea and many others, as perfect. 'Let us', saith he, 'as many as be perfect, be thus minded.'

4. In order therefore to remove the difficulty arising from this seeming contradiction, as well as to give light to them who are pressing forward to the mark, and that those who are lame be not turned out of the way, I shall endeavour to show,

First, in what sense Christians are *not*, and

Secondly, in what sense they *are*, perfect.

I.1. In the first place I shall endeavour to show in what sense Christians are *not perfect.* And both from experience and Scripture it appears, first, that they are not perfect in knowledge: they are not *so* perfect in this life as to be free from ignorance. They know, it may be, in common with other men, many things relating to the present world; and they know, with regard to the world to come, the general truths which God hath revealed. They know likewise (what 'the natural man receiveth not', for these things 'are spiritually discerned') 'what manner of love it is wherewith the Father hath loved them, that they should be called the sons of God'. They know 'the mighty working of his Spirit' in their hearts, and the wisdom of his providence directing all their paths, and causing all things to work together for their good. Yea, they know in every circumstance of life what the

Lord requireth of them, and how 'to keep a conscience void of offence both toward God and toward man'.

2. But innumerable are the things which they know not. 'Touching the Almighty himself', 'they cannot search him out to perfection.' 'Lo, these are but a part of his ways; but the thunder of his power who can understand?' They cannot understand, I will not say, how 'there are three that bear record in heaven, the Father, the Son, and the Holy Spirit, and these three are one;' or how the eternal Son of God 'took upon himself the form of a servant'; but not any one attribute, not any one circumstance of the divine nature. Neither is it for them 'to know the times and seasons' when God will work his great works upon the earth; no, not even those which he hath in part revealed, by his servants the prophets, since the world began. Much less do they know when God, having 'accomplished the number of his elect, will hasten his kingdom'; when 'the heavens shall pass away with a great noise, and the elements shall melt with fervent heat.'

3. They know not the reasons even of many of his present dispensations with the sons of men; but are constrained to rest here, though 'clouds and darkness are round about him, righteousness and judgment are the habitation of his seat.' Yea, often with regard to his dealings with themselves doth their Lord say unto them, 'What I do, thou knowest not now; but thou shalt know hereafter.' And how little do they know of what is ever before them, of even the visible works of his hands! How 'he spreadeth the north over the empty place, and hangeth the earth upon nothing.' How he unites all the parts of this vast machine by a secret chain which cannot be broken. So great is the ignorance, so very little the knowledge of even the best of men.

4. No one then is so perfect in this life as to be free from ignorance. Nor, secondly, from mistake, which indeed is almost an unavoidable consequence of it; seeing those who 'know but in part' are ever liable to err touching the things which they know not. 'Tis true the children of God do not mistake as to the things essential to salvation. They do not 'put darkness for light, or light for darkness', neither 'seek death in the error of their life'. For they are 'taught of God', and the way which he teaches them, the way of holiness, is so plain that 'the wayfaring man, though a fool, need not err therein.' But in things unessential to salvation they do err, and that frequently. The best and wisest of men are frequently mistaken even with regard to facts; believing those things not to have been which really were, or those to have been done which were not. Or suppose they are not mistaken as to the fact itself, they may be with regard to its circumstances; believing them, or many of them, to have been quite different from what in truth they were. And hence cannot but arise many farther mistakes. Hence they may believe either past or present actions which were or are evil to be good; and such as were or are good to be evil. Hence also they may judge not according to truth with regard to the characters of men; and that not only by supposing good men to be better, or wicked men to be worse, than they are, but by believing them to have been or to be good men who were or are very wicked; or perhaps those to have been or to be wicked men who were or are holy and unreprovable.

5. Nay, with regard to the Holy Scriptures themselves, as careful as they are to avoid it, the best of men are liable to mistake, and do mistake day by day; especially with respect to those parts thereof which less immediately relate to practice. Hence even the children of

God are not agreed as to the interpretation of many places in Holy Writ; nor is their difference of opinion any proof that they are not the children of God on either side. But it is a proof that we are no more to expect any living man to be *infallible* than to be *omniscient.*

6. If it be objected to what has been observed under this and the preceding head that St. John speaking to his brethren in the faith says, 'Ye have an unction from the Holy One, and know all things' (1 John 2:20), the answer is plain—'Ye know all things that are needful for your soul's health.' That the Apostle never designed to extend this farther, that he could not speak it in an absolute sense, is clear first from hence: that otherwise he would describe the disciple as 'above his Master'; seeing Christ himself, as man, knew not all things. 'Of that hour', saith he, 'knoweth no man, no, not the Son, but the Father only.' It is clear, secondly, from the Apostle's own words that follow: 'These things have I written unto you concerning them that deceive you,' as well as from his frequently repeated caution, 'Let no man deceive you,' which had been altogether needless had not those very persons who had that unction from the Holy One been liable not to ignorance only but to mistake also.

7. Even Christians therefore are not *so* perfect as to be free either from ignorance or error. We may, thirdly, add: nor from infirmities. Only let us take care to understand this word aright. Let us not give that soft title to known sins, as the manner of some is. So, one man tells us, 'Every man has his infirmity, and mine is drunkenness.' Another has the infirmity of uncleanness; another of taking God's holy name in vain; and yet another has the infirmity of calling his brother, 'Thou fool,' or returning 'railing for railing'. It is plain that all you who thus speak, if ye repent not, shall with your infirmities go quick into hell. But I mean hereby not only those which are properly termed 'bodily infirmities', but all those inward or outward imperfections which are not of a moral nature. Such are weakness or slowness of understanding, dullness or confusedness of apprehension, incoherency of thought, irregular quickness or heaviness of imagination. Such (to mention no more of this kind) is the want of a ready or of a retentive memory. Such in another kind are those which are commonly in some measure consequent upon these: namely slowness of speech, impropriety of language, ungracefulness of pronunciation—to which one might add a thousand nameless defects either in conversation or behaviour. These are the infirmities which are found in the best of men in a larger or smaller proportion. And from these none can hope to be perfectly freed till the spirit returns to God that gave it.

8. Nor can we expect till then to be wholly free from temptation. Such perfection belongeth not to this life. It is true, there are those who, being given up to work all uncleanness with greediness, scarce perceive the temptations which they resist not, and so seem to be without temptation. There are also many whom the wise enemy of souls, seeing [them] to be fast asleep in the dead form of godliness, will not tempt to gross sin, lest they should awake before they drop into everlasting burnings. I know there are also children of God who, being now 'justified freely', having found 'redemption in the blood of Christ', for the present feel no temptation. God hath said to their enemies, 'Touch not mine anointed, and do my children no harm.' And for this season, it may be for weeks or months, he causeth them to 'ride on high places'; he beareth them as on eagles' wings, above all the fiery darts of the wicked one. But this state will not last always, as we may

learn from that single consideration that the Son of God himself, in the days of his flesh, was tempted even to the end of his life. Therefore so let his servant expect to be; for 'it is enough that he be as his Master.'

9. Christian perfection therefore does not imply (as some men seem to have imagined) an exemption either from ignorance or mistake, or infirmities or temptations. Indeed, it is only another term for holiness. They are two names for the same thing. Thus everyone that is perfect is holy, and everyone that is holy is, in the Scripture sense, perfect. Yet we may, lastly, observe that neither in this respect is there any absolute perfection on earth. There is no 'perfection of degrees', as it is termed; none which does not admit of a continual increase. So that how much soever any man hath attained, or in how high a degree soever he is perfect, he hath still need to 'grow in grace', and daily to advance in the knowledge and love of God his Saviour.

II.1. In what sense then are Christians perfect? This is what I shall endeavour, in the second place, to show. But it should be premised that there are several stages in Christian life as well as in natural: some of the children of God being but new-born babes, others having attained to more maturity. And accordingly St. John, in his first Epistle (1 John 2:12 etc.), applies himself severally to those he terms little children, those he styles young men, and those whom he entitles fathers. 'I write unto you, little children', saith the Apostle, 'because your sins are forgiven you;' because thus far ye have attained, being 'justified freely', you 'have peace with God, through Jesus Christ'. 'I write unto you, young men, because ye have overcome the wicked one;' or (as he afterwards adds) 'because ye are strong, and the word of God abideth in you.' Ye have quenched the fiery darts of the wicked one, the doubts and fears wherewith he disturbed your first peace, and the witness of God that your sins are forgiven now 'abideth in your heart'. 'I write unto you, fathers, because ye have known him that is from the beginning.' Ye have known both the Father and the Son and the Spirit of Christ in your inmost soul. Ye are 'perfect men, being grown up to the measure of the stature of the fullness of Christ'.

2. It is of these chiefly I speak in the latter part of this discourse; for these only are properly Christians. But even babes in Christ are in such a sense perfect, or 'born of God' (an expression taken also in divers senses) as, first, not to commit sin. If any doubt of this privilege of the sons of God, the question is not to be decided by abstract reasonings, which may be drawn out into an endless length, and leave the point just as it was before. Neither is it to be determined by the experience of this or that particular person. Many may suppose they do not commit sin when they do, but this proves nothing either way. 'To the law and to the testimony' we appeal. 'Let God be true, and every man a liar.' By his Word will we abide, and that alone. Hereby we ought to be judged.

3. Now the Word of God plainly declares that even those who are justified, who are born again in the lowest sense, do not 'continue in sin'; that they cannot 'live any longer therein' (Rom. 6:1, 2); that they are 'planted together in the likeness of the death of Christ' (Rom. 6:5); that their 'old man is crucified with him, the body of sin being destroyed, so that thenceforth they do not serve sin'; that 'being dead with Christ, they are freed from

sin' (Rom. 6:6, 7); that they are 'dead unto sin', and 'alive unto God' (Rom. 6:11); that 'sin hath not dominion over them', who are 'not under the law, but under grace'; but that these, 'being made free from sin, are become the servants of righteousness' (Rom. 6:15, 18).

4. The very least which can be implied in these words is that the persons spoken of therein, namely all real Christians or believers in Christ, are made free from outward sin. And the same freedom which St. Paul here expresses in such variety of phrases St. Peter expresses in that one: 'He that hath suffered in the flesh hath ceased from sin; that he no longer should live . . . to the desires of men, but to the will of God' (1 Pet. 4:1-2). For this 'ceasing from sin', if it be interpreted in the lowest sense, as regarding only the outward behaviour, must denote the ceasing from the outward act, from any outward transgression of the law.

5. But most express are the well-known words of St. John in the third chapter of his first Epistle (verse eight, etc.): 'He that committeth sin is of the devil; for the devil sinneth from the beginning. For this purpose the Son of God was manifested, that he might destroy the works of the devil. Whosoever is born of God doth not commit sin; for his seed remaineth in him, and he cannot sin, because he is born of God.' And those in the fifth, verse eighteen: 'We know that whosoever is born of God sinneth not. But he that is begotten of God keepeth himself, and that wicked one toucheth him not.'

6. Indeed it is said this means only, he sinneth not *wilfully*; or he doth not commit sin *habitually*; or, *not as other men do*; or, *not as he did before*. But by whom is this said? By St. John? No. There is no such word in the text, nor in the whole chapter, nor in all this Epistle, nor in any part of his writings whatsoever. Why, then, the best way to answer a bold assertion is simply to deny it. And if any man can prove it from the Word of God, let him bring forth his strong reasons.

7. And a sort of reason there is which has been frequently brought to support these strange assertions, drawn from the examples recorded in the Word of God: 'What!', say they, 'did not Abraham himself commit sin, prevaricating and denying his wife? Did not Moses commit sin when he provoked God "at the waters of strife"? Nay, to produce one for all, did not even David, "the man after God's own heart", commit sin in the matter of Uriah the Hittite, even murder and adultery?' It is most sure he did. All this is true. But what is it you would infer from hence? It may be granted, first, that David, in the general course of his life, was one of the holiest men among the Jews. And, secondly, that the holiest men among the Jews *did sometimes commit sin*. But if you would hence infer that *all Christians do, and must commit sin, as long as they live*, this consequence we utterly deny. It will never follow from those premises.

8. Those who argue thus seem never to have considered that declaration of our Lord: 'Verily I say unto you, among them that are born of women there hath not risen a greater than John the Baptist. Notwithstanding, he that is least in the kingdom of heaven is greater than he' (Matt. 11:11). I fear indeed there are some who have imagined 'the kingdom of heaven' here to mean the kingdom of glory. As if the Son of God had just discovered to us that the least glorified saint in heaven is greater than any man upon earth! To mention

this is sufficiently to refute it. There can therefore no doubt be made but 'the kingdom of heaven' here (as in the following verse, where it is said to be 'taken by force') or, 'the kingdom of God', as St. Luke expresses it, is that kingdom of God on earth whereunto all true believers in Christ, all real Christians, belong. In these words then our Lord declares two things. First, that before his coming in the flesh among all the children of men, there had not been one greater than John the Baptist; whence it evidently follows that neither Abraham, David, nor any Jew was greater than John. Our Lord, secondly, declares that he which is least in the kingdom of God (in that kingdom which he came to set up on earth, and which 'the violent' now began 'to take by force') is greater than he. The plain consequence is, the least of these who have now Christ for their King is greater than Abraham or David or any Jew ever was. None of them was ever greater than John. But the least of these is greater than he. Not 'a greater prophet' (as some have interpreted the word), for this is palpably false in fact, but greater in the grace of God and the knowledge of our Lord Jesus Christ. Therefore we cannot measure the privileges of real Christians by those formerly given to the Jews. 'Their ministration' (or dispensation) we allow 'was glorious'; but ours 'exceeds in glory'. So that whosoever would bring down the Christian dispensation to the Jewish standard, whosoever gleans up the examples of weakness recorded in the law and the prophets, and thence infers that they who have 'put on Christ' are endued with no greater strength, doth 'greatly err, neither knowing the Scriptures nor the power of God'.

9. 'But are there not assertions in Scripture which prove the same thing, if it cannot be inferred from those examples? Does not the Scripture say expressly, "Even a just man sinneth seven times a day"?' I answer, No. The Scripture says no such thing. There is no such text in all the Bible. That which seems to be intended is the sixteenth verse of the twenty-fourth chapter of the Proverbs, the words of which are these: 'A just man falleth seven times, and riseth up again.' But this is quite another thing. For, first, the words 'a day' are not in the text. So that if a just man falls seven times in his life it is as much as is affirmed here. Secondly, here is no mention of 'falling into sin' at all: what is here mentioned is 'falling into temporal affliction'. This plainly appears from the verse before, the words of which are these: 'Lay not wait, O wicked man, against the dwelling of the righteous; spoil not his resting place.' It follows, 'For a just man falleth seven times, and riseth up again: but the wicked shall fall into mischief.' As if he had said, 'God will deliver him out of his trouble. But when thou fallest, there shall be none to deliver thee.'

10. But, however, in other places, continue the objectors, Solomon does assert plainly, 'There is no man that sinneth not' (1 Kgs. 8:46; 2 Chron. 6:36); yea, 'there is not a just man upon earth that doth good, and sinneth not' (Eccles. 7:20). I answer: Without doubt, thus it was in the days of Solomon. Yea, thus it was from Adam to Moses, from Moses to Solomon, and from Solomon to Christ. There was *then* no man that sinned not. Even from the day that sin entered into the world there was not a just man upon earth that did good and sinned not, *until* the Son of God was manifested 'to take away our sins'. It is unquestionably true that 'the heir, as long as he is a child, differeth nothing from a servant.' And that 'even so' they (all the holy men of old who were under the Jewish dispensation) 'were', during that infant state of the church, 'in bondage under the elements of the world. But when the fullness of the time was come, God sent forth his Son, made under the law,

to redeem them that were under the law, that they might receive the adoption of sons'; that they might receive that 'grace which is now made manifest by the appearing of our Saviour, Jesus Christ, who hath abolished death, and brought life and immortality to light through the gospel' (2 Tim. 1:10). Now therefore they 'are no more servants, but sons'. So that, whatsoever was the case of those under the law, we may safely affirm with St. John that since the gospel was given, 'He that is born of God sinneth not.'

11. It is of great importance to observe, and that more carefully than is commonly done, the wide difference there is between the Jewish and the Christian dispensation, and that ground of it which the same Apostle assigns in the seventh chapter of his Gospel, verse thirty-eight, etc. After he had there related those words of our blessed Lord, 'He that believeth on me, as the Scripture hath said, out of his belly shall flow rivers of living water,' he immediately subjoins, 'This spake he of the Spirit,' οὗ ἔμελλον λαμβάνειν οἱ πιστεύοντες εἰς αὐτόν, 'which they who should believe on him were afterwards to receive. For the Holy Ghost was not yet given, because that Jesus was not yet glorified.' Now the Apostle cannot mean here (as some have taught) that the miracle-working power of the Holy Ghost was not yet given. For this was given: our Lord had given it to all his apostles when he first sent them forth to preach the gospel. He then gave them 'power over unclean spirits to cast them out', power to 'heal the sick', yea, to 'raise the dead'. But the Holy Ghost was not yet given in his sanctifying graces, as he was after Jesus was glorified. It was then when 'he ascended up on high, and led captivity captive', that he 'received those gifts for men, yea, even for the rebellious, that the Lord God might dwell among them.' And 'when the day of Pentecost was fully come', then first it was that they who 'waited for the promise of the Father' were made more than conquerors over sin by the Holy Ghost given unto them.

12. That this great salvation from sin was not given till Jesus was glorified St. Peter also plainly testifies, where speaking of his 'brethren in the flesh' as now 'receiving the end of their faith, the salvation of their souls', he adds: 'Of which salvation the prophets have inquired and searched diligently, who prophesied of the grace (i.e. the gracious dispensation) that should come unto you; searching what, or what manner of time, the Spirit of Christ which was in them did signify, when it testified beforehand the sufferings of Christ and the glory (the glorious salvation) that should follow. Unto whom it was revealed that not unto themselves, but unto us they did minister the things which are now reported unto you by them that have preached the gospel unto you with the Holy Ghost sent down from heaven' (viz., at the day of Pentecost, and so unto all generations, into the hearts of all true believers). On this ground, even 'the grace which was brought unto them by the revelation of Jesus Christ', the Apostle might well build that strong exhortation, 'Wherefore, girding up the loins of your mind, . . . as he which hath called you is holy, so be ye holy in all manner of conversation' (1 Pet. 1:9, 10, etc.).

13. Those who have duly considered these things must allow that the privileges of Christians are in no wise to be measured by what the Old Testament records concerning those who were under the Jewish dispensation, seeing the fullness of times is now come, the Holy Ghost is now given, the great salvation of God is brought unto men by the revelation of Jesus Christ. The kingdom of heaven is now set up on earth; concerning which

the Spirit of God declared of old (so far is David from being the pattern or standard of Christian perfection), 'He that is feeble among them at that day, shall be as David; and the house of David shall be as God, as the angel of the Lord before them' (Zech. 12:8).

14. If therefore you would prove that the Apostle's words, 'He that is born of God sinneth not,' are not to be understood according to their plain, natural, obvious meaning, it is from the New Testament you are to bring your proofs; else you will fight as one that beateth the air. And the first of these which is usually brought is taken from the examples recorded in the New Testament. 'The Apostles themselves (it is said) committed sin; nay the greatest of them, Peter and Paul: St. Paul by his sharp contention with Barnabas, and St. Peter by his dissimulation at Antioch.' Well; suppose both Peter and Paul did then commit sin. What is it you would infer from hence? That *all the other apostles* committed sin sometimes? There is no shadow of proof in this. Or would you thence infer that *all the other Christians* of the apostolic age committed sin? Worse and worse. This is such an inference as one would imagine a man in his senses could never have thought of. Or will you argue thus?—'If two of the apostles did once commit sin, then *all other Christians, in all ages,* do, and will commit sin as long as they live.' Alas, my brother! a child of common understanding would be ashamed of such reasoning as this. Least of all can you with any colour of argument infer that any man *must* commit sin at all. No; God forbid we should thus speak. No necessity of sinning was laid upon *them.* The grace of God was surely sufficient for them. And it *is* sufficient for *us* at this day. With the temptation which fell on *them* that *was* a way to escape, as there *is* to every soul of man in every temptation; so that whosoever is tempted to any sin *need* not yield; for no man is tempted above that he is able to bear.

15. 'But St. Paul besought the Lord thrice, and yet he could not escape from his temptation.' Let us consider his own words literally translated: 'There was given to me a thorn, to the flesh, an angel or messenger of Satan, to buffet me. Touching this I besought the Lord thrice, that it (or he) might depart from me. And he said unto me, My grace is sufficient for thee: for my strength is made perfect in weakness. Most gladly therefore will I rather glory in these my weaknesses, that the strength of Christ may rest upon me. Therefore I take pleasure in weaknesses . . . ; for when I am weak, then am I strong.'

16. As this Scripture is one of the strongholds of the patrons of sin, it may be proper to weigh it thoroughly. Let it be observed then, first, it does by no means appear that this thorn, whatsoever it was, occasioned St. Paul to commit sin, much less laid him under any necessity of doing so. Therefore from hence it can never be proved that any Christian *must* commit sin. Secondly, the ancient Fathers inform us it was bodily pain: 'a violent head-ache', saith Tertullian (*De Pudicitia,* [§ 13]), to which both Chrysostom and St. Jerome agree. St. Cyprian expresses it a little more generally, in those terms, 'many and grievous torments of the flesh and of the body' ('*Carnis et corporis multa ac gravia tormenta*', *De Mortalitate*). Thirdly, to this exactly agree the Apostle's own words, 'A thorn to the flesh to smite, beat, or buffet me. . . . My strength is made perfect in weakness'—which same word occurs no less than four times in these two verses only. But, fourthly, whatsoever it was, it could not be either inward or outward sin. It could no more be inward stirrings than outward expressions of pride, anger, or lust. This is manifest beyond all possible exception

from the words that immediately follow: 'Most gladly will I glory in these my weaknesses, that the strength of Christ rested upon me.' What! Did he glory in pride, in anger, in lust? Was it through these 'weaknesses' that the strength of Christ rested upon him? He goes on: 'Therefore I take pleasure in weaknesses; for when I am weak, then am I strong;' i.e. when I am weak *in body*, then am I strong *in spirit*. But will any man dare to say, When I am weak by pride or lust, then am I strong in spirit? I call you all to record this day, who find the strength of Christ resting upon you, can *you* glory in anger, or pride, or lust? Can *you* take pleasure in *these* infirmities? Do *these* weaknesses make you strong? Would you not leap into hell, were it possible, to escape them? Even by yourselves, then, judge whether the Apostle could glory and take pleasure in them! Let it be, lastly, observed, that this thorn was given to St. Paul 'above fourteen years' before he wrote this Epistle, which itself was wrote several years before he finished his course. So that he had after this a long course to run, many battles to fight, many victories to gain, and great increase to receive in all the gifts of God and the knowledge of Jesus Christ. Therefore from any spiritual weakness (if such it had been) which he *at that time* felt, we could by no means infer that he was never made strong, that Paul the aged, the father in Christ, still laboured under the same weaknesses; that he was in no higher state till the day of his death. From all which it appears that this instance of St. Paul is quite foreign to the question, and does in no wise clash with the assertion of St. John, 'He that is born of God sinneth not.'

17. 'But does not St. James directly contradict this? His words are, "In many things we offend all" (Jas. 3:2). And is not *offending* the same as *committing sin*?' In this place I allow it is. I allow *the persons here spoken of* did commit sin; yea, that they *all* committed *many* sins. But who are 'the persons here spoken of'? Why, those 'many masters' or 'teachers' whom God had not sent (probably the same 'vain men' who taught that 'faith without works' which is so sharply reproved in the preceding chapter); not the Apostle himself, nor any real Christian. That in the word 'we' (used by a figure of speech common in all other as well as the inspired writings) the Apostle could not possibly include himself or any other true believer appears evidently, first, from the use of the same word in the ninth verse: 'Therewith (saith he) bless *we* God and therewith curse *we* men. Out of the same mouth proceedeth blessing and cursing.' True; but not out of the mouth of the Apostle, nor of anyone who is in Christ a new creature. Secondly, from the verse immediately preceding the text, and manifestly connected with it: 'My brethren, be not many masters (or teachers), knowing that *we* shall receive the greater condemnation: for in many things *we* offend all.' 'We'! Who? Not the apostles, not true believers; but they who know they should 'receive the greater condemnation' because of those many offences. But this could not be spoke of the Apostle himself, or of any who trod in his steps, seeing 'there is no condemnation for them who walk not after the flesh, but after the Spirit.' Nay, thirdly, the very verse itself proves that 'we offend all' cannot be spoken either of all men, or of all Christians; for in it there immediately follows the mention of a man who 'offends not', as the 'we' first mentioned did; from whom therefore he is professedly contradistinguished, and pronounced 'a perfect man'.

18. So clearly does St. James explain himself and fix the meaning of his own words. Yet, lest anyone should still remain in doubt, St. John, writing many years after St. James,

puts the matter entirely out of dispute by the express declarations above recited. But here a fresh difficulty may arise. How shall we reconcile St. John with himself? In one place he declares, 'Whosoever is born of God doth not commit sin.' And again, 'We know that he which is born of God sinneth not.' And yet in another he saith, 'If we say that we have no sin, we deceive ourselves, and the truth is not in us.' And again, 'If we say that we have not sinned we make him a liar, and his word is not in us.'

19. As great a difficulty as this may at first appear, it vanishes away if we observe, first, that the tenth verse fixes the sense of the eighth: 'If we say we have no sin' in the former being explained by, 'If we say we have not sinned' in the latter verse. Secondly, that the point under present consideration is not whether we *have or have not sinned heretofore*, and neither of these verses asserts that we *do sin, or commit sin* now. Thirdly, that the ninth verse explains both the eighth and tenth: 'If we confess our sins, he is faithful and just to forgive us our sins, and to cleanse us from all unrighteousness.' As if he had said, 'I have before affirmed, "The blood of Jesus Christ cleanseth us from all sin." But let no man say, I need it not; I have no sin to be cleansed from. If we say "that we have no sin", "that we have not sinned", we deceive ourselves, and make God a liar. But if we confess our sins, he is faithful and just, not only to forgive our sins, but also to cleanse us from all unrighteousness, that we may go and sin no more.'

20. St. John therefore is well consistent with himself, as well as with the other holy writers; as will yet more evidently appear if we place all his assertions touching this matter in one view. He declares, first, 'The blood of Jesus Christ cleanseth us from all sin.' Secondly, 'No man can say I have not sinned, I have no sin to be cleansed from.' Thirdly, 'But God is ready both to forgive our past sins and to save us from them for the time to come.' Fourthly, 'These things I write unto you', saith the Apostle, 'that ye may not sin: but if any man should sin', or 'have sinned' (as the word might be rendered) he need not continue in sin, seeing 'we have an advocate with the Father, Jesus Christ the righteous.' Thus far all is clear. But lest any doubt should remain in a point of so vast importance the Apostle resumes this subject in the third chapter, and largely explains his own meaning. 'Little children', saith he, 'let no man deceive you' (as though I had given any encouragement to those that continue in sin); 'he that doth righteousness is righteous, even as he is righteous. He that committeth sin is of the devil; for the devil sinneth from the beginning. For this purpose the Son of God was manifested, that he might destroy the works of the devil. Whosoever is born of God doth not commit sin; for his seed remaineth in him, and he cannot sin, because he is born of God. In this the children of God are manifest, and the children of the devil' (1 John 3:7-10). Here the point, which till then might possibly have admitted of some doubt in weak minds, is purposely settled by the last of the inspired writers, and decided in the clearest manner. In conformity therefore both to the doctrine of St. John, and to the whole tenor of the New Testament, we fix this conclusion: 'A Christian is so far perfect as not to commit sin.'

21. This is the glorious privilege of every Christian; yea, though he be but 'a babe in Christ'. But it is only of those who 'are strong in the Lord', and 'have overcome the wicked one', or rather of those who 'have known him that is from the beginning', that it can be affirmed they are in such a sense perfect as, secondly, to be freed from evil thoughts and

evil tempers. First, from evil or sinful thoughts. But here let it be observed that thoughts concerning evil are not always evil thoughts; that a thought concerning sin and a sinful thought are widely different. A man, for instance, may think of a murder which another has committed, and yet this is no evil or sinful thought. So our blessed Lord himself doubtless thought of or understood the thing spoken by the devil when he said, 'All this will I give thee if thou wilt fall down and worship me.' Yet had he no evil or sinful thought, nor indeed was capable of having any. And even hence it follows that neither have real Christians; for 'everyone that is perfect is as his master' (Luke 6:40). Therefore, if he was free from evil or sinful thoughts, so are they likewise.

22. And indeed, whence should evil thoughts proceed in the servant who is 'as his master'? 'Out of the heart of man (if at all) proceed evil thoughts' (Mark 7:21). If therefore his heart be no longer evil, then evil thoughts can no longer proceed out of it. If the tree were corrupt, so would be the fruit. But the tree is good. The fruit therefore is good also (Matt. 12:33). Our Lord himself bearing witness: 'Every good tree bringeth forth good fruit. A good tree cannot bring forth evil fruit, as a corrupt tree cannot bring forth good fruit' (Matt. 7:17-18).

23. The same happy privilege of real Christians St. Paul asserts from his own experience: 'The weapons of our warfare', saith he, 'are not carnal, but mighty through God to the pulling down of strongholds; casting down imaginations' (or 'reasonings' rather, for so the word λογισμούς signifies: all the reasonings of pride and unbelief against the declarations, promises, or gifts of God) 'and every high thing that exalteth itself against the knowledge of God; and bringing into captivity every thought to the obedience of Christ' (2 Cor. 10:4, etc.).

24. And as Christians indeed are freed from evil thoughts, so are they, secondly, from evil tempers. This is evident from the above-mentioned declaration of our Lord himself: 'The disciple is not above his master; but everyone that is perfect shall be as his master.' He had been delivering just before some of the sublimest doctrines of Christianity, and some of the most grievous to flesh and blood: 'I say unto you, love your enemies, do good to them which hate you: and unto him that smiteth thee on the one cheek, offer also the other.' Now these he well knew the world would not receive, and therefore immediately adds, 'Can the blind lead the blind? Will they not both fall into the ditch?' As if he had said, 'Do not confer with flesh and blood touching these things, with men void of spiritual discernment, the eyes of whose understanding God hath not opened, lest they and you perish together.' In the next verse he removes the two grand objections with which these wise fools meet us at every turn: 'these things are too grievous to be borne,' or, 'they are too high to be attained,' saying, 'The disciple is not above his master.' Therefore if I have suffered be content to tread in my steps. And doubt ye not then but I will fulfil my word: 'For everyone that is perfect shall be as his master.' But his Master was free from all sinful tempers. So therefore is his disciple, even every real Christian.

25. Every one of these can say with St. Paul, 'I am crucified with Christ: nevertheless I live; yet not I, but Christ liveth in me'—words that manifestly describe a deliverance from inward as well as from outward sin. This is expressed both negatively, 'I live not'—my evil nature, the body of sin, is destroyed—and positively, 'Christ liveth in me'—and

therefore all that is holy, and just, and good. Indeed both these, 'Christ liveth in me,' and 'I live not,' are inseparably connected; for 'what communion hath light with darkness' or 'Christ with Belial?'

26. He therefore who liveth in true believers hath 'purified their hearts by faith', insomuch that 'everyone that hath Christ in him, the hope of glory', 'purifieth himself even as he is pure' (1 John 3:3). He is purified from pride; for Christ was lowly of heart. He is pure from self-will or desire; for Christ desired only to do the will of his Father, and to finish his work. And he is pure from anger, in the common sense of the word; for Christ was meek and gentle, patient and long-suffering. I say, 'in the common sense of the word'; for all anger is not evil. We read of our Lord himself that he once 'looked round with anger' (Mark 3:5). But with what kind of anger? The next word shows, συλλυπούμενος, being *at the same time* 'grieved for the hardness of their hearts'. So then he was *angry at the sin*, and in the same moment *grieved for the sinners*; angry or displeased *at the offence*, but sorry *for the offenders*. With anger, yea, hatred, he looked upon *the thing*; with grief and love upon the *persons*. Go thou that art perfect, and do likewise. 'Be thus angry, and *thou* sinnest not:' feeling a displacency at every offence against God, but only love and tender compassion to the offender.

27. Thus doth Jesus 'save his people from their sins': and not only from outward sins, but also from the sins of their hearts; from evil thoughts and from evil tempers. 'True', say some, 'we shall thus be saved from our sins, but not till death; not in this world.' But how are we to reconcile this with the express words of St. John? 'Herein is our love made perfect, that we may have boldness in the day of judgment: because as he is, so are we *in this world*' (1 John 4:17). The Apostle here beyond all contradiction speaks of himself and other living Christians, of whom (as though he had foreseen this very evasion, and set himself to overturn it from the foundation) he flatly affirms that not only at or after death but 'in this world' they are as their Master.

28. Exactly agreeable to this are his words in the first chapter of this Epistle: 'God is light, and in him is no darkness at all. If we walk in the light, as he is in the light, we have fellowship one with another, and the blood of Jesus Christ his Son cleanseth us from all sin.' And again, 'If we confess our sins, he is faithful and just to forgive us our sins, and to cleanse us from all unrighteousness' (1 John 1:5 etc.). Now it is evident the Apostle here also speaks of a deliverance wrought 'in this world'. For he saith not, 'the blood of Christ will cleanse' (at the hour of death, or in the day of judgment) but it 'cleanseth (at the time present) us (living Christians) from all sin.' And it is equally evident that if *any sin* remain we are not cleansed from *all sin*: if *any* unrighteousness remain in the soul it is not cleansed from *all* unrighteousness. Neither let any sinner against his own soul say that this relates to justification only, or the cleansing us from the guilt of sin. First, because this is confounding together what the Apostle clearly distinguishes, who mentions first, 'to forgive us our sins', and then 'to cleanse us from all unrighteousness'. Secondly, because this is asserting justification by works in the strongest sense possible. It is making all inward as well as outward holiness necessarily previous to justification. For if the cleansing here spoken of is no other than the cleansing us from the guilt of sin, then we are not cleansed from guilt; i.e. are not justified, unless on condition of 'walking in the light, as he is in the light'. It

remains, then, that Christians are saved in this world from all sin, from all unrighteousness; that they are now in such a sense perfect as not to commit sin, and to be freed from evil thoughts and evil tempers.

29. Thus hath the Lord fulfilled the things he spake by his holy prophets, which have been since the world began: by Moses in particular, saying, 'I will circumcise thine heart, and the heart of thy seed, to love the Lord thy God with all thy heart, and with all thy soul' (Deut. 30:6); by David, crying out, 'Create in me a clean heart, and renew a right spirit within me;' and most remarkably by Ezekiel, in those words: 'Then will I sprinkle clean water upon you, and ye shall be clean; from all *your* filthiness, and from *all* your idols will I cleanse you. A new heart also will I give you, and a new spirit will I put within you, and cause you to walk in my statutes, and ye shall keep my judgments, and do them. . . . Ye shall be my people, and I will be your God. I will also save you from all your uncleannesses. . . . Thus saith the Lord your God, In the day that I shall have cleansed you from all your iniquities . . . the heathen shall know that I the Lord build the ruined places; . . . I the Lord have spoken it, . . . and I will do it' (Ezek. 36:25, etc.).

30. 'Having therefore these promises, dearly beloved', both in the law and in the prophets, and having the prophetic word confirmed unto us in the gospel by our blessed Lord and his apostles, 'let us cleanse ourselves from all filthiness of flesh and spirit, perfecting holiness in the fear of God.' 'Let us fear lest' so many promises 'being made us of entering into his rest' (which he that hath entered into 'is ceased from his own works') 'any of us should come short of it.' 'This one thing let us do: forgetting those things which are behind, and reaching forth unto those things which are before, let us press toward the mark for the prize of the high calling of God in Christ Jesus;' crying unto him day and night till we also are 'delivered from the bondage of corruption into the glorious liberty of the sons of God.'

58. THE GENERAL DELIVERANCE

November 30, 1781

An Introductory Comment

Impressed by an essay from John Hildrop, D.D., who had been appointed to the rectory of Wath, near Ripon, Yorkshire (ODNB), Wesley crafted this sermon on November 30, 1781, and it was published the following year in the *Arminian Magazine* in two installments (January and February) under the title "Free Thoughts on the Brute Creation" (O, 2:436). In 1742, Hildrop had published a work that sought to prove animals' souls are corrupted because of the fall of humanity, an idea derived from Guillaume Hyacinthe Bougeant's *Philosophical Amusement* (ODNB). Developing a more eschatological theme, Wesley changed the earlier title found in the *Arminian Magazine* to the familiar "The General Deliverance," when he reprinted this piece in the 1788 edition of his collection (O, 2:436).

In the course of this sermon Wesley developed three basic themes. First of all, taking into account the political image of the *imago Dei,* he affirmed that humanity is God's "viceregent upon earth," the "governor of this lower world," and "the channel of conveyance between his Creator and the whole brute creation" (O, 2:440–42). With this implied chain of being in place, at least in some sense, the fall of humanity, therefore, had consequence for the rest of the animal realm. Second, Wesley maintained that the distinguishing trait of humanity, in comparison with other living beings, is not reason or understanding but that humanity is wonderfully "capable of God" (O, 2:441). And third, Wesley engaged in a bit of speculation that at the culmination of all things God may then make the animals what humanity now is, in other words, "creatures capable of God" (O, 2:448). If that were the case, then how poignant would be the loss of those who had neglected the glorious image of God in which they had been created. Not surprisingly, Wesley concluded this sermon with an exhortation: "Rest not till you enjoy the privilege of humanity—the knowledge and love of God" (O, 2:450).

The General Deliverance

I. 1.–2. What was the original state of brute creation?

A. Adam had an innate principle of *self-motion*, created in God's likeness

B. He also had perfect *understanding, will*, and *liberty*

3. To Adam, God gave dominion over all the animals and all the earth

4. What was the original state of those brute creatures when they were created?

A. They also had an innate principle of self-motion

B. They had *understanding, will*, and *liberty*, which they still enjoy today

5. What then makes the barrier between human beings and brutes?

A. Human beings are capable of God; the inferior creatures are not

6. God saw everything that was made, and 'behold it was very good'

A. This directly refers to brute creation. But in what state is it at present?

II. 1. After the Fall, human beings could not transmit God's blessings to brutes

A. Every creature was subject to sorrow, to pain, and to evil of all kinds

2. What did the creatures suffer when Adam rebelled against God?

A. They suffered loss in their strength and even more in understanding

3. How little shadow of good or benevolence can now be found in brute creation!

4. Is not the outward appearance of these creatures as horrid as their dispositions?

5. By one man sin and death entered the world and passed upon all creatures

6. Both feebler and stronger creatures now have a common enemy—man

III. 1. But will brute creation always remain in this condition?

2. They shall be delivered from the bondage of corruption into glorious liberty

3. The whole of brute creation will be restored to the vigour it had at creation

4.–7. Their beauty and their happiness will return

8.–9. But what end does it answer to dwell upon such a subject?

A. It serves to illustrate the mercy of God, which is over all his works

10. One more excellent end may result from the preceding considerations

A. They may encourage us to imitate him whose mercy is over his works

11. From this I cannot but draw one inference, which no one of reason can deny

A. Whoever is without God in the world is degraded into a beast

12. Let those who are of a nobler turn of mind assert the dignity of their nature

Sermon 60: The General Deliverance, 1781

Romans 8:19-22

The earnest expectation of the creature waiteth for the manifestation of the sons of God.

For the creature was made subject to vanity, not willingly, but by reason of him that subjected it.

Yet in hope that the creature itself also shall be delivered from the bondage of corruption, into the glorious liberty of the sons of God.

For we know that the whole creation groaneth, and travaileth in pain together until now.

1. Nothing is more sure than that, as 'the Lord is loving to every man', so 'his mercy is over all his works'—all that have sense, all that are capable of pleasure or pain, of happiness or misery. In consequence of this 'he openeth his hand and filleth all things living with plenteousness:' 'he prepareth food for cattle,' as well as 'herbs for the children of men.' He provideth for the fowls of the air, 'feeding the young ravens when they cry unto him'. 'He sendeth the springs into the rivers that run among the hills,' to give drink to every beast of the field, and that even 'the wild asses may quench their thirst.' And suitably to this he directs us to be tender of even the meaner creatures, to show mercy to these also. 'Thou shalt not muzzle the ox that treadeth out the corn'—a custom which is observed in the eastern countries even to this day. And this is by no means contradicted by St. Paul's question, 'Doth God take care for oxen?' Without doubt he does. We cannot deny it without flatly contradicting his word. The plain meaning of the Apostle is—Is this all that is implied in the text? Hath it not a farther meaning? Does it not teach us we are to feed the bodies of those whom we desire to feed our souls? Meantime it is certain God 'giveth grass for the cattle', as well as 'herbs for the use of men'.

2. But how are these Scriptures reconcilable to the present state of things? How are they consistent with what we daily see round about us in every part of the creation? If the Creator and Father of every living thing is rich in mercy towards all; if he does not overlook or despise any of the works of his own hands; if he wills even the meanest of them to be happy according to their degree—how comes it to pass that such a complication of evils oppresses, yea, overwhelms them? How is it that misery of all kinds overspreads the face of the earth? This is a question which has puzzled the wisest philosophers in all ages. And it cannot be answered without having recourse to the oracles of God. But taking these for our guide we may inquire,

I. What was the original state of the brute creation?

II. In what state is it at present? And

III. In what state will it be at the manifestation of the children of God?

I.1. We may inquire, in the first place, What was the original state of the brute creation? And may not we learn this even from the place which was assigned them, namely, the garden of God? All the beasts of the field, and all the fowls of the air, were with Adam in paradise. And there is no question but their state was suited to their place: it was paradisiacal, perfectly happy. Undoubtedly it bore a near resemblance to the state of man himself. By taking therefore a short view of the one we may conceive the other. Now 'man was made in the image of God.' But 'God is a spirit.' So therefore was man. Only that spirit, being designed to dwell on earth, was lodged in an earthly tabernacle. As such he had an innate principle of *self-motion.* And so, it seems, has every spirit in the universe; this being the proper distinguishing difference between spirit and matter, which is totally, essentially passive and inactive, as appears from a thousand experiments. He was, after the likeness of his Creator, endued with *understanding,* a capacity of apprehending whatever objects were brought before it, and of judging concerning them. He was endued with a *will,* exerting itself in various affections and passions; and, lastly, with *liberty,* or freedom of choice, without which all the rest would have been in vain, and he would have been no more capable of serving his Creator than a piece of earth or marble. He would have been as incapable of vice or virtue as any part of the inanimate creation. In these, in the power of self-motion, understanding, will, and liberty, the natural image of God consisted.

2. How far his power of self-motion then extended it is impossible for us to determine. It is probable that he had a far higher degree both of swiftness and strength than any of his posterity ever had, and much less any of the lower creatures. It is certain he had such strength of understanding as no man ever since had. His understanding was perfect in its kind; capable of apprehending all things clearly, and judging concerning them according to truth, without any mixture of error. His will had no wrong bias of any sort, but all his passions and affections were regular, being steadily and uniformly guided by the dictates of his unerring understanding; embracing nothing but good, and every good in proportion to its degree of intrinsic goodness. His liberty likewise was wholly guided by his understanding: he chose or refused according to its direction. Above all (which was his highest excellence, far more valuable than all the rest put together) he was a creature capable of God, capable of knowing, loving, and obeying his Creator. And in fact he did know God, did unfeignedly love and uniformly obey him. This was the supreme perfection of man, as it is of all intelligent beings—the continually seeing and loving and obeying the Father of the spirits of all flesh. From this right state, and right use of all his faculties, his happiness naturally flowed. In this the essence of his happiness consisted; but it was increased by all the things that were round about him. He saw with unspeakable pleasure the order, the beauty, the harmony of all the creatures: of all animated, all inanimate nature—the serenity of the skies, the sun walking in brightness, the sweetly variegated clothing of the earth; the trees, the fruits, the flowers,

> And liquid lapse of murmuring streams.

Nor was this pleasure interrupted by evil of any kind. It had no alloy of sorrow or pain, whether of body or mind. For while he was innocent he was impassive, incapable of suffering. Nothing could stain his purity of joy. And to crown all, he was immortal.

3. To this creature, endued with all these excellent faculties, thus qualified for his high charge, God said, 'Have thou dominion over the fish of the sea, and over the fowl of the air, and over every living thing that moveth upon the earth' (Gen. 1:28). And so the Psalmist: 'Thou madest him to have dominion over the works of thy hands; thou hast put all things under his feet: all sheep and oxen, yea, and the beasts of the field; the fowl of the air, and the fish of the sea, and whatsoever passeth through the paths of the seas!' (Ps. 8:6-8) So that man was God's vicegerent upon earth, the prince and governor of this lower world; and all the blessings of God flowed through him to the inferior creatures. Man was the channel of conveyance between his Creator and the whole brute creation.

4. But what blessings were those that were then conveyed through man to the lower creatures? What was the original state of the brute creatures when they were first created? This deserves a more attentive consideration than has been usually given it. It is certain these, as well as man, had an innate principle of *self-motion*; and that at least in as high a degree as they enjoy it at this day. Again: they were endued with a degree of *understanding* not less than that they are possessed of now. They had also a *will* including various passions, which likewise they still enjoy. And they had *liberty*, a power of choice, a degree of which is still found in every living creature. Nor can we doubt but their understanding too was in the beginning perfect in its kind. Their passions and affections were regular, and their choice always guided by their understanding.

5. What then makes the barrier between men and brutes? The line which they cannot pass? It was not reason. Set aside that ambiguous term: exchange it for the plain word, understanding, and who can deny that brutes have this? We may as well deny that they have sight or hearing. But it is this: man is capable of God; the inferior creatures are not. We have no ground to believe that they are in any degree capable of knowing, loving, or obeying God. This is the specific difference between man and brute—the great gulf which they cannot pass over. And as a loving obedience to God was the perfection of men, so a loving obedience to man was the perfection of brutes. And as long as they continued in this they were happy after their kind; happy in the right state and the right use of their respective faculties. Yea, and so long they had some shadowy resemblance of even *moral goodness*. For they had gratitude to man for benefits received, and a reverence for him. They had likewise a kind of benevolence to each other, unmixed with any contrary temper. How *beautiful* many of them were we may conjecture from that which still remains; and that not only in the noblest creatures, but in those of the lowest order. And they were all surrounded not only with plenteous food, but with everything that could give them pleasure; pleasure unmixed with pain; for pain was not yet—it had not entered into paradise. And they too were immortal. For 'God made not death: neither hath he pleasure in the death of any living.'

6. How true then is that word, 'God saw everything that he had made: and behold it was very good.' But how far is this from being the case now! In what a condition is the whole lower world! To say nothing of inanimate nature, wherein all the elements seem to be out of course, and by turns to fight against man. Since man rebelled against his Maker, in what a state is all animated nature! Well might the Apostle say of this, 'The whole creation groaneth together, and travaileth together in pain until now.' This directly refers to the brute creation. In what state this is at present we are now to consider.

II.1. As all the blessings of God in paradise flowed through man to the inferior creatures; as man was the great channel of communication between the Creator and the whole brute creation; so when man made himself incapable of transmitting those blessings, that communication was necessarily cut off. The intercourse between God and the inferior creatures being stopped, those blessings could no longer flow in upon them. And then it was that 'the creature', every creature, 'was subject to vanity', to sorrow, to pain of every kind, to all manner of evils. 'Not' indeed 'willingly'; not by its own choice, not by any act or deed of its own; 'but by reason of him that subjected it'; by the wise permission of God, determining to draw eternal good out of this temporary evil.

2. But in what respects was 'the creature', every creature, then 'made subject to vanity'? What did the meaner creatures suffer when man rebelled against God? It is probable they sustained much loss even in the lower faculties, their vigour, strength, and swiftness. But undoubtedly they suffered far more in their understanding, more than we can easily conceive. Perhaps insects and worms had then as much understanding as the most intelligent brutes have now; whereas millions of creatures have at present little more understanding than the earth on which they crawl or the rock to which they adhere. They suffered still more in their will, in their passions, which were then variously distorted, and frequently set in flat opposition to the little understanding that was left them. Their liberty likewise was greatly impaired, yea, in many cases totally destroyed. They are still utterly enslaved to irrational appetites which have the full dominion over them. The very foundations of their nature are out of course, are turned upside down. As man is deprived of *his* perfection, his loving obedience to God, so brutes are deprived of *their* perfection, their loving obedience to man. The far greater part of them flee from him, studiously avoid his hated presence. The most of the rest set him at open defiance, yea, destroy him if it be in their power. A few only, those we commonly term domestic animals, retain more or less of their original disposition, and (through the mercy of God) love him still and pay obedience to him.

3. Setting these few aside, how little shadow of good, of gratitude, of benevolence, of any right temper is now to be found in any part of the brute creation! On the contrary, what savage fierceness, what unrelenting cruelty, are invariably observed in thousands of creatures, yea, are inseparable from their natures! Is it only the lion, the tiger, the wolf, among the inhabitants of the forest and plains; the shark and a few more voracious monsters among the inhabitants of the waters; or the eagle among birds; that tears the flesh, sucks the blood, and crushes the bones of their helpless fellow-creatures? Nay, the harmless fly, the laborious ant, the painted butterfly, are treated in the same merciless manner even by the innocent songsters of the grove! The innumerable tribes of poor insects are continually devoured by them. And whereas there is but a small number, comparatively, of beasts of prey on the earth, it is quite otherwise in the liquid element: there are but few inhabitants of the waters, whether of the sea or of the rivers, which do not devour whatsoever they can master. Yea, they exceed herein all the beasts of the forest, and all the birds of prey. For none of these have been ever observed to prey upon their own species,

> *Saevis inter se convenit ursis—*
> Even savage bears will not each other tear.

But the water savages swallow up all, even of their own kind, that are smaller and weaker than themselves. Yea, such at present is the miserable constitution of the world, to such 'vanity' is it now 'subjected', that an immense majority of creatures, perhaps a million to one, can no otherwise preserve their own lives than by destroying their fellow-creatures.

4. And is not the very form, the outward appearance of many of the creatures, as horrid as their dispositions? Where is the beauty which was stamped upon them when they came first out of the hands of their Creator? There is not the least trace of it left: so far from it that they are shocking to behold! Nay, they are not only terrible and grisly to look upon, but deformed, and that to a high degree. Yet their features, ugly as they are at best, are frequently made more deformed than usual when they are distorted by pain, which they cannot avoid any more than the wretched sons of men. Pain of various kinds, weakness, sickness, diseases innumerable, come upon them, perhaps from within, perhaps from one another, perhaps from the inclemency of seasons, from fire, hail, snow, or storm, or from a thousand causes which they cannot foresee or prevent.

5. Thus 'as by one man sin entered into the world, and death by sin; even so death passed upon all men.' And not on man only, but on those creatures also that 'did not sin after the similitude of Adam's transgression'. And not death alone came upon them, but all of its train of preparatory evils: pain, and ten thousand sufferings. Nor these only, but likewise all those irregular passions, all those unlovely tempers (which in men are sins, and even in the brutes are sources of misery) 'passed upon all' the inhabitants of the earth, and remain in all, except the children of God.

6. During this season of 'vanity', not only the feebler creatures are continually destroyed by the stronger; not only the strong are frequently destroyed by those that are of equal strength; but both the one and the other are exposed to the violence and cruelty of him that is now their common enemy—man. And if his swiftness or strength is not equal to theirs, yet his art more than supplies that defect. By this he eludes all their force, how great so ever it be; by this he defeats all their swiftness, and notwithstanding their various shifts and contrivances, discovers all their retreats. He pursues them over the widest plains, and through the thickest forests. He overtakes them in the fields of air, he finds them out in the depths of the sea. Nor are the mild and friendly creatures who still own his sway, and are duteous to his commands, secured thereby from more than brutal violence, from outrage and abuse of various kinds. Is the generous horse, that serves his master's necessity or pleasure with unwearied diligence, is the faithful dog, that waits the motion of his hand or his eye, exempt from this? What returns for their long and faithful service do many of these poor creatures find? And what a dreadful difference is there between what they suffer from their fellow brutes and what they suffer from the tyrant, man! The lion, the tiger, or the shark, give them pain from mere necessity, in order to prolong their own life; and put them out of their pain at once. But the human shark, without any such necessity, torments them of his free choice; and perhaps continues their lingering pain till after months or years death signs their release.

III.1. But will *the creature*, will even the brute creation, always remain in this deplorable condition? God forbid that we should affirm this; yea, or even entertain such a thought! While 'the whole creation groaneth together' (whether men attend or not) their groans are not dispersed in idle air, but enter into the ears of him that made them. While his creatures 'travail together in pain', he knoweth all their pain, and is bringing them nearer and nearer to the birth which shall be accomplished in its season. He seeth 'the earnest expectation' wherewith the whole animated creation 'waiteth for' that final 'manifestation of the sons of God': in which 'they themselves also shall be delivered' (not by annihilation: annihilation is not deliverance) 'from the' present 'bondage of corruption, into' a measure of 'the glorious liberty of the children of God.'

2. Nothing can be more express. Away with vulgar prejudices, and let the plain word of God take place. They 'shall be delivered from the bondage of corruption into glorious liberty'; even a measure, according as they are capable, of 'the liberty of the children of God'.

A general view of this is given us in the twenty-first chapter of the Revelation. When he that 'sitteth on the great white throne' hath pronounced, 'Behold I make all things new;' when the word is fulfilled, 'The tabernacle of God is with men, [. . .] and they shall be his people, and God himself shall be with them and be their God;' then the following blessing shall take place (not only on the children of men—there is no such restriction in the text—but) on every creature according to its capacity: 'God shall wipe away all tears from their eyes. And there shall be no more death, neither sorrow nor crying. Neither shall there be any more pain: for the former things are passed away.'

3. To descend to a few particulars. The whole brute creation will then undoubtedly be restored, not only to the vigour, strength, and swiftness which they had at their creation, but to a far higher degree of each than they ever enjoyed. They will be restored, not only to that measure of understanding which they had in paradise, but to a degree of it as much higher than that as the understanding of an elephant is beyond that of a worm. And whatever affections they had in the garden of God will be restored with vast increase, being exalted and refined in a manner which we ourselves are not now able to comprehend. The liberty they then had will be completely restored, and they will be free in all their motions. They will be delivered from all irregular appetites, from all unruly passions, from every disposition that is either evil in itself or has any tendency to evil. No rage will be found in any creature, no fierceness, no cruelty or thirst for blood. So far from it that 'the wolf shall dwell with the lamb, the leopard shall lie down with the kid, the calf and the young lion together; and a little child shall lead them. The cow and the bear shall feed together, and the lion shall eat straw like the ox. [. . .] They shall not hurt or destroy in all my holy mountain' (Isa. 11: 6, 7, 9).

4. Thus in that day all the 'vanity' to which they are now helplessly 'subject' will be abolished; they will suffer no more either from within or without; the days of their groaning are ended. At the same time there can be no reasonable doubt but all the horridness of their appearance, and all the deformity of their aspect, will vanish away, and be exchanged for their primeval beauty. And with their beauty their happiness will return; to which there can then be no obstruction. As there will be nothing within, so there will

be nothing without, to give them any uneasiness—no heat or cold, no storm or tempest, but one perennial spring. In the new earth, as well as in the new heavens, there will be nothing to give pain, but everything that the wisdom and goodness of God can create to give happiness. As a recompense for what they once suffered while under 'the bondage of corruption', when God has 'renewed the face of the earth', and their corruptible body has put on incorruption, they shall enjoy happiness suited to their state, without alloy, without interruption, and without end.

5. But though I doubt not that the Father of all has a tender regard for even his lowest creatures, and that in consequence of this he will make them large amends for all they suffer while under their present bondage, yet I dare not affirm that he has an *equal regard* for them and for the children of men. I do not believe that

> He sees *with equal eyes,* as Lord of all,
> A hero perish or a sparrow fall!

By no means. This is exceeding pretty; but it is absolutely false. For though

> Mercy, with truth and endless grace,
> O'er all his works doth reign,
> Yet chiefly he delights to bless
> His favourite creature, man.

God regards his meanest creatures much; but he regards man much more. He does not *equally regard* a hero and a sparrow, the best of men, and the lowest of brutes. 'How *much more* does your heavenly Father care for you'! says he who is 'in the bosom of the Father'. Those who thus strain the point are clearly confuted by his question, 'Are not ye *much better* than they?' Let it suffice that God regards everything that he hath made in its own order, and in proportion to that measure of his own image which he has stamped upon it.

6. May I be permitted to mention here a conjecture concerning the brute creation? What if it should then please the all-wise, the all-gracious Creator, to raise them higher in the scale of beings? What if it should please him, when he makes us 'equal to angels', to make them what we are now? Creatures capable of God? Capable of knowing, and loving, and enjoying the Author of their being? If it should be so, ought our eye to be evil because he is good? However this be, he will certainly do what will be most for his own glory.

7. If it be objected to all this (as very probably it will): 'But of what use will those creatures be in that future state?' I answer this by another question—'What use are they of now?' If there be (as has commonly been supposed) eight thousand species of insects, who is able to inform us of what use seven thousand of them are? If there are four thousand species of fishes, who can tell us of what use are more than three thousand of them? If there are six hundred sorts of birds, who can tell of what use five hundred of those species are? If there be four hundred sorts of beasts, to what use do three hundred of them serve?

Consider this; consider how little we know of even the present designs of God; and then you will not wonder that we know still less of what he designs to do in the new heavens and the new earth.

8. 'But what end does it answer to dwell upon this subject which we so imperfectly understand?' To consider so much as we do understand, so much as God has been pleased to reveal to us, may answer that excellent end—to illustrate that mercy of God which is 'over all his works'. And it may exceedingly confirm our belief that much more he is 'loving to every man'. For how well may we urge our Lord's word, 'Are not ye much better than they?' If then the Lord takes such care of the fowls of the air and of the beasts of the field, shall he not much more take care of *you*, creatures of a nobler order? If 'the Lord will save' (as the inspired writer affirms) 'both man and beast' in their several degrees, surely 'the children of men may put their trust under the shadow of his wings'!

9. May it not answer another end, namely, furnish us with a full answer to a plausible objection against the justice of God in suffering numberless creatures that never had sinned to be so severely punished? They could not sin, for they were not moral agents. Yet how severely do they suffer! Yea, many of them, beasts of burden in particular, almost the whole time of their abode on earth. So that they can have no retribution here below. But the objection vanishes away if we consider that something better remains after death for these poor creatures also! That these likewise shall one day be delivered from this bondage of corruption, and shall then receive an ample amends for all their present sufferings.

10. One more excellent end may undoubtedly be answered by the preceding considerations. They may encourage us to imitate him whose mercy is over all his works. They may soften our hearts towards the meaner creatures, knowing that the Lord careth for them. It may enlarge our hearts towards those poor creatures to reflect that, as vile as they appear in our eyes, not one of them is forgotten in the sight of our Father which is in heaven. Through all the vanity to which they are now subjected, let us look to what God hath prepared for them. Yea, let us habituate ourselves to look forward, beyond this present scene of bondage, to the happy time when they will be delivered therefrom into the liberty of the children of God.

11. From what has been said I cannot but draw one inference, which no man of reason can deny. If it is this which distinguishes men from beasts, that they are creatures capable of God, capable of knowing, and loving, and enjoying him; then whoever is 'without God in the world'—whoever does not know, or love, or enjoy God, and is not careful about the matter—does in effect disclaim the nature of man, and degrade himself into a beast. Let such vouchsafe a little attention to those remarkable words of Solomon: 'I said in my heart concerning the estate of the sons of men, . . . they might see that they themselves are beasts' (Eccles. 3:18). *These* sons of men are undoubtedly beasts—and that by their own act and deed. For they deliberately and wilfully disclaim the sole characteristic of human nature. It is true they may have a share of reason—they have speech and they walk erect. But they have not the mark, the only mark, which totally separates man from the brute creation. 'That which befalleth beasts, the same thing befalleth them.' They are equally without God in the world, 'so that a man' of this kind 'hath no pre-eminence above a beast.'

12. So much more let all those who are of a nobler turn of mind assert the distinguishing dignity of their nature! Let all who are of a more generous spirit know and maintain their rank in the scale of beings. Rest not till you enjoy the privilege of humanity—the knowledge and love of God. Lift up your heads, ye creatures capable of God. Lift up your hearts to the Source of your being!

Know God, and teach your souls to know
The joys that from religion flow.

Give your hearts to him who, together with ten thousand blessings, has 'given you his Son, his only Son'! Let your continual 'fellowship be with the Father, and with his Son, Jesus Christ'! Let God be in all your thoughts, and ye will be men indeed. Let him be your God and your all! The desire of your eyes, the joy of your heart, and your portion for ever!

November 30, 1781

59. THE GREAT ASSIZE

1758

An Introductory Comment

Retiring for a few days to the home of his friend Ebenezer Blackwell at Lewisham, Wesley penned this sermon at the request of William Cole, the High Sheriff of Bedfordshire, who had invited him to deliver the assize sermon at Bedford (S, 2:398). This brief title, not initially understood by modern readers, is actually a reference to the Last Judgment and can be found as early as 1340 in Richard Rolle of Hampole's *Pricke of Conscience* (O, 1;355).

Taking Romans 14:10 as his text, Wesley preached this sermon at St. Paul's church before Sir Edward Clive, who by 1753 had succeeded Sir Thomas Burnet as "a puisne justice of the common pleas" (ODNB). This was the same Edward Clive who had a caricature made of him as displayed in Hogarth's plate "The Bench" (S, 2:399). The congregation on this solemn occasion was, in Wesley's own words, "large and attentive" (WH, 21:137), and he noted twenty years later in his *Journal* on September 1, 1778, that "I cannot write a better [sermon] on the Great Assize than I did twenty years ago" (WH, 23:104).

The sermon is one of Wesley's more important vehicles by which he developed strong eschatological and undoubtedly weighty themes. For his part Outler noted that it contained "an implicit statement about the Christian *ordo salutis*" (O, 1:355), demonstrating its greatest extent, and that God's ultimate purposes for human creation are "already validly revealed in Jesus Christ" (O, 1:355). The design of this composition is also evident in its three principal points: (1) the chief circumstances that precede standing before the judgment seat of Christ; (2) the judgment itself; and (3) the circumstances that follow. Such a reckoning, whereby "every appetite, passion, inclination, [and] affection" (O, 1:363) will be revealed and whereby everyone "shall there 'give an account of his own works'" (O, 1:362), constitutes a second justification (by the evidences of saving faith), a notion that Wesley had earlier rejected but ultimately embraced.

The Great Assize

I. What circumstances precede our standing before the judgment seat?
  1. And first, God will show signs in the earth beneath
  2. At the same time the Son of man shall send forth his angels
    A. They shall gather his elect from the four winds
    B. The Lord himself shall come with clouds
    C. Before him shall be gathered all nations, and he shall separate them
    D. The dead will be judged according to their works

II. What will happen in the judgment itself?
  1. God will judge the world by his only-begotten Son
  2. This is called the great and the terrible day, or the day of the Lord
  3. We do not know where humankind shall be judged
  4. Nor can we count the persons to be judged
  5. Every person will give an account of his own works
  6.–7. God will reveal hidden works of darkness and the thoughts of the heart
  8.–10. Then the king will say to those on the right, 'Come, ye blessed of my Father'
  11. The righteous will then rejoice with joy unspeakable
  12. The king will then turn to those on his left, and they shall be judged
    A. He will pronounce the dreadful sentence of condemnation upon them

III. What circumstances will follow the judgment?
  1. Some shall go away into eternal life, others into eternal punishment
  2.–4. Then the heavens will be shriveled up as a parchment scroll
    A. All works of nature, art, and human industry will be destroyed
  5. We will then see a new heavens and a new earth

IV. It remains only to apply the preceding to all who are here present before God
  1. How beautiful are the feet of those who execute justice on earth
  2. May you not be compared to the spirits who will attend the coming Judge?
  3. Should you not approve yourselves the servants of God?
  4. Should you not bear it in your minds all day that an awful day is coming?
  5. What manner of persons ought we to be, in all holy conversation and godliness?
    A. Be diligent that ye may be found in peace, without spot and blameless

Sermon 15: The Great Assize, 1758

Romans 14:10

We shall all stand before the judgment seat of Christ.

1. How many circumstances concur to raise the awfulness of the present solemnity! The general concourse of people of every age, sex, rank, and condition of life, willingly or unwillingly gathered together, not only from the neighbouring, but from distant parts: *criminals*, speedily to be brought forth, and having no way to escape; *officers*, waiting in their various posts to execute the orders which shall be given; and the *representative* of our gracious Sovereign, whom we so highly reverence and honour. The *occasion* likewise of this assembly adds not a little to the solemnity of it: to hear and determine causes of every kind, some of which are of the most important nature; on which depends no less than life or death—death, that uncovers the face of eternity! It was doubtless in order to increase the serious sense of these things, and not in the minds of the vulgar only, that the wisdom of our forefathers did not disdain to appoint even several minute circumstances of this solemnity. For these also, by means of the eye or ear, may more deeply affect the heart. And when viewed in this light, trumpets, staves, apparel, are no longer trifling or insignificant, but subservient in their kind and degree to the most valuable ends of society.

2. But as awful as this solemnity is, one far more awful is at hand. For yet a little while and 'we shall all stand before the judgment seat of Christ. For, As I live, saith the Lord, every knee shall bow to me, and every tongue shall confess to God.' And in that day 'every one of us shall give account of himself to God.'

3. Had all men a deep sense of this, how effectually would it secure the interests of society! For what more forcible motive can be conceived to the practice of genuine morality? To a steady pursuit of solid virtue, an uniform walking in justice, mercy, and truth? What could strengthen our hands in all that is good, and deter us from all evil, like a strong conviction of this—'The judge standeth at the door,' and we are shortly to *stand before* him?

4. It may not therefore be improper, or unsuitable to the design of the present assembly, to consider,

I. The chief circumstances which will precede our standing before the judgment seat of Christ.

II. The judgment itself, and

III. A few of the circumstances which will follow it.

I. Let us, in the first place, consider the chief circumstances which will precede our standing before the judgment seat of Christ.

And first, 1. 'God will show signs in the earth beneath' (Acts 2:19): particularly, he will 'arise to shake terribly the earth'. 'The earth shall reel to and fro like a drunkard, and shall be removed like a cottage.' 'There shall be earthquakes' κατὰ τόπους (not in divers only, but) 'in all places' (Luke 21:11)—not in one only, or a few, but in every part of the habitable world—even 'such as were not since men were upon the earth, so mighty earthquakes and so great'. In one of these 'every island shall flee away, and the mountains will not be found' (Rev. 16:20). Meantime all the waters of the terraqueous globe will feel the violence of those concussions: 'the sea and waves roaring' (Luke 21:25), with such an agitation as had never been known before since the hour that 'the fountains of the great deep were broken up,' to destroy the earth which then 'stood out of the water and in the water'. The air will be all storm and tempest, full of dark 'vapours and pillars of smoke' (Joel 2:30); resounding with thunder from pole to pole, and torn with ten thousand lightnings. But the commotion will not stop in the region of the air: 'The powers of heaven also shall be shaken.' 'There shall be signs in the sun and in the moon and in the stars' (Luke 21:25, 26)—those fixed as well as those that move round them. 'The sun shall be turned into darkness and the moon into blood, before the great and terrible day of the Lord come' (Joel 2:31). 'The stars shall withdraw their shining' (Joel 3:15), yea and 'fall from heaven', being thrown out of their orbits. And then shall be heard the universal 'shout' from all the companies of heaven, followed by 'the voice of the archangel' proclaiming the approach of the Son of God and man, 'and the trumpet of God' (1 Thess. 4:16) sounding an alarm to all 'that sleep in the dust of the earth'. In consequence of this all the graves shall open, and the bodies of men arise. 'The sea also shall give up the dead which are therein' (Rev. 20:13), and everyone shall rise *with his own body*—his own in substance, although so changed in its properties as we cannot now conceive. For 'this corruptible will then put on incorruption, and this mortal put on immortality' (1 Cor. 15:53). Yea, 'death and Hades', the invisible world, shall 'deliver up the dead that are in them' (Rev. 20:13); so that all who ever lived and died since God created man shall be raised incorruptible and immortal.

2. At the same time 'the Son of man shall send forth his angels' over all the earth, 'and they shall gather his elect from the four winds, from one end of heaven to the other' (Matt. 24:31). And the Lord himself shall 'come with clouds, in his own glory and the glory of his Father, with ten thousand of his saints, even myriads of angels', and 'shall sit upon the throne of his glory. And before him shall be gathered all nations, and he shall separate them one from another, and shall set the sheep' (the good) 'on his right hand, and the goats' (the wicked) 'upon the left' (Matt. 25:31-33). Concerning this general assembly it is that the beloved disciple speaks thus: 'I saw the dead' (all that had been dead) 'small and great, stand before God. And the books were opened (a figurative expression, plainly referring to the manner of proceeding among men), and the dead were judged out of those things which were written in the books according to their works' (Rev. 20:12).

II. These are the chief circumstances which are recorded in the oracles of God as preceding the general judgment. We are, secondly, to consider the judgment itself, so far as it hath pleased God to reveal it.

1. The person by whom God 'will judge the world' is his only-begotten Son, whose 'goings forth are from everlasting', 'who is God over all, blessed for ever'. Unto him, 'being the out-beaming of his Father's glory, the express image of his person' (Heb. 1:3), the Father 'hath committed all judgment, [. . .] because he is the Son of man' (John 5:22, 27); because, though he was 'in the form of God, and thought it not robbery to be equal with

God, yet he emptied himself, taking upon him the form of a servant, being made in the likeness of men' (Phil. 2:6-7). Yea, because 'being found in fashion as a man, he humbled himself' yet farther, 'becoming obedient unto death, even the death of the cross. Wherefore God hath highly exalted him,' even in his human nature, and 'ordained him' as man to try the children of men, to be the 'judge both of the quick and dead'; both of those who shall be found alive at his coming, and of those who were before 'gathered to their fathers'.

2. The time termed by the prophet 'the great and the terrible day' is usually in Scripture styled 'the day of the Lord'. The space from the creation of man upon the earth to the end of all things is *the day of the sons of men.* The time that is now passing over us is properly *our day.* When this is ended, the day of the Lord will begin. But who can say how long it will continue? 'With the Lord one day is as a thousand years, and a thousand years as one day' (2 Pet. 3:8). And from this very expression some of the ancient Fathers drew that inference, that what is commonly called 'the day of judgment' would be indeed a thousand years. And it seems they did not go beyond the truth; nay, probably they did not come up to it. For if we consider the number of persons who are to be judged, and of actions which are to be inquired into, it does not appear that a thousand years will suffice for the transactions of that day. So that it may not improbably comprise several thousand years. But God shall reveal this also in its season.

3. With regard to the place where mankind will be judged we have no explicit account in Scripture. An eminent writer (but not he alone; many have been of the same opinion) supposes it will be on earth, where the works were done according to which they shall be judged, and that God will in order thereto employ the angels of his strength,

> To smooth and lengthen out the boundless space,
> And spread an area for all human race.

But perhaps it is more agreeable to our Lord's own account of his 'coming in the clouds' to suppose it will be above the earth, if not 'twice a planetary height'. And this supposition is not a little favoured by what St. Paul writes to the Thessalonians. 'The dead in Christ shall rise first. Then we who remain alive shall be caught up together with them, in the clouds, to meet the Lord in the air' (1 Thess. 4:16-17). So that it seems most probable the 'great white throne' will be high exalted above the earth.

4. The persons to be judged who can count, any more than the drops of rain or the sands of the sea? I beheld, saith St. John, 'a great multitude which no man can number, clothed with white robes, and palms in their hands'. How immense then must be the total multitude of all nations, and kindreds, and people, and tongues! Of all that have sprung from the loins of Adam since the world began, till time shall be no more! If we admit the common supposition, which seems noways absurd, that the earth bears at any one time no less than four hundred millions of living souls—men, women, and children—what a congregation must all those generations make who have succeeded each other for seven thousand years!

Great Xerxes' world in arms, proud Cannae's host, . . .
They all are here, and here they all are lost:
Their numbers swell to be discerned in vain;
Lost as a drop in the unbounded main.

Every man, every woman, every infant of days that ever breathed the vital air will then hear the voice of the Son of God, and start into life, and appear before him. And this seems to be the natural import of that expression, 'the dead, small and great': all universally, all without exception, all of every age, sex, or degree; all that ever lived and died, or underwent such a change as will be equivalent with death. For long before that day the phantom of human greatness disappears and sinks into nothing. Even in the moment of death that vanishes away. Who is rich or great in the grave?

5. And every man shall there 'give an account of his own works', yea, a full and true account of all that he ever did while in the body, whether it was good or evil. O what a scene will then be disclosed in the sight of angels and men! While not the fabled Rhadamanthus, but the Lord God Almighty, who knoweth all things in heaven and earth,

Castigatque, auditque dolos; subigitque fateri
Quae quis apud superos, furto laetatus inani,
Distulit in seram commissa piacula mortem.

Nor will all the actions alone of every child of man be then brought to open view, but all their words, seeing 'every idle word which men shall speak, they shall give account thereof in the day of judgment.' So that, 'By thy words' (as well as works) 'thou shalt be justified; or by thy words thou shalt be condemned' (Matt. 12:36-37). Will not God then bring to light every circumstance also that accompanied every word or action, and if not altered the nature, yet lessened or increased the goodness or badness of them? And how easy is this to him who is 'about our bed and about our path, and spieth out all our ways'! We know 'the darkness is no darkness to him, but the night shineth as the day.'

6. Yea, he 'will bring to light' not 'the hidden works of darkness' only, but the very 'thoughts and intents of the heart'. And what marvel? For he 'searcheth the reins', and 'understandeth all our thoughts'. 'All things are naked and open to the eyes of him with whom we have to do.' 'Hell and destruction are before him' without a covering; 'how much more the hearts of the children of men!'

7. And in that day shall be discovered every inward working of every human soul: every appetite, passion, inclination, affection, with the various combinations of them, with every temper and disposition that constitute the whole complex character of each individual. So shall it be clearly and infallibly seen who was righteous, and who unrighteous; and in what degree every action or person or character was either good or evil.

8. 'Then the king will say to them upon his right hand, Come, ye blessed of my Father. For I was hungry and ye gave me meat; thirsty and ye gave me drink; I was a stranger and ye took me in; naked and ye clothed me.' In like manner, all the good they did upon

earth will be recited before men and angels: whatsoever they had done either 'in word or deed, in the name', or for the sake 'of the Lord Jesus'. All their good desires, intentions, thoughts, all their holy dispositions, will also be then remembered; and it will appear that though they were unknown or forgotten among men, yet God 'noted' them 'in his book'. All their sufferings likewise for the name of Jesus and for the testimony of a good conscience will be displayed, unto their *praise* from the righteous judge, their *honour* before saints and angels, and the increase of that 'far more exceeding and eternal weight of glory'.

9. But will their evil deeds too—since if we take in his whole life 'there is not a man on earth that liveth and sinneth not'—will these be remembered in that day, and mentioned in the great congregation? Many believe they will not, and ask, 'Would not this imply that their sufferings were not at an end, even when life ended? Seeing they would still have sorrow, and shame, and confusion of face to endure?' They ask farther, 'How can this be reconciled with God's declaration by the Prophet, "If the wicked will turn from all his sins that he hath committed, and keep all my statutes, and do that which is lawful and right; . . . all his transgressions that he hath committed, they shall not be once mentioned unto him"? (Ezek. 18:21-22). How is it consistent with the promise which God has made to all who accept of the gospel covenant, "I will forgive their iniquities, and remember their sin no more"? (Jer. 31:34). Or as the Apostle expresses it, "I will be merciful to their unrighteousness, and their sins and iniquities will I remember no more"?' (Heb. 8:12).

10. It may be answered, it is apparently and absolutely necessary, for the full display of the glory of God, for the clear and perfect manifestation of his wisdom, justice, power, and mercy toward the heirs of salvation, that all the circumstances of their life should be placed in open view, together with all their tempers, and all the desires, thoughts, and intents of their hearts. Otherwise how would it appear out of what a depth of sin and misery the grace of God had delivered them? And, indeed, if the whole lives of all the children of men were not manifestly discovered, the whole amazing contexture of divine providence could not be manifested; nor should we yet be able in a thousand instances to 'justify the ways of God to man'. Unless our Lord's words were fulfilled in their utmost sense, without any restriction or limitation, 'there is nothing covered that shall not be revealed, or hid that shall not be known' (Matt. 10:26), abundance of God's dispensations under the sun would still appear without their reasons. And then only when God hath brought to light all the hidden things of darkness, whosoever were the actors therein, will it be seen that wise and good were all his ways; that he 'saw through the thick cloud', and governed all things by the wise 'counsel of his own will'; that nothing was left to chance or the caprice of men, but God disposed all 'strongly and sweetly', and wrought all into one connected chain of justice, mercy, and truth.

11. And in the discovery of the divine perfections the righteous will rejoice with joy unspeakable; far from feeling any painful sorrow or shame for any of those past transgressions which were long since blotted out as a cloud, washed away by the blood of the Lamb. It will be abundantly sufficient for them that 'all the transgressions which they had committed shall not be once mentioned unto them' to their disadvantage; that 'their sins and transgressions and iniquities shall be remembered no more' to their condemnation.

This is the plain meaning of the promise; and this all the children of God shall find true, to their everlasting comfort.

12. After the righteous are judged, the king will turn to them upon his left hand, and they shall also be judged, every man 'according to his works'. But not only their outward works will be brought into the account, but all the evil words which they have ever spoken; yea, all the evil desires, affections, tempers, which have or have had a place in their souls, and all the evil thoughts or designs which were ever cherished in their hearts. The joyful sentence of acquittal will then be pronounced upon those on the right hand, the dreadful sentence of condemnation upon those on the left—both of which must remain fixed and unmovable as the throne of God.

III.1. We may, in the third place, consider a few of the circumstances which will follow the general judgment. And the first is the execution of the sentence pronounced on the evil and on the good. 'These shall go away into eternal punishment, and the righteous into life eternal.' It should be observed, it is the very same word which is used both in the former and the latter clause: it follows that either the punishment lasts for ever, or the reward too will come to an end. No, never, unless God could come to an end, or his mercy and truth could fail. 'Then shall the righteous shine forth as the sun in the kingdom of their Father,' and shall 'drink of those rivers of pleasure which are at God's right hand for evermore'. But here all description falls short; all human language fails! Only one who is caught up into the third heaven can have a just conception of it. But even such an one cannot express what he hath seen—these things 'it is not possible for man to utter.'

'The wicked', meantime, 'shall be turned into hell,' even 'all the people that forget God'. They will be 'punished with everlasting destruction from the presence of the Lord, and from the glory of his power'. They will be 'cast into the lake of fire burning with brimstone', originally 'prepared for the devil and his angels'; where they will 'gnaw their tongues' for anguish and pain; they will 'curse God, and look upward': there the dogs of hell—pride, malice, revenge, rage, horror, despair—continually devour them. There 'they have no rest day or night, but the smoke of their torment ascendeth for ever and ever.' 'For their worm dieth not, and the fire is not quenched.'

2. Then the heavens will be shrivelled up 'as a parchment scroll', and 'pass away with a great noise'; they will 'flee from the face of him that sitteth on the throne, and there will be found no place for them' (Rev. 20:11). The very manner of their passing away is disclosed to us by the Apostle Peter: 'In the day of God, the heavens, being on fire, shall be dissolved' (2 Pet. 3:12). The whole beautiful fabric will be overthrown by that raging element, the connection of all its parts destroyed, and every atom torn asunder from the others. By the same 'the earth also and the works that are therein shall be burnt up' (2 Pet. 3:10). The enormous works of nature, 'the everlasting hills', mountains that have defied the rage of time, and stood unmoved so many thousand years, will sink down in fiery ruin. How much less will the works of art, though of the most durable kind, the utmost efforts of human industry—tombs, pillars, triumphal arches, castles, pyramids—be able

to withstand the flaming conqueror. All, all will die, perish, vanish away, like a dream when one awaketh!

3. It has indeed been imagined by some great and good men that as it requires that same almighty power to annihilate things as to create, to speak into nothing or out of nothing; so no part of, no atom in the universe will be totally or finally destroyed. Rather, they suppose that as the last operation of fire which we have yet been able to observe is to reduce into glass what by a smaller force it had reduced to ashes; so in the day God hath ordained the whole earth, if not the material heavens also, will undergo this change, after which the fire can have no farther power over them. And they believe this is intimated by that expression in the Revelation made to St. John: 'Before the throne there was a sea of glass like unto crystal' (Rev. 4:6). We cannot now either affirm or deny this; but we shall know hereafter.

4. If it be inquired by the scoffers, the minute philosophers: 'How can these things be? Whence should come such an immense quantity of fire as would consume the heavens and the whole terraqueous globe?' we would beg leave, first, to remind them that this difficulty is not peculiar to the Christian system. The same opinion almost universally obtained among the *unbigoted* heathens. So one of those celebrated 'free-thinkers' speaks according to the generally received sentiment:

Esse quoque in fatis reminiscitur, affore tempus,
Quo mare, quo tellus, correptaque regia coeli
Ardeat, et mundi moles operosa laboret.

But, secondly, it is easy to answer, even from our slight and superficial acquaintance with natural things, that there are abundant magazines of fire ready prepared, and treasured up against the day of the Lord. How soon may a comet, commissioned by him, travel down from the most distant parts of the universe? And were it to fix upon the earth in its return from the sun, when it is some thousand times hotter than a red-hot cannon-ball, who does not see what must be the immediate consequence? But, not to ascend so high as the ethereal heavens, might not the same lightnings which give 'shine to the world', if commanded by the Lord of nature give ruin and utter destruction? Or, to go no farther than the globe itself, who knows what huge reservoirs of liquid fire are from age to age contained in the bowels of the earth? Aetna, Hecla, Vesuvius, and all the other volcanoes that belch out flames and coals of fire, what are they but so many proofs and mouths of those fiery furnaces? And at the same time so many evidences that God hath in readiness wherewith to fulfil his word. Yea, were we to observe no more than the surface of the earth, and the things that surround us on every side, it is most certain (as a thousand experiments prove beyond all possibility of denial) that we ourselves, our whole bodies, are full of fire, as well as everything round about us. Is it not easy to make this ethereal fire visible even to the naked eye? And to produce thereby the very same effects on combustible matter which are produced by culinary fire? Needs there then any more than for God to unloose that secret chain whereby this irresistible agent is now bound down, and lies quiescent in every particle of matter? And how soon would it tear the universal frame in pieces, and involve all in one common ruin?

5. There is one circumstance more which will follow the judgment that deserves our serious consideration. 'We look', says the Apostle, 'according to his promise, for new heavens and a new earth, wherein dwelleth righteousness' (2 Pet. 3:13). The promise stands in the prophecy of Isaiah: 'Behold, I create new heavens and a new earth. And the former shall not be remembered' (Isa. 65:17); so great shall the glory of the latter be. These St. John did behold in the visions of God. 'I saw', saith he, 'a new heaven and a new earth; for the first heaven and the first earth were passed away' (Rev. 21:1). And only 'righteousness dwelt therein.' Accordingly he adds, 'And I heard a great voice from' the third 'heaven, saying, Behold, the tabernacle of God is with men, and he will dwell with them, and they shall be his people, and God himself shall be with them, and be their God' (Rev. 21:3). Of necessity, therefore, they will all be happy: 'God shall wipe away all tears from their eyes, and there shall be no more death, neither sorrow, nor crying; neither shall there be any more pain' (Rev. 21:4). 'There shall be no more curse; but [. . .] they shall see his face' (Rev. 22:3, 4), shall have the nearest access to, and thence the highest resemblance of him. This is the strongest expression in the language of Scripture to denote the most perfect happiness. 'And his name shall be on their foreheads.' They shall be openly acknowledged as God's own property; and his glorious nature shall most visibly shine forth in them. 'And there shall be no night there; and they need no candle, neither light of the sun; for the Lord God giveth them light, and they shall reign for ever and ever.'

IV. It remains only to apply the preceding considerations to all who are here before God. And are we not directly led so to do by the present solemnity, which so naturally points us to that day when the Lord 'will judge the world in righteousness'? This, therefore, by reminding us of that more awful season, may furnish many lessons of instruction. A few of these I may be permitted just to touch on. May God write them on all our hearts!

1. And, first, 'how beautiful are the feet' of those who are sent by the wise and gracious providence of God to execute justice on earth, to defend the injured, and punish the wrongdoer! Are they not 'the ministers of God to us for good', the grand supporters of the public tranquillity, the patrons of innocence and virtue, the great security of all our temporal blessings? And does not every one of these represent not only an earthly prince, but the Judge of the earth; him whose 'name is written upon his thigh, King of Kings, and Lord of Lords'! O that all these sons 'of the right hand of the Most High' may be holy as he is holy! Wise with the 'wisdom that sitteth by his throne', like him who is the eternal wisdom of the Father! No respecters of persons, as he is none; but 'rendering to every man according to his works': like him inflexibly, inexorably just, though pitiful and of tender mercy! So shall they be terrible indeed to them that do evil, as 'not bearing the sword in vain'. So shall the laws of our land have their full use and due honour, and the throne of our King be still 'established in righteousness'.

2. Ye truly honourable men, whom God and the King have commissioned in a lower degree to administer justice, may not ye be compared to those ministering spirits who will attend the Judge coming in the clouds? May you, like them, burn with love to God and man! May you love righteousness and hate iniquity! May ye all minister in your several spheres (such honour hath God given you also!) to them that shall be heirs of salvation,

and to the glory of your great Sovereign! May ye remain the establishers of peace, the blessing and ornaments of your country, the protectors of a guilty land, the guardian angels of all that are round about you!

3. You whose office it is to execute what is given you in charge by him before whom you stand, how nearly are you concerned to resemble those that stand before the face of the Son of man! Those 'servants of his that do his pleasure', 'and hearken to the voice of his words'. Does it not highly import *you* to be as uncorrupt as *them*? To approve yourselves the servants of God? To do justly and love mercy; to do to all as ye would they should do to you? So shall that great Judge, under whose eye you continually stand, say to you also, 'Well done, good and faithful servants: enter ye into the joy of your Lord!'

4. Suffer me to add a few words to all of you who are this day present before the Lord. Should not you bear it in your minds all the day long that a more awful day is coming? A large assembly this! But what is it to that which every eye will then behold—the general assembly of all the children of men that ever lived on the face of the whole earth! A few will stand at the judgment seat this day, to be judged touching what shall be laid to their charge. And they are now reserved in prison, perhaps in chains, till they are brought forth to be tried and sentenced. But we shall all, I that speak and you that hear, 'stand at the judgment seat of Christ'. And we are now reserved on this earth, which is not our home, in this prison of flesh and blood, perhaps many of us in chains of darkness too, till we are ordered to be brought forth. Here a man is questioned concerning one or two facts which he is supposed to have committed. There we are to give an account of all our works, from the cradle to the grave: of all our words; of all our desires and tempers, all the thoughts and intents of our hearts; of all the use we have made of our various talents, whether of mind, body, or fortune, till God said, 'Give an account of thy stewardship; for thou mayest be no longer steward.' In this court it is possible some who are guilty may escape for want of evidence. But there is no want of evidence in that court. All men with whom you had the most secret intercourse, who were privy to all your designs and actions, are ready before your face. So are all the spirits of darkness, who inspired evil designs, and assisted in the execution of them. So are all the angels of God—those 'eyes of the Lord that run to and fro over all the earth'—who watched over your soul, and laboured for your good so far as you would permit. So is your own conscience, a thousand witnesses in one, now no more capable of being either blinded or silenced, but constrained to know and to speak the naked truth touching all your thoughts and words and actions. And is conscience as a thousand witnesses? Yea, but God is as a thousand consciences! O who can stand before the face of 'the great God, even our Saviour, Jesus Christ'!

See, see! He cometh! He maketh the clouds his chariots. He rideth upon the wings of the wind! A devouring fire goeth before him, and after him a flame burneth! See, he sitteth upon his throne, clothed with light as with a garment, arrayed with majesty and honour! Behold his eyes are as a flame of fire, his voice as the sound of many waters!

How will ye escape? Will ye call to the mountains to fall on you, the rocks to cover you? Alas, the mountains themselves, the rocks, the earth, the heavens, are just ready to flee away! Can ye prevent the sentence? Wherewith? With all the substance of thy house, with thousands of gold and silver? Blind wretch! Thou camest naked from thy mother's womb, and [shalt move] naked into eternity. Hear the Lord, the Judge! 'Come ye blessed of my Father! Inherit the kingdom prepared for you from the foundation of the world.' Joyful sound! How widely different from that voice which echoes through the expanse of heaven, 'Depart, ye cursed, into everlasting fire, prepared for the devil and his angels!' And who is he that can prevent or retard the full execution of either sentence? Vain hope! Lo, 'hell is moved from beneath' to receive those who are ripe for destruction! And the 'everlasting doors lift up their heads' that the heirs of glory may come in!

5. 'What manner of persons (then) ought we to be, in all holy conversation and godliness?' We know it cannot be long before the Lord will descend 'with the voice of the archangel, and the trumpet of God'; when every one of us shall appear before him and 'give account of his own works'. 'Wherefore, beloved, seeing ye look for these things', seeing ye know he will come and will not tarry, 'be diligent that ye may be found of him in peace, without spot, and blameless.' Why should ye not? Why should one of you be found on the left hand at his appearing? He 'willeth not that any should perish, but that all should come to *repentance*'; by repentance to faith in a bleeding Lord; by faith to spotless love, to the full image of God renewed in the heart, and producing all holiness of conversation. Can you doubt of this when you remember the Judge of all is likewise 'the Saviour of all'? Hath he not bought you with his own blood, that ye might 'not perish, but have everlasting life'? O make proof of his mercy rather than his justice! Of his love rather than the thunder of his power! 'He is not far from every one of us'; and he is now come, 'not to condèmn, but to save the world'. He standeth in the midst! Sinner, doth he not now, even now, knock at the door of thy heart? O that thou mayst know, at least '*in this thy day*', the things that belong unto thy peace! O that ye may now give yourselves to him who 'gave himself for you', in humble faith, in holy, active, patient love! So shall ye rejoice with exceeding joy *in his day*, when he cometh in the clouds of heaven.

60. THE NEW CREATION

1785

An Introductory Comment

In many respects this sermon is the culmination of the collection. It represents Wesley's mature judgment in terms of the height, depth, and extent of salvation. It offers a cosmic vision (which however quickly devolves upon the earth) that embraces the redemption of the relationships of humanity to (1) God, (2) self, (3) the planet, and (4) the animal realm. He drafted it specifically for inclusion in the November and December issues of the *Arminian Magazine* in 1785 (WWS), and it was placed in volume V of the *Sermons on Several Occasions.* Wesley had employed the text, Revelation 21:5, two years earlier in 1783 and one last time in 1790 (O, 2:500).

Drawing upon his well-worked distinction between real and nominal Christians in the area of eschatology as well, and late in his career, Wesley noted at the beginning of this sermon that this topic, filled with promises, is hardly thought of or understood "by the generality of Christians" (O, 2:501). Beyond this, Wesley specifically took issue with the dull, flat ascription of these cosmic promises to the reign of Constantine as constituting "a miserable way . . . of making void the whole counsel of God" (O, 2:501). Indeed, the key agent here is not the Roman emperor but no one less than "the Creator and Governor of the universe" (O, 2:502).

Obviously aware of the work *On Nature* written by Empedocles (495–435 [H] b.c.[P]), Wesley observed what changes will be brought about by a sovereign God in terms of fire, air, water, and the earth (O, 2:504–6) with respect to the coming new heavens and the new earth. What's more, there will be "no more death, and no more pain or sickness preparatory thereto" (O, 2:510). And "to crown it all," Wesley concluded, the grace of God will triumph, and "there will be a deep, an intimate, an uninterrupted union with God; a constant communion with the Father and his Son Jesus Christ, through the Spirit" (O, 2:510).

The New Creation

1. What a strange scene is here opened to our view
    A. How remote from all our natural apprehensions
    B. It is little thought of or understood by both heathens and Christians
2. After our researches our knowledge of this truth is short and imperfect
3. The Apostle tells us in the first verse of the chapter:
    A. 'I saw a new heaven and a new earth'
4. Many entertain a strange opinion that this relates only to present things
    A. This prophecy does not end with the present world
    B. It shows us the things that will come to pass when this world is no more
5. A new heaven: the original word in Genesis is plural
    A. And indeed this is the constant language of Scripture
    B. Not *heaven,* but *heavens*; the ancient Jews speak of three heavens
    C. The third heaven is the immediate residence of God
6. We cannot think that this heaven will undergo any change
7. Meanwhile, the lower heaven, with the elements will melt in fervent heat
8. There will be no blazing stars, no comets there
9. We may more easily conceive the changes wrought in the lower heaven
    A. It will no more be torn by hurricanes or agitated by furious storms
10. All the elements will be new indeed; entirely changed as to their qualities
    A. *Fire* is at present the general destroyer of all things under the sun
    B. But it will destroy no more; consume no more
11. There will be no more rain
12. What change will the element of *water* undergo when things are made new?
    A. It will in every part of the world be made clear, limpid, and pure
13. It seems an even greater change will be wrought in the *earth*
14. It will no more be bound up with intense cold, nor parched with extreme heat
15. It will contain no jarring or destructive principles within its bowels
16. The earth shall be a more beautiful paradise than Adam ever saw
17. On the new earth no creature will kill or hurt or give pain to another
18. Most glorious of all will be the change on poor, miserable human children
    A. Hence will arise an unmixed state of holiness and happiness

Sermon 64: The New Creation, 1785

Revelation 21:5

Behold, I make all things new.

1. What a strange scene is here opened to our view! How remote from all our natural apprehensions! Not a glimpse of what is here revealed was ever seen in the heathen world. Not only the modern, barbarous, uncivilized heathens have not the least conception of it; but it was equally unknown to the refined, polished heathens of ancient Greece and Rome. And it is almost as little thought of or understood by the generality of Christians: I mean, not barely those that are nominally such, that have the form of godliness without the power; but even those that in a measure fear God and study to work righteousness.

2. It must be allowed that after all the researches we can make, still our knowledge of the great truth which is delivered to us in these words is exceedingly short and imperfect. As this is a point of mere revelation, beyond the reach of all our natural faculties, we cannot penetrate far into it, nor form any adequate conception of it. But it may be an encouragement to those who have in any degree tasted of the powers of the world to come to go as far as we can go, interpreting Scripture by Scripture, according to the analogy of faith.

3. The Apostle, caught up in the visions of God, tells us in the first verse of the chapter, 'I saw a new heaven and a new earth;' and adds, 'He that sat upon the throne said (I believe the only words which he is said to utter throughout the whole book), Behold, I make all things new' (Rev. 21:5).

4. Very many commentators entertain a strange opinion that this relates only to the present state of things, and gravely tell us that the words are to be referred to the flourishing state of the church, which commenced after the heathen persecutions. Nay, some of them have discovered that all which the Apostle speaks concerning the 'new heaven and the new earth' was fulfilled when Constantine the Great poured in riches and honours upon the Christians. What a miserable way is this of making void the whole counsel of God with regard to all that grand chain of events, in reference to his church, yea, and to all mankind, from the time that John was in Patmos unto the end of the world! Nay, the line of this prophecy reaches farther still. It does not end with the present world, but shows us the things that will come to pass when this world is no more.

5. Thus saith the Creator and Governor of the universe, 'Behold, I make all things new:' all which are included in that expression of the Apostle, 'a new heaven and a new earth'. 'A new heaven': the original word in Genesis (chapter one) is in the plural number. And indeed this is the constant language of Scripture—not *heaven*, but *heavens*. Accordingly the ancient Jewish writers are accustomed to reckon three heavens. In conformity to which the apostle Paul speaks of his being 'caught up into the third heaven'. It is this, the third heaven, which is usually supposed to be the more immediate residence of God—so far as any residence can be ascribed to his omnipresent Spirit, who pervades and fills the whole universe. It is here (if we speak after the manner of men) that the Lord sitteth upon his throne, surrounded by angels and archangels, and by all his flaming ministers.

6. We cannot think that this heaven will undergo any change, any more than its great inhabitant. Surely this palace of the Most High was the same from eternity, and will be world without end. Only the inferior heavens are liable to change; the highest of which we usually call the starry heaven. This, St. Peter informs us, is 'reserved unto fire, against the day of judgment and destruction of ungodly men'. In that day, 'being on fire', it shall first shrivel as a parchment scroll; then it shall 'be dissolved', and 'shall pass away with a great noise'; lastly it shall 'flee from the face of him that sitteth on the throne', 'and there shall be found no place for it.'

7. At the same time 'the stars shall fall from heaven,' the secret chain being broken which had retained them in their several orbits from the foundation of the world. In the meanwhile the lower or sublunary 'heaven', with 'the elements' (or principles that compose it), 'shall melt with fervent heat,' while 'the earth with the works that are therein shall be burnt up.' This is the introduction to a far nobler state of things, such as it has not yet entered into the heart of men to conceive—the universal restoration which is to succeed the universal destruction. For 'we look for', says the Apostle, 'new heavens and a new earth, wherein dwelleth righteousness' (2 Pet. 3:7, etc.).

8. One considerable difference there will undoubtedly be in the starry heaven when it is created anew; there will be no blazing stars, no comets there. Whether those horrid, eccentric orbs are half-formed planets, in a chaotic state (I speak on the supposition of a plurality of worlds) or such as have undergone their general conflagration, they will certainly have no place in the new heaven, where all will be exact order and harmony. There may be many other differences between the heaven that now is and that which will be after the renovation. But they are above our apprehension: we must leave eternity to explain them.

9. We may more easily conceive the changes which will be wrought in the lower heaven, in the region of the air. It will be no more torn by hurricanes, or agitated by furious storms or destructive tempests. Pernicious or terrifying meteors will have no more place therein. We shall have no more occasion to say,

> There like a trumpet, loud and strong,
> Thy thunder shakes our coast;
> While the red lightnings wave along,
> The banners of thy host!

No; all will be then light, fair, serene—a lively picture of the eternal day.

10. All the elements (taking that word in the common sense for the principles of which all natural beings are compounded) will be new indeed; entirely changed as to their qualities, although not as to their nature. *Fire* is at present the general destroyer of all things under the sun; dissolving all things that come within the sphere of its action, and reducing them to their primitive atoms. But no sooner will it have performed its last great office of destroying the heavens and the earth (whether you mean thereby one system only, or the whole fabric of the universe—the difference between one and millions of worlds being nothing before the great Creator); when, I say, it has done this, the destruction

wrought by fire will come to a perpetual end. It will destroy no more; it will consume no more; it will forget its power to burn, which it possesses only during the present state of things, and be as harmless in the new heavens and earth as it is now in the bodies of men and other animals, and the substance of trees and flowers; in all which (as late experiments show) large quantities of ethereal fire are lodged—if it be not rather an essential component part of every material being under the sun. But it will probably retain its vivifying power, though divested of its power to destroy.

11. It has been already observed that the calm, placid *air* will be no more disturbed by storms and tempests. There will be no more meteors with their horrid glare, affrighting the poor children of men. May we not add (though at first it may sound like a paradox) that there will be no more rain. It is observable that there was none in paradise; a circumstance which Moses particularly mentions: 'The Lord God had not caused it to rain upon the earth. But there went up a mist from the earth,' which then covered up the abyss of waters, 'and watered the whole face of the ground' (Gen. 2:5-6) with moisture sufficient for all the purposes of vegetation. We have all reason to believe that the case will be the same when paradise is restored. Consequently there will be no more clouds or fogs; but one bright, refulgent day. Much less will there be any poisonous damps or pestilential blasts. There will be no sirocco in Italy; no parching or suffocating winds in Arabia; no keen north-east winds in our own country,

> Shattering the graceful locks of yon fair trees;

but only pleasing, healthful breezes,

> Fanning the earth with odoriferous wings.

12. But what change will the element of *water* undergo when all things are made new? It will be in every part of the world clear and limpid, pure from all unpleasing or unhealthful mixtures; rising here and there in crystal fountains to refresh and adorn the earth 'with liquid lapse of murmuring stream'. For undoubtedly, as there were in paradise, there will be various rivers gently gliding along, for the use and pleasure of both man and beast. But the inspired writer has expressly declared, 'there will be no more sea' (Rev. 21:1). We have reason to believe that at the beginning of the world, when God said, 'Let the waters under the heaven be gathered together unto one place, and let the dry land appear' (Gen. 1:9), the dry land spread over the face of the water, and covered it on every side. And so it seems to have done till, in order to the general deluge which he had determined to bring upon the earth at once, 'the windows of heaven were opened, and the fountains of the great deep broken up.' But the sea will then retire within its primitive bounds, and appear on the surface of the earth no more. Neither indeed will there be any more need of the sea. For either as the ancient poet supposes,

Omnis feret omnia tellus—

every part of the earth will naturally produce whatever its inhabitants want—or all mankind will procure what the whole earth affords by a much easier and readier conveyance. For all the inhabitants of the earth, our Lord informs us, will then be ἰσάγγελοι, 'equal to angels'; on a level with them in swiftness as well as strength; so that they can quick as thought transport themselves or whatever they want from one side of the globe to the other.

13. But it seems a greater change will be wrought in the *earth* than even in the air and water. Not that I can believe that wonderful discovery of Jacob Behmen, which many so eagerly contend for, that the earth itself with all its furniture and inhabitants will then be transparent as glass. There does not seem to be the least foundation for this, either in Scripture or reason. Surely not in Scripture: I know not one text in the Old or New Testament which affirms any such thing. Certainly it cannot be inferred from that text in the Revelation, chapter the fourth, verse the sixth: 'And before the throne there was a sea of glass, like unto crystal.' And yet, if I mistake not, this is the chief, if not the only Scripture which has been urged in favour of this opinion! Neither can I conceive that it has any foundation in reason. It has indeed been warmly alleged that all things would be far more beautiful if they were quite transparent. But I cannot apprehend this; yea, I apprehend quite the contrary. Suppose every part of a human body were made transparent as crystal, would it appear more beautiful than it does now? Nay, rather it would shock us above measure. The surface of the body, and in particular 'the human face divine', is undoubtedly one of the most beautiful objects that can be found under heaven. But could you look through the rosy cheek, the smooth, fair forehead, or the rising bosom, and distinctly see all that lies within, you would turn away from it with loathing and horror.

14. Let us next take a view of those changes which we may reasonably suppose will then take place in the *earth.* It will no more be bound up with intense cold, nor parched up with extreme heat; but will have such a temperature as will be most conducive to its fruitfulness. If in order to punish its inhabitants God did of old

> Bid his angels turn askance
> This oblique globe,

thereby occasioning violent cold on one part, and violent heat on the other; he will undoubtedly then order them to restore it to its original position; so that there will be a final end, on the one hand of the burning heat which makes some parts of it scarce habitable; and on the other of

> The rage of Arctos, and eternal frost.

15. And it will then contain no jarring or destructive principles within its own bo-

som. It will no more have any of those violent convulsions in its own bowels. It will no more be shaken or torn asunder by the impetuous force of *earthquakes*; and will therefore need neither Vesuvius nor Etna, nor any *burning mountains* to prevent them. There will be no more horrid rocks or frightful precipices; no wild deserts or barren sands; no impassable morasses or unfaithful bogs to swallow up the unwary traveller. There will doubtless be inequalities on the surface of the earth, which are not blemishes, but beauties. For though I will not affirm that

> earth hath this variety from heaven
> Of pleasure situate in hill and dale;

yet I cannot think gently rising hills will be any defect, but an ornament of the new-made earth. And doubtless we shall then likewise have occasion to say:

> Lo there his wondrous skill arrays
> The fields in cheerful green!
> A thousand herbs his hand displays,
> A thousand flowers between!

16. And what will the general produce of the earth be? Not thorns, briars, or thistles. Not any useless or fetid weed; not any poisonous, hurtful, or unpleasant plant; but every one that can be conducive in any wise either to our use or pleasure. How far beyond all that the most lively imagination is now able to conceive! We shall no more regret the loss of the terrestrial paradise, or sigh at that well-devised description of our great poet;

> Then shall this mount
> Of paradise by might of waves be moved
> Out of his place, pushed by the horned flood,
> With all its verdure spoiled, and trees adrift,
> Down the great river to the opening gulf,
> And there take root, an island salt and bare!

For all the earth shall then be a more beautiful paradise than Adam ever saw.

17. Such will be the state of the new earth with regard to the meaner, the inanimate parts of it. But great as this change will be, it is little, it is nothing, in comparison of that which will then take place throughout all animated nature. In the living part of the creation were seen the most deplorable effects of Adam's apostasy. The whole animated creation, whatever has life, from leviathan to the smallest mite, was thereby 'made subject' to such 'vanity' as the inanimate creatures could not be. They were subject to that fell monster, death, the conqueror of all that breathe. They were made subject to its forerunner, pain, in its ten thousand forms; although 'God made not death, neither hath he

pleasure in the death of any living.' How many millions of creatures in the sea, in the air, and on every part of the earth, can now no otherwise preserve their own lives than by taking away the lives of others; by tearing in pieces and devouring their poor, innocent, unresisting fellow-creatures! Miserable lot of such innumerable multitudes, who, insignificant as they seem, are the offspring of one common Father, the creatures of the same God of love! It is probable not only two-thirds of the animal creation, but ninety-nine parts out of a hundred, are under a necessity of destroying others in order to preserve their own life! But it shall not always be so. He that sitteth upon the throne will soon change the face of all things, and give a demonstrative proof to all his creatures that 'his mercy is over all his works.' The horrid state of things which at present obtains will soon be at an end. On the new earth no creature will kill or hurt or give pain to any other. The scorpion will have no poisonous sting, the adder no venomous teeth. The lion will have no claws to tear the lamb; no teeth to grind his flesh and bones. Nay, no creature, no beast, bird, or fish, will have any inclination to hurt any other. For cruelty will be far away, and savageness and fierceness be forgotten. So that violence shall be heard no more, neither wasting or destruction seen on the face of the earth. 'The wolf shall dwell with the lamb' (the words may be literally as well as figuratively understood) 'and the leopard shall lie down with the kid.' 'They shall not hurt or destroy,' from the rising up of the sun to the going down of the same.

18. But the most glorious of all will be the change which then will take place on the poor, sinful, miserable children of men. These had fallen in many respects, as from a greater height, so into a lower depth than any other part of the creation. But they shall 'hear a great voice out of heaven, saying, Behold, the tabernacle of God is with men, and he will dwell with them, and they shall be his people, and God himself shall be their God.' Hence will arise an unmixed state of holiness and happiness far superior to that which Adam enjoyed in paradise. In how beautiful and affecting a manner is this described by the Apostle! 'God shall wipe away all tears from their eyes; and there shall be no more death, neither sorrow nor crying, neither shall there be any more pain: for the former things are done away' (Rev. 21:3-4). As there will be no more death, and no more pain or sickness preparatory thereto; as there will be no more grieving for or parting with friends; so there will be no more sorrow or crying. Nay, but there will be a greater deliverance than all this; for there will be no more sin. And to crown all, there will be a deep, an intimate, an uninterrupted union with God; a constant communion with the Father and his Son Jesus Christ, through the Spirit; a continual enjoyment of the Three-One God, and of all the creatures in him!

NOTES

General Introduction

1. The notable exception during this early period is the sermon "The Circumcision of the Heart," which was produced in 1733 and published in the first collection of 1746. It represents one of Wesley's best expressions of the doctrine of Christian perfection. For more on Wesley's early sermons, see Richard P. Heitzenrater, "John Wesley's Early Sermons," *The Proceedings of the Wesley Historical Society* 37 (1969–70): 110–28.

2. For those interested in such a question that eventually grew into a lively debate we refer them to the works of both Thomas C. Oden and Richard P. Heitzenrater that are listed in the abbreviations section preceding this introduction.

3. Note that the term *way* as employed in the sermon "The Scripture Way of Salvation" refers not to the notion of path but to that of manner. In other words, in Wesley's reckoning and emphasis in this context it is the *Scripture* way of salvation as opposed to some other way, such as a *rational* or *traditional* way of salvation.

4. We recognize, as Wesley did, that God is free to work in a variety of ways. In other words, we do not regard the notion of an *ordo salutis* as somehow restricting the Christian journey to an eternally fixed blueprint. On the contrary, we celebrate the freedom and ingenuity of the Holy Spirit at every step along the way. However, we also agree with the classical notion that, *for the purpose of teaching*, there is an order that helps people reflect on and make progress in the Christian journey as displayed, for example, in the key sermon, "The Scripture Way of Salvation."

10. The Almost Christian

1. ['Good men avoid sin from the love of virtue; wicked men avoid sin from the fear of punishment,' Cf. Horace, *Epistles*, I.xvi. 52–53.]

2. ['Thou shalt not be hanged,' Horace, *Epistles*, I.xvi.48.]

3. Homily on the Salvation of Man [Pt. III].

52. On Sin in Believers

1. What follows for some pages is an answer to a paper published in the *Christian Magazine* [1762], pp. 577–82. I am surprised Mr. [William] Dodd should give such a paper a place in his magazine which is directly contrary to our Ninth Article.